PIMLICO

191

CHRISTINA ROSSETTI

Jan Marsh is the authority on the Pre-Raphaelite women. Her ground-breaking biographies include *Pre-Raphaelite Sisterhood, Jane and May Morris,* and *The Legend of Elizabeth Siddal.* She lives in London.

CHRISTINA ROSSETTI

A Literary Biography

JAN MARSH

PIMLICO

PIMLICO
An imprint of Random House
20 Vauxhall Bridge Road, London SW1V 2SA

Random House Australia (Pty) Ltd
20 Alfred Street, Milsons Point, Sydney
New South Wales 2061, Australia

Random House New Zealand Ltd
18 Poland Road, Glenfield
Auckland 10, New Zealand

Random House South Africa (Pty) Ltd
PO Box 337, Bergvlei, South Africa

Random House UK Ltd Reg. No. 954009

First published by Jonathan Cape 1994
Pimlico edition 1995

1 3 5 7 9 10 8 6 4 2

Printed and bound in Great Britain by
Mackays of Chatham PLC

ISBN 0–7126–7437–3

Contents

PART THREE: 1861–70

PART FOUR: 1871–94

PART ONE:

1830–50

1

Nursery Days

AS SHE LATER recreated in her own nursery poem, Christina Rossetti's earliest memory was of her father crowing like a cock to wake his children:

> Kookoorookoo! Kookoorookoo!
>   Crows the cock before the morn;
> Kikirikee! Kikirikee!
>   Roses in the east are born.
>
> Kookoorookoo! Kookoorookoo!
>   Early birds begin their singing;
> Kikirikee! Kikirikee!
>   The day, the day, the day is springing.

It came of course, from Italian, as she recaptured when translating her verse back into her father's tongue:

> Cuccurucu – cuccurucu –
>   All 'alba il gallo canta.
> Chicchirichi – chicchirichi –
>   Di rose il ciel s'ammanta.

Nursery memories also included childish versions of other animal noises made to amuse the youngsters – donkeys braying, pigs grunting, geese hissing. Born and reared in London, the Rossetti children heard real farmyard sounds only when staying with their grandparents in the country, where, at the age of one, Gabriel was scared by the mooing of a real-life cow.

Our first recorded glimpse of Christina is in the country, aged eighteen months, when her father pictured his skittish baby daughter, with rosy cheeks and sparkling eyes, taking tentative steps in the garden 'like a little butterfly' among the flowers and currant bushes. It was time Christina be weaned, he suggested, though there was no other baby on the way.

As the youngest, she was cradled at the breast while the older children played, with that sense of utter security later invoked in her children's verses, *Sing-Song*:

> You are my one and I have not another;
> > Sleep soft, my darling, my trouble and treasure;
> Sleep warm and soft in the arms of your mother,
> > Dreaming of pretty things, dreaming of pleasure.

Soon, she would learn her first words. When their mother reported the amusing sayings of the other children, their father promised picture books and a box of figs, to 'reward their good behaviour and satisfy their small greed'. The picture books contained traditional rhymes like 'Ding, dong, bell' and 'Ladybird, ladybird', whose echoes fill *Sing-Song*, while a faint memory of the figs also reached its pages:

> Currants on a bush,
> > And figs upon a stem
> And cherries on a bending bough
> > And Ned to gather them.

At home, Christina's brother William recalled, their plump, balding, good-humoured father would often take a child on his knee and clap their hands together, repeating 'with his Italian intonation and clear-cut delivery', the pat-a-cake, pat-a-cake rhyme, transformed in *Sing-Song* into lines whose accompanying gestures may easily be imagined:

> Mix a pancake,
> Stir a pancake,
> > Pop it in the pan;
> Fry the pancake,
> Toss the pancake –
> > Catch it if you can.

The Rossettis lived in central London, in a tall house behind the grander Portland Place, a short walk from the newly-opened Regents Park. No. 38 Charlotte Street had no garden, so the children played indoors, and in a family with four children born within five years, there was naturally much squabbling and crying. 'Hop o' my thumb and little Jack Horner, What do you mean by tearing and fighting?' asks *Sing-Song* in hornbook mode. William was the least assertive of the four – in his own words, 'a demure little boy, not quarrelsome and not teazing'. To his mother he was my own 'Willie-wee', and his childhood ambition was long-remembered:

> Little Willie in his heart
> Is a sailor on the sea,

And he often cons a chart
With sister Margery.

Maria, nicknamed Maggy, was an energetic and bossy big sister, rising four at the time of Christina's birth. She learnt to read and write early, a jealous edge to her warm disposition no doubt sharpened by having three siblings born in quick succession. She made the most of her superior knowledge and was always regarded as the cleverest child, who 'might have topped us all', as Gabriel recalled, and as she remained to Christina. In respect of sex, looks and behaviour however, Maria was outdone by Gabriel, Christina and William respectively, and in all other ways she was challenged and eclipsed by Gabriel – 'a fiery spirit not lightly to be rebelled against'; in William's words: 'in anything wearing the garb of mischief he counted for all, and Maria for nothing'. A charming as well as favoured eldest son, he dominated the nursery, encountering no opposition, and little resentment. He was also precociously gifted: one day in 1834 the milkman expressed astonishment at such a 'baby making a picture!', as he sat scribbling in the hallway. Mamma carefully kept the drawing, of a toy rocking horse, as she did all their youthful productions, in what Christina later called her proud 'maternal store'.

Christina and William, with just over a year between them, were small allies against their teasing and often imperious elders. But Christina was also aligned with Maria by gender and, perhaps more enticingly, with Gabriel by a shared spiritedness. Where William was placid, pretty little Christina was volatile and fractious: 'hardly less passionate than Gabriel and more given to mere tantrums', with a formidable will. Their father called her an 'angelic little demon', and in 1836 wrote of her and Gabriel with their mother in the country as two little rascals brawling and bawling, while at home Maria and William were good as gold. Gallantly he offered to exchange the 'two storms for two calms'.

But vehemence in Gabriel was considered 'snappishness' in Christina. From infancy she had a reputation for wilfulness and temper, lamented by her father despite a certain admiration for her spirit. Before she was two years old, he compared her lack of docility to the recalcitrant House of Lords, unwilling to pass the 1832 Reform Bill. 'They will make all the outcry and resistance that Cristina is wont to make when you force her teeth, medicine glass in hand' he wrote, 'but what is the end of the performance? Cristina gulps the medicine.' She remembered this in *Sing-Song*, with Papa's voice echoing in the Italian version:

Baby cry –	*Ohibò piccina*
Oh, fie! –	*Tutto atterita!*
At the physic in the cup:	*La medicina*
Gulp it twice	*Bever si de'*
And gulp it thrice	*Uno, due, tre,*
Baby gulp it up.	*Ed è finita.*

Toys included the little rocking horse, a spinning top, ninepins and a teetotum like a large dice with letters. The girl had dolls, and a treasured dolls' tea-set, but from an early age the children were most happily occupied with colouring books and 'penny plain' theatrical prints. Partly with an educational purpose there were card games like beggar-my-neighbour, which William's memory linked to arithmetic, for in Mamma's hands, games and pictures were usually more than play, and *Sing-Song* contains several 'learning rhymes' to teach children about time, or the months of the year, or the coins of the realm:

> What will you give me for my pound?
> Full twenty shillings round.
> What will you give me for my shilling?
> Twelve pence to give I'm willing.
> What will you give me for my penny?
> Four farthings, just so many.

Numbers came in rhyme, too, as did colours, starting with a pink rose and ending with 'just an orange!' that is like nothing else. All around Christina, in her baby years, there was such instructional rhyming.

Letters soon followed, in alphabet verses like her own, running from Antelope and Bear to Zebra and Zebu. Y was a yellow yacht or, according to Papa, noting that the letter was unknown in Italian, the shape made by the cat as she stretched her paws on the fender before the fire.

There were various pets: always a tabby cat, usually a cage-bird and also for a while a pet squirrel with a wheel. The children were fond of all furry animals, but the exotic inhabitants of the Zoological Gardens were a major delight. Newly-established in Regents Park, this was the best destination for a walk, where sloths, armadilloes and screaming parrots were their favourites. Here, one of the alphabet animals was a species then called by its African name, the Sing-Sing Antelope, which Papa took a childlike pleasure in addressing with the words: 'Sing, sing, antelope; antelope, sing, sing!' To his great satisfaction, no song was ever heard. Once at the Zoo, Christina was bitten by a peccary, a sort of wild pig with strong teeth and tusks. He does not feature in her alphabet.

There were other injuries and sorrows too, and it has been re-marked that *Sing-Song* contains some 'inappropriate' verses about sadness and death, which makes the book unsuitable for the modern nursery. But grief is part of childhood, and painful whether the cause be trivial or deep. There is mourning in *Sing-Song* for a broken doll as well as for a baby who blossomed and died like a flower; the author of such lines knew that early intimations of loss are as significant to a child as to an adult. She knew, too, that some sorrows have no cause:

> Under the ivy bush
>   One sits sighing,
> And under the willow tree
>   One sits crying: –

> Under the ivy bush
>   Cease from your sighing,
> But under the willow tree
>   Lie down a-dying.

The family was bi-lingual: Mamma spoke English, Papa always Italian. He could speak English fairly enough when he chose, said William, 'but he never did choose *en famille*' and to him as to his children it was a language to be learnt and laughed at, full of inconsistencies and paradoxes like the oddly-named antelope. His linguistic delight was a lasting inheritance: throughout her life Christina loved riddles and puns. *Peter Puzzlepate's New Riddle Book*, typical of those the Rossetti children read, had numerous rhymes whose echoes are heard in *Sing-Song*:

> The peacock has a score of eyes
>   With which he cannot see;
> The cod-fish has a silent sound,
>   However that might be.

> No dandelions tell the time
>   Although they turn to clocks;
> Cat's cradle does not hold the cat
>   Nor foxglove fit the fox.

Peter Puzzlepate contains this conundrum:

A well-known word in the English language the first two letters of which signify a male, the three first a female, the four first a great man, and the whole a great woman. Answer: HEROINE.

and when she was over fifty Christina offered her young nephew one she herself had invented 'in byegone days':

My first is a donkey. My second is a donkey. My third is a donkey. My fourth may be composed of donkeys. My whole is an act of which a donkey may be ashamed. Answer: ASS-ASS-I-NATION.

This playful pleasure in words provided an apt grounding in language for a prospective poet. Christina's very first verses, composed before she had learnt to write –

Cecilia never went to school
Without her gladiator.

– were informed by pure liking for the sounds, and perhaps also by the fact that the rest of the family were always using long words she did not know.

Whimsicality is close to imagination. If a mouse could fly what would he do? wonders *Sing-Song*; if a crow could swim he might turn grey. What about the things you can't see?

Who has seen the wind?
Neither you nor I:
But when the trees bow down their heads,
The wind is passing by.

Both silly rhyming and philosophical inquiry were heard in the Charlotte Street parlour-cum-playroom. Papa was fond of aphorisms. '*Cosa fatta capo ha*' ('no end without a beginning') was one Italian saying his daughter remembered to the end of her life, together with the Voltairean: '*Nemico del bene è il meglio*' – 'the best is the enemy of the good'. And even when the sense was lost on the children, there was always the sound of Italian phrases, rising and falling around them.

Christina herself, when pressed on the origins of her poetic training, offered an alternative explanation. 'If any one thing schooled me in the direction supposed,' she wrote, 'it was perhaps the delightful idle liberty to prowl all alone about my grandfather's cottage grounds some thirty miles from London, entailing in my childhood a long stage coach journey!' This was the cottage with the currant bushes, where Mamma took the children to visit her parents, and for recuperative country air, on a six-hour journey westwards beyond Uxbridge. At High Wycombe in Buckinghamshire they changed to the local coach, and halfway to Amersham lay the crossroads and pond of Holmer Green, a hamlet of scattered dwellings on the edge of the

Chiltern woodlands, amid lanes and fields, orchards and copses. It was an area of historic Protestantism, not far from John Hampden's village and Milton's cottage at Chalfont St Giles, with William Penn's ancestral home a mile or two away on the other side of the great Penn Wood.

All that remains of Grandpapa's house is the garden cottage of rust-red brick and white sash windows, with its tiled well; the main house and large garden have been lost to modern building. Here, holly, blackthorn and cherry trees sheltered the wrens and robins of *Sing-Song*. 'The grounds were quite small and on the simplest scale,' Christina insisted later, with the realism of adulthood; 'but in those days *to me* they were vast, varied, worth exploring', offering 'inexhaustible delight'. There was an orchard, a garden pond, a pig-sty and a large spaniel named Delta. Was there also a peach tree against the southern wall, like the one in *Sing-Song*?

> A peach for brothers, one for each,
> A peach for you and a peach for me;
> But the biggest, rosiest, downiest peach
> For Grandmamma with her tea.

Beyond the garden lay fields and lanes:

> A frisky lamb
> And a frisky child
> Playing their pranks
> In a cowslip meadow:
> The sky all blue
> And the air all mild
> And the fields all sun
> And the lanes half shadow.

She remembered watching the cows come home for milking, and the boy who kept sheep out of the clover, and longer excursions across fields and stiles. 'I have an impression (for I will not relate my adventure more positively),' she recalled in adulthood, 'that in my youth, being at that time too young to appreciate such a rarity, in one of my country walks I found what I can only call a four-leaved trefoil. *Now* I would give something to recover that wonder: *then*, when I might have had it for the carrying, I left it.'

Later she used Holmer Green as the setting for a children's story whose heroine is 'a little girl who thought herself by no means such a little girl, and at any rate as wise as her elder brother, sister and nurse'. A picnic tea in the woods is planned, but bored with waiting little

Edith sets out alone, intending to start the fire, and is found weeping by the nursemaid:

'Oh my dear child, run indoors as fast as you can: for your mother, father, brother and sister are hunting up and down all over the house looking for you; and cook is half out of her wits because she cannot find the kettle.'

Was there a comparable incident in real life, when little Christina wandered off into Penn Wood?

Adjoining the house Grandpapa had a workshop, from where he shot wood pigeons. The boys enjoyed catching frogs, and on the dusty roadway by the tree-fringed village pond where the coaches passed she saw many a mangled frog, flattened by a waggon-wheel like a cartoon character, whom she later celebrated in facetious rhyme. In the garden, she was once frightened by a frog who jumped unexpectedly, and once she frightened a frog by poking it with her warm finger so that it covered its head with its hands, as if in fear.

She liked all creepy-crawlies – spiders, earwigs, slugs. A woman who was herself a child when Christina visited her family in Surrey wrote wonderingly of,

the way in which she would take up and hold in the hollow of her hand cold little frogs and clammy toads, or furry many-legged caterpillars, with a fearless love that we country children could never emulate.

But it was with a small creature at Holmer Green that Christina had her 'first vivid experience of death', when she found a dead mouse in the orchard, who moved her sympathy:

I took him up, buried him comfortably in a mossy bed, and bore the spot in mind.

It may have been a day or two afterwards that I returned, removed the moss coverlet and looked . . . a black insect emerged. I fled in horror, and for long years ensuing I never mentioned this ghastly adventure to anyone . . .

It was an intimation of corruption that she was able to disinter only years later, for the purpose of religious contemplation. At the time it was a secret horror, concealed in silence.

Holmer Green was the site of another memorable lesson:

To this hour I remember a certain wild strawberry growing on a hedge-row bank, watched day by day while it ripened by a little girl and by my yet younger self.

My elder instructed me not to pluck it prematurely, and I complied.

I do not know which of us was to have had it at last, or whether we were to have halved it. As it was, we watched, and as it turned out, we watched in vain: for a snail, or some such marauder, must have forestalled us at a happy moment. One fatal day we found it half-eaten and good for nothing.

Thus, then, we had watched in vain: or was it altogether in vain? On a very lowly level we had obeyed a counsel of prudence, and had practised self-restraint. . . .

For there was another side to the sunny childhood celebrated in *Sing-Song*, represented here by Maria, the always-instructive elder sister, imparting the approved counsels of prudence, obedience and self-restraint.

According to the moral and social values of the time, childish desire had to be curbed, with a strong sense of duty instilled in its place, inculcated with the assistance of exemplary lyrics such as those of Isaac Watts that Lewis Carroll was later to parody:

> How doth the little busy bee
>   Improve each shining hour,
> And gather honey all the day
>   From every opening flower!
>
> In works of labour, or of skill,
>   I would be busy too;
> For Satan finds some mischief still
>   For idle hands to do.

First published in 1715, Watts's collection enjoyed renewed popularity a century later, in keeping with the Evangelical tenor of the age. Infant idleness or misdemeanour were threatened with death and damnation. In 1827 *The Thief* was illustrated with a woodcut of a public hanging, and frequent reminders of judgement pulled no punches:

> 'Tis dangerous to provoke a God!
>   His pow'r and vengeance none can tell!
> One stroke of his Almighty rod
>   Shall send young sinners quick to hell.

There were no rods at Charlotte Street, however, where discipline was upheld by moral reproach:

> Seldom 'can't',
>   Seldom 'don't':

> Never 'shan't',
> Never 'won't'.

Occasionally, a slap was administered by their mother, and still sel-domer the threat of 'a nominal whipping', which was sufficient to provoke screams of terror. But moral reproach can be powerful: obedience, penitence and perseverance remained the keynotes of Christina's childhood training. Watts's *Good Resolution* was hers in sentiment, if not in scansion:

> I'll not willingly offend,
>   Nor be easily offended;
> What's amiss I'll strive to mend
>   And endure what can't be mended.

This was a lesson learnt at some cost by a passionate, wilful child given to tears and tantrums. 'To have a temper of her own was perhaps her right,' wrote William, 'to be amiable and affectionate along with it was certainly her endowment.' Christina herself felt that she spent many years subduing her spirit:

> Not to be first: how hard to learn
>   That lifelong lesson of the past;
> Line graven on line and stroke on stroke,
>   But, thank God, learned at last.

Other moral teaching came from the nursery poems of Ann and Jane Taylor, which laid particular stress on the love owed to one's mother and on the duty of compassion – a lesson Christina faithfully repeated in *Sing-Song*:

> There's snow on the fields
>   And cold in the cottage,
> While I sit in the chimney nook
>   Supping hot pottage.
>
> My clothes are soft and warm,
>   Fold upon fold,
> But I'm so sorry for the poor
>   Out in the cold.

Another book she may have known was *Pretty Lessons in Verse for Good Children*, written by Sara Coleridge, daughter of the poet, whose teaching was similar to Frances Rossetti's moral training against wilfulness, vanity, impatience. There was naturally nothing stolid about their mother, wrote William; her feelings were warm and her 'temper might have been less unruffled than it was, but for a lifelong practice of moderating self-control'. Self-control was, quintessentially, a feminine lesson: far more than their brothers, girls were taught to suppress desire and ambition, told that wishing and wanting were greedy and selfish, and schooled to internalise the values of denial and docility. Moral instruction was founded on aphorisms such as: Since we cannot have what we like, let us learn to like what we have. In a family magazine she encouraged to combat boredom and bickering, Mamma offered her own slightly softer version: 'If we cannot do all that we would like, let us do all that we can.'

With Christina's passionate nature, childish desire was difficult to conquer – perhaps especially so since Gabriel was seldom thwarted in his wishes. The wild strawberry incident was an emblem of the monitory check to her natural impulse, forbidding her to pick, insisting on patience. But postponement can also mean disappointment, and the deferred and finally lost fruit was an early intimation of what came to feel like a lifetime's experience of keen disappointment. 'Hope deferred' is a phrase Christina was to use repeatedly, like an insignia; it comes from chapter thirteen of the Book of Proverbs, where the 'soul of the sluggard' is damned and that of the diligent rewarded:

Hope deferred maketh the heart sick; but when the desire cometh, it is a tree of life.

Christina felt 'quite at home in the first clause' she noted later, acknowledging the bitterness that came from often experiencing the heartsickness of disappointment and seldom the pleasure of gratified desire, whether secular or spiritual.

Mamma, in catechetical mode, explained that the 'tree of life' in the second clause referred to the Cross, which satisfied 'the world's heartsick hope'. But while this 'explanation', promising compensation for present sorrows in the fulfilled desires of heaven, was a commonplace of religious instruction, it was also a lesson in suppressing personal grief in what would now be considered the vain hope of drawing its sting.

So the loving, lively security of infancy, where cuddles and hugs abounded and Christina was teased for her tantrums, was moderated by moral seriousness and a wholly middle-class sense of deferment. It was, too, explicitly religious in tone, for the elements of the Christian faith were deemed essential teaching from the earliest years. Among Mamma's favoured picture books was a volume of sacred prints, and she reported that at three and two years of age Maria and Gabriel knew most of the holy stories by heart. Moreover, she added with affectionate pride, she had told Maria that if she were good God would take her to heaven. Anxiously, Maria asked 'but will you be there?' and 'how shall I get up to the sky, will God come down to fetch me?'

Both heaven and an all-seeing God who would reward and punish like a supernatural parent were major features of contemporary religion. For her sixth birthday Christina received a bible inscribed by her father – a sign she had attained years of discretion. A year later the family acquired the version illustrated by Martin and Westall, with its vivid engravings. And among her first serious achievements, Christina learnt by heart the Lord's Prayer closely followed by the Catechism and the Creed with their questions and answers: 'Dost thou not think thou art bound to believe?' 'Yes, verily: and by God's help so I will . . . And I pray unto God to give me His grace, that I may continue in the same unto my life's end.'

2

Family Life

GRADUALLY AS CHRISTINA grew out of babyhood, she learnt more about the world and her own family history. From the start she had the sense of belonging to a family with special qualities, with high social and intellectual attainments. She was 'certainly born with a marked antipathy to anything which savoured of vulgarity,' wrote William, 'and with an instinctive disposition to "hold her head high" ', though without any taint of snobbery. She herself described her parents as 'clever and cultivated', and the family as close as well as high-minded, for 'neither nursery or schoolroom secluded their children from them; indeed our household was too small for any such separate system'. Naturally it centred on Mamma, whose own family filled the next circle of affection, with grandparents and especially aunts.

Born in 1800, Frances Mary Lavinia (Fanny to her family and *cara Francesca* to her husband) was the fourth of the seven surviving children of Anna Maria and Gaetano Polidori. So though English-born, she too was bi-lingual and half-Italian.

Grandpapa Polidori, of Tuscan origin, had been secretary to the poet and diplomat Count Alfieri and had witnessed the storming of the Bastille. He then settled in Britain as teacher and translator; among his works were an Italian-French-English dictionary and an edition of Milton. He was physically robust and 'of the most sturdy and independent character', with very blunt opinions. In the early years of his grandchildren's lives he retained rooms in London, but in 1835 he retired to Holmer Green, where his English wife, born Anna Maria Pierce, was already living, and where his large library led to the house being nicknamed 'Holmer College'. With her brothers and sisters, however, Frances had been born and raised in the parish of St James' Piccadilly.

Her eldest brother John studied medicine and was briefly famous as Byron's physician – he was present at the Villa Diodati on Lake Geneva when Byron composed *The Prisoner of Chillon* and Mary Shelley began *Frankenstein*, and himself wrote a Gothick tale called *The Vampyre*. In 1820 however, Dr Polidori killed himself with poison, owing to gambling debts. It was a 'death most painful' to his family, and the grandchildren were warned that Grandpapa could not bear to hear uncle John's name mentioned. Frances however nurtured warm memories of her favourite brother, whose suitably Byronic portrait hung in her marital home, though the stigma of suicide was a social liability in an age when insanity was believed to be hereditary.

John's brothers were hardly less of a disappointment to their father, for Philip was slow-witted and remained at home, while Henry (who later Anglicised his name to Polydore) pursued an unsuccessful legal career, spent largely as a conveyancing clerk. So, though the Rossetti children always showed respect to their uncles, they learnt early that the world did not. The aunts were another matter, for all four Polidori daughters – Frances, Margaret, Charlotte and Eliza Harriet – were educated to be governesses (their father's savings were earmarked to establish his sons in the professions) and endowed with a resourceful self-sufficiency. Frances took her first job at the age of sixteen, in Leatherhead, while Margaret spent thirteen years with a family in Gloucestershire, and Charlotte secured posts with the nobility travelling in Europe with her employers. To Eliza, the youngest, fell the duty of staying home to manage the household and nurse her mother, but she too was markedly independent in spirit.

Grandmamma, suffering from a nameless 'internal complaint', seldom left her bed; the grandchildren recalled being taken up to see her, as into a presence chamber. She was dignified and austere, an old-fashioned High Tory and earnest Anglican, in which faith her daughters were raised. The sons followed their father's religion, which he did not practise, and Henry became a mindful, meticulous Catholic. Grandmamma's family was genteel, with a great-uncle in the Indian Army and an unmarried great-aunt, known to the Rossetti children as 'Granny Pierce', who lived in comfort in London; said to be the Earl of Yarborough's secret wife, she had presumably been his mistress. Beyond these relatives lay a further realm, of Mamma's English cousins, whom the children knew mainly by repute. They included Mrs Bray, a clergyman's wife in Devon, who had some success as an author.

As a young governess Frances Polidori taught French and Italian in addition to religion and the three Rs. She lacked music (her father disapproved of singing as well as dancing) and according to her son had no talent for domestic arts such as dressmaking, though like all women she was competent in plain sewing. The ambiguous social position of a governess was not always awkward: many middle-class girls without money became governesses in order to earn their keep and to mix with superior company, where they might attract an eligible spouse; if not, teaching provided a respectable and secure career. Frances's marriage prospects arose in 1825, when she caught the attention of her employer's brother, Colonel Macgregor, who would have proposed – according to Frances – had she not, at the end of the year, accepted an offer from Gabriele Rossetti.

This was a far more romantic match. Seventeen years her senior, Gabriele was a poet and political exile, who had fled from the kingdom of Naples with a price on his head. In tune with her fraternal association with Lord Byron (who had died the year before in the cause of Greek liberty) Frances's idealism chimed with that which had driven Signor Rossetti into exile. She had an Italian heritage, admired eminence of mind, and looked more favourably on a talented albeit penniless poet than a military man, however advantageous the latter might seem in the eyes of the world. 'I always had a passion for intellect,' she confessed later, 'and my wish was that my husband should be distinguished for intellect, and my children too.'

She was nearly twenty-six and Gabriele forty-three when they married in April 1826. Their first child, Maria Francesca, was born on 17 February 1827, and the others followed at fifteen month intervals: Gabriel Charles Dante on 12 May 1828; William Michael on 25 September 1829; and Christina Georgina on 5 December 1830.

Years afterwards, Christina read a letter from her father announcing her arrival to the aunts:

You now have another niece, born at the due time, last Sunday night, at ten minutes past three. Her mother suffered little, and now lies nursing her dear pledge who, to judge by her appetite, could not be doing better. She is considered to be the very picture of Maria, but more beautiful. She is fairer, and looks with that round face of hers, like a little moon risen at the full. All the rest of the family is well.

'How could my dear Father give such a report?' wrote Christina indignantly in the margin. 'Dearest Mamma had a fearful time with me.' Yet perhaps Gabriele was not intentionally misleading: both mother and child had escaped the very real dangers that frequently attended childbirth. It may be significant, however, that Christina believed her birth to have been a painful one: in later life she always showed a protective tenderness towards her mother.

All four children were baptised into the Church of England, in the parish of their birth, All Souls, Langham Place. The godmothers of baby Christina Georgina (for whom she was named) were Lady Dudley Stuart, formerly Princess Christina Bonaparte, niece of the great Napoleon, whose acquaintance Gabriele had recently made, and Georgina Macgregor, Frances's former pupil. What benefits were intended to flow from such sponsors is unknown; neither seems to have featured in their goddaughter's later life, though one is thought to have given as christening gift a coral necklace she always treasured.

'Four children only Heaven conceded me in the four opening matrimonial years,' recorded Gabriele, and one can only speculate as to why there were no more. Perhaps, with four infants under five and an income that allowed for only a single servant, Frances decided that prudence commended a halt to child-bearing. (As it was, the doctor and his wife at Holmer Green offered to adopt William, evidently regarding the Rossettis as overburdened.) Perhaps she was advised that further births would affect her health; this was a contemporary medical concern. Whether the end of child-bearing was effected by any form of contraception or by simple abstinence cannot now be known, but it is possible that this marked the end of sexual relations. Gabriele's regret at having no more children suggests it was not his choice.

But his love for Frances showed no diminution. 'I needn't ask you to look after the children,' he wrote to Holmer Green in 1832, 'I know you too well:

I doubt whether there lives a better mother than you; and a wife more amiable and affectionate has yet to be born. And so your husband idolizes you and his sincerest love increases with years, and he considers himself fortunate in possessing so rare a woman.

He was effusively uxorious. 'I love above all your lovely soul, and ten years of possession and scrutiny have only shown me its worth more clearly,' he wrote in 1836. 'The morning you left, I felt as if my heart was torn from my bosom.' Such flowery expressions were less typically English than Italian, the language they were written in, and they also contain more than a hint (in the word 'possession') of traditional masculine values. Frances did not dispute these and, for all her own reserve, took pleasure in her demonstrative husband; late in life she nostalgically regretted the loss of his conjugal greeting: 'Cara Francesca moglie mia'. Gabriele was appreciative, too, of his wife's genius in subduing chaos. 'At the touch of her industrious hand, order ever flourishes around me,' he wrote.

Frances was not especially good with babies – thirty years later a young couple, seeking her advice for their sick infant, were surprised that a mother of four could only refer them to a doctor – but undertook the whole of her children's earliest education. Under her guidance they learned to read, write and cipher, to know the Bible and begin French through the familiar medium of L'ami des enfants. Her sisters assisted: when William was slow in reading, aunt Margaret intervened, with swift success. Having now given up governessing, Margaret was always the most present of all the aunts.

Above all, Frances set an example of correct conduct. She was, in William's words, 'the most womanly of women', full of commonsense and modesty, with no ambitions beyond home, church and family.

'Day and night she attended to the household – doing needlework, teaching her girls, keeping things in order, etc.' In that 'etc' her self-effacement is expressed: evidently William could remember little more than his mother's constant presence in the house. 'No butcher nor baker nor candlestick maker ever had a claim upon us for a sixpence unpaid,' he added in a remark infused with nursery memories to illustrate her prudent housekeeping. Her only recreation was reading; she never went out in the evening, took no interest in fashion but a little in politics, inclining to Liberal views, and was 'unpretentiously religious'. In the children's earliest years she took them to Holy Trinity Church, Marylebone Road, until bullied by the rector 'on some flimsy pretext of pew rent' (which reserved the best seats in church for the well-to-do); she then removed her family to St Katherine's Chapel, Regents Park, an independent foundation established by Queen Matilda in the twelfth century and exempt from episcopal control. Her husband, like her father a nominal Catholic, did not attend.

Anything savouring of self-regard was to be avoided as inimical to the virtue of a Christian gentlewoman. Yet her admitted desire for intellectual excellence in husband and children indicates that Frances's own desires were exchanged for ambition on their behalf. Disappointed in many things – and Christina on her own deathbed told William that she did not think their mother's life could be called happy – she took great satisfaction in her children's achievements, and was always proud to see their names in print. Such sublimated hopes are sometimes hard to live up to; all four children felt a deep need to repay their mother's affection, as if in compensation for her own undeveloped talents.

In *Sing-Song* Christina depicted maternal care as a fat white hen sheltering her chicks. She also celebrated the full domestic group:

> Mother shake the cherry-tree,
>   Susan catch a cherry;
> Oh, how funny that will be,
>   Let's be merry!
>
> One for brother, one for sister,
>   Two for mother more,
> Six for father, hot and tired,
>   Knocking at the door.

and Christina's sight of her father must often have been of his home-coming thus at the end of the day. 'In all my earlier years,' wrote

William, 'I used frequently to see my father come home in the dusk rather fagged with his round of teaching.' After dinner, in late afternoon, he would lie flat on the hearthrug and sleep for an hour or two, snoring vigorously – as, one supposes, a sort of delayed siesta. Beside him, the cat warmed her furry front, making a Y with her paws. There was always a blazing fire in the parlour: Papa never adapted to British temperatures.

Born in Vasto in the Abruzzi region in the kingdom of Naples, Gabriele had prospered through adaptability. His first patron, the local *marchese*, took him to Naples for education and a career in court service. After Ferdinand I was deposed by the Bonapartes, Rossetti lived by his wits, writing for the operatic theatre, working in the museum of antiquities, and establishing himself as poet-orator, composing extempore on public occasions. It is thought he had a wife or at least a woman in Naples, and also a child who died young, but this was not acknowledged in England. On the restoration of Ferdinand in 1815, he applied without success to become Professor of Eloquence, a failure which fuelled a certain resentment allied to ardent but essentially simple political sympathies. These led him into the ranks of the Carbonari, a quasi-revolutionary group which in 1820 took up arms demanding the return of constitutional government, in which uprising Rossetti became the voice of the people, renowned for patriotic odes on freedom and justice. With support from the Papacy, Ferdinand used Austrian troops to defeat the constitutionalists and in March 1821 Gabriele went into hiding. Carbonarism was made a capital offence and, being closely linked to freemasonry, was excommunicated. Rescued by the British admiral Sir Graham Moore, whose wife admired his odes, Rossetti was smuggled aboard ship dressed in naval uniform; years later his children were regularly regaled with the tale of how King Ferdinand gnashed his teeth in rage, swearing to capture and execute Papa. He found sanctuary in Malta, under the patronage of retired diplomat John Hookham Frere, and in 1824 was conveyed for greater safety to Britain, at a time when Italian nationalist exiles were scattered in clusters throughout Europe. Here, in his forties, he had perforce to adopt a new career, there being no equivalent of the *improvisatore* in Britain, even had he been fluent in English. In any case he soon learnt that in London public performing did not add to social status: 'in the long run a man who does it for pay loses dignity,' he gravely informed Lady Moore.

He tried at first to find creative work, composing *libretti* for Italian opera, but teaching quickly became his main resource. Whereas in Naples his pupils had been aspiring *improvisatori*, in London they were well-to-do ladies and gentlemen, acquiring Italian as an accomplishment. Soon Gabriele identified scholarship as the better path of advancement, explaining at the time of his marriage – a somewhat imprudent step for a penniless immigrant, but by no means a foolish one – that a more regular system of life was necessary 'in order to give proper attention to my studies'.

He embarked on the study of Dante, partly in honour of Polidori's Tuscan inheritance and partly because Dante was a special interest of his chief patron Charles Lyell, father of the celebrated geologist, who provided financial support for his first work, a commentary on the *Inferno*, published by subscription in 1825/6 – both Gaetano and Frances were listed as subscribers – as part of a projected study of the whole *Divina Commedia*. This, Gabriele believed, would bring fame and fortune – or at least a respectable reputation, for the works of Dante were relatively unknown in Britain. By 1828 he was so far immersed in the subject that his first-born son received Dante as his third baptismal name.

Shortly after Christina's birth, Gabriele obtained the chair of Italian at Kings College London, which brought social and intellectual status, and gratified his wife's desire for excellence. It brought no salary, however, for professors were paid a proportion of students' fees, and in Italian there were never many students. Hence the continuing need for peripatetic language teaching, which indeed the professorship was designed to encourage, prospective pupils preferring an eminent instructor. In this respect Professor Rossetti was well regarded, with wealthy and well-connected friends. He worked hard, at both teaching and research, taking full financial responsibility for the household. As *Sing-Song* explains:

> What does the bee do?
>   Bring home honey.
> What does Father do?
>   Bring home money.
> And what does Mother do?
>   Lay out the money.
> And what does baby do?
>   Eat up the honey.

According to both English and Italian custom, the spheres of husband and wife were complementary but separate: it was Father's duty to bring home money and Mother's to lay it out on honey and other necessities. But as it emerged, Gabriele and Frances differed in their attitudes to spending. Frances was careful, in the cautious middle-class mode of the time, while her husband was typically impulsive.

Passing a closing-down sale in Oxford Street, he once bought a dozen pairs of stockings and some gloves for his wife as well as socks and a silk handkerchief for himself. 'I hope on the whole you won't be displeased,' he wrote, pride mixed with misgiving.

He was physically affectionate and unlike the cold, distant paterfamilias of Victorian legend, was happy to allow the four children 'to litter and rollick about the room while he plodded through some laborious matter of literary composition' as William recalled – though always careful to observe Italian superstition and never step over them as they played, lest ill luck befall. And in marked contrast to the style favoured by many English fathers, he was apt to be emotional where the family was concerned. 'Every word you wrote pierced me like a dagger,' he replied to news of childish ailments from Holmer Green. 'My sweetest Gabriel, then, is so ill!' Christina was teething and had bumped her forehead: 'Oh, my poor children! ... Who knows but what the figs I sent may have done them harm!' Then he added more soberly, to himself as much as Frances: 'but take heart, my wife, it may turn out to be nothing serious.'

He was generous too, enjoying the way his youngsters clustered round expectantly on his arrival home, eager for the trifles he brought, though his readiness to buy lollipops did not please Mamma. He also bought toys and strawberries and other fruits in season, perhaps nostalgic for Neapolitan abundance. And whenever Frances was summoned to Holmer Green, owing to Grandmamma's ailments, the children were accustomed to being left in Papa's indulgent care. On one such occasion Granny Pierce called; she gave each child a bright shilling and confirmed that they were not fretting. Two years later, when Frances was again away, Gabriele noted that nevertheless the children were calculating the days till her return, the most steady reckoner being five-year-old Christina:

> This morning, barely out of bed, she came in great glee into the room where I was working, and the first words she spoke were: 'not counting today, only three days remain'.

He had recently bought Christina a little chest of drawers – perhaps a belated birthday present, or to match one Maria had received from Grandpapa. It had four drawers and a key with which, one imagines, she delighted to lock treasures away from prying eyes and fingers; as youngest she was doubtless taunted by 'secrets' the others refused to reveal, and equally often teased into disclosing her own.

Generally speaking, all four were treated equally. Once, after seeing Mamma off on the coach, Papa took the two older children to a café, mindful to also buy cakes for William and Christina at home. 'Not one of us ever felt any sense of unfairness in family life,' William reported confidently, adding however that 'dazzling' Gabriel was their father's favourite, and he their mother's. Maria and Christina were 'evenly balanced, by contrasting qualities' – Maria diligent and eager, Christina clamorous, spirited, pretty. In Papa's letters and conversation each child had a customary epithet: *carissima* (dearest) Maria, *ingegnoso* (clever) Gabriel, *saggio* (wise) William and *vivace* (lively) Christina.

But poor Maria understood early that she was no beauty, which may have aggravated the jealous streak William so clearly recalled. When she was rising seven Granny Pierce remarked hopefully that her nose was looking smaller, and Gabriele commented that from 'the mixture of amazement and satisfaction she betrayed, I judged how hideous she must have thought the poor child before'. Everyone knew Christina was prettier, whispered Maria on hearing a family friend praise the *bellezza perfetta* (perfect beauty) of her own *fisonomia tutta Italiana* (wholly Italian features). At an early age Maria was nicknamed Moony, from the roundness of her face. In compensation, Papa praised her intellectual abilities, addressing his first-born (*primogenita*) in verse as 'daughter of Clio', the conventional figure for the muse of history and scholarship. At other times, he called her a youthful Sappho, after the first female poet, and as with her namesake some fragments survive. *Epitaph on a Thrush* is dated 9 July 1837, when Maria was ten, and seems to have been written at Holmer Green:

> O listen, listen to my lay
> About a thrush that died today.
> This little Bird with snails was fed
> And straw composed its humble bed.

A memory of this, seasonally-transposed, informs one of *Sing-Song's* more melancholy rhymes:

> Dead in the cold, a song-singing thrush,
> Dead at the foot of a snow-berry bush –
> Weave him a coffin of rush,
> Dig him a grave where the soft mosses grow,
> Raise him a tombstone of snow.

Perhaps this was the same summer that Christina laid her dead mouse to rest in his mossy bed. Certainly she always associated poetry with both Holmer Green and death.

There was hardly a time when the children did not know their father himself was a poet. For the two girls, he composed a short ode of lyrical sweetness:

Cristina e Maria	Christina and Maria
Mie care figliuole	My dear daughters
Son fresche viole	Are fresh violets
Dischiusse all'albor.	Opened at dawn.
Son rose nudrite	They are roses nurtured
Dall'aure novelle	By the earliest breezes,
Son tortore belle	Lovely turtle-doves
Nel nido d'amor.	In the nest of Love.

As rhetorician and librettist, the histrionic style came naturally. With a fine voice, he was apt to break into song and splendid declamation, quoting from Italian authors or his own verses with a gusto that warmed the children's early years.

So, unlike Mamma, Papa was certainly not modest or self-effacing. Somewhat to William's later embarrassment, he was inordinately 'fond of name and fame', with a distinct tendency to self-glorification. Yet the flamboyance was moderated with humour and kindness – his natural temper was 'lively and ardent, not without excitability, yet essentially placid,' wrote William. He was seldom angry with the children, and never cruel or cold. But though none of the four was ever afraid of Papa, his authority was nevertheless considerable, and from an early age they learnt to do their best to please him. Indeed, the concomitant of paternal indulgence was loving obedience to his wishes: no whining or disrespect was permitted. Despite the warmth, he exuded 'a perceptible tone of *patria potestas*', reflecting the patriarchal status commonly accorded the male head of the household in both Italian and British society. He had the authority, too, of ancestry and age, bringing from Naples a reputed family motto: *frangas non flectas* (break not bend) with its intimations of antiquity, and himself belonged to an older generation: before Christina was three years old, her father was over fifty.

Family life thus combined affection and security. Fatherly exuberance was balanced by maternal steadiness, and her firmness softened by his generosity. And if Christina's 'baby' status made her fight even harder for her rightful share of the cakes, she had the advantage in that the burden of setting an example rested elsewhere. Without sentimentality, her childhood can be judged exceptionally happy and companionable.

From birth the children were accustomed to eminent callers – members of the Bonaparte entourage, Italian counts and generals and writers, one of whom gave Christina a locket containing a picture of the Virgin. 'It seems hardly an exaggeration to say that every Italian staying or passing through London, of a liberal mode of political opinion, sought out my father,' recalled William later, listing fifty such exiles by name. On one occasion, Papa joked, three young compatriots had sought him out as if he were a holy relic, but this was an index of his reputation – as was the invitation from the Turkish ambassador to orate at a glittering social event, in Neapolitan style.

At the end of 1835, when Christina was just five, the family moved across the road to a slightly larger house at no. 50 Charlotte Street. Every evening visitors called to exchange political news in the small parlour amid lively debate and vainglorious appeals to the heroic past. The enemies, cursed with rhetorical vigour, were the King of Naples, the King of France *Luigi Filippo*, the Pope and above all, Metternich and the Austrians, whose forces occupied large parts of Italy. In old age William recreated in his mind's eye the familiar sight:

> My father and three or four foreigners engaged in animated talk on the affairs of Europe, from the point of patriotic aspiration, and hope long deferred ... with frequent and fervent recitations of poetry ...
>
> My mother quiet but interested, and sometimes taking her mild womanly part in the conversation; and we four children – Maria more especially, with her dark Italian countenance and rapt eyes – drinking it all in as a sort of necessary atmosphere of the daily life, yet with our own little interests and occupations as well – reading, colouring prints, looking into illustrated books, nursing a cat, or whatever.

In keeping with Italian custom, the Rossetti children were not shooed upstairs but expected to greet visitors, the girls bobbing a curtsey and no doubt having their cheeks squeezed. In such a context, the British style of icy politeness, lest others 'presume', was unknown; William remembered chiefly warmth and volubility among his father's friends, qualified only by envy, intrigue and self-applause. To the youngsters, the most exciting exile was one Sangiovanni, who had been captain of a band hunting down brigands and was reputed to have killed a man in a knife-fight.

Among the callers there were also 'numerous relays of tatterdemalions' who came for handouts. Callers offering a Masonic handshake were immediately relieved, while in the street Papa would speak to pedlars and organ-grinders, asking what region they came from, and offering hospitality. He could nevertheless be brisk as to their merits, saying that any such caller was either *un cercatore* (a beggar) or *un seccatore* (a bore). Mamma made gifts of food or clothing to exile families in need, sometimes repaid in kind. Signor Parodi gave dancing lessons to Maria and Christina (an accomplishment they seldom had occasion to use) while Signor Pistrucci painted portraits of all four. Christina's shows nothing of her lively, skittish nature, being a conventional rendering of a pretty child, in the chocolate-box manner of the time, though its steady, wide-eyed gaze may reflect her open, mettlesome character. Grandpapa averred that she would be the most spirited of them all.

At home Mamma's choice of books for her children included two by Mrs Hofland significantly titled *The Son of a Genius* and *The Daughter of a Genius*, indirectly reflecting her estimate of their father. In later life, Christina was to demur in mock horror when her nephew was over-praised, saying there had already been enough geniuses in the family. She herself felt always outdone by the others, later describing herself as the family dunce. 'I may pretty well say that from first to last I was a dead weight on the hands of those who would fain have taught me,' she insisted, claiming to have picked up more than she learnt. Indeed, though she did not neglect her lessons, she lacked application and her education was limited, if not desultory, with a thorough grounding in reading, French and religion, but little serious study and no under-standing of maths or science. William described her as 'naturally rather indolent' and disinclined to stick to any occupation. To their mother's regret, though surely not surprise, neither she nor Maria manifested any musical ability whatsoever: years later, Christina hailed such talent in her niece, trusting it would compensate Mamma for her own unmusical daughters. With literature, however, Mamma's passion for poetry and prose surely shaped her children's predilec-tions. From the start of her career as governess, she had kept a Com-monplace Book, into which striking and edifying passages were entered, and to which the children were in time encouraged to con-tribute. As well as stanzas by her husband, her brother and Byron, this held extracts from Crabbe, Southey, Paley's *Natural Theology* and a summary of Magna Carta. In 1838 Maria copied out a poem 'To a Dying Infant' from *Blackwoods' Magazine*, and some months later Wil-liam added a passage from *Oliver Twist*. The tales of Maria Edgeworth were a maternal standby – fictions which, in the author's words, 'shall display examples of virtue, without initiating the young reader into the ways of vice', and though William remembered disliking these, Christina returned to them with pleasure in middle life.

She claimed to read 'only what hit her fancy': in William Hone's *Everyday Book* she first met Keats' *Eve of St Agnes*, and Shelley's *Skylark* was an early favourite. However, Perrault's *Fairy Tales* were a family passion – Cinderella, the Sleeping Beauty and especially Bluebeard – as were the inexhaustible *Arabian Nights*, in imitation of which Chris-tina composed her earliest remembered story, narrated aloud, about a dervish called Hassan.

In daily life, stories were accompanied by chores. 'Come sit round me, my dear little girls, and I will tell you a story,' begins the storytelling aunt in Christina's own collection of tales, dedicated to Frances 'in grateful remembrance of the stories with which she used to entertain her children':

> Each of you bring her sewing, and let Ella take pencils and colour-box and try to finish some one drawing of the many she has begun. What Maude! pouting over that nice clean white stocking because it wants a darn? Put away your pout and pull out your needle, my dear; for pouts make a sad beginning to my story . . . Silence! Attention! All eyes on occupations . . .

All too clearly, when she was the same age as her fictional listeners, Christina regarded sewing as a baleful duty, for the aunt's stories are punctuated by commands: 'Jane and Laura, don't *quite* forget the pocket-handkerchiefs you sat down to hem . . . Yes, Maude, that darn will do: now your task is ended, but if I were you I would help Clara with hers.'

In these tales, her childhood self was re-created in the figure of Flora, the plump, pink-cheeked, youngest member of a perfect storybook family, who wakes to happiness on her birthday – for it is sheer pleasure 'to be eight years old when last night one was merely seven, [and] to hope for birthday presents without any doubt of receiving some.' Presents are followed by a party, but the day's bliss is ruined by squabbling:

> Flora accused Alfred of tripping her up, Richard bawled that George broke away when fairly caught, Anne when held tight muttered that Susan could see in spite of bandaged eyes . . .

Things get worse: the youngsters turn into monsters, tormenting Flora and preventing her from tasting the birthday tea, piled high with sweets and fruits. In the end, she is imprisoned in a glass house as the others begin throwing stones – only to wake and find the hateful party was after all a nightmare, reflecting the day's discord. She is duly chastened, with 'a conscious look in her little face', and before long nestles up close, to whisper that she is sorry to have been so cross. The narrator's moral lesson is surely that of Frances Rossetti, gently rebuking a child

> who, with dear friends and playmates and pretty presents, yet scarcely knew how to bear a few trifling disappointments, or how to be obliging and good-humoured under slight annoyances.

Christina later noted that it was better to have brothers and sisters than to be an only child. William conjured a picture of four youngsters seldom apart and seldom in the company of others, but they mixed frequently at tea parties and social visits with children of their own age. 'I knew a Serena once,' comments the storytelling narrator in relation to one of Flora's young friends who kisses and gushes with effusive affection, adding: 'She was not at all like this Serena, I am happy to say.' All her life Christina herself disliked gush, and would seem to have been a child who found intimate, effusive friendship hard to handle, preferring the rough and tumble of family life.

Later, in relation to her own nieces and nephew, Christina commented ruefully on the lot of females to play second fiddle, and eight-year-old Flora is well aware of gender difference. In her nightmare party, the characters have names and attributes according to sex, the boys being endowed with aggressive masculine qualities such as their author observed, or remembered. In *Hunt the Pincushion*, poor Flora is the quarry, attacked from all sides, by Quills, Angles and Hooks. In *Self Help*, the boys are 'the players, the girls the played' – an apt though glancing definition of gender disparity and tacit recognition that however egalitarian the ideal home, boys and girls were differently placed in the world. And in a second tale that reintroduces the same hateful children there is also a monster Mouth-Boy, with no eyes but a gaping, wheedling mouth, who demands the heroine's chocolate – a vivid image of maleness. Reading such stories, one cannot doubt that as she grew older Christina had a less idyllic image of the world, where a small girl might be a victim instead of an adored daughter – or rather that she might be both, anger and fear alternating with presents and pleasure as she learnt to adjust to life's complexities.

Steadily her experience widened. She recalled the excitement of her first rail journey – then itself a novelty – down to Greenwich, and back by river steamer. They were taken to the British Museum, and to Madame Tussauds, where she was put out of countenance by the waxworks, blushing at her own boldness, for well-brought-up children were taught never to stare. There were also visits to the Italian opera, with complimentary tickets for *il professore* and his family, recalled in one of Christina's later stories describing a *diva* 'pouring forth her soul in passion' as she weaves lilies into a garland, and the storm of applause that greets her curtain call.

The first major change in family life came in autumn 1836 when the boys started at a local day school, to learn Latin, which was beyond their mother's competence. This was in preparation for Kings College School, junior department of Papa's college, which they entered together in late summer 1837. The main emphasis, as at other schools for boys of the middle ranks, was on maths and the classics – but there was another branch of learning too, for 'there is always some nasty-

thinking boy to egg-on his juniors upon a path of unsavouriness,'
noted William primly, recalling his introduction to the rude bits of the
Bible. This was reported at home, where nothing that was not high-
minded was ever heard, and after Papa spoke to the principal the
offending boy was admonished. But it was a symptom: henceforth
Gabriel and William were in contact with a coarser world.

At ten years old, the bright, diligent Maria might also have been
regarded as having reached an educational level beyond their
mother's capacity. But she, of course, was not destined for a school
career, where she would have shone. Girls did not learn Latin or
Greek, or algebra, or anything approaching science, so she knew
nothing of the subjects her brothers were now studying. Her response
was to join and, if possible, beat them, using their textbooks. By 1839,
Papa reported to Lyell, the boys were doing well but Maria was doing
better; 'gifted by nature with a quite uncommon intelligence', she had
set herself to the study of Greek, with astonishing progress. She herself, at Holmer Green with their mother, feared she was slipping
behind, until William wrote to assure they had not yet started on
Greek verbs but were still doing nouns.

To assist, Grandpapa read Greek legends with her in Italian and, aided
by the fact that Polidori was ultimately a Greek name (and Polydorus
one of the sons of Priam) Maria's earlier enthusiasm for Napoleon was
replaced with a passion for all things Homeric. Unlike her brothers, to
whom the language was a chore and the legends of less interest than
their home-made tales of bandits and brigands, she conceived a lifelong passion for the heroes of *The Iliad*, which in childhood was far
stronger than religion, and still active twenty-five years later when
she breathlessly recounted her admiration for the 'magnificent passage' describing Achilles 'shining and shouting from the ramparts'.
He was her hero and Book 17 the most precious, she asserted: 'really
the more I think about it the more I warm to these heroes . . .'

Gabriel obliged her classical fervour by drawing a sequence of warriors, but not everyone approved. In 1839, visiting the home of Papa's
friend Swynfen Jervis MP, Maria recognised the classical figures in a
print and proudly declared that she had read the story several times,
thereby alarming their hostess, who felt that detailed knowledge of
Greek legends was indelicate in a young girl. But Papa disagreed.
'Bravo! bravo!' he replied to the news that she was now reading
Euripides in translation. 'Everybody is afraid that too much application may injure her heath, but I have no such fear, for when voluntary
application produces so much pleasure it cannot do any harm; rather,
it becomes food for the mind, which in turn does the body good.'

This sensible atttude was against the received wisdom of the time,
which held that mental exertion was harmful to females, especially in

adolescence – a theory that effectively infantilised girls, restricting them to juvenile educational levels when their brothers were being urged to serious study. According to the 1840 edition of Buchan's *Domestic Medicine*, issued for family use, intense thinking was so generally destructive to health that 'few instances can be produced of studious persons who are strong and healthy', and it was considered additionally injurious to the already weaker female physiology. Strength was needed either for study or for child-bearing: girls' bodies would be fatally enfeebled by too much schooling.

Some few years earlier, Elizabeth Barrett, another talented girl, lost Latin and Greek lessons when her brother went away to school, and without proper lessons Maria's classical studies could not progress far. More seriously, she gave up competing; by the time she reached her mid-teens, her desire for achievement was tamed, as she 'settled down into religion' and good works. Aware of her ability, Gabriel never ceased to regret this decline into devotion.

Christina's favourite hero was not Achilles but Ajax, who was surpassed in each feat of arms by his companions and with whom she shared a secret sympathy at being the perpetual secondranker. 'I certainly for one,' she wrote later, 'care more now for Ajax than for those who at some point excelled him.' She had learnt another important, if contradictory lesson: though Mamma urged everyone to excellence, girls were not expected to surpass. Ironically, the boys did not much like school, always preferring their own imaginative games based on the Waverley Novels, a bowdlerised Shakespeare – source of much energetic acting – stirring *Stories from English History* about Druids burning their victims in wicker cages, and illustrated forerunners of the comic book called *Tales of Chivalry* and *Legends of Terror*. Christina's second recorded story, for an ambitious family tetralogy of romantic tales, was 'Retribution', about a Crusader knight. In time, the Gothick tales by Ann Radcliffe, *The Mysteries of Udolpho* and *The Italian* became her own favourite reading. In this British literature, it may be noted, Italy, their ancestral land, featured as a place of wild and bloodthirsty adventure – a romantic setting for improbable action – where the protagonists were often young women. As Gabriel grew older, he shared with the others the comparable delights of Edgar Allan Poe and Charles Robert Maturin.

During this period, too, the children expanded their juvenile repertoire of card games, and each appropriated a suit. Gabriel took the favourite hearts, Christina the sharp, flame-like diamonds, William the solid clubs, while Maria demonstrated her maturity by adopting the despised spades – a figuration which was echoed later in life, as Christina explained:

My dear sister used to say that *she* had the good sense, William the good nature, Gabriel the good heart and I the bad temper, of our beloved father and mother.

This memory – intentionally self-deprecating – was perhaps unintentionally revealing, for no other reminiscence records the short fuse which was one aspect of Papa's volatile temperament. This perceived affinity, however, made the fiery nature of the red diamonds that Christina claimed for her own an appropriate emblem for her juvenile self. A few years later, when phrenology was all the rage, Christina's bumps were interpreted as indicative of 'pugnacity', a diagnosis hailed with teasing delight by her siblings, who knew the intensity of her tantrums.

3

First Poems

COUNTRY HOLIDAYS CAME to an end in autumn 1839, when Grandpapa moved his family back to London, taking a house in Park Village East on the northern corner of Regents Park, where Regency villas meet Camden Town. It was quarter of an hour from Charlotte Street: William recalled the regular walk up past the Nash terraces, which their mother characteristically used for instruction in the architectural orders. In picturesque contrast, Park Village is semi-Gothick stucco. Maria, displaying her classical learning, wanted to call the house 'Myrtle Cottage' in allusion to the legend that the Trojan Polydorus was turned into a myrtle tree. It housed their grandparents, Uncle Philip and Aunts Eliza and Margaret. Aunt Charlotte worked for the Marchioness of Bath, and came home only for holidays.

In Christina's stories for children her small heroines begin to learn the lessons of life at the age of eight, and looking back on her own childhood, she recalled how from the same age she had been 'pent up in London' until she was 'a great girl' of fourteen. Her imprisonment metaphor is telling as well as Keatsian, for in general Christina did not consider herself a reluctant Londoner, later claiming kinship with those 'hundreds and thousands' of cityfolk who rarely escaped from the metropolis. 'As we are bred, so we live,' she said; 'what is more, I am fairly sure that I am in the place that suits me best.' Yet now she felt immured, the more so perhaps because she was increasingly conscious of the limitations imposed on girls. Hitherto content with the security of home and small excursions *en famille*, she now acquired a vague sense of constraint and narrowed opportunities.

The change, however, meant that from this date Grandpapa played a larger role in the girls' lives, giving Maria educational guidance and instructing both sisters in Italian. His large library was alluring too, though equally fascinating was the servant Mrs Catchpole, whose husband was said to have been murdered by his workmates. Also employed was an Italian compositor who cooked snails, and operated a printing press, enabling Gaetano to encourage his grandchildren's literary ambitions.

'Maria's first "book" was quite a *booklet*, a translation of an Ode on the death of Lady Gwendalina Talbot,' as Christina later told an inquiring bibliophile, adding with customary precision that the achievement (a funeral tribute to the exemplary benevolence of Prince

Borghese's English-born wife) was mainly their mother's work.
Gabriel's first effort was *Sir Hugh the Heron*, a ballad based on the
Legends of Terror, which he later said was 'absurd trash' showing
'absolutely no promise at all – less than should exist even at twelve'.
It was followed by Maria's *The Rivulets: A Dream not all a dream*, an
allegory about four children named Love, Sloth, Conceit and Selfishness, who are variously rewarded, corrected and condemned. There
are no prizes for recognising the least desirable qualities in Mamma's
moral scheme.

Christina's earliest poem was written when she was eleven, copied
out in a large copperplate hand on pencilled lines that were then
erased, and given to Mamma on 27 April 1842, with a posy:

> *To my Mother on her Birthday*
> Today's your natal day
>   Sweet flowers I bring;
> Mother accept I pray,
>   My offering.
>
> And may you happy live,
>   And long us bless
> Receiving as you give
>   Great happiness.

As a birthday gift, it far surpassed more commonplace offerings of
laboriously stitched needlework. Much later, on her mother's eightieth
birthday, Christina told her own niece that if she had poetic talent, she
would find that 'almost if not quite its brightest point is that it kindles
a light of pleasure in your Mother's eyes', and this was to prove a
lifelong motivation. No doubt the birthday gift was also proudly
shown to visitors, giving the author her first taste of the praise that
could be won from verse. Some time later the lines were copied out by
Mamma into a tiny notebook, with a note:

> NB. These verses are truly and literally by my little daughter, who scru-
> pulously rejected all assistance in her rhyming efforts, under the impres-
> sion that in that case they would not really be her own. The first was
> written when she was eleven.

This conjures a vivid picture of Christina jealously guarding her compositions, so that no one else could interfere. Now the boys were at
school, Maria's influence was inescapable; as Gabriel later remarked,
'Maria was a born leader, Christina a born apostle', and she had need
of something 'really her own'.

Her second poem, also written in 1842, reflected Mamma's earliest teaching and prefigured a major theme:

> What is heaven? 'tis a country
>   Far away from mortal ken;
> 'Tis a land, where by God's bounty,
>   After death live righteous men.
>
> That that blest land I may enter,
>   Is my humble, earnest cry;
> Lord! Admit me to Thy presence,
>   Lord, admit me, or I die.

Like the birthday verse, this is bookish in diction, and both pieces are the work of a 'good child', voicing approved pieties. *To my Mother* has a certain charm, though the controlling correctness nearly cancels out the simple feeling, while *Heaven* gains, just a little, from its ingenuous pastiche of Protestant hymn-making.

Not copied into the notebook was an earlier effort, later regarded by William as Christina's second real poem and produced in response to the boys' homework assignment to celebrate British victory in the 1842 Opium War. Hearing them grumble, Christina took up the patriotic challenge, drawing on imagery from political cartoons of the day:

> 'Centre of Earth!' a Chinaman he said,
> And bent over a map with his pig-tailed head –
> That map in which, portrayed in colours bright,
> China, all dazzling, burst upon the sight:
> 'Centre of Earth' repeatedly he cried,
> 'Land of the brave, the beautiful, the wise!'
> Thus he exclaimed; when lo his words arrested
> Showed what sharp agony his head had tested.
> He feels a tug – another, and another –
> And quick exclaims, 'Hallo! what's now the bother?'
> But soon, alas, perceives. And 'why, false night,
> Why not from men shut out the hateful sight?
> The faithless English have cut off my tail,
> And left me my sad fortunes to bewail.
> Now in the streets I can no more appear,
> For all the other men a pig-tail wear',
> He said, and furious cast into the fire
> His tail: those flames became its funeral pyre.

Roughly contemporaneous was a satirical couplet that William never forgot:

> 'Come cheer up, my lads, 'tis to glory we steer!'
> As the soldier remarked whose post lay in the rear.

Vigorous, dramatic and funny, these verses show a sharper side to Christina's writing, which was perhaps most truly her own. Despite piety, Christina was seldom sentimental.

Almost from the cradle the young Rossettis knew a true metre from a false one, in both English and Italian, and they grew up with a knowledge of couplet, lyric and ode, to add to the rhymes of the nursery and the hymns at church. On her deathbed Christina surprised William by claiming that before *The Chinaman* she had already written 'various other small things' which were not apparently preserved. Then, as Gabriel recalled, there came a 'memorable Sunday afternoon' when Maria pronounced a poem of Christina's to be so good that 'she would be the poet in the family'. Thus, somewhere around her twelfth birthday, her vocation was established; indeed this may mark the date that Maria began filling the notebook on her sister's behalf, with the proud title-page inscription 'Poems by C. G. Rossetti'. In truth, Maria's poetic debut on the dead thrush showed more promise than Christina's stilted lines for her mother, but the choice was made: henceforth, poetry was her speciality, just as painting was Gabriel's.

There is unfortunately no record of their father's response. Despite his own pride and proficiency, poetic encouragement did not come from Papa. One reason may have been his faltering career. It is difficult to judge when Christina became aware of this, for Gabriele continued to applaud his renown and anticipate his triumphal return to Naples (affectionately transmuted in a tale Christina wrote about a Neapolitan couple in England, dreaming of going back to 'Vascitammo') but by the early 1840s this prospect was still distant, and compounded by worse worries.

For one thing, the young Queen's marriage to Prince Albert of Saxe-Coburg brought German into vogue, reducing the popularity of Italian, the number of prospective pupils and consequently the Professor's income. This downturn in fortune was then accompanied by attacks on Rosseti's competence as a scholar. As was customary, his professorship had been secured by patronage not merit and though some readers admired his commentary on *The Inferno*, others described it as 'sublime and perfect nonsense', a judgement supported by later, more impartial critics. In response, with the support of Frere in Malta and Lyell in Scotland, together with author Thomas Keightley – in whose books on European mythology Maria read the classical legends that startled Mrs Jervis – he had embarked on a more ambitious enterprise in the shape of a vast study of Dante and his contemporaries, as forerunners of the Reformation and freemasonry. This was published in two fat volumes translated in 1834 under the full title of *Disquisitions on the Anti-Papal Spirit which produced the Reformation: Its Secret Influence on the Literature of Europe in General and of Italy in Particular*, whose thesis, insofar as it could be divined, was that the essence of Love in the poems of the Ghibellines was anti-papalism, necessarily concealed from the Inquisition. As Lyell explained, Professor Rossetti argued that 'an anti-papal sect existed under the disguise of the Sette d'Amore, with its secret object founded on the plan of the ancient mysteries which originated in Egypt and handed down to us in the rites of modern masonry'. Dante's language had always a double meaning, literal and allegorical, ostensible and secret, after the model of the ancient philosophers. His works were thus written in a code, where everything is symbolically displayed to initiates. Most importantly, Beatrice was not a real beloved or historical figure, but a personification of the *summum arcanum*, the secret mystery at the heart of religious worship. Similarly, Petrarch's Laura stood for a Masonic lodge.

With hindsight one can see that this argument was essentially anti-papal in a contemporary political sense, written by one who had sufficient reason to be hostile to the Vatican, following events in his homeland. By aligning Dante with a supposed spirit that heralded the Reformation, Professor Rossetti was moreover protecting himself from current anti-papist feeling in Britain, where civil restrictions on Catholics were being abolished amid a good deal of alarmist controversy over the Pope's presumed desire to undermine the English Church and crown. Finally, in the implicit parallel between himself and Dante, also exiled, was a barely disguised claim to eminence.

Whatever his motives, however, Gabriele Rossetti was undone by his method, with its incoherent paraphernalia of scholarly (or more properly scholastic) erudition, that reads like a parody of academic discourse. Each sentence spawns a page of finely-argued footnotes, designed to impress and intimidate. According to Lyell, this exegesis was profound and original, but non-freemasons have been unimpressed. As his biographer commented, esoteric interpretation attracted absurdities as a magnet gathers iron filings, and if the arguments were never fully refuted, this was only because no scholar had undertaken so thankless a task. One who has, more recently, is the Italian writer Umberto Eco, who studied the work as part of his own research into the clandestine 'Templar tradition', for his novel

Foucault's Pendulum and confirmed the essential nonsense of Rossetti's ideas, which Eco places firmly in a line of obsessional paranoid readings, betrayed at last by deliberate fudging of footnotes – the scholar's final act of desperation.

Rossetti was indeed paranoid, constructing an increasingly obsessional case to justify his own political position. Onto Dante, he painted his own dislike of despotism and papal power, together with nationalistic Italian fervour; in every age, he proclaimed, patriotism was punished by banishment. And he anticipated opposition. No doubt, he wrote, critics would dismiss him as a crazy interpreter 'who tells us that we're all wrong ... that hell is Rome, Paradise is Rome, Dante did not love a lady called Beatrice; and, more than all that, that ladies are men...' – all of which was 'quite enough to render my sanity a matter of doubt'. But criticism made him only more certain – truth had been suppressed down the ages. He therefore began work on a further *magnum opus* entitled *Il Mistero dell'Amor platonica del medio evo derivato da' misteri antichi*, which in his son's words 'meandered through the thickets of very audacious thought', in five interminable volumes, arguing for an ancient, 'true religion' or doctrine of divine love driven underground by the official Church, whose teachings were thus revealed as an imposture to oppress the unlettered.

Where the *Anti-Papal Spirit* had at least chimed with contemporary politics and religion, *Amor Platonica*, which owed something to Gnosticism and more, it is said, to ideas current in nineteenth-century Italian freemasonry, was both heretical and ill-advised. Frere and Lyell took fright, fearing they might be charged with blasphemy as well as folly in supporting such a crackpot professor. Both advised against publication; it would end Rossetti's career as a teacher. Not to publish, on the other hand, would destroy his reputation as a scholar. Finally Lyell paid for the work to be printed on condition that it was not distributed. Frere thought it should be burnt, but copies went instead into permament storage. This, to Gabriele, was further proof of the suppression of truth, and his letters to his patrons are filled with a terrible agitation that certainly places his sanity in doubt.

Christina is unlikely to have understood much of this aspect of her father's work in childhood. Nor did she read deeply in his prose works in adulthood, not least because of the implications of heresy. Yet their influence on her life was considerable; indeed none of the Rossetti family can be understood without reference to this arcane paternal activity, which for several years 'saturated the household air'. William thought of Dante as a kind of spectral presence whom he half-expected to meet on a dark corner of the staircase, and later as a sort of banshee, whose shriek was 'audible even to familiarity', but whose message was unintelligble. Increasingly they saw their father surrounded by 'ponderous folios in italic type, *libri mistici* and the like (often about alchemy, freemasonry, Brahminism, Swedenborg, the Cabbala etc)' as in his miniscule handwriting he filled page after page, 'full of underscorings, interlineations and cancellings. We contemplated his labour with a certain hushed feeling, which partook of respect and also of levity, but were assuredly not much tempted to take up one of his books.'

As the controversy raged, Papa's health deteriorated. He began to suffer from insomnia. The threat of having the fruits of his eight years' labour destroyed made him feel persecuted, terrified of his own shadow. By the summer of 1840, his patrons were informed, he was spitting blood, suffering from recurrent fever and diabetic nausea.

And there were other troubles, as he was ousted from his position as doyen of the exile community by Mazzini, whose Young Italy movement forged a new and militant campaign for national liberation under a republican banner. In London *La Giovane Italia* organised a network of clubs that functioned as a political powerbase. Lyell wrote jocularly but surely in warning about the Professor's precarious position in John Bull's Britain in 1841, where:

> the pot can only be kept boiling by giving lessons. I then ponder on the wrongheadedness of the Bull family which with toryism, whiggism, radicalism, romanism, evangelicalism, independentism is really half mad at present ... and the possibility of some jesuitical fellow whispering in the ear of Mrs Bull that G. R. is a very personification of la Giovane Italia – and, pray, what is that? to which he will reply, Madame, la Giovane Italia is *gergo* [code] for the devil. The deuce it is, says she, then never shall G. R. give another lesson to Miss Bull ... no fire in the grate, no pot boiling, Maria Francesca & Co hungry and calling out for their macaroni ...

Sticking to his constitutional principles, Rossetti refused to give public support to the republican slogan 'May God and the People be the Salvation of Italy!' – with some reason, for the British government was sympathetic to Hapsburg hegemony. So although in 1843 Rossetti was honoured alongside Mazzini for services to Italian freedom, he had been effectively sidelined. Henceforth, the callers at Charlotte Street were more likely to be beggars and bores.

His health continued to worsen. By 1842 it was 'seriously impaired'. There followed 'some troubles of a different kind', which may refer to depression or to the ridicule that greeted his latest publication, an essay on the purely allegorical role of Dante's beloved Beatrice. And having since his escape from Naples had a lively conviction that political enemies were conspiring to kill him, so increasing paranoia

accompanied declining health. In 1843 he suffered a crisis so serious
and painful that he expected to die. Hitherto, whatever the financial
uncertainties, 50 Charlotte Street had been a cheerful and sociable
home. Now it became a place of sickness and worry. The boys, who
were out all day – William at school, Gabriel now attending a private
art school – were perhaps less affected than the girls, who helped
Mamma look after a despondently sick man. While a colleague
covered his teaching commitments, Maria acted as amanuensis, taking responsibility for collecting outstanding tuition fees. This summer, as a diversion, Mamma began a 'home magazine', with the title
Hodge Podge or Weekly Efforts. The first issue, dated 20 May, opened
with a pious, not to say priggish admonition against 'conceit – a
monster of so frightful mien, that to be hated it needs but to be seen' –
followed by items on the death of Paul and Virginie and on Joan of
Arc, 'the most extraordinary female character ever recorded in history'. She and aunt Charlotte then took Papa to Hastings, while aunt
Margaret stayed with the children.

Christina's first surviving letter – written to her father in June when
she was twelve and a half – is composed in a nervous Italian. She
apologised in advance for mistakes, and listed various visitors who
had called to ask after Papa – the Radical MP J. L. Leader; Dr Heimann
of University College who was teaching the children German; Signor
Parodi the dancing master; and Signor Rovedino, musician – and
concluded with love from Maria, aunt Margaret and herself. It is an
empty and formal letter, especially when compared with Gabriel's
lively communication to his mother (in English) of the previous day,
in which he described how Dr Heimann had brought his bride-to-be,
who had looked through the children's Scrapbook of drawings and
compositions. Maria and Christina had been invited to return the call:
did they have their mother's permission to accept? This, as it turned
out, was the start of a lifelong friendship for Christina, for Adolf
Heimann married Amelia Barnard, 'a very pretty pleasant young
English Jewess', who became a lifelong friend.

A few days after her stiff epistle, Christina composed the third poem
to merit inclusion in the notebook, a brief hymn 'to the God who
reigns on high', which parrots the Lord's Prayer but may also be
accounted a propitiatory prayer to accompany those said for Papa's
recovery. From Hastings, Frances and Gabriele proceeded to Paris,
sending back reports of their visits to la Madeleine, les Invalides and
Père la Chaise. At home, the children, who were more than usually
confined to the house, continued with their Scrapbook, into which
Gabriel inserted his 'choicest specimens of sketching' and Christina
'two poetic effusions ... both of which are very good'. The first was
a worldly-wise pastoral, *Corydon's Lament and Resolution*, in which

Corydon unromantically decides not to pine over Chloe's inconstancy but to wed Amaryllis instead – a piquant subversion of sentiment. The second was *Rosalind*, a melodramatic ballad about a lady whose husband is seized by pirates. On her entreaties to pity, the pirate leader hurls the husband into the sea; Lady Rosalind thereupon expires. Combining vividness with bathos, it was a vigorous pastiche for a twelve-year-old author, owing something to the British love of pirates, and something to *Sir Hugh the Heron* as well as to Gottfried Bürger's *Lenore* (which the young Rossettis were reading with Dr Heimann) and to Gabriel's own melodrama *Sorrentino* in which the Devil impersonates a lady's lover. But Christina's depiction of a woman violently lamenting the loss of a husband who is borne away by sea also suggests displaced fear. This was the first time she had been separated from both parents, in circumstances of extreme anxiety.

Papa returned home safely however, 'as good as cured', and family life was restored. Early in October 1843 Christina wrote a lyric poem of great accomplishment for one so young, which reads conventionally enough as a devotional piece but more poignantly as a wishful propitiation of her own fears:

> Love for ever dwells in heaven –
>   Hope entereth not there,
> To despairing man Love's given –
>   Hope dwells not with despair.
> Love reigneth high and reigneth low and reigneth everywhere.
>
> In the inmost heart Love dwelleth,
>   It may not quenched be;
> E'en when the life-blood welleth
>   Its fond effects we see
> In the name that leaves the lips the last, fades last from memory . . .

The long, bold last line barely compensates for the poeticisms; but the sentiment is of more interest than the form. Here, Love is eternal, unquenchable, secure.

But it proved a vain invocation, for this same month saw alarming deterioration in Papa's state. Overnight, at the end of October, his sight failed, virtually disappearing in one eye and dimming markedly in the other. He was obliged to give up nearly all teaching. If he went out, he had to be guided, like a blind man. His abstruse studies were abandoned, and he became more or less confined to the house, bereft of spirits, health, occupation and social status. He fell into voluble despair, and his loudly anticipated blindness, sickness and imminent death 'cast a thick mantle of gloom for months and years,' as William recalled, 'not only over my father's own feelings but over those of the entire family'. It was a catastrophic transformation within a previously happy household.

4

Breakdown

THIS FURTHER AND as it proved permanent breakdown in Gabriele's health underlined and perhaps partly resulted from his realisation at age sixty that the fame and fortune for which he had striven were never to be attained. With the failure of his scholarly and political ambitions, the hopes he had fostered in twenty years' exile were now utterly deferred; and physical debility served to console or conceal the bitterness. For Frances too, it marked the end of any illusions of husbandly distinction she may still have cherished and the unspoken transfer of ambition to the children.

Family finances plunged into an acute state. There was never any lack of primary necessities, but a perpetual economy and many unwelcome changes, not least the end of most treats and excursions. An anxious Christmas followed Christina's thirteenth birthday. Her grandfather could help only by advancing money on Frances's inheritance from her mother, but risked disadvantaging his other dependants by eating into the capital. Frances also had hopes of Granny Pierce, but this did not meet immediate needs. Aunt Charlotte provided more direct assistance, in the shape of a position for Maria, who therefore went away, sometime around her seventeenth birthday in February 1844, to be nursery governess to Gertrude Thynne, Lady Bath's five-year-old niece.

She did not dislike the job, but hated being away from home. 'I thank God for having given me talents which enable me to assist my dear father by removing the burden of my maintenance which he has borne for so many years with such loving care' she wrote a few months later, the stiff syntax and dutiful phrases barely concealing a resentment she surely did not intend to express, with pious quotations that implicitly admonished Papa to be more prayerfully stoical in adversity. Significantly, moreover, the letter demonstrates the psychological reversal that had taken place, as the child assumed the role of consoling the parent, and contributing to his maintenance.

For the time being, Gabriel continued at art school, 'costing something and earning nothing' in his brother's words, while William carried on at KCS, knowing that his hopes of entering the medical profession were now unrealisable. Most crucially of all, however, Frances Rossetti resumed employment, going out to work as a daily governess. It was a considerable descent for the wife of a professor,

especially since women's paid employment outside the home signified loss of gentility. Frances was no snob, but it was necessity that
promoted this return to teaching. It also doubled her workload, for
domestic responsibilities remained, and there was no money for extra
household help.

With Maria away and the boys and Mamma out for most of the day,
Christina's allotted role was to look after her father, or at least keep
him company. But the confident, energetic father of her childhood had
changed into a depressed and ailing invalid, who constantly lamented
his misfortunes, daily anticipated blindness and often wished, albeit
rhetorically, that he was dead. His despair, William recalled, caused
the family more unhappiness than their material poverty.

One is reminded of the young Virginia Woolf some fifty years later,
when after his wife's death Sir Leslie Stephen groaned and wept
openly, ignoring and usurping his teenage daughters' own need to
grieve with his unassuagable demands for sympathy. Christina of
course had not lost her mother, and her father was not an emotional
tyrant, but the position of adolescent daughter and distressed father is
comparable, and was further compounded by the loss of Maria's
companionship, by her sense of Mamma's increased burden and perhaps most importantly by the way in which the sufferings of father,
mother and sister overshadowed and eclipsed Christina's own needs.
She had no legitimate reason to complain – that there were no more
treats or that she was 'pent up' in the city. Others' troubles were far
greater. Like a good child in Mrs Edgeworth's stories, she was required to show gratitude and obedience, and expected only to feel
thankful, like Maria, that she was able to help her 'dear father' in his
time of need. Any natural resentment could be neither expressed nor
felt. And in this situation poetry proved an invaluable emotional
resource.

On 4 March 1844 she completed her first long fantasy poem, *The Water
Spirit's Song*, running to 68 lines in three rolling periods, with a wave-like
rhythm and conspicuous feminine endings. The story is that of a
naiad who departs each evening from her daytime station under a
waterfall to join her sister, Queen of the Ocean, in the vast depths, where

> the mermaidens sing plaintively
> Beneath the deep blue ocean,
> And to their song the green fishes dance
> With undulating motion.
> And the cold bright moon looks down on us . . .

Truth to tell, up to this point Christina's verse displayed little real
promise. Had it not been so self-consciously copied into the notebook,

it would hardly be taken to presage an exceptional talent. And in many ways this piece too is naive and derivative, inspired by Tennyson's mermaids and mermen, who frolic 'merrily' all night, and by water-nymph stories such as *Undine*. But the skill that enabled Christina, at age thirteen, to imitate such works is less striking than the expression of feeling, through intense mesmeric rhythms and cool, watery imagery. The atmosphere is cold but compelling, and vividly conveys the desire to float amid swaying waves. Moreover, the twin motifs of this fantasy – the wish to escape and be reunited with a sister – surely point to recent events, notably Maria's departure.

The next samples of her work were Italian imitations, exercises in the pastoral style favoured by her father and grandfather. Papa had indeed returned to poetic composition as his eyesight failed, abandoning the *libri mistici*. In Christina's *Pitia a Damone* (20 April 1844), the shepherd declares himself ready to die for his beloved. In *The Faithless Shepherdess* (17 June 1844), he complains of her inconstancy. In *Ariadne to Theseus* (18 June 1844) the deserted Ariadne bewails the king's perfidy in lines of operatic mimicry, to which Maria added a prim note reading: 'The reader may perhaps detect in these verses a resemblance to an idea in one of Pietro Metastasio's dramas'. With sudden enthusiasm Christina was losing herself in the writing of this eighteenth-century court poet whose works included *La Clemenza di Tito* and *Dido Abandonata*. Clearly, Metastasio's baroque world of declamatory outpourings over love and betrayal offered a model for legitimate expression of grief in her own pieces, indirectly lamenting the woes that had befallen the family.

Another important influence was the work of Maturin, whose novels Christina now read for herself – wild historical adventure-romances, with elaborate plots, vivid characterisation a good deal of sexual feeling, and a beguiling if tinselly blend of worldly wisdom and moral sensibility that barely modifies the sensationalism. They were similar to the romances mocked by Jane Austen in *Sense and Sensibility* and several, including *The Wild Irish Boy* and *Melmoth the Wanderer* contain strong male and female characters, offering readers of both sexes a focus of identification, with stirring action and superbly doomed love interest. (Teenage readers seem the most appropriate audience, although the books were of course written for adults and had powerful influence throughout Europe, on Balzac, Baudelaire, Oscar Wilde.)

Melmoth, Christina's favourite, was a fierce and fantastical three-decker drama, whose shape-shifting central character has sold his soul to the Devil and is searching for love to redeem it. It also includes gruesome torture by the Spanish Inquisition, and tales of valour among lords and ladies in the 'olden dayes'; but Christina's imagination was caught by the tale of beautiful Immalee, heroine and child of nature, reared on a tropical island, who is seduced by Melmoth and transported to Spain where she is discovered to be Isidora, daughter of a nobleman. Like Eve or Miranda she is introduced to knowledge of the world, and learns to weep and fear, dreaming always of her lost innocence. Melmoth is a version of the demon lover, and after many sufferings Isidora is imprisoned in a dungeon where she kills her daughter and dies with absolution on her lips. The priest promises palm-wreaths in paradise. 'Paradise!' utters Isidora with her last breath in a mixture of fear and longing – 'Will he be there?' It was an ending that had a long-lasting hold on Christina's creative imagination, strangely but strongly linked to some deep emotion.

Such works clearly supplied a need, but their sensationalism did not occlude her sense of the absurd. The melodramatic poem on Ariadne, for example, was followed by a mordant quatrain on Albinia:

> The roses lingered in her cheeks
>   When fair Albinia fainted;
> O gentle reader, could it be
>   That fair Albinia painted?

Satire was another neo-classic resource, and this ironic strain acted as counterpoint to both the 'high poetic' and devotional verses of Christina's adolescence. In August she completed a ballad called *Despair*, in which a medieval squire operatically laments his lost love, whose ghost he sees returning, until she is revealed as the maidservant bearing a lamp along the corridor. Whatever the consolations of melodrama, wit and humour also helped make things bearable.

Compositions poured forth in this period, reflecting immediate reading but also foreshadowing the motifs of Christina's life's work. Pious shepherds replaced faithless ones in an unseasonal Christmas hymn at midsummer, followed on 2 July by *Love and Death* – a title encapsulating her poetic obsessions – describing Lady Bianca's elopement in a sea-going gondola. Clasped to each other, the fantasy lovers sink to a watery grave, the first of many to suffer such fate in Christina's verse. This too owed something to the story of Undine (Maclise's painting of the water-spirit was the star of this year's Royal Academy, bought by the Queen for Prince Albert) but it also betrays the powerful influence of Gabriel's translation of *Lenore*, in which a ghostly horseman returns to claim his wife:

The churchyard troop – a ghostly group –
  Close around the dying girl;
Out and in they hurry and spin
  Through the dance's weary whirl . . .

Gothick tales of love and death in this very mode were to be constant themes throughout Christina's writing.

It was now even clearer that she was following her father's footsteps, for it was to poetic composition that he returned as his sight failed. 'To live and nought to do I cannot brook,' he lamented. 'A poet I began, a poet end'. He revised earlier pieces and then started a new long work entitled *Il Veggente in Solitudine (The Seer in Solitude)*. Other members of the family had to copy out these texts. Although Gabriele did not lose his sight, taking instead to strong spectacles, he never lost the fear that he would do so; acting as amanuensis was one way the children could assist and also relieve Mamma, who also undertook much copying.

In *Il Veggente*, Gabriele paid tribute to '*Francesca, i miei martiri*', and eulogised the 'four tokens' of their fruitful love, including dark-haired Maria, whose fervid eyes reflected her father's ardent soul, and Christina, cast in her mother's image. Both girls, he declared, reminded him of Francesca as a young woman; from her they inherited a soul in harmony with the Muses which, combining with his own, shone with doubled splendour. This rather convoluted image suggests both an acknowledgement of Christina's literary gift, and a sense of her approaching womanhood.

In December 1844 William gave his sister – as a birthday or Christmas gift, or because, having discovered Shelley, he was shedding religious books – a little anthology entitled *The Sacred Harp*, earlier presented to him at school for good conduct and evidently now considered more appropriate for a girl. Piously, she noted 'beautiful' lines and sentiments in its pages, many by Mrs Hemans, and it was probably here that she first read George Herbert, whose *Misery and Virtue* she copied out into her mother's commonplace book, supplementing them with stanzas of her own entitled *Charity*, to which Maria added a careful note, explaining that that they were 'imitated from that beautiful little poem "Virtue" by George Herbert'.

The boys were growing up and away. For the second year running, Gabriel was in Boulogne, with old exile friends of Papa. He wrote William enviable letters about excursions and engravings, and contracted mild smallpox, which prevented his return at Christmas. At the beginning of February he rejoiced to hear that 'the prospect of employment' had been secured for William who, it had been decided, must leave school, aged fifteen. Through the patronage of a family friend a job was found in the government tax office, where he reluctantly started work on 6 February 1845, at an annual salary of £80.

It was thought that Gabriel, too, should start earning, and he was sent to one of the new railway telegraph offices in search of a similar post. But such prospects formed no part of his plans, and he simply declined to alter his position as favoured son. He continued at art school, aiming for the Royal Academy Schools but not working especially hard, and tending to ignore family demands. He was, he confessed later, temperamentally unable to undertake anything imposed as an obligation: 'what I *ought* to do is what I can't do,' he said. In the evenings William, making no friends at work, fell in with his brother's circle, so the boys were less at home. Papa no longer commanded the domestic scene. 'I am always alone, for everybody in this house has undertaken work of one kind or another to earn a living,' he told a compatriot, adding with a touch of his old vainglory 'and yet all of them put together cannot make the half of what I used to make myself' – which was true but pathetic and partly inaccurate, since he was not 'all alone', but with Christina. Later, William recalled that she was good at chess, like their father who had taught them to play and it is probable that she was encouraged to play with him in these difficult years to keep him from brooding on his troubles. As at cards, she was a spirited player, keen to win.

Thus Christina and her father were daily companions. A visitor's glimpse into the front parlour at Charlotte Street a little later gives a vivid picture of how they spent their time. Here, one dark afternoon, there was to be seen

an old gentleman sitting by the fire in a great chair, the table drawn close to his chair, with a thick manuscript book open before him and the largest snuff box I ever saw beside it . . . He had a black cap on his head furnished with a great peak or shade for the eyes . . .

By the window was a high narrow reading desk at which stood writing a slight girl with a serious regular profile, dark against the pallid wintry light without. [She] turned on my entrance, made the most formal and graceful curtsey, and resumed her writing, and the old gentleman signed to a chair for my sitting down.

In her poems, Corydon and Phillis and their British ballad equivalents continued to feature, alongside pious pieces on the transient beauties of earth and the eternal joys of heaven. All were superficially sophisticated but conveyed little sense of true feeling. Perhaps they served more importantly to conceal emotion, or keep untractable feelings at bay. In March 1845 came two very sombre pieces – *The Last*

Words of St Telemachus and *Burial Anthem* – treated of death as a consummation devoutly to be wished. 'Oh! wherefore mourn that I at last should be at liberty?' asks the martyr, while *Burial Anthem* envies the dead, for the living have still 'our weary race to run, In doubt and want and sin and pain'. Given Gabriele Rossetti's self-dramatising tendency to lament his approaching end, these verses – for whose occasion William later, unconvincingly, proffered the death of 'some young clergyman esteemed in our household' – seem to represent in part a poetic resolution of the fears aroused by the idea that Papa was dying. Submerged in the piety, however, are hints of resentment at being abandoned, together with the reiterated statement that life is dreary and desolate, as it may well have seemed to the author.

Unacknowledged resentment – repressed because too unfilial to allow – has often coloured the experience of daughters obliged to attend their parents. While there is no evidence of overt resistance on Christina's part, there are also surprisingly few expressions of affection for her father, especially in comparison with her lifelong devotion to her mother which almost amounted to worship. In her work, mothers are idealised, fathers are absent, a configuration that may have its origin in her conflicting feelings during these adolescent years, when she felt resentful, and ashamed of so feeling, as her father's cheerful boasts and hugs were replaced by embarrassing frailty and wheedling self-pity. Perhaps, too, Papa made excessive demands, confusing Christina's companionate role with that of his absent wife, whom she so resembled in his eyes (though William denied the likeness) – behaviour that in a previously loved and admired father would be truly pitiable but also frightening to his bewildered daughter. Outwardly, she maintained a daughterly dutifulness, and indeed for the rest of her life showed what William called 'a rather unusual feeling of deference for "the head of the family", whoever he might be, which was more Italian than English' – largely, it seems, in reaction to the waning of paternal strength in her teenage years when she felt its lack most keenly.

Gabriel, by contrast, was openly disrespectful, provoking Papa to anger. To soothe matters Mamma extracted an apology, but the decay of authority was plain.

These difficult years coincided with those in which Christina reached puberty, and had to adjust to the physical signs of womanhood in a culture that – so it seems – suppressed all mention of budding breasts, bodyhair and monthly bleeding. 'Females generally begin to menstruate about the age of fifteen,' noted *Domestic Medicine*, though in fact menstruation is also linked to body weight and, as

Christina was well-developed for her age, it is likely that she had her first periods in 1845. This was considered a highly critical time by the medical profession, in which the whole future health of a woman might be determined, and the mood changes of adolescence were treated as incipient illness. Some doctors prescribed powdered steel, or iron filings steeped in beer (to counteract anaemia) together with potions made from bitter aloes and myrrh, and recommended that girls undergoing difficult or delayed menstruation be kept indoors. *Domestic Medicine* advised otherwise, suggesting fresh air, wholesome food, sufficient exercise and pleasant amusements. There was detailed advice on diet and on the dangers of catching cold while 'out of order'. Moreover, girls should be kept cheerful, as 'anger, fear, grief and other affections of the mind' caused incurable obstructions to the menstrual flow. Amenorrhoea seems to have been the chief worry; excessive menstruation was treated with a reduced diet and blood-letting, by cup or leech.

Christina was familiar with leeches: later she joked that they made for the door whenever faced with her flesh. And by the spring of 1845 something was seriously wrong with her. In *Lines to my Grandfather*, composed on 1 May, she apologised for lack of inspiration:

> My muse of late was not prolific;
> And sometimes I must feel
> To make a verse a task terrific,
> Rather of woe than weal.

She was forcing herself. It was a strained poem, and the last for several months.

'In innate character she was vivacious, and open to pleasurable impressions,' wrote William, 'and during her girlhood, one might readily have supposed that she would develop into a woman of expansive heart, fond of society and diversions and taking a part in them of more than average brilliancy. What came to pass was of course quite the contrary.'

Many subsequent biographers have felt the same sense of disappointment, watching Christina change from 'a quick-tempered but very affectionate little girl, full of whims and fancies' to a painfully controlled young woman, 'retiring, introverted, mistrustful of the world and of her own self'. The transformation is mirrored in her own story *Hero*, where the lively fifteen-year-old heroine, who mistakenly thinks her father and sweetheart do not love her as they did, undergoes a similar alteration. Her demeanour darkens, and 'her face, always beautiful, lost its expression of gay sweetness; her temper became capricious, and instead of cheerful airs she would sing snatches of plaintive or bitter songs'. She pines away in inexplicable discontent, 'sick alike of herself and others'.

Christina's moodiness was accompanied by occasional violent outbursts that recalled her juvenile tantrums and were themselves the cause of self-lacerating guilt. These explosions were long remembered, and she retained the memory of a protracted struggle to attain a properly subdued temper. 'Ask William, who knew me in my early stormy days,' she said at the age of fifty-two, 'he could a tale unfold.'

One of the tales William knew but did not unfold was related when his daughter Helen was guilty of 'an outburst of unseemly temper' as a child. 'You must not imagine,' Christina told her sobbing niece, 'that your Aunt was always the calm and sedate person you now behold:

> I, too, had a very passionate temper . . . On one occasion, being rebuked by my dear Mother for some fault, I seized upon a pair of scissors, and ripped up my arm to vent my wrath.

Such violent self-mutilating gestures are more characteristic of troubled adolescence than childhood, and frequently allied to self-hatred, as anger is turned in on the self. It seems likely that Christina's ungovernable explosions of rage and remorse were keenly felt as failures in self-control in her teenage years, when philosophic calm was most needed but hard to attain. Maria and William had cause for grievance, but remained good-tempered, as did poor Mamma, whose worries were only increased by Christina's outbursts. So she buried her anger and resentment, only to find them erupting on inappropriate occasions, causing more grief and guilt. Ripping her arm was an eloquent gesture of self-hatred.

Virtual silence surrounds the breakdown in her health over the summer of 1845: William said only that she was 'ill'. But the distress, violence and personality change were accompanied by physical symptoms not easy to diagnose. She was examined by a number of eminent physicians, including Sir Thomas Watson, former professor of medicine at King's College Hospital, the acknowledged doyen of the medical world, and Sir Charles Locock, the Queen's gynaecologist. Also consulted were Dr Latham, who had a double career in medicine and letters, and Dr Charles Hare, who became a distinguished physician. None seemed able to identity the problem. William understood only that in the end they decided that she was suffering from 'angina pectoris (actual or supposed) of which after some long time she seemed cured'. This diagnosis seems unlikely, for though heart disease occurs in the young, it is not readily cured; but presumably it indicated her symptoms: chest spasms and constriction, a feeling of suffocation, palpitations, possibly fainting fits. There is no evidence that she lost weight, but she certainly lost all stamina and animation, falling into extreme weakness and lassitude. At this distance it is not possible to offer a definitive diagnosis, but hysteria and depression suggest themselves. At the age of fourteen she was suffering a severe nervous breakdown, just eighteen months after her father's collapse.

Around this time, as if in identification, she copied into her mother's commonplace book two long extracts from Wordsworth's *The Excursion* – evidently the result of current reading – which describe despair and personality change in young women. The first passage is that known as 'The Ruined Cottage', a sad tale of a woman whose rustic felicity is blighted by her husband's desertion. Margaret's spirits sink, home and garden and child are neglected:

> . . . I many days
> About the fields I wander, knowing this
> Only, that what I seek I cannot find;
> And so I waste my time: for I am changed,
> And to myself", said she, "have done much wrong
> And to this helpless infant. I have slept
> Weeping, and weeping have I waked; my tears
> Have flowed as if my body were not such
> As others are . . .

Teenagers are apt to prefer melancholy themes but a personal element enters into the choice: was Christina trying to tell Mamma how she was feeling? Her second extract covered ten further pages, relating the tragic tale of Ellen, who is betrayed by her village swain, bears an illegitimate child and then dies of shame, 'a weeping Magdalene' waiting only for God to take her 'into that pure and unknown world of love Where injury cannot come'. On the face of it, this was an unexpected extract to choose, turning as it does on sexual transgression. But evidently something in both Margaret's depression and Ellen's distress answered to Christina's need.

In September she was sent away on holiday – the first time she had been out of London for six years, as she so clearly recalled with that memory of being pent up until 'a great girl of fourteen'. Still far from well, she sent a shaky letter to William, twice repeating what a labour it was to write, yet trying to summon some sprightliness by joking that 'all sorts of accomplishments' had showered down on his talented sister. She had learnt backgammon, and had 'coursed gallantly' on a sedate pony, who had broken into a trot. But after two paragraphs the letter was abandoned, to be briefly completed the next day, with apologies. Reading it, one can hardly doubt that she had been very sick.

She was in the country with the Read family, to whose daughters Maria was now governess, having left the Rev. Lord Charles Thynne's household after little more than a year. The Reads, who also had a London house in the city, were a pleasant family whose daughters Lucy and Bessie were not much younger than Christina. 'I knew her when I was fourteen and she about twelve', she reminded William when some forty years later she received a visit from the now middle-aged Lucy, adding with affection that there was something very agreeable in seeing such an old acquaintance. At the time, helping Maria entertain the girls with board games, pony rides and the like must have provided a welcome break from the gloom of Charlotte Street. On her return home, Christina began saving used stamps for Bessie's collection and six months later sent a hundred specimens, with a complimentary poem to her young friend.

However, the holiday did not restore Christina's health, which grew worryingly worse. More medical consultations followed. In November Dr Hare became her physician, and a month later wrote a memorandum on her condition, which was preserved and partly published by her first biographer. This noted that she was 'fully the middle stature; appears older than she really is – 15; hair brown; complexion brunette; but she is now pale (anaemic). Conformation good.' More intimate observations would have been withheld from publication for the sake of decorum, so this tells us little except that Christina was physically mature for her age, but appeared pale and listless; perhaps iron filings steeped in ale were prescribed. But the memorandum contained further, unpublished, remarks, according to a later informant:

> a question arose ... while this biography was being written ... as to whether a notice should be inserted of the fact that the doctor who attended on Christina Rossetti when she was about 16–18 said that she was then more or less out of her mind (suffering, in fact, from a form of insanity, I believe a kind of religious mania); and for obvious reasons it was determined that this fact should be omitted, tho' the doctor's good faith was not impugned.

Was Christina insane in her mid-teens? Today, an adolescent breakdown might not be seen as a form of insanity, though Virginia Stephen's comparable collapse at thirteen, following the death of her mother, was the first manifestation of her recurrent mental derangement. In the 1840s, however, 'religious mania', the form of insanity suggested by Hare, was a recognised medical diagnosis, given to states of excessive self-blame. Papa alluded to the tendency in himself, noting that insomnia and anxiety had caused him to become 'like one of those people of exaggerated piety who think that in their most insignificant action they have committed a mortal sin' and *Domestic Medicine* glossed 'religious melancholy' in terms that are similar to modern accounts of clinical depression:

> A perpetual gloom hangs over their countenances, while the deepest melancholy preys upon their mind. At length the fairest prospects vanish, everything puts on a dismal appearance, and those very objects which ought to give delight afford nothing but disgust . . .

Depression is commonly linked to half-perceived guilt and children sometimes feel obscurely responsible for catastrophes afflicting their family, blaming themselves for having been selfish, disobedient or angry. As the incident with the scissors suggests, Christina's melancholy was allied to self-castigation, and all her life she was apt to think of herself as sinful. This recurrent motif expressed itself in poems of extreme hatred for her loathsome, leprous self, in the attempt to exercise the evil lurking within like a horned and abominable beast.

The religious tenor of the time placed a great value on the virtues of self-denial, and William remembered that his sister, who had been so 'fond of society and diversions', soon determined never again to go to plays and operas, and also gave up playing chess, which she loved, 'simply because it made her too eager for a win' – though this sacrifice of an innocent amusement may have concealed a different problem if, at the chessboard, Papa did not like losing to his daughter. Over the next few months she retreated behind a mask of external self-control, and polite stiffness. Like all girls she had been trained in the arts of courtesy and conversation, which were now employed to hollow excess. Henceforth, her true feelings were almost always concealed from others – and even, one sometimes feels, from herself – by habitual reserve. All impetuosity and openness vanished, and William watched as her 'naturally warm and free temperament' became as 'a fountain sealed' – a quotation Christina repeatedly invoked in allusion to the Bride of the Canticles: 'A garden inclosed is my sister, my spouse, a spring shut up, a fountain sealed.'

Curiously, the author of *Domestic Medicine* advised those sinking into religious melancholy not to dwell on their faults but to 'write a book', as an infallible remedy. Was this Dr Hare's advice? On 3 December 1845, after six months' poetic silence, Christina again took up her pen, and the first poem to be entered into the notebook after her breakdown, headed *Hope in Grief*, expressed an anguish that is still painful to read:

> Tell me not that death of grief
> Is the only sure relief.
> Tell me not that hope when dead
> Leaves a void that naught can fill,
> Gnawings that may not be fed.
> Tell me not there is no skill
> That can bind the breaking heart,
> That can soothe the bitter smart,
> When we find ourselves betrayed,
> When we find ourselves forsaken,
> By those for whom we would have laid
> Our young lives down, nor wished to waken.
> Say not that life is to all
> But a gaily coloured pall,
> Hiding with its deceitful glow
> The hearts that break beneath it,
> Engulphing as they anguished flow
> The scalding tears that seethe it.
> Say not, vain this world's turmoil,
> Vain its trouble and its toil,
> All its hopes and fears are vain,
> Long unmitigated pain.
> What though we should be deceived
> By the friend that we love best?
> All in this world have been grieved,
> Yet many have found rest.
> Our present life is as the night,
> Our future as the morning light:
> Surely the night must pass way
> And surely will uprise the day.

The sophisticated use of rhetorical denial and inversion does not obscure the desolate emotion of these couplets, written on the eve of Christina's fifteenth birthday, at the end of a long and painful year.

5

Sin and Sisterhoods

A DOLESCENT BREAKDOWN was not uncommon among Victorian girls, as they struggled to tailor their natures to fit the prescribed mould. At the age of fifteen, Elizabeth Barrett, who had been a robust child, developed a disabling illness, suffering convulsive paroxysms, palpitations and chest pain, which turned her into an invalid and was accompanied by a personality change from childish self-assertion to habitual self-restraint. At a similar age Catherine Booth suffered a mysterious 'spinal attack' and fell into invalidism before finding her vocation as co-founder of the Salvation Army. At seventeen, Florence Nightingale went through a crisis caused by her desire for meaningful work, and for several years suffered recurrent collapses, fainting fits and strange trances in which she had vainglorious fantasies of heroic deeds. Counselled against selfishness, she sought refuge in religious submission, only to feel guilty of nameless sins.

Wilful in childhood, Christina had enjoyed a relatively egalitarian upbringing, and it is perhaps understandable that her adolescent breakdown coincided with the reining in of her spirited personality to fit the requirements of Victorian femininity, with its stress on sweetness, submission, self-sacrifice. But it was also her fate to experience this under the powerful religious influence of the Tractarian preachers Edward Bouverie Pusey and William Dodsworth, which explains why her breakdown took the form of religious melancholy and sense of sinfulness. For the religious atmosphere fermented by these men and their colleagues was particularly targeted at young women.

In the Church of England the evangelical zeal of the 1820s had been replaced by the nascent High Church or Oxford Movement headed by Pusey, John Keble, William Manning and John Henry Newman. Frances Rossetti remained a deep but simple believer, stirred neither by fervour nor doubts and with enough commonsense not to trouble over inconsistencies in the Bible, nor to become 'the slave of every irrational dogma propounded by old women in or out of cassocks,' as the freethinking William put it. But in 1843 she moved her allegiance from St Katherine's Chapel to Christ Church, Albany Street – still conveniently close to Park Village – which had been established on a rising tide of High Anglican ardour. Located between the stuccoed terraces of Regents Park and the slum terraces of Cumberland Market, Christ Church soon became a main London centre of the movement, under Rev. Dodsworth, Pusey's intense, passionate and persuasive disciple.

The boys were hardly affected and neither went forward to confirmation. William, shocked in childhood by God's commendation of Jehu's treachery, decided at fourteen that he believed nothing of Christian doctrine, and soon ceased churchgoing entirely. No one in the family, he noted, ever mentioned this backsliding. Both sisters, however, with Maria leading the way, were swept into the Anglo-Catholic persuasion, which argued that the Church of England was direct heir to the apostolic succession, rather than to the Lutheran tradition; as stated in the Creed, it was part of 'the Holy Catholick Church', believing inter alia in the Communion of Saints and the Remission of Sins. There followed attempts to return to the liturgical traditions of the pre-Reformation Church, with the reinstatement of weekly communion preceded by confession, with vestments, crucifixes, candles, incense, a sung liturgy and other practices associated with the Roman Church – 'smells and bells' as it was dubbed by opponents. The accompanying theology was elaborated in *Tracts for the Times*, chiefly promoted by Newman, together with published sermons and volumes of sacred verse such as his *Lyra Apostolica* (1836) and Keble's hugely popular *The Christian Year* (1827) and his more explicitly Tractarian *Lyra Innocentium* (1846). As in other forms of religious evangelism, the Tractarians proselytised among the young, aiming to attract both men and women through a mission of spiritual renewal.

The influence of pietism on Christina's own work was already evident. Derived originally from Evangelical hymns, this was then reinforced by Tractarian verse and seventeenth-century writers rediscovered by the High Anglicans. This tradition was important, since it gave moral legitimacy to poetry which otherwise, in the wake of the Romantics, was accused of sensuousness, freethought and immorality; aunt Margaret once intervened when she heard that Gabriel was proposing to read Shelley. Keble by contrast laid out a devotional path which Christina's literary impulses could commendably follow. As indeed she read in Maria's well-thumbed *Christian Year*, those whose 'hearts beat with the pulse of poetry' were urged to sing for God's sake, as the earthly equivalent of angelic harps. Indeed, Christina's desperate lines 'Tell me not that death of grief' were clearly written in direct response to the homilectic instruction contained in Keble's *St John's Day* to trust in the Lord's 'sure relief'. 'When the shore is won at last, Who will count the billows past?' he assured those in sorrow and pain.

At Christ Church, where the congregation included many titled and eminent persons, Dodsworth was a charismatic figure, a man of 'great force of character' and 'telling eloquence'. He instituted daily services and saints' days, employed curates and built up an atmosphere of pioneering piety, in which an essential ingredient was his success in attracting other notable Anglo-Catholic preachers.

'We have had Pusey and Manning preaching here lately, the former three times,' noted parishioner Sara Coleridge in July 1845, giving a vivid account of Pusey's style:

> He is certainly, to my feelings, more impressive than anyone else in the pulpit, though he has not one of the graces of oratory. His discourse is generally a rhapsody, describing with infinite repetition and accumulativeness, the wickedness of sin, the worthlessness of earth, and the blessedness of heaven. He is as still as a statue all the time he is uttering it, looks as white as a sheet, and is as monotonous as possible in delivery. While listening to him, you do not seem to see and hear a *preacher*, but to have visible before you a most earnest and devout spirit, striving to carry out in this world a high religious theory.

If Pusey's fervour had such impact on the middle-aged and rational Mrs Coleridge, one may imagine how it would have been for an impressionable girl, listening in a depressed and anxious state. Rather uncannily, the chief qualities of Christina's mature verse can be described in similar terms: rhapsody, repetition, accumulativeness, the worthlessness of earth and the blessedness of heaven.

Whoever the preacher, the Sunday sermon at Christ Church was an important weekly event. To Dodsworth, who had been a millenarian before he was a Tractarian, Advent was a key church season, signalling the imminence of the Second Coming. Under his influence Maria confessed to looking with horror on the Egyptian mummies in the British Museum, lest while she watched the General Resurrection took place, a vivid intimation of chiliastic thought. Christina too was directly influenced: the day after the anguished *Hope in Grief*, she concluded one of two long songs with the adjuration to those 'dreary with a cureless woe' to think upon the End of Time, followed by *Mother and Child*, a pious piece in which the child longs for heaven and in March by *Lady Isabella* who is already dead, all her sins forgiven.

In addition to menacing admonitions, Anglo-Catholics urged worshippers to consecrate their lives to God, using rediscovered hagiography and saints' stories as models of Christian sacrifice. Virgin martyrs were particularly praised in a book by Rev. J. M. Neale, comparing the higher destiny offered to women by the Holy Chuch, with the pagan slavery of wifehood. Grisly descriptions of the tortures suffered by SS. Lucy, Agnes, Agatha and the rest were concluded with the pious hope that the grace that enabled them to endure was still mighty, to work in a different manner but to the same end. 'God grant that England may see many such, if not in circumstances, yet in spirit!' Neale declared.

Pusey's particular mission was the restoration of religious orders within the Anglican church, and specifically the revival of conventual life for women, unknown in England since the Dissolution. He earmarked his own daughter Lucy for the religious life and although she died before this could be accomplished, on the day of her funeral in 1844 he held a meeting with Dodsworth and others to discuss proposals for a holy community of women living under a religious Rule. It thus came about that the first Anglican Sisterhood was planned in the Christ Church parish, and located in Park Village West, not far from the Polidoris' home, inspired, in the words of the Christ Church historian, by Pusey's 'opinion of Dodsworth, his sense of the exceptional zeal of some members of the congregation, and his knowledge of the many poor in this populous district'.

Postulants were sought by word of mouth, in an atmosphere of semi-clandestine excitement owing to hostility to nunneries as a sort of papist fifth column, or a furtive challenge to parochial and parental control. But precisely because women drawn to vows by their spiritual fathers in Christ often faced family opposition, sisterhoods offered not only a life of service that accorded with the feminine ideal but also the glamour of being pioneers, even martyrs, in a holy cause. Admittedly, much of this was manufactured by the clerics. Dodsworth for instance wanted to keep the rules at Park Village secret. 'People have no business to inquire how the Sisters regulate their dress or diet – or their devotions,' he wrote to Pusey. 'Confession should not be *required*, but I suppose it will be practised.'

In spring 1845, the Park Village Sisterhood came into existence, with three members, received in floods of tears by Pusey and Dodsworth, who made their first appearance at Christ Church on Easter Sunday, dressed in simple black habits, cloaks and bonnets. One can imagine the thrill and awe this caused among fellow worshippers, including the Polidori and Rossetti sisters. A month earlier, Christina had written her lines on the martyr St Telemachus, ending with an invocation of faith. A month or so later she suffered the breakdown that her doctor diagnosed as religious mania. The time and place were evidently conducive to an adolescent crisis taking a religious cast.

As William later remarked, in all seriousness, Maria would gladly have gone to the stake for any tenet of faith she held sacred, such as the Real Presence of Christ in the Eucharist, and was strongly drawn towards taking the veil. 'Mamma, should you mind my being a nun?' asks Maude Foster, the heroine of Christina's first full-length story.

'Yes, my dear; it would make me miserable,' comes the firm reply, no doubt echoed in life by Frances Rossetti. Christina herself confessed to a 'romantic impulse' towards the convent 'like many young people' and her story was in part a dramatisation of the impulse in its complexities. Maude and her cousin Agnes discuss a friend who has taken vows:

'. . . perhaps you are not aware that poor Magdalen has done with albums and such like, at least for the present: she has entered on her noviciate in the Sisterhood of Mercy established near our house.'

'Why poor?' said Maude. 'I think she is very happy.'

'Surely you would not like such a life,' rejoined her cousin. 'They have no proper clothes on their beds, and never go out without a thick veil, which must half blind them. All day long they are at prayers, or teaching children, or attending the sick, or making things for the poor, or something. Is that to your taste?'

Nevertheless, Agnes admiringly obtains a lock of Magdalen's shorn hair, saying, 'It makes me sad to look at it; yet I know she has chosen well; and will, if she perseveres, receive hereafter an abundant recompense for all she has foregone here.'

In practice, the Park Village Sisterhood only admitted adult women, Pusey being well aware that to recruit young girls would bring instant charges of abduction. And in practice the Rossetti sisters were pulled into parochial work, just as Maude's friends embroider lectern cloths, rise at six to make garments for the poor and save their pocket money to help sick children. Aunt Eliza took on district visiting in the Christ Church area, with which her nieces assisted, and it is possible that like Maude Christina was offered a parish 'district' of her own, which she declined, feeling ill-equipped to 'talk to the poor people' or do the slightest good in this field.

Poor Maude, indeed, feels unworthy of everything pertaining to goodness, and the novella is largely the history of her spiritual crisis, at the age of fifteen. Like her author she is obscurely troubled, and painfully preoccupied. She envies her cheerful cousins, and on Christmas Eve is found alone in her room, in distress. She cannot receive holy communion, she asserts:

I will not profane Holy Things. I will not add this to all the rest . . . I have gone over and over, thinking I should come right in time and I do not come right . . .

You partake of the Blessed Sacrament in peace, Agnes, for you are good; and Mary, for she is harmless: but . . . I am neither the one nor the other. Some day I may be fit again to approach the Holy Altar, but till then I will at least refrain from dishonouring it.

Baffled, Agnes beseeches her to reconsider, but Maude is desperately stubborn, repeating only, 'It is of no use; I cannot go tomorrow; it is of no use.'

Her sense of unworthiness has no clear cause in the story; but the Prayerbook text for Holy Communion, which Christina studied in preparation for confirmation, states plainly: 'for as the benefit is great ... so is the danger great if we receive the same unworthily. For then we be guilty of the body, and blood of Christ our Saviour. We eat and drink our own damnation...'

Later Christina alluded to her breakdown in such a way as to suggest it was a spiritual crisis well known in the family. When near the end of his life Gabriel suffered acute remorse regarding his long-past act of filial disrespect, she wrote to comfort him, saying:

> I want to assure you that, however harassed by memory or by anxiety you may be, I have (more or less) heretofore gone through the same ordeal. I have borne myself till I became unbearable to myself, and then I have found help in confession and absolution and spiritual counsel, and relief inexpressible. Twice in my life I tried to suffice myself with measures short of this, but nothing would do; the first time was of course in my youth before my general confession.

Both this account and Maude's agonised self-criticism indicate the importance placed by the Puseyites on coming 'holy and clean' to communion, for central to High Church theology was a wholly Puritan sense of sinfulness, as in the Commination which heralded Lent:

> For now is the axe put unto the root of the tree, so that every tree that bringeth forth not good fruit is hewn down and cast into the fire. It is a fearful thing to fall into the hands of the living God: He shall pour down rain upon the sinner, snares, fire and brimstone, storm and tempest ...

Taken to extremes, this was matter for masochism. As Pusey declared in 1844:

> I am scarred all over and seamed with sin, so that I am a monster to myself ... I loathe myself; I can feel of myself only like one covered with leprosy from head to foot.

The need to cleanse the soul in order to receive joy with forgiveness, like a ray of light in darkness was the constant theme of his preaching. In a born-again manner, young and old were exhorted to repent, repent!

At the time of her breakdown, Christina was being prepared for confirmation, by Dodsworth or one of his curates. Her collapse intervened and it was probably not until the following year that she returned for instruction, with its heavy stress on self-abasement. Into her mother's commonplace book she copied a telling passage by Mrs Coleridge's father on the humble acceptance of poverty and in praise of George Herbert (quoting the lines 'Who would have thought my shrivel'd heart Could have recovered greenness' which her own work was often to echo), followed by two poems on Mary Magdalene, the biblical model of the repentant sinner, which focused on 'the leprous state' of sin. Her own poem on Mary Magdalene, dated 8 February 1846, depicted the saint as a young woman weeping for her 'great transgression':

> Trembling betwixt hope and fear,
>   She sought the King of Heaven,
> Forsook the evil of her ways,
>   Loved much, and was forgiven.

Identification with the Magdalene was a popular theme in Victorian pietism, and too much need not be made of a fifteen-year-old girl's choice of a saint known chiefly for sexual sin, especially as it is difficult to judge what a well-brought-up young woman knew of sexual transgression; most probably she simply used the saint as a conventional trope for contrition. But it had a powerful impact, and six weeks later she reworked the motif in *Divine and Human Pleading*, where the penitent is cast as a man rewarded with a vision of Mary Magdalene with holy fire in her eyes and a crown on her golden hair, who describes her sin as a heavy chain and clog, binding her to earth. 'It was a stain upon my hands, A curse upon my hearth,' she says feelingly.

The Magdalene, as it happens, was Dodsworth's favourite saint. He was currently busy with the inauguration of a daughter church with this dedication in the poorer part of the parish, where a prostitute had been murdered. Many years later William omitted *Divine and Human Pleading* from his edition of Christina's collected poems, on the grounds that they were rather 'preachy' – which was true but rather puzzling since the same might be said of much of her verse. Perhaps he recalled some direct link with his sister's troubles at this date, which made him distrust the poem. For it is clear that the subject spoke directly to her heart, giving expression to the burden of obscure guilt and self-blame that chained her soul.

Maude Foster describes the sequel to her spiritual crisis as follows:

the truth is, for a time I avoided as much as possible frequenting the parish church, for fear of remarks. Mamma, knowing I love St Andrew's, let me go there very often by myself ... I wanted resolution to do right; yet, believe me, I was very miserable; how I could say my prayers at that period was a mystery. So matters went on; till one day as I was returning from a shop, I met Mr Paulson. He enquired immediately whether I had been staying in the country. Of course I answered, No. Had I been ill? Again, No. Then gradually the whole story came out. I shall never forget the shame of my admissions; each word seemed forced from me, yet at last, all was told. I will not repeat all we said then, and on a subsequent occasion when he saw me at church: the end was that I partook of the Holy Communion on Easter Day. That was indeed a Feast.

Filled with a sense of sin and guilt during her breakdown, did Christina avoid the eloquent, forceful Dodsworth by attending another church? She was ill, and Christ Church was not her parish of residence; she was not bound to worship there. Closer to home was St Andrew's, Wells Street, where the choral music was much admired. Did Christina later meet Dodsworth in the street and confess her dereliction? Did he then counsel her, and offer forgiveness as a prelude to confirmation in 1846, thereby lifting her burden? As she wrote in *Divine and Human Pleading*:

> There is a mighty Power and Grace
>   Can loose the heavy chain,
> Can free the feet, can cleanse the hands,
>   Can purge the hearth again.
>   . . . .
> Weeping I sought the Lord of life,
>   Bowed with my shame and sin;
> And thereunto my wondering heart
>   Love's searching fire came in.

Confession and absolution was a contested Anglo-Catholic practice, regarded by many as Romanist and by the same token attractive to devotees, who sought out eminent figures as father confessors. One early Anglican Sister recalled the devices that were used to gain an audience with Pusey, for example, saying that 'the lady (few men went to Confession) who could obtain the privilege, was looked upon with more or less holy envy and felt correspondingly elated'. But it was provided for in the Prayerbook and offered in Pusey's eyes a means to 'trace out sin in the lurking corners of our hearts', as a prelude to all that the penitent craved 'full present absolute universal forgiveness and release'. Christina's gratitude for 'confession and absolution and spiritual counsel' shows the value she later placed on the practice. And although we can only guess at what made her feel 'unbearable to herself' and unable to 'come right' in these distressful months, it is probable that like Maude she felt the shame of her admissions, and found relief in clerical forgiveness.

For his part, Dodsworth no doubt stressed the prospective benefits of confessing each and every sin. Recently, Pusey had told Manning of a fourteen-year-old girl, who had been 'almost miraculously changed' by confession. 'All who knew her *before* ask "What magic has been practised with her",' he wrote. He also ascribed most youthful ills to sins against the seventh commandment, by which he meant 'impurity' in thought or deed. Most controversially of all, Pusey accompanied absolution by penance, a Catholic practice hardly seen in the English Church. He promoted fasting, especially before Easter, when devotees went without food for three days, he also advocated mortification of the flesh, sending one of his followers a hair shirt telling her it was 'very penitential', and also procuring the five-tailed whip known as the 'discipline' for two Anglican Sisters to use daily 'in memory of the scourging of our Lord'. He studied the spiritual exercises devised by the priest who exorcised devils at the convent of Loudun, and in 1848 was persuaded that a young woman who came to him for confession had herself been tried by such forces; indeed, he believed she had actually seen demons.

Things were less hysterical at Christ Church, but still highly charged. In May 1846 Christina completed a dramatic fantasy in which a youthful martyr is led to the stake, all too obviously betraying the sublimation of physical longing in religious arousal:

> Quickened with a fire
> Of sublime desire,
> She looked up to heaven and she cried aloud:
>   'Death, I do entreat thee,
>   Come! I go to meet thee,
> Wrap me in the whiteness of a virgin shroud.'
>   . . .
>
> On she went, on quickly,
> And her breath came thickly
> With the longing to see God coming pantingly:
>   Now the fire is kindled . . .
>
> Higher, higher mounting,
> The swift moments counting –
> Fear is left beneath her, and the chastening rod:
>   Tears no more shall blind her;

> Trouble lies behind her;
> Satisfied with hopeful rest, and replete with God.

Spiritually, Christina was marked for life by exposure to Puseyite thought. But an enigma remains. As William noted, Maria became 'serenely or even exuberantly happy' in her inner self as a result of her faith. Christina, by contrast, acquired 'an awful sense of unworthiness, shadowed by an awful certainty' of the reality of hell. For her, Satan's demons were almost as real as they were to Pusey. Why two sisters, growing up in the same environment, should respond so differently to the same religious influences is a question not easily answered.

6

Portrait of the Artist as
Young Poetess

Having SUFFERED ANOTHER bout of ill-health, in late summer 1846 Christina was sent for her first seaside holiday, to Folkestone in Kent. She took a load of books – Ariosto and Tasso and Dante and Petrarch – although, as she left behind the list of 'prohibited' passages (presumably on account of indecency) she was unable to read much of Ariosto. She enthused over Tasso, however, admiring Armida's parting and reunion with her lover, and finding Clarinda's defence of her honour 'exquisite and sublime'. This reading resulted in several Italian poems and it is possible that her studies were intended to improve her command of the language in preparation for employment as a governess. She was still destined, as William explained, to adopt 'the family vocation'. Poetry as yet was not an alternative career. Maria had somewhat reluctantly returned to the Thynnes' household, her employment with the Reads having ended.

Though lonely – it was painful to be separated from family and friends by illness, she told Mrs Heimann – Christina greatly enjoyed the seaside, as she was to do for the rest of her life. 'It is a pretty sight in brilliant holiday weather to watch the many parties of health or pleasure-seekers which throng the beach,' she later wrote:

> Boys and girls picking up shells, pebbles and star-fishes, or raising with hands and wooden spades a sand fortress, encircled by a moat full of sea-water, and crowned by a twig of seaweed as a flag; mothers and older sisters reading or working beneath shady hats, whilst after bathing their long hair dries in the sun and wind. Hard by, rock at their moorings bannered pleasure-boats, with blue-jerseyed oarsmen or white sails; and if the weather is oppressively hot and sunny, a gaily-coloured canopy is reared on light poles, for the protection of voyagers.

It was a 'never-failing pleasure' to walk along the shore searching for coloured stones, seaweeds and sea-creatures. In the late 1880s she wrote that even out of season the beach would retain its attraction for her, if she could 'potter along stone-hunting as of yore ... To this day I think I could plod indefinitely along shingle, with my eyes pretty well glued to the ground ...'

From strand and rockpool, trophies were carried home: bright pebbles that dulled in the air, seaweed for amateur weather forecasting, shells for drawing-room displays, and live creatures for salt water aquariums. And like so many holiday places, the seaside came to symbolise freedom and pleasure and escape from the duties of normal life. But at the same time, in her writing, the shore is haunted with intimations of horror and fear. The margins of sea and land became evocative coastlands where brides were drowned and ghosts came to reclaim their lovers. In one of her later stories the heroine flees inland when long walks on the beach raise intolerable visions of her drowned father; and towards the end of her life Christina identified several sea-creatures as personifications of evil and carnality, being particularly fascinated and repelled by sea-anemones, soft, dark red, fleshy excrescences in air that became waving tendrils underwater. Like the terrifying Mouth-Boy of her children's tale they had only a voracious mouth that gulped all into its chasm, and were emblems of sensuality, she asserted later, in a curiously sexual analogy, swelling in the lower element but shrivelling out of it, like the base desires they symbolised.

Towards the end of her stay at Folkestone, she wrote several poems, including *The Dead Bride* (10 September 1846) a figure who was to become a familiar inhabitant of her verse, followed by *Sappho* (11 September 1846), an extended effusion of juvenile yearning for oblivion. It is unlikely that Christina had been reading Sappho. Classical scholarship was at a low ebb in Britain, and Sappho's surviving verses were not widely read either in the original or in translation. But her reputation as 'the tenth Muse' made her a symbolic figure, both as the woman poet of unhappy love – her work was at this date taken to express heterosexual love, addressed to a faithless man – and as a name commonly bestowed on any woman with literary gifts. Once, Papa had so addressed Maria. Now Christina claimed the title for herself. She may, just possibly, have been reading Mme de Stael, who was renowned for her portrayals of creative classical figures, in art and life. Portrait engravings showed de Stael on Sappho's clifftop, in Greek chiton, holding a lyre. In her most famous novel *Corinne* the heroine is an Italian *improvisatrice*, who represents the Romantic genius in female form, and offered a role model for Christina, given her paternal inheritance. 'At a time when the reality barely existed, de Stael created the myth of the woman poet and thus made the reality imaginatively possible,' writes a recent critic. 'In *Corinne* women read the story of their own ambitions or, maybe, discovered ambitions to match its story'. As an artist, Corinne is so transported by emotion that her poetic voice issues forth in apparent spontaneity; as a lover, she is one for whom death is not defeat, but a final gesture of liberation, in defiance of the world.

The last poem written at Folkestone was *To A Murderer* (16 September 1846), in which a terrible deed has been done:

> And who is this lies prostrate at thy feet?
> And is he dead, thou man of wrath and pride?
>   Yes, now thy vengeance is complete,
>   Thy hate is satisfied . . .
>
> See where he grasped thy mantle as he fell,
> Staining it with thy blood; how terrible
>   Must be the payment due for this in hell!

With vigorous imprecation the murderer is told he will be forever haunted, and everywhere 'the air shall smell of blood'. It is a vengeful poem – quite lacking in Christian forgiveness – and some months later was retitled *Will these Hands Ne'er be Clean?* in acknowledgement of its Shakespearean source. Biographically, however, the interesting question is why Christina should have chosen such a subject, and given it such powerfully punitive force through nearly fifty violent lines, threatening the guilty man with the inescapable 'curse of memory'. Anger was not an allowable female emotion, and this fierce assault on a stage villain evidently served as a means of handling turbulent but forbidden feelings.

At the same time, however, a poem like this is also a conscious work of art. As well as masks for the self, *Sappho* and *To a Murderer* were dramatic creations. Steadily Christina was extending her range, and developing her role as 'poet of the family'. Earlier in the year she had punctuated her flow of pious verse with mock heroic lines, *On the Death of Aunt Eliza's Cat, aged ten years and a half.* Inspired by Gray's elegy on the cat drowned in the goldfish tub, this also registered her duty to record events of note. On the one hand, poetry represented something intensely private, 'really her own'; on the other, as her pieces accumulated, numbering over fifty by the time of her sixteenth birthday, it was public, copied out for all to admire. So the poems can be read both as strategies in the handling of personal emotion during some difficult years and as self-conscious steps in the construction of individual identity. If at one level they served to voice painful feelings in an indirect but allowable manner, at another they also gave their author an 'impersonal' role and potential career. Maria was a governess, William a civil servant. Gabriel was now at the RA School training to be a painter – and Christina was learning to be a poetess.

The feminine ending is significant, because poetry was 'gendered' both in production and reception. There were separate literary spheres for men and women and to an extent separate traditions too.

Alongside Tractarian and neo-classical Italian authors, contemporary women writers thus determined the poetic modes open to Christina as a girl with literary gifts.

Generally speaking the eminent women poets of the 1840s were those of feeling, sentiment and romance. There was Mrs Howitt, who sang of 'love for flowers, and Christ, and little children'. There was Mrs Southey, the laureate's widow, renowned for deathbed pathos. There was Miss Landon, or L. E. L., who defined her subjects as passion and sadness, love and sorrow, and had recently died in pathetic circumstances. Felicia Hemans, the most renowned, was praised for delicacy, pathos, and the 'spontaneous offspring of intense and noble feeling'. Some critics complained that women writers exuded too much mournfulness. Eliza Cook, with her charmingly sentimental hymn to mother's old arm-chair, was often preferred; or Charlotte Yonge, whose melancholy was deemed to be 'healthy' rather than morbid. Nevertheless all occupied the poetic territory marked out for the fair sex – a realm of feeling, beauty, piety and sorrow. Woman's faculties were held to be intuitive rather than investigative, sympathetic rather than knowledgeable. Formed for 'softness and sweet attractive grace', the woman poet should trust to tender emotion and simple thought. Her themes were nature, domestic affection, deathbeds and devotional religion. As a reviewer remarked, Mrs Hemans's charming and seemingly unstudied 'effusions' were 'in fine keeping with the sex of the writer'.

The younger generation was represented by Elizabeth Barrett, who this year became Mrs Browning after a romantic elopement. She was considered rather learned owing to her knowledge of Greek and Hebrew, but her *Poems* of 1844 were much admired for their emotional and imaginative qualities, in mock-medieval works like *The Romaunt of Margret* and *The Lay of the Brown Rosary*, a Gothick tale of an immured nun. She had also written elegies on Felicia Hemans and L.E.L, praising the 'silver song' that still rang sweetly in their readers' ears.

With her deathbed laments and spontaneous-seeming effusions of feeling, young Christina was already part of this female tradition. Its formative influence on her work is a warning against taking her expressions of sorrow too literally, but also shows how the role of poetess was defined as she took up the melody. However, though the most obvious influence on her juvenile work is undoubtedly Mrs Hemans, the writers Christina openly acknowledged seldom included the women listed here. This was in part simple denial: writers wish to be original, not imitative. It was also strategic: as Maude Foster is told, excessive melancholy was considered mannered; above all, the woman writer had to be sincere. Nor did Christina invoke

Keats, the great poet of mournfulness, while Tennyson was not yet the overweening influence on verse he later became. Her admitted models included Gray and Crabbe, whose two-volume *Poems and Tales* she gave to William on his birthday this year, some three weeks before the completion of an imitative poem. And behind these lay the eighteenth-century 'graveyard school' with its meditations on mortality:

> When I die, oh lay me low
> Where the greenest grasses grow . . .

The heroine of *Maude*, who so transparently resembles her author, is just fifteen when her story starts. She writes poems full of sorrow, that are handed about and discussed:

> some pronounced that she wrote very foolishly about things she could not possibly understand; some wondered if she really had any secret source of unhappiness; while some simply set her down as affected. Perhaps there was a degree of truth in all these opinions.

But if Maude has a secret source of sorrow, it is not revealed. Like her author, she has undergone a personality change, from animated child to languid and withdrawn adolescent 'who, without telling lies, was determined not to tell the truth'. She also knows that people think her clever, and admire her verses. Her religious crisis over holy communion is intermingled with painful self-consciousness that centres on her writing. She is conceited, dissembling, wicked, she avers: and 'sick of display, and poetry, and acting'.

Yet she is deeply proud of her writing. As the girls prepare for a party, cousin Agnes introduces a surreptitious sprig of bay into Maude's garland, in allusion to her talent. Maude disclaims the honour, but does not remove the bay, and her narrator notes that 'when placed on her dark hair it well became the really intellectual character of her face'. She then shows off by insisting on a party game that involves writing extempore sonnets. The other girls protest, but beg her compositions for their albums, prophesying that in the future Maude's 'name will be known'. Her portrait is thus, at least in part, that of the artist as young poetess.

As such *Maude* affords a glimpse of Christina's habits of composition. According to William, throughout her life her writing was 'entirely of the casual and spontaneous kind . . . If something came into her head which she found suggestive of verse, she put it into verse.' She 'scribbled the lines off rapidly enough,' he wrote, adding however that he could not recall ever seeing her in the act of composition. She did not talk about her work, or ask advice, but what she wrote was 'pretty well known in the family' as soon as the impeccably neat lines appeared in the notebooks.

Yet *Maude* contains a different account, in which the young writer, far from dashing off her verses rapidly, keeps them hidden until the work is finished. When the story opens, she is 'surrounded by a chaos of stationery'; as her mother enters, she slips the scrawls out of sight. Once more alone, she resumes composition, in a writing book containing 'original compositions not intended for the public eye, pet extracts, extraordinary little sketches, and occasional tracts of journal'. This is the sole surviving hint that Christina herself wrote poems not shown to others, and kept some sort of diary. Maude's manuscript book has a key, and when Agnes finds her in despair on Christmas Eve she has just locked it against prying eyes. No such volume of Christina's has survived, only the impeccable notebooks, but like her youthful heroine she had no taste for preservation. When Maude is dying she asks Agnes to destroy all that is 'evidently not intended to be seen'. The locked book is placed unopened in the coffin, and all other scraps – 'mere fragments, many half-effaced scrawls, some written on torn backs of letters, and some full of incomprehensible abbreviations' – are consigned to the fire. In thus imagining her own death, Christina clearly feared lest her own unfinished writings be read by others. Hence in part the absence of preliminary drafts for her poems; all must have been destroyed.

When interrupted by her mother, Maude is copying out a world-weary sonnet. Having completed it, she yawns, leans back in her chair, and wonders how to fill up the time till dinner – a mocking comment on the poetic affectation of melancholy. This recurs later in the story when friends again raise the subject, evidently au fait with the morbid female mode:

> Did she continue to write? Yes. A flood of ecstatic compliments followed this admission: she was so young, so much admired and, poor thing, looked so delicate. It was quite affecting to think of her lying awake at night meditating those sweet verses – ('I sleep like a top', Maude put in, drily) – which so delighted her friends and would so charm the public if only Miss Foster could be induced to publish. At last the bystanders were called upon to intercede for a recitation.

Gracelessly, Maude refuses to recite. Presumably Christina experienced similar requests. Young ladies were expected to sing or play the piano at social gatherings; as Christina had no music, recitation may well have been her recourse. Yet to recite one's own verses savoured of display.

And this is Maude's problem, and by extension her author's. As William noted in publishing his sister's story, Maude's only fault seems to be that when she has written a good poem, she thinks it is good. Pride, of course, was a snare, and hardly distinguishable from Mamma's bugbear, conceit. Young women should not brag about their talents; 'display' was a grievous fault. As Mrs Hemans had written regarding the allure of Fame:

> Thou hast green laurel leaves that twine
> Into so proud a wreath;
> For that resplendent gift of thine
> Heroes have smiled in death –
> AWAY! to me – a woman – bring
> Sweet waters from affection's spring;
> Give *me* from some kind hand a flower –
> The record of one happy hour!

True femininity was incompatible with public acclaim.

The social world of young ladies' tea parties, albums and competitive devotions depicted in *Maude* also offers a partial picture of Christina's teenage friendships, which are otherwise shadowy. We know however that they included the Misses Townsend, named by William as the models for Maude's cousins, whose family later went to New Zealand. There were too, the Misses Harrison, daughters of a well-known flower painter, whose circumstances were not unlike the Rossettis', for after the collapse of her husband's health Mrs Harrison maintained twelve children by means of her brush. Three at least of the daughters – Emily, Harriet and Fanny – were trained in the same art, and on Mrs Harrison's death in 1875 Christina recalled that she had known the family for some thirty years.

When Maude's cousins come to London and are invited to tea by Mrs Strawdy, an old friend of her mother's, conversation is awkward and stilted. Polite inquiries about mutual acquaintances are exchanged and a cake is dissected with mathematical precision. Under the table Maude twists her finger in an agony of boredom. When she is among her friends, however, girlish chatter flows, on Sister Magdalen's vows, and church embroidery, and more frivolous matters. 'Who did you think was the prettiest girl in the room last night? Our charming selves, of course, excepted,' asks Mary, proceeding to analyse the complexions of each guest in turn. Maude, incidentally, is described like her authoress as having been very pretty as a child, but now less so, owing to 'a habitual shrugging stoop' in .true teenage mode, and an expression 'languid and preoccupied to a painful degree'. With the addition of Christina's habitual reserve that suggested haughtiness, this sounds very like a self-portrait.

In later life, Christina was renowned for her lack of fashion consciousness; indeed as William wrote, all the female members of his family were likely to dress in the style of ten or twenty years past, without apparent awareness. Vanity, of course, was frowned on, but in youth Christina showed a natural interest in fashion, obliquely revealed in two pencil portraits by her brother. One shows her hair in the current style, with two braids that curl down round the ear to loop up with a plaited chignon. A few months later, this had given place to ringlets, held behind the ears with a comb, in another portrait that so pleased the sitter it was affectionately presented to Mrs Heimann. One would guess that ringlets were not an everyday occurrence, requiring time and assistance with curling tongs and papers. Perhaps they were worn for a special occasion, and kindly recorded for posterity by Gabriel.

Like Maude, Christina may have blushed when asked to recite, and feared poetry was a source of pride, but she also knew it gave her mother pleasure and, when devotional, was pleasing to God. Grandpapa, operating at a more secular level, promised to have her poems printed on his private press. This gave her a new sense of purpose, visible from early 1847 in the poems that continued to fill the notebook pages. One was *The Solitary Rose*, completed on 15 March and the first to celebrate the flower she chose as her emblem, no doubt prompted by the early Victorian passion for flower language and symbolism. Maria adopted the myrtle and Christina the rose, which amongst other things was also sacred to Sappho. In Christina's hands it became an ambiguous self-image, combining beauty with a sharp, wounding thorn derived both from tradition and from her own sense of buried injury and anger – or, as Maude puts it, of not being as she appeared.

At the beginning of April she completed her longest and most ambitious poem to date, *The City of Statues*. This opens in a prelapsarian world, as the speaker rambles through a wood filled with birds and bubbling streamlets. After twelve stanzas, a blight falls and darkness covers the land. The narrator then travels across a desert drear and cold, past a heap of ruins old, before entering a silent city, where doors and windows swing in the wind. Another fifteen stanzas, and she reaches a shady avenue of flowers and a splendid banquet on gold and jewelled dishes:

> In green emerald baskets were
> Sun-red apples, streaked and fair;

> Here the nectarine and peach
> And ripe plum lay, and on each
> The bloom rested everywhere.
>
> Grapes were hanging overhead,
> Purple, pale, and ruby-red;
>   And in panniers all around
>   Yellow melons shone, fresh found,
> With the dew upon them spread.
>
> And the apricot and pear
> And the pulpy fig were there,
>   Cherries and dark mulberries
>   Bunchy currants, strawberries,
> And the lemons wan and fair . . .

Finally, the banqueters are revealed, all turned to stone in the midst of feasting. Like waxworks they stare silently at the narrator, who drops her gaze. When she looks up, all have vanished. So, suddenly, the poem ends, as she returns to the ordinary world, and immediately kneels to pray.

Some sources for this dream-fantasy are easily discerned. The opening passages recall the first pages of *Melmoth*, where Immalee wanders through her paradise island, as well as Tennyson's version of the Sleeping Beauty, *The Day Dream*, which likewise features a royal court arrested in mid-banquet. Somewhere here, too, is a memory of that disconcerting visit to Madame Tussauds.

The theme, however, is moral allegory. The poem, soon retitled *The Dead City*, begins in Edenic innocence, where 'life-begetting sun' always shines. Light is then withdrawn, first intimation of the blight caused by sin. The false glamour of pleasure is seen in the splendid city's golden palaces, images of spiritual nullity. The voluptuous fruits represent soul-destroying pleasure, for which the frozen banqueters have forfeited eternal life, and is an antipole of the feast of holy communion. Thus petrifying self-indulgence ensnares young and old, man and maiden; the faithful must shut their eyes to its allure, whereupon they will awake to the sunlight of true joy, giving thanks through prayer.

This is the first in a genre of mixed moral and fantasy Christina was to make especially her own. But its dreamy sequences lead directly into the emotional domain of mysterious, unconscious feeling, as the speaker moves from one strange landscape to another. Most conspicuous of all is the choice of fruit to represent temptation – 'fruits of every size and hue, Juicy in their ripe perfection'. Some carry infantile memories of cherry trees and currant bushes at Holmer Green. Others are Mediterranean fruits familiar to Papa, brought home as treats and indelibly linked with her own relish for exotic sweetness, often against Mamma's wishes. They therefore seem to represent greedy pleasures of which Christina, as a child, had never been able to have enough.

Fruit is eminently consumable, as an emblem of fleshly lust, with immediate sensuous appeal to sight, smell, touch and taste. It also, of course, contains an implicit image of corruption. Ripe fruit is soon rotten: the bloom on the peach grows mouldy, the fat currants shrivel, the rosy apples harbour worms, as the rose conceals a thorn. What seems fair can also be foul.

The poem was a major achievement – a long and fully achieved poetic allegory – and must signal the start of Grandpapa's printing project. Perhaps, initially, he thought of printing the piece singly, as with *Rivulets* and *Hugh the Heron*. Soon, however, it grew into a small collection; the printed booklet contains four poems that are not in the notebook, evidently written during May or June. They included yet another deathbed fantasy, another lament for lost joy alluding to 'concealed indifference' and 'a covered ill' – the recurrent motif of hidden hurt – and the first of Christina's poems based on the denunciation of vanity in the Book of Ecclesiastes ('Vanity of vanities, saith the Preacher . . . I have seen all the works that are done under the sun; and, behold, all is vanity and vexation of spirit') which reads like a warning against pride.

For *Verses* by Christina G. Rossetti, printed by Gaetano Polidori at Park Village East, was a source of much pride and pleasure. *The Dead City* held premier place, followed by *The Water Spirit's Song* – the mermaid fantasy of 1844 – and forty others, a significant achievement for sixteen years.

Grandpapa prefaced the text with 'A Few Words to the Reader' explaining that the booklet was printed for his own gratification, not that of 'the authoress', a decorous denial of vanity that was no less genuine for being conventional. It was underlined by the dedicatory verse from Metastasio which, translated, reads:

Why should I fear? My songs I know are inexperienced; but my mother will not therefore refuse this first homage; indeed the lowly simplicity of the gift will tell her all the better how grateful I am to her.

Thus sanctioned, *Verses* was a filial offering to mother and grandfather, rather than self-display. And on the day of publication, Gaetano presented his 'remarkable granddaughter' with a bouquet and a *canzonetta* paying tribute to her 'pure and noble song' beginning

Queste rose ch'io ti dono	These roses I give you
Simbol sono	are a symbol
Nel diverso lo colore	in their different colours
Del tuo spirito e del tuo core	of your spirit and your heart

Her first appearance in print was thus marked by old-fashioned courtesy and warm praise. Not surprisingly, as William recalled, Christina always felt much affection for her grandfather.

Though it appears altogether a family affair, the issue of *Verses* was not as different from 'real' publication as has been thought. Private publishing of various kinds still flourished. Patrons frequently paid authors' printing costs even when books were produced by commercial firms, and proud parents like Elizabeth Barrett's father regularly arranged for their precocious productions to be printed and circulated. As was well known, Felicia Hemans was thirteen when her first volume appeared. So while *Verses* was a gesture of grandfatherly indulgence towards a favourite granddaughter, it also marked Christina's formal literary debut, and was distributed outside the family. Dr Hare, for instance, received a copy inscribed by his patient, perhaps in recognition that he had indeed encouraged her to write as an antidote to depression.

Another recipient was Mamma's relative in Devon. This led to an unforeseen result, for cousin Eliza's husband the Reverend Mr Bray, now nearly seventy, had pretensions to poetry himself, and on 24 July returned thanks for *Verses* in a 'semi-amatory vein' evidently intended to compliment the young author:

What! can a maid so young
  Feel the fond force of love?
Or childhood's harp be strung
  Most women's power above?

Yes. For what's stranger still,
  I feel my heart, so old,
If passion prompt its will
  Has never yet been cold.

The first and last to beat,
  The heart – by God's own breath
Of life and love the seat –
  Is ever young at death.

When these 'equivocal compliments' arrived, Christina was enjoying a holiday with her parents, at Herne Bay in Kent. She was filled with dismay, perhaps exacerbated by the fear that she had invited such a response by writing on passion like any juvenile Sappho. With facetious self-consciousness, she told William of her 'illimitable and indescribable' contempt for Mr Bray. Maria was equally outraged. 'I can only say,' she wrote

> I am provoked that anyone who could write such stuff, equally below the dignity of a man and a clergyman, should ever have had anything half as nice as your poems to write about. I return the lines with disgusted thanks and adequate astonishment.

Gabriel was of the same opinion, advising her to 'consign the fool and his folly to utter mental oblivion'. But it was a warning, against self-exposure.

At Herne Bay, Christina was again enjoying the seashore. As she later wrote in *Hero*, there were many treasures to be found washed up on the beach: a rose-coloured shell with wings, a jewelled starfish, a branch of satiny seaweed, or wet pebbles glowing like gold and ivory. She was not without company of her own age, for also holidaying at Herne Bay was a friend of Mamma's named Mrs Marsh, together with a young relative named Anna Mary Fourdrinier, whom Christina found very cordial. Here too, she met Emily Newton and her sisters, pious members of the local church, with whom she kept up a lifelong acquaintance.

Verses evidently acted as a stimulus to further composition, and the autumn of 1847 was an extremely productive season. Between September and December nineteen new pieces were copied into the notebook. The last half dozen were written out by Christina herself, indicating self-confidence and the fact that poems were flowing too fast to await her sister's visits home. Whatever the reason, there was now no doubt that Christina was 'the poet in the family', as Maria had prophesied.

She was still enjoying the Gothick tales of Maturin, and this year saw no fewer than five poems based on his characters, including two for the child of nature seduced by the satanic Melmoth. Now Christina depicted the moment of her death in the dungeon, still ready to sacrifice her immortal soul to save his. 'Yea from hell I would look up' she tells her demon lover, 'And behold thee in my place, Drinking from the living cup.' As William noted, something extraordinarily strong drew his sister to this story. It blended with the strong thread of heartache and hidden pain, silenced or stony emotion disguising inner terror, that seems to reflect the continuing impact of her breakdown, and was prominent in the new poems. In time, this gloominess became something of a family joke, which Christina shared, and regretted without being able to alter. As she later explained to Dr Heimann, this was more or less how her poems came. Thus in *The Last Hope* on 22 September, exploring a sense of dual consciousness:

> What time I am where others be
>   My heart seems very calm –
> Stone calm: but, if all go from me,
>   There comes a vague alarm,
> A shrinking in the memory
>   From some forgotten harm.
>
> And often through the long long night,
>   Waking when none are near,
> I feel my heart beat fast with fright,
>   Yet know not what I fear . . .
>
> Sometimes I can nor weep nor pray,
>   But am half-stupefied;
> And then all those who see me say
>   Mine eyes are opened wide
> And that my wits are gone astray: –
>   Ah would that I had died!

Thus, too, in *Anne of Warwick* on 27 September, as the widowed noblewoman grieves for her dead husband:

> Who hath talked of weeping? – yet
>   There is something at my heart
> Gnawing, I would fain forget,
>   And an aching and a smart –

The temperature is always chill – Christina's poems are typically wintry – with a repeated motif of stoical self-silencing:

> Then cried I to my heart: If thou wilt, break,
> But be thou still; no moaning will I make.

and death is always calling. A long devotional piece in December contained the lines

> Mourn not, my Father, that I seek
> One who is strong when I am weak . . .

His care for me is more than mine,
Father; His love is more than thine.
Sickness and death I have from thee,
From Him have immortality . . .

Although she does not seem to have discussed poetry with her father, his example was constantly before her, and around this time she wrote lines now entitled *Sognando* (*Dreaming*) which she said were 'fired by Papa's calling this metre difficult'. The metre was that of his published volume *Il Tempo* (1843), into which she later copied her own verses, beginning

Ne' sogni ti veggo
amante ed amico . . .

Earlier this year Papa had finally acknowledged that he could no longer teach, and had relinquished his Professorship. 'God has seen fit to afflict me with a terrible calamity and I resign myself to his supreme will,' he wrote to the college authorities. In despondency, he too turned to religion and repentance. 'Remember me, O Lord, of sinners me the woefullest,' he wrote in one poem devoted to contrition. But he was still loud in lamentation. He was old, toothless and nearly blind, he told Lyell a few months later; it was a miracle he was not already in his grave. He sat daily hunched at his desk, with his eyeshade and snuff box, writing in his microscopic hand and shaking surplus ink from his nib. One of Christina's tasks was to fill the inkwell and provide pen-wipers. On 30 November, one of these came with Lines: *Given with a Pen-Wiper* – orotund verses in the voice of the lowly wiper:

I have compassion on the carpeting
   And on your back I have compassion too.
The splendid Brussels web is suffering
   In the dimmed lustre of each glowing hue;
And you the everlasting altering
   Of your position with strange aches must rue.
Behold, I come the carpet to preserve
And save your spine from a continual curve.

The satire must have raised a smile: surely the threadbare Charlotte Street carpet was no splendid 'Brussels web'. But the lines have pathos too, for behind the humour lies a sense of all the other ills the poet-penwiper was unable to remedy. But at least the situation had stabilised. It was now five years since her father's collapse, and under Mamma's careful management the family had survived. Christina too was recovering – aided by the publication of *Verses*, and something of her spirit was returning. In company she was often quiet, occasionally bursting out with a strong or unexpected remark that hinted at vehemence beneath the skin.

7

The PRB

POLITICALLY, THERE HAD been encouraging developments in Italy, where the newly elected Pope Pius IX had threatened to excommunicate the Hapsburg Emperor and his subjects in protest against the continuing occupation of Italian territory. While Christina was at Herne Bay, the Heimanns went to hear the Swedish soprano, Jenny Lind, and reported that a hymn had also been sung in honour of the Pope's patriotism. By the spring of 1848 optimism was surging throughout Europe, making this 'the year of revolutions' everywhere except Britain (where, in April, William and his colleagues were issued with truncheons to defend government offices against the expected Chartist mob, which in the event dispersed quietly). In Italy, the Austrian army was driven from Milan and Venice, bringing a real prospect of liberation from autocracy. By April things looked hopeful too in Naples – 'so leave London and come back to your country where you will be received with rejoicing,' wrote General Pepe, Gabriele's old comrade. Papa began to look forward to a homecoming in late summer, when things had settled down.

This prospect seems not to have disturbed the Charlotte Street household; probably they knew only too well that he was unlikely to travel far again. Had it been a real possibility, no doubt he would have wished all to return after his quarter century in exile, and though Gabriel and William might have declined, both Maria and Christina would have been expected to accompany their parents. Yet none seems even to have contemplated such a move. In any case, political events intervened. 'I cannot tell you how uneasy my heart is over the delays and the uncertainties of Italy's fortunes,' Gabriele wrote urging his compatriots to strike while the iron was hot; otherwise, he feared he would die 'in the land of mists' after all. Things got worse: constitutional government collapsed in Naples and autocracy returned; now he swore not to return until Ferdinand was dead. Pius IX became 'Pio? No! No!', execrated for pusillanimity. In August the Austrians regained control of Milan and eventually retook Venice. Britain and France refused to act. 'Horrible, horrible!' wrote Gabriele. 'Even that hope has failed me! I had clung to it as a raft in the miserable shipwreck of my life.' And in October he acknowledged that hopes of Italian freedom were over, informing Lyell it was providential that he had resisted the calls to return.

Some restiveness seems to have rubbed off on Gabriel however, who had chafed against the Royal Academy training, based on disciplines devised for students a century before. In the spring of 1847, using William's money, he bought a manuscript by William Blake with jottings and jeerings against artists like Rubens and Rembrandt and especially Reynolds, whose *Discourses* on painting formed the backbone of art training in Britain. 'Reynolds thinks that Man learns all that he knows,' wrote Blake scornfully in relation to artistic aptitude. 'I say on the contrary that Man Brings All that he has or can have Into the world with him ... Man is Born Like a Garden ready Planted & Sown ... What has Reasoning to do with the Art of Painting?' Inspiration was the key to all creativity. This appealed to Gabriel far more than the tedious exercises in outline and shading, anatomy and perspective, and he thought seriously of abandoning art for literature, where more Romantic notions already ruled.

As often happens in adolescence, Christina's relationship with her elder brother had grown more distant. Now, the appearance of *Verses* alerted him to the fact that his kid sister was growing up with a distinct gift. He was inspired to emulation, in several lyrics that betray rivalry. *My Sister's Sleep*, for instance, is a deathbed item with her very own wintry chill:

> Without, there was a cold moon up,
>   Of winter radiance sheer and thin;
>   the hollow halo it was in
> Was like an icy crystal cup.

The religio-Romantic *Blessed Damozel* followed, imitative of her dialogues across death's threshold.

In the event, Gabriel decided not to take up poetry, persuaded that painters made more money. But for a while he pursued the two arts, and this brought sister and brother into a new alliance. As Maria relinquished her role in copying out Christina's verses, Gabriel stepped forward as a partner in composition. Henceforth, though Christina remained devoted to her sister, it was her brother with whom she shared a more significant identity as fellow artist.

He showed a renewed brotherly affection, too. Somewhere around this time he took her to the Zoo, where he whimsically wondered what the animals were saying to each other. Characteristically, Christina thought the birds sang plaintive songs, but Gabriel made her laugh by inventing comic biographies for the different creatures. As they walked home through Regents Park there was a magnificent sunset, which he declared was setting fire to the distant trees and rooftops. Some little while later, she dreamt of walking in the Park before dawn

> and just as the sun rose, she saw what looked like a wave of yellow light sweep from the trees. This 'wave' was a multitude of canaries. Thousands of them rose, circled in a gleaming mass and then dispersed in every direction. In her dream it was borne in upon her that all the canaries in London had met and were now returning to their cages!

The image of escape is striking, for one who felt 'pent up' in the city, but the sequel is significant, for as with the sunset Gabriel's imagination was fired: he declared the dream to be symbolic, with 'some strange personal significance', and announced that he would paint it, showing the dreamer as a visionary clad in yellow, with the ground underfoot covered in primroses, as the yellow canaries wheeled overhead. He promised to write a poem too, saying Christina should do the same, though she waited in vain for both his painting and poem. 'I don't believe there was anything but whim behind his words,' she said later. 'He was always like that as far back as I can remember.'

But if airy, Gabriel's whims were stimulating, and an essential encouragement. It may be said that from father and grandfather Christina received training in prosody and diction; from mother and sister religion and morality; and from Gabriel the vital freedoms of fantasy and invention – the liberation of imagination. And there was practical encouragement, too, for towards the end of 1847 he made Christina and William try their hand at the *bouts rimés* parlour game described in *Maude*, where contestants write verses to a prescribed rhyme-scheme, competing against each other and the clock – playful but productive practice in composition.

Perhaps also newly aware of her relatively restricted life, Gabriel also began to discuss contemporary poetry with his sister, sharing books and broadening her literary knowledge in a way that neither Papa nor Grandpapa, with their essentially backward-looking interests, was able to do.

In 1847, for instance, he came across 'beautiful and original' poems by the unknown author William Bell Scott, sharing his enthusiasm with the family and sending off a letter of admiration, with copies of his own work. Scott, who was a painter as well as poet, was intrigued; now principal of the School of Design in Newcastle, he visited London regularly, and so it was he who on a winter afternoon called at 50 Charlotte Street, and found Christina and her father by a blazing fire in the front parlour, he an old gentleman bent over a thick manuscript book and she a slight girl standing at a desk, who curtseyed and then resumed writing. Gabriel was not at home and Scott soon took his leave. Later, he learnt that she had already written, like her brother, 'some admirable lyrics, nearly all overshadowed with melancholy'. At that moment however she is more likely to have been polishing the penwiper's lines.

Another new acquaintance was the painter Ford Madox Brown, to whom Gabriel also wrote a fulsome letter. The story goes that, fancying the flattery to be sarcastic, Brown took a stout walking stick to Charlotte Street, where he was at once disarmed by Gabriel's sincerity, and agreed to take him as a pupil. Gabriel then abandoned the RA, induced aunt Charlotte to provide funds and moved into Brown's studio. This tuition also proved too conventional, however, and within a few months Gabriel had decamped to the studio of a fellow student named Holman Hunt. His erratic progress was no doubt a cause for concern – he was still earning nothing and costing something – but his brother and sisters benefitted from his expanding network.

Gabriel had admired Hunt's painting of a scene from Keats's *Eve of St Agnes* and found him idealistic, ambitious, and full of boisterous energy; within a short while they were firm friends. During August they took sketching excursions together, when Gabriel all too frequently abandoned drawing in favour of verse-writing, and discovered that Hunt too had literary aspirations. They knew other artists who also wrote: sculptors Thomas Woolner and John Hancock, and painters Walter Deverell and James Collinson. Soon, they had formed the nucleus of a proposed literary club, with the idea of eventually including 'all the nice chaps we know who do anything in the literary line'. Christina, Gabriel told Hunt, would also be a member, and the first full meeting would be held at Charlotte Street.

She and Maria had been in Brighton for more than a month, in order to benefit from the sea air during Maria's vacation. Maria enjoyed bathing, from a machine, but Christina was forbidden this pleasant activity, presumably on medical grounds. Instead they spent long mornings on the beach with their needlework, fending off hawkers and snobbishly voting the pier 'rather dreary' – this year's favourite adjective. Later Mamma, Grandpapa and William came to Brighton, while Maria returned to London to keep house for Papa.

Christina declined to join the literary club. 'When I proposed that my sister should join, I never meant that she should attend the meetings, to which I know it would be impossible to persuade her,' Gabriel told Hunt rather lamely. 'I merely intended that she should entrust her productions to my reading; but must give up the idea, as I find she objects to this also, under the impression that it would seem like display, I believe – a sort of thing she abhors'. 'Display' was of course close cousin to conceit, but it was more probably the indecorum of a mixed group that frightened her. It was one thing for Maude Foster to be asked for a bashful recitation in the drawing-room, but to join young men, even by proxy, was to risk being considered immodest as well as boastful. No doubt this was sincerely felt, yet the objection came from a girl who was at this very moment reading L. E. L.'s *The Improvisatrice*, based on Mme de Stael's *Corinne*, about a female figure whose very forte is display and self-proclaimed genius. However, she was also shy and sensitive to criticism: could she lay her work open to the young men's comments? They were certainly loud in their likes and dislikes. The recently published *Life and Letters of Keats* was greeted with enthusiasm, but other poets were mocked. One evening, as darkness fell in Woolner's studio, they began a collective parody of those considered most vapid, Hunt's lines partaking 'of the meta-physico-mysterioso-obscure,' as Gabriel told William, urging him not to forget the literary club's next meeting. 'Does Christina write? Love to Mamma, etc.,' he concluded.

Christina was certainly writing, if *bouts rimés* can be so dignified. Partly because it was wet and dull at dreary Brighton, she and William bombarded Gabriel daily with rhymes and sonnets. She was adept and speedy, William wrote later, noting that her first sonnet in this series was done in nine minutes and the ninth in five. Altogether, she composed twenty such, each in under ten minutes, scribbled on small sheets of ruled paper where the rhyme words were already pencilled and showing few visible fumblings or second thoughts. At the end of each poem she noted the time taken, which was half the point of the game. Seven of the twenty sonnets were deemed good enough to be copied, with minor alterations, into the notebook; the remainder were rejected but not destroyed. Owing to the rapid composition, the texts are almost in the nature of automatic writing, their themes were always prompted by the rhyme words, and although generally dis-missed as insignificant compositions, they reflect very present concerns.

One was surely inspired by Maria, and must refer to the thrush whose elegy she had composed:

> Listen and I will tell you of a face,
>   Not lovely but made beautiful by mind;
>   Lighted up with dark eyes in which you find
> All womanly affections have their place . . .
>
> And when I think upon her bosom heaving,
> And her full glistening eyes looking on me

> When the poor bird was struggling; I still see
> The throbbing tenderness of virgin glow ...

Ennui is the theme of others, in heartfelt Romantic pastiche. 'I sit alone all day, I sit and think – I watch the sun arise, I watch it sink,' proclaims one despondently. A third laments lost happiness in a manner that recalls regret for Holmer Green:

> The spring is come again not as at first
> For then it was my spring: & now a brood
> Of bitter memories haunt me, & my mood
> Is much changed from the time when I was nursed
> In the still country. Oh! my heart could burst
> Thinking upon the long ago: the crude
> Hopes all unrealised ...
> And though I know the kingcups are as fine
> As they were then, my spirit cannot soar
> As it did once ...

This was, Gabriel judged, as good as anything she had written, and well worthy of revision.

Not all were so lugubrious, for Gabriel's high spirits had rewoken the wry humour in Christina's verse. One sonnet rebuked the typical English summer:

> And is this August weather? nay not so
> With the long rain the cornfield waxeth dark,
> How the cold rain comes pouring down! and hark
> To the chill wind whose measured pace and slow
> Seems still to linger, being loth to go.
> I cannot stand beside the sea and mark
> Its grandeur; it's too wet for that ...
> And since its name is August all men find
> Fire not allowable ...

'Hath the sun ever shone?' this ends mournfully. 'Cheer up, there can be nothing more to mind.'

Another sonnet featured a 'gnashing madman', whose body is carelessly chucked into a common plaguepit. Gabriel was delighted. 'I grinned tremendously over Christina's *Plague*,' he wrote to William, returning a 'howling canticle' of his own that mimics his sister's most dismal tones. 'Apropos of death,' he continued, 'Hunt and I are going to get up among our acquaintance a Mutual Suicide Association' – a proposal whereby any member, 'may call at any time upon another to cut his throat for him'. Like his poem, this seems to have been in satiric response to mortuary affectation, in which cultured persons – including his sister in so many poems – declared themselves weary of life. 'It is all of course to be done very quietly, without weeping or gnashing of teeth,' he explained. 'I, for instance, am to go in and say, "I say, Hunt, just stop painting that head a minute and cut my throat"; to which he will respond by telling the model to keep the position as he shall only be a moment, and having done his duty, will proceed with his painting.' In her *Plague* poem mood, Christina probably grinned tremendously at this idea.

The literary club did not meet in William's absence, though Deverell sent something about 'a distressingly ideal poet yearning for the inane' and Collinson, who had been sketching in the Isle of Wight, had finished a poem on Jesus's childhood. But in Hunt's Cleveland Street studio the young artists drew up a list of 'Immortals, forming our creed', and planned to transcribe various passages from their favoured poets to be stuck up about the walls. The Immortals included some thirty writers, from Homer and Isaiah to Mrs Browning and Coventry Patmore, and nineteen artists, from Phidias to Wilkie. The ranking suggests that the criteria were more literary than artistic, for three stars were awarded to Shakespeare and the author of Job, and two to Dante, Chaucer, Goethe, Keats, Shelley, Landor, Thackeray and Browning. Leonardo had two stars, Fra Angelico and Raphael one each.

This last name has a somewhat ironic presence among the young painters' list of heroes, for a short time later the poetic club was dissolved in favour of a new grouping, the now-famous Pre-Raphaelite Brotherhood, a fraternity devoted in the first instance to rubbishing Raphael and his influence. Curiously, considering its fame, the exact formation of the PRB is obscure and undocumented, but to the original group of Gabriel, Hunt, Woolner and Collinson was soon added Hunt's friend John Millais, a prize-winning student at the Academy and a 'very good fellow'; William – by virtue of his attendance at a life class where, in Hunt's words, he regularly executed rigid transcripts of the nude; and Hunt's protégé Fred Stephens, who had hardly made more progress in art than William but who was assured that 'he also, with the whirl of enthusiasm in operation' might become an active artist. Their art was to be modern but sincere, spirited and sharing the lyric piety of early Italian and Flemish art. At an inspired moment no one could specifically recall, they chose the name Pre-Raphaelite Brotherhood, devised the monogram 'PRB' to add to their signatures, and swore themselves to secrecy.

All this was related with great glee at Charlotte Street. At the age of twenty, Gabriel was in his element as acknowledged leader. In practice, he was not the best painter, but in imagination and ambition he led the way, exhibiting a good deal of his father's expansiveness and charm. And indeed, a glow of general exhilaration seems to have been cast over the whole band, in which Christina was also caught: her later verses on the 'great PRB' for all their gentle mockery show with what delight she responded to her brothers' new Brethren.

They were occasionally invited to dine at Charlotte Street, where the Brotherhood met in the boys' upstairs room. In the parlour Fred Stephens remembered the shrunken figure of Signor Rossetti, looking 'like an old and somewhat imperative prophet', his voice having a 'slightly rigorous ring' when speaking to his sons. Beside the fire sat Mamma, 'erect, comely and very English'. Hunt's impressions give a vivid portrait of the family, as he recalled his first visit, and his embarrassment when Papa failed to register his name:

> The father arose to receive me from a group of foreigners around the fire, all escaped revolutionists from the Continent, and addressed me in English with a few words of welcome as "Mr Madox Brown", a slip on which his eldest daughter rated him pleasantly. He was so engrossed in a warm discussion going on that some minutes afterwards he again made the same mistake. The conversation was in Italian, but occasionally merged into French ... The tragic passions of the group round the fire did not in the slightest degree involve either the mother, the daughters, or the sons, except when the latter explained that the objects of the severest denunciation were Bomba, Pio Nono and Metternich, or, in turn, Count Rosso and his memory; with these execrated names were uttered in different tones those of Mazzini, Garibaldi and Louis Napoleon, who had once been a visitor at the house.

Events in Italy were confused. By mid-November there was chronic unrest in the Papal States, causing Pio Nono to flee to Neapolitan territory. The Austrians still held Lombardy and Venetia, with control in Tuscany and Parma. Mazzini and Garibaldi were in Rome, with uncertain prospects. Not understanding the content of the political discussion, Hunt was nevertheless drawn into its atmosphere. As each new orator took up 'the words of mourning and appeal to the too tardy heavens, the predecessor kept up the refrain of sighs and groans'.

> Gabriel and William shrugged their shoulders, the latter with a languid sign of commiseration, saying it was generally so. As the dinner was being put on the table some of the strangers persisted, despite invitation, in going; some still stayed round the fire declaring solemnly that they had dined

and when the meal was over, the young men adjourned upstairs, leaving the rest of the company, including Christina, to dominoes, chess and other sedate pursuits.

The young women of her own social world, with their churchgoing, albums, embroidery and what she called 'perpetual talk of *beaus*', could hardly compete with her brothers' new friends with their exciting ideas of astonishing the Academy and winning global renown. And even though she could not join in directly, her vicarious participation was considerable, especially since neither Gabriel nor William were accustomed to excluding women from general conversation. Moreover, amid the excitement that attended the early days of the PRB, literary ambition was not forgotten. Somewhat unexpectedly, William was the first to appear in print, when his poem *In the Hill Shadow*, written at Brighton, was accepted by the *Athenaeum*, the major literary weekly of the time and published on 23 September. Following this triumph, Gabriel declared something of Christina's must be despatched. Publication was apparently not the same as 'display', and she allowed him to choose two poems from the notebooks that had not been selected for *Verses*. Both were accepted. *Death's Chill Between* appeared on 14 October, and *Heart's Chill Between* the following week, over the initials 'C. G. R.'.

To have two poems in a national paper at the age of seventeen was a remarkable achievement, the literary equivalent of a prestigious debut at the RA, and throws some doubt on Christina's fear of showing off, for such public success was hardly appropriate to a shrinking violet. The coup no doubt owed much to Gabriel's boldness, and also to his imaginative retitling of the poems, for *Death's Chill Between* was Anne of Warwick's lament and *Heart's Chill Between* had formerly been *The Last Hope*, with its haunting evocation of a dissociated consciousness and inexplicable terror. It is not known what prompted Gabriel to include the word 'chill' in his titles, except perhaps the reference to 'cold rain' in the first. Yet his choice was perceptive, for Christina's poetic signature was already written in icy tones and petrified emotional states. The titles of her first published work thus prefigure her dominant poetic themes in a strikingly apt manner, foreshadowing the mode by which she would be best known to her audience.

For once, there is evidence of Papa's reponse, as he proudly informed Lyell how some poetry by his second son and youngest daughter had been received with 'great praise'. Apart from this, surviving family letters make no mention of either event. Nor was there any sequel. The editor, apparently, rejected further submissions on the grounds that they were 'too infected with Tennysonian mannerisms'. Nevertheless, it was gratifying early success.

And amid the excitement of this eventful autumn, Christina became engaged to James Collinson. This was unexpected, because she had been unaware of his feelings, and happened rather quickly despite several obstacles.

A year or so older than Gabriel, James Collinson had been a fellow student at the RA. He was further advanced professionally, having first exhibited in 1847 with a genre scene called *The Charity Boy's Debut*, whose moral flavour was in keeping with the tenor of the times. It is said that Gabriel was so impressed by this picture that he sought out the artist, but Collinson was already known to the family as a member of the congregation at Christ Church, Albany Street where, William noted, 'he was remarked by my female relatives for his heedful and devout bearing'. It is possible that the scene in his painting, which showed a parish lad putting on his uniform, was taken from one of the Christ Church schools, where the children wore a distinctive livery. If so, the subject had a special appeal for his fellow-worshippers.

Collinson came from Mansfield in Nottinghamshire where his late father's bookselling business was carried on by an elder brother. He lived on a modest allowance in Somers Town, lodging in a square inaptly named the Polygon, where the landlady was reputedly a 'dragonness'. In 1848, his picture for the RA was a sentimental scene of a little girl and two boys, with the coy title *The Rivals*, which was presumably saleable but sounds very like the sort of thing the Brotherhood deemed 'sloshy'. Around this time, James joined the Church of Rome, under the influence of Cardinal Wiseman and possibly one of the Christ Church curates, who had 'gone over'. He remained a member of the artists' circle however, and was thus among those swept into both the poetic club and the PRB by Gabriel's enthusiasm. By late August the two were on very friendly terms, going to hear Grisi sing, and to see a melodrama, where one of the pirates was observed to be wearing trouser-straps. Hunt, who remembered that the *Charity Boy* had caused a great stir among the critics, described how Gabriel 'took possession' of Collinson, declaring he was a painter of great promise. This was typical of Gabriel, but also indicates what his friendship may have meant to James, who was somewhat lonely in his lodgings. No doubt too the Rossetti home struck him as unusual and welcoming as it did Hunt, with the boys' genial companionship and the sisters' warm interest in each visitor. And knowing that young Mr Collinson was as devout as themselves, albeit of now a different persuasion, the women's sympathy towards the young provincial painter would have been considerable.

His current work in progress testified to his seriousness, for the subjects included 'The New Curate' and 'the Novitiate to a Nunnery', perhaps inspired by the Park Village Sisterhood. His main project was an ambitious figure group showing itinerant Italian image-sellers displaying statuettes of the Virgin at a wayside inn, which combined a genre style (James was not yet a convert to the 'Pre-Raphaelite' manner, which was indeed hardly yet in existence) with a religious (and Catholic) theme. In other ways, however, it was rather mundane. By contrast Hunt, in homage to political events in Europe (and perhaps to his new friendship with the Rossettis) had chosen the heroic *Rienzi* in which an early liberator of Italy vows to avenge the victims of tyranny. Millais, even more pictorially ambitious, had composed a foreshortened group for Keats's *Lorenzo and Isabella*, and Gabriel, though no churchgoer, was working on a picture of Christina and Mamma as the Virgin and St Anne, in 'early Italian' style. These were the paintings with which the PRB were to astonish the staid and sloshy Academy next spring.

For the literary club, Collinson had written a poem called *The Child Jesus*, a five-part narrative 'emblematical of the "five sorrowful mysteries" of the Atonement'. Set beside the Sea of Galilee, each part recounts a supposed incident in Christ's childhood prefiguring his Passion. Highly Tractarian in its typology, the poem was also notable for its placing of biblical incidents in a pastoral English landscape – around the Holy Family's humble home grow honeysuckle and mossrose as well as a sunny vine, and Jesus's playmates gather English flowers. Both subject and handling seem to have influenced Gabriel, for in his *Girlhood of Mary Virgin*, St Joachim is seen tending a vine such as grows in James's poem, just as the dove that hovers over Mary in Gabriel's picture surely belongs to the same family as those in *The Child Jesus*. Indeed poem and painting seem to be interlinked, at the moment when Gabriel's friendship with Collinson was at its height, and Christina was sitting for the figure of the Virgin, so that all three were implicated in a cluster of artistic projects with devotional meaning. It is therefore not surprising that, sometime during October, encouraged by the warmth he felt towards the whole family, James found himself attracted to the quiet younger sister, and that he expressed his admiration to Gabriel, who immediately urged Christina to accept.

Whatever expressions of mutual regard had passed between the pair this was probably more precipitate than either had intended. Moreover, according to social convention, a proposal should first have been sanctioned by the suitor's family and then communicated to the young woman's father, whose formal consent was required while she was under age. Christina was not yet eighteen, and James was hardly in a position to offer marriage, being still dependent on his family. The whole thing, one suspects, was chiefly Gabriel's doing, carried along by his liking for James and his wish for Christina to enjoy more of the activities of the Brotherhood. Perhaps, too, he wanted to save her from having to go away as a governess or stay home to care for Papa, so that the prospect of her becoming affianced to one of the Brethren presented itself as a brilliant solution. There was no thought of immediate marriage, rather a long engagement until James was established in his career.

Of all the PRBs, James Collinson was certainly the most eligible suitor, having already begun to make his name. He came from a respectable, if provincial family. But there were two snags: Christina was not in love with him, and he was a member of the Catholic Church.

When he came, over half a century later, to make public the details of this affair, William's account was carefully worded. 'I cannot say that she was in love with James Collinson in any such sense that she would, before knowing him to be enamoured of her, have wished him to become so,' he wrote. 'In breeding and tone of mind, not to speak of actual genius or advantages, she was markedly his superior.' Moreover, 'though not indisposed to his suit on general grounds, [she] was unwilling to marry a member of a religious communion other than her own.'

She therefore declined his offer. But was this the real reason? William, indeed, was puzzled by his own explanation, knowing that his sister was never hostile to Catholics, considering them as 'authentic members of the Church of Christ, although in error upon some points'. Nor was she prejudiced against inter-faith marriages – indeed both her parents and grandparents offered examples of successful Anglican-Catholic partnerships. But currently there was a great deal of turbulent ecclesiastical feeling, which she herself had alluded to in a poem a few months earlier, citing rifts within the Holy Church. The powerfully unsettling influence of Newman, who joined the Church of Rome in 1845 was now effectively creating schism in High Anglican circles, as members strove to encourage or prevent others from 'going over'. Many years later, Christina penned a memorial sonnet to Newman, recalling his impact and commending the depth of his faith, but at the time she, like her female relatives, withstood the 'flood' that wished to wash all Tractarians towards Rome. Simultaneously she and Maria also resisted the overt endeavours of uncle Henry to draw them into the Catholic fold. So she had already signalled her Anglican loyalties.

There was moreover another very strong reason why she could not accept a Catholic marriage proposal, which was her father's decided hostility towards the Papacy. To Papa, hopes of returning in honour to his homeland had been first betrayed by Pio IX and then 'quenched in blood', and he was now vociferously anti-Catholic. Indeed, he was attaching himself to the Protestant faith, with a volume of verse entitled *L'Arpa Evangelica* and contributions to *L'Eco di Savonarola*, a magazine dedicated to preventing the Church of Rome from 'recovering' Britain and thence 'Romanising' the whole world. Politics and religion were of course intertwined, and sections of the Anglican Church – which then represented the most powerful nation in the world – were already evangelising in the Catholic countries of Europe, in order to 'rescue' them from superstition. Spiritual and material support was offered to those who would deconvert, as it were, in order to proselytise in their own countries and also minister to Protestant congregations – a major concern for pious British tourists. After the liberalisation of political affairs in early 1848, thousands of copies of the vernacular Diodati Bible were distributed in Tuscany, until with returning autocracy such Protestant propaganda was prohibited. Italian nationals were forbidden to attend Protestant worship; some were harassed and arrested, and even celebrated in Britain and America as true Christian martyrs. It was against this background that Gabriele Rossetti became involved with what his son called 'anti-Papal protestantizing religionists ... disfrocked priests and semi-Waldensian semi-simpletons' who 'got a good deal about him when his broken health and precarious eyesight enfeebled his mental and bodily powers'.

He would not therefore have looked favourably on his daughter marrying a papist, and the difference of religion allowed Christina to decline James's offer without obliging him to break off all family friendship or making Gabriel look foolish. But if, as one presumes, her reply was polite and gentle, it had an unforeseen effect. 'Collinson, upon receiving this refusal, set about considering whether he really was so firmly a Catholic as to be unable to revert to his original membership of the Church of England,' wrote William; 'he thought he *could* do this, resumed attending an Anglican place of worship, and renewed his suit to Christina, as being no longer a Roman Catholic. Hereupon he was accepted.'

Her acceptance has often puzzled biographers, who feel that Collinson was hardly a worthy suitor. But he was a member of the PRB, whom Gabriel proclaimed would do great things. And a proposal of marriage was naturally romantic and flattering. Christina knew, from novels if nowhere else, that an offer was not to be turned down lightly. It was a daughter's duty to marry as well as was compatible with happiness, especially when family circumstances were straitened. Mamma must have approved, perhaps hoping an engagement would stabilise Christina's mental and physical health. Moreover, she was scrupulously honest: having given one reason for refusal, she may have felt that she could not in honour refuse Mr Collinson once that objection was removed. Shy and uncertain, she may have trusted that love would follow, and that her suitor was at any rate gentle and as timid as herself. Whatever the reason, she accepted James Collinson without being exactly in love with him and then proceeded, in William's words, to 'freely and warmly' bestow her affections upon him.

There seems to have been no formal announcement, no exchange of gifts, no introductions. If Papa, in typical fashion, lamented the loss of a daughter, or rejoiced in her good fortune, it was not recorded. One wonders how much he was actually told.

In appearance James was somewhat insignificant, small and rather dumpy in stature, with a thick neck according to William, although his own self-portrait shows a more refined figure, with straight nose, thin lips and receding hair. He was not unintelligent, and talked good sense, but did not shine in conversation, for his manner was subdued. To Holman Hunt, who later disclosed the engagement to Christina's first biographer, Collinson appeared 'tame and sleepy'. He joined in the studio gatherings but could 'rarely see the fun of anything, although he sometimes laughed in a lachrymose manner'. In the manner of young men who do not have to go to work in the morning, the others stayed up convivially late, but James tended to go home, or fall asleep. One incident stuck in Hunt's memory:

Once, concluding a meeting at my studio, on going to the door with him near midnight, we discovered that it was a magnificent moonlit night, and we resolved that, instead of going to bed, we would take a long walk in the country. He pleaded that he must go home to bed, and when we pointed out that for a real change, which might be of great permanent benefit to him, he should consider that he had had enough sleeping, he insisted that he must really go back to change his boots; and eventually we let him depart with the promise that he would be ready for us when we should call in half an hour. We arrived punctually, but knocked for a time in vain. In ten minutes a voice from the second floor window thundered out to ask why we went on knocking when we knew that Mr Collinson had long since been in bed ... Collinson came to his window sleepily entreating to be left alone; but we explained that we had chosen a northerly course solely on his account, and that he must not now disappoint us. He gave in, and came with us on our walk ...

Eagerly they set off through the fast emptying streets towards Hampstead Heath, climbing up through the Vale of Health and then down to the hamlet of North End, where they rested around the village pump. When they decided to start back, they had again to wake

Collinson, setting up a lusty shout that brought nightcapped heads to all the cottage windows.

Christina's own record of Collinson includes a less adventurous walk, probably in Regents Park, commemorated in a sonnet written some weeks into the engagement:

> Have you forgotten how one Summer night
>   We wandered forth together with the moon,
>   While warm winds hummed to us a sleepy tune?
> Have you forgotten how you praised both light
> And darkness; not embarrassed yet not quite
>   At ease? and how you said the glare of noon
>   Less pleased you than the stars? but very soon
> You blushed, and seemed to doubt if you were right.
> We wandered far and took no note of time;
>   Till on the air there came the distant call
> Of church bells: we turned hastily, and yet
> Ere we reached home sounded a second chime . . .

Poetic licence must have dictated the season, for no summer night would conclude with the summons to evensong, but the other elements ring true: James's blushes and hesitancy, her own romantic expectation tempered by scrupulous observation. If this was true love, it was also awkward and often 'not embarassed yet not quite at ease'. Romance had not clouded her candour.

8

James and *The Germ*

ONE IMMEDIATE RESULT of the engagement was an oil portrait of Christina by James, probably done from careful drawings at Charlotte Street and possibly while she was sitting to Gabriel for the *Girlhood of Mary Virgin*, for something of the same, slightly forward-leaning posture and inward gaze is visible in both works. James's oval canvas shows a nervous, almost frightened young woman, hair braided over the ears, wearing a white lace-edged collar and a small crucifix, which William later described as 'a true likeness, but an ordinary one'. It seems to partake of the artist's natural timidity as well as the sitter's and contrasts with Gabriel's oil portrait of around the same time (for which the preliminary drawing also shows a crucifix) where she is depicted a good deal more confidently, her eyes holding the viewer's with a steady gaze. The ringlets, incidentally, had passed out of fashion, and Christina's hair was now looped under the ears to a loose chignon in the demure style of the time.

In November, James went home to Mansfield in order to give an account of his engagement, taking with him his portrait and William acting as it were *in loco parentis* to vouch for his sister's background and prospects. A copy of *Verses* went too. Graciously, James's mother and sister commented on the 'thoughtful and pleasing expression' depicted in the portrait. Anxiously, Christina surmised that they had also been 'profusely banqueted', if not surfeited, with her poems. She was surprised to hear that Mrs Collinson was very prim, though kind-hearted, but pleased that William liked James's sister, whom she apprehended was nevertheless 'dreadfully clever'. 'Is either of these ladies *alarming*?' she asked; 'not to you, of course, but would they be so to me? I wish they could be convinced that the celebrated portrait is flattering.' She demanded a detailed account of James's sister-in-law and baby, for the prospect of lifelong female relationships stretched before her. She joked that the Collinson's bull-terrier sounded hideous enough even for her taste, and concluded nervously:

> Pray, if you think it expedient, present my respects to Mrs Collinson and love to Miss C. Why I have left off calling the latter Mary is not easily explained except on the score of feeling awkward. Mamma sends her love. Will you remember me most particularly to Mr Collinson?

Custom rather than feeling prescribed he should not become 'James' until after their wedding, yet clearly she was not wholly comfortable in her new position.

While he was away, she wrote a nameless *Song*, which with its peculiarly serene pathos was to become one of her most famous poems:

> When I am dead, my dearest,
>   Sing no sad songs for me;
> Plant thou no roses at my head,
>   Nor shady cypress tree:
> Be the green grass above me
>   With showers and dewdrops wet
> And if thou wilt, remember,
>   And if thou wilt forget.
>
> I shall not see the shadows,
>   I shall not feel the rain;
> I shall not hear the nightingale
>   Sing on as if in pain:
> And dreaming through the twilight
>   That doth not rise nor set,
> Haply I may remember,
>   And haply may forget.

A few weeks later came another untitled lyric blending sweetness and sadness; together they represent the flowering of her art in exquisite melodies just as her initially hesistant love for James was unfolding:

> Oh roses for the flush of youth,
>   And laurel for the perfect prime;
> But pluck an ivy branch for me
>   Grown old before my time.
>
> Oh violets for the grave of youth,
>   And bay for those dead in their prime;
> Give me the withered leaves I chose
>   Before in the old time.

The laurel and the bay, though disclaimed, are of course the marks of fame, here entwined with the delicate melancholy so favoured in the feminine mode, in musical cadences that were more poetical than personal. Alert to the disjunction between private and public, Christina begged William, some little while later, not to hand round any of her pieces which the most imaginative person could construe into 'love personals' adding: 'you will feel how more than ever intolerable it would be now to have my verses regarded as the outpourings of a wounded spirit.' It had happened before, she warned, in allusion to Rev. Bray. Nevertheless the tender expressions of melancholy seem to reflect something of the current state of her heart.

When James returned to London, the courtship resumed its sedate progress. If he called at Charlotte Street, it was always in company, and the occasions on which the young couple could be alone were limited to the occasional decorous walk on Sundays, after listening to Dodsworth's fulminations on the 'Signs of the Times'. These were his Advent sermons devoted to the exposition of a millenarian scenario, on which, a church publication noted, he was 'always full and edifying', and which this year identified current events throughout Europe – revolutions, earthquakes, cholera, Irish famine, eclipses of the sun and moon – as prophetic of divine visitation. 'Take ye heed, watch and pray, for ye know not when the time is,' he began:

> What the special character of that trial shall be is uncertain; whether of outward bitter persecution or of subtil delusion; whether it is to come from the strong hand of power or from the insidious blandishments of the world – this we cannot know . . . But whatever it may be, there is one and but one way of preparing for it, and that is by living nearer to God and farther from the world . . .

Never did Advent offer stronger reasons for consecrating one's life to religion; never had the Church more pointedly taught 'the value of eternity and the nothingness of all this world'. And on the four Sundays before Christmas the correct responses were spelt out: constant expectation, confession of sins, propitiatory penance.

Both Christina and James were intimidated by such preaching. In the course of her life Christina wrote upwards of thirty poems on the Second Coming, as well as a commentary on the Book of Revelations, the key millenarian text. One of the most disturbingly violent of her poems came early in the New Year, under the title *Symbols*.

> I watched a nest from day to day,
>   A green nest full of pleasant shade,
>   Wherein three speckled eggs were laid:
> But when they should have hatched in May,
>   The two old birds had grown afraid
> Or tired, and flew away.
>
> Then in my wrath I broke the bough
>   That I had tended so with care,

> Hoping its scent should fill the air;
> I crushed the eggs, not heeding how
> Their ancient promise had been fair:
> I would have vengeance now.

Perhaps recalling an actual event, the crushed eggs were an image of divine retribution. 'And what if God, Who waiteth for thy fruits in vain, Should also take the rod?' the poem concludes, threateningly.

Like Pusey, Dodsworth took penance and self-mortification seriously, initiating debates at Christ Church over austerities such as fasting; some while earlier a general day of 'fasting and humiliation' was held in recognition of Irish famine. As it happened, James Collinson was among those who took mortification of the flesh even more literally, for under Dodsworth's influence he began to flagellate himself, no doubt using a discipline like that procured by Pusey. Perhaps he wore a hairshirt too; possibly even a chain beneath his clothing. And no doubt he rose early to prove himself no sluggard, which would incidentally explain his late-night sleepiness. Most contemporaries regarded self-flagellation as excessive, but at this date there was a sizeable minority within the Church to whom such practices were a central part of their faith.

Shortly before Christmas, the Rossettis made another interesting acquaintance, when William Bell Scott paid his second visit to Charlotte Street. 'I well remember his first appearance, in the evening,' wrote William, describing Scott as tall, handsome and striking, with black bushy brows and eyes of piercing blue, in a manner rather suggestive of Maturin's satanic heroes. Years later, travelling in Italy, a woman in the same carriage was transfixed by the steely brightness of Scott's gaze, whispering that he surely had 'the evil eye'. 'We in Charlotte Street did not think so,' commented William, 'but took very warmly indeed to Mr Scott, and found him not only attractive but even fascinating.' Indeed, the whole family was captivated and 'WBS' or 'Scotus' as he was familiarly known (though not to his face, proprieties being always observed) was soon regarded with the utmost partiality. They were not alone: Holman Hunt found 'the visitor from the North' both handsome and interesting, despite his Mephistophelean appearance, while Madox Brown commented with exasperation on how all women were enchanted by Scott. Of the Rossettis, Maria seems to have shown the most partiality, notwithstanding his religious scepticism, a mutual regard acknowledged by Scott many years later, when he wrote all four Rossettis were 'very near and dear' from the day of their meeting but that between himself and Maria there existed a particular affinity. On this first acquaintance, Scott did not mention a wife, and it is possible that Maria's warm emotions were stirred by this visitor whom all found so fascinating. Though the Rossettis were not enslaved by social convention, there was still a strong feeling that elder daughters should marry before their sisters.

Scott's appearance so soon after Christina's engagement has been used to construct a scenario in which her unripe heart was smitten by this compelling figure, causing a lifetime's anguish. But there is no evidence that this was so. Though thirty years later she asserted that her admiration for Scott began while she was still in her teens, she was at first intimidated and then rather prickly towards him; true liking took time to develop.

In the spring of 1849, her health again gave rise to anxiety, though no specific ailment is recorded, and she was despatched to stay with Mrs Marsh in Clapham. In 'this my banishment' she read a novel 'whose improbablities only yield in enormity to its absurdities', and declared her preference for Leigh Hunt's *Men, Women and Books*. She wrote in sprightly mood to William with elaborate puns based on character studies by a handwriting analyst, referring to Collinson as William's 'absent brother' (he must have been away from London again) and invoking her own 'double sisterhood'. Annotating this letter, William commented that 'it should not be inferred that she was in any way enrolled in the Brotherhood' but the allusion is eloquent, particularly as this moment marked the public debut of the PRB. Afraid of being rejected by the Academy, Gabriel sent the *Girlhood* to another exhibition without consulting his Brethren in what was a supposedly collective plan to surprise the RA. Happily his picture was well received, the critic of the *Athenaeum* especially liking the depiction of the Virgin, which reminded him of St Thomas's statement that no man could gaze amorously on Mary, so much beauty and holiness shone in her face. Neither the author of this notice nor the family of the artist made the vulgar error of confusing subject and sitter, yet these remarks must have been gratifying. As it turned out, when the Academy opened in May, the reception accorded Millais and Hunt was less generous, and no one noticed the PRB monogram on each canvas. Collinson's *Image Makers* attracted little attention and altogether the grand scheme to startle the world of art was rather a damp squib. The Brotherhood responded by reformalising the group, and appointing William as official scribe.

Christina's output remained high: twenty-two poems in the six months to April 1849, including one with the memorable title *What Sappho would have said had her leap cured instead of killing her* (7 December 1848) which has more than a touch of L. E. L. or one of Maturin's heroines, but little to do with the Greek poet. There was a sonnet in homage to Keats, written on the eve of St Agnes, and several mortuary verses, including a gruesome deathbed monologue by an old man, with unintentional comic effects. On 24 January, she wrote some charming lines to her little cousin Henrietta Polydore, who was pretending to read:

> Darling little cousin
>   With your thoughtful look
> Reading topsy-turvy
>   From a printed book.
>
> English hieroglyphics
>   More mysterious
> To you, than Egyptian
>   Ones would be to us.

Uncle Henry had married a woman from Cheltenham, also called Henrietta, and their daughter was the Rossettis' first and only cousin. For a while the Polydores lived in north London, but soon they moved to Gloucester, and the rest of Christina's life was punctuated by family visits thither and thence.

By June, she was 'so sick she could not even write out her own poems', and the task of copying them into the notebook was assigned to Mamma. But she was not too sick to devise several puzzles for a pocket diary which solicited charades and enigmas, and she also wrote seriously, in July composing an accomplished and justly famous valediction forbidding mourning entitled *Remember*:

> Remember me when I am gone away,
>   Gone far away into the silent land;
>   When you can no more hold me by the hand,
> Nor I half turn to go yet turning stay.
> Remember me when no more day by day
> You tell me of our future that we planned:
>   Only remember me; you understand
> It will be late to counsel then or pray.
> Yet if you should forget me for a while
>   And afterwards remember, do not grieve:
>   For if the darkness and corruption leave
> A vestige of the thoughts that once I had,
> Better by far you should forget and smile
> Than that you should remember and be sad.

It is hardly surprising if the author of this, who was engaged to be married and might be expected to be planning 'our future' with her beloved, did not wish such verses to be circulated and interpreted as 'love personals'. Nevertheless in this and the earlier *Song* there is something troubling about the preoccupation with posthumous relations. It is almost as if, unconsciously, she did not expect to reach, or survive, marriage.

She was certainly apprehensive, for in August she was due to spend a month with the Collinsons. She went alone, because James was painting landscapes in the Isle of Wight. 'As various affairs obliged her son to be away for several weeks, she invited me to visit,' says a character of her future mother-in-law in one of Christina's stories that seems to reflect her own experience. 'I'm afraid she was deceived in this but I must say she is very amiable. Although not young, she retains a dignified beauty which inspires respect and love; her conversation is full of spirit and goodness. She very much resembles her son, of whom she speaks with tender affection.'

Christina herself found Mrs Collinson an active old lady of sixty, despite a touch of rheumatism. Her daughter Mary was amiable, over thirty and disfigured by an 'eruption' on her face; she played chess and bagatelle with their guest.

To William, Christina wrote frankly, saying that though tolerable, Nottinghamshire was tedious:

Local converse wearies me somewhat; yet this advantage it possesses – I cannot join in it; so may, during its continuances, abandon myself to my own meditations ... the talk of *beaus* here is as perpetual as at Mrs Heimann's: however, fewer jokes (?) have been passed on me than might have been anticipated; and of these Mary is entirely innocent. Do you know, I rather like Mary; she is not at all caressing, and seems real.

All her life, Christina was averse to being embraced in the gushing manner Victorian women used to express female friendship. She much preferred the Collinsons' hideous bull-terrier, but even this affectation could hardly disguise metropolitan ennui:

In my desperation I knit lace with a perseverance completely foreign to my nature. Yesterday I made a dirt pudding in the garden wherein to plant some slips of currant ...

Ah Will! if you were here we would write *bouts rimés* sonnets, and be subdued together ...

In response, William sent some rhyme endings, and Christina turned out a 'rather intense sonnet' in her now hackneyed melancholic vein but filled with disturbingly violent images that suggest unconscious protest against being pressed into a social role she did not enjoy, with no congenial company.

She was at Pleasley Hill, a village just outside Mansfield where James's mother and sister now lived, with a single servant and immediate neighbours of a lower social class (including the framework-knitting Strawdy family whose unusual name Christina borrowed for Maude's story). Mary Collinson was amiable but rather unapproachable; one cannot but suspect that they disapproved, not of Christina herself but of James's imprudence, while still establishing his career, in proposing marriage to one so young, inexperienced and stiff. As her family knew, Christina's shyness was easily taken for disdain. Nevertheless the Collinsons endeavoured to amuse Christina, amongst other things organising a picnic excursion to nearby Hardwick Hall.

Hardwick and its ruined Old Hall was virtually required visiting for anyone in the vicinity, and almost certainly the 'real live castle' with tumbling parapets that William had visited the year before. In the epistolary tale Christina composed a few months later, a picnic party to a similar site takes place, with romantic embellishments. 'The day was brilliant' she wrote; the sun shone with Italian splendour and a light breeze refreshed the air, spreading the scent of wild flowers. Their destination was 'a ruined castle about two miles from here', all that remained of a baronial hall in the middle of a great park. At first it seems dark and sombre, but as her fictional narrator climbs the mossy stairs, passes down long corridors, and glimpses daylight through the stained glass of the half-ruined oratory, she feels 'all the majesty of the scene'. In a large roofless chamber known as the giants' hall on account of its height, with ivy-hung window embrasures, they lunch on cold meats, salad and fruit, and at five o'clock the party starts for home.

From Pleasley Hill, a visit to Mr and Mrs Charles Collinson in Mansfield was also scheduled. Mary predicted that her elder brother would admire Christina's 'unalterable self-possession' – the mask which was her defence against social encounters. 'Fancy the inflated state in which I shall re-enter London, should this flattering preference result from my visit,' she wrote waspishly to William. As if Christina was already a member of the family, Mary also asked her to 'kindly remember, or something of the sort, "us" to you', when writing home. But she did not feel she belonged to them, and perhaps never would.

Contrary to expectations, however, she enjoyed her week in Mansfield, largely because of all those she had met, Mrs Charles was the most to her taste; perhaps this was because Anne Collinson and her sister Carrie were closer than Mary to her own age, and therefore less intimidating. She made no comment on baby Maud, whose name she borrowed for her poetic heroine, but had the satisfaction of finding herself more or less evenly matched in several games of chess with Mr Charles.

Altogether, she reported on her return home, she had received 'unvarying kindness and hospitality' from all in Nottinghamshire. She called on her grandparents and on the Heimanns (where she dreaded the bold questions they would ask) and was busy with some needlework to present to Anne, having sent Mary a portfolio case in place of the intended ring: she had discovered that Mary wore no jewellery. But this brought an unexpected response: Mary Collinson desired the correspondence to cease, saying her brother's affairs were so unpromising as to render their continuing to write not pleasant. 'Does this not sound extraordinary? We are all much surprised,' wrote Christina to William, who had gone to the Isle of Wight for his annual holiday. Small wonder, for James had just called at Charlotte Street, on his own return to London. No further explanation of Mary's action was committed to paper, so her reason for regarding James's affairs in so dismal a light remains a mystery. He himself seems to have shown no doubts, and had begun a picture of a young woman sitting by a stile with a child whose bonnet she is trimming with wild flowers. This suggests he was already casting his bride-to-be in the role of wife and mother for, though not a portrait, in demeanour and features the young woman resembles Christina. The background was painted in the Isle of Wight, and artistic practice was to paint in the figures over the winter, using studio models and preparatory studies such as Christina was used to sitting for.

At Gabriel's instigation the Brotherhood had decided to produce a magazine, in a renewed attempt to draw the reluctant world's attention to their work. Each Brother was to contribute, with poetry, prose, criticism or illustration, and solicit support from associates and friends. During Christina's absence the idea had taken off: Coventry Patmore promised a poem, Madox Brown and Walter Deverell were involved, Hunt was busy devising a two-part illustration for Woolner's double poem, and Stephens was wrestling with an article on early Italian art. In Ventnor William was composing a blank verse narrative on a modern theme, which he hoped would not be too long for inclusion, as well as exchanging more *bouts rimés* with his sister. As contributions mounted, William was designated editor-in-chief, and plans were laid for future issues, which were to include Collinson's poem *The Child Jesus*. It seems to have been taken for granted that Christina would contribute, and her breezy letters to

William around the time of his birthday reveal her happy sense of participation.

James showed her his poem, and also spoke to her about Charles Kingsley's drama *The Saint's Tragedy*, which had used the life of the thirteenth-century noblewoman St Elizabeth of Hungary as the basis for a polemical attack on 'Romish' practices in the English Church and was currently causing some ripples in Anglo-Catholic circles. In Catholic teaching, the saint was revered for renouncing husband and throne in favour of the religious life – a sacrifice that might, from an English Protestant viewpoint, be regarded as dangerously threatening to state and family, and emblematic of Catholic aggression – while Kingsley's text had the declared aim of deterring young men from following those clerics who promoted religious celibacy, 'depreciating as carnal and degrading those family ties to which they owe their own existence ... insulting thus their own wives and mothers, nibbling ignorantly at the very root of that household purity which constitutes the distinctive superiority of Protestant over Popish nations'. The villain of his book was accordingly Elizabeth's confessor, a supposedly power-hungry priest usurping the authority of her lawful husband.

In this controversy, the PRB were firmly on St Elizabeth's side. Millais drew her washing pilgrims' feet, Gabriel sketched a design of her at prayer, Collinson planned to paint her renunciation and in conversation with Christina is unlikely to have commended Kingsley's book; more probably the Anglo-Catholic community was alerting its members to what was perceived as a hostile text.

Gabriel and Hunt were about to leave for Paris and Belgium, and Christina expected to see Mr Collinson at the Heimanns'; otherwise, she told William, her own urgent business consisted of 'nothing more important than needlework and such like'. In the context of this chatter, it is startling to read the *bouts rimés* sonnet she forwarded to Ventnor:

> So I grew half delirious and quite sick,
> And thro' the darkness saw strange faces grin
> Of monsters at me. One put forth a fin,
> And touched me clammily: I could not pick
> A quarrel with it: it began to lick
> My hand, making meanwhile a piteous din
> And shedding human tears: it would begin
> To near me, then retreat. I heard the quick
> Pulsation of my heart, I marked the fight
> Of life and death within me; then sleep threw
> Her veil around me; but this thing is true:
> When I awoke, the sun was at his height,

And I wept, sadly, knowing that one new
Creature had love for me, and others spite.

'This thing is true': was it a real dream, or a half-waking vision, or a actual experience of fear, graphically rendered? Why did William's rhyme words prompt such a macabre scene? What was the pitiful monster with its clammy fin, and why did it so frighten her? In some obscure way the poem seems to refer back to her breakdown, with its invocation of delirium, sickness, fainting. As with the vision of canaries, all her life Christina was apt to mark and remember dreams, and often made poems from them. This encounter with something that causes the pulse to race as it licks or kisses her hand is one of the most striking, and all the more so for having been composed at speed. Doubtless it made her brothers 'grin tremendously' once more.

Papa was poorly again this autumn, though this did not much dampen spirits at Charlotte Street. Gabriel and Hunt enjoyed themselves in France and Flanders and the PRB continued to meet, William recording matters of moment. Millais's new subject was *Christ in the House of his Parents*, while Collinson had chosen two contemporary subjects, one showing an old soldier in his Chelsea Hospital uniform, the other a genre piece with overtones of social comment entitled *Answering the Emigrant's Letter*, showing 'a smoky picturesque little interior' with a poor but honest family at the kitchen table, poring over a map of Australia.

He had moved his studio to Brompton, and by December was also thinking of starting on St Elizabeth. First however he completed his etching for *The Child Jesus*, to appear in *The Germ*. The style was distinctively Pre-Raphaelite, with angular poses and dry draughtsmanship and a Latin text from the Vulgate: *ex ore infantium et lactentium perfecisti laudem* – out of the mouths of babes and sucklings hast thou ordained praise. Somewhat oddly, he placed Jesus and his playmates mid-way between Jerusalem and a landscape of chalk cliffs, making it look as if Nazareth was in the Isle of Wight. Like the text, however, the illustration was symbolic rather than literal.

December 1849, the month of Christina's nineteenth birthday, marked the highest and happiest period of her association with the Brotherhood and also of her engagement. Indeed the two things were closely linked, forming the context in which her feelings for James developed and deepened, and gaining an added impetus from *The Germ*. She could not be a casual visitor at the studios nor join in the men's late-night perambulations, but the magazine allowed for vicarious involvement. As Christmas approached, excitement mounted, for the first issue was due in January, but a title had not yet been chosen –

The Germ was picked from sixty-five suggestions on the evening of 19 December at Gabriel's studio in Newman Street – and some contributions were not ready. Gabriel stayed up all night to complete *Hand and Soul*, his story about a medieval artist in search of fame and faith, who enters into a dialogue with his soul, figured as a fair woman with loose hair. Eventually all was done, and the first number was printed, with a sonnet by William on the cover, outlining the aims: originality, sincerity, truth. At this stage no contributors were named, and Gabriel seems to have chosen Christina's pieces, *DreamLand* and the much-admired *An End*, both from a clutch of poems about youthful death written earlier in the year, repeating in mournful cadences a lament that is more than half desire:

> Love, strong as death, is dead.
> Come, let us make his bed
> Among the dying flowers:
> A green turf at his head;
> And a stone at his feet,
> Whereon we may sit
> In the quiet evening hours . . .
>
> To few chords and sad and low
> Sing we so:
> Be our eyes fixed on the grass
> Shadow-veiled as the years pass,
> While we think of all that was
> In the long ago.

The second issue, dated February 1850, contained James's poem and etching, together with Christina's *Song*: 'Oh! roses for the flush of youth, And laurel for the perfect prime', and an earlier poem on disappointment and desire, now retitled (by Gabriel) *A Pause of Thought*:

> I looked for that which is not, nor can be,
>   And hope deferred made my heart sick in truth:
>   But years must pass before a hope of youth
>   Is resigned utterly.
>
> I watched and waited with a steadfast will:
>   And tho' the object seemed to flee away
>   That I so longed for, ever, day by day,
>   I watched and waited still.

Sometimes I said – "This thing shall be no more;
  My expectation wearies, and shall cease;
  I will resign it now, and be at peace:"
    Yet never gave it o'er.

Sometimes I said: "It is an empty name
  I long for; to a name why should I give
  The peace of all the days I have to live?"
    Yet gave it all the same . . .

This is Christina's authentic poetic voice: lucid speech rhythms, with complex yet simple-seeming ideas articulated in a manner that implies more than it states. What, for instance, is the speaker searching for, and why does she not name it? To William, the lines demonstrated that 'even at that early age she aspired ardently after poetic fame, with a keen sense of "hope deferred" ' but though this chimes also with Gabriel's subject in *Hand and Soul* it seems too determinate a reading; the meaning of the verses lies precisely in the not-naming of the thing desired, which thus stands for all such hopes.

Her third piece in this issue was *A Testimony*, written while she was in Mansfield, on the familiar theme 'all is vanity', with ringing homilectic phrases:

We build our houses on the sand
  Comely withoutside and within;
  But when the wind and rains begin
To beat on them, they cannot stand:
They perish, quickly overthrown,
Loose at the hidden basement stone . . .

Why should we hasten to arise
  So early, and so late take rest?
  Our labour is not good; our best
Hopes fade; our heart is stayed on lies.
Verily we sow wind; and we
Shall reap the whirlwind, verily.

In the first issue all contributions had been anonymous; now Gabriel devised the poetic pseudonym Ellen Alleyn for his sister. This reduced the number of Rossettis on the title page, where his own *Blessed Damozel* appeared, alongside a number of William's *bouts rimés*, as well as items by Scott, Deverell and Woolner, but also identified her contributions as the work of a single hand. And it was on these pieces, read and remembered by fit readers though few, that her early reputation rested.

As it happened, after sharing in the preliminary pleasures, Christina was away from home during much of *The Germ's* short existence, paying an extended visit to Longleat House in Somerset, where aunt Charlotte was governess to Lady Louisa, daughter of the widowed Marchioness. Through the autumn she had been troubled by a persistent cough, to which London fogs were inimical. But though the invitation was gracious, she was reluctant to exchange the excitements of the capital for a month in the country; for grand Longleat was literally freezing. 'You should see me rushing about the house shivering in a blanket shawl,' Christina reported; 'large lofty rooms, endless galleries and grand halls are at this season magnificent rather than cosy.' Lady Bath interested herself in the affairs of Miss Polidori's gifted nieces and nephews; she had bought Gabriel's *Girlhood* at an inflated price, and had also no doubt been shown the poems in the *Athenaeum*, as well as a copy of the new magazine, hot from the press. But polite conversation in the drawing-room, at which Christina never excelled, was poor substitute for daily gossip and visitors at Charlotte Street.

The park surrounding Longleat was beautiful, she acknowledged in her somewhat world-weary letters home, but she was not inspired. 'Were you in this lovely country,' she told William, 'you could hardly fail to gush poetry; with me the case is altogether different. The trees, the deer, the scenery, and indeed, everything here, seems to influence me but little, with two exceptions, the cold and the frog.' The frog was especially splendid: sere yellow, black-spotted and very large; he appeared to be leading a calm and secluded life. So was she, eager to hear what was chosen for the *The Germ* 's second number, and relying on William to send news of the other subject that interested her – Mr Collinson's affairs. Though engaged, it seems she and James did not correspond.

In return William forwarded a copy of Edgar Allen Poe's poem *Annabel Lee* which she professed to dislike, claiming to have at first thought the whole thing one of Gabriel's parodies. But one can see why William thought she would like the gloomy ballad, lamenting a lost beloved 'in the sepulchre there by the sea'. Poe, who died in mysterious circumstances the previous autumn, possessed cult status among the young Romantics of the Brotherhood, but his overweighted rhymes and repetitions stood as a warning: the doom-laden fantasy of *Annabel Lee* is uncomfortably close to Christina's mortuary mode.

Subsequent letters were full of *Germ* matters. Aunt Charlotte wanted copies for several potential subscribers, and on her own account Christina suggested sending one to Swynfen Jervis, who had recently published a slim volume of his own. She offered to pay, but had only thirteen and a half pence to her name – a note that serves to underline how young women had virtually no disposable income of their own –

and when she received the poems Mr Jervis submitted her uncompromising vote was that they should on no account be accepted. But she was delighted to learn Mr Scott's sonnet was to be printed; what was it about? She approved the pseudonym Gabriel had chosen for her, and earnestly asked Mrs Heimann whether the magazine seemed likely to prove successful, offering her own opinion that it was rather too serious. 'If an amusing tale could regularly come out in each number, it seems to me its prospects might improve,' she wrote; 'what say you?' And to William she made a similar suggestion, advocating more prose and less poetry, before waxing facetious, in a manner partly derived from reading Lady Bath's novels and Court Circulars:

> Should all other articles fail, boldly publish my letters; they would doubtless produce an immense sensation. By hinting that I occupy a high situation in B-ck——-m, P-a-e, being in fact no other than the celebrated Lady ——, and by substituting initials and asterisks for all names, and adding a few titles, my correspondence might have quite a success.

Though she claimed to enjoy the solitude, and also the gales that kept all indoors – 'Do you not like the noise of the wind?' William was asked, 'I rank it next after that of the sea' – the days at Longleat were empty. Her cough had not improved, and references to blisters and leeches indicate she was undergoing some distinctly old-fashioned treatment. So the idea of an amusing tale seems to have prompted the production of her own story, somewhat in the style of Charlotte Yonge, on whose autobiographical heroine she bestowed the fashionable name of Maude, and whose adolescent troubles resemble her own. The manuscript is in a school exercise book and from the evidence of the names must have been written after the visit to Pleasley Hill. Mrs Strawdy's nieces are named Annie and Caroline Mowbray after Mrs Charles Collinson and her sister while several surnames allocated to Maude's friends, such as Hunt and Deverell, came directly from *The Germ* circle, as did that of Mr Herbert, cousin Mary's husband, borrowed from the painter John Rogers Herbert, whom James had recruited to support the magazine.

Amongst its other elements, *Maude* articulates the choices available to girls like Christina. There was pious self-sacrifice, as practised in the nunnery by Sister Magdalen. There was conventional courtship and marriage, the role allotted to cousin Mary. And there was authorship, as conflictingly experienced by Maude. Her dilemma – how to reconcile feminine docility with desire for excellence and fame, or to find a role that combined piety, poetry and love – is resolved only by Maude's melodramatic death, as if to say literary ambition is incompatible with female fulfilment. Her penultimate act is a sonnet articulating the demands made on the faithful, echoing Christ's command to 'Take up the Cross, and follow Me'. This was a debate Christina was having, or hearing about, from James, who aimed to depict a similar resolution in his picture of St Elizabeth renouncing her throne. So at Longleat, Christina discussed *The Saint's Tragedy* with Lady Bath, who lent her the alternative version of St Elizabeth's life by Count Montalembert, and copied out extracts for William to pass to James, saying 'if the painting of St Elizabeth's life is ever completed, all details may be useful'. When completed, James's picture indeed followed Montalembert rather than Kingsley, and it would thus seem to be Christina who introduced the artist to the French author.

In her letter she concentrated on Montalembert's description of Elizabeth's appearance, which James duly used for his painting. But other details may have been of equal interest, for though the saint later took the veil, Montalembert's story of Elizabeth and her husband Louis is mainly one of exemplary Christian marriage:

> Despite her extreme youth and the almost childish vivacity of her love for her husband, Elizabeth never forgot that he was her head, as Jesus Christ is the head of the Church, and that she should be submissive to him in all things as the Church is to Jesus Christ. She united therefore to her ardent affection a great respect for him; she responded eagerly to the least sign or word from him; she was scrupulously careful that no action or word of hers, even the most insignificant, should wound or even annoy him . . .

As an exemplary husband, however, Louis supported her with tender solicitude, objecting only when her zeal seemed too great. 'To the frequent demonstrations of mutual tenderness which they gave one another were added sweet exhortations to advance together in the way of perfection and this holy emulation strengthened and maintained them in the service of God'.

It was Elizabeth's habit to spend the night praying, or sleeping on the bare floor, and self-mortifications of various kinds fill a whole chapter. Under her fine garments, she wore a hair shirt. Every Friday and throughout Lent, 'she whipped herself severely in secret', in reparation for Christ's scourging, and often rose at night to 'compel her attendants to chastise her rigorously', afterwards returning to her husband's bed 'full of gaiety and sweetness'. The flagellation never made her morose, wrote Montalembert; on the contrary, she was always joyful. 'They seem to want to frighten God,' she remarked of those who prayed mournfully; 'why do they not give him what they have to offer cheerfully and with good heart?' – an admonition Christina was to ponder and endorse.

We do not know what she thought of the saint's self-inflicted suffering, though we can guess why Collinson was interested in these displays of Christian discipline. It is however clear from her study of Montalembert that Christina looked forward to being James's pious helpmate in art as well as marriage, just as her epistolary heroine Clorinda hopes to assist her curate-husband in the discharge of his vocation. But anxieties loomed: why had Charles Collinson still failed to reply to William's letter? 'C. C's silence astonishes me,' she wrote; perhaps he wished the acquaintance to cease. Was this too in reference to James's 'unpromising affairs'? There are indications of family discord, for James's allowance had been withdrawn, and around this time he borrowed small sums from William and Gabriel. He was mixing with 'some rather influential Catholics', William told Fred Stephens, who feared lest the controversial symbolism of the *The Child Jesus* should deter new subscribers; on the contrary, William replied, it would prove popular among Catholics and Puseyites, and controversy could only help the magazine.

Greater assistance was needed. By the time Christina came home from Longleat, *The Germ*'s finances were already critical, and the prospect of bringing out a third number was distinctly slim. However, the printing firm offered to keep it going, and issues 3 and 4 were duly prepared, appearing at the end of March and April respectively, after which the project was abandoned. To No. 3, 'Ellen Alleyn' contributed *Repining* – a shortened version of a long poem written in December 1847, and *Sweet Death* – her final offerings to what proved a brief but legendary enterprise.

Inspired by her rustic sojourn, Christina celebrated her return home with a nature exercise notable chiefly for its inclusion of gnats and slugs – creatures not normally invoked in pastoral odes – followed by a Tennysonian monologue in response to *Annabel Lee*, in which a modern paragon of piety lies in her grave and *Three Moments* on 23 March, which dramatised three experiences of loss: the first by a Child whose bird has died (Maria's thrush cast a longer shadow than has been perceived); the second by a Girl who weeps emblematically for the loss of her flower; and the third by a Woman grieving beside a bed, unable to weep. The same emotional blockage reappeared in *Is and Was*, describing the transformation of a peasant girl into a noble lady,

> With calm voice not over loud;
> Very courteous in her action,
>   Yet you think her proud;
> Much too haughty to affect;

> Too indifferent to direct
> Or be angry or suspect:
> Doing all from self-respect.

The last line had personal significance. 'Much about the time when the poem was written, a lady told my sister that [she] seemed to "do all from self-respect", not from fellow-feeling with others, or from kindly consideration for them,' William explained. 'Christina mentioned the remark, with an admission that it hit a blot in her character ... She laid the hint to heart and, I think, never forgot it.'

Ever since her breakdown, Christina had presented this mask of reserve and 'unliveable-with politeness'. It was the subject of teasing at home, and now perhaps Lady Bath, or possibly Mary Collinson, with her remark about unalterable self-possession, had mortifyingly noted that this gave the impression of standoffishness – a grievous fault in any well-brought up girl. Moreover it was true: in her manner 'a certain amount of reserve and distance, not remote from hauteur, was certainly at that date perceptible,' wrote William, adding that in her punctilious courtesy some people suspected affectation or even sarcasm.

With this demeanour, and sense of her true self concealed, she was not easy to know or to like. In part, the awkwardness stemmed from genuine teenage shyness, politeness being a strategy against self-consciousness and was exacerbated by the fear of emotional exposure, lest her true feelings or temper burst out. Like the transformed peasant-girl in her poem, the blush upon her cheek would otherwise tell of much Christina could not or should not speak, and throughout her life one has the impression of a shuttered personality, a fountain deliberately sealed, lest the waters of emotion should flow.

It was nearly five years since she had visibly changed from a high-spirited child into a painfully withdrawn young woman. And there was soon another wound and more pain to endure in silence, for James had reverted to the Catholic faith.

The first surviving evidence of this came at Whitsuntide, when he announced his resignation from the Brotherhood in a letter to Gabriel:

> I feel that, as a sincere Catholic, I can no longer allow myself to be called P. R. B. in the brotherhood sense of the term, or to be connected in any way with the magazine ...
>
> I love and reverence God's faith, and I love His holy Saints; and I cannot bear any longer the self-accusation that, to gratify a little vanity, I am helping to dishonour them, and lower their merits, if not absolutely to bring their sanctity into ridicule.

It was a decision of devastating consequence for Christina.

9

Heartbreak

JAMES'S REVERSION TO the Catholic faith meant the end of the engagement. At least, the two events have always been seen as interdependent, the engagement being broken off, William wrote 'at some such date as May or June 1850, owing to his having reverted from the Anglican to the Roman Church'. But this does not seem to be quite the whole story. Both James's letter of resignation and William's earlier remark about his influential friends indicate that he had been a Catholic for some weeks if not months already, and that this adherence had not initially caused any conflict. Other details support this inference – his friendship with J. R. Herbert, a Catholic convert, his *Child Jesus* quotation from the Vulgate rather than the Authorised Version, and his interest in St Elizabeth of Hungary. Even his move to Brompton, where London Catholicism now centred, may relate to his change of allegiance, which would also account for his family's withdrawal of funds.

Why then was the engagement not terminated earlier? Christina had already once refused to marry a Catholic, so both were aware that his reversion was incompatible with their continuing relationship. Did she hope once again to dissuade him? Or did he, perhaps, assume that as his spouse-to-be she would faithfully follow where he led, according to the model not just of Christian marriage but also Victorian Britain? William thought Rome her natural spiritual home and both she and Maria were at this date closely associated with the clergy at Christ Church, where one curate had already gone over and the incumbent seemed likely to follow. Was she asked to make such a move?

When disclosing the broken engagement some half century later, William stated that his sister suffered greatly in forming and maintaining her resolve, which implies reluctance. The result was 'a blight on her heart and spirits', he added:

> I will not harshly condemn James Collinson for [his] successive tergiversations: he was a right-meaning man of timorous conscience. But he had none the less struck a staggering blow at Christina Rossetti's peace of mind on the very threshold of womanly life, and a blow from which she did not fully recover for years.

Her participation in the discussions and research on St Elizabeth reveals no weakening of her affection. What happened after her return from Longleat, by which time James's reversion was well known? Is the sonnet on the conflict between love and faith that she added to *Maude* an oblique expression of the demands James was then making?

> What is it Jesus saith unto the soul?
> 'Take up the Cross, and come, and follow Me.'
> This word He saith to all; no man may be
>   Without the Cross, wishing to win the goal . . .

> He will be with thee, helping, strengthening,
> Until it is enough: for lo, the day
> Cometh when He shall call thee . . .

Christina did not want to join the Church of Rome, but she had by now fully committed herself to James. Did he make it a condition of their continuing engagement? Or did he rather use it as a means to extricate himself from a situation which was now looking rather misconceived?

From the story of Elizabeth of Hungary, James had chosen to depict the episode when, after the death of her devout spouse, the saint refuses to remarry, throws down her crown before the effigy of Christ and symbolically consecrates her nuptial gown before entering a convent. This renunciation had evident personal resonance. Just as Sisterhoods were thought to entice young women from their filial duties, so fervent young men were encouraged to sacrifice family ties and worldly advancement in order to consecrate their lives to God. And it seems this was the choice James was both making for himself and imposing on Christina. Love had once kept him from the true faith, but now he put religious conscience above personal affections. Had not Christ commanded his followers to forsake father and mother, wife and children (Luke 14:26), and St Paul specifically stated that it was better not to marry (I Corinthians 7:32–38)? And as James came to his decision he presented Christina with a sonnet spelling it out in the form of a dialogue between Christ and his heart:

> 'Give Me thy heart'. I said: Can I not make
> Abundant sacrifice to Him Who gave
> Life, health, possessions, friends, of all I have
> All but my heart once given? Lord, do not take
> It from its happy home or it will break,
> 'Give Me thy broken heart'. Can love enslave?

> Must it be forced to look beyond the grave
> For its fruition? Lord, for Thy Love's sake
> Let this thing be: as two streams journeying on
> Melt into one and widen to the sea,
> So let two souls love-burdened make but one
> And one full heart rest all its love on Thee.
> 'Alas, frail man, for thine infirmity!
> Thy God is Love'. – Then, Lord, Thy will be done.

The somewhat implacable deity conjured by Collinson clearly won the argument, forbidding the two love-burdened souls to join in marriage. No doubt James was sincere, but it was an unkind message to a girl whom he had caused to love him, against her initial feelings, and who was now being effectively jilted.

Christina destroyed but did not forget the words, later turning them to contemplative use. 'Many years ago a friend wrote and gave me a sonnet, which now, as best I may, I reproduce from memory,' she wrote in 1885. 'I think it devotional.' Devotional it may have been, but it was also devastating.

When exactly did this happen? It appears that the crisis which caused Collinson to resign from the Brotherhood was precipitated by the sudden notoriety of the PRB following this year's exhibitions, when 'the mystic letters with their signification appeared in all kinds of papers'. With the revelation came the critical attack, in which Gabriel's *Ecce Ancilla* (which again used Christina's features for those of the Virgin) and Millais's *The Carpenter's Shop* bore the brunt of virulent hostility from all major papers. As a result Millais had difficulty finding a buyer, while the pictures by Gabriel, Hunt and Collinson remained unsold.

The critical assault was levelled against the perceived Romanism of the paintings – all (with the ironic exception of Collinson's *Emigrant's Letter*) contained sacred symbolism that was read as covertly Catholic – and also against their 'realism' or unideal rendering of sacred personages. Here was the Virgin in bed, without bedclothes; here was the Holy Family in a workshop, looking like dirty undernourished manual workers. Not surprisingly, *The Carpenter's Shop* was described as 'pictorial blasphemy'. Poor Collinson thus found himself, for the sake of ambition and to 'gratify a little vanity', associated with artists who, however honest their intentions, had in his view helped to dishonour holy personages and bring their sanctity into ridicule. And in addition, he was publicly associated with artists whose pictures would not sell, when he had no money. 'You know I am a good deal in debt,' he told William on 21 May when the final reckoning for *The Germ* left each proprietor liable for the sum of £3.14.

Sometime subsequently Collinson entered a Catholic community. This seems to have been a later decision, not even hinted at in his letter to William, but he may have forewarned Christina that such was his ultimate aim. Or perhaps, being a man 'of timorous conscience' he had spoken only of consecrating his life to holy service, leaving her in doubt as to his meaning. Was the despair of *Three Moments*, written at Eastertime, an early apprehension of this? If James chose celibacy, there was no future for her in marriage:

> The Woman knelt, but did not pray
> Nor weep nor cry; she only said,
> 'Not this, not this!' and clasped her hands . . .
>
> . . .
>
> 'Not this, not this!' tears did not fall;
> 'Not this!' it was all
> She could say; no sobs would come;
> The mortal grief was almost dumb –

On 10 May, she completed a long and confused poem called *Three Nuns* which seems to rehearse the same fear and incomprehension:

> I loved him; yes, where was the sin?
>   I loved him with my heart and soul;
>   But I pressed forward to no goal,
> There was no prize I strove to win.
> Show me my sin that I may see:
> Throw the first stone, thou Pharisee . . .
>
> . . .
>
>   I prayed for him; was my sin prayer?
> I sacrificed, he never bought;
> He nothing gave, he nothing took;
> We never bartered look for look
>
> . . .
>
> I only prayed that in the end
>   His trust and hope may not be vain;
>   I prayed not we may meet again:
> I would not let our names ascend
> No not to Heaven, in the same breath;
> Nor will I join the two in death . . .
>
> . . .
>
> While still the names rang in mine ears
>   of daughter, sister, wife,
> The outside world still looked so fair
>   To my weak eyes and rife

With beauty, my heart almost failed;
  Then in the desperate strife
I prayed, as one who prays for life . . .

Did Christina spend the early summer waiting for James to make his meaning clear, hoping that their love would, somehow, survive his change of faith? Was she torn, as this suggests, between her love for him and for her family, knowing them incompatible? Did she finally release him from the engagement, knowing her decision to be a polite fiction, commonly practised in a culture which still regarded a rejected woman as soiled or unwanted merchandise in the marriage market place?

From 25 May to 26 September no new poems were entered in Christina's notebook. But at some stage *Three Nuns* was added to the manuscript of *Maude*, with the addition of a running epigraph in Italian that translated reads 'This heart sighs, and I know not why. It may be sighing for love but to me it says not so. Answer me, my heart, why do you sigh? It replies: I want God, I sigh for Jesus.' Elliptically this seems to refer to James's decision.

Christina's immature heart had thus been awakened, only to be cruelly broken. The love she had bestowed on James now had to be revoked and suppressed. Moreover, her response could not be one of anger, or even open sorrow, for he had chosen a 'higher' vocation, in giving his heart to Christ rather than Christina.

As was usual practice, all letters and tokens of affection were returned, and Mamma insisted all communication cease between the young couple, even though James remained on friendly terms with her brothers despite his defection from the Brotherhood. No doubt this decree was wise, but it was hard. And in the immediate aftermath of the affair, Christina was sent to stay with the Polydores in Gloucester, where she was taken on several excursions – up Robin Hood's Hill, and out along the Severn Estuary to the pretty village of Hempstead and the ruined priory of Llanthony Secunda. Then in August, she went again to Brighton with Maria, where she suffered an acute attack of neuralgic migraine that led her to distrust the resort ever after, but which seems a natural reaction to emotional shock and distress. She wrote clandestinely to William's office, pathetically seeking news:

Have you seen the *St Elizabeth* lately? and do you yet know what is to be done with the figure of the old woman whose position was not liked? Whilst I am here, if you can manage without too much trouble, I wish you would find out whether Mr Collinson is as delicate as he used to be: you and Gabriel are my resources, and you are by far the more agreeable.

I direct this to the Excise that Mamma may not know of it. Do not be shocked at the concealment; this letter would not give her much pleasure. Do have patience with the trouble I occasion you and with myself. I am ashamed of this note, yet want courage to throw it away; so must despatch it in its dreary emptiness.

A week later she wrote more openly to Charlotte Street, thanking William 'for the St Elizabeth news':

it must be very beautiful. Is it intended to be ready for next Exhibition? I quite wish to see it, and examine into all its beauties.

She guessed that William would sit for one of the figures, and inquired whether a model had been found for the saint's indignant mother-in-law. And from his account she deduced that Elizabeth herself was to be painted from the same model as one of her maids of honour: 'Is this the case? I hope not.' Surely she herself had once expected to sit for the saint's image.

Brighton was dull: she and Maria had called on the Sangiovannis and the Pistruccis, and managed to borrow some books – Layard's *Nineveh*, a Life of Crabbe and a book on China. Three weeks later she was still valiantly but vainly attempting to suppress her desire for news of James, in a letter to William that was opened by Mamma, who was 'so totally disgusted' that Christina speedily destroyed the missive on her own return home.

Gradually some glimpses of humour reappeared. Priscilla Townsend called to say farewell before her family emigrated to New Zealand; Christina promised to write sometimes, 'which cannot fail to console her for all privations. But nonsense apart I sincerely regret losing her: she was a very nice girl,' she told William. She enjoyed the doggerel verses William was shown by a beggar in Edinburgh during a Royal visit, protesting the essential similarity between Queen and pauper before the last trump. Rather too late to be useful, a favourable review of the defunct *Germ* appeared in the High Church *Guardian*, which also mentioned Gabriel's *Ecce Ancilla* and awarded high, if not unmixed praise to the Pre-Raphaelite school. Mamma was particularly gratified, because 'pre-eminence of *mind* is not attributed to Mr Millais'. Christina was well aware of her mother's affectionate partiality. With becoming modesty, she did not allude to the high praise awarded to her 'very fine poem' *Repining* or the long quotation from *DreamLand*.

William went to visit Scott, and brought back a glowing account that included some unexpected news, as least as far as his new friends in the Brotherhood were concerned. 'I was surprised to hear you were

married, I had not the slightest idea of it,' wrote Woolner; 'what a
pleasant life yours must be, with your calm philosophic mind, and a
happy home...' William, later, was more discreet about this discovery, which nevertheless altered the Rossettis' view of Scott, especially as William's report of his wife was not encouraging. Letitia was
a chatterbox, 'constantly talking in a pattering sort of way', voicing
whatever thoughts passed through her head and always with a prompt
opinion on every topic, and many foolish whimsies. She also had
what he later described vividly as 'a knack of pirouetting around
religious subjects' and over the years tried her luck 'in every doctrinal
camp from secularism to Roman Catholicism'. His final judgement
was more balanced, however, for Mrs Scott proved a steady friend,
and 'we prized her in the long run much better than we had done at
first'.

   If anyone was upset to learn that Scott already had a wife, it was
probably Maria. There is no substance in the idea that Christina was
devastated on her own account, having broken her engagement with
James because of her feelings for Scott. Indeed, she was far too heart-
broken to pay attention to anyone else. Meeting James by chance in
Regents Park this autumn was such a shock that she collapsed in a
faint. The wound was still raw, and on 21 November she completed a
sonnet on the one subject indelibly associated with James, St Elizabeth
of Hungary, which gives a mournful self-portrait of disappointment:

> She gave up beauty in her tender youth,
> Gave all her hope and joy and pleasant ways;
> She covered up her eyes lest they should gaze
> On vanity, and chose the bitter truth.
> Harsh towards herself, towards others full of ruth,
> Servant of servants, little known to praise,
> Long prayers and fasts trenched on her nights and days:
> She schooled herself to sights and sounds uncouth
> That with the poor and stricken she might make
> A home until the least sufficed
> Her wants; her own self learned she to forsake,
> Counting all earthly gain but hurt and loss.
> So with calm will she chose and bore the cross
> And hated all for love of Jesus Christ.

With the saintly example before her, Christina was learning to school
herself to accept 'hurt and loss' as a cross and a blessing.

The end of the year saw a number of changes, both at church and at home. Dodsworth finally followed James into the Roman communion, leaving the Christ Church congregation in some disarray, only held together, in Maria's view, by one of the curates. It was a time of turmoil in Anglo-Catholic circles, with the Gorham judgement asserting the power of the state over the Church and anti-ritualist riots taking place at St Barnabas Pimlico, (whose high Gothick interior James had used for the background of *St Elizabeth*). But according to Christ Church's new incumbent, Rev. Henry Burrows, Dodsworth's long wavering had alienated many parishioners, 'which partly accounted for his secession not drawing many after him'; clearly some preventive anti-romanising influence had been exerted. None of the Polidori or Rossetti women seem to have been tempted to join him, which may throw an oblique light on Christina's relation to James's conversion, all her female relatives being staunch in Anglican allegiance. Rector Burrows proved pragmatic and conciliatory and succeeded in retaining many High Church practices without causing further dissension. So though less forceful than his predecessor, he was soon more esteemed, and certainly so by Christina, for the remainder of her life.

In November, the decision was taken to leave Charlotte Street, when Mamma elected to purchase a small day school situated at 38 Arlington Street, towards Camden Town. The result is visible in the household's Census entry in April 1851.

Gabriele Rossetti: Head of household: Married: age 66:
   occupation – Professor of Italian: place of birth – Italy
Frances Rossetti: Wife: Married: age 50:
   occupation – Mistress of Day School: place of birth – Middlesex,
   London
Maria Rossetti: Daughter: Unmarried: age 24:
   occupation – Daily Governess: place of birth – Middlesex, London
William Rossetti: Son: Unmarried: age 21:
   occupation – Clerk (Inland Revenue): place of birth – Middlesex,
   London
Christiana [sic] Rossetti: Daughter: Unmarried: age 20:
   occupation – Assistant in the school: place of birth – Middlesex, London
Ann Carter: Servant: Widow: age 30:
   occupation – General Servant: place of birth – Ireland.

The house possessed a garden in which Papa could take the air. Hardly had the move taken place, however, than he suffered a stroke, which added to his disability. But a day school enabled Mamma to attend to husband and household while still earning a living, and gave Christina an added share of responsibility. Pupils were never expected to number more than a handful: the house was too small for anything else, but in retrospect William saw little improvement, writing bleakly of 1851 as a time of privation and pessimism, with his father incapacitated, Maria giving Italian lessons at two or three houses, his mother and Christina 'fagging over the unremunerative attempt' at a school and the whole household more or less dependent on his meagre salary.

He did not mention Gabriel, who was absent from home on the night of the Census, perhaps sleeping at the studio he now shared with Walter Deverell. And the general mood of the time seems to be reflected in the title of the first poem entered in Christina's manuscript book in 1851 – *A Dirge*. The notebook was not opened again till early summer, just about a year from James's defection with the words 'Oh for my love, my only love, Oh for my lost love far away!' This was a well-worn but heartfelt theme, the only disguise a transposition of gender:

> Therefore we parted as we met
>   She on her way, and I on mine,
> I think her tender heart was set
>   On holier things and more Divine: –
> We parted thus and gave no sign.

Her heart was still tender, for James's painting of a saint set on holier things was currently on view at the Portland Gallery. William, now writing for the *Spectator*, gave it a long and generally favourable review, showing that he at least was still well disposed towards the artist. The scene depicted, he explained, was that of high mass on the feast of the Assumption, 'when it is told of St Elizabeth that, kneeling before the crucifix, she took the coronet from her head'. The canvas exhibited very refined feeling, he judged, but had some flaws, in particular the use of the same model for so many of the female figures – just as Christina had feared.

The *Athenaeum* was openly hostile, sneering at the picture's 'attitudinizing, affectation and error'. A prostrate nun looked like a bundle of rags, and there was blasphemous clumsiness in the way St Elizabeth's cheek rested on the nailed life-size feet of the crucified Christ in effigy. 'What a bitter pill this row will be for Collinson,' commented Stephens, writing to William in some agitation lest the review signal a further attack on the PRB as a 'Catholic conspiracy', a fear that seemed justified when the *Times* poured renewed scorn on the 'juvenile artists who style themselves P. R. B.', who painted 'faces bloated into apoplexy or extenuated to skeletons, with colour borrowed from the jars in a druggist's shop'. Luckily the critic John Ruskin – then known to the Brotherhood as author of *The Stones of Venice* and *Modern Painters* – came to the PRB's defence with a vigorous, disinterested critique of Millais and Hunt, and the threatened storm did not break. London had other distractions this summer, notably the Great Exhibition in Paxton's glass palace in Hyde Park, though this was scant consolation to Christina, who had hoped so much of the St Elizabeth and its painter.

A month later, on 15 June, she completed *The Three Enemies*, an important and impressive dialogue between the soul and its tempters, the Flesh, the World and the Devil. The Flesh speaks first:

> "Sweet, thou art pale."
> "More pale to see,
> Christ hung upon the cruel tree
> And bore His Father's wrath for me."
>
> "Sweet, thou art sad."
> "Beneath a rod
> More heavy, Christ for my sake trod
> The winepress of the wrath of God" . . .

The World appeals to youth and beauty:

> "Sweet, thou art young."
> "So He was young
> Who for my sake in silence hung
> Upon the Cross with Passion wrung."
>
> "Look, thou art fair."
> "He was more fair
> Than men, Who deigned for me to wear
> A visage marred beyond compare."

The Devil offers fame:

> "Thou shalt win Glory."
> "In the skies,
> Lord Jesus, cover up mine eyes
> Lest they should look on vanities."
>
> "Thou shalt have Knowledge."
> "Helpless dust!

In thee, O Lord, I put my trust:
Answer Thou for me, Wise and Just."

"And Might – "
 "Get thee behind me. Lord,
Who hast redeemed and not abhorred
My soul, oh keep it to Thy Word."

It was bitter to have lost the partner with whom such spiritual trials
were to have been shared, and halved.

PART TWO

1850–60

10

The Bouquet

CHRISTINA THUS REACHED her twenty-first year in a rather bruised emotional state. The distress of her father's illness and her own breakdown, from which she had emerged without recovering her vivacity and with a permanent sense of guilt and unspoken injury, had been compounded by the abrupt termination of her engagement, against the wishes of her heart. She sought refuge in verse and in religion, and had absorbed lasting doctrines of grace through repentance, but depression was seldom far away. 'I wrote such melancholy things when I was young that I am obliged to be unusually cheerful and robust in my old age,' she said later, half acknowledging the inner source of her sadness. Precocious literary acclaim contrasted with private grief, hidden behind a stiff mask that seemed excessive to her contemporaries: what made the younger Miss Rossetti so distant, and her poems so mournful?

With the ending of *The Germ* and her relationship with James, Christina lost some of the social stimulus that meant a good deal to her. Though the PRB continued to meet from time to time, its collective energy had dispersed, and she no longer had a share in it. But in the autumn of 1850 a new circle of friends opened up, through Emily Patmore's sister Eliza Orme, wife of a prosperous distiller who had a great liking for the society of artists and writers, and a warm sympathy that helped both Christina and William gain self-confidence. The Ormes had two teenage daughters, Helen and Rosalind, who kept albums like the girls in *Maude* – on one occasion Papa inserted a gallant verse in Rosalind's volume – and lived in Avenue Road, to the north of Regents Park, where there was 'nothing but green fields between it and Hampstead – fields with hawthorn hedges, white stiles and yellow buttercups,' as Christina recalled later. On summer Sundays family and friends gathered in the garden to stroll along the gravel paths till sunset faded into dusk, as Holman Hunt remembered doing once in 1850, 'when the fortunes of the PRB looked most dismal'. Here Christina met Tennyson's lively and outspoken sister, Emily Jesse, who had been betrothed to Arthur Hallam and took a 'marked fancy' to young Miss Rossetti, though no friendship ensued. This was the year of *In Memoriam*, Tennyson's extended elegy for Hallam. Perhaps Christina derived some comfort from Mrs Jesse's emotional survival; more probably, she looked askance at a woman who had married after losing such a beloved. Romantic notions of lifelong espousal were very powerful. She was also shy – years later she recalled her gratitude towards Mrs Macmillan, wife of the publisher, who had kindly talked to her at a party at the Ormes'.

Other new acquaintances included the Irish poet William Allingham; Charles Cayley, a quiet young man previously known to them as one of Papa's last pupils, who had now produced a 'remarkably literal' *terza rima* translation of Dante; and Charley Collins, painter brother of the writer Wilkie Collins, who in 1851 exhibited *Convent Thoughts*, depicting a novice nun in a walled garden, inscribed with quotations praising virgin vows. Like James, Charley was prone to self-imposed penances: on a painting excursion Millais teased him for refusing blackberry pudding, saying it was a 'preposterous rule of superrogation which you have adopted ... no doubt you will think it necessary to have a scourge and take the discipline for having any dinner at all.'

In pursuit of a new interest, or perhaps with the unconscious desire to keep in touch with James at least in spirit, Christina enrolled in a class for young ladies at the North London School of Drawing in Camden Town, established by Madox Brown. Here she was glimpsed by Scott trying to draw wood shavings such as had notoriously featured in the super-realism of Millais's *The Carpenter's Shop*. But though she persevered, and later tried her hand at portraits and animals, she had little natural facility and virtually no 'eye' for art; indeed, despite fraternal influence, she later confessed to being quickly bored by looking at paintings.

This year Scott introduced his wife to the Rossettis. She was pronounced scatterbrained but amiable, despite her religious vagaries. Letitia Scott's garrulity was impervious to Christina's aloofness, or rather she took no notice of it, with that 'habit of running on with long-winded, perfectly harmless commonplaces', later ascribed by Christina to a fictional character with Letitia's chattering habit of dipping and darting across conversations. She noted Christina's peculiar stiffness, however, and much preferred Maria, who returned the cordiality. For her part, Christina's liking for Mrs Scott was never as warm as that of Maria, but like William she came to esteem her good heart and transparently open feelings, and over the years the womenfolk became good friends.

Through the Scotts, the Rossettis also met the extended Epps family, including the homeopathic Dr Epps with the 'decidedly odd' habit of kissing all female visitors; as William remarked, this was doubtless pleasing to himself, but led Maria and Christina to declare him 'cracked'. They pronounced his wife Ellen to be 'most fascinating', albeit a Dissenter; this, according to William, proved his sisters were no religious bigots. Later this year Mrs Scott also introduced Johannes Ronge, a disfrocked priest from Silesia, who had denounced a famous relic known as the Holy Coat of Treves and 'for a while was talked of as almost a new Luther'.

Another new acquaintance was an Italian cousin named Teodorico Pietrocola, who arrived in Britain towards the end of 1850 with various unsettled aspirations. Although the family were welcoming, finding him 'truly estimable', they were hardly able to offer assistance. To Teodorico, his illustrious great-uncle, poet and *professore*, seemed prematurely aged, with few teeth, bent back and slow, stumbling steps. His mind was still active, however, as he waxed warm about his homeland, recalling 'its beauties, its history, its glories!'

In July Christina was again invited to Longleat, where Lady Bath read *Maude* with its poetic additions, and judged it lacking in elevation. 'The conversation she objects to, not as unnatural,' Christina told William, 'but because the commonplaces of conversation she considers not worth recording – only the striking or the beautiful. The verse, however, appears more to her taste.' The criticism rankled: years later Christina was to assert the importance of the commonplace.

William suggested sending *Maude* to *The Germ*'s publisher, as a girls' story in the Miss Edgeworth mode. But Christina was discouraged, replying that the manuscript was now lying in a drawer, 'several removes from undergoing a revise'. She hoped some day to write something better, but it was beyond her power to do anything more with the tale.

Life at Longleat was still sedate, though Christina's listless mood was mainly responsible for the lack of animation in her letters. She tasted bread-fruit from the greenhouse, comparing it to 'an indifferent pear', and was still taking tonics, mixing her wine with hop-tea, an 'unpleasant but salutary compound'. One Sunday, when it rained, Lady Bath graciously insisted that Christina ride back from church in the carriage; she was thus 'very amiable in certain little everyday matters', however damning in literary ones. They were reading a journal kept by Aunt Charlotte in Italy ten years before, and had briefly seen Maria's former pupil Gertrude. But the liveliest companions were the pet monkeys who clambered about their chained perch and groomed their whiskers 'as anyone else might his shirt collar'. William was urged to write with 'all interesting news'.

Back in London in August she began a poem that she fancied might prove good. Called *A Fair World though a Fallen* and finished on 30 August, it was perhaps a response to those who deplored her poetic melancholy; its composition over several days confirms that, though Christina could seldom revise, her poems were not thrown off spontaneously and complete. When the impulse came, she worked to make the result as good as possible, often preferring 'the genuine lyric cry', but not despising other forms, nor believing in any sort of vatic inspiration.

Her chief task was to assist Mamma with the young pupils at Arlington Street, most of whom were local shopkeepers' children not long out of the nursery. Little Fanny Grey made them smile in a counting exercise, she reported, by saying that a goose had no legs, a cat two and a canary four. Some time later, Christina fictionalised her teaching experience in the figure of Mrs Grey, whose name was perhaps unconsciously borrowed from young Fanny. In her story, Fanny's counterpart is Jane, whose homework is being scrutinised:

> The addition sum was produced, worked at last without one blunder; the blotted B elicited a mild rebuke; a flower-pot added to the sampler was inspected and approved. Next Jane, who had, in preparation, read it over by herself, was questioned on the parable of the lost sheep . . .
> 'What is a wilderness?'
> 'A barren place, without houses, or trees, or grass, or water.'
> 'But what were the sheep to eat?'
> Some moments spent in thought. 'Did they have manna, ma'am?'
> 'No, I do not suppose they had manna. In a wilderness there are certain spots where water springs out of the ground; and round about this water or fountain the ground is fertile, fruit-bearing and other shady trees grow, and grass springs up. I recollect once reading of a traveller who found a single most beautiful lily blooming by such a fountain. Doubtless the good shepherd fed his flock on a fruitful spot of the wilderness, as the Psalm says – "He shall feed me in a green pasture, and lead me forth beside the waters of comfort".

'Did the shepherd fall asleep at night and let the wolf come and catch them?' continues Mrs Grey. 'No,' replies little Jane. 'No indeed,' repeats Mrs Grey. 'He kept a watch over his flock by night: if he saw a roaring lion or a great heavy bear coming to tear them, he rose and killed it or drove it away'.

The parable of the lost sheep was important to Christina: its imagery informs much of her verse as, does the parable form which, like Aesop's fables, was widely used in Victorian teaching. Mrs Grey then offers a brief discourse on the purpose of parable, before asking the hidden meaning of the lost sheep story. Jane correctly identifies the shepherd as Christ, but mistakes his flock:

> 'Not every one. He has "other sheep". The wilderness where they lived is this world. What was the fruitful spot where he pastured them?'

No answer. 'It is the Church', continued Mrs Grey; 'the fold or pen if we speak under emblem, the Church if we speak plainly. So the flock is not all people, but – ?'

'Christian people'.

and so the catechism continues.

As it happened, the image of Christ as Shepherd was in others' minds this autumn, too, for Holman Hunt, painting in Surrey with Millais and Charley Collins, had been working on a parable-painting called *The Hireling Shepherd*. He now began a new picture of Christ as a nocturnal visitor, inspired by the text from Revelation: 'Behold, I stand at the door and knock'. News of this was carried back to Arlington Street, and the idea must have struck Christina, for on 1 December she completed a poem with the same title. Instead of Christ, she saw a homeless widow, a destitute old man and a ragged child, needily knocking at a well-to-do door. All are refused, before Christ appears to chastise the confortable householder for her lack of charity.

The theme reflected contemporary concern for the condition of the urban poor revealed by social investigators and articulated by poets with a social conscience such as Elizabeth Barrett Browning, whose latest volume included *The Cry of the Children*. Christina's protest was addressed to those within the Christian fold who directed the sick and needy to the Poor Law and parish workhouse, rather than heeding the sacred duty of alms-giving. Politically, Christina inherited the Liberal compassion of her class, while at Albany Street Rev. Burrows was proving an incumbent with a conscience, promoting Sunday schools, an orphanage, a refuge for outcast women and a network of district visiting whereby parishioners became voluntary social workers. As she confessed in *Maude*, Christina was not drawn to such work, but aunt Eliza took on a district, and Maria was prominent among 'the more devout young women of the congregation' who ran a Friendly Society for servant girls, offering tea and Bible study to those with nowhere to go on their free afternoon. In the history of Christ Church there is mention too of a class for Italian urchins, sons of street hawkers and organ-grinders, which was possibly the work of aunts Margaret and Eliza.

It was probably through some of the more well-connected worshippers at Christ Church that Christina was introduced to a group of aristocratic young women who lived on the far side of Regents Park and had started a magazine entitled *The Bouquet from Marylebone Gardens*. This was a female version of *The Germ*, without its intellectual pretensions, launched in June 1851. The origin of *The Bouquet* was outlined in its opening number in a dialogue between three young ladies – 'Mignonette', 'Kingcup' and 'Bluebell' – whose anxieties illustrate the conflict between female modesty and 'display':

M. Do you ever write poetry, Kingcup?

K. Occasionally; my sister does. I prefer stories.

M. So do I. Have you seen my German story?

K. No; I should like very much to do so. Is it to be published?

M. Oh! no; I only write for amusement; it is very horrible; I should feel rather ashamed to see it in print.

B. I do not think you have any reason to be so; all German stories are horrible.

M. By the bye; what do you think of getting up a little work amongst ourselves, and printing it. Would either of you write?

K. I should be delighted to do so, provided it be not published; and I am sure my sister would join. Would you not do so, Bluebell?

B. Yes, but how are we to get it printed? We could not manage that part of it.

M. That could easily be done. I have often thought of this; I have arranged it all in my own mind. I propose that the name should be "A Bouquet of Wild Flowers, culled in Marylebone Gardens", by us, under fictional names . . .

The magazine was funded by subscriptions, and to protect ladylike anonymity each contributor took the name of a flower. 'Bluebell', for instance, was Lady Hester Browne, daughter of the Marquess of Sligo, and 'Mignonette' Miss Hume Middlemass, of St Andrews Place. When invited to contribute, Christina became 'Calta', which is marigold in Italian, because her pieces were in that language – *The Bouquet* being partly for the discreet display of accomplishments. After a short while male contributors appeared, over vegetable names, together with brief comments on previous issues.

Christina's first contributions, in October 1851, were some *Versi* in the pastoral style, in which a mother warns her daughter to beware of love, although the girl is already dreaming of 'when, how, whom'. This was followed by *L'Incognita*, on Christina's favourite rose image. Calta had written some 'very elegant and pointed Italian verses', noted *The Bouquet* in response. 'The clever authoress dwells, like Heliotrope, on the theme "Men are deceivers ever", but it is cruel to revile the whole sex for the faults of a small portion.'

Thus encouraged, Christina began a prose composition, which occupied her for the first months of 1852 and in its depiction of the aristocratic world of *The Bouquet's* circulation gave scope for the satirical wit and ironic observation that had been strong elements in her writing from the start. This was the epistolary novel that began appearing in instalments in April under the title *Corrispondenzia Famigliare* (Family Correspondence), whose central characters are two girls not unlike their author: Angela-Maria de' Ruggieri, daughter of a political refugee, and her English cousin, Emma Ward. On the basis of William's dismissive reference to *The Bouquet* as a young ladyish enterprise, unworthy of consideration, the story has been overlooked, but it is in fact a sprightly composition that offers an intriguing glimpse of its author's literary and social aspirations.

Angela-Maria, aged fifteen, attends a school for young ladies in the country (Nottinghamshire or Wiltshire suggest themselves to the informed reader), and her first letter describes the school's proprietor Mrs Sharp and the other pupils, who range 'from the hateful to the passable'; they include one named Gertrude Orme. Angela has a sharpish sense of superiority, but is not happy: 'It was different in Italy, where everyone admired and courted me,' she laments. 'Ah, if only Papa was not involved in politics . . .'

Cousin Emma responds with a long account from her social diary, which includes an invitation to the Duchess of Bridport's garden party. Three dressmakers and two maids are required to produce a perfect toilette, described in glowing detail. The other guests are pale with envy. The Misses Fairfax look ghastly in green and Clorinda Knight is pitiful in purple. In the evening, Emma dresses entirely in white, with pearls at her throat, ears and wrist; every eye turns as she enters the room. When she drops her posy three peers of the realm rush to retrieve it, while poor Clorinda sits talking to a curate. Unfortunately, on leaving Emma trips and twists her ankle – pride must have a fall – and is thereafter confined to the house, obliged to miss two more splendid parties.

A note in the next issue of *The Bouquet* complimented Calta on her 'lively and satirical Italian letters', or one might have feared that the gushing snobbery of Miss Emma Ward were directed against the well-born editors of *The Bouquet*, who certainly numbered duchesses among their acquaintance. In fact, one can detect some wishfulness amid the satire, for certainly Emma's author never had such stunning gowns or jewels as she describes. Aunt Charlotte was knowledgeable on aristrocratic matters of precedence and pedigree, and it is refreshing to find Christina expressing, albeit indirectly, a desire to share in the delights of Society. Was she once invited to some grand event where she felt as out of place as poor Clorinda?

Pious Clorinda, soon engaged to her curate, describes the visit to her mother-in-law, but Emma is the livelier correspondent, who in the next epistle laments her desperate experience at another party where an old bore talks interminably of literature and philosophy. Then Countess Crawley – she who was a nobody until she married the richest man in Ireland, old enough to be her grandfather, but gives the best dances of the season – requests some Italian verses for her album, and for the sake of an introduction Emma volunteers. 'I have always thought that anyone can write Italian verses, that the rhymes come by themselves, and that not even improvisation is difficult in that fine language,' she explains to Angela in a self-referential commentary on her author's literary heritage. 'Alas! I have been struggling for three hours and have only produced four and a half verses, without even a single rhyme.'

Angela, whose father has mysteriously disappeared, sends two stanzas such as Christina was accustomed to compose for Grandpapa. Presented to Countess Crawley, they excite admiration from the Neapolitan ambassador and his equerry: the more Emma disclaims all worthiness, the more compliments flow. The next day arrives, with verses of its own, beginning:

> Queste rose ch'io ti dono
> Simbol sono
> Nel diverso lo colore
> Del tuo spirito e del tuo core

The roses come from the young equerry, but the lines were written, as we already know, by Christina's grandfather, to salute the appearance of *Verses*. (And indeed, 'Calta' added a scrupulous footnote explaining that they were borrowed from her honoured friend 'Prezzemolo', or Parsley. Did she or Grandpapa choose this pseudonym?) Emma is suitably abashed, before concluding briskly that she cannot be blamed if the true author refuses to be named. She trusts Angela will soon hear from her father, and promises a full account of the Countess's next party.

Thus the instalments cease, in August 1852, just as the story is getting into its stride; a total of eight letters, spread over five months. The characters are vividly drawn and the storyline is quite as lively and picaresque as that of *Maude*, whose sequel it effectively forms. Moreover, the tone of the episodes – by turns bitchy, gushing and stiffly formal – dramatises the situations in which young ladies found themselves. Emma is spirited and lively, with a sharp sense of mockery, yet trained in polite formality. Angela's account of schoolgirl relations alternates between affectionate teasing and effusive emotion, with a touch of religiose sensibility in the visit to the castle with its ruined oratory.

All the figures reflect something of their author, from Emma's aspirations to shine in society, Clorinda's devotion to her curate, to Angela's poetic talent and Italian ancestry. Moreover, Angela's keen delight in her verses, coupled with the modesty that forbids taking credit, articulates the very difficulty expressed by the editors of *The Bouquet* over reconciling ambition with vulgar display. With the demise of *The Germ*, Christina had few outlets for her talent. It is a pity that something intervened to break off her contributions so abruptly.

William attributed this to the 'withering of *The Bouquet*', though as the magazine continued for several more years and Miss Rossetti was listed among subscribers until March 1853, this cannot have been the cause. Perhaps the social gulf became too great: a contributor to *The Germ* can hardly have felt much affinity with a journal that printed the scorecard of the Eton and Harrow match. Or perhaps some private censure of subject or treatment made her abandon the project, mortified by the realisation that 'to gratify a little vanity' her mockery had overstepped the bounds of decorum. It was not easy to be a woman and a writer.

While her social life was spent largely among young women, her brothers were spreading their wings. The contrast in their situations is illustrated by the fact that in February 1852 William went alone to hear Mazzini address the Friends of Italy – a group established 'to foster a correct appreciation of the Italian question in England' – at a public meeting to which his sister could never have gone unescorted and probably not even under male protection, for political gatherings were generally off limits for women. In the same manner, William and Gabriel were both able to accept casual invitations: this year they met William and Mary Howitt, an indefatigable literary couple who had admired *The Germ*, while Gabriel succeeded in gaining an introduction to his hero Robert Browning – whose wife, he reported, looked wasted by illness.

Late in 1851 Gabriel, now painting in Brown's studio, began a picture of Tibullus and Delia, for which he first asked Brown's young companion Emma Hill to sit and then found a better model in Elizabeth Siddall. She was a young dressmaker who was currently sitting to various members of the Brotherood, most memorably, to Millais, for the figure of Ophelia, drowning in the river – for which, in the studio, a tin bath was substituted. Christina did not meet 'Miss Sid' as she was familiarly known among the painters, for she did not often visit the studios and models were not asked to Arlington Street. As Hunt recalled, Gabriel showed no particular interest in Lizzie at first, and although by the summer of 1852 her name was more and more on his lips, it is not clear when the Misses Rossetti learnt of her existence. They were probably also unaware that the widowed Madox Brown had fathered a daughter on the teenage Emma, whom he was now supporting in quasi-marital state, away from public view. Such gossip was not for girls' ears.

Millais's *Ophelia* was the success of the season, though Hunt's *Hireling Shepherd* also sold well, fetching 300 guineas. This year the Brotherhood was depleted by Woolner's departure for Australia, then in the midst of a gold rush. For a few weeks Gabriel, who did not exhibit, shared a small studio cottage in the garden of the Howitts' home in Highgate, with a friend named Edward Bateman. Christina was no doubt voicing family anxieties when she expressed the hope that he would apply himself to work, in order to 'shine superior at the next Exhibition', rather than be eclipsed by his PR Brothers. In July she went to stay with the Jervis family at Darlaston Hall in Staffordshire, from where she wrote to William in her characteristically mannered style, revealing how her interest still centred on the men's activities and how governed by others were her own:

Many thanks for your unexpected, most welcome letter. I had no idea of your writing to me unless I commenced the correspondence . . .

I am heartily glad of Hunt's success; and if you like to tell him so (with the information that I will paint a picture on considerably lower terms, if he would kindly name this to his patrons), you are at liberty to do so. Another feeling of yours in which I cordially sympathize is regret at Woolner's departure for the diggings; poor fellow, I hope he will come back safe and well, and not estranged from his old friends by any amount of gold . . .

Your projected visit to the Scotts promises much enjoyment: let me beg of you betimes to remember me to both with genuine cordiality. I hope you will find pleasant occupation for the remainder of your holidays; mine are passing very satisfactorily; the improvement of health is really surprising.

The Ronges did not in the least take my fancy. I could imagine myself being described as a *quaint girl*. I should not think our *Germ* peculiarly adapted to the social evening . . . I should much have enjoyed boating with you and party, but have no idea I shall return to London before you quit it. Perhaps too, after your insulting mention of my cheerful disposition, female dignity would require me to reject your proffered company.

Our resident party has been increased, expressly for the picnic, by the arrival yesterday of a Captain Jacob, a young man with lightish hair, a very florid complexion, and no particular reputation for talent. My picknicking promises to be limited to some 10 minutes; the rest of the time to be devoted to fern-hunting with Mr J. A rather absurd arrangement, is it not? – but Mrs J. considers it the best attainable. What say you to your correct sister having taken a very short drive yesterday perched on the footman's board behind a carriage? Florence and Margherita shared my elevation; and, as we all escaped tumbling off, the expedition was quite satisfactory. The fact is, we met a carriage not far from the house, belonging to a neighbour and proceeding to Darlaston; so, as the vehicle was full and the coach box preoccupied, our only resource (except walking) was perching, and Florence preferred the latter. I fancy you would like Margherita; and we have given up *Missing* each other. She is 19. Mr Jervis has returned. On Monday a Dr Holland is expected, and Mr Philip Jervis back again, I believe.

Will you – or will you not? – convey my love to Papa and Mamma, Maria and Gabriel, and believe me

Ever your affect. sister
Christina G. Rossetti

All her life Christina used this signature, to family and friends alike. It was of course a more formal age, and it is nice to know she relaxed sufficiently to address Margherita, a young governess, by her first name and to perch with Florence Jervis on the back of a carriage, though her disdain for the rest of the company is clear. Besides Mr Jervis's parliamentary career, the family's main claim to fame, or notoriety, was due to the elder daughter, Agnes, who was wife to G. H. Lewes and mistress to Thornton Hunt, having children by both men – a scandalous situation unmentionable in polite society.

Darlaston was in the 'shady and inviting' Trent Valley. Christina enjoyed rambles in the woods, boating on the river, and a day excursion to the historic city of Chester. Writing to Maria, she unexpectedly received a reply from Gabriel, who forwarded the vital information that Mamma considered half a crown sufficient tip for the Jervises' maidservant, and sent a caricature of his sister crouching before her host, quill in hand; behind, a bust of Shakespeare smiles at Jervis's pretensions to poetry. He went on to wax lyrical about 'the Sid' in a playful manner that hinted at serious developments, saying he now had a lock of her hair 'radiant as the tresses of Aurora, a sight of which may perhaps dazzle you on your return', comparing her to Tennyson's 'meek unconscious dove' and warning his sister not to rival Lizzie in drawing, for she too was taking lessons, from himself. He added that both Mrs Howitt and her artistic daughter Anna Mary were anxious to meet Christina. Having admired her poems in *The Germ*, they invited her to contribute to 'an intelligent magazine' edited by Howitt.

Christina duly forwarded some pieces. She produced only a handful of new poems this year – suggesting that most of her creative energy went into *The Bouquet* – including a devotional monologue entitled *The Bruised Reed shall He not Break*, in which she herself was the bruised soul, and yet another poem on St Elizabeth of Hungary, in which she paid tribute to James's image of the saint kneeling to lay her crown 'careless on the cushions down'. Shortly after her return from Darlaston

she wrote *After a Picture in the Portland Gallery* (where James's St
Elizabeth had been on show) in which the speaker struggles to accept
things, invoking Christ's words at the moment of his betrayal, with
their implied continuation 'Father, if thou be willing, remove this cup
from me; nevertheless, not my will, but thine, be done'. The poem
ends with a plea:

> Ah, will it ever dawn, that day
>   When calm for good or ill
> Her heart shall say: "It is enough . . .
>
> It is enough, O Lord my God,
>   Thine only blessed Will".

It was now over two years since the end of the engagement, but her
heart had not healed.

Her next production was an entirely new departure, inspired by the
stories she was reading with the young pupils at Arlington Street –
the old tales of Jack the Giantkiller, Red Riding Hood and the rest.
Christina had grown up with Thomas Keightley's mythologies
and Perrault's Fairy Tales, and now knew those collected by the Brothers Grimm or newly-minted by Hans Andersen, whom the Howitts
had introduced to English readers. Her own story, *Nick*, was about a
poor man who dwelt in a small village, not a thousand miles from
Fairyland. But 'when I call him poor' she explained 'you must not
suppose he was a homeless wanderer, trusting to charity for a night's
lodging:

> on the contrary, his stone house, with its green verandah and flower-
> garden, was the prettiest and snuggest in all the place, the doctor's only
> excepted. Neither was his store of provisions running low: his farm
> supplied him with milk, eggs, mutton, butter, poultry and cheese in
> abundance; his fields with hops and barley for beer, and wheat for bread;
> his orchard with fruit and cider; and his kitchen-garden with vegetables
> and wholesome herbs. No, I call him poor because, with all these, he was
> discontented and envious.

Instead of enjoying his own prosperity, and being glad when his
neighbours prosper, Nick grumbles, as if other men's riches were his
poverty. And thus it was that one day he leans over Giles Hodge's
gate, envying his cherries, wishing he were a flock of birds to eat them
up or a blight to kill the trees altogether. The words are hardly uttered
before Nick is cursed by a rosy woman no bigger than a butterfly, who
announces that he must henceforth become everything he wishes, for
at least an hour.

Nick is thus an archetypal curmudgeon, and his curse the traditional 'gift', in the Mother Goose mode. First he becomes a flock of sparrows, who devour the envied cherries but are themselves blasted by Farmer Giles's shotgun and chased by a tabby cat, from whom he escapes by turning into a snarling bulldog:

A shake, a deep bite, and poor puss was out of her pain. Nick, with immense satisfaction, tore her fur to bits, wishing he could in like manner exterminate all her progeny.

Then chased by a man with a cudgel, Nick forms wish after wish – that he were a viper only to get trodden on, a thorn to run into some one's foot, a man-trap in the path, even the detested bludgeon to miss its aim and break. This duly comes to pass, and when placed on the hearth, Nick takes revenge by burning down the house, for 'it was provocation enough to be burned; but to contribute by his misfortune to the well-being of his tormentors was still more aggravating.'

Ravenous birds, bulldog, bludgeon, flames – the chain is forged of violent links, each ferociously crushed in turn. Buckets of water douse the fire, reducing Nick's malice to a small flame amid wet ashes, smouldering with suppressed fury. Eventually he forgoes revenge and turns himself into the village miser. Then the house is burgled and the miser felled by a crowbar. In a Gothick twist, Nick realises that he is dead, as he listens to his attackers ransacking the house:

Nick felt quite discouraged by his ill success, and now entertained only one wish – that he were himself again. Yet even this wish gave him some anxiety; for he feared that if the servants returned and found him in his original shape they might take him for a spy, and murder him in downright earnest. While he lay thus cogitating two of the men reappeared, bearing a shutter and some tools. They lifted him up, laid him on the shutter and carried him out of the room, down the back-stairs, through a long vaulted passage, into the open air. No word was spoken; but Nick knew they were going to bury him.

An utter horror seized him while, at the same time, he felt a strange consciousness that his hair would not stand on end because he was dead. The men set him down, and began in silence to dig his grave. It was soon ready to receive him; they threw the body roughly in, and cast upon it the first shovelful of earth.

But the moment of deliverance had arrived. His wish suddenly found vent in a prolonged unearthly yell. Damp with night dew, pale as death, and shivering from head to foot, he sat bolt upright, with starting, staring eyes and chattering teeth. The murderers, in mortal fear, cast down their tools, plunged deep into a wood hard by, and were never heard of more.

Under cover of night Nick made the best of his way home, silent and pondering . . .

Next day he makes amends for all damage his rage and envy have caused. And of course he is never again heard to utter a wish.

In this fairytale mode Christina found at a stroke the narrative style through which to speak in her own voice which had eluded her previous attempts at fiction. Loosened from realist constraints, the genre allowed for accomplished storytelling, with a message that is saved from sanctimoniousness by humour and imagination. At the same time, *Nick* also has levels of personal meaning, from the exploration of Christina's graveyard fantasies about what it would be like to be buried alive – a familiar image of dissociated feeling – to the double pleasure so often used in children's writing, of both indulging and condemning bad behaviour. *Nick* is obviously and ostensibly a moral tale, warning against envy and anger, and therefore also a self-admonition, in which Christina castigated her own faults, as she perceived them. More importantly, it also expressed her own anger and envious discontent, which were otherwise buried – like the miser, alive but unable to speak – thus voicing her repressed desires to hurt others as she herself had been hurt. Through Nick's malevolence, she was able to both enjoy and punish all her 'bad' feelings, of anger, envy, gloating, spite, hatred. The hero with the Satanic name is chastened and transformed by the folk wisdom of describing what is most proscribed, and his author's own corrosive rage and shameful fantasies thereby expressed and exorcised.

She had much to be angry about, though little that could legitimately be voiced, and the imaginative linking of Nick's rage with his consciousness of being dead suggests the depth to which her injury was buried. She could not be openly envious of others' good fortune, as long as Mamma, Maria and William shouldered their burdens uncomplainingly. But there is no doubt that inwardly, if not consciously, Christina felt profoundly discontented and aggrieved. 'Hope deferred maketh the heart sick', she had learnt at her mother's knee; but would her wishes never come true?

Wishfulness was strong this autumn. On 15 October the notebook received a revenge ballad in which the unresponsive lover is reproachfully warned of lifelong guilt. On 24 October came a dialogue with the self, ending with resignation: 'I must unlearn the pleasant ways I went: Must learn another hope, another love . . .' And 23 December saw the completion of the poignantly-titled *The heart knoweth its own bitterness* in which the poet vainly tries to assuage her grief in silence:

Weep, for none shall know
　Why sick at heart thou weepest . . .

Weep, sick and lonely,
　Bow thy heart to tears,
For none shall guess the secret
　Of thy griefs and fears . . .

'To what purpose is this waste?' she asked in the New Year:

A windy shell singing upon the shore:
A lily budding in a desert place,
　Blooming alone
　With no companion
To praise its perfect perfume and its grace . . .

There had been a depleted reunion of what William described as 'our long-forgotten PRB' at Arlington Street, with Hunt and Stephens as guests. Collinson was of course neither present nor invited; he had in fact recently decided to enter the Jesuit community at Stonyhurst – 'as a "working brother", I am told, whatever that may mean,' wrote William with a sneer, though in fact James had begun training for the priesthood.

Gabriel and William had taken an apartment on the river, by Blackfriars Bridge, where Gabriel spent most of his time and William sometimes slept. It was convenient for William's office in Somerset House, but even closer to Lizzie's home in Southwark. This was an unorthodox relationship – Gabriel admitted no more than that Miss Sid was his student – and probably not advertised at home. Here the little school had folded, and Papa was again poorly, having spent October in Hastings with Mamma in a vain attempt to restore his strength. Christina continued 'ploddingly enough at her drawing studies,' William recalled, where she was joined by Rosalind Orme, whom she described as pretty, clever and 'indescribably winning', and who was soon to marry the young scholar David Masson, secretary of the Friends of Italy. She wrote some sepulchral stanzas for Rosalind's album, in her most inappropriate mortuary mode, and together they visited the Patmores, now living in uncle Henry's old house. The Polydores came to visit, too, for on 21 February Christina wrote some gloomy verses for little cousin Henrietta, whose day was just beginning, while her own was nearly done.

All her life Christina associated winter with emotional gloom, and frozen feeling, in recurrent images of inner and outer bleakness that shroud a dismal sense of pain. She was of course often ill in the winter, yet this association seems more figurative than literal – or perhaps her disabling fits of depression and neuralgia were less easy to bear in winter, if only because summer held out the promise of holidays, and therapeutic searchings for windy shells and sea-creatures on the beach.

In March 1852, rather suddenly, Mrs Rossetti took a swift decision. 'My dear Mrs Heimann,' wrote Christina:

> Our London school having failed, Mamma has felt it her duty to avail herself of what appears a good opening for one at Frome in Somerset-shire; so next Thursday (that is tomorrow week) we expect to leave town for that place. On the following Monday our school is to open; so you may imagine we shall have plenty to do in arranging our house during the few intervening days. Maria, Gabriel and William will continue here; and Papa also just for the present; though he is finally to join us, if the school answers.
>
> Now I am going to be quite brazen. As I cannot well spend an evening away from home, because our time together threatens to be so short, and as I also want to see you before our departure, would you kindly tolerate me to luncheon next Monday or Tuesday . . . when I could say good-bye to some of my kindest old friends, and ask permission to write to you when away?

'There's self-inviting impudence,' she concluded affectionately, knowing the Heimanns would not be offended.

11

Frome Forlorn Hope

FROME IS A small country town close to Longleat. Aunt Charlotte and Lady Bath had put themselves about to find this 'opening', perhaps to save Mamma from going back to governessing. They hoped too that country air and tranquillity would benefit Papa, and get him away from excitable acquaintance like Johannes Ronge. Christina and her mother went ahead on 8 April, staying at an inn until they found a suitable house in Brunswick Place, Fromefield, a terrace of tallish houses out on the Trowbridge road. Here they established a school, and advertised for pupils; and here in a sheltered corner Christina planted some fig-tree seedlings presented by Fred Stephens, with a view to consoling her father for what meant renewed exile, far from all compatriots.

'We have discovered some beautiful country hereabouts; abundance of green slopes and gentle declivities; no boldness or grandeur, but plenty of peaceful beauty,' she reported on 22 April. She had been trying to draw Mamma's portrait, and requested an account of the Royal Academy summer show. There was no real news from Frome, but she had discovered an inn whose name chimed with her boredom – the Blue Boar. 'Is it not quite a prevision of my sparkling self?' she asked ironically.

Joking apart, she was truly unwilling to leave London. It was akin, in her view, to being buried alive, or consigned to limbo, beyond the river of oblivion. With humorous invocation of Charon and Cerberus, she wrote a few near-nonsense lines beginning 'In my cottage near the Styx' in parody of the popular song 'In a cottage in a wood' and in punning allusion to the London habit of disparaging rural England as 'out in the sticks', where nothing happens. The verses, relayed home, made Maria grin. William, who had wholly forgotten the doggerel, was surprised to hear his sister recite the lines forty years later. They were, he recalled, 'more dreary than jocular'.

No sooner had the school opened than Frances Rossetti was summoned back to her mother's deathbed. 'My precious Mamma' wrote Christina on 28 April,

Thank God indeed that dear Grandmamma died without pain, and also that you left Frome when you did; another delay would have made you too late ... I am very glad she mentioned me, but hardly hope she understood my love.

She proposed to defer her own journey for a few days, in order to call on pupils' parents, ensure the cook was able to look after the house, and complete some promised shopping for aunt Charlotte. She hoped, however, that she might see her grandmother for the last time, 'unless the lapse of so many days renders it inadvisable'. Despite her many mourning poems, this was the first death she had directly experienced.

Grandmamma was buried in St Pancras churchyard, and towards the end of May Christina and her mother returned to Frome, taking Papa with them. The only other resident they knew was the vicar, Rev. W. J. E. Bennett, whom Lady Bath had recently installed amid some controversy, for Bennett had been drummed out of his cure at St Barnabas, Pimlico following the anti-ritualist riots there, when in his own words, he had been 'assailed in the church in my public office of preaching God's word, by hissing, yells, shouting – blasphemies within, a mob without.' The government did not intervene and the magistrates before whom the rioters were brought 'turned theologian' and denounced Puseyism. *Punch* carried a comic comment:

> Hushaby Bennett on the Church top
> When your bells cease the outcry will stop.
> If you don't stop when reason shall call
> Down will go Bennett, bell-ringing and all.

Bennett did go down, glorying in his 'persecution'. Not surprisingly, his induction at Frome was opposed locally, where rumours as to his closet Romanism flourished, but in the event he proved an energetic, popular and long-standing incumbent. Curates were recruited and it has been suggested that Frances Rossetti was invited to Frome under his aegis. There is no evidence this was so, however; her connection was directly with Lady Bath, via aunt Charlotte. Given their name, it is surprising that the Rossettis were not assumed to be Catholics too, which was ironic if one reason for being in Frome was to remove Papa from the baleful influence of anti-papist agitators in London.

'Do you know that I am seventy years old?' he wrote to a friend, having just received a birth certificate from Vasto:

> My wife, excellent woman, has come here to set up a school for young ladies, and I hope it will succeed. My two sons have stayed in London; one is an able painter and makes a good deal of money; the other is employed at the Excise Office with the fine salary of £250 a year, in addition to which he makes £50 more by writing very fine articles on the arts for a magazine . . .

William's salary alone was sufficient to support the family, he continued, but his wife wished to leave the young people in possession of their own earnings. 'Even my two daughters can already support themselves,' he added: 'the older one earns about £80 a year. The other assists her mother.' This gives a lucid picture of family finances, yet is still puzzling. No one, least of all William and Maria, wanted the family to be split up, nor to retain their own earnings. William ascribed the move to their mother's sense of duty, but she may simply have been heeding medical advice regarding Papa's health.

His friends tried to cheer him. 'So you are alone with your wife and Christina?' wrote old Pistrucci, 'but *corpo di Baccho*, those two are worth two hundred.' Thomas Keightley feared Gabriele would be lonely with no one to call by as in London, but declared that he had often thought him 'by far the happiest of all the exiles who have sought these shores', for he alone enjoyed domestic happiness. Moreover, his children were all talented: could he have hoped for greater bliss under the brilliant sky of Naples?

Her father was in better spirits than had been feared, Christina told Mrs Heimann. One of the curates had travelled in Spain and Italy, and promised agreeable conversation. Their young scholars were pleasant and well-behaved and they had attended the prize-giving at the parish school. Aunt Margaret came for four weeks, and cousin Teodorico arrived too, having taken and left a teaching post in Devon. (He had also joined the Plymouth Brethren and abandoned his native faith for noisy Protestant proselytism. Both papacy and tyranny were doomed, he wrote in apocalyptic vein a few months later, for the end of the world was nigh 'when all the despots, with all the priests, shall be destroyed!') Later in the summer the other aunts would come to stay, as well as Maria and William. But Christina's main concern was a baby thrush, which had fallen from the nest and was not fully fledged:

so I took it home with me to bring it up till it could take care of itself, when of course I should have restored it to liberty: but the poor little creature refused to eat or drink; so next day I took it out again, and deposited it in a field near a hedge, in the hope that either it could manage to maintain itself, or that some parent birds would take care of it. I only hope that neither cat nor cruel boy found it.

All her life Christina's tender heart was moved by the plight of vulnerable creatures.

William came to Frome, en route for Paris, and Gabriel visited the Scotts in Newcastle. In London Madox Brown introduced his elder daughter Lucy to Maria, 'for the advantage of her acquaintance'; having earlier in the year quietly married Emma Hill he was now preparing to unite both parts of his family. Christina and Mamma visited Wells, made thirteen jars of blackcurrant jam, and were reading the work of a juvenile author commended by Mrs Heimann. 'How very grand to be published in Germany and New York as well as in England,' she wrote wistfully. 'I wonder if I shall ever attain such eminence.' She was still sketching, but doubted her ability to gain fame in that particular art.

On her behalf her brothers sent *Nick* to their friend James Hannay, currently enjoying success as a novelist, in the hope that he would commend it to his publishers, Messrs Cundall and Addey. On this slight foundation Christina built a financial fantasy – a 'first-rate scheme for rebuilding the shattered fortunes of our house' – in which Hannay would forward the story with her portrait, to the firm's general manager ('a susceptible individual of great discernment') who would at once send her a cheque for £20 and set the story into type.

> Addey returns; is at first furious; but, seeing the portrait, and with a first-rate business head perceiving at a glance its capabilities, has it engraved, prefixed to "Nick", and advertized all over the civilized world. The book spreads like wild-fire. Addey at the end of 2 months, struck by a late remorse, and having an eye to future contingencies, sends me a second cheque for £200; on which we subsist for a while. At the publication of the 20th edition Mrs A (a mild person of few words) expires; charging her husband to do me justice. He promises with one suppressed sob. Next day a third cheque for £2000 reaches me. This I divide; assigning half to Maria for her dowry, and handing the rest to Mamma. I then collapse. Exeunt Omnes.

Jesting often conceals true desires. As well as money, Christina wished for fame, yet knew such wishes could not be openly expressed. On the death of Sara Coleridge a few months earlier, her obituarist set out conventional wisdom in regard to women and writing, noting how Mrs Coleridge's 'intellectual powers were held in harmony with that feminine delicacy and gentleness, which sometimes are injured by pride or vanity attendant on the notoriety of authorship'. This was all very well, but notoriety of authorship had not damaged James Hannay.

Though also jocular, the reference to Maria's dowry is one of very few allusions to her marriage prospects. Was any romance budding? According to William, the nearest approach to a 'preference' that Maria entertained was bestowed on Charley Collins, close friend of John Millais, whose latest painting was devoutly entitled *Thoughts of Bethlehem*. Slight in stature, with bright orange hair and chiselled

features, he was considered by male friends to be a good fellow full of
unexpected perplexities caused by religion; in 1853 his widowed
mother was thinking of retiring to the country, and this might have
seemed an appropriate time for Charley to consider marriage, especially now Maria was virtually on her own in Arlington Street, with
William often at Blackfriars. Christina's glancing allusion may therefore betray her knowledge of a potential romance. Beyond this, however, nothing is known of the relationship, though Charley remained
on good terms with the family until at least 1855, and his brother
Wilkie later used Papa as the model for Professor Pesca in *The Woman
in White*.

There was no response, let alone a cheque, from Mr Addey. Christina
asked William to retrieve *Nick*; she now thought of sending it to Mrs
Howitt. She was still bored and homesick. 'Pray remember me anywhere you like,' she wrote; 'I really do remember absent friends,
though I do not gush.' And when Maria returned to London, Christina, though sorry, was also glad her sister was not obliged to stay and
swell 'the Frome forlorn hope'.

Later in life Christina always disavowed any special knowledge of
the country, and despite her happy memories of Holmer Green she
always regarded the city as her true home, partly it seems in reaction
to the 'banishment' of Frome. To chime with the season she was
feeling morosely autumnal, not even roused by the news that some of
the *Germ* poems were to be reprinted in an anthology called *Beautiful
Poetry*. What a ghastly fate, she wrote, to be ranked amongst the
'beautiful poets' of England; worse still, the authors' names were to be
published. She was probably pleased, nevertheless, at this small token
of fame, as also with Mrs Howitt's inclusion of 'O Rose thou flower of
flowers' in a forthcoming Christmas annual.

Over the summer she had written several new poems, including an
interminable ballad called *Annie*, and some pieces copied out in September under the heading *Odds and Ends*. Most harped on about hope
deferred and love betrayed. In London there was talk of an anthology
by new writers, and Christina sent her latest offerings for Gabriel to
read. He replied tactfully but judiciously. What did the title *Something
like Truth* mean? Was it true, or not? Parts were excellent, but lines like
' "dreaming of a lifelong ill" (etc etc ad libitum) smack rather of the
old shop'. Instead of such repetitious dreamings, why did she not try
narrative, or writing from 'real abundant nature'? This was evidence
of his serious interest in her work, and acute advice: *Something like
Truth* was immediately retitled *Sleep at Sea*, from its image of heedless
souls heading towards shipwreck. But the original title hinted at
something deeper than allegory, for she was still using verse to express her own adolescent desire for oblivion:

'Wake' call the spirits again:
But it would take
A louder summons
To bid them awake . . .

Gabriel's news underlined her isolation. Anna Howitt had introduced a new friend, rich and buxom Miss Barbara Smith, who, in Gabriel's words was 'blessed with large rations of tin, fat, enthusiasm and golden hair', and as an aspiring artist thought nothing 'of climbing up a mountain in breeches, or wading through a stream in none, in the sacred name of pigment'. She had invited them all to lunch and was 'quite a *jolly fellow*'. Millais had been elected an Associate of the Royal Academy, Hunt was planning to travel to Egypt, and Gabriel himself had acquired a new patron, Mr MacCracken of Belfast. He sent a comic sonnet on the subject, parodying Tennyson's *Kraken*. In reply Christina followed up an unfinished tribute to the PRB with another on its 'decadence', now that Woolner was in Australia, Hunt yearning for 'the land of Cheops', and

the champion great Millais,
Attaining academic opulence
Winds up his signature with A. R. A.
So rivers merge in the perpetual sea . . .

She more than anyone regretted the Brotherhood's demise.

From William, who had been promoted, she received 'a real live five pound note' for her birthday in December – a large sum for one whose disposable income was usually measured in shillings. And once again she held the fort, while Mamma was in London visiting her father. The lease on Arlington Street having expired, William and Maria took weekly lodgings, until the future was settled. Bravely, Christina offered to take care of Papa throughout the Christmas break. But he missed his wife, as always. 'Today will be the third night I shall sleep without you,' he wrote on 15 December. 'Dear Christina does everything she can to make me happy, but you are not there . . . Come back, my soul.'

Frances replied rather briskly, because poor Grandpapa was in a coma, having suffered a stroke. The shock was sudden, for though nearly ninety, he had been remarkably fit and well. 'Oh, my dear Grandpapa!' Christina cried out on reading the letter, with such anguish that Gabriele thought Gaetano was already dead. He lingered only a day, without regaining consciousness, and the whole family grieved. 'He was one of the people in the world for whom I had a real affection,' Gabriel told Scott. 'Our family may wait long now for so stout a branch.'

Christina was deeply affected, for Grandpapa had been her most constant friend, tutor, consoler and critic. Only three weeks earlier she had sent him a poem, soliciting comments. Indeed, William remembered, she had more warmth of feeling for him than for her father, and the loss added to the forlornness of Frome.

'When are you going to return, when?' Gabriele asked querulously a week later. 'Cristina and I await you with open arms.' Would *cara Francesca* now agree to reunite the family in London? 'Oh, what a joy it will be if I can have all my children around me, as we do in Italy.' In fact, Papa was himself dying, and although Frances returned to Frome and to the school, at the end of January he suffered a paralytic seizure so alarming that Maria, Gabriel and William hurried to his bedside. He survived, but the decision was finally taken to return to London. Combining William and Maria's earnings with Mamma's small inheritance, the household could live economically together. So a new house was sought, and packing commenced, Christina wishing she had the arms of Briareus or the legs of a centipede; the joke shows how much the prospect brightened her spirits.

Her last letter to William from Frome was full of chatter about selling off old copies of *The Germ* and schoolmistressy jokes about her brothers' use of slang. 'Wherever we settle, permit me to adjure you never under any circumstance to designate our abode as a "crib". Your vocabulary would gain by the eradication of that and sundry other such temperate facetiae,' she wrote. Would William look out for a vacancy in 'the combustible department' of the Revenue office (which employed a team of 'firelighters') and had he noticed a piece in the *Athenaeum*, evidently far inferior to their own efforts, about 'a supposed being, wholly spiritual, seeing without eyes or light another given supposed being, visible in perfect darkness'. Finally, in honour of returning sprightliness, she sent off some *bouts rimés* endings. A month later, the family was together again in London, after less than a year apart, at 45 Upper Albany Street, close to Christ Church.

For a fortnight, Papa's condition remained stable. He was slowly sinking, however, and on Easter Sunday his condition worsened. Dr Stewart was called, and then Dr Hare, who diagnosed infection on top of diabetes. To the last he remained conscious though often confused, as when he fancied he saw his mother, or asked if his old comrade General Pepe was in bed with him. But he recognised the family and responded when Frances read the liturgy. Friends called to pay their respects – among them cousin Teodorico and Papa's former pupil Charles Cayley. According to a deathbed diary kept collectively, his last words were '*Ah Dio, ajuatami Tu!*' whose meaning may not be fully conveyed by the English equivalent 'God help me!', but was clear evidence that, as Christina later wrote firmly, her illustrious father after long years of exile, 'died a patient Christian'. The end came early on the morning of 26 April and the death certificate gave the cause as old age and wasting disease.

Seven days later the family accompanied the coffin to the new cemetery at Highgate, where Frances had purchased a grave-plot. She vetoed a patriotic send-off by the exile community, almost as if wishing to close that chapter, and quietly ordered all remaining copies of *Amor Platonica* to be burnt. The family went into mourning, of course, but though this meant refusing invitations, the fact that there was now no invalid at home brought as much relief as grief. In a sense, as husband and father, Gabriele had been dead for some time, his funeral the mere formality. In years to come, his presence would come back to haunt the family, rather like the banshee to which William eloquently likened his Dante studies, but at the time death seemed a welcome deliverance. With it came too the resumption of old friendships with the Heimanns and Ormes, and the introduction of new acquaintances made by Maria and William. As far as Christina was concerned, her father's dying coincided with a return to the land of the living.

Henceforth the presence of Maria – bright, pious, forceful, full of humour, goodwill and unshakeable views – was constant and crucial to Christina. Perhaps something of Maria's bustling activity was also a defence against depression, but William at least was in no doubt as to her essentially equable temper. She knew herself to be physically ill-favoured, and made a virtue out of perceived deficiences, remarking on one occasion (in an age that valued delicate sizes) 'What a good thing my feet are so large – for so anyone can wear my boots!' Christina long admired this throwaway remark. 'If only we could estimate every such blemish in ourselves, not as a personal hardship, but as a helpful possibility,' she wrote earnestly.

It is conjectured that around this date Maria declined a proposal from Charley Collins though the evidence for this is as yet unrevealed. It would have been considered an inappropriate moment for an engagement, and perhaps the moment passed. William, however, was now paying decorous court to Miss Rintoul, daughter of the *Spectator*'s editor, who was introduced and liked, while Gabriel was manifestly in love with Miss Siddall. Almost the first message to Christina on her return to London was an invitation to meet Lizzie and view 'that Gug's emanations', or drawings. 'Gug' and 'Guggums' were pet names for Gabriel's 'dear dove divine', though what Christina made of this intimacy can only be guessed, for the family were not informed of his intentions. They knew only that Gabriel was with Lizzie at Hastings while Papa was dying, and that Barbara Smith thought it quite natural for him to share Lizzie's sitting-room without a chaperone –

evil be to him who evil thinks was the subtext of this letter home. But he drew Lizzie with eloquent tenderness, and was carelessly imperious in his enthusiasm, for without asking he had declared that he and Allingham would select some of Christina's poems for a volume, which Lizzie would illustrate. 'I have no doubt we shall get a publisher,' he added airily. There was always something magisterial in Gabriel's dispositions.

Silence surrounds the actual meeting between Christina and Lizzie in 1854. But six months later she recorded her impressions in a little poem that adopted her brother's own image of Lizzie as a dove, seeing her as sweet and shy:

> And downcast were her dovelike eyes,
> And downcast was her tender cheek;
> Her pulses fluttered like a dove
> To hear him speak.

'Not fair as men would reckon fair', this continued – Lizzie had red hair and protruding teeth – 'Nor noble as they count the line' – her father was an ironmonger – but very much in love. Indeed, the Patmores and Ormes were freely gossiping that both Rossetti brothers now had sweethearts – but what could their sister say to friendly inquiries about Miss Siddall, when Gabriel made no announcement and had not even introduced her to his mother? Not surprisingly, Christina's admiration for Lizzie was not as fulsome as Gabriel expected.

He was also eager to introduce his other new friends, Anna Howitt, Barbara Smith and Bessie Parkes – to whom he sent a copy of Christina's *Verses*, because she too was a poet. All three hoped soon to meet handsome Mr Rossetti's talented sister. It was another sign that Christina had returned from beyond the Styx, and heralded her introduction to members of a new and stimulating circle, in the emergent women's movement.

'Dear old Mrs Howitt – I am glad you recollect her with so much friendship,' wrote Christina to a friend many years later. 'She and her home circle and her two successive pretty little houses at Highgate linger among my agreeable memories'. And at the first of these homes, romantically named the Hermitage, Christina was now introduced to the poet, translator and editor – the first professional woman writer she knew – who had already accepted *The Rose and The Trees Counselling*, and was also promising to put *Twilight Calm*, the revised and renamed pastoral containing gnats, into a special issue of a magazine designed to introduce new English poets to German readers, alongside a witchcraft ballad by Gabriel, named *Sister Helen*.

As well as offering a model of female achievement, Mary Howitt thus actively assisted the younger generation. On occasion she could be mildly discouraging, as when Bessie asked how much time to devote to writing and was told that Mrs Howitt was never without some work in hand; though Bessie earnestly wished to succeed, this was daunting. In manner Mrs Howitt was eminently modest, but her achievements were considerable, for as well as her own writing, she worked alongside her husband, a veteran Radical journalist, as an active campaigner in the anti-slavery movement; recently, the Howitts had hosted Harriet Beecher Stowe, author of the best-selling *Uncle Tom's Cabin* on a tour of Britain.

Mrs Howitt's daughter Anna Mary, some five years older than Christina also set a stimulating example. Indeed, the energy and high aspirations of Anna and her friends matched those of the PRB, with the significant addition of gender equality. 'Oh, how terribly did I long to be a man so as to paint there,' Anna exclaimed to Barbara Smith after visiting the Royal Academy Schools a year or so earlier; 'one seemed stepping into a freer, larger, and more earnest artistic world ... which one's *womanhood* debars one from enjoying'. But this exclusion prompted action, not complaint. 'Instead of lamenting that we *are* women' she added, 'let us earnestly strive after a nobler state of things.' With Jane Benham, Anna had then gone to study with Kaulbach in Munich, publishing on her return a lively account of their time there, as well as a long magazine story called *Sisters in Art*, which conjured a vivid picture of mutual support in artistic endeavours.

When introduced to Christina, Anna had just made her exhibition debut with *Margaret returning from the Fountain*, from *Faust*, and was planning a further exploration of the fallen woman theme, entitled *The Castaway*, with lilies trampled in the mud as symbolic accessories; as Gabriel remarked, it was a bold subject for a female artist. Enthusiastic and volatile, Anna was rather given to gush, on the evidence of her literary style, but at the same time sincere and sympathetic.

In terms of feminist consciousness, Anna was also well ahead of her new friend. The previous summer, while Christina entertained the aunts in Frome, Anna, Jane and Bessie had lodged alone in a village inn in order to paint and write, pursuing art and independence just as the young men of the Brotherhood were accustomed to do, in delicious, unaccustomed female freedom. Here they earnestly discussed issues of the day, especially the debates over 'woman's right and fitting sphere'. At the top of Leith Hill, Anna set up her easel, commanding Bessie to write a poem and swearing that one day they would be famous. Back in London they gathered in the garden studio at the Hermitage – where Gabriel had briefly lodged during the Howitts' absence – a picturesque Gothick cottage 'buried in exuberant growth of ancient ivy . . . where Anna now covered her canvas with some of the most delicate, beautiful drawings ever done by a woman's hand', and where they talked of all they aspired to achieve.

They dreamt in particular of a 'beautiful sisterhood in Art' which would support their endeavours. Barbara Smith, who enjoyed an independent income from her progressively-minded father and was also an eager if impatient artist, had even grander aims of an Associated Home like a college, where women could live in comradely independence, and of a large scheme for an Outer and Inner Sisterhood with artistic rather than religious aims. Here, the Inner group would consist of Art-sisters, painters and poets, supported by the Outer Sisterhood of working women, 'all striving after a pure moral life, but belonging to any profession, any pursuit'. All would contribute according to their abilities: one assisting with the sewing, to keep the Art-sisters' stockings mended; another to produce cakes and preserves. And in the evenings, they would gather and talk . . .

Such ideas were in the vanguard of a new feminism, challenging accepted notions. Generally speaking, the women were not separatist, and Anna in particular protested against the common calumny that men thwarted women's every effort to attain eminence, insisting that whenever she had needed help with the 'sharp stones and thorns which peculiarly beset a woman upon the path of Art', it had come from 'strong, manly hands', with generous words prophesying happy achievement. Emotionally, things had been less happy; like Christina her engagement to a fellow artist, Gabriel's friend Edward Bateman, had foundered. When he left with Woolner for Australia, and did not write, Anna knew the relationship was over. 'She has been so stripped and sorrowful,' her mother wrote in the summer of 1854, hoping that the success of her painting would lift her spirits.

As poet Bessie Parkes gave voice to the women's shared idealism in lines inscribed 'To all True Artists', which Mrs Howitt had also published in her annual:

> Thou that wouldst enter here
> Fashion thy being with an Art austere;
> Leave thou thy bitterness of heart behind . . .
> All base ambitions see that thou forsake –
> All the bright armour of a Christian take –
> Turn thy face forward ever . . .

Christina would have admired the views, if not the verse. And in Bessie's first volume she also found homage to Mrs Browning, as a role model:

>Yet oh! how I rejoiced that you were great,
>And all my heart exulted in your fame;
>A woman's fame, and *yours!*

This summer Bessie and Barbara were away in Wales, again painting and writing and relishing their freedom to indulge in brave exploits, such as bathing naked in a mountain pool, 'in the most utterly crazy, Diana-like way', with only sheep as audience, until scared by their own boldness into imagining that Barbara's father had been magically summoned to rebuke them. They were active too in the political field, Bessie writing on girls' education and Barbara composing a commentary on the iniquitous legal position of women. As yet suffrage was not on the agenda – many men were still without the vote – but their aspirations were high, and particularly encompassed the desire for egalitarian marriage. Moreover, they were dedicated to what would later be called feminist networking, and when Christina finally came to meet them the following year, she 'had so long heard and known of' their activities that formalities were unnecessary.

Such an atmosphere of ambition and idealism among women was stimulating, after the sleepiness of Frome, but also alarming, to one schooled in Tractarian theology. Towards the end of June came a sudden burst of composition, as Christina entered three poems in the notebook in two days, starting with a forceful warning entitled *The World*:

>By day she woos me, soft, exceeding fair:
> But all night as the moon so changeth she;
> Loathsome and foul with hideous leprosy,
>And subtle serpents gliding in her hair.
>By day she woos me to the outer air,
> Ripe fruits, sweet flowers, and full satiety:
> But thro' the night a beast she grins at me,
>A very monster void of love and prayer.
>By day she stands a lie: by night she stands
> In all the naked horror of the truth,
> With pushing horns and clawed and clutching hands,
>Is this a friend indeed, that I should sell
> My soul to her, give her my life and youth,
>Till my feet, cloven too, take hold on hell?

Repudiation of worldly desires (represented by fruit and flowers, as in the *Dead City*) here combines with Puseyite fascination, to produce a nightmarish image of terror reminiscent of the groping monster of the *bouts rimés* sonnet, or the opposing figures of Coleridge's *Christabel*.

As she had struggled to express elsewhere, Christina had a strong sense of having a true self behind a false one, a hidden, leprous enemy within, whether possessed of Nick's malevolence or the obscure guilt that makes Maude fear to profane holy things. Here she conveys a real sense of danger – that as the 'foul' self triumphs, the speaker's feet *will* be revealed as the devil's, that she *will* wake to find she has sold her soul.

Worldliness, in religious terms, was commonly glossed as the desire for esteem, and two conflicts seem to be at work in *The World*, whose horned beast is satanically masculine, yet fair and feminine in gender, almost as if foulness were defined by male desires in a female body. The struggle between good and bad, between 'fair' self-denial and 'foul' self-realisation, is thus heavily gendered. Women were supposed to serve others. Female ambition and secular temptation, were therefore projected on to an unnatural and evil monster, with soft, wooing ways, and cloven hoofs.

Like Anna Howitt, Christina had generally received support and encouragement from men, and was far from regarding them as obstacles to female achievement. But she could hardly fail to mark the disparity between the sexes, and her next poem, *From the Antique* (the title designed to deflect attention from personal application) contained a plain protest, which fortuitously echoed Anna Howitt's frustration:

> It's a weary life, it is; she said: –
>   Doubly blank in a woman's lot:
> I wish and I wish I were a man;
>   Or better than any being, were not:

This struggle echoes throughout Christina's writing and indeed her life, regarding the correct balance between female advancement and withdrawal.

On 25 July, she returned again to the theme of disappointment and desire, adding a new section to *A Pause for Thought*, as she hovered on the verge, as it were, of launching forth:

> So will I labour, but will not rejoice:
> Will do and bear, but will not hope again . . .
>
> I said so in my heart: and so I thought . . .
>
> But first I tired, and then my care grew slack,
> Till my heart dreamed, and maybe wandered too: –

I felt the sunshine glow again, and knew
　The swallow on its track:

Full pulse of life, that I had dreamed was dead;
Full throb of youth, that I had deemed at rest . . .

I may pursue, and yet may not attain,
Athirst and panting all the days I live:
Or seem to hold, yet nerve myself to give
　What once I gave, again.

Less than a week later, encouraged by Mrs Howitt's example, Christina nerved herself to submit six poems to *Blackwood's*, the most prestigious magazine of the day, accompanied by a long and earnest letter of justification such as new authors are apt to send. 'Sir,' she began, addressing herself to William Aytoun as a fellow poet:

As an unknown and unpublished writer, I beg leave to bespeak your indulgence for laying before you the enclosed verses.

I am not unaware, Sir, that the editor of a magazine looks with dread and contempt upon the offerings of a nameless rhymester, and that the feeling is in nineteen cases out of twenty a just and salutary one. It is certainly not for me to affirm that I am the one-twentieth in question, but speaking as I am to a poet, I hope that I shall not be misunderstood as guilty of egotism or foolish vanity when I say that my love for what is good in the work of others teaches me that there is something above the despicable in mine; that poetry is with me, not a mechanism, but an impulse and a reality, and that I know my aims in writing to be pure, and directed to that which is true and right. I do not blush to confess that, with these feelings and beliefs, it would afford me some gratification to place my productions before others, and ascertain how far what I do is expressive of mere individualism, and how far it is capable of approving itself to the general sense. It would be a personal favour to me if you would look into the enclosed with an eye not inevitably to the waste paper basket, and a further obligation if, whatever the result, you would vouchsafe me a few words as to the fate of the verse. I am quite conscious that volunteer contributors have no right to expect this of an editor; I ask it simply as a courtesy. It is mortifying to have done something sincerely, offer it in a good faith; and be treated as a 'non-avenue'.

　　　　　I am, Sir, your obedient servant, Christina G. Rossetti

This was either a bold or a misconceived move, for *Blackwood's* was generally detested by the PRB for its truculent attacks on Keats,

Tennyson and Arnold and Aytoun himself, as a notable parodist of Mrs Browning's pseudo-medieval lays, was hardly likely to appreciate Christina's intense and dreamy productions. Yet the letter is an important document, showing clearly how at the age of twenty-three she regarded her poetic calling. Despite the incurable female fear of 'foolish vanity' in putting her work forward, she had distinct self-confidence. She knew she wrote well, in response to something that was both 'an impulse and a reality', not mere affectation. Perhaps she was too modest in describing herself as a 'nameless rhymester', for she had a respectable beginner's provenance. But in any case *Blackwood's* duly consigned the poems to the wastepaper basket, and there is no evidence that Aytoun respected her request for an opinion.

Like writers before and since, she was hurt by the rejection, but determined to try again, and three months later made an approach to *Fraser's*, this time using William as intermediary. 'The poems are by Miss Christina G. Rossetti at this address,' he wrote to the editor, adding that she did not necessarily expect to be paid, and would like to appear half-anonymously as 'Christina G. R.'. When *Fraser's* also turned them down, however, she was sufficiently discouraged to abandon the attempt. Her only success was with *Our Paper*, a church magazine for young women, which accepted the unexceptionably pious *Dead Bride* for its first issue. The experience was instructive: to reach print, female poets must behave in a 'feminine' manner.

It is just possible that one editor did send some comments, for much later Christina explained how she had first aimed at 'conciseness' in composition. Her youthful work was notable rather for prolixity and repetition, as Gabriel had noted; was it now returned with advice to write more crisply? Curiously enough Elizabeth Barrett had sent an aspiring poet some words that would have been useful to Christina at this point, commending 'the labour and discipline without which no artist can excel', before seeking publication:

> I do not say – *she would be a happier woman if she did not try it* ... because my words would probably be said in vain ... But I take courage ... to advise her to think more, to read more, and dream somewhat less ... to study hard our English poets, and even prose writers of the graver reasoning order, to write with compression and concentration of meaning (and more thoughts in proportion to the sentiments) ... It is a mistake to think that a true poet (whatever his gifts!) can sing like a bird; he must work on the contrary like an artist.

Up to this point, Christina had tended to sing like a bird rather than like an artist. She continued to dream rather more than was wise, but her poetic ambitions were starting to become as earnest as those of

Mrs Browning. As yet however they did not offer much in the way of fulfilment. And so in the autumn of 1854, freed from domestic and teaching duties, and with a new sense of opportunity, Christina volunteered to nurse sick and wounded soldiers in the Crimea.

12

Hero

THE WAR AGAINST Russsia declared by Britain and France earlier in the year had been largely ignored until the assault on Sebastopol in the autumn. The first major engagement, the battle of the Alma, was fought on 20 September – Christina herself gave the news to Madox Brown, when he happened to call at Albany Street on 5 October – and by 9 October first-hand despatches began appearing in the *Times*, as casualties were shipped back to base hospitals at Scutari, telling of shocking conditions and lack of medical care, with insufficient surgeons, no nurses, not even linen to make bandages. The wounded were left to die in agony and epidemic diseases were rife: of over twenty thousand losses, only one in seven died of battlefield injuries.

A tide of indignation swept the British public, with the possible exception of William Rossetti. 'Don't you find the war an ever-recurring and supreme bore?' he asked Scott in November. Most people were appalled. 'Hundreds were dying whom the Russian shot and sword had spared and whom the hospitals at Scutari were utterly unable to shelter or their inadequate staff to attend to,' noted Mary Seacole, a veteran supplier to British soldiery overseas. The response was immediate: 'In every household busy fingers were working for the poor soldiers – money flowed in golden streams – and Christian ladies, mindful of the sublime example "I was sick and ye visited me", hastened to volunteer their services.' With tears streaming down his face, the Poet Laureate saluted *The Charge of the Light Brigade*, decimated in the valley of death. Florence Nightingale, who had recently found her vocation after years of nervous prostration and was now superintendent of a sanatorium, was equally roused, at once offering to lead a team of British nurses out to Scutari.

Within a week of the first press reports, an appeal went out for qualified volunteers. Catholic and Anglican sisterhoods were applied to, and several women found themselves volunteered by their orders, in an atmosphere of urgency. Sister Sarah Terrot and four colleagues summoned from Devon, conjectured they were being sent to nurse cholera victims but at four in the morning were greeted by their superior with the words: 'Our soldiers in the East want nurses – I wish to send eight – are you willing?' The next day the Secretary of State for War gave out contracts and instructions, emphasising the duties of modesty and endurance. The nurses then met Miss Nightingale, and left Britain the next day, arriving at Scutari just as casualties began coming in from Balaclava and Inkerman. 'In the course of a few days, all who had been entrusted to us were gone, succeeded by others who equally seemed doomed to die,' wrote Sister Sarah. 'All we did seemed of no avail, except that at their last hours, they had acts and words of kindness which otherwise they had wanted.' When these reports reached London, new volunteers flocked to apply. 'Need I be ashamed to confess that I shared in the general enthusiasm?' wrote Mary Seacole, 'and longed more than ever to carry my busy fingers where the sword or bullet had been busiest, and pestilence most rife.' She applied to the War Secretary's house in Belgrave Square, waiting in the hallway watching the powdered flunkeys, until informed that all vacancies were filled; she then organised her own passage to the Crimea.

Mrs Seacole, who had references from many military figures, was rejected on grounds of class and race – 'did these ladies shrink from accepting my aid because my blood flowed beneath a somewhat duskier skin than theirs?' she inquired, rhetorically but correctly. But Miss Eliza Polidori was accepted and joined the second group of women who left London under the direction of Miss Mary Stanley in the last week of November. This was quite an adventure, for Eliza had nursed her mother over many years but never taken employment outside the home. Since her parents' deaths she had been living in lodgings near Albany Street with her servant Sarah Catchpole, and undertaking parochial tasks in the slums of Cumberland Market.

Christina's simultaneous application to join the Crimean party, prompted more by the national sense of emergency than any sense of vocation, was turned down on grounds of age and inexperience. As she had no particular desire to nurse, and her own health was perceived as precarious, the rejection was probably no great surprise or disappointment. But however fruitless, the attempt underlines her desire for a wider sphere, and her current situation as a young woman with no clear direction in life. Her literary aspirations were getting nowhere, and her ideals of Christian service sought a more heroic outlet than the parish was able to offer. Already Florence Nightingale was a national heroine, and emulation of her endeavours was one form that female ambition could legitimately follow.

Eliza Polidori proved an efficient and reliable member of the team at the Barrack Hospital. Put in charge of stores and supplies, hers was a key position in the chaotic situation. Later she played down her role, claiming to have done little actual nursing, but since one of Nightingale's chief victories was over the Army's requisition system, her work was invaluable in the struggle. After a week in post, it felt less of a 'whirlpool', she wrote home as she sorted out useful stores from inappropriate items such as baby clothes sent by well-wishers in Britain. Miss Nightingale was 'here there and everywhere, it is quite a trouble to catch her', but the doctors were now convinced of the value of female nurses and though the wounded arrived deplorably verminous, they were soon made clean and comfortable, and given a dose of arrowroot in wine. News of a change of government in London was worrying, however: would the nurses be recalled?

At Albany Street, it was a source of pride to have a relative engaged in such a newsworthy venture: at church there were many admiring inquiries and messages for Miss Polidori. Temporarily Maria and Christina took over her parish duties, receiving a share of reflected glory. From Scutari aunt Eliza (using the family names from childhood) thanked her 'vice-Visitors', Mi and Chris. In July, when morale was low, Nightingale was tempted to leave. But, she wrote to her family,

> If Miss N goes to England, says my troop, she will never come back – and all my best, Revd. Mother and her crew, Roberts, Polidori, Hawkins and several nurses, Robbins etc., have announced their intention of not staying if I go. This is not so selfish as it first appears . . . without a central authority, they would not be able to do any good here.

Writing to her family the same week, Eliza mentioned no such prospect, but listed eight colleagues who were the only ones from Miss Stanley's group to have brought no discredit to the party; the rest had all moaned or misbehaved. She had been on an excursion and seen the Sultan in a splendid caique rowed by a dozen oarsmen, on a dais trimmed with gold lace.

In September, Sebastopol was seized and the military operation began to wind down. In November, by which time aunt Eliza had probably returned, a large public meeting was held to thank Miss Nightingale and her nurses, and a concert by Jenny Lind at the time of the Peace Treaty the following March attracted a full house; possibly Christina was in the audience. Not everyone, however, saw Nightingale as a model of heroic womanhood. 'Since the siege of Troy and earlier, we have had princesses binding wounds with their hands; it's strictly the woman's part and men understand it so,' wrote Elizabeth Barrett Browning to Anna Jameson:

> Every man is on his knees before ladies carrying lint, calling them 'angelic she's' whereas, if they stir an inch as thinkers or artists from the beaten lane (involving more good to general humanity than is involved in lint) the very same men would curse the impudence of the very same women

and stop there. I can't see on what grounds you think you see here the least gain to the 'woman's question' . . .

She concluded: 'I do not consider the best use to which we can put a gifted and accomplished woman is to make her a hospital nurse. If it is, why then woe to us all who are artists!' Perhaps in retrospect Christina was glad not to have gone to Scutari: as her letter to *Blackwood*'s shows, she had a higher view of her calling as an artist.

Some time later, in indirect homage to Lind and Nightingale, Christina wrote another story of forbidden desires, frankly voicing the wish for glory. Inspired by the tales of Hans Andersen, *Hero* was a Cinderella fantasy of female transformation that articulated all the ambition and aspiration that was desired by and denied to women. It was therefore set in an imaginary realm, and began thus:

> If you consult the authentic map of Fairy-land (recently published by Messrs Moon, Shine, and Co.) you will notice that the emerald-green line which indicates its territorial limit, is washed towards the south by a bold expanse of sea, undotted by either rocks or islands. To the north-west it touches the work-a-day world, yet is effectually barricaded against intruders by an impassable chain of mountains; which, enriched throughout with mines of gems and metals, presents on Man-side a leaden sameness of hue, but on Elf-side glitters with diamonds and opals as with ten thousand fire-flies.

On the frontier with this alluring land live a hardy fisherman named Peter Grump, his only child Hero, 'beautiful, lively, tender-hearted', and Forss, her sweetheart, as sturdy a young fellow as ever cast a net in deep water.

Foolishly, Hero is discontented, believing her father and Forss do not love her as they should. One day on the seashore she finds a magic shell, with the power to fulfil dreams. Unlike Nick, Hero does not wish ill on others, but good fortune to herself, asking only to be made 'the supreme object of admiration'.

This is of course the great female fantasy – to be the fairest of all. Hero – an odd name for a heroine, we may think, though there is classical and Shakespearean precedent – then journeys to fairyland, absorbed by 'ambitious longings', where despite misgivings the Fairy Queen confirms her wish:

> In you every man shall find his taste satisfied. In you one shall recognise his ideal of loveliness, another shall bow before the impersonation of dignity. One shall be thrilled by your voice, another fascinated by your wit and inimitable grace. He who prefers colour shall dwell upon your

complexion, hair, eyes; he who worships intellect shall find in you his superior; he who is ambitious shall feel you to be a prize more august than an empire . . .

First, Hero becomes a great diamond: 'a glory by day, a lamp by night, and a world wonder at all times' – probably the Koh-i-noor, on view at the Great Exhibition and hailed as a symbol of supreme value. Fought and bargained over, as a jewel Hero eclipses even beautiful and beloved Princess Lily on her wedding day.

Her next port of call is the voice of a great *diva*, Melice Rapta, who recalls the Italian opera singers of Christina's youth:

In another moment Hero was singing in the unrivalled songstress, charming and subduing every heart. The play proceeded; its incidents, its characters developed. Melice outshone, out-sang herself; warbling like a bird, thrilling with entreaty, pouring forth her soul in passion. Her voice commanded an enthusiastic silence, her silence drew down thunders of enthusiastic applause. She acknowledged the honour with majestic courtesy; then, for the first time, trembled, changed colour: would have swept from the presence like a queen, but merely wept like a woman.

It was her hour of supreme triumph.

Of course, in the end Hero tires of adulation, though its pains are not very persuasively drawn, and when she voices the wish to return home she is instantly transported back to her family, where she marries Forss and lives happily ever after. In later years, sitting by the fireside, Hero tells the tale to her children:

And when their eyes kindled while she told of the marvellous splendour of Fairyland, she would assure them, with a convincing smile, that only home is happy: and when, with flushed cheeks and quickened breath, they followed the story of her brief pre-eminence, she would add that though admiration seems sweet at first, only love is sweet first, and last, and always.

Nevertheless, even five minutes of fame is very sweet. Of course, the magic gift is salutary: true contentment comes only with renunciation of desire – but until such time, this tale tells us, worldly acclaim is stunning. And if its heroine must renounce pre-eminence, at least she is not punished for her ambition. Nick's desires are selfish and wicked; Hero's vanity is forgiven. She has dared to dream, too, not only of being admired for her beauty – a passive feminine aspiration – but of being a great performer, an international star whose forte is display. Like Jenny Lind, she can renounce glory without losing renown. Her story is thus a fitting one for women of Christina's generation, and shares something of the naive delight that bubbles through Anna Howitt's account of the projected Art-sisters, devoting themselves to idealism and achievement.

Now that the painful years of her father's decline were over, Christina could legitimately look to her own interests and needs. New friendships and possibilities were opening, and the pious dilemmas that exercised poor Maude had given way to a more judicious optimism. Visions of 'marvellous splendour' were no longer exclusively those of heavenly glory. To find pleasure in life and the exercise of one's gifts did not mean being in thrall to the world.

Mamma, who preached contentment with whatever God ordained, also encouraged excellence. She had fed her daughters on stories of heroic women, and encouraged their achievements – for while the Church might teach submission, there was also the parable of the talents, and the Victorian doctrine of self-realisation. 'Let me say there are two kinds of ambition; one wholly blameable, the other laudable,' Carlyle had written in his essays on *Heroes*. The 'selfish wish to shine over others' was altogether miserable, but the earnest cultivation of one's abilities was a different matter, for 'the meaning of life here on earth might be defined in consisting in this: to unfold your *self*, to work that thing you have the faculty for'. This was 'a necessity for the human being, the first law of our existence ... proper, fit, inevitable; nay, it is a duty and even the summary of duties for a man'. Of course, such self-realisation was not quite the summary of duties for a woman, but in the right spirit it was not forbidden.

In Gloucester, aunt Henrietta Polydore solved the contradiction between self-sacrificial feminine ideals and self-realising individual needs by simply walking out on her husband – what an unhappy marriage in every respect, commented aunt Eliza. The Rossettis were neither surprised nor shocked, for they had long regarded uncle Henry as a nervous old fusspot, whereas his wife was an energetic and resourceful woman, who found her husband's habits and temper quite incompatible with her own. They were surprised and dismayed some little while later, however, when she left for America with her daughter, to join the Mormons at Salt Lake City.

Various travellers returned from the East and the Antipodes – Woolner and William Howitt from Australia, and Holman Hunt's companion Tom Seddon from Egypt and Palestine. In January 1855 there was a large party at the Seddons' where Brown noted that Mary Howitt was 'unaffected and dresses nicely, two rare qualities in a Poetess', and that Christina was unusually animated, wearing a Syrian costume brought back by Seddon, who himself spent the evening in 'full Arabicals'. A

few weeks later, there was an exhibition of his Middle Eastern landscapes, and though Christina may not have been to see it – she was
intermittently unwell this winter – the Middle East featured largely in
a vivid dream-image that appeared as it were unbidden, on 6 March
in a long poem simply entitled *My Dream*:

Hear now a curious dream I dreamed last night,
Each word whereof is weighed and sifted truth.

   I stood beside Euphrates while it swelled
Like overflowing Jordan in its youth:
It waxed and coloured sensibly to sight;
Till out of myriad pregnant waves there welled
Young crocodiles, a gaunt blunt-featured crew,
Fresh-hatched perhaps and daubed with birthday dew,
The rest if I should tell, I fear my friend
My closest friend would deem the facts untrue;
And therefore it were wisely left untold;
Yet if you will, why hear it to the end.

   Each crocodile was girt with massive gold
And polished stones that with their wearers grew:
But one there was that waxed beyond the rest,
Wore kinglier girdle and a kingly crown,
Whilst crowns and orbs and sceptres starred his breast.
All gleamed compact and green with scale on scale,
But special burnishment adorned his mail
And special terror weighed upon his frown;
His punier brethren quaked before his tail,
Broad as a rafter, potent as a flail.
So he grew lord and master of his kin:
But who shall tell the tale of all their woes?
An execrable appetite arose,
He battened on them, crunched and sucked them in,
He knew no law, he feared no binding law,
But ground them with inexorable jaw.
The luscious fat distilled upon his chin,
Exuded from his nostrils and his eyes,
While still like hungry death he fed his maw;
Till every minor crocodile being dead
And buried too, himself gorged to the full,
He slept with breath oppressed and unstrung claw.

   Oh marvel passing strange which next I saw:
In sleep he dwindled to the common size,

And all the empire faded from his coat.
Then from far off a winged vessel came,
Swift as a swallow, subtle as a flame:
I know not what it bore of freight or host,
But white it was as an avenging ghost.
It levelled strong Euphrates in its course;
Supreme yet weightless as an idle mote
It seemed to tame the waters without force
Till not a murmur swelled or billow beat:
Lo, as the purple shadow swept the sands,
The prudent crocodile rose on his feet
And shed appropriate tears and wrung his hands.

What can it mean? you ask. I answer not
For meaning, but myself must echo, What?
And tell it as I saw it on the spot.

What indeed is the meaning of this strange and partly comic poem, that insists each word is 'weighed and sifted truth'? Much later Christina pencilled 'not a real dream' beside the text, as if feeling the need for absolute honesty. But the distinction is not crucial, for such Coleridgean poems are dreams of the imagination rather than sleep. If not 'real', this dream-poem is nevertheless as mysterious as any true dream. Ten days after completing it, she sketched three little illustrations in her naive manner – showing the dreamer asleep under a tree from which the monarch crocodile dangles; the gorged creature sleeping 'with unstrung claw'; and rearing up in front of the winged vessel, wringing his hands – all of which suggest that whether a sleeping or waking dream it was a vivid image in her mind.

It was an instant hit with the family, and became one of her own favourites. Jokingly, Gabriel asked Holman Hunt to bring back a crocodile for Christina from Cairo, and over the years printed images of crocodiles large and small were seized on with delight. Such domestication is partly what the poem is about – the taming of a monster, who not only lords over his fellows but crunches them like a cannibal. When the winged boat arrives to avenge the devoured kin, the prudent reptile weeps, in mock contrition, for his power has been curbed.

As with real dreams, he seems to derive from a variety of sources, both incidental and profound. Tom Seddon's pictures of Egypt and Palestine clearly provided the setting – though, as Hunt pointed out, crocodiles were only to be found further south, and certainly not in the Jordan or Euphrates. Historically, they were legendary creatures that shed tears to allure the victim they would then consume, and in

Bacon's essay on self-love, for example, crocodiles illustrate the dark side of human nature – an apt image for Christina, with her sense of a divided self. During the nineteenth century, as the lands of the Nile were explored, the crocodile acquired a monstrous metaphorical presence as a fearful foreign beast who, like the 'Bengal tiger', figured the ineradicable savagery of the Orient. As such he lodged in the collective consciousness as an image of terror, appearing in comic guise at the end of the century inexorably pursuing Captain Hook in *Peter Pan*. Internalised, as with the nursery bogeyman, he became the evil and frightening 'other', onto whom all hatred could be displaced. In the early 1850s he appeared vividly in Thomas Beddoes's *Crocodile*, whose iambic rhythms are those of Christina's dream, and more grotesquely in *Death's Jest-Book*, a Rossetti favourite. Most notoriously, in *Confessions of a Opium-Eater* crocodiles were hideous beasts swarming through de Quincey's drugged 'oriental dreams', self-created creatures of loathing by which he was pursued. 'Sometimes I escaped, and found myself in Chinese houses,' he wrote. 'All the feet of the tables, sofas, etc soon became instinct with life: the abominable head of the crocodile, and his leering eyes, looked out at me, multiplied into ten thousand repetitions; and I stood loathing and fascinated.' It was surely from such sources that Christina, whether she knew it or not, derived her cannibal crocodile, half human, half monster.

In her imagination he became strikingly patriarchal, with kingly sceptre and orbs. He swells phallicly until his incestuous urge is satisfied, and then 'dwindles to the common size' – lines that could only have been written without a blush in a pre-Freudian age. He is also a tyrant and a transgressor, who flouts the law in devouring his own kind. In part this imperious figure seems to represent the dominance of all males, but he also brings to mind the role played by Papa in his last years, weeping as he exacted the sacrifice of other family members. The luscious fat on his chin is like the dribbling of an invalid, while the winged vessel has a distinctly maternal character, restoring order and silently rebuking the beast. At the same time, the crocodile is also the monstrous 'bad self' whose infantile appetite threatens to overwhelm the dreamer (whose imagination indeed creates the image). Like the horned and clutching figure of *The World*, the crunching creature personifies that which the dreamer fears and loves within herself.

He appeared again this year in another guise, in a real dream, which left Christina with the powerful feeling it was her duty to record it visually, as if she were a painter. Instead she described it in words:

Night but clear with grey light. Part of a church in the background with the cloud side towards the spectator. In the churchyard many good sheep with good innocent expressions: one especially heavenly. Amid them with a full face a Satan-like goat lying with a kingly look and horns. Three white longish-haired dogs in front, confused with the sheep though somewhat smaller than they; one with a flattering face, a second with a head almost entirely turned away, but what one sees of the face, sensual and abominable.

Again, the image derives partly from the Middle East, for the goat is clearly a relative of the biblical scapegoat described in Leviticus, which Holman Hunt was currently planning to paint, after a visit to the Dead Sea. He had recently sent back an account of this project, which would have been of particular interest to Christina on account of its scriptural subject. Hunt's conception of the accursed animal 'bearing all the sins of the children of Israel' was as a type of Christ, however, whereas Christina's dream was dualist: the Satanic king of darkness surrounded by innocent, heavenly souls – the biblical division of sheep and goats. There are however, some intermediate animals, the white dogs that look like sheep but are sensual and corrupt, with 'flattering' and half-glimpsed abominable faces. Again, the recurrent image of a divided self, outer and inner, upper and lower, fair and foul.

Whether in dreams or poems, such images have many layers of potential meaning. In Christina's case they often seem to rise unbidden, as if from an unrecognised reservoir of feeling, below the level of memory. Frequently, they were associated with periods when she was ill; rather like the sudden onset of neuralgia, it is as if they were similarly triggered by some unknown agency.

Other poems this season continued to smack of what Gabriel had called 'the old shop' – familiar images of lost love, lamentation, unassuaged pain, icy sterility. The cold weather chimed with her inward mood, though the motifs are too recurrent in Christina's work to have local application: at some deep level she felt herself everlastingly frozen and barren. And soon after writing the crocodile poem she fell into a prolonged bout of illness and despondency, which gave rise to two poems of suicidal depression amidst the renewal of spring, one of which makes the specific link between mental and physical health with a note saying it was 'written in sickness'.

This coincided with the first anniversary of her father's death and may therefore have some oblique connection to suppressed grief or guilt. William asserted that Christina's life and character could not be understood without recognising the fact that she was almost constantly invalid and often very ill, but in retrospect many of her bouts of illness seem to have been accompanied if not caused by depression, rendering her sufficiently listless for doctors to be called and sickness diagnosed. Certainly, she believed her health to be precarious, and this was a crucial factor in her self-image. Yet often there were few distinct symptoms, and a general sense that no one really knew what caused her maladies. Though not above using it on occasion, Christina did not actively cultivate illness. But it occupied an ambiguous place in her life, freeing her from some unwelcome duties. While affording space in which to write, it restricted her activities and also caused guilt. Like many young women, she struggled with the contradictions.

13

Wrestlings in the Soul

GABRIEL WAS IN expansive mood, for he had acquired Ruskin as his patron, and also successfully introduced Lizzie, to whom Ruskin had promptly offered an allowance of £150 a year. 'This is no joke but fact,' Gabriel told William, 'I shall bring her on Saturday to tea.' At last, Lizzie was being introduced to their mother.

Unfortunately, the visit to Albany Street did not go well. Miss Siddal (who had dropped the last 'l' from her name) was shy and stiff, with a silence that seemed frosty rather than dovelike. Christina might have recognised a fellow-sufferer, or Maria deployed her warmth to make the visitor feel at home; perhaps they did, but Lizzie did not thaw. No doubt, in her eyes, both mother and sisters were as formidable as Christina had feared the Collinsons would be, and she retreated behind a foolishly disdainful mask when a more gushing manner would have gained their sympathy. So no friendship flourished, though Mamma graciously offered to take Lizzie to see Dr Hare – an invitation Lizzie avoided by pleading toothache. She went instead to Oxford, at Ruskin's insistence, where she was introduced to Miss Pusey, who 'seems to have been the one she liked best', as Gabriel informed his family in a remark calculated to impress. After this, on Ruskin's money, he and Lizzie proceeded to Clevedon, for a seaside holiday.

Some weeks later, Madox Brown noted in his diary that a certain coldness had developed between Gabriel and Christina, 'because she and Guggums do not agree'. As the two women can seldom have met, the chill probably stemmed from Christina's inability to share her brother's high estimate of Miss Siddal's looks and talent. In this she was not alone. Though taken with the romance of Gabriel's relationship, the Howitts could never discern the artistic genius he ascribed to Lizzie's naive drawings. Perhaps too Christina felt some dismay towards a family connection with shopkeepers, just as despite herself she had looked down on the Collinsons as provincial booksellers. Not that Gabriel spoke of marriage – but his intimacy with Lizzie precluded other possibilities, such as were suggested by the distinct partiality shown towards him by both Anna Howitt and Bessie Parkes.

As prospective sister-in-law Christina much preferred Henrietta Rintoul, William's intended, who although rather dull was amiable and interested in literature. She had also taken up photography and this year made several portrait studies of Christina, one done on a little balcony up on the roof at Albany Street, which the sitter described as 'perhaps the most satisfactory ever done of me', but sadly does not survive. Also taken this year were some studio portraits of their mother with both daughters, Maria looking very 'moony' with one hand on her sister's shoulder, and Christina crouched by Mamma's knee, with a fixed and blank expression like a scared rabbit. The group possesses a certain austere charm, but the effect on Lizzie can easily be imagined.

At the Royal Academy this year, Millais was the talk of the town with his *Rescue*, in which a heroic firefighter saves two children from the flames. It was, in Ruskin's generous words, 'the only *great* picture exhibited this year', and Millais was fulfilling all his early promise; indeed 'Titian could hardly head him now'. There was however a rival sensation, in *A Florentine Procession*, depicting Giotto and Cimabue, 'by a new man, living abroad, named Leighton – a huge thing, which the Queen has bought, and everyone talks of', as Gabriel reported, and which seemed designed to outdo the Pre-Raphaelites at their own game. They were indeed rather overshadowed, not least because Holman Hunt was still in the Holy Land, and Gabriel, again, did not exhibit. But there was a surprise. 'What do you think?' Gabriel told Allingham

> Collinson is back in London and has two pictures in the RA. The Jesuits have found him fittest for painting and restored him to an eager world.

The tone was ironic, for the Pre-Raphaelite world was certainly not eager to renew Collinson's acquaintance. And his unexpected reappearance – he had left Stonyhurst at the end of 1854 – was awkward for Christina, since there was always the possibility of an unexpected social encounter. As it turned out, James avoided his former friends, seeking instead to restart his career on commercial lines, with saleable genre subjects.

Shortly after the opening of the exhibition, Christina and her mother went to Hastings, for their first holiday since Papa's death. On their return, they learnt that Johnny Millais had quietly married Effie Ruskin, and that Maria's warm heart had been stirred by Effie's former husband. Since the annulment of his marriage on grounds of impotence the year before, Ruskin had maintained a dignified magnanimity towards Millais – as in his comparison of the living artist to the old master – tending privately to pity him for having been ensnared. Though not without a shaft of malice in feeling that if there was anything like visible retribution in this life, there were 'assuredly dark hours in the distance' for Effie, he on the whole felt a sense of deliverance from a tiresome, frivolous and ungrateful wife. Introduced by Gabriel, he was politely attentive to Maria, in such a way as to engage her affections. Gabriel of course had a tendency to matchmake and may have mistakenly thought to promote his intelligent sister's friendship with a man who, in the eyes of the world, needed a new and worthy wife. Maria was approaching thirty, and in the eyes of the same world was equally in need of a husband, for whom she would have proved a loyal and supportive spouse. Moreover, her homeliness, devotional habits and cheerful modesty would have pleased old Mrs Ruskin.

But it was not to be. Ruskin was not seeking a new helpmate. Writing discreetly of her sister's feelings in *Time Flies*, Christina described how 'one of the most genuine Christians I ever knew once took lightly the dying out of a brief acquaintance which had engaged her warm heart, on the ground that such mere tastes and glimpses of congenial intercourse on earth wait for their development in heaven'. A note pencilled in the margin of aunt Eliza's copy reads: 'Maria with Ruskin'.

Knowing something of disappointment herself, Christina was perhaps more hurt on her sister's behalf. Maria evidently realised her error quickly, yet her remark about future fulfilment is curious: did she think all aborted courtships were to be resumed in the hereafter? The observations on either side of this entry in *Time Flies* commend cheerful acceptance of God's will, and it was Maria's ability to greet reverses with a rueful smile that Christina most admired. For Maria did not mope, and in late summer went to visit the Scotts, spreading characteristic cheerfulness. 'Your name is often heard in our house,' reported William to Scotus 'and none the less since the return of Maria, who never tires of your virtues and fascinations and Mrs Scott's kindness, and looks upon everything connected with dingy Newcastle in rose-coloured light.' If Maria could not have what she liked, she made the best of what she had.

Christina had no such resilience or liveliness. Invited to spend a few days with the Madox Browns, she sat with her cross stitch embroidery – the Victorian gentlewoman's constant occupation – and spoke sparingly, as her host commented. This was hardly surprising, for she had little to say to Emma Brown, who was rather overwhelmed with caring for five-year-old Cathy and new-born Oliver, and in any case William was a fellow guest, and no doubt male conversation predominated.

A month later, she answered a plea from Lady Frances Lindsay, one of aunt Charlotte's connections, who needed a temporary governess for her four young children. Christina therefore spent two months at Haigh Hall in Lancashire, attributing the damp and misty climate to the 'coaliness' of the district, though by the same token fires were strong and plentiful. There were a number of pictures in the house, she told William, and her duties were not onerous – they included an anniversary celebration of the battle of Inkerman, organised by two of her charges – but she was not tempted to seek other such work. As she told her brother,

> I hope you are glad to know that I am very comfortable in my exile; but at any rate I know I am rejoiced to feel that my health does really unfit me for miscellaneous governessing *en permanence*. For instance yesterday I indulged in breakfast in bed, having been very unwell the day previous: now I am very tolerable again, but do not feel particularly to be depended upon.

Amongst other things, she was reading a book about Russia, which contained some 'particularly bad plates' signed F. Harrison; could this be the work of the fair Fanny, daughter of Mrs Harrison? Christina could do better herself. However, the book had one wonderful piece of information: 'To wit, the Chinese have three words signifying death; *sze* (?) for the vulgar, *pang* for the emperor, but for princes and such like *hung!!!* I am so pleased.'

This leisurely letter suggests she had a good deal of time on her hands, even when not breakfasting in bed, and the evident satisfaction she felt in being unfitted for governessing is a reminder of Christina's propensity to idleness. This partly explains her lack of occupation in the mid-1850s after her escape from the schoolroom, which has led biographers to describe her as a virtual invalid and recluse. As William wrote, despite a strong sense of duty, she was naturally indolent, 'often better pleased to be doing nothing than anything'. Outward inactivity, however, concealed an intense inner life which, without being constantly occupied with composition, nevertheless did not admit serious competition; of this her work is the evidence. Like many writers, Christina preferred to do 'nothing' rather than anything that made other demands on the mind. And it was perhaps indolence of this kind that prompted the return of her poetic impulse, after six months' abeyance, with a clutch of poems in December and January, including one in which she imagined Eve sorrowing for the loss of Eden, while simultaneously the trees of paradise weep for loss of Eve. It was a subject to which she would return, in both poetry and prose, pondering the problem of Eve's transgression and punishment, and suggests that in her own 'exile' from home, Christina had been reading Elizabeth Barrett Browning's *A Drama of Exile*, in which among other things the trees of Eden bid farewell to Adam and Eve.

Expulsion was the theme of her boldly-titled first poem of 1856, *What Happened to Me* completed on 21 January, expressing her own sense of exclusion from joy:

> The door was shut, I looked between
>   Its iron bars; and saw it lie,
>   My garden, mine, beneath the sky,
> Pied all with flowers bedewed and green:
>
> From bough to bough the song-birds crossed,
>   From flower to flower the moths and bees;
>   With all its nests and stately trees
> It had been mine, and it was lost.
>
> A shadowless spirit kept the gate,
>   Blank and unchanging like the grave.
> I peering through said: "Let me have
> Some buds to cheer my outcast state."
>
> He answered not. "Or give me, then,
>   But one small twig from shrub or tree;
>   And bid my home remember me
> Until I come to it again."
>
> The spirit was silent; but he took
>   Mortar and stone to build a wall;
>   He left no loophole great or small
> Through which my straining eyes might look:
>
> So now I sit here quite alone
>   Blinded with tears; nor grieve for that,
>   For nought is left worth looking at
> Since my delightful land is gone.
>
> A violet bed is budding near,
>   Wherein a lark has made her nest:
>   And good they are, but not the best;
> And dear they are, but not so dear.

This is in the metre of *In Memoriam*, and like everyone else she had also been reading Tennyson's new poem, *Maud*, the literary event of 1855, with its dramatic and tender story of love, violence, joy and pain. It confirmed Tennyson's pre-eminence and was greeted with great 'flurry and skurry' in the Rossettis' circles, as elsewhere. All her adult life Christina wrote in the shadow of the Laureate, and though as yet the influence of *Maud's* innovative variety, with a different verse form for each of its 28 sections, was not visible in her verse, its impact on the younger generation can hardly be overestimated.

Not long before this, her brothers had been invited to hear Tennyson read *Maud* at the Brownings' house, after which Browning read from his own forthcoming collection *Men and Women*. Gabriel, who had an advance copy, sang its praises loudly, saying it was an 'elixir of life'. So *Men and Women* was soon read at Albany Street too, and indeed Christina's first poem *Cobwebs* seems to have been inspired by the desolate landscape of *Childe Roland*.

Christina admired both Brownings, later identifying *Cleon* and *Karshish* as her own favourites among Robert's work, but more warmly describing Elizabeth as 'that great poetess and (I believe) loveable woman, whom I was never, however, so fortunate as to meet', betraying regret at the lost opportunity. For her brothers gave a favourable account of their hostess, stressing her lack of conceit. 'What a delightfully unliterary person Mrs B. is,' Gabriel told Allingham, describing how she had left Tennyson with her husband, William and himself 'to discuss the universe, and gave all her attention to some certainly not very exciting ladies in the next room'. Here was a lesson for Christina: lady poets, however gifted, should put their duties to dull guests above the pleasures of discussing the universe with the Poet Laureate. Sadly, unlike their brothers, the Misses Rossetti were not invited to meet Tennyson and Browning – or they might have enjoyed withdrawing with Mrs B. and the other ladies, to talk about the universe too.

Early in 1856 ten-year-old Lucy Brown joined 'the domestic circle' at Albany Street on a daily basis, so that she might be educated by Maria and share in their household activities. She was bright and attentive, and came to be regarded with much affection, especially when, later, uncle Henry obtained his daughter's return from America and brought her on regular visits to London, when Lucy proved an invaluable companion. Around this same time William became formally engaged to Henrietta Rintoul. No wedding date was set, however: while as yet needed at home, Henrietta felt unable to contemplate marriage, and William, now twenty-six, was still on a junior salary, at a time when it was deemed prudent for men to delay marriage until firmly established in their career.

Gabriel by contrast was becoming increasingly wayward. Lizzie had spent the winter in the south of France, on Ruskin's instructions and money, chaperoned by one of Mamma's cousins named Mrs Kincaid, of whom nothing more is known. In her absence, Gabriel's affections began to wander, though few realised anything was amiss. In the spring Holman Hunt returned from the Holy Land, bearing his tent and many tales of adventure in the desert, together with several canvases, including the *The Scapegoat*. Ruskin said it was fit only for an inn sign, but Woolner thought it stupendous. Tom Seddon was now married and living in Highgate, and around this time Christina became better acquainted with his sister Emily, herself an aspiring artist. She also met Ellen Heaton, who lived in Leeds, a wealthy and warm-hearted woman, whom Ruskin introduced to Gabriel as a prospective patron and who became a better friend of his sisters, being ecclesiastical as well as artistic in her interests. Miss Heaton also offered another link to the Brownings, with whom she kept up an avid friendship, being something of a lion-hunter too. Indeed, Scott sourly complained after meeting her in Newcastle that while speaking to him her eyes sought more eminent figures over his shoulder, as she darted about the gathering in pursuit of celebrities.

Some little while later, Christina wrote a sparkling new story called *The Lost Titian*, inspired by memories of the PRB, Ruskin's comparison of Millais to the great Venetian, and the old problem of ambition and envy. It drew on her Italian inheritance too, with a light and witty display of erudition, and was prompted by the fact that William had been asked to recruit writers for *The Crayon*, an American magazine devoted to the fine arts; to this Anna Howitt had already sent two items, on the theme of 'Unpainted Pictures'. In a different sense, this was the subject of Christina's story.

Set in the High Renaissance, *The Lost Titian* is about the great painter and his two companions, 'Gianni the successful and Giannuccione the universal disappointment' – a trio with a passing resemblance to the three leaders of the PRB. Like Millais, Titian is virtually unrivalled; Gianni ranks second, like Holman Hunt, stoutly asserting Titian's supremacy; and Giannuccione, 'who had promised everything and fulfilled nothing', has about him a certain touch of Gabriel Rossetti:

> At the appearance of his first picture ... Venice rang with his praises, and Titian forboded a rival: but when, year after year, his works appeared still lazily imperfect, though always all but perfect, Venice subsided into apathetic silence ...

It was over six years since the *Girlhood of Mary Virgin* and five since *Ecce Ancilla*. Asked when he was going to exhibit again, Gabriel tended to say he wished to show nothing less than perfect, but how would that day come? The comparison, however, should not be taken further: in other respects Christina's characters do not resemble the men she knew.

Titian has completed a new masterpiece, in which

> The orange drapery was perfect in its fruit-like intensity of hue; each vine-leaf was curved, each tendril twisted, as if fanned by the soft south wind; the sunshine brooded drowsily upon every dell and swelling upland: but a tenfold drowsiness slept in the cedar shadows. Look a moment, and those cymbals must clash, that panther bound forward; draw nearer, and songs of those ripe, winy lips must become audible. The achievement of his life glowed upon the easel, and Titian was satisfied.

The description has Pre-Raphaelite precision, but the image was derived from Titian's own canvas of *Bacchus and Ariadne*, in the National Gallery, which contains raised cymbals and a panther, or at least a leopard. The subject of the fictional painting is deliberately obscured, however:

> some spoke of it as an undoubted *Vintage of Red Grapes*, others maintained it to be a *Dance of Wood Nymphs*; while an old gossip whispered that, whatever else the painting might contain, she knew whose sunset-coloured tresses and white brow would figure in the foreground . . .

The masterpiece is centred on a beautiful female form, but was surely intended as an allegory of the senses, carefully constructed to represent in writing the allure of sight, sound, touch, taste and smell. For in Titian's brushwork is combined 'the softness of a dove's breast with the intensity of an October sunset', to create 'a picture of which the light almost warmed, and the fruit actually bloomed and tempted'. Once more, ripe fruits epitomise luxurious desire, in an Italian setting. They are also emblems of art's imitative power, looking real enough to eat.

The three painters spend a festive evening in the studio, with music, laughter, wine. They are merry, yet obscurely troubled. Gianni takes up a lute, and we hear

> cries of passion, desolate sobs, a wail as of one abandoned, plaintive, most tender tones as of the *solitario passero*. The charm worked: vague uneasiness was melting into delicious melancholy . . .

The senses are, of course, snares, like the daylight loveliness of *The World*, and Gianni's music leads on to the sound of dice – 'more fascinating, more ominous, than a snake's rattle'. Begun in conviviality, the game grows serious: Gianni stakes his whole self – his artistic soul – against

Titian's masterpiece, and wins. The jesting falls away, as Gianni revels in his gain – or rather in his rival's loss – with destructive *schaden-freude*.

And worse follows, for Gianni is also guilty of theft. His studio contains many trophies, including Giannuccione's early, admired canvas – 'how obtained, who knows?' – pictures by Giorgione and Tintoretto, and a golden goblet by Benevenuto Cellini. His manners, however, are so good that his delinquencies are overlooked; some call him a defaulter but all agree he is a thorough gentleman. Presciently, he seems to foreshadow the Whistler or Wilde of a later decade:

> his sketches sold with unprecedented readiness, his epigrams charmed the noblest dinner-givers, his verses and piquant little airs won him admission into the most exclusive circles . . . If he now committed follies, they were committed in the best society; if he sinned, it was at any rate in a patrician *casa*; and, though his morals might not yet be flawless, his taste was unimpeachable.

To prevent repossession of the canvas and keep his rival from the pinnacle of fame, Gianni overpaints the image with 'a flaming, clawed, preposterous dragon', symbolic of his own malice. Nevertheless his career does not prosper. Soon his creditors are upon him, and all assets must go, even Titian's masterpiece, 'that prize for which he had played away his soul, by which, it may be, he had hoped to acquire a worldwide fame, when its mighty author should be silenced for ever . . .'

Rather than reveal it, Gianni lets the dragon go for an inn-sign, and with his own death, the work vanishes for ever. Titian goes on to fresh greatness, but never regains the perfection achieved in the lost canvas, and the story ends with an elegant whimsy:

> Reader, should you chance to discern over wayside inn or metropolitan hotel a dragon pendent, or should you find such an effigy amid the lumber of a broker's shop, whether it be red, green or piebald, demand it importunately, pay for it liberally, and in the privacy of home scrub it. It *may* be that from behind the dragon will emerge a fair one, fairer than Andromeda, and that to you will appertain the honour of yet further exalting Titian's greatness in the eyes of a world.

Only the unusualness of that final phrase, 'a world', indicates the author's moral position – that worldly ambition is not the highest aim in life.

Polished wit and fastidious language almost conceal the satirical intention of this apparent *jeu d'esprit*, with its learned historical allusions and apposite Italian phrases. The cadences are stylish, with rare flourishes that simultaneously undercut the meaning, so that elegant writing is indistinguishable from ironic intent. Above all the story's success lies in its subtlety: nowhere else did Christina camouflage a parable with such devastating delicacy.

Behind or beyond the wit, of course, lay an inwardly-directed message against the temptations not primarily of the senses but of ambition and envy. As in *Nick*, this also allowed the expression of such desires, but with greater complexity, for while Titian's high ideals carry him above such snares, other artists must beware, lest their abilities be perverted by envy or wasted by laziness. Far from eschewing ambition, this tale defines the glory of true excellence, and the legitimate pursuit of fame. As the great Reynolds had declared in his influential *Discourses*, studied by every aspiring artist: 'Without the love of fame you can never do anything excellent' and Gabriel later defined ambition as 'the feeling of pure rage and self-hatred when anyone else does better than you ... This in an ambitious mind leads not to envy in the least, but to self-scrutiny ... and that to something, if anything can'. In modified form this was Christina's experience too. In *Hero* she had acknowledged and exorcised the desire for admiration. Here, with great felicity, she tamed the preposterous dragon of envy. Excellence should be its own reward.

In due course *The Lost Titian* was despatched to *The Crayon* in New York. His sister had talent, William told the editor, and would be gratified if it were liked. She was: the story was accepted and published in July, though *The Crayon's* circulation was too small for it to make much impact. It seems to have answered a need, for despite the accomplishment of the tale, Christina did not pursue this vein of prose fiction in which she now showed such skill. Perhaps the paragraphs were a little mannered and over-full of adjectives, but they were also assured and compelling. Moreover, the style intriguingly anticipates the sensuous quality of her brother's paintings in his 'Venetian' phase, which is often contrasted with the ascetic purity of her own characteristic style. As here, she was often in the vanguard, developing an aesthetic mode ahead of the age.

When Lizzie returned from France in May she discovered that Gabriel had been rhapsodising over actress Ruth Herbert and escorting Hunt's model Annie Miller to places of amusement. Though not privy to all details, the family must have been aware of the ensuing sequence of quarrels and reconciliations recorded in Brown's diary. On one occasion, to show he was sorry, Gabriel bought Lizzie a fine evening cloak, to display at the theatre. 'They had better marry,' was Brown's eloquent comment. No such ideas were suggested at home.

When Christina called on Emma one day, Brown recorded only that they talked of Carlyle, whom she was reading with Mamma. But on 12 July she completed a long and hectic poem in forty-five urgent triplets, based in part on one of Maturin's novels but also reflecting her perception of what was happening to Gabriel, as the male speaker struggles between duty and dalliance:

> I wish we once were wedded – then I must be true;
> You should hold my will in yours to do or to undo:
> But now I hate myself Eva when I look at you.
>
> You have seen her hazel eyes, her warm dark skin,
> Dark hair – but oh those hazel eyes a devil is dancing in: –
> You my saint lead up to heaven, she lures down to sin.

Although not close to Lizzie, Christina seemed able to enter imaginatively into her experience, as she watched her brother renege on his promises.

   On 30 September, she finished an even longer work, of nearly a hundred forceful quatrains – the most substantial poem she had yet produced – in which she struggled to resolve the female conflict between self-denial and self-realisation in a dramatised debate, largely free of dreamings. It owed much to Browning's example, but came, surely from her own, unsatisfactory experience as a young woman, trying to reconcile the desire for achievement with the feminine ideal as promoted by Church and society. Called *A Fight over the Body of Homer*, this opened with an assertion that the struggle was over:

> Amen: the sting of fear is past,
>   Cast out and no more burdensome;
> There can be no such pang as this
>   In all the years to come.
>
> No more such wrestlings in my soul,
>   No more such heart-break out of sight,
> From dawning of my long-drawn day
>   Until it draws to night.

In fact, the text enacts a fight rather than a resolution, for this conclusion, repeated at the end, is at odds with much of the argument, which is cast as a dialogue between two sisters regarding contemporary gender positions. How could women fulfil their ambition and aspirations to excellence? How could they relate to the world of masculine endeavour and achievement?

The elder sister complains that women are like sequestered flowers, excluded from life's possibilities. She pleads for a greater destiny:

> Oh what is life, that we should live?
>   Or what is death, that we must die?
> A bursting bubble is our life:
>   I also, what am I?

– an expression of *weltschmerz* which suggests that among the works of Carlyle's that Christina had been reading this summer was *Heroes and Hero-Worship*, in which is set out the fundamental problem of being: 'What am I? What *is* this unfathomable thing I live in, which men name Universe? What is Life; what is Death? What am I to believe? What am I to do?'

The elder sister has been reading Homer, whose heroes have stirred her sluggish pulse. Why must women always come second, she protests, confessing to impotent envy of both male strength and past valour:

> I cannot melt the sons of men,
>   I cannot fire and tempest-toss: –
> Besides, those days were golden days,
>   Whilst these are days of dross.
>   . . .
> Then men were men of might and right,
>   Sheer might, at least, and weighty swords;
> Then men in open blood and fire
>   Bore witness to their words

Had Christina also been reading Carlyle's *Past and Present*, with its vigorous indictment of the nineteenth century, as well as *Heroes* with its praise of savage valour, might as right and the 'everlasting duty' whereby 'a man shall and must be valiant'?

On her warriors she also bestowed the Rossetti family motto *frangas non flectas* – who broke but would not bend – linking herself with the heroes of antiquity as well as invoking Maria's juvenile passion for the *Iliad*. Indeed, like Maria the speaker lauds Achilles, defending his passion for Briseis on the grounds that he valued a slave-girl more than contemporary men did their wives. Gently, this outburst is checked by the other sister, in whose manner is a memory of Mamma's response to young Maria's ardour.

For this is the real problem, with its echo of Barbara Smith's essay on the legal status of women. The stirring stanzas contain not just a Carlylean complaint against the modern world, but a female protest against exclusion from that modern, male, military world. 'Oh better then be slave or wife Than fritter now blank life away,' continues the elder sister, protesting against her own aimless life, as she and her sister stitch endless holes in a 'waste of white' – an apt image of the vast amount of time-filling and often superfluous needlework Victorian women spent their days completing, and against which feminists complained, urging women to more worthwhile occupations.

Just as Maria had relinquished her ambitions in favour of religious submission, so this argument is answered by the gentler sister, who offers the alternative solution of service as true heroism. 'Shall not the Sevenfold Sacred Fire suffice to purge our dross?' she asks. 'Who dooms me I shall only be the second, not the first?' Christ is the true role model.

The rebuke is welcomed, heralding the elder sister's submission and self-judgement:

> She never guessed her words reproved
>   A silent envy nursed within –
> A selfish, souring discontent,
>   Pride-born, the devil's sin

To prove the moral, the younger sister is rewarded with marriage and motherhood, while the narrator remains single, duly punished for her erstwhile ambition:

> While I? I sat alone and watched;
>   My lot in life, to live alone
> In mine own world of interests
>   Much felt but little shown.
>
> Not to be first: how hard to learn
>   That lifelong lesson of the past;
> Line graven on line and stroke on stroke;
>   But, thank God, learnt at last.

These verses are often quoted as the *leit-motiv* of Christina's life – learning the lesson of female self-abnegation and religious submission. Yet they also convey a virtually contrary sense, denying what is ostensibly said. These are the approved pieties, but they only repress discontent, and indeed the poem concludes almost blasphemously that the burdensome lessons of life will be reversed in heaven, when 'all deep secrets shall be shown, And many last be first' – deservedly so, as the narrator evidently believes.

Under pressure from Gabriel, Christina later revised this text, altering its emphasis by renaming it *The Lowest Room* (thereby asserting what it does not quite endorse), and omitting the opening stanzas about wrestlings in the soul. But cancelling the lines did not end the argument. The wrestling continued within, between self-realising 'masculine' ambition, and self-denying 'feminine' submission, with Christ as the unsurpassable example. If the latter wins the argument, the former has the best lines; the poem enacts its own conflict. It is truly *A Fight*, though over the body of woman rather than Homer; the feminist text is no less powerful for being so heavily occluded at the end. Like her narrator Christina struggled with contradictions. Outwardly, she would be satisfied with the lowest place, but in her heart, and in her art, she cherished a heroic secret self.

Her friends were wrestling with the same problems. Barbara Smith was this year spreading a renewed feminist message in her essay *Women and Work*, urging purposeful service on all those whom gentility condemned to aimlessness and embroidery but even she was not in control of her destiny, and had been peremptorily plucked from an unsuitable 'free relationship' by her otherwise progressive father. And this year Christina's closer friend in feminist circles, the talented and ambitious Anna Howitt, had been virtually destroyed by disappointment and inner conflict.

Following the success of *Margaret* and *The Castaway*, Anna had aimed even higher for the 1856 RA show, with a large oil that was 'to embody her ideals' and be her masterpiece. Depicting Boadicea brooding over her wrongs, it was truly sublime, wrote her mother. Barbara Smith had sat for Boadicea, defeated in battle by the invading Romans, and the subject was contemporary as well as historical, with the conquered British Queen a symbol of oppressed womanhood. The feminist message was clear.

It was rejected by the RA and sent instead to the Crystal Palace exhibition, where the artist requested a second opinion from the influential Mr Ruskin. She was at the Hermitage when the answer arrived:

Annie snatched and tore open the letter. Then came a cry of grief and anger as from a wounded creature – one could never forget it nor how she read out – almost screamed, the words 'What do *you* know about Boadicea? Leave such subjects alone and paint me a pheasant's wing'. Waving the letter, she rushed into the house crying "a pheasant's wing – I'll paint him a pheasant's wing!" and then as the family gathered round sank down in a passion of hopeless grief.

This signalled the end of her career. She began to hear voices and when her aunt commissioned a picture of a bluebell wood she covered

the ground with snakes, which the spirits told her to draw. The family
was horrified:

> was Annie mad? Had Ruskin's letter, coming after the broken engage-
> ment, affected her mind? Her nerves were utterly shaken; her ambition as
> an artist dead. They were in despair. She shunned her painter friends.
> Barbara begged her to rest at Scalands; she refused; the place was too full
> of memories of the past. Rap, rap, went the spirits in her head and Annie
> grew paler and thinner . . . It was a dark time about which the Howitts
> said little .

The following year, the Howitts left the Hermitage, moving further up
Highgate Hill. Christina, who remained on friendly terms, was certainly aware of Mrs Howitt's belief that 'over-exertion' and artistic
ambition were the cause of her daughter's breakdown. Probably, too,
she read the story, published this year, in which Anna dramatised the
conflict of ambition and despair in the figure of a young male artist.
And it seems possible that *A Fight over the Body of Homer*, which
indirectly invokes heroic figures like Boadicea, was in part a response
to Anna's breakdown, commending domesticity in order to curb dangerous ambition. Safety and happiness lay in contentment with a
lower place.

Christina had a lifelong struggle with feminist desires. However
much she sought them, ambition and autonomy frightened her, for
they seemed always at odds with the feminine ideal. When Gabriel
objected, violently, to the retitled *Lowest Room*, on the grounds that it
was infected with the 'falsetto muscularity' of Barrett Browning's
work – he must chiefly have had in mind *Aurora Leigh*, which dealt
with the same problems of modern womanhood, artistic ambition and
feminine fulfilment. Aurora herself defines ambition in Carlylean
terms of self-realisation, and intriguingly makes the same comparison
in her modern, female epic, between Homeric heroes and the present
age:

> every age
> Appears to souls who live in't (ask Carlyle)
> Most unheroic. Ours, for instance, ours:
> The thinkers scout it, and the poets abound
> Who scorn to touch it with a finger-tip:
> A pewter age – mixed metal, silver-washed;
> An age of scum . . .

Christina cannot have read this before writing *A Fight*, because *Aurora
Leigh* was published more than a month after her poem was com-

pleted. Both poems were of their time. It is possible however that she heard something of *Aurora*'s subject, for Gabriel and William were again frequent guests of the Brownings while the text was going through the press, and probably received an advance copy in late October before the Brownings left for Italy. 'O the wonder of it!' wrote Gabriel at the end of the year, whatever his later views. Christina herself regarded the author as virtually unsurpassable. 'I doubt whether the woman is born, or for many a long day, if ever, will be born, who will balance, not to say outweigh Mrs Browning,' she told a friend. If Tennyson was a bugbear, as she later joked, Barrett Browning was a beacon.

Other shared concerns began to appear in her work. The sub-plot of *Aurora Leigh*, concerning the seamstress Marian Erle, who is raped and cast out of society with her infant, is echoed in *Light Love* (28 October 1856), the first of several ballads Christina wrote about seduction, desertion and illegitimacy. Like female emancipation, this was essentially a social problem of unequal gender relations. In art the woman was often treated as victim, although in life she and her child were more likely to be held responsible for their fate – a contradiction that reflected conflicting attitudes. *Light Love* ends with the single mother calling for divine retribution, being unlikely to receive much from men.

And just as *Aurora Leigh* dramatised different types of womanhood in the shape of Aurora, Marian and the worldly Lady Waldemar, so in *A Triad*, written in December, Christina set out three figures – 'sluggish wife', shameful mistress and 'famished' spinster – to conclude that all were 'short of life'. Her critique of wifehood ('droning in sweetness like a fattened bee') is of particular interest, for though marriage might not retain its rapture in real life, lyric poetry seldom broke the illusion.

Some of Christina's ambivalence on gender issues had its roots, like much else, in her youthful experience of male abdication. Her 'rather unusual feeling of deference for the "head of the family" whoever he might be', which placed her in the traditionalist rather than feminist camp, was in part a demand that male dominance be accompanied by responsibility. Having felt its lack at a crucial period in her youth, she desired the protection of dependence. Hence her exaggerated, and as it turned out largely misplaced, respect for 'the head of the family', and perhaps also her reluctance to seek economic independance as a governess. Or maybe, like many artists, she was tacitly determined to let nothing interfere with her life's work.

Something of this reached the pages of the notebook. *In the Days of the Sea-Kings* (20 December 1856) is a ballad avowedly unegalitarian in its fantasy of male dominance. In it, the heroine is betrothed to a soft, southern lover. At the altar, she is rescued by the man of her dreams:

> He was a strong man from the north,
>   Light-locked, with eyes of dangerous grey:
> 'Put yea by for another time
>   In which I will not say thee nay'.
>
> He took me in his strong white arms,
>   He bore me on his horse away
> O'er crag, morass, and hairbreadth pass,
>   But never asked me yea or nay.
>
> He made me fast with book and bell,
>   With links of love he makes me stay;
> Till now I've never heart nor power
>   Nor will nor wish to say him nay.

In *Aurora Leigh*, Mrs Browning had urged her fellow poets to recognise the character of glory in the present rather than look backwards to sing of black border chieftains or some 'beauteous dame, half chattel and half queen'. But the gipsy rover genre retained its hold over the imagination. Besides being a deft variation on a single rhyme-word, Christina's poem-fantasy of a magnetic stranger has antecedents in *Jane Eyre* and *Wuthering Heights* as well as that most powerful figure from her adolescent reading, the demonic lover Melmoth, while his Viking attributes come from the Northern mythologies that everyone was reading in the mid-1850s. In personal terms, the theme expresses the common desire for true romance, rather than sluggish marriage or sterile spinsterhood. When would a man appear for whom she would have 'neither heart nor power Nor wish nor will' to refuse?

Her final poem of the year came on Christmas Eve, after a visit to Gabriel's apartment where dozens of drawings of Lizzie were on view but she herself was absent. The exact state of the relationship was still puzzling to outsiders for, although Gabriel told Brown that he 'intended to get married at once to Guggum and then off to Algeria!!!' he had failed to do either. Lizzie then stormed out of London, vowing to have no more to do with him. Gabriel followed, spending most of December in Bath, before returning to Chatham Place in time for Christmas. How much of this tumultuous history was known to Christina is hard to judge, but her sonnet *In an Artist's Studio* reflects somewhat sadly on the gulf between male and female perceptions:

One face looks out from all his canvases,
  One selfsame figure sits or walks or leans:
  We found her hidden just behind those screens,
That mirror gave back all her loveliness.
A queen in opal or in ruby dress,
  A nameless girl in freshest summer greens,
  A saint, an angel – every canvas means
The same one meaning, neither more nor less.
He feeds upon her face by day and night,
  And she with true kind eyes looks back on him,
Fair as the moon and joyful as the light:
  Not wan with waiting, not with sorrow dim;
Not as she is, but was when hope shone bright;
  Not as she is, but as she fills his dream.

14

Full Powers

IF ROMANTIC FULFILMENT was still lacking in her own life, Christina was now coming into her full poetic powers. She was, of course, careful never to boast. 'Upon her reputation as a poet she never presumed,' wrote William, 'nor did she ever volunter an allusion to any of her performances: in a roomful of mediocrities she consented to seem the most mediocre and the most unobtrusive of all.' Yet she knew she was a poet, and a good one, he added and was resolute in setting 'a line of demarcation between a person who is a poet and another person who is a versifier', deaf to all special pleadings.

And she was stimulated by competition. Recently, Gabriel had made some new friends whose idealism recalled that of the Brotherhood. Mainly university men preparing to give up sober careers for the uncertain pathways of art, these 'nicest young fellows in – Dreamland', also happened to be producing a magazine modelled on *The Germ*. The *Oxford and Cambridge Magazine* was the brainchild of Edward (or Ned) Jones, who wanted to be a painter, and William Morris, who wrote 'capital tales' and glorious poems. Indeed, though Morris had been writing for little more than a year, he already had 'enough poetry for a big book'. Returning the compliment, the young men reprinted *The Blessed Damozel*. Gabriel offered more poems and urged his sister to do likewise.

'I cannot quite recollect about the Oxford and Cambridge Mag.,' Christina wrote years later to an inquirer. ' I certainly have an idea of having contributed something to it . . . If I did so (and I think I did), my pieces must have appeared under my own name.' In fact, all contributions were unsigned, but in any case nothing by Christina appeared. Yet clearly she imagined it had. Was something offered, but not printed owing to the early demise of the journal? In its year of existence it carried Gabriel's new ballad, *The Staff and Scrip* which Christina later singled out for praise, and six poems by Morris, all in medieval vein, which he was now planning to publish in volume form.

She herself had more than enough poetry for a 'big book' of her own, but little hope of publishing one. New poets were accustomed to guarantee publisher's costs, and she had no such funds. Her attempts at magazine publication show she sought an audience, however, and Mrs Browning's lines on their common muse in *Aurora Leigh* were ones to make Christina pause:

> O life, O poetry,
> – Which means life in life! . . .
> – poetry, my life,
> My eagle, with both grappling feet still hot
> From Zeus's thunder, who hast ravished me
> Away from all the shepherds, sheep, and dogs,
> And sent me in the Olympian roar . . .

Her father had commended poets to soar like eagles, not hop like sparrows.

Until such time, she had other tasks in hand – contributions to the grandly-named *Imperial Dictionary of Universal Biography*, for which Mrs Howitt had recruited both Christina and William to write on Italian men of letters and politics, and helping with a translation of Mallet du Pan's memoirs, which seems to have run into the sand, though not on her account. Christina was glad of the work, but developed no interest in scholarship. And she was naturally always occupied with domestic matters: helping Mamma write letters, pay calls, supervise the housework, cooking and laundry and especially take her share of the mending, to make sure that William had no missing buttons or holes in his socks. He, in turn, earned the money on which the household depended.

One morning late in 1856, Lucy brought the sad news of Tom Seddon's death in Cairo. Christina was deputed to send condolences on Mamma's behalf. In response, the Seddons circulated Tom's last letters home, which Christina acknowledged with a second sympathetic note to Emily. They also indulged in modest entertaining, for Mamma now presided over regular 'at homes', but some other friendships were in abeyance. Anna Howitt still shunned society, and Barbara Smith was again wintering in Algiers, where early in 1857 Bessie learned that she had found a soul-mate in Eugene Bodichon, a French doctor working among the Algerian people, whom her family thought almost as unsuitable as a free union but was at least single. In May Barbara brought him back to Britain to marry, on the understanding that they would live at least half the year in Algeria. Bessie meanwhile went to Edinburgh, where with Isa Craig she joined the staff of a ladies' magazine, which they aimed to make into a feminist journal.

Gabriel's relationship with Lizzie was breaking up. He had, Brown noted in March, got as far as borrowing money for a wedding licence, but failed to use it. Lizzie was angry and upset in lodgings in Hampstead, though in June she participated in a private Pre-Raphaelite *salon*, showing work alongside Gabriel, Brown, Millais, Hunt, Arthur Hughes and a new man called John Brett. Immediately afterwards Gabriel left for Oxford, to join Jones and Morris in a high-spirited scheme to decorate the university debating chamber with Arthurian murals of Knights of the Round Table.

The same month saw the death of Rosalind's sister Helen Orme, and shortly afterwards the Browns' new baby, not yet weaned, sickened and died in one dreadful week. Again Lucy bore the bad tidings, and again Christina was deputed to write. 'Mamma unites with me in affectionate sympathy with you on the loss of poor Arthur,' she began:

> indeed I was quite grieved at the news Lucy brought us this morning; and cannot forbear telling you so, though it seems almost a mockery to talk of *my* sorrow to his parents. I hope we shall all follow Nolly's advice and go and see him some day – yet it is a relief poor little dear to think he is now out of all his pain for ever.

This seems a touch unfeeling, though such condolences were regarded as entirely appropriate in the Victorian age. Like her contemporaries, Christina had been brought up to believe in literal reunion with loved ones; in her cosmogony heaven was indeed a place where one could 'go and see' the dead some day, as three-year-old Oliver fondly imagined.

Her verse continued to invoke paradisal consolation, though equally often the commerce between living and dead was more troubled. Earlier, she had imaged herself lying in the grave, unwept or sadly lamented. Now spectral figures returned from limbo to reclaim their lost ones. *The Hour and the Ghost*, for example, is a supernatural ballad featuring a long dialogue between bride, bridegroom and a ghost who may be regarded as the woman's former lover, now dead, or as death itself, drawing her away. It is a poem of haunting imagery and metrical freedom, in lines whose irregular stress seldom stumbles, and whose varying lengths hold off the insistent closure of the rhymes, in tension with the sense. Only Coleridge and Tennyson had approached this flexibility in versification, although each of the Brownings was moving in the same direction. Christina's poem ends with the ghost's victory that brings no respite from grief:

> O fair frail sin,
> O poor harvest gathered in!
> Thou shalt visit him again
> To watch his heart grow cold;
> To know the gnawing pain
> I knew of old;
> To see one much more fair
> Fill up the vacant chair,
> Fill his heart, his children bear: –

> While thou and I together
> In the outcast weather
> Toss and howl and spin.

The final image echoes that in Dante's second circle of hell, where the souls of illicit lovers swirl in the wind like flocks of starlings, or cranes crying with dolorous notes, and the final words echo those of Gabriel's translation of *Leonore*. Together, they suggest that Christina was unconsciously returning to the ghosts of that troubled time in the 1840s, to evoke a shadowy, suggestive realm of strange, estranging love.

Her intense inner life is glimpsed in several poems from this period. 'Few things contain more of her innermost self,' wrote William of *The Heart Knoweth its Own Bitterness*, an expression of desolation and desire completed on 27 August. The title is taken from the Book of Proverbs, and the poem contains several 'signature' phrases, including the sealed fountain from the *Song of Solomon*. The urgent address recalls John Donne's wrestlings with his maker, and the verse has an angry undertow barely balanced by the devotional elements, together with an erotic urgency that mixes sacred and sexual yearning. Above all, it articulates the female sense of unfocused dissatisfaction, powered by indefinite or inadmissable cravings:

> How can we say 'enough' on earth;
>   'Enough' with such a craving heart:
> I have not found it since my birth
>   But still have bartered part for part.
> I have not held and hugged the whole,
>   But paid the old to gain the new;
>   Much have I paid, yet much is due,
> Till I am beggared sense and soul.
>
> I used to labour, used to strive
>   For pleasure with a restless will:
> Now if I save my soul alive
>   All else what matters, good or ill?
> I used to dream alone, to plan
>   Unspoken hopes and days to come: –
>   Of all my past this is sum:
> I will not lean on child of man.
>
> To give, to give, not to receive,
>   I long to pour myself, my soul,
> Not to keep back or count or leave
>   But king with king to give the whole:

> I long for one to stir my deep –
>   I have had enough of help and gift –
>   I long for one to search and sift
> Myself, to take myself and keep.
>
> You scratch my surface with your pin;
>   You stroke me smooth with hushing breath; –
> Nay pierce, nay probe, nay dig within,
>   Probe my quick core and sound my depth.
> You call me with a puny call,
>   You talk, you smile, you nothing do;
>   How should I spend my heart on you,
> My heart that so outweighs you all?

A month earlier she had written *introspective*, with its powerful opening:

> I wish it were over, the terrible pain,
> Pang after pang again and again:
> First the shattering ruining blow,
> Then the probing steady and slow.
>
> Did I wince? I did not faint:
> My soul broke but was not bent...

'Not another the sight must see', this concluded. She was determined to conceal her innermost feelings, and her chatty letters to the Heimanns and others at this date show no signs of distress – a reminder that Christina's poetry did not necessarily reflect immediate moods, but at its deepest sprang from buried and partly inexplicable emotions.

It is perhaps as well for posterity that Christina's brilliant career did not prosper as her early success might have seemed to predict, or she might then have remained in the same groove, producing verses that were 'the same thing in blue, green, red, yellow' as Sara Coleridge said of Felicia Hemans, with 'a sentiment or moral like the large bead of a rosary'. As it was, she wrote with the freedom to take risks, to wait for the necessary fusion in the crucible of the imagination, without feeling that the public was waiting to read and judge each piece.

She was now writing with full assurance. And although many single women chafed against the emptiness of being merely 'a daughter at home', the position rather suited a poet. She was growing a little more at ease socially, as Letitia Scott noted in July 1857 when she invited the Rossetti sisters to join her on a visit to Warlingham in Surrey, where

the Eppses had a country cottage. Christina was now 'much less peculiar' and more 'suited to visit', she told her husband. They went for an
excursion on the Downs, with a donkey for the children to ride, and
Maria caused much mirth by sitting down to descend a steep slope,
accompanied by Christina and Ellen Epps. No doubt all three were
hampered by steadily widening skirts, the crinoline was about to
flounce into fashion.

Not long after this a tide of fury swept through Britain in response to
insurrection and mutiny among sepoy regiments in India, in a flood
of indignation that few were able to ignore or challenge.

Following the murder of Europeans in Meerut, rebellion spread like
bushfire to military stations large and small, where British officers and
their families were outnumbered by the local troops under their command. The most terrible events, from the British perspective, took
place at Cawnpore in June and July where mutiny and siege were
succeeded by the massacre of several hundred European women
and children. Though the details are confused and disputed, the
news provoked outrage when the lurid accounts began to reach Britain during August. 'These hordes of savage mutineers seem to
have cast aside the commonest feelings of humanity,' wrote Cardinal
Wiseman in a pastoral letter, going on to invoke 'the ferocity of the
tiger in his jungle' and 'unchecked excesses of fiendish fury', all in
a land 'which we called our own and thought we had blessed with
earthly happiness'. The *Times* concurred, overcome with excessive
metaphor in excoriating the insurgents' frenzy, as they swarmed
with 'voracious relish to the pollution of the sanctuary ... to soil the
marble surface of the temple with vilest filth, to spit in the face of
Majesty'.

As well as a betrayal of the loyalty Indian subjects were deemed to
owe the British crown, the actions were perceived as anti-Christian,
for although the spark that ignited the rebellion was a calculated
insult to the Hindu and Islamic religions – the order to grease cartrid-
ges with animal fat – the reaction was interpreted as a display of
heathen aggression. The Queen issued a proclamation calling on God
to restore lawful authority and ordering a national day of prayer to
implore 'His blessing and assistance on our arms', while the Society
for the Propagation of the Gospel resolved to double the number of
missionaries to India. The Bishop of London's Prayer for our
Countrymen in the East, which was read at Christ Church on Sundays
in August included a plea for divine assistance:

O Lord we beseech Thee to watch over the helpless women and children
who are perchance even now exposed to cruel assaults of enemies at once

infuriated and treacherous, and strengthen those whom Thou hast armed to defend them . . .

In early August came brief reports of a new atrocity at Jhansi in June where mutineers were said to have murdered all European men, women and children. A month later, on 5 September, this was confirmed, with vivid details in the *Illustrated London News*:

> Through the gloom of the Indian news the heroism of our countrymen, and countrywomen too, shines brightly out . . . The following account of the death of Captain Skene, superintendent of Jhansi district, and of his noble wife, also of Captain Gordon, assistant superintendent, will be read with thrilling interest: –
> It is all true about poor Frank Gordon. He, Alick Skene, his wife and a few peons managed to get into a small round tower when the disturbance began; the children and all the rest were in other parts of the fort – altogether sixty. Gordon had a regular battery of guns, also revolvers; he and Skene picked off the rebels as fast as they could fire, Mrs Skene loading for them. The peons say they never missed once, and before it was all over they killed thirty seven, beside many wounded. The rebels, after butchering all in the fort, brought ladders against the tower and commenced swarming up. Frank Gordon was shot through the forehead and killed at once, Skene then saw that it was no use going on any more, so he kissed his wife, shot her and then himself.

Within two days, Christina had written her poem:

In the Round Tower at Jhansi, 8th June 1857:

A hundred, a thousand to one; even so;
  Not a hope in the world remained;
The swarming, howling wretches below
  Gained, and gained, and gained.

Skene look'd at his pale young wife: –
  'Is the time come?' 'The time is come.'
Young, strong, so full of life;
  The agony struck them dumb.

'Will it hurt much?' 'No, mine own;'
  I wish I could bear the pang for both'.
'I wish I could bear the pang alone:
  Courage, dear, I am not loth'.

Kiss and kiss: 'It is not pain
  Thus to kiss and die.

> One kiss more.' 'And yet one again.'
> 'Good-bye.' 'Good-bye.'

This was the first time she had taken up her pen in response to a political event, perhaps prompted by the *ILN's* observation that India was 'sure to be the all-engrossing subject connected with literature for the remainder of the year'. Though the Laureate was unaccountably silent, magazine versifiers poured out venomous and vengeful items. By comparison, Christina's piece was restrained. It spoke not of atrocity but of courage, with great spareness of poetic means.

Christina was proud of the poem, and her high regard was shared by William, who was no jingoist and yet rated it 'among her masterpieces'. We would not now reckon it so highly, seeing it as too dependent on clichés. It suffers, too, from the altered meaning of 'pang', which has devalued into facetiousness; this was one of Christina's favourite words and time has not served her well in its regard. Nevertheless, the imagination that responded with such quickness to the reported plight of the Skenes can still be felt. Concentrating on their affective, conjugal relationship, the poem presents them as modern-day martyrs, heroically choosing to die together in a long moment of mutual resolve amid the tumult.

Politically, of course, the poem espouses the imperialist view of British bravery versus Indian 'savagery', which formed the basis of all reporting of events in India. It also possesses a sexual dimension supplied by the context that would have been apparent to the poem's original readers. For alongside the horror inspired in Britain by the image of upright Englishmen being slaughtered by infidels, lay the fear, much fanned by the press, of pure English women being violated by sensual hordes in an orgy of lust – an essential element in European demonology regarding Asian races. The *ILN*, for instance, published an engraving (drawn from imagination, since no illustrators were on the spot) showing the sister of Cawnpore's commander using a pistol to defend her virtue against sabre-wielding sepoys – an event that had no basis in reported fact, while one of the key images of the conflict was *Punch's* depiction of a 'British Lion' leaping upon a 'Bengal Tiger' in order to rescue a half-naked white woman. This was the fate worse than death awaiting Mrs Skene, had her husband not shot her first.

Beyond this, Christina gave Mrs Skene a voice, taking from the newspaper report just enough information about her courage for an imaginative leap, and helping to underline public perception of female heroism as a key element in the terrible events. Christina had no interest or competence in military matters, but her nightmare poems had given her practice in the evocation of terror; here she used her pen to salute a brave woman, and in doing to so speak on behalf of her countrywomen. War might be outside female experience, in life and literature, but in *Jhansi* Christina found modern valour worthy of the epic celebration she had wished for in *A Fight over the Body of Homer*.

When, some years later, the press accounts of Jhansi were shown to be untrue, Christina declined to change or suppress the poem. To her, its emotional impulse remained authentic. And she also sketched an illustration to the text, showing a part-imperial, part-romantic image: a raised standard with the conjugal motif of two caressing doves, and a broken staff, the flag stained with blood. Here, as elsewhere, love, fear and death were entwined in her imagination.

In the Round Tower at Jhansi was to prove a turning-point in her career. Immediately afterwards she began a second composition based on the evocation of terror, in a strange and disturbing poem explicitly called *A Nightmare* (12 September 1857):

> I have a love in ghostland –
> Early found, ah me how early lost! –
> Blood-red seaweeds drip along that coastland
> 　By the strong sea wrenched and tost.
> In every creek there slopes a dead man's islet,
> 　And such an one in every bay;
> All unripened in the unended twilight:
> 　For there comes neither night nor day.

Two more long stanzas describe the watery place where ghosts drift in flocks and shoals amidst spectral towns before moving to an unexplained dialogue:

> How know you that your lover
> 　Of death's tideless waters stoops to drink? –
> Me by night doth mouldy darkness cover,
> 　It makes me quake to think:
> All night long I feel his presence hover
> 　Thro' the darkness black as ink.

> Without a voice he tells me
> 　The wordless secrets of death's deep:
> If I sleep, his trumpet voice compels me
> 　To stalk forth in my sleep;
> If I wake he rides me like a nightmare:
> 　I feel my hair stand up, my body creep:
> Without light I see a blasting sight there,
> 　See a secret I must keep.

This is the third of Christina's major nightmare poems, following the monster with clammy fin of August 1849, and the weeping crocodile of March 1855. It is the most mysterious and least self-explanatory. Somehow, watery seas or rivers are linked to each poem, and also to a male figure who is both frightening and pitiful but only half-human. Here the unseen lover is felt as a hovering presence in inky darkness. He speaks 'without a voice', and yet compels the dreamer to wake. Her scalp prickles with fear, and though there is no light she 'sees' something unsayable, knowing only that the secret must be kept.

This powerful piece confirmed the access of poetic strength. Between September and December this year, Christina completed eleven new poems, of which several were to be those on which her reputation was founded. These included *Memory*, whose theme and title seem to refer to the self-silencing that accompanied the end of her engagement to James, and the slow self-murder of her love:

> I nursed it in my bosom while it lived,
>   I hid it in my heart when it was dead.
> In joy I sat alone; even so I grieved
>   Alone, and nothing said.
>   . . .
> None know the choice I made; I make it still,
>   None know the choice I made and broke my heart,
> Breaking mine idol ...

There were also two significant poems about keeping secrets: *Day Dreams*, in which the poet muses on the silence of her innermost soul, wondering if its secret is worth guessing; and *Nonsense*, later retitled *Winter: My Secret*, in which she teasingly promises disclosure:

> I tell my secret? No indeed, not I:
> Perhaps some day, who knows?
> But not today; it froze, and blows, and snows,
> And you're too curious: fie!
> You want to hear it? well:
> Only, my secret's mine, and I won't tell.
>
> Today's a nipping day, a biting day;
> In which one wants a shawl,
> A veil, a cloak, and other wraps:
> I cannot ope to every one who taps,
> And let the draughts come whistling thro' my hall;
> Come bounding and surrounding me,

Come buffeting, astounding me,
Nipping and clipping thro' my wraps and all.
I wear my mask for warmth: who ever shows
His nose to Russian snows
To be pecked at by every wind that blows?
You would not peck? I thank you for good will,
Believe, but leave that truth untested still . . .

Perhaps some languid summer day,
When drowsy birds sing less and less,
And golden fruit is ripening to excess,
If there's not too much sun nor too much cloud,
And the warm wind is neither still nor loud,
Perhaps my secret I may say,
Or you may guess.

What was the secret around which these poems circled? In *Nightmare* the dreamer wakes to 'know she must not tell'. In *Day Dreams* the speaker is unable to guess. In *Winter: My Secret* keeping the secret has itself become the subject.

Yet the poem would not work unless the reader received a strong impression that the secret *is* about to be told. The emotional movement of the verse repeatedly offers and withdraws, in a flirtatious manner whose light touch charms even as it annoys, in the manner of real teasing. The mode is consciously juvenile, yet this is not a child's poem; it is about adult privacy, insecurity and distrust. It is also, obliquely, about something that must be concealed yet is so important that it must be advertised. As every child knows, a secret has no value unless others know you have it.

The prospect of disclosure however fills the speaker with bitingly cold fear. Secrecy is a shawl, a cloak, 'a mask for warmth', against questions that nip and peck like blackbirds in the nursery rhyme. And the nursery rhythms, strung on an irregular but firm conversational metre, maintain the delicious balance between teasing humour and serious undertow, between the sparkling surface of the verse and its half-concealed intentions, just as the abrupt changes of direction contribute to the double sense of enjoyment and discomfort. Its success is to convince the reader that there is indeed a secret, while the final line positively encourages the biographer to guess what this is. Of course, we are not altogether surprised to be cheated at the end, for a secret told is no secret at all.

Like the other poems of the season, this is not necessarily about an actual secret but about the sense of having a secret – a sense that was familiar to Christina who, without telling lies, was like Maude determined not to tell the truth, describing herself as 'a fountain sealed'. Only she knew what was being concealed – or perhaps did not quite know, for all the powerful poems of this period convey the impression of something seeking expression that nevertheless cannot be described, bound in with half-glimpsed fear. As critics have perceived, the texts contain obscure, unidentified referents, 'something unknown and inexplicable both to speaker and reader' around which meaning nevertheless takes shape. Biographers, too, have been intrigued by this baffling sense of secrecy at the heart of Christina's life, which she was unwilling or unable to reveal. In these poems, she at least came close to admitting there was a secret, even if she did not know herself what it was. And together these poems make 1857 something of an *annus mirabilis* in her career.

15

No Thank You, John

IN OCTOBER CHRISTINA resurrected the old story of the envious curmudgeon with which she had once fantasised gaining fame and fortune and submitted it to the *National Magazine*, one of the many new illustrated magazines launched in this period. The idea may have come from Bessie Parkes, who had published an account of Algiers in its pages; or it was prompted by the appearance of a tale called *The Wicked Old Woman in the Wood: a Child's Story* in the September issue. *Nick: a Child's Story* appeared in October. No one seems to have taken much notice.

The first poem of 1858 was *Maude Clare*, in Border Ballad style, in which a rejected woman watches her false lover marry another woman. At the wedding breakfast, Maude Clare upbraids Lord Thomas with his betrayal and returns the tokens of their betrothal:

> 'Lo, I have brought my gift, my Lord,
>   Have brought my gift,' she said:
> 'To bless the hearth, to bless the board
>   To bless the marriage bed.
>
> 'Here's my half of the golden chain
>   You wore about your neck
> That day we waded ankle deep
>   For lilies in the beck . . .

Lord Thomas quails before her scorn, for his is a mercenary marriage and Maude Clare a wronged woman of heroic demeanour, whose pride echoes through the incantation of her name.

Christina's repeated choice of the name Maude for her literary personae clearly had some personal significance, even if this was in origin no more than girlish sentiment. And Maude Clare's high drama of confrontation reads quite straightforwardly as revenge-fantasy, as if to cauterise an old wound. Other poems of heartbreak, like the recent *Memory*, showed that the relationship with James Collinson cast a long shadow; here the poet who had herself been first courted and then rejected at last played out her own proud repudiation.

Since Collinson's reappearance in the world of art, it had been difficult to forget the past, for his name was visible each season in exhibition reviews; indeed the magazine that printed *Nick* had unwittingly alluded to their early days of happiness by recalling the early promise of *The Charity Boy's Debut*. James's Academy pictures of 1857 had caught the attention of a wide if undiscerning public, one being published as an engraving shortly before Christina began *Maude Clare*. Moreover, two new pictures were currently on view at the British Institution, reviewed by William in the *Spectator* and providing another reminder of the past.

But there was a more immediate reason for Christina's dramatic expression of disdain, for with somewhat uncanny aptness the national marriage registers reveal that on 9 February 1858, at Brompton Oratory, James Collinson, aged 32, artist, of Queens Road, Chelsea, married Eliza Alvinia Henrietta Ann Wheeler, 40, spinster, of South Parade, Chelsea.

No doubt artistic success enabled him to take the step he had renounced eight years earlier. Probably also Miss Wheeler, with such an array of baptismal names, had some fortune of her own; her deceased father was a man of independent means. Like James she was a Catholic, related by marriage to his friend J. R. Herbert. James's portrait of his wife, done soon after their wedding, shows a plainly dressed woman of vigorous, attractive character. Their first and only child, Robert, was born in 1859.

At age forty Eliza was late finding a husband. It would be improper to assume that this was a mercenary marriage on James's part, but easy to see how it could be so interpreted – especially since he was peculiarly associated with the idea of mercenary marriage through his successful works at the 1857 RA, *To Let* and *For Sale*, which depicted women advertising their charms by means of commercial analogy. The first showed a young widow offering lodgings in her house, the second a girl opening her purse at a charity sale; in both the objects available are themselves. Opinion is still divided as to whether the subjects were intended as a satire on the marriage-market or as coarsely coy portrayals of nubile young women, but there is little doubt that the double entendre was immediately understood by the public. So James might have jilted Christina for the sake of religion rather than wealth, but recent pictures showed him much concerned with money matters. And in this context, Maude Clare's scornful arraignment of her faithless lover does indeed begin to look like a revenge fantasy. Moreover, it was immediately followed by a poem called *Jealousy is cruel as the grave*, which Christina later tore from the notebook and destroyed – an eloquent gesture in the context, albeit now indecipherable in detail.

It seems hardly likely that she had consciously nurtured hopes that, having left Stonyhurst, James would one day return to her. In

Memory she had described her love as cold and crushed, buried deep in her heart 'where it used to live', as if all were over. Yet *Maude Clare* suggests she was both shocked and jealous, and perhaps surprised by the vehemence of her feelings. She may not by this date have wished to marry James, but she could still feel hurt. In their scornful cadences, Maude Clare's words conveyed all the pain and anger she would have liked to heap on his head.

A decade later, she returned to the subject in fiction. The heroine of *Commonplace*, Lucy Charlmont, has enjoyed a decorous flirtation with Alan Hartley and is hopeful of a happy conclusion. Suddenly, she reads of his marriage in the *Times*. Lucy's dismay from 'unavowed heart-sorrow' – she will let no one see her anguish – echoes the self-silencing of *Memory* and *Introspective* and was surely based on Christina's experience of learning, perhaps also from a newspaper announcement, that her former sweetheart was now another's husband:

> Lucy, ready to cry, but ashamed of crying for such a cause, thrust the Supplement out of sight, and sitting down, forced herself to face the inevitable future. One thing was certain, she could not meet Alan – in her thoughts he had long been Alan, and now it cost her an effort of recollection to stiffen him back into Mr Hartley – she must not meet Mr Hartley till she could reckon on seeing him and his wife with friendly composure . . . Then came the recollection of a cracker she had pulled with him, and kept in her pocket-book ever since; and of a card he had left for her and her sister or, as she fondly fancied, mainly for herself . . . Treasures no longer to be treasured, despoiled treasures – she denied herself the luxury of a sigh, as she thrust them between the bars of the grate and watched them burn.

Contemptuously, Maude Clare returns her love gifts. How long had Christina held on to the remaining tokens of James's affection? In her heart at least she had cherished his memory, destroying but never forgetting the poem he had given her.

The very act of writing *Maude Clare*, however, suggests that she had in fact now come to terms with her heartbreak, and was ready to dismiss James as disdainfully as Maude Clare does her fickle swain. Perhaps James's marriage helped, for reality is sometimes able to lay fantasies to rest. Henceforth Christina was no longer nursing dead love in her bosom, but once again open to romantic possibilities.

She was too secretive to make this public, but even now a new romance was kindling, between herself and the painter John Brett.

The details are difficult to retrieve. In 1860 Christina wrote a humorous poem *No Thank You, John*, in which the speaker teasingly but firmly rejects a rather spoony suitor. 'I'd rather answer "No" to fifty Johns,' she says, 'than answer "Yes" to you.' In reprinting this piece in 1875, Christina told Gabriel there was no risk of emotional exposure, because 'no such person exists or existed'. But in 1890, making notes on a new edition of her works, she pencilled in: 'The original John was obnoxious, because he never gave scope for "No thank you"!'

William reconciled the statements as meaning that 'John' did exist but had never proposed, identifying him as 'the marine painter John Brett' who around 1852 had 'appeared to be somewhat smitten with Christina'. In return, he implied, Christina was certainly not smitten. But perhaps it was not as simple as that, just as 1852 was not the date of Brett's ardour.

Today John Brett is best known as a Pre-Raphaelite landscapist and painter of striking Alpine scenes. He entered the Royal Academy Schools in 1853 and was subsequently introduced by the Patmores to Holman Hunt and others in the Pre-Raphaelite circle, making his RA debut in 1856 with three portraits. Over the previous winter he was lodging in Camden Town, and though he was probably already acquainted with the Rossettis – William recalled meeting him at the Ormes' house and he also knew the Eppses – he made little or no impression until he read the works of Ruskin, nailed his artistic colours to the Pre-Raphaelite mast and towards the end of 1856 asked Gabriel to look at his new pictures, painted in Switzerland in direct response to Ruskin's essay on Mountain Beauty.

Brett's studio was now in Gloucester Road, about five minutes from Albany Street. Gabriel liked his *Glacier of Rosenlaui*, as did Ruskin and Hunt, and in April it was accepted by the RA, together with an interior scene called *Faces in the Fire*. He was then invited to join the small Pre-Raphaelite *salon* at Russell Place organised by Madox Brown in June 1857, and included in an exhibition of British Art partly selected by William to tour North America in the autumn. To this he sent *The Glacier*, together with a picture of three peaks in the Bernese Oberland, and a careful nature study entitled *The Bank whereon the Wild Thyme Grows*.

Physically, Brett was a stocky fellow, with square features, bushy fair hair, a full flaxen beard and bright eyes under beetling brows. His manner of speaking was open and forthright, sometimes opinionated, with an abrupt humour; though not conceited, he was also ambitious, and determined to make his way in the world. His family lived in Kent, where his father had retired after serving as an Army vetinerarian, and his early career had been promoted by his older sister Rosa, herself a talented painter with whom John had formed a quasi-professional partnership; both were disciples of Ruskin, whose valuable patronage they hoped to attract. There is no doubt that knowing the

Rossettis was advantageous to John, both through Gabriel's contact with patrons and William's work as art critic. Born in December 1831, he was almost exactly a year younger than Christina.

His friendship with the family developed during the first half of 1857, when he was probably amongst those invited to Mamma's Thursday evening 'at homes'. He and Christina may also have met at the opening of the Russell Place show, at a visit to Marlborough House to see the Turners, and at social gatherings hosted by Ormes and Patmores. By July he was in Surrey, working on the landscape background for his next year's canvas. His subject was *The Stonebreaker* and the location Mickleham, looking south towards Box Hill.

Now in the possession of Brett's descendants is a small, unfinished oval oil head of a young woman, reproduced on the back jacket of this book, with a pencilled note identifying it as a portrait of Christina Rossetti, done at Mickleham in 1857. Behind the sitter's head is a large feather which seems intended to carry symbolic significance, perhaps as the quill pen of her vocation.

There is no record of Christina visiting Mickleham in 1857. But she was less than ten miles away while visiting the Eppses at Warlingham with Letitia and Maria. Around this time Brett gave drawing lessons to young Laura Epps and her sisters, and it seems very possible that while Christina was in Surrey there was an excursion to John's lodgings below Box Hill, or that he came to Warlingham, as a guest of the Eppses, making sketches of her for the portrait, to be completed in the studio.

Though not mentioned by William in his list of Christina's portraits, Brett's bears a striking similarity to that done by Collinson some nine years earlier. Brett's granddaughter, the family archivist, made the identification apparently from detailed notes of conversations with her mother, John's daughter Daisy. Though he had long since lost contact with the Rossetti circle, Brett did not die until 1902; no doubt in later life he spoke of days long past and his friendship with members of the famed Brotherhood and their sister.

When they met John and Christina were tackling similar themes in art. While John was working on *The Stonebreaker* he was also reading *Aurora Leigh* and on 9 September drew a detailed ink study of Marian Erle and her illegitimate child; ten weeks later Christina completed *Apple Gathering* with the same motif of seduction and desertion. *The Stonebreaker* itself was originally conceived with an overt religious message, in a composition that was both landscape and moral subject, comparable to Hunt's *Scapegoat* and Millais's *Blind Girl*. Pencilled notes to Brett's preliminary sketches for the figure of the pauper boy breaking flints by the roadside as a terrier puppy plays with his cap, allude to the expulsion from Eden and 'the wilderness of the world', from the opening line of *Pilgrim's Progress*. Echoes of both themes sound through Christina's work, and it is possible that Brett – who was not otherwise pious – conceived his subject knowing that an image combining social concern with religious symbolism regarding life's pilgrimage would match her views of the spiritual aims of art. The site chosen, incidentally, was close to the Pilgrim's Way from Winchester to Canterbury (and thus also on the way from Mickleham to Brett's home in Kent, via Warlingham). In the withered tree, on whose single leafy branch a bullfinch sings, may also be detected a reference to spiritual or emotional rebirth, shadowing the many symbolic allusions to barrenness and sudden bursts of joy in Christina's poems. 'Hy heart is like a singing bird,' she wrote suddenly, this November, in what would become one of her best-known lyrics, *A Birthday*.

By the early weeks of 1858 the families were in close contact. 'Will you remember my mother and sisters (as well as myself) kindly to your sister and brother, whom they were very happy to see on their call the other day,' wrote William to John in January. Neither Frances Rossetti nor her daughters were in the habit of superfluous social visiting, so some genuine reason must have taken them to call at his lodging, where Rosa now kept house for John and their younger brother. The most obvious reason would be an invitation to view *The Stonebreaker* as it neared completion, and possibly also John's half-finished portrait of Christina. In the studio they would also have seen Rosa's picture of a tabby cat asleep in a hayloft, with which she made her RA debut, a subject with especial appeal to Christina, who always preferred tabbies.

By this time, Christina was presumably aware of John's admiration. She knew too of the artistic partnership that existed between him and Rosa, whose sisterly affection matched her own. Although she may not have so formulated it to herself, Christina needed a marriage in which her own talents would develop alongside, rather than be subordinate to, those of her spouse. If John, too, were seeking a wife of similar metal, this would be an added reason for mutual regard. Nor did she immediately snubb him with a cool 'No thank you!', or the visit to his studio would not have taken place.

The Stonebreaker was one of the Academy stars this year, indifferently hung but well received. Ruskin's appreciation included the observation that if Brett could 'paint so lovely a distance from the Surrey downs and railway-traversed vales, what would he not make of the chestnut groves of the Val d'Aosta!', and very soon afterwards the artist left for Italy, where he set to work painting not only the chestnut groves of Aosta but also the snowy peaks of the Alps. When he returned in the autumn, his friendship with the Rossettis had faded.

What happened? Many years later, the daughter of the painter Alfred Hunt claimed to have been told by 'Mr John Brett RA' that he had proposed to and was refused by Miss Rossetti. This is not conclusive – Violet Hunt was a renowned embroiderer of facts, and although the reputed conversation must have taken place before William's remark about John being smitten, it may have developed from it, together with the words of Christina's poem, which if taken literally support such a statement. As she wrote, with witty seriousness:

> I never said I loved you, John:
>   Why will you tease me day by day,
> And wax a weariness to think upon
>   With always 'do' and 'pray'?
>
> You know I never loved you, John;
>   No fault of mine made me your toast:
> Why will you haunt me with a face as wan
>   As shows an hour-old ghost?
>
> I dare say Meg or Moll would take
>   Pity upon you, if you'd ask:
> And pray don't remain single for my sake
>   Who can't perform that task.
>
> I have no heart? – Perhaps I have not;
>   But then you're mad to take offence
> That I don't give you what I have not got:
>   Use your own common sense.
>
> Let bygones be bygones:
>   Don't call me false, who owed not to be true:
> I'd rather answer 'No' to fifty Johns
>   Than answer 'Yes' to you.
>
> Let's mar our pleasant days no more,
>   Song-birds of passage, days of youth:
> Catch at today, forget the days before:
>   I'll wink at your untruth.
>
> Let us shake hands, as hearty friends;
>   No more, no less; and friendship's good:
> Only don't keep in view ulterior ends
>   And points not understood

In open treaty. Rise above
  Quibbles and shuffling, off and on
Here's friendship for you if you like; but love –
  No, thank you, John.

Just a year after this was written in March 1860, Christina had no hesitation in publishing it, clearly not fearing it would be construed as a 'love personal'; and no member of the family demurred on these grounds. But given her annotation regarding the 'original John', and Gabriel's remark that it was 'open to comment', it must hold some biographical significance. What happened between them? If Brett was smitten, did he propose? The optimum moment to do so would have been shortly after the opening of the exhibition, when his picture was receiving praise. But Christina's statement that he was 'obnoxious' because he never gave her scope to say No seems to deny this. She was a woman of utter scrupulosity, who could hardly have penned a lie to save her life, even if she could and did conceal the truth. Was she led to believe he would propose, only to find that while she was away during June, he had decided to leave for Italy without declaring himself? Or was she led to believe that if he proposed, she would refuse?

It is all something of a puzzle, and one cannot feel that this flicker of romance represents a major chapter in the history of Christina's affairs of the heart. Yet it was certainly more than a mere schoolboy crush on John's part, and raises the possibility that, if he was obnoxious for not speaking, she was not wholly indifferent. Some unexpected intimation of romance certainly seems to have prompted the sudden outburst of joy in *A Birthday*. Does *No Thank You, John!* conceal the fact that, had he asked, she would have considered saying 'Yes'?

There were two curious sequels. On his return from Italy Brett went home to Kent, from where he sent *The Val d'Aosta* to the 1859 RA. It flopped, and Ruskin was obliged to buy it when no one else would. The following year he returned to English landscape, with a successful picture of a woodman laying a sapling hedge amid bluebells. He then took a studio in the Temple, where in the spring of 1861 he invited the Misses Rossetti to see his new work, an ambitious painting of *Warwick Castle*. 'We have been quite artistic of late in our manners and habits; visiting the studios of Mr Holman Hunt and Mr Brett', Christina told a friend. 'Have you seen Mr Brett's picture? Some of it I like, some I dislike: two small works by his sister which I also saw appeared to me very rich in merit.' The visit presumably took place on 'Show Sunday', when artists opened their studios before works were despatched to the Academy. Though by no means private, this suggests that whatever had happened three years before left no bitterness – another puzzle to the whole affair. If John proposed, Christina evidently caused no offence by saying No.

A year later, Gabriel spoke of Brett with surprising malignity to a mutual friend, declaring he was 'insufferable' and had 'no more eye for colour than a pig' – a judgement not universally shared. Later William too spoke disparagingly about him, as if something had soured their earlier liking, for both Rossetti brothers had previously done much to assist his career. Christina's interest did not falter, however. At the RA in 1864 she sought out a small work, hung in an obscure corner, which she had seen in the catalogue. 'What a grand *Arctic* picture that is by Sir Edwin Landseer, and are not his *Piper and a Pair of Nutcrackers* delightful?' she wrote to Mrs Heimann. 'Simeon Solomon's *Deacon* is a fine thing, and so is Whistler's *Wapping*, and so (in my eyes) is John Brett's small *Wave* picture in one corner of the miniature room . . .' Others' eyes might be on the great Landseer's chilling image of polar bears prowling round the remains of Sir John Franklin's expedition, or on the up-and-coming Whistler, but she did not fail to find and commend a little picture of a squall at sea, painted by someone whose youthful attentions she had not forgotten, perhaps with a touch of regret that the brief blaze of attraction had not flamed into something warmer.

In the summer of 1857 around the time of John's conjectured proposal, Christina spent three weeks in Newcastle, now she was considered 'more suited to visit' by the Scotts. They did not regard her as a great social asset, for the younger Miss Rossetti was neither as amiable as her sister nor as interesting as her brothers. She wrote poetry, it was true; but then so did many people, including her host and hostess; she had published very little and nothing that was likely to impress Newcastle society. Nor did she sparkle conversationally, although a sharp wit lay beneath a shyness which could still be taken for superciliousness. Nevertheless, the Scotts exerted themselves to entertain her, and their warm hospitality was the basis of Christina's lifelong affection for both husband and wife.

Their first excursion was with a party of friends to Sunderland, on a chilly day commemorated by Christina in doggerel verse that was lamentable even as doggerel (as she herself recognised, she had no gift for such writing) and after listing the participants ended abruptly with the picnic consumed en route:

> From Newcastle to Sunderland
> Upon a misty morn in June
> We took the train: on either hand
> Grimed streets were changed for meadows soon.

> Umbrellas, tarts and sandwiches
> Sustained our spirits' temperate flow
> With potted jam, and cold as snow
> Rough-coated sun-burnt oranges.

This 'historical fragment', sent with Christina's letter of thanks, suggests a rustic outing. But Sunderland is as industrial as Newcastle and a most unlikely spot for a picnic. The Scotts must have been taking the party to meet Thomas Dixon, a workingman with literary aspirations, whom Scott had 'discovered' some years before and enjoyed introducing to friends; he is best known as recipient of the tracts Ruskin published as *Time and Tide by Wear and Tyne*. Dixon's class position made it difficult for him to play host, especially to such a large group as the Scotts brought: a picnic hamper presumably solved the problem of hospitality.

Dixon remembered Christina's 'quiet face and calm quiet voice', but much preferred Maria, whose cordial words made him feel welcome when he in turn visited London. And it seems Christina was comparably ill-at-ease. Soon afterwards she wrote *After the Picnic*, not like the doggerel to record an actual event but rather to convey the feeling of isolation that sometimes strikes in the midst of social jollity. In these verses the poet imagines herself as a wraith, looking on as friends feast 'beneath green orange-boughs' – a rather more poetic repast than the actual sandwiches and tarts of the Sunderland outing, yet recognisably related to that occasion:

> From hand to hand they pushed the wine
> They sucked the pulp of plum and peach;
> They sang, they jested and they laughed
> For each was loved of each.

Present but unseen, the spirit listens to the chatter, as the company discuss plans for the next day and, in a psychological transposition of the unseasonable cold of the original picnic into an inner state, shivers comfortless, as she watches her shadow 'cast no chill across the table-cloth'. The oblivious merrymaking continues as she leaves the room, like the brief 'remembrance of a guest That tarrieth but a day'. Was this how Christina felt among the Scotts and their friends, shy and perhaps ignored amid the laughter and gossip?

The next expedition was to Wallington, about an hour's train ride north-west of Newcastle, where Scott was painting eight large scenes from Northumbrian history for the country seat of Sir Walter and Lady Trevelyan. Despite the ancient lineage the Trevelyans were untypically aristocratic, Sir Walter being of a scholarly bent, with an immense knowledge of geology, botany, folklore and fossils, and his wife Pauline a clergyman's daughter with artistic talent. Through Ruskin, they had patronised the Pre-Raphaelites, commissioning works from Woolner and fellow sculptor Alexander Munro, and a watercolour from Gabriel; no doubt they were graciously pleased to meet the artist's literary sister. To Scott, as to Ruskin and the young Algernon Swinburne from the neighbouring estate, Pauline Trevelyan was a most sympathetic and intelligent friend, with a penetrating but warm manner, able to tease stiffness out of the shyest guest. Not all were charmed, for the Trevelyans' high thinking was matched by plain living: their rooms were sparsely furnished, and meals consisted of artichokes and cauliflowers, according to one discomfited visitor. Sir Walter's dislike of luxury was legendary, and he had poured the contents of his ancestral wine-cellar into the lake; he was also rather a bore, knowing 'every book and every ballad that ever was written, every story of local interest that ever was told, and every flower and fossil that ever was found'. Pauline, by contrast, was lively and informal, taking a flattering interest in others' affairs. Scott later teased Christina, saying that at luncheon she had sat silently, looking like the grave of buried hope (an allusion to one of her own lines) but she responded warmly to Pauline, admiring house, garden and estate village, and willingly ordering lace collars for her aunts from the lacemakers on the Trevelyans' estate in Devon, whose work Pauline promoted.

She was invited to admire the decoration of the new central hall, for which Scott's pictures were destined, but most enjoyed making friends with Pauline's little dog Peter, later sending warm wishes that he remained 'well and waggish'. Scott's new dog Olaf was the favourite, however. 'I wish I could see him, poor dear, wagging and drumming, pawing at me with dubious paws and flattening my dress unblamed,' Christina wrote afterwards, reminding us of one hazard caused by the voluminous crinoline; as yet one would guess Christina's own dresses were free of hoops, but even she could not ignore fashion entirely. She added in mock disgust that all her enthusiasm had failed to convince Maria of Olaf's canine charms.

Back in Newcastle, they took another trip, to the coast south of the city where the waves had hollowed out part of the cliff, leaving an arch standing out to sea, and on the eve of Christina's departure they attended the first viewing of Scott's latest picture for the Trevelyans, showing a Viking raid. William believed that on this visit, too, his sister met the poetess Dora Greenwell, 'a slim dark rather tall woman, of an elegant serious type', with a sweet rippling voice, who lived with her clerical brother in the cathedral city of Durham, and had published her first volume in 1848. In fact, it was a few years before they met in person, but no doubt at this date if not before the Scotts introduced Christina to Miss Greenwell's verse, which was 'quite above mere mediocrity' and had many points of comparison with her own.

Christina travelled to and from Newcastle alone. The return journey was trouble-free, if hot and inevitably full of smoke and smuts. 'My travelling companions were sufficiently agreeable,' she reported to her hostess; 'but I did not meet a fatal individual with whom to play at chess or exchange poems' – presumably the subject of some joking allusion – 'in fact the dust and heat kept my mental eye intent rather on water and a towel than on reciprocity of soul'. One fellow traveller was a 'polite Prussian' whom she had subsequently chanced to meet again in Regents Park – pleased this time to be in possession of a clean face.

Her expansiveness shows how much she had enjoyed the visit, and suggests that between them Pauline and Letitia – who remained 'my dear Mrs Scott' despite increasing intimacy – had melted some of Christina's reserve. She found proofs awaiting her, presumably for the *Biographical Dictionary*, as well as domestic news and the latest ecclesiastical gossip, and sent 'special cordialities' from the family along with her own affectionate and even effusive thanks.

She made no mention of her affairs of the heart, and indeed it is tantalising not to know when – by his account – John Brett proposed and was refused, or – by hers – failed to give her the opportunity to decline. There is just time for them to have met, and parted again, before he left for Italy. *Goodbye* was the title of a short poem written on the rail journey:

> Parting after parting
>   All one's life long . . .
> Parting after parting
>   Sore loss and sore sore pain:
> Till one dreads the pang of meeting
>   More than of parting again . . .

The intensity of feeling is excessive in lines ostensibly addressed to friends she was soon to see again, as William noted. However indefinite her feelings towards John Brett may have been, as with her sense of being a spectre at the feast she felt doomed to permanent disappointment – parting after parting and 'sore loss and sore sore pain'.

The proofs that greeted her return to London contain one startling statement nowhere else recorded, laying claim to a remarkable poetic heritage which she had now decided to reveal. Most of her initialed contributions to the *Imperial Dictionary of Universal Biography*, (a grandiose partwork subtitled 'A Series of Original Memoirs of Distinguished Men of All Ages and All Nations, by Writers of Eminence in the Various Branches of Literature, Science and Art') were minor figures from Italian history, such as Francesco Guerrazzi, statesman and author born in Leghorn in 1805, who took a leading part in the Tuscan uprising of 1848 and was later exiled; or Ottavio Rinuccini, the Florentine poet 'called the inventor of modern opera'. She was, however, also asked to compile the entries for Leopardi, and for Petrarch, who warranted meticulous research and an extended essay, composed with stylish elegance.

Although the Dictionary was chiefly concerned with his political career, Petrarch was later an important influence on Christina's work, so her account of his life has a significant place in the story of her own. The startling claim lay in Christina's description of Petrarch's love and muse, the 'incomparable golden-haired Laura' as 'the daughter of Audebert de Noves, sydic of Avignon, and the wife of Hugh, son of Paul de Sade; and ... in fact my own ancestress, as family documents prove'.

Was Christina descended from Petrarch's Laura? No record of such illustrious ancestry is known, and in any case, as Christina herself went on to explain, the identity of Laura is disputed. Boccaccio believed she represented the laurel wreath of fame, rather than a real woman, while to Papa (as Christina did not mention) she was symbolic of a Masonic lodge. Critical scholarship however is here less important than the fact that Christina believed herself a descendant of Laura, in a family tradition presumably handed down by her grandfather – a belief that surely shaped her self-image. In describing her supposed ancestress as one whose 'habitual reserve and exceptional piety inspired poem after poem', for example, was Christina inscribing her own attributes onto Laura, or had she in part modelled herself on this glamorous forebear? What were the family documents she believed proved the descent? Why have they not survived, and why is no other mention made of this claim? If, as it seems, there was little solid foundation for the belief, why did Christina choose to assert it in this public manner? The Victorian fondness for claiming noble ancestry and lost titles had its basis in social insecurity, and Rossetti family aspirations had always been high: was this Christina's way of establishing significance in the world? However much she told herself to take the lowest place, her instinct was always for fame and whether true or legendary, the reputed lineage from Petrarch's beloved Laura was inspiring for someone whose chosen vocation was poetry.

She had it seems been incubating poems in Newcastle, for on 19 June, three were copied into the notebook together, making this a red-letter day, especially as one was *Up-hill*, which became her most oft-quoted poem. This Puritan death text is succinct and sombre, though to modern tastes a touch macabre – the beds which the traveller is promised are too clearly coffin-shaped for comfort. It marked a new maturity in her poetic voice, confirming the significant creativity of this period of intense composition.

It was followed within the week by a very different piece, a long and hectic monologue called *On the Convent Threshold*, with an arresting opening:

> There's blood between us, love, my love,
> There's father's blood, there's brother's blood;
> And blood's a bar I cannot pass . . .

The reader expects something derived from Shakespeare or from Tennyson's *Maud*, whose heroine's predicament it would appear to reflect. A woman is confessing to a Lady Macbeth-like sense of guilt: her white feet are soiled with scarlet mud, and a similar stain is on her heart. No tale unfolds, however. For thirty lines the speaker contrasts her heaven ward gaze with that of her earth-bound lover, exhorting him to repent. Both are guilty of some unnamed sexual crime. 'You sinned with me a pleasant sin,' she says, going on to invoke the aid of visions, in which first a transfigured spirit rises towards the hosts of cherubim in what can only be termed an orgasmic manner, followed by a Gothick nightmare in which a Melmothian spectre returns from beyond the grave:

> It was not dark, it was not light,
> Cold dews had drenched my plenteous hair
> Through clay; you came to seek me there,
> And 'Do you dream of me?' you said.

Half asleep, she answers:

> 'My pillow is damp, my sheets are red,
> There's a leaden tester to my bed:
> Find you a warmer playfellow,
> A warmer pillow for your head . . .

> 'All night long I dreamed of you,
> I woke and prayed against my will,
> Then slept to dream of you again,
> At length I rose and knelt and prayed,
> I cannot write the words I said . . .

Through the dark her silence speaks 'like thunder'; in the morning her hair is grey, and frozen blood is on the threshold. After this horror, the final lines simply rehearse the bland delights of heaven, where the lovers will meet again. Why they cannot do so on earth – how they are to expiate the crime whose blood is on the doorstep – is left utterly unexplained.

When compared to *Up-hill*, this poem seems hysterical and regressive, reminiscent of Poe, Beddoes and romances by Barrett Browning about immured nuns. Its story, however, is that of the love between Heloise and Abelard, taken without acknowledgement from Alexander Pope's version *Eloisa to Abelard*:

> Ev'n here, where frozen chastity retires,
> Love finds an altar for forbidden fires,
> I ought to grieve, but cannot what I ought:
> I mourn the lover, not lament the fault;
>
>   . . .
>
> Now turn'd to heaven, I weep my past offence,
> Now think of thee and curse my innocence . . .
>
> How shall I lose the sin, yet keep the sense
> And love th'offender, yet detest th'offence?

Like Christina's nameless protagonist, Eloisa is disturbed by shameful visions of her beloved: 'father, brother, husband, friend', and struggles with guilty memories.

Pope is not normally a poet associated with Christina Rossetti. Yet she responded feelingly to Eloisa's story. At the end of his poem Pope appealed to 'some future bard' to take up Eloisa's tale, and this challenge may have prompted *On The Convent Threshold*. But evidently it also answered some emotional need – as it did, when published, to the young Gerard Manley Hopkins, with his own burden of Puseyite guilt. Some similarly powerful sense of sexual transgression haunted Christina's imagination. In the context of unsanctioned passion between Heloise and her priestly father-confessor however, the opening reference to father's and brother's blood also hints at a more unmentionable sin than murder, namely a submerged Byronic incest theme – the blood bar the speaker 'cannot pass' being a metonym for consanguinity. This would help explain both the 'unsayable' nature of the sin and the hope that the lovers may find their 'old familiar love' in heaven – lawful affection uncontaminated by carnal attraction.

Nothing in Christina's outer life corresponds with the melodrama of her imagination. This summer she stayed in London with Mamma, while William went with the Rintouls to the Isle of Wight, from where, she flatteringly noted, his letters cheered those at home, producing a 'moon-like content'. Maria, whose nickname was here alluded to, was also away, en route for the Scotts, where she experienced for herself the charms of Olaf. Christina's diversion was the Zoo, where she spotted a tree-frog exactly like the tin toy that follows a magnet in a bowl of water, and watched a fight between a wombat and a porcupine. She drew some portraits of the wombat, having been the first to 'discover' it earlier in the year when, as William recalled, she caught sight of *phascolomys ursinus* in an outlying enclosure and exclaimed in delight at the hitherto unknown creature. Whenever they went to the zoo, she always took 'a goodly bag of eatables' for the inmates.

She also received a visit from young Simeon Solomon, who called under the mistaken impression that he could see Gabriel's work at Albany Street. 'He is an unsightly little Israelite' replied William unkindly: 'but a youth of extraordinary genius in art and perhaps otherwise.' Oddly enough, a month before Christina had written *Christian and Jew* (9 July 1858) a dialogue poem in which a Christian voice expatiates on the paradise unattainable to the Jewish respondent, who in turn laments 'forsaken Zion'. The poem is not overtly hostile to the Jewish faith – as it might have been given the proselytising zeal of the Victorian Church of England and the generally-held view that British Jews should apostatise and assimilate – but it does advocate conversion. Times change, and Christina cannot be held to sympathise wittingly or unwittingly with any later form of anti-semitism, but it is dismaying nevertheless to register this point of view, and to reflect that among the author's oldest and dearest friends were Amelia Heimann and her family. When the poem was published Christina was sufficiently alert to draw the Heimanns' attention to it. 'I cannot bear to be silent on the all-important topic of Christianity,' she wrote anxiously:

> indeed, how could I love you and yours as I do, having received so many favours at your hands, and felt so often your good example, without longing and praying for faith to be added to your works? Dear old friend, do not be offended with me; but believe that the love of Christ and of you all constrains me. If aught I have said offends you, be sure the offence lies in the words, not in the heart from which they come warm.

The generous Heimanns did not take offence, but we may feel less tolerant; in this instance Christina's faith blotted out her profession of Christian lovingkindness.

The autumn of 1858 was an extremely mournful season for some reason – the only evidence being her poems, and the lack of all other information on her activities. To read the poems in full sequence is indeed to experience a dismaying and largely unrelieved impression of deep spiritual despair, epitomised by *Sorrow not as those who have no hope*, finished on 19 November:

> That night destroyed me like an avalanche;
> One night turned all my summer back to snow . . .
>
>   . . .
>
> Then with a cry like famine I arose,
>   I lit my candle, searched from room to room,
> Searched up and down; a war of winds that froze
>   Swept through the blank of gloom.
>
>   . . .
>
> I saw a vision of a woman, where
>   Night and new morning strive for domination;
> Incomparably pale, and almost fair,
>   And sad beyond expression.
>
>   . . .
>
> She bled and wept, yet did not shrink; her strength
>   Was strung up until daybreak of delight:
> She measured measureless sorrow toward its length,
>   And breadth, and depth, and height . . .

William ranked this one of Christina's 'most manifest masterpieces' and 'a personal utterance too plain to need exposition'. Like the rest of the sequence, it showed 'a spirit sorely wrung, and clinging for dear life to a hope not of this world'. In explanation of this mood, he cited her unhappy love affair with James Collinson, from which he claimed she had still not recovered. But one can hardly credit that James was responsible for such an outpouring of grief. These are poems of spiritual distress not a broken heart, and Christina had been prone to depression before loving and losing James. At the start of the year, she had looked back despondently at all the 'pains and pleasures and crises' of her life; now on the last night of 1858, as was her custom, she wrote a devotional New Year poem that articulates not only loneliness but also unloveableness: in her selfabnegating moods Christina found it hard to love herself.

She knew her poems to be gloomy. When kindly Dr Heimann responded to her first volume and its ambiguous apology, he drew attention to the sorrowful themes, which implied she was unloved. She guessed that poems like *After the Picnic* had grieved her friends, she replied, adding in extenuation that surely everyone had sorrowful experiences, and her poems had been written over a long period. Moreover, they were not necessarily profound, but merely the passing record 'of sensation, fancy, and what not, much as these came and went'. She would however accept 'shame and blame' if they displayed facile or affected melancholy, for this would make her 'unmindful of the daily love and mercy' lavished upon her; and finally promised that her next volume would show an 'improved tone of mind and feeling'. But all these arguments were disingenuous: while melancholy might not be the colour of her daily life amid loving family and friends, it was the wellspring of her writing.

Yet there was a way out of depression. As it happened, at this year-end Christina was on the threshold of a new departure in her life, which was comparable to the convent. The road might wind uphill, but now it in some ways had a new destination.

16

Highgate Penitentiary

THROUGH THE 1850s feminist writers urged women to undertake more purposeful work, for the sake of themselves and society. Anna Jameson, Harriet Martineau, Barbara Bodichon and others – many in the pages of the *English Woman's Journal* launched in spring 1858 by Bessie Parkes with Barbara's money – argued forcefully for professional employment for ladies, in a variety of fields.

'Women must, as children of God, be trained to do some work in the world,' declared Barbara. 'We go on talking as if it were still true that every woman is, or ought to be, supported by father, brother, husband,' wrote Martineau. On the contrary, every individual should aim for self-reliance. Moreover, argued Bessie, it was 'our plainest duty to feed the hungry and clothe the naked and afford shelter to the aged . . . remembering the story of the good Samaritan who when he saw that the stranger was wounded, did not stop to speculate on the best way of rendering roads secure from thieves, but *went up to him and bound his wounds*'.

Mrs Jameson promised deliverance from aimlessness. 'Send such a woman to her piano, her books, her cross-stitch; she answers you with *despair!*' she wrote. 'But send her on some mission of mercy, send her where she may perhaps die by inches in achieving good for others, and the whole spirit rises up strong and rejoicing . . .' And Mary Carpenter argued eloquently for voluntary work in reformatories:

> We call then, on Christian women, who are not bound by their pecuniary circumstances to work for their own living . . . and those who are mothers in heart, though not by God's gift on earth, will be able to bestow their maternal love on those who are more to be pitied than orphans, those most wretched moral orphans whose natural sweetness of filial love has been mingled with deadly poison . . .

Christina disliked teaching. 'I myself feel like an escaped governess, for had I only learnt my lessons properly at the proper age I too might have taught some one something – and doubtless I should have had to do so,' she wrote later. Nor was she drawn to social work or nursing. But as *The Lowest Room* made clear she was in need of more meaningful occupation beyond housekeeping and needlework. So early in 1859 she became a voluntary worker at the St Mary Magdalene

Penitentiary in Highgate, supervising young prostitutes who wished to relinquish a life of shame.

Prostitution, or 'the great social evil', had caused a moral panic such as periodically sweeps British society, largely on account of the hordes of harlots who thronged the streets of central London, dressed in fine clothes no working girls could afford, accosting gentlemen and rendering such areas unsafe for respectable women. According to William Acton's 1858 study, *Prostitution considered in its Moral, Social and Sanitary Aspects, in London and other large cities: with Proposals for the Mitigation and Prevention of its Attendant Evils*, there were nearly nine thousand prostitutes in the capital, of whom a third walked the West End in their finery, usually drinking with their clients at a place of entertainment such as the Alhambra in Leicester Square before resorting to the divans and nighthouses of the Haymarket. According to Acton, the causes of prostitution were chiefly poverty and poor housing, though vanity and idleness also played a part, as well as the simple folly that made girls prey to seduction. He claimed too that the fee expected by a whore of the 'better-dressed class' was two or three sovereigns (vastly higher than the average weekly wage and an obvious inducement if true). The newspapers began to carry reports of public meetings about this growing menace, together with despatches from the street, as it were, featuring the history and opinions of these 'unfortunates' who, in most cases were enjoying lives of leisure and luxury otherwise unattainable. One bricklayer's daughter, for example, described in detail her social rise as a result of her sexual fall, and claimed to be training her sister to follow the same profession. More widely believed however was the idea that, once launched on the primrose path, it was but a short slide to the gutter, and that the common fate following a 'fall' was a more literal and fatal leap into the Thames.

To deal with the 'problem' the diocese of London opened a refuge for the reception of fallen women, aiming to retrain them for respectable employment in domestic service. As the prospectus argued:

> This great metropolis with its teeming population and monstrous growth of corruption has not one home for the fallen where their Sisters in Christ can labour for their restoration and guide the feeble steps of their penitence to peace . . . We earnestly hope that ladies who act as Sisters will be led by God's grace to join this work.

Established in 1855, the St Mary Magdalene home was located in Park House at the top of Highgate Hill, where late in 1856 Rev. John Oliver became Warden. Day-to-day supervision was carried out by a Lady Principal and unpaid lady Sisters. Inmates stayed for two years, learning habits of obedience, sobriety and industry, and those who thought this too long were invited to compare two years with the eternity that awaited the unrepentant sinner. Laundry and kitchens were used for training as well as to service the community and contribute to its funds. But, the first annual report noted, the Council was 'unwilling to press either kind of labour as a means of profit, lest an excess of work should give inmates an aversion to the discipline of the house'. St Mary Magdalene was not a House of Correction but a House of Mercy. There was no system of coercion as in reformatories; instead, the influence of the Sisters would be felt through their concern for the wrongdoers in this 'new effort of the Church of England to recover some of her lost daughters, so that many who now walk the streets of this our Babylon as outcasts, may one day be found within the gates of the New Jerusalem, being cleansed from their sins and made whole in the Blood of the Lamb'.

Rev. Burrows was one of thirteen clergy on the management council, and the annual reports also record a donation of one pound from William Rossetti in 1857 – perhaps paid on his sister's behalf, as she had no independent income. Appeals for money were continuous – it cost some £20 a year to maintain each penitent – and local churches held collections on its behalf. Staff were also sought: Rev. Oliver appealed regularly for volunteers who for the love of Christ would undertake the blessed work of reclaiming their fallen sisters, and

who by sympathy, by cautious discipline, by affectionate watchfulness, will teach them to hate what has been pleasant to them, and to love what they have despised, that so after a while they may go forth again into the world and be able to serve amid the ordinary temptations of life, the merciful Saviour whom they have learnt to serve and love in retirement.

A vivid picture of how the Penitentiary appeared to Christina on her first visit was given in the first issue of the *English Woman's Journal*, in an an unsigned article probably by Mary Howitt. Escorted round by the Warden, she saw in the laundry ten girls clad in grey or blue gingham dresses and white caps, working in silence. Others were sewing in the classrooms used for religious and domestic training. In the dormitories each inmate had a sleeping cubicle with bedstead and washstand, which they were allowed to decorate with holy mottoes and pictures; one print, showing Christ on a narrow bridge over a deep chasm stretching out his hands to a frail girl on the tottering plank, particularly struck the writer as 'not bad in an artistic point of view' and very moving when one knew it was placed over her pillow by the poor penitent herself. Each dormitory also contained a bedroom with

an interior window allowing night-time surveillance by the resident
Sister.

The chapel, where penitents gathered for prayers several times a
day, had Christ's words of forgiveness to Mary Magdalene emblaz-
oned over the altar. And, the visitor went on,

> Kneeling amidst these unhappy girls snatched from a hell upon earth,
> with the sunshine streaming in through the clear windows upon the
> white capped heads, and bowed grey and lilac forms, and in the hushed
> silence to hear the Warden's voice chant forth 'O God the Father of
> Heaven, have mercy upon us miserable sinners!', and then those young
> penitent voices reply 'O God the Father of heaven, have mercy upon us
> miserable sinners!' brought sudden tears to my eyes . . .

At the time of her visit, two Sisters were on duty, each in charge of a
separate class. They wore muslin caps and black dresses, with a string
of black beads and a crucifix (not a rosary, since this was an Anglican
house). Both spoke with touching devotion of their mission and the
'heavenly peacefulness of their own lives'; and one put out yet another plea for assistance, saying

> I only wish that we could persuade more ladies to join us in our labour.
> They do not know how much their aid is wanted; how holy is the life, or
> what an internal joy would animate their souls. And many ladies need
> sacrifice no really sacred worldly tie by joining us, for we can return to the
> world whenever we cease to feel our duty is here. At any time of sickness
> of sorrow in our own families we can return to our homes, for we are
> bound by no vow.

It was an appeal of this kind that Christina heeded in becoming an
Associate at Highgate. Here she was known as 'Sister Christina',
though the Penitentiary was in no sense a formal religious order. The
work took up a major part of her time for several years, yet has
received little attention in accounts of her life – chiefly, one supposes,
because she did not advertise her work there. William mentioned it
briefly to her biographer, and in editing her letters he added a note to
1861, saying that 'Highgate' referred to an institution for 'the reclamation and protection of women leading a vicious life: Christina stayed
there from time to time, but not for lengthy periods together, taking
part in the work'. In the memoir prefacing her collected poems he
made no reference at all to the Penitentiary.

It was not a secret, however. The exact date of her joining the staff
remains unknown, but by summer 1859 she was spending relatively
long periods on duty, for in August she told Mrs Heimann that she

had hardly seen Mr Scott during his annual visit to London because she had been 'away almost the whole time at Highgate'. Mrs Heimann clearly knew what this meant.

Curiously enough, at this date Gabriel was also involved with street-walkers. He had finally brought the relationship with Lizzie to an end, and in early summer 1858 returned to London, fancy free. Soon after-wards, strolling in one of the riverside pleasure gardens – known places of assignation and sexual commerce – his attention was caught by a buxom, golden-haired young woman, who laughingly tossed nutshells in his direction. She went under the name of Fanny Corn-forth and was immediately taken back to his apartment in Chatham Place, to sit for his picture of a 'fallen woman', untouched since 1854. In the months that followed, with Fanny and fellow painters George Boyce and Val Prinsep, Gabriel took to exploring London's low life – the drinking and dancing establishments around Piccadilly Circus, the cigar divans, the little shops in the arcades, and the disreputable theatres with *poses plastiques*, the contemporary equivalent of strip shows – all the many locations where respectable women did not go. He painted Fanny regularly, enjoying her company, and teased his friends for their primmer attitudes. Once, he paid a prostitute to accost Ned Jones, telling her the young man was eager but shy. And he completed a poem with a sympathetic portrayal of a whore:

> Lazy laughing languid Jenny,
> Fond of a kiss and fond of a guinea . . .

who is contrasted with the narrator's pure cousin:

> Of the same lump (as it is said)
> For honour and dishonour made,
> Two sister vessels, here is one,
>
> It makes a goblin of the sun,
> So pure – so fall'n!

To make the subject discreetly plain, he added as epigraph a truncated quotation from Shakespeare: 'Vengeance of Jenny's case! Fie on her! Never name her, child, [if she be a whore]!'

He was pleased with the poem, but knew the subject was too bold for publication; and we do not know when or indeed whether the female members of the family became aware of Fanny's profession. It is ironic therefore that within a short while Christina's acquaintance with prostitutes was probably equal to her brother's, albeit very dif-ferent in kind.

The work at Highgate centred on domestic training and spiritual instruction in the Sunday School manner. Religion, it was discovered, had invariably been 'neglected if not quite forgotten' by penitents. This was hardly a surprise, the religious census having shown in 1853 how godless Britain's urban poor had become. So particular attention was paid to prayers, scripture readings and holy conversation – moral guidance to bring the inmates to Christ as well as improve their conduct. In this respect the chief problem, according to the Warden, was lack of self-control and the outbreaks of temper to which the girls were 'so much tempted'. To make the point he described to visitors and no doubt also to new Sisters the exemplary cases of three girls who had been tempted to relapse by stealing apples from the Park House garden – a symbolic but serious infraction of the rules. Each had heeded a personal plea to confess the fault and ended by repudiating the fruit. Considering the inmates' waywardness and violent outbursts when thwarted, he explained it was impressive that so few 'inexperienced ladies' had succeeded in retaining – not to say reclaiming – forty-three out of the forty-nine penitents received in the first year. Some inmates found the discipline irksome, and absconded to former haunts, but the drop-out rate does not seem to have been high. A book was kept of each inmate's conduct, and a dull but respectable life in domestic service was held out as the reward. Many wished to start a new life overseas, though emigration was not easy since assisted passages were only available to those of 'unblemished character'.

Christian reclamation rather than vocational training was the paramount aim; as well as chalking up the success of those discharged into employment, the Penitentiary listed the numbers baptised and confirmed – equal if not better evidence of success. From this perspective, the Sisters were engaged in mission work, where every penitent redeemed from a life of sin was a lamb brought back to safety, and every one who relapsed was a soul lost to perdition. And the voluntary nature of the Sisters' work was itself important. 'No paid matron or housekeeper with a good salary can win souls for Christ in the same way as they who are able to plead with the penitent: "We love, labour and strive for you without money and without price, because for Christ's sake we love you, care for you, long to rescue you",' wrote Rev. Oliver.

To mark the start of their 'new life', penitents received new clothes and a new name. They chose ill-advised poetic names, according to the author of the EWJ article: Gertrudes, Rosalines, Helenas, instead of Ruths, Marthas, Marys; surely, she wrote, it was injudicious to foster the love of 'romantic distinction in these poor, frail, ignorant human breasts'. She also heard with some wonderment that there appeared to be 'a latent love of poetry' in many of the girls, who brought among their possessions various volumes of verse. Being mainly gifts from former associates, these were 'dangerous reminders of the forbidden past' and confiscated; in their place a new Bible and Prayerbook were given to each departing penitent, together with 'fresh pure garments prepared for her re-entrance into the outer world'.

During Christina's time at the Penitentiary Mrs Oliver acted as Lady Principal until replaced by Scottish-born Miss Janet Walker, listed in the Census of 1861 together with Sisters Margaret Wilkinson and Annie Warman, and Charlotte Wright, porteress. According to the annual reports, there were 'seven devoted women' working as Sisters, but without fuller staff details it is not possible to say what their periods of residence were. It would seem that a fortnightly 'sleeping-in' rota operated, and that like her colleagues Christina spent regular periods on duty, in what was a serious and demanding commitment, which could not be lightly neglected.

Associate Sisters at Highgate were also urged 'to promote by every means in their power the Institution in the several spheres of life and society to which they belong'. The annual reports list various donations presumably secured by Christina, from William, aunt Eliza, Mrs Scott and Emily Seddon, now married to H. V. Tebbs. In 1860 she helped raise funds towards the purchase of Park House, at an open day held for this purpose in July. 'Though the show of company was small, the influx of funds was I believe more liberal,' Christina told Lady Trevelyan, who took an interest in a similar scheme run by the Shipmeadow Sisters. 'I mustered a tolerable array of friends for the occasion, including our dear Mrs Scott, who gave us two days of her stay in London.' This was the first time Letitia saw Christina wearing the quasi-conventual dress, with veil; in Letitia's view it was 'very becoming', though such was scarcely the Sisters' priority. She also noted that Christina was spending increasing amounts of time at Highgate, suggesting this curtailed her social availability. Some time later, presumably when Miss Walker retired, 'Sister Christina' was asked to become Lady Principal, but she declined on grounds of health, and thereafter Mrs Oliver resumed the post.

The 1861 Census provides a snapshot view of the Penitentiary during her time there, providing virtually the only information available on the inmates, who now numbered thirty-seven. Under the column headed 'Rank, Profession or Occupation' was a composite entry: 'Penitents have all been Prostitutes, for that reason their profession is not mentioned in the schedule', this is a pity, for it would be illuminating to see from which occupations the young women were predominantly drawn. Their ages ranged from sixteen to twenty-four with one exception, and most were under twenty on admission. This supports the Penitentiary's statement that it dealt not with 'hardened' whores, but with those who had made one disastrous slip. All except one were unmarried.

The Census recorded the girls' true names – Elizas, Sarahs, Ellens – but the only other information given was their place of birth. Nearly half came from London or its suburbs, a sprinkling from other southern counties, and a few from further afield, including the solitary married woman, born in Scotland, who had perhaps taken to the streets after being deserted, far from home. A number had more than one baptismal name, which was generally a sign of middle-class status, and this confirms a note in the annual reports to the effect that 'of the inmates admitted to St. Mary Magdalene Penitentiary, several have been of the higher class as regards birth and education'. Presumably their reclamation was felt to be particularly worthwhile. The absence of Irish-born penitents is explained by the fact that this was an Anglican establishment.

By this date the burgeoning Magdalen movement, as it may be called, encompassed various types of institution and outreach initiatives such as 'midnight meetings' where streetwalkers were offered tea and an introduction to the penitentiary of their choice. By 1860 there were some twenty establishments in London offering reclamation, and a 'Penitents' Guide' described the Diocesan Penitentiary at Park House, as having accommodation for a hundred girls and admitting those 'received chiefly from other Refuges, or on recommendation of a clergyman'. Denominational recruitment was certainly part of the intention, but active proselytism was never mentioned; the emphasis was on reclamation of strays to the Christian flock rather than any particular sheepfold.

We can surmise that, in 1861, what brought Ellen Pope, Emma Smith, Jemima Osbourne and the rest to Highgate was some folly or misfortune that left them destitute, unable or unwilling to return home, and reluctant to remain on the streets. Perhaps they had accepted a man's 'protection', only to find themselves deserted, without means of support. They now hoped to erase the past, to emigrate and to marry. Those with a high degree of motivation could expect to find employment, since the demand for hardworking and obedient servants – who would also be shackled by their employers' knowledge of their past – far exceeded the supply. Highgate admitted neither pregnant girls nor those with illegitimate children, for whom the workhouse and the Foundling Hospital were seen as appropriate alternatives, while those with venereal infections were sent to the Lock Hospital.

What impelled Christina to choose this field, out of the range of voluntary occupations available? Though a worthy arena for good works, it was also controversial. For one thing, prostitutes were not universally seen as either needy or deserving. For another, their profession was not a subject of which ladies should have any knowledge, let alone experience; in *Jenny*, Gabriel wrote of it as a book 'in which pure women may not look', lest its base pages 'crush the flower within the soul'. Generally speaking, penitentiary work was regarded as especially unsuitable – even contaminating – for unmarried women. Other fields of endeavour were open: around this same time, Maria for instance began working with the All Saints Sisters of the Poor, an Anglican order in Marylebone, that ran a ragged school, infirmary and hospice, while Adelaide Procter, Bessie Parkes's friend and fellow poet, much given to good works, chose to concentrate her efforts on a night shelter for homeless women.

Still in her twenties, Christina would have been considered by many too innocent to mix with social casualties of this particularly sordid kind. However, as Mary Carpenter argued in the *EWJ*, 'a true woman will surmount all obstacles by the God-sent strength of her very weakness [and] know how to keep the privacy of her individual nature guarded by an invisible but impenetrable shield'. Moral reclamation could also be seen as pre-eminently 'women's mission to women': as Emma Shepherd wrote eloquently in *An Outstretched Hand to the Fallen*, 'the purer, the more ignorant of vice the lady is who seeks them, the greater the influence she has'.

From her later life and writings, it is clear that Christina felt much compassion for the poor, but had a particular horror of moral evil. Her guiding parable was not the Good Samaritan but the Lost Sheep. Unlike those who, according to Acton, believed that 'once a harlot, always a harlot', she regarded all the strays of Highgate as reclaimable lambs.

She felt a deeper sympathy, too, despite a formidable moral sense that in nowise condoned or excused their conduct. When a few years later Gabriel objected to one of her poems on illegitimacy, her defence was spirited. The subject might be unpleasant, but that was no reason for censoring it, she replied, for

whilst it may truly be argued that unless white could be black and Heaven Hell my experience (thank God) precludes me from hers, yet I don't see why "the Poet mind" should be less able to construct her from its own inner consciousness than a hundred other unknown quantities.

A number of ballads written during the years of her association with Highgate show that her creative imagination or 'poet mind' was also able to enter into the experience of seduction and betrayal that was commonly held to start young harlots on the road to ruin. Penitents were generally forbidden to talk of their past activities and though

Christina must have been aware of their case histories, she was not encouraged to discuss such matters outside the institution. Hence in part the cloak of secrecy that still surrounds her work there, but also the oblique impact on her writing. Indirectly, she recognised a certain relation between herself and the Highgate penitents, such as did not preclude her from understanding their 'inner consciousness' even if she did not share their actual experience of sin, which surely stemmed from her own religious formation under Pusey and Dodsworth, that placed particular emphasis on the dangers of temptation and the blessings of penitence. 'Fallen girls' like Jemima Osbourne and the rest were seen by the sisters as weak and culpable sinners who easily succumbed to tempting desires. These took a sexual form but were seldom attributed to carnal impulses; rather, the girls were believed to have 'fallen' through more mundane or worldly lusts – for fine clothes, jewellery, good food, an easy life. Vanity, greed, envy and sloth rather than concupiscence were the underlying faults. Indeed, one writer went further, asserting that most fallen women were guilty of much less, having yielded to sexual desires only 'from a weak generosity that cannot refuse anything to the passionate entreaties of the man they love'.

As with the servant class in general, wayward young women such as those at Highgate were held to be impulsive, inattentive, given to instant gratification and outbursts of rage. Christina's poems and stories show how vividly she interpreted moral injunctions and how gravely she censured herself for sins of vanity, indolence and anger. While she knew she was 'precluded' from the penitents' experiences, she felt in other ways equally susceptible to sin – there but for the grace of God! Her nightmares had a carnal quality and it is possible, given the way in which the 'social evil' was generally discussed, that she felt, obscurely, that any self-indulgence or ill-temper paved the way for greater transgression. Many of her poems convey a powerful sense of being outcast by sin, just as they express the deep disgust and self-loathing that was urged upon young penitents. Consistently, her God was Christ the Redeemer who rescued strayed sheep and cleansed them with his suffering, so that they might be reborn in innocence and purity. The Highgate girls could not hope for quite such ecstasy in domestic service, or even in Australia, but spiritual reclamation was undoubtedly the key to success, and the Sisters were fully conscious of the redemptive Christ-like nature of their task.

In *The Magdalen's Friend*, a journal for those involved in rescue work, which Christina was perhaps encouraged to read while working at Highgate, Emma Shepherd appealed emotionally for women to join the cause:

English Ladies, have you ever analysed these two words – 'a Sister' – though 'fallen'? Yes, high-born, gently-bred, delicately-nurtured Ladies, that poor Outcast, upon whom you cast an eye of scorn and loathing as perhaps she tramped up Regent Street this morning, looking wistfully at your luxurious carriage, with its warm wrappings from the cold, carrying you from shop to shop in quest of some small trifle; – that poor, weary, outwardly-hardened, sin-debased creature – a victim to man's brutal requirements – is, in the sight of our most holy God, your *Sister* . . .

. . . think for ten minutes of midnight streets, cold pavements, dreary door-steps, dark corners, on which, perhaps, the eye of God alone then looks; – picture these filled with women, young girls, your Sisters, once fair and loved as you, now debased and humbled and degraded to the level of the brutes, either cursing or drinking or quarrelling or following deeds of darkness such as your mind never*can* picture; and then turn your head on your pillow, and bless that gracious God who has kept you *unfallen* in the eyes of the world, though perhaps equally guilty in the sight of Him to whom sin is sin, and who will visit for an unholy thought as much as for an unholy deed; 'whose eyes are in *every* place, beholding the evil and the good'. Yes, your *Sister*; despise her not; – loathe her not; let the poet's words be proved *untrue*:

And every woe a tear can claim

Except an erring sister's shame.

Oh, pity her; look kindly on her; perhaps such a kindly look may yet win her!

One can only wonder whether Christina ever felt moved to suggest to Gabriel that those 'erring sisters' of hers who served as model for *Jenny* or the fallen women in his paintings would be greeted with much compassion, as well as firmness, if they applied to the retraining programme at Highgate.

17

Girls and Goblins

OWING TO WORK at Highgate, Christina wrote relatively little verse during the first half of 1859. But on 27 April – her mother's birthday and thus exactly seventeen years since her first preserved poem – she completed her longest composition to date and eventually her most famous work. She called it *A Peep at the Goblins* and dedicated it to her sister: 'to M.F.R.' reads the line below the title in the notebook. Better known under its final title *Goblin Market*, this was directly inspired by the work of the Penitentiary, though its composition also included many other autobiographical elements. It has always attracted critical attention, appropriate to its intrinsic literary importance, but as Christina's masterpiece it also represents a major event in her life story, as well as the key event in her poetic career. Without this poem, she would have been an accomplished poet; with it, she became an exciting one.

It is a poem about two sisters, who live like Hero on the frontier with fairyland, and are forbidden to have dealings with fruit-selling goblins. Laura succumbs to temptation, and then wastes away, inwardly poisoned. To save her, Lizzie risks her own life in securing a second taste of the fruit, by which intervention Laura is restored to health. Later, Christina insisted that the poem was not an allegory, but it is not simply a fanciful tale either, and though its full meanings are the subject of endless debate, the overall message is relatively straightforward: it is a poem about temptation, resistance and redemption. The girl who succumbs, choosing the goblin delights she knows are prohibited, suffers the spiritual effects of wrongdoing, as her blighted soul sickens and dies. She is saved only through the action of her heroic sister, who risks and withstands temptation on her behalf and thereby defeats the power of evil. Like Jesus in the Christian gospels, the redeeming figure participates in the sinful world but remains undefiled; through this agency the fallen soul can regain grace and blossom again. In essence therefore the poem is a simple expression of the redemptive beliefs that took its author to work with repentant prostitutes at Highgate.

It is however presented not as parable but as fairytale in the manner of Mother Goose or the German *Sagen und Märchen* that the young Rossettis had read with Dr Heimann. In origin, all such tales were exemplary, devised for moral purposes, so a long tradition lay behind the choice of genre, although by the mid-nineteenth century there was a strong competing interest in the purely folkloric elements of such stories, from which Christina's goblins derive. One source for this lay in the *Fairy Mythology*, compiled by Papa's friend Thomas Keightley, with whom the family were still in touch; indeed, some time in the late 1850s Christina and William went to visit Keightley at his home in Kent. His book was illustrated with dwarves, elves and pixies, and included long quotations from *A Midsummer Night's Dream* in which Titania's elves feed Bottom on some of the same delicious fruits as appear in the goblins' baskets: 'apricocks and dewberries ... purple grapes, green figs and mulberries'. In one of the folktales cited, moreover, humans are warned against fairy merchants, for death is the traditional penalty for eating fairy food.

In 1850, Keightley's anthology was reissued with new material taken from *Traditions, Legends, Superstitions and Sketches of Devonshire on the Borders of the Tamar and Tavy*, a collection compiled by Anna Eliza Bray. Now the Rossettis knew not only Mr Keightley but also Mrs Bray, who was Mamma's cousin and wife of the Tavistock clergyman whose 'equivocal compliments' on *Verses* had caused Christina such mortification. When Rev. Bray died in 1857, his widow removed to London and renewed acquaintance with her relatives, but in any case Christina was familiar with Mrs Bray's later book, *A Peep at the Pixies, or Legends of the West*, published with illustrations by Phiz in 1854. Later, Christina confirmed the deliberate emulation in her own poem. 'In the first instance I named it "A Peep at the Goblins" in imitation of my Cousin Mrs Bray's "A Peep at the Pixies"', 'she wrote, 'but my brother Dante Gabriel Rossetti substituted the greatly improved title as it now stands.'

This title change rather usefully deflected comparison with Mrs Bray's volume, for within *A Peep at the Pixies* is one tale bearing a striking resemblance to *Goblin Market*. While travelling to a distant chapel, Serena of Tintagel hears fairy music and is so beguiled by the sight of the fairy musician that she fails to complete her prayers at the appointed time. She then falls into a decline, wracked by desire to hear the music again. Her father confessor confirms that this is a pixie snare; pixies have a spiteful power over those negligent of religious duty. Serena consults a wizard who gives her a spell to say when she reaches a waterfall; in doing so she topples into the pool and drowns. There is no happy moral ending, but the germ of *Goblin Market* is surely here.

In 1859 Mrs Bray reissued her late husband's *Poetical Remains*, which included a fairy tale called *The Rural Sisters* in which beautiful but selfish Mira loses the Prince to plain but high-souled Flora, through the intervention of a fairy godmother not unlike the rosy applewoman in *Nick*. This theme of two sisters also went into the making of *Goblin Market*, and as the *Remains* incidentally included Bray's embarrassing lines on Christina's *Verses*, it is ironic that her masterpiece should thus link up with his unfortunate response to her juvenile work.

A third immediate source for the storyline was *The Fairy Family*, published in 1857 with an illustration by Gabriel's friend Ned Jones, in which *The Pixies* is a Devonshire tale of two similar sisters, industrious Mary and idle Alice. Like Rev. Bray's poem, this is a straightforward reworking of traditional material. But the preface contains a statement that connects with *Goblin Market*'s moral purpose, in which the author complained that while 'fairy lore' was supremely attractive for young readers, it was all too often 'moral poison', full of indelicacies and excess. Moreover, moral instruction should be worked into the structure of a story, not tacked to the end. Like *Goblin Market*, *The Fairy Family* had higher aims, for 'from the Nursery to the Study is a wide step ... the Author will have somewhat mistaken his purpose and failed in his efforts, if they be not read with profit by the intelligent child, and with interest by the indulgent reader of maturer years.'

Pixies are not goblins, however, nor do goblins feature in the *Fairy Mythology* or the Devon tales. Indeed, traditionally, goblins are not fairies at all, but full-size devils, and as such are named among Satan's crew in *Paradise Lost*. In *A Winter's Tale*, Mamillius offers to tell a seasonally sad tale, of sprites and goblins, set in a graveyard. In *Jenny* Gabriel had written of the whore's shame making 'a goblin of the sun', turning fair to foul, but I suspect that Christina's goblins came more directly from *Comus*, where the sorcerer's crew are 'headed like sundry sorts of wild beasts but otherwise like men', and the action describes a similar contest between evil and innocence.

The goblins' wares of course invoke the symbolic fruits of the Bible – the forbidden fruit with which the serpent tempts Eve, as well as the 'fruits that thy soul lusted after' in Revelation, which have departed with the fall of Babylon leaving the merchants of the earth, incidentally, to weep and mourn, 'for no man buyeth their merchandise anymore'. Fruit in the form of ripe pears was a symbol of the primal choice between good and evil in the *Confessions* of St Augustine, while, as it happened, apples in the gardens of Park House also featured in Rev. Oliver's account of the penitents' moral training at Highgate.

However, the goblins' enticing cries come from the street pedlars of Christina's childhood, recalling, as from *The Dead City* onwards, the mouthwatering delights brought home by Papa for his eager children. One of their earliest books, William Hone's *Everyday Book*, illustrated a London barrow woman, crying her wares:

> Round and sound,
> Two-pence a pound
> Cherries! rare ripe cherries!
>   . . .
>
> Cherries a ha'penny a stick!
> Come and pick! come and pick!
> Who comes? who comes!

and other childhood recollections permeate the poem. It has been suggested that the goblin men recall the inviting but forbidden street life of Charlotte Street, with Laura's susceptibility figured on Christina's own wilful, impulsive nature, disciplined by Maria's stronger sense of duty. There was a closer parallel still, described by Christina herself in the wild strawberry incident at Holmer Green when she, immediately tempted to pick and eat, was restrained by Maria, only to find the ripe berry hollowed out by a slug, transformed from a delightful treat into a rotten husk, rather like the goblins' fruit, fair without but foul within.

Memories of Holmer Green were in her mind when *Goblin Market* was being written. 'Certain destructions are so miserably irreparable,' she told Pauline Trevelyan. 'Some of my pleasantest early recollections are of a little cottage in Buckinghamshire which we frequented as children: and I have just now learned with disgust that an unconscientious steward has bodily made away with Penn Wood near where it stood.' This fear was exaggerated – part of Penn Wood survived – but it reveals her nostalgia for lost childhood delights.

All the ingredients that went to the making of *Goblin Market*, however, do not explain its overall effect, and in particular the powerful undercurrent of eroticism that drives the verse. This dimension needs teasing out delicately: for one thing, it can be reasonably argued that any such approach is anachronistic, raised by post-Freudian ideas of psychological repression and given rein in recent responses – notoriously that which reprinted *Goblin Market* in 1965 with erotic illustrations in *Playboy* magazine, but also evident in scholarly articles. Moreover, unlike criticism, biography should not concern itself with the work's reception today; erotic readings of *Goblin Market* are our creations, not Christina's. Goblin fruit was not intended by the author as a symbol of sexual desire, nor received as such by her original audience, for both Christina and her readers were accustomed to interpret 'forbidden fruit' as pleasures and self-indulgences of various kinds. In this context, the mouth-watering urgency of Laura's longing for the ripe fruits, which now seems so expressive of sexual desire, is also that of childish greed, the passionate hunger for instant gratification, which like Lizzie adults learn to withstand. In this figuration the goblin fruits are 'all that infantile libido yearns for, pleasure unlimited, eternal dessert'. This is also the essence of desire: once attained, it ceases to satisfy, vainly driving the sensual urge to repetition, seeking to regain that first, orgasmic joy. By denying gratification, the ascetic soul triumphs over desire, and is no longer in thrall to the senses. Contentment thus comes, paradoxically, from self-denial.

But the poem's cadences are nevertheless erotic, and the excitement of the work resides not in its allegory (William 'more than once heard Christina say that she did not mean anything profound by this fairy tale – it is not a moral apologue') but in its tensions, shifts and layers of suggestive meaning, amongst which the sexual dimension is barely buried. As William also noted, cautiously, the incidents were 'at any rate suggestive, and different minds may be likely to read different messages into them'. Sex is indeed glimpsed when the sisters recall the case of Jeanie, poetic sister to her near-namesake in Gabriel's poem, who in accepting goblin gifts tastes the 'joys brides hope to have' and dies – a clear allusion to pre-marital experience. When Lizzie goes to trade with the goblins, she politely offers her penny, 'mindful of Jeanie', and is described in metaphors used of sexual conquest in a long Renaissance tradition. Most importantly, moreover, the goblin assault on Laura is a seduction, while that on Lizzie is attempted rape. Laura succumbs to the sensuous appeal of the fruit – figs 'to fill your mouth', so 'sweet to tongue', 'sweeter than honey, stronger than wine' – in a manner vividly expressive of female desire. She 'sucked and sucked and sucked the more . . . sucked until her lips were sore'. By contrast, when they cannot tempt, cajole or bully Lizzie, the men turn to violence in order to force their fruit into her mouth:

> Lashing their tails
> They trod and hustled her,
> Elbowed and jostled her,
> Clawed with their nails . . .
> Twitched her hair out by the roots,
> Stamped upon her tender feet,
> Held her hands and squeezed their fruits
> Against her mouth to make her eat . . .

As an image of ejaculation, the 'juice that syruped all her face' after this assault is the more powerful for being also the infant experience of refusing to eat, with spoonfuls dribbling against clenched lips. Indeed, the picture itself is reminiscent of Papa's early reference to little Christina refusing to open her mouth to take her medicine.

Finally when Laura gains a second taste from her sister's lips, the imagery is again orgasmic: she is

> Like the watchtower of a town
> Which an earthquake shatters down,
> Like a lightning-stricken mask,
> Like a wind-uprooted tree
> Spun about,
> Like a foam-topped waterspout
> Cast down headlong in the sea . . .

Laura's payment for the fruits with a golden curl is traditionally sexual, consciously echoing the amorous conquest in Pope's *Rape of the Lock*. If, as *On The Convent Threshold* reveals, Christina had been reading *Eloisa and Abelard*, it is likely that she also read the story of Belinda, and the assault on her virtue by the Baron:

> He saw, he wished, and to the prize aspired.
> Resolved to win, he meditates the way,
> By force to ravish, or by fraud betray . . .

As my own schoolbook edition of *The Rape of the Lock* indicates, it has been possible to read this 'most airy, ingenious and delightful of Pope's works' as a simple burlesque on 'the fashions and foibles of the reign of Queen Anne' rather than a comic account of aristocratic rape. In much the same way *Goblin Market* half-conceals its sexual meaning in an ostensible fairytale, as a similar violation is suffered by Laura at the cost of a lock of hair. Amongst other things *Goblin Market* is thus a moral and poetic answer to Pope. Both Belinda and Laura are beguiled by worldly delights, and both 'fall', but whereas Belinda sees her ravished curl vanish forever among the stars, Laura's virtue is restored by Lizzie's intervention – as Victorian morality replaced Augustan cynicism. *The Rape of the Lock* is also in part a fairy fantasy, peopled with airy sylphs and dismal gnomes – figures which suggest an additional source for Christina's goblins.

At some level, therefore, the sexual dimension was intentional. We can't guess whether Christina, who at the age of twenty-eight had never experienced so much as a sexually passionate kiss, would necessarily have recognised sexual desire in herself; had she done so, she might not have been able to write as she did. Her deployment of erotic feeling in *Goblin Market* was therefore largely unconscious, derived from childish memories of sensual desire and perhaps other arousals. As some critics argued, this is a poem about the unconscious fantasy life of children, drawn 'from the night side of the Victorian nursery ... where childish cruelty and childish sexuality come to the fore', or from the sexual romping of the Rossetti children, evoking the archetypal desire to violate the sibling incest taboo.

But there was an area of the author's adult life where ideas of temptation and pleasurable self-indulgence were openly linked to sexuality, and from where she could draw deliberate, if figurative, links. This was her work at Highgate. Here, it was believed that young girls 'fell' from virtue into prostitution not from innate wickedness but from weakness and vanity. Like Laura, they were coaxed and bullied into unsanctioned sex by smooth-tongued seducers, who sounded 'full of loves' until, having gained their ends, goblin-like, they deserted their victims, deaf to all appeals.

It therefore seems very probable that *Goblin Market* was conceived as an engaging but moral tale for the Penitentiary, designed to delight and instruct and pitched midway between the nursery and the study, in order to be accessible both to intelligent children and imaginative adults. And if not written explicitly for the girls at Highgate – there is no evidence that such storytelling formed any part of the Sisters' instruction – it surely evoked their situation, and the relation of fallen and redemptive 'sisters'.

Technically, the poem demands that it be read aloud, with its swift pace, colloquial phrases and free-wheeling rhymes; half the pleasure of the verse is lost if read silently, as the response of more than one audience indicates. Christina's publisher Alexander Macmillan read the poem to his wife and family, for example, to see if they liked it as much as he did. Then, he told Gabriel, he read it to an evening class of working-men. 'They seemed at first to wonder whether I was making fun of them; by degrees they got as still as death, and when I finished there was a tremendous burst of applause,' he wrote. 'I wish Miss Rossetti could have heard it.'

Furthermore, the message of *Goblin Market* was appropriate not only to the girls at Highgate, who were perceived to have the moral immaturity of children, but also to more sophisticated readers like the staff at Highgate, especially those schooled in Tractarian exegesis. For the poem's sisters are also Sisters in Christ, able to interpret accurately such things as moral temptation and spiritual sickness. Rescued from the fate of Jeanie by a sister's love, a regenerated Laura becomes at the conclusion a wife, mother and also herself a teller of exemplary tales, and thus 'a model of aspiration for anyone with the desire to change for the better and the belief that with the help of a "sister" good can be brought out of evil'.

Rev. Oliver used the orchard apples at Park House with just such didactic aim. One day, he explained, he found on the ground an apple with a bite out of it, and demanded a confession, from 'some one whose conscience must now be reproaching them with falsehood'. Almost at once the culprit cried out: 'Oh, Warden! I did it! I did it! Oh, why did I disobey for a nasty apple? I don't know why I took it . . . Oh, forgive me!' Indeed the poor girl was so stricken that she lost her appetite, and fell ill from 'distress of mind'. But the story of the third apple was most compelling, for it concerned a girl 'of most violent passions' who appeared at times fairly possessed with a devil and whose temper had been curbed, only to suddenly return. Rev. Oliver was convinced there must be a reason. So he asked what had happened to change her thus unaccountably. After a pause she blurted out, 'The nasty apple! I have not had a moment's peace since I took it'. Her 'evil spirit' had evidently again been aroused, and it seemed no easy matter to dispel him. Oliver warned that there was no use her remaining in the Penitentiary, 'but that if she returned to her old courses she knew well enough what waited her – *death, death, body and soul!*'. Nevertheless the girl preferred to leave, and was given back her old clothes. When the moment of discharge came, however,

she dashed about her dress with her hands as though she would have forced it from her body, and followed me to the outer gate in a most excited state of feeling. As I applied the key to the lock I reminded her of God's mercy to her, of the doom awaiting her . . . The door stood wide open, and the street was before her. A most agonising cry burst from her, as if it would rend her frame; such a cry as that I had never heard before; a cry that was unearthly, it seemed stifled in her throat, yet as if it burst forth through every pore of her skin. She threw herself from before the door against the adjoining fence, clutched at her clothes, buried her face in them, and stood convulsed from head to foot.

I instantly closed the gate and, after standing for a short time, took her by the arm and led her back into my room . . . She has been since then very quiet.

In *Goblin Market*, Laura is similarly convulsed by remorse in a violent struggle of the soul. Like the girl in Oliver's simple allegory, her decline exemplifies the Pauline teaching that the wages of sin are death, while her final domestic happiness is an emblem of the promise held out to the penitents at Highgate. Lizzie's redemption of Laura thus both enacts the moral aspects of the Highgate training – firmly but politely decline goblin invitations to what you know is lax or dangerous; refuse to take what has not been paid for; mount a stout defence against cajolery, insult and force – and makes explicit the high Anglican typology of the Virgin Mary who redeems the error of sinful Eve. Like Eve, Laura is sentenced to suffer, while Lizzie wears the Virgin's colours of white, blue and gold. In enjoining Laura to 'eat me, drink me, love me' Lizzie also typifies Christ in the Eucharist as the means of salvation, in a symbolic meal that reverses the taste of forbidden fruit. 'For Christ's sake we love you, care for you, long to rescue you' were the words used by the Highgate Sisters, in an almost exact replication of rhythm.

The double meaning of sister in *Goblin Market* thus gains a dimension from Sister Christina's role at Highgate, but leaves in limbo the explicit dedication of the poem to her real sister: 'M. F. R.' on the manuscript. Is the poem's conclusion that 'there is no friend like a sister ... To fetch one if one goes astray, To lift one if one totters down...' to be read personally as well as professionally? Disclosing the dedication William commented: 'Christina, I have no doubt, had some particular occurrence in her mind, but what it was I know not,' adding rather ominously that the poems immediately preceding - *Goblin Market* were marked by a 'more than normal amount of melancholy and self-reproach', as if to hint that Maria had saved her sister from going astray in some specific instance. To Christina's biographer he added privately that while he couldn't remember any actual circumstances, he certainly agreed that the lines 'indicate *something*: apparently Christina considered herself to be chargeable with some sort of spiritual backsliding, against which Maria's influence had been exerted beneficially'. This has led to some rather sensational speculations, to the effect that Maria prevented Christina eloping with James Collinson after his marriage, or intervened to break her supposed infatuation with Scott after her Newcastle trip. Neither seems the least plausible. There are two other possibilities. Firstly, Maria may simply have asked her sister for a poem with a happy ending. The family teased Christina about her poetic gloominess, and at some stage Maria also criticised her opacity. 'Perhaps the nearest approach to a method I can lay claim to was a distinct aim at conciseness,' wrote Christina to a later inquirer; 'after a while I received a hint from my sister that my love of conciseness tended to make my writing obscure, and I then endeavoured to avoid obscurity as well as diffuseness.' This advice would have made a grateful dedication altogether apt, as would a second possibility, that Maria had encouraged Christina to seek work at Highgate, arguing that such godly and meaningful occupation would help lift her despondency. Christina certainly regarded Maria as a spiritual guide, who acted as a sisterly shepherd. Beyond this may also lie shared memories of Holmer Green raised by the threatened destruction of Penn Wood. Perhaps around this time they recalled the wild strawberry, making Maria an appropriate dedicatee for a 'childish' poem about tempting fruit and sisterly intervention.

Certainly, though prompted by the work at Highgate, *Goblin Market*, with its wealth of imagery drawn from childhood, tapped deep emotional and autobiographical roots. In her inner heart, Christina felt a strong affinity with the sister who succumbs, in the twilight world of blurred boundaries that spell danger. In this sense, the poem enacts a spiritual struggle for clarity. The goblins are neither men nor animals, and are seen at dusk from the rushy margins of the brook; they are both charming and baneful, furry yet cooing like doves, with ambivalent 'demure grimaces', whatever these may be. The maidens themselves are between childhood and maturity, without parents yet not orphans. They live on the borderland between the natural and supernatural world, which is always exposed to risk; this is the territory of uncertainty, where things seem what they are not. In the encounter with the goblins there is for Laura no clear line between good and evil: dizzy with confusion, she cannot tell whether it is day or night. The story thus inhabits a confused, unstable realm, part domestic, part magical, part moral and part evil, part safe and part life-threatening. It is both fecund and barren, ripe and wasted, according to viewpoint; as the moon waxes, Laura wastes and is then restored. The goblins are seen and unseen, victorious and (finally) vanquished; like the clammy monster and prudent crocodile they are both frightening and fascinating, inconstant, changeable, switching from coaxing to cuffing, as caresses turn to violence. And the poem itself is neither fish nor fowl, but switches vertiginously between fairytale and moral fable, balancing simultaneously between the genres before coming breathlessly to rest. It is difficult to guess what exact significance this invocation of liminality with its frightening yet exhilarating mix of danger and desire had for its author, yet, as in her nightmare poems, Christina seems here to have been grappling with something of profoundly ambiguous meaning, which at some level was resolved through the narrative conclusion, as Lizzie, representing the 'good self', returns to confront and defeat the goblins and thereby rescues and as it were absolves her sister. Laura's scarlet sins are not only forgiven: they are washed and made 'white as wool', just as her grey hair turns golden. On some level *Goblin Market* is also a poem of self-forgiveness for obscure trangressions.

18

Sister and Sisters

MARIA'S CONSTANT PRESENCE in Christina's life must in some ways have been oppressive – Christina never escaped being the younger sister of a more knowledgeable, virtuous and industrious woman. As Letitia observed at Warlingham, she was 'so devoted' to Maria, looking up to her with a lifelong admiration that she later expressed in several acutely sententious tributes. To Edmund Gosse, Maria appeared a harsh moral custodian over her sister, but the truth was more complex, for while Maria was certainly a spiritual guide, her cheerful energy did much to dispel Christina's mopish tendencies; indeed, as William remarked, her religious faith made her even exuberantly happy. She was no sobersides, and her robust sense of humour can be glimpsed in a letter she wrote to Scott's dog, some time after making his shaggy acquaintance. On receiving a new *carte de visite* from 'WBS', Maria replied to his companion, B. W. Olaf, Esq:

My dear Olaf,
   A thousand thanks for that dogged perseverance in the remembrance of an old friend, which has prompted you to afford me the pleasure of your own and your master's company at this morning's breakfast table. Your beaming and speaking eye, aspiring nose, feathering tail and universal shagginess, are happily rendered by the skilful photographer whom, with your never-failing discernment you have selected from among the crowd of competitors, panting to transmit to posterity your expressive features. Your master looks a thought sleepier than you would consider it wise to allow when he is in such immediate proximity to yourself; but what of that? This time he is at least bona fide W. B. Scott, not Maddens of Warsaw, still less an Italian brigand. Pray, my dear Olaf, recommend the proposer of that last hideous perpetration, the work of his worst enemy, to replace it with this; and to adorn their walls with two friends instead of one.
   Your affectionate admirer Christina sends you her tender and respectful love. She also joins my mother and myself in love to your happy possessors. Did you ever chance to meet with a work once maliciously described as 'Half hours with the worst authors'? A copy of it is here and I promise myself much pleasure and instruction from its perusal.
   Christina desires me to tell you that she is fortunate enough to own three portrait sketches of Wombats, framed and glazed. They emulate

your hairy exuberance, but your intellectual development leaves them far behind, in distance too dim to be discerned by the naked eye. Pray ask, in my name, for an extra biscuit this evening, and believe me,

Your grateful friend, Maria F. Rossetti

This teasing – not without its own shaft of malice regarding Charles Knight's book *Half Hours with the Best Authors* – is testimony both to Maria's warm affection for Scott and to her wit, which here surpassed her sister's. For despite its sprightly aspects, in correspondence Christina's attempts at humour were more often heavy-handed.

Professionally, Christina believed her sister to be 'a born teacher', and one can easily imagine that Maria was both lively and rigorous with pupils. Her education of Lucy Brown, which came to an end around 1860 when Lucy was sixteen, proved thorough and durable, though not in all ways she would have hoped: in later life Lucy rejected the religious beliefs Maria had aimed to instil. And her Italian lessons continued to be in demand, though here her skills may not have been perfect, for she admitted to some difficulty in getting pupils to any stage of fluency. 'How shall their ear be trained instinctively to feel what is not Italian even before they are sufficiently advanced to discover for themselves what is?' she asked in the preface to a text-book she later placed with an educational publisher. The answer was an ingenious and idiosyncratic system of her own devising, consisting of exercises based on retranslating passages into Italian from ultra-literal English versions. Though she claimed this method was effective, it suggests some degree of teacher's desperation.

At home, the three women shared domestic duties. As Christina explained to Mrs Heimann in the summer of 1859, William's not leaving town obliged Mamma, Maria and herself 'to divide our forces, so that one of us may always be at home keeping house for him'. In little more than a week she would be in London again 'to take Maria's place, who will then join Mamma for a month at the seaside' – where, incidentally Maria would as usual enjoy sea-bathing and 'disport herself like a fish'. Housekeeping was necessarily a female task, which had to be juggled with other duties such as Christina's spells at Highgate and Maria's commitment to the Sunday Bible Class at Christ Church which had evolved into an educational session for young women who sought self-improvement – one member, for instance, was a pupil teacher who used the class to prepare for her qualifying exam in scripture – though its purpose remained strictly devotional. As well as her Italian textbook, Maria also published a small volume, *Letters to My Bible Class* which reveal that the level of textual study was relatively high, and the tone both theological and practical. Indeed, they suggest that but for the accident of gender Maria would have made a capital ordinand, with a typical Victorian blend of biblical sternness and sympathy, tailored to the circumstances of her audience.

'Are we getting rid of our old bad habits as we get rid of dirty linen on Saturday?' she asked in a lesson on Sabbath-keeping:

> and are we putting on new and holy habits as on Sunday we put on clean clothes? . . . let us instantly set about correcting our faults and pleasing God; we have not an hour, not a minute to lose . . . Let us do well for Him the very next disagreeable duty we have to do, though it be but a very small one, perhaps nothing more than rising to fetch something wanted by another, when we should like better to be still . . .

The lasting impact of Dodsworth's millenarism was as strong on Maria as on her sister. So too was the influence of Pusey. Towards Lent, her lessons began to focus more and more fiercely on extirpating sin – 'probably the fault we have oftenest been told of at home and at school – the fault which whenever we think of death rises up first before us to make us afraid to die . . . the fault which led to the first childish sin we can remember . . .' She exhorted her pupils to confess all, and the sin she chose to dwell on reveals how firmly admonitions against self-regard had been instilled in both Rossetti sisters. 'What are the occasions of my besetting sin?' Maria asked her Bible class rhetorically:

> Perhaps I am proud; what tempts me to pride? Is it the praise of others? Then I will never say or do anything in order to obtain praise; I will conceal, as far as I can, whatever might lead anyone to praise me; if I cannot help hearing myself praised, I will inwardly beg God at the moment to keep me humbled; and then I will try to think of my sins or anything else that may humble me.
>
> Or do I feel proud when in the company of those who are less pretty or less clever or less careful of their behaviour than myself? Then I will say to myself: 'Many that are first shall be last, and the last shall be first'.

'Not to be first: how hard to learn': even more than Christina, Maria had taken this injunction to heart in relinquishing her childhood ambitions. And though it is as well to remember Maria's kindly good humour when reading this programme of self-interrogation, and to be reminded that the style was typical of contemporary practice, it is also painful to think that whenever friends commended Maria's goodness or Christina's verse, each was instantly obliged by such training to think on her sins and beg God to keep her humble. Maria was undoubtedly more able and virtuous than many around her, yet was never allowed the pleasure of being pleased with herself.

Women's ministry was a current topic of interest, particularly to those with a clear vocation for religious teaching. It was practised in a modest way by all Sunday school teachers and by those who took the scriptures out into the community – one of the Rossettis' fellow parishioners, Mrs Sara Tomlinson, regularly held prayer meetings for the female inmates of St Pancras workhouse for example. In most Churches, however, there was a bar on anything approaching public ministry, though in 1859 a pair of American evangelists named Palmer caused a minor sensation in Britain, largely owing to Mrs Palmer's preaching. This in turn prompted Catherine Booth to the defence of women's right to ministry, with a manifesto and series of prayer meetings and sermons of her own, from which she went on with her husband to found the Salvation Army. Here, gender was at least partially dissolved in the quasi-military structure and uniforms, and Mrs Booth was enabled to overcome the restrictions of her position to achieve a satisfactory public role.

No such satisfaction awaited Maria, for she was obedient to a Church that promoted women's service rather than leadership; yet all histories point to religion as a major arena for women in the Victorian age, which allowed active participation in public life without loss of gentility. Like many others, Maria was constantly alert to the possibility of 'doing good', though perhaps like Dora Greenwell she lamented the fact that all too often endeavours to help the poor proved futile: those who most needed assistance were least able to benefit from it. After Maria's death, Christina wrote up two examples of her sister's work in this field, under the title *True in the Main*. One described Mrs Bates, a valiant working woman with a chronically sick husband, whose plight first came to the attention of aunt Eliza, who 'loved souls in general and babies in particular', and made a layette for the Bates babies. Maria – 'Miss M' as she is named in the narrative – in turn befriended the family with such good effect that in time she led both husband and wife to confirmation. In return Mrs Bates was employed as a church cleaner, and also 'washed and more particularly ironed for a small connexion of paying customers' – including no doubt the Rossetti household. Thus were the deserving poor encouraged to be also devout.

A less deserving family was that of Mr Meads, a drunken and violent husband, who once kicked his wife out to shiver on the doorstep all night. Eight-year-old son Jack became a crossing sweeper, an occupation not far above begging undertaken by the most ragged children. Maria did her utmost to persuade such boys to attend school by offering to pay their fees: but 'their idleness baffled her energetic good will and to school they would not go with any approach to regularity'. Young Jack was happily more receptive:

touching his cap and looking shy and pleasant he one day accosted kind Miss M, who had already given him many a penny at his post, and asked her whether she could tell him of a night school into which he might gain admittance, 'after his day's work', said he stoutly, ready to forego even coveted book learning if incompatible with duty.

Miss M. stood still to listen. Yes, she knew of a night school kept by certain Sisters who devoted their lives to praying, teaching and other holy pursuits. She would speak to the Head Sister and pay his weekly fee ... On his part she required regularity, painstaking and strict obedience to rules. All this Jack promised.

It was a turning-point in his life. By the time of his benefactress's death, Jack was under-butler in a wealthy home; when Christina wrote to inform him that his 'staunch friend Miss M.' had died, he called to express his gratitude and sympathy.

The Sisterhood that assisted young Jack was that based at All Saints', Margaret Street, under the Rev. Upton Richards and Mother Harriet Brownlow Byron. Started in 1856, this now became the main focus of Maria's good works; in February 1860, she became an Associate Sister, making a weekly contribution to the costs of the community, and taking part in devotional and pastoral activity. Steadily, as the years passed, she aspired to the full religious life, as she had done in her teens. She had now relinquished hopes of marriage, for in February 1858 she had passed what Dora Greenwell described as 'the rubicon of thirty' – the age that was held to mark the transition from marriageability into the 'long descent' as an elderly spinster or 'old maid'. The single woman in her thirties was highly conscious of the change, wrote Greenwell, speaking from experience:

> Among men of her own age, there may be some with whom she would gladly place herself on a footing of cordiality; yet she fears to be misunderstood, lest, where she is but following a kindly social impulse, she should be suspected of looking out for a husband ... in general it would be curious, if it were not so touching, to watch the woman 'of no particular age' fading into a neutral tint long before the setting in of her autumn need have compelled the change, studiously obliterating herself from the busy foreground of life, taking up less and less room in the world, and seeming to apologize to it for even the little space she occupies.

The census of 1851 had shown a population surplus of women over men, raising the cry 'What shall we do with our Old Maids?'. Though answered constructively by many, this nevertheless meant that spinsters regarded their situation as a problem and yet recoiled from drawing attention to it. For as long as the primary role of women was seen as marriage and motherhood, it was hard for single women to avoid being labelled as those who had 'lost' in the competition for a man. 'Married life is a woman's profession,' pronounced the *Saturday Review* in 1859. 'Of course by not getting a husband, or losing him, she may find that she is without resources. All that can be said of her is that she has failed in business.' But it was not in the interests of society to assist spinsters to find independent means of support, for this would undermine the basis of marriage.

And so the sociable, ardent and able Maria devoted the best years of her maturity to teaching Italian, to God's work among the needy, and to her family and friends. Scott, who shared none of his wife's devotionalism, nevertheless felt a strong affinity with Maria that is testament to her gift for friendship. As he wrote on her death, there was something in her 'way of untiring industry, and continually doing something in the way of duty, that made, I used to fancy, a kind of bond between us – and then she was always ready to come down to us in Newcastle, and make sunshine in a shady place . . .'

As it transpired, in the spring of 1859 Scott gained a new friend, who rather displaced Maria in his affections, and it is a measure of his friendship with the Rossettis that Miss Boyd soon became one of their friends too. She was, as he told Pauline Trevelyan, 'a lady who came to me about learning to paint and whom I have in friendly way been doing my best to make an artist'. Recently bereaved, she was weak but 'full of spirits and enthusiastic' about the new pleasure she had discovered in painting. 'Such an amiable good soul she is and such a sweet candid expression she has!' Born in 1825, Alice Boyd was already past the rubicon. Paternally she belonged to the Scottish gentry – her brother was hereditary laird of a decaying castle on the Ayrshire coast – but she lived with her maternal grandfather in Newcastle. Introduced to WBS as a potential pupil, she was made welcome by Letitia and at once recognised by Scott as soul-mate; theirs was, he wrote, a true marriage of minds, 'the perfect friendship, the ambition of my life'. Alice reciprocated his feelings, but she was also a devout churchgoer and eminently respectable woman, who wished to compromise neither Letitia or herself, and there was no sense in which the friendship was clandestine.

In time, the Scotts and Alice became known to their friends as the Sun, Moon and Star. Curiously, however, in October 1859 Christina accepted another invitation to visit Newcastle, and in subsequent weeks composed a clutch of poems on romantic triangles, female rivalry and unkind sisterhood. The first, completed on 18 November, was a ballad now known as *Cousin Kate* in which one woman 'falls' while her cousin becomes his lordship's bride. The betrayed woman is bitter towards her rival, claiming that had the roles been reversed, she would have spurned such a suitor:

O cousin Kate, my love was true,
  Your love was writ in sand:
If he had fooled not me but you,
  If you stood where I stand,
He'd not have won me with his love
  Not bought me with his land;
I would have spit into his face
  And not have taken his hand.

She is also triumphant that she has a son while her ennobled cousin is childless.

Coming so soon after *Goblin Market*, this might seem an appropriate piece for the Highgate inmates, with its cautionary tale of folly and betrayal in accessible language. But the final claim that a love-child is better than a wedding-ring was hardly an exemplary moral, and the cruelty of the verses is disturbing. Why is Kate so reviled and mocked? Where is the sisterly sympathy she surely deserves even if – especially because – she has 'won' this noble blackguard?

Similar unkind imaginings appeared again in *Noble Sisters*, a ballad dialogue in which one speaker is secretly in love with a young squire, whom the other turns away, falsely saying her sister is already married – malice that is barely justified by her allegation that an elopment will shame the family name. And in the third poem, *Sister Maude* the drama is even more vicious: jealous Maude has both betrayed her sister's love and caused her lover's death:

Who told my mother of my shame,
  Who told my father of my dear?
Oh who but Maude, my sister Maude,
  Who lurked to lie and peer ...

You might have spared his soul, sister,
  Have spared my soul, your own soul too:
Though I had not been born at all,
  He'd never have looked at you.

The conclusion is maledictory as Maude is roundly cursed:

My father may wear a golden gown,
  My mother a crown may win;
If my dear and I knocked at Heaven-gate
  Perhaps they'd let us in:
But sister Maude, O sister Maude,
  Bide you with death and sin.

Not surprisingly, perhaps, both *Sister Maude* and *Cousin Kate* were later suppressed by Christina. Yet something prompted their melodramatic texts, so strongly oppositional to the sisterly theme of *Goblin Market*. Perhaps something in the Scott-Boyd relationship, or Maria's displacement by Alice, prompted this dramatisation. Or perhaps at a deeper level Christina was casting out some demon of her own. By naming the evil sister Maude, perhaps she was bidding farewell to the wicked 'little sister' that dwelt within and had always envied Maria's greater goodness and loveability, and thereby taking responsibility, at the end of a year of good sisterhood, for the base feelings once entertained by the creator of Maude Foster, Maude Clare and Sister Maude? This was her last heroine bearing that name.

Shortly before *Goblin Market*, Christina wrote a poem acknowledging her poetic sisters, or foremothers. In keeping with the female tradition, this was a poignant lyric, each stanza containing the same fourth line, like a refrain:

> Downstairs with friends I laugh, I sport, I jest
>   But in my solitary room above
> I turn my face in silence to the wall;
>   My heart is breaking for a little love.

Though heartfelt, the familiar melancholy was more importantly a homage, for to the manuscript is attached a footnote reading 'LEL by EBB', in reference to Barrett Browning's poem, *LEL's Last Question*. This in turn referred to a poem written by Letitia Landon on her last voyage, with the appeal: 'Do you think of me as I think of you, My friends, my friends?' 'We all do ask the same,' Barrett Browning responded:

> And little in the world the Loving do
> But sit (among the rocks) and listen for
> The echo of their own love evermore –
> 'Do you think of me as I think of you?'

But, she went on, speaking to her readers:

> How think ye of her? warm in long ago
> Delights? – or crowned with budding bays? No so.
> None smile and none are crowned where lieth she,
> With all her visions unfulfilled . . .

In her late teens Christina had devoured Landon's books; now she paid tribute, consciously invoking the silver chain of literature stretching back beyond Barrett Browning and Landon to Felicia Hemans – for Barrett Browning had also paid homage to Landon's mourning ode to Felicia Hemans in saluting the 'bay-crowned living one that o'er the bay-crowned dead art bowing'.

In a now-famous letter, the young Elizabeth Barrett had remarked pertinently 'England has had many learned women ... and yet where are the poetesses? ... I look everywhere for grandmothers, and see none.' She herself offered a magnificent example as Christina's invocation of both 'EBB' and 'LEL' acknowledged. As a final touch, her own poem deliberately echoed Barrett Browning's *The Mask*, which contains the lines:

> I have a smiling face, she said,
> I have a jest for all I meet;
> I have a garland for my head
> And all its flowers are sweet –
> And so you call me gay, she said.
> Grief taught me this smile, she said.

Christina was again seriously thinking of publication. It was five years since the unsuccessful approach to *Blackwood's*. This time she approached *Once a Week*, a newly-launched literary magazine whose first issue contained a poem on the French victory at Magenta, illustrated by Millais. On Christina's behalf William then wrote to his erstwhile PR Brother, who replied generously, offering to forward any submissions to the editor. 'Some poem of your Sister's I am sure would be gladly received, and I could illustrate it,' he wrote on 13 July. A day or two later the third issue of *Once a Week* carried Tennyson's *The Grandmother's Apology*, a mawkish tale in which an elderly woman relates the sorrows of her life, including a contretemps involving her cousin Jenny, who was known to have 'tript in her time' – another example of the fascination with 'fallen' women and the name that seems to have been attached to their fate. Some perceived similarity between this and *Goblin Market*, as well as Millais's mention of a short poem, perhaps discouraged Christina from sending her newest work; instead she sent earlier items, including the lines on the Indian Mutiny from 1857, clearly prompted by those on Magenta.

On 13 August 1859, *The Round Tower at Jhansi: June 8, 1857* was printed in *Once a Week*. It was not illustrated, and its position at the foot of the final page suggests that it was included as a space-filler, though this need not imply any adverse view of its quality on the part of editor Samuel Lucas; Christina's name was not well-known, and the magazine's reputation depended to a great extent on attracting eminent contributors. Unfortunately, her name was so unknown that it was given as 'Caroline G. Rossetti' – a blow to her beginner's pride which one hopes she was able to laugh at, though ever after she showed a distinct touchiness regarding her by-line.

Perhaps for this reason, the poem's publication has been entirely overlooked. But it marks an important step in Christina's career: her first success as a poet in commercial terms since the *Athenaeum* over a decade before.

What happened next is open to some conjecture. Political conflict in Italy this year had involved brutalities by Papal States troops against the citizens of Perugia, during a short insurrection. Soon after *Jhansi's* appearance in *Once a Week*, Christina completed a new topical poem entitled *The Massacre of Perugia*, which began:

> A trumpet pealed thro' France. Then Italy
> Stirred, shook, from sea to sea.
> Then many cities broke
> Their lawful yoke.
> Then in an evil hour
> Perugia on her fort-crowned hill . . .

Later, she cut the rest of the text from the notebook, but both the high rhetorical style of the opening and the fact that it occupied ten manuscript pages indicate that it was intended as a long, public poem. On the face of it both subject and style were tailor-made for publication. However, it has never been found in either printed or manuscript form, and is now believed to have been destroyed – on William's surmise that it cast odium on the Pope in what his sister came to regard as an unChristian manner. But was it perhaps sent to *Once a Week* and rejected, in a way that soured Christina's relations with the magazine? For there followed an awkward incident that can only partially be reconstructed. As well as *Jhansi*, Lucas had accepted *Maude Clare*, offered in drastically shortened form that significantly reduced the personal aspect. This was accorded full-page status, with an illustration. As a regular contributor Millais was the obvious choice as illustrator, but it looks as if Gabriel now intervened, insisting that he provide the woodblock. There followed some argument with the magazine, during which Gabriel reported that *Once a Week* objected to paying 'so high a price' as he asked (he was renowned for demanding exorbitant fees and as a result did little illustrative work) and he would only be able to illustrate her poem if he made it a small drawing.

It appears that Lucas declined to negotiate, and then hastily applied to Millais to fill the allocated gap. On 5 November *Maude Clare* (this time over the author's correct name) appeared in *Once a Week*, with a half-page picture by Millais, showing the heroine striding proudly through the crowd, a hound at her side. It was, William commented later, one of his worst designs; though true, this was poor recompense for the artist's earlier generosity. Did Lucas then return *Perugia*, requesting no more submissions from this quarter? Certainly something abruptly ended Christina's relationship with the magazine after her auspicious debut, for later she referred to herself as 'the pariah of *Once a Week*'– a term that suggests she had been cast out of its pages.

Though the renewed attempt at publication thus ended once more in relative failure, the poetic company she aspired to keep shows that she had confidence in the calibre of her work. Her name might be unknown, and humility forbad boasting, but her poems were good. She had the satisfaction of another success, too, in seeing her lyric *An End* from *The Germ* included in an anthology called *Nightingale Valley*, a selection of 'the Choicest Lyrics and Short Poems in the English Language'. Published by Routledge for the Christmas market, this was the forerunner, by a year, of the vastly more popular *Golden Treasury*, and reflected contemporary taste for melody in poetry.

Since the editor of *Nightingale Valley* was William Allingham, his inclusion of her poem among two hundred others was not quite the impartial honour it seemed, although at least one of the anthology's readers, unknown to Christina, was impressed. 'But – who is Christina Rossetti, pray?' he asked Allingham. 'Her idiom is a little outlandish, but that poem of hers is a perfect gem.' It was a mark of the general approbation her work received; but why was wider recognition so elusive?

19

The Rubicon

WHATEVER HER LATER doubts about the poem, the bold rhetoric of Christina's lines on Perugia suggest that ancestral feelings were stirred by the liberation of Italy that was now taking place, thanks to Cavour and the French army in the north and the *risorgimento* of Garibaldi in the south, culminating in autumn 1860. Christina did not trust Louis Napoleon. 'I do not want to judge him rashly,' she wrote cautiously on his death a dozen years later; 'but some of his acts – the December coup at least – seem to speak with unmistaken voices.' She left no record of her views on Garibaldi, but admired Cavour as statesman and monarchist, for at heart she remained a Liberal constitutionalist, like her father deploring both violence and despotism. And her English nationalism was probably strong enough for her to have mixed feelings about Mrs Browning's polemical *Poems before Congress* – a copy came to Albany Street, for William – which caused offence by praising Napoleon III at the very time when the British militia was being mobilised against possible French invasion.

The chief domestic event of spring 1860 was an unexpected announcement in April from Gabriel in Hastings that he and Lizzie were going to be married at last, 'in as few days as possible', for all the world as if there had been no hiatus in the relationship. He added that her health was a cause of great anxiety, but thankfully his financial prospects were good.

The news was a surprise to all. 'Who, think you, is married?' wrote Christina to Mrs Heimann, announcing the event. The exact reason for the long-delayed decision is still unknown, but it is probable that in illness Lizzie appealed to Gabriel and he, believing she was dying, pledged to make good his former promises. To William's brotherly congratulation he replied with a frank account of Lizzie's continual vomiting, saying it seemed doubtful she would get to church and adding remorsefully: 'If not, I should have so much to grieve for, and what is more so much to reproach myself with, that I do not know how it might end for me.' In the circumstances, no family or friends were invited to the wedding, which took place on 23 May, and all adopted a deceptively casual tone. To Allingham, who inquired about summer lodgings, William replied with a long list of addresses, written on the very day of the ceremony, saying only that Gabriel was 'not *very* likely to be using the rooms in Chatham Pl. for some little while . . .' To Scott (who was openly astonished, having watched Gabriel become entangled with Fanny and others during the past two years) he sent the news with studied blandness, confessing briefly that the family had not been forwarned, while Christina deployed something of the same style in reply to Lady Trevelyan's inquiries in July, informing her that 'Gabriel and his Lizzie' had returned from their honeymoon in Paris, and adding carefully: 'Some years ago I knew her slightly; she was then extremely admired for beauty and talent'. But, she went on, unable to conceal disapproval,

> His marriage would be more of a satisfaction to us if we had seen his
> bride; but owing I dare say in great measure to the very delicate state of
> her health, we have not yet met. She suffers much from illness . . . I hope
> we shall be good friends some day.

It was scandalous, as Letitia was quick to note, that Mrs Gabriel had not been taken to meet her in-laws. Etiquette if not affection decreed that a new spouse be formally introduced to all relatives and close acquaintance. Not so long ago, Anna Howitt had brought her husband Alaric Watts to meet all at Albany Street. Yet by August, as Maria confirmed on her visit to Newcastle, Lizzie and Gabriel had still not called, though lodging not far away in Hampstead.

The spring had been very wet and cold, and the weather remained unseasonable. 'What a dreary summer we have had, if indeed we can be said to have had a summer at all,' Christina remarked to Pauline in August, confessing that even 'the seaside itself lacks charm this dim wet chilly season'. Her tender heart had been sufficiently moved by news of Lakeland shepherds using teapots to feed lambs orphaned by the cold to pen a curiously topical poem on the subject, but after a poignant lyric called *Mirage*, in which she again evoked her foremothers' silver song and explicitly hung her 'silenced harp' on a weeping willow – the conventional figure of the poetic voice lost through grief – she wrote no poems for the rest of the year. This was presumably because Highgate claimed her attention. At midsummer, she took Letitia to the Penitentiary's open day, as part of a fundraising drive to buy the property at Park House and enlarge the accommodation. The event was 'a tolerable success as regards money', she informed Pauline, and the high point of the day was her introduction to the Bishop of London. But, she noted hastily, lest this sound like boasting: 'I cannot help suspecting that he may have taken me for someone else, which tempered my elation at the incident!' This was false modesty – Christina is likely to have been presented to his Lordship as the very sort of Associate Sister the Penitentiary wished to recruit. Ellen Heaton would have understood, however, for in church circles

bishops were celebrities, and personal acquaintance with the hier-
archy was eagerly cultivated.

On 14 August Barbara Bodichon called on Christina, bearing one of
her own works. It was the first picture she had ever possessed, Christina wrote afterwards, 'I wish you could see us all admiring and
enjoying your beautiful gift . . . as a fine painting, as the transcript of a
wonderful scene and as your handiwork and most kind present.' In
exchange she offered something of her own, courteously disparaged
to avoid any hint of pride. 'Will you think me very conceited if I
supplement "Refuge" with another trifle?' she wrote. 'No, think me
desirous to give you pleasure.'

Barbara's gift was probably an Algerian scene similar to those she
had exhibited at the French Gallery in 1859. Among Christina's possessions at her death was a framed watercolour described as 'Cactus'.
It signalled Barbara's serious commitment to art, but the habit of
bestowing works on others was also part of her networking style, and
her call was indicative of resumed feminist friendships in the 'set'
centred around Bessie and herself, loosely known as the Langham
Place circle. This now encompassed a spread of activities ranging
from the *English Woman's Journal* to Social Science Association, a
women's reading room and employment bureau, a women's press
and a more informal grouping of painters and poets known as the
Portfolio Society, founded by Barbara, Bessie and Barbara's sister
Anne (usually known as Nannie) in 1859. There is no evidence of
Christina's participation in the Portfolio at this date, but it is very
likely that Barbara urged her to join; just possibly Christina's unidentified trifle was offered as a contribution, with a promise that, should
she take up her silenced harp again, she would in due course join the
group. Later, she claimed to have been only on the edge of the Langham Place set, but friendships kept her in touch. In 1860, for instance,
Bessie remembered meeting Christina in the street soon after hearing
the news of Gabriel's marriage. London literary and artistic circles
were relatively small.

Full of warm goodwill, Barbara had invited Christina to spend a
Sunday at Scalands, the Leigh Smith estate in Sussex, and Christina
was in some embarrassment at having accepted, evidently without
full consultation. 'I clean forgot that I am not sufficiently devout to
render Sunday visiting a safe practice for me,' she apologised, adding
the more plausible excuse that too many of her fellow Sunday school
teachers were on holiday for her to defect. In normal circumstances
she and her sister could cover for each other, but this very morning
Maria had left for a month's visit to Newcastle. 'Are you acquainted
with W.B.S., painter and poet?' she asked. 'He is charming, and his
wife ranks among the dearest and most affectionate of our friends.'

This year Scott went to stay with Miss Boyd and her brother at Penkill Castle, arousing everyone's intense curiosity. 'What right has such a grave philosopher as he to flirt with pretty women?' Tommy Woolner asked Lady Trevelyan in mock indignation. William had been to Tuscany, where the political situation was now calmer and where he made a special pilgrimage to Grandpapa Polidori's birthplace. After vain house-hunting, Gabriel and Lizzie decided to stay at Chatham Place, renting an additional apartment. At an unknown date, possibly on William's return from Italy, they accepted an invitation to one of the regular 'at homes' at Albany Street, though subsequent correspondence suggests that this was repeatedly postponed, as was a reciprocal invitation to Blackfriars. 'I find everything will be in disorder on Saturday next, as we have failed in getting things made up,' wrote Gabriel on 28 November, not disclosing that the other guests, including the Browns and Morrises, were still coming. Lizzie's health was weak, and she was dependent on laudanum, an opiate drug causing mood-swings that made social events intimidating. By this date she was also pregnant, which was an additional excuse. But one cannot doubt that the family were rebuffed and displeased. They were willing to welcome Lizzie, but she did not seem to want to know them.

There were other anxieties at Albany Street. Maria suffered an attack of erysipelas so severe that by December she could no longer take her Bible Class. Her affliction was a fiery skin infection causing painful inflammation on face, hands and feet. According to contemporary medical opinion it was caused by 'violent passions or affections of the mind' or by sudden cooling after exertion. Attacks began with fever and swelling, with acute tenderness, swollen eyes and angry blotches on the face, followed by cracked and scaling skin. Treatment kept the patient indoors, avoiding extremes of temperature, on a bland diet, bathing affected parts in tepid water. In chronic cases, sufferers were advised to guard against all extreme emotions and abstain from strong liquor – prescriptions of little use (but perhaps some mirth) to Maria. Today, the condition is treated with antibiotics, but the psychosomatic Victorian diagnosis may have some symbolic application, in suggesting that Maria's susceptibility to erisypelas signalled strong but repressed desires, its symptoms mimicking the ardour that marked her youthful personality and the perceived ugliness of her appearance. The plain child, with her passion for Homeric heroes, was now a middle-aged woman with inflamed skin burning as if in mockery of past fervour. Likewise, the prescribed remedies of tranquillity and self-denial can be seen as those she adopted as devotional as well as medical regimen, to curb swelling ambition alongside physical discomfort. As she perceived it, however, erysipelas was simply an affliction to be borne with patient good humour – one of the many trials to test one's submission to God's will.

William, who had vastly enjoyed his journey to Italy, returned home to learn that Henrietta Rintoul's mother had died, leaving her free to marry at last, after five years' engagement. But in November, as he recalled stiffly, she announced that, consequent upon her grief for her mother's death, she 'viewed with dismay the idea of forming any new ties, and she preferred that the engagement should be regarded as at an end. Against myself no sort of complaint was made or suggested.' William found this development 'not entirely reasonable' and 'determined to remain a bachelor'; he never saw Henrietta again.

This was not the whole truth, however, for William's daughter was later told that Henrietta, then in her mid-thirties, requested a celibate marriage, which he refused. Certainly she was very upset, which would not have been the case had she simply decided to remain single. On 30 November, returning some books – a formal mark of the end of the engagement – Christina found Henrietta distraught. 'I never saw anything like her misery,' she told her brother, preferring to write rather than speak of such a delicate matter. 'She held me fast kissing me and crying, and I could feel how thin she is and how she trembled in my arms.' They talked, or rather Christina listened as Henrietta told her 'a great deal about what is past and what now is; poor dear, I pity her beyond what words can express'. If there was anything she herself could do to restore the relationship, she wished to offer it, but doubted whether William's happiness was compatible with Henrietta's – which certainly suggests conditions had been set – and ended by assuring him of her full support.

This letter has been used to construct a scene in which Christina rushed over to comfort Henrietta and 'the two repressed virgins held each other fast'. In fact Christina's role was that of messenger. She was fond of Henrietta, but firmly on William's side. And in some ways, the outcome brought him closer to his sisters, who had also been disappointed in love; all three now faced a future without marriage.

As a family the Rossettis, with so many other advantages, seemed singularly unsuccessful in the wedding stakes. Only Gabriel was married, and even this was more a cause for commiseration, given his wife's precarious health. Why, one wonders, did the four siblings have such difficulty, when their parents' marriage was so happy? This could have been due to Frances's high expectations, but in fact she was neither exacting nor censorious. Rather, perhaps, the reason lay in the way all four offspring felt a strong protective impulse towards their mother which at an unconscious level was incompatible with marriage. At the time of her husband's collapse, Mamma had shouldered burdens for the whole family, engendering in her children a shared need to repay her – chiefly by the pursuit of excellence – with a filial loyalty that tended to inhibit attachment to other partners.

It was now Christina's rubicon. Five days after the tearful meeting with Henrietta came her own thirtieth birhday. Filled with apprehension, she was 'relieved and exhilarated' when she gazed into the looking-glass and found no visible change, as she confessed to William thirty years later, and exactly as attributed to her heroine Lucy Charlmont as the dreaded date approaches:

> This birthday had loomed before her threateningly for months past, but now it was over; and it became a sensible relief to feel and look at thirty very much as she had felt and looked at twenty-nine. Her mirror bore witness to no glaring accession of age having come upon her in a single night. 'After all', she mused, 'life isn't over at thirty'.

But prospects were definitely diminishing. In the course of a picnic outing in *Commonplace*, 'poor Lucy' feels her age and isolation keenly as she sits, talking and laughing but sensing herself becoming 'more and more worn-looking as she talked and laughed on, getting visibly older and more faded...' Poor Christina: though the mirror might show no grey, the spectre of ageing spinsterhood loomed.

Earlier in the year she had written another story – a compelling tale entitled *Case 2: Folio Q* about a man doomed to have no reflection in a looking-glass. It was, in William's words, 'perhaps the best tale she ever wrote', but when in 1861 Gabriel proposed submitting it to a magazine, it transpired that Christina had destroyed the manuscript, because 'it turned out to raise – or seem to raise – some dangerous moral question'.

It is hard to guess what dangerous moral question could have been inadvertently contained in such a tale which sounds more like a spooky story than an exemplary one, perhaps comparable to the ghost tales that were currently tumbling from Mrs Gaskell's pen. The title suggests that it took the form of an archaic text reputedly discovered in an old folio – the kind of distancing device often used for works of Gothick imagination. And in 1860 she thought it good enough to send to the newly-launched *Cornhill*, which had just published Gaskell's *Curious if True*, whose characters are drawn from nursery tales in a manner that is sure to have appealed to Christina. She submitted her own story under the odd pseudonym C. G. Redlets, and when it was returned she tried again in the autumn, this time sending it to *Blackwood's*.

Blackwood's also turned it down. Did the editor perhaps remark on some risky moral question? Maybe the man in her story had no reflection because he had no soul, having forfeited it to the devil like

Melmoth, or maybe he was already dead, like uncle John Polidori's *Vampyre*; perhaps the objectionable issue was communication from beyond the grave, which spiritualism made so controversial. If so, the tale belonged to the shadow side of Christina's imagination, inspired by Maturin and Poe, inhabited by ghosts, goblins, nightmares and other horrors with invisible features or inaudible voices. But the idea of a blank looking-glass may also be seen as a variation on Lucy Charlmont's fear: as a woman grew older, she faded socially as well as physically, becoming more and more 'invisible' and insignificant. There may therefore have been a buried connection between Christina's tale of a mirror that showed no reflection and the thirty-year-old woman who was afraid to look at her own image.

In this respect Lucy Charlmont was certainly her author's self-portrait, and it is somewhat startling as well as oddly moving to see Christina scrutinising the glass for wrinkles and white hairs. Somehow, her reputation is of one who was above such vanities. We forget what importance was accorded to beauty in women at this date, despite the simultaneous ban on admiring one's appearance. In his memoir, William indeed felt obliged to devote a long paragraph to the question 'as to the amount of good looks' with which his sister could be credited, saying that while she was neither 'a beauty', nor 'handsome', nor 'pretty', she was nevertheless 'assuredly much nearer to being beautiful than ugly' and in youth had sometimes been called lovely, 'if a refined and correct mould of face, along with elevated and deep expression, is loveliness'. This rather convoluted account is far from conclusive – certainly insufficient to claim, as some writers have done, that Christina had a 'Pre-Raphaelite beauty' – but suggests why she worried about growing old. Of course, such anxiety was vain, in both senses of the word, but clearly thirty marked a climacteric in her life.

Like her author, Lucy suffers from severe depression, spent partly in solitary walks on the shoreline. Like Christina too, she is troubled with nightmares:

> By day she could forbid her thoughts to shape themselves, even mentally, into words . . . But by night, when sleep paralysed self-restraint, then her dreams were haunted by distorted spectres of the past; never alluring or endearing – for this she was thankful – but sometimes monstrous and always impossible to escape from. Night after night she would awake from such dreams, struggling and sobbing, with less and less conscious strength to resume daily warfare.

In the story, these monstrous spectres are ascribed to Lucy's disappointment in love, though the connection is not explained. And further details of her haunting indicate a more subliminal source, as she plods along the lonely beach

> to and fro, to and fro, at once listless and unresting, with wide, absent eyes fixed on the monotonous waves, which they did not see. Gradually a morbid fancy grew upon her that one day she should behold her father's body washed ashore, and that she should know the face: from a waking fancy, this began to haunt her dreams with images unutterably loathsome. Then she walked no more on the shingle, but took to wandering along green lanes and country roads.

Lucy's father was lost at sea some twenty years before, so the idea has psychological plausibility, but again it is not explained why this should be linked to disappointment in love, and the incident plays no further part in the plot. Nor is it clear why Lucy should so morbidly fear the reappearance of his drowned body as to provoke 'unutterably loathsome' images in her dreams. Did this idea come from Christina's experience, or her imagination? Something connected both with turning thirty and with romantic loss certainly has power to haunt and disturb. It cannot be faced, and Lucy flees from the sea to the pastoral security of the countryside, evocative of Holmer Green.

From the goblin merchants and the Satanic goat to the weeping crocodile and the ghost-lover of *A Nightmare* set on the coast where blood-red seaweeds drip, Christina's recurrent dreams and waking visions had a monstrous, masculine, inescapable, incomprehensible aspect, where innocence and sensuality, terror and desire, fear and pity were mixed. Lucy fears her dreams will be alluring; they become loathsome. The ghost who rides his beloved amid death's tideless waters is a variant of the spectre that causes Lucy to wake sobbing and struggling, and which turns the imagined sight of her father's long-lost face into a hideous image. The morbid linking of lost father and lost lover gives this passage a power out of all significance to its narrative role, as if it were a theme too urgent to suppress yet not fully understood by its author, who therefore cannot adequately integrate it into her tale.

This recurrent imagery in Christina's work, which in *A Nightmare* is a terrifying secret that must be kept, and in *Commonplace* the source of unspeakable yet inescapable thoughts, is a matter of personal psychology as well as literary criticism. It is of course true that everyone has nameless fears that the creative imagination can put to artistic use. But what shaped Christina's particular terrors? Where did these images come from, and what do they represent?

The clammy, tearful monster of the 1849 sonnet, who grins through the darkness, came almost unconsciously in *bouts rimés* at Brighton, when Christina was suffering from something like Lucy Charlmont's depression:

> I could not pick
> A quarrel with it; it began to lick
> My hand, making meanwhile a piteous din,
> And shedding human tears: it would begin
> To near me, then retreat. I heard the quick
> Pulsation of my heart, I marked the fight
> Of life and death within me. Then sleep threw
> Her veil around me . . .

When she wakes, the dreamer weeps, knowing that the creature loves her.

In psychotherapeutic circumstances such recurrent images are often indications of suppressed sexual trauma, indirectly disclosed. They suggest an experience to which the victim has responded with both fear and love, without full comprehension, and which has been successfully repressed but resurfaces in inexplicable dreams and flashbacks. As Lucy Charlmont finds, thoughts that by day could be forbidden rose at night when self-restraint was released. Throughout Christina's verse, ghostly lovers return in the dark, frighteningly intent on reclaiming their loved ones. Monsters rise and fall, like the cannibal crocodile who also weeps. Secrets must be kept, or cannot be told.

Once raised, the suspicion that Christina was the victim of sexual trauma has to be explored and defended. Is it likely that her nightmares, morbid fancies, neuralgic migraine and recurrent depressions had a psychological origin in some such experience? If so, how was this related to her breakdown at age fourteen? The conjectured experience cannot simply be reconstructed from the nightmare texts: such evidence is at best oblique even when it does hint at some undeniable 'truth'. But the circumstances of her life made such a history possible.

Christina's infancy was especially happy and secure, with much demonstrable affection, both at Charlotte Street and Holmer Green. When she was twelve, however, the security fractured, with her father's illness, professional failure and financial loss. The following year her sister was away, her mother out at work and her brothers at school, leaving Christina alone in the house with Papa, who had changed from an indulgent parent, provider of sweets and strawberries, into a self-pitying invalid, convinced of impending blindness, prone to despair and loudly imploring comfort that no one could give, least of all his bewildered younger daughter. In part, she may have blamed herself for the family's troubles, as children often do, vainly hoping to repair the damage.

Did something else happen at this time? In his distress, did Christina's father, like the terrifyingly blind Mouth-Boy in her children's story, demand something she knew she ought not to give? In the worst years 1844–5 she was physically mature for her age, according to her doctor, but in other respects still an obedient child. In his autobiography Gabriele described his daughters at this age as mirror-images of their mother. He also maintained a patriarchal sense of *patria potestas* and authority within the family even as he became its weakest member. Without *cara Francesca* at the hearthside, domestic order and emotional restraint were lacking. The opportunity was thus there for paternal abuse of some kind.

The alteration in Christina's demeanour – her retreat behind a mask of stiff reserve, keeping emotional distress to herself to avoid adding to others' – could simply be a response to the catastrophic change in family circumstances. Something of the same seems to have happened to William, whose dull, undemonstrative exterior was in part the result of concealing his own feelings at this troubled time. But it does not seem sufficient cause for Christina's breakdown, nor recurrent depression, nor for what are now read as the 'Freudian' aspects of her dreams – the crocodile who swells and devours his kin, the monster with the clammy fin that advances and retreats, the kingly goat and dog with abominably sensual features.

Did Christina's father in his despair make sexual advances or requests she could not refuse? When a fin came forth, in the sonnet, she 'could not pick a quarrel' as it licked her hand piteously, shedding tears. Her heart beat fast, as the fin came closer. Then she slept, or forgot, but when she woke, she wept, knowing it was true. In the dream of the Satanic goat, the horned patriarchal figure lies beside sheep with innocent expressions. When the crocodile has gorged his fill, he sleeps 'with unstrung claw' and dwindles in size, before the white vessel approaches, restoring order, as Mamma was wont to do. He then wakes, weeping and wringing his hands. 'What can this mean?' the poet asks, for she herself does not understand. But the figure of a crocodile who sheds tears to allure his victim, is an apt image for a sexually abusive father.

The goblins lure Laura to transgress by means of luscious fruit wholly reminiscent of the treats Papa provided against Mamma's wishes, and press and squeeze these against Lizzie's tight-closed lips. In *Hero*, the father yearns to share his daughter's deathbed. In *On The Convent Threshold* the woman is pursued across the bar of blood by an illicit lover, who is piteous, angry, inescapable; when she wakes, her hair is grey. Lucy Charlmont's days and nights are haunted by a morbid fancy of seeing her father's drowned body, that swells into an unutterably loathsome image. Was Christina unwillingly implicated in some sexual activity at the age of twelve or thirteen that left a permanent sense of guilt? 'My lily feet are soiled with mud, with scarlet mud which tells a tale', she made Eloise say. Incest can of course only be inferred, not proved, for direct evidence is lacking; moreover, the true facts of such cases are often impossible to establish. But incestuous abuse of some kind – possibly in the form of mutual masturbation that gave Christina unwanted knowledge of arousal – offers a convincing explanation of the dark and disturbed aspects of her inner life that would account for her teenage breakdown, personality change, inexplicable rages and recurrent depression. That it probably coincided with puberty made it all the more disabling.

Whatever the actual experience, it was not something that could be talked about, and perhaps like many abuse victims she banished the knowledge from conscious memory. But the nightmare texts and the account of Lucy's morbid imaginings as she turns thirty – which have so little to do with the rest of the story – look like oblique 'disclosure' of something Christina needed to express without knowing what she was trying to say. Her sense of having a secret, and of being haunted by a lover who insists she must keep the secret, have their place in this outline. So does her pervasive sense of sin and a black double within, the self-loathing that led her to slash her arm with scissors, and the repetitive compulsion to penitence.

The physical symptoms of her nervous collapse – which served the immediate purpose of getting her away from Charlotte Street, at least temporarily – were all suggestive of a hysterical causation. Her natural vivacity vanished, and for years afterwards death and petrifaction were her obsessional themes: figures lying on their deathbeds or in the grave, frozen like statues. Warmth was craved; wintry cold and emotional ice were dominant. Believing herself blameworthy, she was vulnerable to the religious teaching of Pusey and Dodsworth, who proffered 'relief inexpressible' when sins were confessed. Yet, if *Maude* is to be trusted, she was unable to believe herself deserving of absolution.

Her poems were copied out for all to read. Was death the only sure relief? she asked in December 1845:

> Tell me not there is no skill . . .
> That can soothe the bitter smart,
> When we find ourselves betrayed,
> When we find ourselves forsaken
> By those for whom we would have laid
> Our young lives down . . .

'What though we should be deceived By the friend we love the best?' these verses inquired of the air. 'Oh! it were better far to die Than thus for ever mourn and sigh' she lamented in Sappho's voice the following year, in a desperate longing for oblivion. And into Mamma's commonplace book she copied out Wordsworth's stories of Margaret and Ellen, as if trying to find an explanation for her feelings of despair.

Her obsessional linking of ripe fruit with desire and guilt, especially in *Goblin Market*, hints at some erotic feeling that is not always threatening, but must not be indulged. As a girl, she must have wished to console her father for his debility while at the same time resenting the demands that his illness imposed upon her, and it is possible that in responding to him, she had feelings of tenderness and even submerged desire, which were 'incestuous' to a certain degree. Such a psycho-scenario would see Christina as passing naturally through this phase in childhood, when Papa petted and hugged his daughters, only to have it frighteningly replayed as she approached adolescence, with her father now perhaps initiating a sexual relationship to compensate for his dwindling authority, in a manner that aroused both love and terror.

Many of Freud's early female patients exhibited similar hysterical symptoms and in many cases the cause was sexual trauma in adolescence, usually perpetrated by the father – though in his case histories Freud frequently changed this to an 'uncle' or more distant figure. Indeed, the disclosure became such a recurrent ingredient in his analyses that, unable or unwilling to acknowledge evidence of such widespread paternal behaviour, Freud developed instead his theory of incestuous fantasy in which girls dream of a seductive father.

Today sexual abuse is more openly acknowledged. The clinical literature on paternal incest is large and increasing, with no great areas of disagreement as regards either the incidence or the adverse effects on the victims, who are mainly female. Characteristic responses include feelings of paralysis and dissociation, of being hypnotised like a frightened animal, or struck dumb, unable to speak. The traumatic experience is usually followed by psychological denial, the child being unable to make sense of what has happened, and therefore developing psychic defences to detach herself from the event. Frequently, victims imagine themselves elsewhere, watching without involvement. Later they 'forget' everything.

Despite considerable efforts to maintain denial, repetitive intrusions nearly always occur, with an involuntary compulsive tendency towards repetition of some aspects of the trauma, notwithstanding strong conscious efforts at avoidance and suppression. These repetitions include nightmares, hallucinations, unbidden images and obsessive ideas; panic attacks and weeping episodes; or re-enactments of some disguised aspect of the trauma in gesture, movement or artistic production. Chronic depression is the most common secondary symptom, accompanied by guilt, low self-esteem and feelings of powerlessness. Attempts at self-mutilation are common and suicidal feelings are frequent. Most distressingly, incestuous sexual trauma can be resistant to therapy; frequently abused women seek help, knowing something is wrong, but are unable to uncover the cause.

Sexual abuse is double-edged if love is experienced by the victim from the abuser. 'There is that enjoyment and need which I felt,' writes one recent victim; 'and at the same time there is the violence of intrusion which is feared and hated and generates a level of rage that is terrifying to the child.' When incest takes place within a context that is otherwise protective, the betrayal of trust causes disproportionate difficulties in later life: victims both seek and fear intimacy, either hurrying into early relationships, or withdrawing into celibacy. Frequently victims believe they have committed some unpardonable sin that leaves them soiled and stigmatised, turning to religion to root out and exorcise the evil. At the same time, incest survivors often have difficulties relating to God the Father, as a patriarchal figure, and seek absolution in the convent, among nuns.

Such understanding illuminates Christina's juvenile fascination with nuns and virgin martyrs, as well as her work at Highgate amongst social outcasts, who could never regain their sexual innocence, but whom she would help atone for their sin. I don't for a moment imagine that any such emotional identity was consciously felt – black would be white and heaven hell before her own experience encompassed anything comparable, as she told Gabriel – but unconsciously she was drawn to work with girls who were weak and culpable, who claimed to love their seducers while hating their sin, to love th'offender yet detest th'offence, as Pope put it.

What, if anything, can she have known about incest? In her relatively sheltered upbringing the word may never have been heard (the solitary incidence in the Bible is that of Lot who lay with his daughters to beget the tribes of Moab and Ammon, but this surely did not feature frequently in Victorian sermons). Shelley was forbidden or censored; there is no evidence she read *The Cenci*. But there was a good deal of perverse sensuality in the melodramatic books of her adolescent reading, much of which inhabited a fantasy world of alluring, demonic males and innocent females. The goblins' twilight world has been interpreted as the Gothick domain of vampires, who feed on maidens, causing them to sicken and though Christina did not read the vampire tale written by uncle John during his Byronic days, it is possible she read Byron's *Giaour*, with its curse:

But first on earth, as Vampire sent
Thy corpse shall from its tomb be rent;
Then ghastly haunt the native place
And suck the blood of thy race;
There from thy daughter, sister, wife,
At midnight drain the stream of life . . .
Thy victims, ere they yet expire,
Shall know the demon for their sire . . .
The youngest, best beloved of all,
Shall bless thee with a father's name –
That word shall wrap thy heart in flame!

The Swiss psychotherapist Alice Miller, whose work centres on emotional injury in childhood, and the ways in which the experience of the 'child within' is manifested in adulthood, has persuasively described the effect of trauma, when mitigated by affection. In the work of creative artists, where profoundly moving themes are powered by feelings outside conscious control, she argues, the inner pain is transmitted into obsessional visual and verbal energy. The trauma may not be sexual – Picasso's experience of earthquake in infancy, resurfacing in images of dismemberment, is one cogent example, as is the familiar case of Dickens's banishment to the blacking factory, which had a lasting impact on his life and work – but it retains an uncanny tendency to reappear even when not remembered, like the snake that is scotched but not killed. For fear of losing a parent's love, children cannot express anger, and are therefore impelled to displace and internalise injury, often later manifested in the idealisation of their childhood and parents and in blaming themselves for all their suffering. Thus they keep the secret from others as well as themselves.

For sexual abuse must nearly always be kept secret. Fathers and other abusers insist on this with threats of the withdrawal of love from the victim, who may otherwise be indulged or treated as a 'little princess'. But with the effort of keeping the secret, the child's personality withers into depressive illness, enacting the silence demanded. At the same time the 'unremembered plight of being vulnerable and abused by a loved person' is perpetuated emotionally, either in an identification with other dumb and damaged creatures, or actively in a punitive approach towards young people. Christina had no children, of course, but her stories for them contain cruel and even sadistic elements; *Nick*, for instance, is a fiercely retributive tale. Anger and pain can be transformed through the creative impulse into art – as in fantasy, fairy stories and myth, where 'censored' ideas are safely expressed. This results in powerful works of the imagination, where obsessive themes are repeatedly explored, yet never conquered: territory to which the artist must return, without knowing why.

This seems to fit Christina's case well. For some as yet undiscovered reason, however, 1860–1 marked a watershed in her writing. In subsequent years she used her creative gifts to come to terms with childhood fears. The healing process had begun.

PART THREE

1861–70

20

Towards Publication

TURNING THIRTY BROUGHT Christina a renewed desire for recognition. 'Passing away, saith the world,' she wrote on the last
night of 1860, lamenting the loss of youth:

> Is the eye waxen dim, is the dark hair changing to grey
> That hath won neither laurel nor bay?

As William noted, she now 'thought that the bay had been kept
waiting quite long enough'. She was perhaps spurred into action by
one of her father's Italian aphorisms, which began

> If you don't know at twenty, you never will know.
> If you don't do at thirty, you never will do . . .

So early in January she again set about getting her work published.

The year began as usual with family affairs, for the mid-winter
holiday was always important to the Rossettis. It seems that on Christmas Day Gabriel and Lizzie joined the family and cousin Henrietta,
who had returned from America to live with her father. On 11 January,
leaving Christina at home with Mamma, who was unwell, William
and Maria joined Ruskin and the Burne-Joneses for an evening with
Lizzie and Gabriel. A few days later Gabriel asked Ruskin to put in a
word for Christina with Thackeray, editor of the *Cornhill*, who was
currently publishing *Unto this Last*, and to this end asked his sister to
send him the notebook containing 'the poem about the two Girls and
the Goblins'. He inquired too about her story *Folio Q*, apparently
unaware of its rejection by the *Cornhill*.

Simultaneously, however, Christina herself sent some shorter poems
to *Macmillan's Magazine*, whose editor David Masson, husband to
Rosalind Orme, was an old friend. Her tone was noticeably less assertive than it had been to *Blackwood's* seven years before. 'My dear Mr
Masson,' she wrote:

Bored as you are with contributions, many of them doubtless being
poems good or bad by unknown authors, I feel ashamed to add the
enclosed to the heap: the more so as personal acquaintanceship might

make it more unpleasant for you to decline them. Will you therefore give me credit for sincerity when I beg you to accept all or any of the enclosed to *Macmillan's Magazine* in case you think them of any use, and to pass upon them a condign sentence of rejection in the (highly probable) opposite case?

Macmillan's Magazine, launched in 1859, was a liberal literary monthly which typically carried articles on Garibaldi, Darwin's *Origin of Species*, Tennyson's *Idylls of the King* and Holman Hunt's *The Finding of the Saviour in the Temple*. Its current serial was *Tom Brown at Oxford*, sequel to the hugely popular *Schooldays*. Contributors known to Christina included Charles Collins, Fred Stephens and Herbert Coleridge, any one of whom might have encouraged her submission, though she made use of no one else's services in approaching Masson. Poetry was the magazine's weakest department, tending to the sentimental and topical. Apart from the Laureate's *Sea Dreams* in the opening number, none of the early verse was of any enduring merit.

Masson responded positively, and *Up-hill* was swifty accepted. A week later, Gabriel was surprised to hear the magazine's proprietor Alexander Macmillan proudly announce he had been congratulated on securing Miss Rossetti's services, and with great satisfaction reading out the poem, already in proof for the February issue. Macmillan, whose publishing business was located in Cambridge, left the magazine mainly to Masson, but paid a weekly visit to London where he held 'open house' each Thursday evening above the editorial office, when political and literary issues of the day were debated in all-male gatherings nicknamed 'tobacco parliaments'. He told Gabriel he would like to see more of Christina's work, including 'the Goblin poem', if it did not go into the *Cornhill*. All this Gabriel duly reported, advising his sister to deal directly with Macmillan, whose judgement he considered as good as Masson's.

It has been widely assumed that Gabriel was responsible for first showing Christina's work to Macmillan, but the correspondence is clear: while he was indirectly addressing Thackeray, her approach to Masson had scored. And her choice was justified, for within a day or two Ruskin gave his verdict on the 'Goblins' saying the poem was full of power but unpublishable because of its 'quaintnesses' and offences against correct form. 'Irregular measure is the calamity of modern poetry,' he told Gabriel pompously; 'your sister should exercise herself in the severest commonplace of metre until she can write as the public like. Then if she puts in her observation and passion all will become precious.'

'Most senseless, I think,' commented Gabriel, forwarding the letter with 'regret and disgust', a view doubtless seconded at home. Undeterred, he proposed sending the poem to Mrs Gaskell, who would surely commend it to Thackeray. But this was unnecessary, now that Christina had a toehold elsewhere. And his mind leaping forward, Gabriel asked her to send copies of all her most suitable pieces, so he could choose those to be included in a collection. 'I believe they would have a chance with Macmillan, or might with others, if they existed in an available form,' he wrote. It would be best to divide the proposed volume into sacred and secular sections, he added, so large a number being devotional; 'what do you think?' He was a little out of date. Disregarding those written before 1848, of Christina's current stock of some two hundred poems, only a third can be described as specifically religious; over the past couple of years the proportion of strictly devotional verse had declined.

Maybe Macmillan had said something about the vast amount of pious poetry offered for publication nowadays. He had certainly expressed interest in *Folio Q*. 'Can you get it or make another copy?' Gabriel inquired; 'or have you got anything else available?' There was no copy, but Christina duly obliged with something else that has not as yet been identified, sending this with her notebooks. 'Many and many thanks for your fair copy just received,' Gabriel replied on 28 January, 'which is *so* fair it almost seems a pity to print it.' As to the poems, having read some out to Swinburne and others, he was pleased to report that the general opinion was excellent. 'Really they must come out somehow,' he insisted. *After the Picnic* was one of the best of all, apart from the title. Could it be called *At Home*? And he forwarded the notebooks for Macmillan to read.

This retitling was one of several examples designed to eliminate awkwardnesses and oddities – in this case appropriately, since the text has nothing to do with picnics. More importantly, it shows Gabriel was reading the work with increased attention now that publishers were showing interest, and realising how it had gained in variety and power in recent years, when he himself had been otherwise occupied. Unnoticed, his younger sister had turned from a promising into an accomplished poet. He was himself preparing for publication two volumes, one of original poems and one of translations, so he was pleased to resume the collaborative spirit they had shared in the days of *The Germ*. Always Christina's warmest admirer as well as sternest critic, he was anxious she do justice to her talent. For her part, Christina sent comments on Gabriel's translations, though when she objected to the use of 'ye' in the objective as well as subjective case, Gabriel dismissed this as a grammarian's quibble, saying 'I'm afraid I don't think it matters much'. Collaboration evidently had its limits.

When *Up-hill* appeared, it 'at once commanded a considerable share of public attention', and proved the break-through she needed; as she modestly told Macmillan when acknowledging the guinea fee, it had been noticed by a pleasingly wide circle – who included an old friend named Mary Haydon, who wrote to solicit an autograph. The joyous *Birthday* then appeared in the April issue, like 'a pennyworth of wheat prominent among the pebbles,' as Gabriel joked to Allingham, raising hopes that a collection would soon be agreed. Macmillan had returned all the notebooks except one – probably that including *Goblin Market*, which he read to his evening class – and when he inquired after new pieces for the magazine Christina reminded him of this, saying she needed the notebook in order to make her selection, and was not writing anything fresh. As to *Folio Q*, this had become 'such a subject of annoyance' that she had burnt it. In ·its place, she sent 'a trifle which I have by me', which can only have been *Hero*, but was not liked.

When Macmillan promptly returned the last notebook, she was 'in great hopes of being able to put a volume together'. Calculations as to length pointed 'in the right direction' – she knew she had sufficient material. Masson still had two poems in hand, she reminded him, before signing off with a lively expression of pleasure and gratitude: 'You may think whether I am not happy to attain fame (!) and guineas by means of the magazine'.

Despite the jocular tone, both fame and guineas were welcome. False modesty was not among Christina's faults, but it must have been especially gratifying to be offered a first collection by a well-respected publishing house on the basis of two lyrics and the unedited contents of several tiny notebooks. Moreover, though no contract was yet produced, Macmillan's terms were good. If a satisfactory selection could be made, the firm would cover all production costs, and offer her half profits thereafter.

A Peep at the Goblins, which Macmillan especially liked, was the obvious choice as lead poem. Over the next few weeks, and in the intervals of work at Highgate, Christina was therefore busy with revising and fair-copying the remainder of her selection. There was not much revision: by and large Christina's poems were printed as written. This illuminates her compositional practice, for where Gabriel was a compulsive reviser, continuing amendments through many proof changes, she regarded works as finished products, which might be better or worse, but were not subject to constant tinkering. Her guiding principles for selection were quality and what has been called 'objectivity' – poems whose presentation annihilates all ordinary and personal reference despite the direct voice, and pursues an aesthetic of conciseness and clarity. She did not want private meaning to be read into her work.

Some pieces were therefore shortened. *Maude Clare* lost a further three stanzas, and *Echo* came down from seven to three. Ten of the sixty-three poems selected were retitled, usually in such a way as to reduce their oddity or whimsy. *The Lambs of Westmoreland* became *The Lambs of Grasmere*, for example, and *A Trio* became *A Triad*. *A Peep at the Goblins* became *Goblin Market* and *Cousin Kate* was substituted for *Up and Down*. *Something like Truth*, a title Gabriel had ridiculed in 1853, became *Sleep at Sea*, and he probably also suggested *Winter: My Secret* in place of the unduly self-deprecating *Nonsense*. *In the Days of the Sea-Kings* became *Love from the North* – ironically giving later critics more rather than less scope for personal interpretation, but certainly showing that this was not seen as a 'love personal' by its author. Later, Gabriel noted that Christina paid too little attention to titles, which again illuminates her mode of composition: for her, the lines dictated the subject, rather than being determined by it. When they were complete, she simply appended a more or less appropriate heading.

The most striking aspect of her overall selection for this first volume was the prominence given to the dramatic and colloquial. She adopted the idea of two sections, but that headed 'Devotional Pieces' contains only eighteen poems. Conspicuously placed in the general section are *Jhansi*, *Cousin Kate*, *Noble Sisters*, *My Dream*, *The Hour and the Ghost*, *Maude Clare*, *Winter: My Secret*, *No Thank you, John!* and *On The Convent Threshold*.

Given these inclusions, the omissions are surprising: *A Nightmare* with its ghostly lover and blood-red seaweed; *Introspective*; *A Blank*; *LEL* – all now considered among her most impressive works. The hectic *On the Convent Threshold* was included, but *A Fight over the Body of Homer* was rejected, presumably at Gabriel's insistence. So too was *In an Artist's Studio*, perhaps because too obviously applicable to the author's sister-in-law, although the most recently written poem to be included might bear the same construction. This was *Wife to Husband*, the only piece in the volume that was composed after Macmillan's initial offer of publication. Copied into the notebook on 8 June 1861, it probably provides the cut-off date for the selection. Its subject takes us back to the previous month, when sorrow struck Lizzie and Gabriel.

In replying to Mary Haydon in February, Christina had given a broad hint. 'Some day I suppose I shall rival you in Auntship if not in infatuation,' she wrote. 'My sister-in-law proves an acquisition now that we know her better ... you cannot think now quaintly and prettily they have furnished their (by courtesy) drawing room.' Harmonious relations between the households had clearly been restored, and the prospect of an addition to the family was welcomed, with the discreet annoucement of Lizzie's pregnancy – 'quite in confidence as such things are better waited for quietly,' as Gabriel told Allingham. But on 2 May came bad news. 'Lizzie has just been delivered of a dead child,' wrote Gabriel to his mother. 'Do not encourage any one to come just now – I mean, of course, except yourselves.' So Christina's propspective Auntship vanished. There was little she could do to help Lizzie, who in any case turned to the young wives among her friends – Emma Brown, Georgie Jones and Janey Morris – but it was an ominous as well as sad event. When Georgie and Ned called soon afterwards, they found Lizzie sitting beside the empty cradle; as they came into the room she cried with 'a kind of soft wildness', saying ' "Hush, Ned, you'll waken it!" '

In Christina's poem, the wife is sinking:

> Goodbye.
> I must drift across the sea,
> I must sink into the snow,
> I must die.
>
> You can bask in the sun,
> You can drink wine and eat;
> Goodbye:

Such sombre tone was not characteristic this season, however, for in April she had produced *Promises like Piecrust*, with a distinctly colloquial tenor reminiscent of *No Thank You, John!* 'Promise me no promises' the speaker says, celebrating freedom:

> Keep we both our liberties,
>   Never false and never true:
> Let us hold the die uncast,
>   Free to come as free to go;
> For I cannot know your past,
>   And of mine what can you know?
>   . . .
> If you promised, you might grieve
>   For lost liberty again;
> If I promised, I believe
>   I should fret to break the chain:
> Let us be the friends we were,
>   Nothing more but nothing less;
> Many thrive on frugal fare
>   Who would perish of excess.

Curiously, Christina never chose to publish this in her lifetime, though it reflects the best of her poetic wit and humour. What made it seem unsuitable?

There is a circumstantial hint to link *Promises* (which like piecrust are made to be broken) with John Brett, for it was written very soon after Christina visited his studio on Show Sunday, and sent Mary Haydon her opinion of *Warwick Castle*. Just possibly, therefore, the poem may be read as the closing of a brief chapter. 'Let us be the friends we were' it says. 'Free to come as free to go'.

In June, Christina went abroad for the first time, on a short trip to France with her mother and William. The itinerary was modest, starting in Paris, where they met up with Mamma's cousin Sarah Austin, and proceeding via Rouen and Caen to Avranches and the Cherbourg peninsula, before sailing home from Jersey.

It was pleasant, if uneventful. 'Boulogne, Rouen, Paris are realities now for me, instead of mere names,' Christina wrote later in the year after attending a lecture on 'Foreign Travel'. But virtually all that is recorded of the trip is that near Avranches they saw a magnificent view of sunlight after thunder, and in one hotel they were particularly taken with a fat Persian cat, who demanded milk from the table and passed into family tradition as the Cat of St Lô. Oddly enough, given their cosmopolitan inheritance, only William among the Rossettis showed any real inclination for foreign travel. Gabriel's travels were limited to northern France and Belgium, while despite her language teaching Maria never left England. To them, Europe was a source of literature, art and history, not tourism.

While they were in France, the death of Elizabeth Barrett Browning was announced in Florence. Returning home, Christina renewed her friendships with the women who centred round Langham Place, the *English Woman's Journal* and the Portfolio Society. It seems likely that their example encouraged her determination to publish, for the *EWJ* carried regular articles on eminent women writers, including her near namesake and compatriot, Christine de Pisan, together with original poems, against which Christina measured her own. The most accomplished of these came from Adelaide Procter, whose famous *Lost Chord* appeared here in March. She was already spoken of as prospective heir to Mrs Browning.

Five years older than Christina, Adelaide was daughter to the well-known author Barry Cornwall, and had been a precocious lover of verse, her first poems having been published when she was only eighteen. *Legends and Lyrics*, her first volume, issued in May 1858, soon reached a fourth edition, much praised for its 'tenderness, devotional feeling and resigned sadness' (which as the *Saturday Review* noted were general characteristics of women's verse) and for its 'rarer merits' of just thought and felicitous language. Rather like Christina's, Adelaide's subjects encompassed conventional mourning lyrics, moral verses on altruism and modesty, and romantic narratives about medieval nuns and heroic maidens. *The Lesson of the War 1855* emphasised the sinking of class conflict in the greater cause of victory in the Crimea, for Procter's values were of a liberal, high-minded kind: true honours, in her view, were accorded those who aided the poor, or triumphed in a glorious cause, or produced a noble poem. With regard to love she displayed a sharp and not at all gushing tongue, in a sceptical mode that may well have influenced *Promises like Piecrust*. But while always intelligent, her verse is not outstanding: its meanings and metaphors carry no complicated harmonies and (to a Rossettian ear) its metres are sometimes false.

Later, Christina told Macmillan she feared no rivalry from Miss Procter; but she admired Adelaide's approach, and also her energetic and cheerful devotion to the night shelter for women and children in the aptly-named Providence Row, Bishopsgate. This was the subject of Adelaide's poem *Homeless*:

> It is cold dark midnight, yet listen
>   To that patter of tiny feet!
> It is one of your dogs, fair lady
>   Who whines in the bleak cold street?
>   . . .
> Nay, our criminals all are sheltered,
>   They are pitied and taught and fed:
> That is only a sister-woman
>   Who has got neither food nor bed –
> And the Night cries 'sin to be living'
>   And the River cries 'sin to be dead'
>   . . .
> Nay, goods in our thrifty England
>   Are not left to lie and grow rotten . . .
> But in counting the riches of Britain
>   I think our poor are forgotten.

Later this year, when Bessie asked for a poem for the *EWJ*, Christina selected the old *Behold I Stand at the Door and Knock*, evidently prompted by Adelaide's example.

Adelaide was also a member of the Portfolio Society, which usually met at the Leigh Smiths' London home but also welcomed 'corresponding members'. These received notification of each month's theme, and sent their sketches and verses for circulation and appraisal. Themes were suitable for both verbal and visual treatment, and sufficiently general to allow for wide interpretation; those known to have been set in 1861–2 include 'Light and Shade', 'Reflections' and 'Strife and Peace'.

It is not known exactly when Christina became a member, and in any case she did not attend the meetings. But one of the Portfolio themes was 'Too Late', and on 11 October she completed a short poem about a Sleeping Beauty, called *The Prince who arrived too late*, which was presumably so prompted. Within the context of family affairs, the piece is also easily read as a poetic extrapolation from the lives of Lizzie and Gabriel, for he too had been a tardy suitor. It was perhaps now too late to save Lizzie, whose disturbed state of mind gave cause for concern. Above all, however, *The Prince who arrived too late* spoke of the confinement of womanhood, condemned to inaction and emotional atrophy unless 'woken' by marriage.

It was followed within eleven days by a poem about another princess, which ran to fifty-two triplets in heroic metre and may have been inspired by the 'strife and peace' Portfolio theme. This was *A Royal Princess*, part courtly fantasy and part political fable, with an unexpectedly feminist and democratic slant.

This princess is also confined, but restive on her royal pedestal, comparing herself to 'an eagle that must not soar' and lamenting her impotent narcissism:

> All my walls are lost in mirrors, whereupon I trace
> Self to right hand, self to left hand, self in every place,
> Self-same solitary figure, self-same seeking face.

Her father is a tyrant who treats his subjects like slaves, just as he keeps his daughter in a jewelled cage, as a docile and decorative object of delight. Then comes a rebellion, with the famished populace 'howling in the streets for bread'. The king commands his troops to smite and spare not, but the rebels storm the citadel and set fire to the palace, shouting for revenge. At this moment, the princess sides with the people, offering her jewels, asking only 'once to speak before the world' and ending with Queen Esther's words: 'I, if I perish, perish: in the name of God I go'.

The poetic form Christina chose, with long lines and strong caesuras, lends itself to over-heated declamation, as the princess moves from her stately palace to the very threshold of freedom. For this was another female fantasy of heroic action, which nevertheless could not go beyond the moment of deliverance. Despite its strong personal and political resonances, it is one of the least-quoted of Christina's works, though unlike *A Fight over the Body of Homer*, there is no concluding retreat into patient domesticity as this heroine prepares to join the revolution:

> A flash of red reflected light lit up the cathedral spire;
> I heard a cry for faggots, then I heard a yell for fire.

The verse is driven by a strongly charged undertow of mounting excitement, as the story surges towards its climax. In it, Christina seems to have been expressing both the excitement of resistance to patriarchal oppression, and also the fear of fame, as she prepared to step into the public arena, and 'speak before the world'.

The subject may also be linked to the American Civil War, which was beginning to engage British consciousness, for in this context *A Royal Princess* is also a poem about slavery. The *EWJ* carried regular articles on this topic, including Barbara's first-hand observations and a reprint of Fanny Kemble's account of a slave sale, and Christina's feelings were equally simple and firm. 'Please do not think I was tepid about the American War,' she later wrote to a friend. 'I cared to go no farther with the rights and wrongs of the question than the one fact that the North struck at slavery. This settled all my partisanship at once, for Slavery I loathe and abhor.' It is therefore significant that the tone of *A Royal Princess* echoes that of *Curse for a Nation* which had appeared in Barrett Browning's latest book:

> 'Therefore' the voice said, 'shalt thou write
>   My curse tonight.
> Some women weep and curse, I say
> (And no one marvels), night and day.
>
> 'And thou shalt take their part tonight,
>   Weep and write.
> A curse from the depths of womanhood
> Is very salt, and bitter, and good.

A little while later, *A Royal Princess* was the poem Christina chose to donate to a fund-raising anthology in support of textile workers in Lancashire, who were suffering the effects of the trade embargo against the Southern slave crop, cotton. If it was too long, she told editor Isa Craig, she had plenty of other pieces, though none 'on so appropriate a theme'.

She spent the first fortnight of November in residence at the Penitentiary, on condition that she had leisure to attend to her proofs. This shows her sense of priorities: the author took precedence over the social worker, and her true vocation was confirmed. But it also suggests that publication was well-advanced, which it was not. Macmillan had not yet approved the manuscript. Indeed, he had not yet seen it, and after the successful appearance of *An Apple Gathering* in the magazine, sent a polite note of inquiry. 'My brother has got my collected verses at present, and means I know to show them to you,' Christina replied tactfully, adding her own excuse that the poems had taken longer 'putting to rights' than expected, which was why she had not answered his previous inquiry. Such uncharacteristic discourtesy suggests Gabriel was at fault; had she already asked him to respond?

In indirect apology Gabriel offered two woodblock designs. Both author and publisher were pleased, but further delay ensued, as Macmillan sought an opportunity to discuss the text. 'I was hoping to have seen you one of these Thursdays to talk about your sister's poems,' he wrote on 28 October. 'I quite think a selection of them would have a chance – or, to put it more truly, that with some omissions they might do. At least I would run the risk of a small edition, with the two designs which you kindly offer.' Clearly, whatever Christina expected in the way of proofs, it was only now that the manuscript was formally accepted. However, Macmillan continued, he hoped to make it 'an exceedingly pretty little volume and to bring it out as a small Christmas book. This would give it every chance of coming right to the public.' If the public proved wise and discerning, the print-run could easily be increased. *Goblin Market* would obviously be the main attraction, and should therefore furnish any designs:

A quaint wood-cut initial – not elaborate and *not* sprawling down the page, but with a queer goblin, say, grinning at a sweet patient woman face – or something else of the kind, would make a nice addition.

Gabriel was in Yorkshire, from where he sent Christina the good news. She was already at Highgate. 'No doubt you heard of Christina's luck with Macmillan,' he wrote to Mamma a day or so later. It cannot have been until his return to London on 7 November at the earliest that the final text was agreed upon and unfortunately there is no record of which poems Macmillan wished to omit, or whether Gabriel persuaded him to include them. But soon all was settled. 'If Christina is away,' wrote Gabriel in his next letter to Albany Street, 'will you forward the enclosed at once, and let me hear to that effect.'

This was probably the formal agreement, together with some samples of cloth for the binding. Was she meant to choose? Christina asked, stating a preference for puce or violet, and adding that, as a very minor grievance in the scale of things, she deplored the looming threat of war with the United States, lest it affect sales. The British government was pledged to a neutral line, but the Union seizure of two Confederate envoys on a British ship was being regarded as a *casus belli*. In the event Prince Albert intervened, and the threat of hostilities was averted.

Goblin Market and Other Poems was quickly set, filling just under two hundred small pages. Second proofs were with Christina by 7 December. But again Gabriel was responsible for delay, for he had no time to attend to the woodcuts – a title page showing the sisters asleep 'golden head by golden head' and a frontispiece showing Laura cutting a lock of hair, surrounded by animals with aggressively fawning faces. At first he promised that both would be drawn well before the end of November, but this proved optimistic, especially as he insisted that the engraving be done by the firm in which he was now a partner, Morris, Marshall, Faulkner & Co, even though they had no professional skills in this field. Several more days elapsed before Charley Faulkner, Oxford don and the firm's accountant, to whom one block had been allocated, could be located. Where was he? Gabriel asked; and would he have time? But, he added:

> Do not be at all fidgetted about it, as Macmillan will put off the publication till February if necessary, and should you not please yourself with this first block, it will be no trouble to me to draw it again. But I dare say you will agree with me that the soonest done is the best if practicable, and that we should try for Xmas. It seems to me that with your steady eye and hand it cannot be too difficult.

Clearly, even with a swift publishing schedule, the book could hardly be out for Christmas if the illustrations were not ready by the beginning of December. It is hard to escape the conclusion that at least half-consciously Gabriel was holding back his sister's volume – perhaps so that it would not compete with his own *Early Italian Poets*, or because he did not want it to appear before his own volume of original work. He was also under much other pressure – Lizzie's erratic behaviour, painting commissions to fulfil, financial problems following the death of a patron, and promised assistance with a new book on Blake. Christina's woodblocks therefore lost out, though she appeared unperturbed. 'Have you seen my brother's designs?' she asked Macmillan sweetly, when they were finally drawn. 'Charming I think.'

In other respects she was anxious, however. She wrote to protest when she saw the book advertised as *The Goblin Market* – 'Please expunge *the* as forming no part of the title' – and to both printer and publisher when on the page proofs she found three errors, at least one of which she was sure had already been corrected. This was so serious, she claimed, she would be greatly vexed if it appeared in print.

There was in the event plenty of time for corrections. For one thing, the woodblocks were still not ready. For another, the Prince Consort died unexpectedly on 14 December, plunging the nation into mourning.

Christina was sufficiently moved by Albert's death to write a funeral ode of her own, if not exactly to order, like the Laureate, then certainly to the occasion. Though dismal as verse, *Our Widowed Queen* was thus on a public theme that struck a chord with the whole country, as if registering Christina's incipient debut as a published poet.

21

Fame

THEN ON 11 February came another sudden death – that of Lizzie. 'You will see about it in the papers, unfortunately – laudanum,' wrote William laconically to Fred Stephens, cancelling an appointment.

In all probability, this was not the first overdose Lizzie had taken. She had been in the habit of taking large doses, to soothe her nerves and help her sleep, and in her disturbed state no doubt such an outcome had been half feared. Mixed with natural grief and shock, there was therefore some sense of relief when the news reached Albany Street early that morning, which Lucy Brown noted and remembered.

The evening before, Lizzie and Gabriel had dined out with young Algernon Swinburne. Gabriel then took his wife home before going on to the Working Men's College in Red Lion Square. Returning home towards midnight, he found Lizzie unconscious, breathing heavily, with the empty laudanum phial beside the bed. Unable to rouse her, he called a doctor who used a stomach pump. A message was sent to Lizzie's family across the river, summoning her sister Clara. Other doctors were called, and at five o'clock Gabriel arrived at Brown's house, taking him back to Chatham Place for the now inevitable outcome. At 7.20 in the morning Lizzie died.

The inquest returned a verdict of accidental death, so a suicide verdict was avoided. Nevertheless, the circumstances were the 'cause of some notoriety,' as Scott remarked, which added to the shock. In the coffin Gabriel placed Lizzie's bible and the manuscript of the poems he had been preparing for publication. The book was already advertised, but William, for one, felt that such a sacrifice was appropriate in the circumstances. Lizzie was laid to rest in the same grave as their father, and the family went into deep mourning. There is however no sign that her death caused Maria or Christina any great distress, not so much from lack of feeling but because none of Gabriel's family had been able to get close to Lizzie; their grief was chiefly on his account. Christina's letter to Mary Haydon about prospective auntship shows that she had looked forward to greater friendship. Now, barely a year later, this hope had vanished; and a certain regret tinged Christina's later references to her sister-in-law.

Staying temporarily at Albany Street, Gabriel took the opportunity to make further improvements to his goblin design. 'You are perhaps already aware of his great loss,' wrote Christina to Macmillan, 'and will imagine that he is little fit for business: he promises however to return it almost immediately.' The title page had already been entrusted to a professional engraver; now, 'with marvellous boldness, not to say impudence', Charley and Gabriel finally succeeded with the frontispiece, and by the beginning of April the book was ready. Christina liked its sober blue binding and absence of proof errors. It was, she wrote rather pointedly, no small satisfaction to appear in public with only her own shortcomings to answer for. A few days later she received her six complimentary copies. 'I have already commenced distributing them, and as two of my recipients are my mother and sister, am quite certain my little book has already given some pleasure,' she told Macmillan, adding that she knew a good many copies were wanted by her friends, so some would sell. However, she trusted it would also be noticed. 'I hope reviewers will say something about G. M. Even being laughed at is better than being ignored,' she wrote.

This was a remarkably confident observation. The prospect of critical reviews is daunting to most new writers, who are often both fearful and yet over-optimistic. For women of Christina's generation, seldom accustomed to emerging from the private sphere, it was immeasurably hard: her phrase 'to know that I appear in public with only my own shortcomings to answer for' carried extra meaning when ladies could be criticised for the very act of appearing in public, with no shortcomings at all. One suspects Christina's brave preference for being laughed at disguised a real fear, for she had reached the age of thirty-one without having had her work publicly assessed by rigorous or impartial standards, let alone hostile or prejudiced reviewers.

She had however received her share of rejections, to say nothing of Ruskin's recent attack on her poetics, as well as valuable criticism of her work from her siblings. And she badly wanted to be noticed: as she had written to William Aytoun, there was nothing worse than being ignored. In this respect her approach was professional, and almost masculine in its boldness. Nevertheless she must have awaited the reviewers' judgements with inner trepidation, perhaps remembering the effect of criticism on her father, and Gabriel's continuing fear of public exhibition. So there was a dilemma: she hoped for recognition, yet pretended her only desire was to please family and friends, lest she be guilty of conceit by seeking praise. As Maria had exhorted her Bible students, if one could not help hearing oneself praised, one should inwardly beg God to keep one humble. Bad reviews would be very humbling. In the event however she had more to fear from pride. The reviews were good.

'Those who are acquainted with Miss Rossetti's fugitive pieces will expect much from this volume, and they will not be disappointed,' began the *London Review* on 12 April in a long, double column critique, with extensive quotation. The volume was thoroughly original, 'the genuine utterance of a richly imaginative mind' and 'of a very high order, that deserves a special place among our favourite books'. The *Spectator*, which commonly did a round-up of fiction and poetry but devoted a full article to the book, had particular praise for the title poem:

> We believe fully that in that border-land of the marvellous – half dream, half awaking intellect, half conscience – . . . Miss Rossetti has found a true field for her genius. She handles her little marvel with that rare poetic discrimination which neither exhausts it of its simple wonders by pushing symbolism too far, nor keeps those wonders in the merely fabulous and capricious stage. In fact, she has produced a true children's poem, which is far more delightful to the mature than to children, though it would be delightful to all.

It is not often that a new author, particularly a poet with her first slender volume, receives such immediate and unanimous critical coverage, for these notices were followed by equally appreciative reviews in *The Critic*, the *Literary Review*, and the *Literary Gazette*. Indeed, only by reading the reviews can we understand how Christina felt when publication was finally achieved – especially when on 26 April the prestigious *Athenaeum* added its commendation:

> To read these poems after the laboured and skilful but not original verse which has been issued of late, is like passing from a picture gallery, with its well-feigned semblances of nature, to the real nature out-of-doors which greets us with the waving grass and the pleasant shock of the breeze.

Goblin Market was dramatic and delightful whether legend or allegory, and the goblins were 'so deliciously painted, that we almost forgive poor Laura for yielding to their seductions'. Above all, Miss Rossetti was 'a mistress of verbal harmony'. In *Love from the North* and *Maude Clare* ideas were 'rendered with a vividness and roundness that leaves nothing to be added or desired'; in *Apple Gathering*, the texture of the verse was so delicate that the reader's own imagination was called into play. Not all the pieces were of equal merit, the reviewer concluded judiciously, but as a whole the collection displayed 'undeniable and unborrowed' imagination and beauty.

Genius – imagination – beauty – originality: 'Altogether I am faring very well amongst the critics,' wrote Christina modestly when Macmillan sent clippings, adding that friends were equally 'goodnatured' in their praises.

My dear Mrs Heimann,

Your's affectionately,

Christina Rossetti

Christina with ringlets, 1847. Pencil portrait by
Gabriel Rossetti, affectionately inscribed by the
sitter to Amelia Heimann (Victoria & Albert Museum)

Aunt Charlotte Polidori, 1853. Pencil drawing by Gabriel, owned by Christina at the time of her death (Birmingham Museum and Art Gallery)

Frances Rossetti, 1852. Pencil drawing by Gabriel, owned by Christina at the time of her death (Birmingham Museum and Art Gallery)

Aunt Eliza Polidori, ink drawing by Gabriel Rossetti, *c.* 1852 (Birmingham Museum and Art Gallery)

Christina at a window. Pencil sketch by Gabriel inscribed by William Rossetti: 'This must be Christina – Date towards 1850' (Iowa Historical Library, Des Moines)

Grandfather Gaetano Polidori, age 90. Pencil drawing
by Gabriel Rossetti, done in 1853 (Private Collection)

Father Gabriele Rossetti, age 70. Pencil portrait by
Gabriel Rossetti (Private Collection)

Brother William, age 17. Pencil drawing by Gabriel
Rossetti (Private Collection)

Brother Gabriel, age 18. Pencil and chalk self-portrait
by Gabriel Rossetti (National Portrait Gallery)

ABOVE Young Woman and Girl, oil painting by James Collinson. Nothing is known of this work except that the landscape was painted around 1849 in the Isle of Wight, during James's engagement to Christina (Paul Mellon Center for British Art)

BELOW The Renunciation of St Elizabeth of Hungary. Detailed study for oil painting by James Collinson, 1850. Work on this picture coincided with James's withdrawal from his engagement to Christina (Birmingham Museum and Art Gallery)

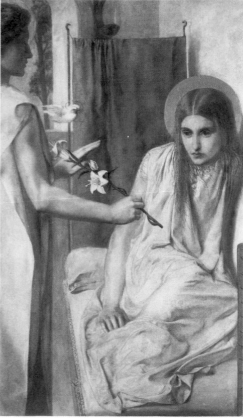

ABOVE The Girlhood of Mary Virgin (detail). Oil painting by Gabriel Rossetti, inscribed 'P.R.B. 1849'. Christina
and her mother sat for the Virgin and St Anne in the
Autumn of 1848 (Tate Gallery)

ABOVE Ecce Ancilla Domini, or the Annunciation
(detail). Oil painting by Gabriel Rossetti inscribed
'D.G.R. March 1850'. (Tate Gallery)

BELOW Christina, 1848. Oil portrait by Gabriel Rossetti,
done around the time of her engagement to James
Collinson (Private Collection)

BELOW Frances Rossetti, 1854. Pencil portrait by
Gabriel Rossetti (Private Collection)

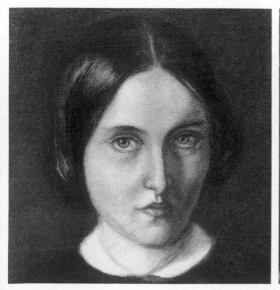

Christina, age 34. Pencil portrait by Gabriel
Rossetti dated 20 May 1865 (National Trust.
Photo: Cliff Guttridge)

Christina, age 26. Unfinished oil portrait by
John Brett, believed to have been begun in 1857
(Private Collection)

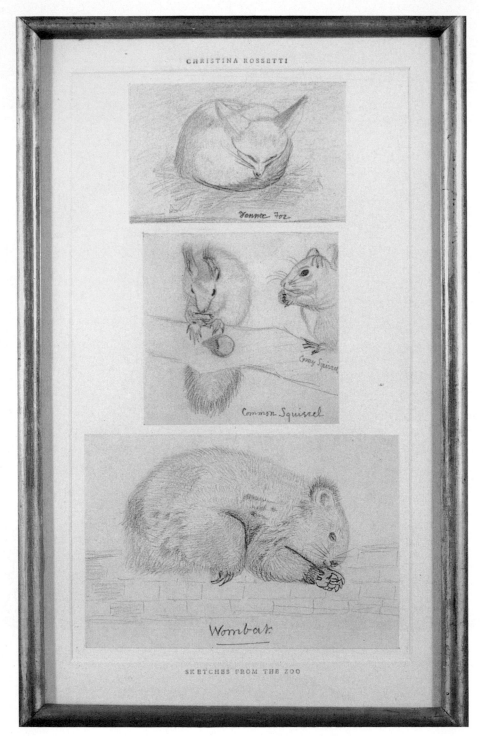

Fennec Fox

Grey Squirrel

Common Squirrel

Wombat

SKETCHES FROM THE ZOO

Animals by Christina. Pencil sketches of fox,
squirrels and wombat (Private Collection)

'If you like these,' gushed the *EWJ*, singling out *Up-hill* and *A Bruised Reed*, 'get the volume, for there are many quite as good. And if you do not like these, then get the volume, for there are many that may please you much better . . .' while Julia Cameron, to whom William had sent a copy, said the book made her feel as if she knew the author already 'and always affectionately as well as admiringly'. Mrs Cameron's importance lay in her friendship with the Laureate, whose opinion was highly desirable, if procurable. Another channel ran through Palgrave, who reported that 'Tennyson when here looked at Miss Rossetti's poems and expressed great pleasure to me at what he read', but added, more discouragingly, that one could never get Tennyson 'to formularise a neat *Saturday* or *London Review* judgment on these matters'. The great bard was well aware how his casual approbation might be used and abused.

The *Saturday Review* had in fact failed to notice the volume on publication, but remedied the omission on 24 May with three long columns of quotation, tempered only by complaint that the story of the goblins was too flimsy to bear the weight of allegory attached to it. The shorter poems, however, were 'as faultless in expression, as picturesque in effect and as high in purity of tone as any modern poem that can be named'. This was Tennyson territory, and there could hardly be greater commendation.

The quarterly journals concurred, with less space but continuing praise. 'The principal poem has a rare delicacy and beauty of a modest kind, and several of the sonnets are fine,' noted the *National Review*. The *British Quarterly Review* liked the devotional pieces best, while the critic of the *Eclectic Review* rather mistakenly believed himself the first to discover the 'rare delight and refreshment' afforded by this 'new and unknown hand', concluding: 'is not this writer a true and most genuine poet?' This review reappeared across the Atlantic, in a Boston weekly digest of British opinion, thereby confirming *Goblin Market* as the critical success of the season, and introducing Christina to a North American audience. In November, the same periodical re-printed *An Apple Gathering*, together with Swinburne's *Song in the Time of Revolution 1860*. A new generation of English poets was claiming its place.

It is clear that reviewers were almost as astonished as pleased to have discovered a new voice, and each individually recognised its excellence. Though some claimed to have remembered poems from *The Germ*, and others were no doubt aware of those in *Macmillan*'s, there was no orchestrated judgement at work. Most praised Christina's originality, while sometimes comparing her work with that of William Morris, or noting echoes of Tennyson; otherwise 'of positive discipleship and imitation there is no trace,' declared the *Eclectic Review*. The volume followed so closely on Barrett Browning's posthumous collection, however, that the issue of poetic succession was unavoidable. 'Simultaneously with the publication of Mrs Browning's *Last Poems*, the legacy of one whose untimely death has robbed us of many a noble thought set to rich music, we receive from a poetess whose name is known to but few, a first work of singular merit,' wrote the *Literary Review*. Moreover, she was well fitted to assume the female mantle, for she handled 'difficult' subjects with exquisite delicacy as well as beauty – in *Goblin Market*, *On The Convent Threshold* and especially *An Apple Gathering* – with none of the 'violation of reserve' that marred work by other 'women of real power', as the *London Review* observed in reference to Mrs Browning, Charlotte Bronte, George Eliot. In Miss Rossetti, no such coarseness was visible.

As if in response to the stress of this general acclaim, Christina fell ill, following in this a well-attested tendency among female authors to sicken after publication – just as later Virginia Woolf would be frequently pushed towards a breakdown on the publication of her books. A century earlier, Maria Jane Jewsbury achieved overnight fame with *Phantasmagoria* and almost immediately collapsed, with a disabling guilt for having been motivated by conceit, while other writers like Elizabeth Gaskell tried to be out of the country on publication or affected not to read reviews. For publishing transgressed the gender rules of the time, in an implicit challenge to male authority in the field of letters. To actively seek recognition and occupy pages of print in the prestigious journals was to trespass on essentially masculine territory. Illness in response to the anxiety thus generated was an affirmation of feminine frailty and dependence, in symbolic denial of the assertive autonomy of entering the literary market place.

Of course Christina had flouted none of the overt rules governing the gendered division of literary labour – her book was short and sweet and lyrical, keeping to the female gardens of religion and fantasy rather than straying into larger political and philosophical fields. But it had drawn attention to itself, threatening uncomfortable notoriety. Her ambivalence is seen in her response to Macmillan's request for a portrait photo of his author. 'I wish I had by me a photograph worthy of a place in your magazine,' she wrote with due modesty, explaining that she was 'not much addicted to sitting for my portrait'. This was true, but she had Henrietta Rintoul's photos from 1855, and also three 'extremely good' *carte de visite* photos taken shortly before the trip to France. And when she realised Macmillan wanted her picture to place in his own copy rather than publish to the world, she was more gracious, forwarding one of Henrietta's, 'perhaps the most satisfactory ever done of me' and claiming it had only just come to hand.

Though no doubt genuine, her ill-health also seems somewhat puzzling. On 3 June, for instance, she was well enough to attend a large and lively evening party at the Parkes' house – a 'great affair' at which 'Dr Bodichon introduced four Algerians, one a splendid Arab in his burnous, camelhair cord round his head,' as Barbara boasted to Allingham, and where Bessie as usual was an excellent hostess. No doubt both women congratulated Christina on her success (Barbara herself had 'been ambitious and had a disappointment – refused at the RA', but insisted she was 'not disheartened at all'). Soon afterwards, however, when Gabriel proposed inviting the whole family to his lodgings to meet Browning, it transpired that 'Christina continues so seedy that it has to be put off'.

She then went to Eastbourne, where she was allowed to try sea-bathing at last, finding it both enjoyable and beneficial. Changes were projected at home, for Gabriel had found a large old house fronting the river in Cheyne Walk, Chelsea, which he wanted the whole family to share. At first they agreed to do so, but then doubts set in, for the short period he had spent at Albany Street had already indicated what tensions might ensue – acutely hinted at by Scott when in confidence to William he contrasted Gabriel's 'unsystematic expenditure' with 'Christina's predetermined notions of things', in combination with William's submission to his mother and sisters' wishes. 'I speak to you rather freely, do I?' Scott wrote. 'The fact is, my own luck in my family was always to be chained up, so I fear in your case.'

'You are too hard upon poor Christina in attributing "predetermined notions" to her,' replied William; 'for she effaces herself very much in all these things and her only notion in questions involving expense is to abstain from it.' It is not clear precisely what inflexible notions were here being alluded to, but the exchange testifies to conflicting attitudes towards money. Christina's extreme caution, reflecting the fact that as she earned virtually nothing, so it behoved her not to spend, was in keeping with what the also-careful William described as general 'family unselfishness' and restraint. Indeed all were as parsimonious as each other: only Gabriel inherited Papa's impulse-buying tendency. But it was a symptom: the whole family could hardly live comfortably under one roof.

William insisted to Scott that in all things that mattered he had 'absolute liberty and suiting of my own taste'. Paradoxically, Christina tended to feel that the womenfolk were constrained by having to housekeep for William, and though none would ever have refused such a duty, in their eyes the Chelsea plan had drawbacks, for Gabriel's nocturnal habits and bohemian friends were not theirs. They were also reluctant to leave aunt Eliza to care for aunt Margaret, who was now extremely frail, while the prospect of taking responsibility for a large house, far from Christ Church, Highgate and All Saints, was an additional deterrent. The women therefore decided to stay in Albany Street, while Gabriel and William took Tudor House, inviting Swinburne and George Meredith to share. William agreed to divide his nights, sleeping sometimes there and sometimes at home. 'We should have missed him very much if he had left us altogether,' Christina explained to Barbara in September.

'I have not forgotten the Portfolio,' she added, for Barbara had called while she was away, reminding her of the earlier promise, 'and my latterly alarmingly barren brain not impeding will with your permission direct my contribution under cover to you at Blandford Square'. The latest theme was 'Reflection', but rather than write a new poem, Christina attached the title to the lines originally called *Day Dreams*. This became her usual habit regarding the Portfolio – 'I used, having received notice of the theme, to look up something apposite amongst my old compositions,' she explained later; as she knew, when she tried to write to order, the results were usually poor.

But the exchange of themes acted as a challenge, to what without exaggeration seemed alarming barrenness. For the excitements of publication had made poetry a sluggish trickle, if not a fountain sealed. In the first three months of the year she had completed nothing, and in the next eight only a handful, mostly marked by extreme religious abasement, which a psychological analysis might suggest was prompted by a prophylactic desire not to let praise make her proud. On 17 December, however, came a new dream poem, deploying a strange vision of love and vulnerability:

> Once in a dream (for once I dreamed of you)
>   We stood together in an open field;
>   Above our heads two swift-winged pigeons wheeled,
> Sporting at ease and courting full in view:
> When loftier still a broadening darkness flew,
>   Down-swooping, and a ravenous hawk revealed;
>   Too weak to fight, too fond to fly, they yield;
> So farewell life and love and pleasures new.
> Then as their plumes fell fluttering to the ground,
>   Their snow-white plumage flecked with crimson drops,
>   I wept, and thought I turned towards you to weep:
>   But you were gone; whilst boundary hedgerow tops
> Bent in a wind which bore to me the sound
>   Of far-off piteous bleat of lambs and sheep.

Symbolically, the ravenous hawk is kissing-cousin to the crunching crocodile. The blood-flecked birds – derived from the turtledoves that featured so frequently as images of love in her father's poetic lexicon – are innocent victims for whom the poet weeps, and for whom she expects her companion or lover to weep also. But he is inconstant and vanishes, leaving her alone.

She wrote no poem for the New Year vigil, as had been her habit, but on 13 January she gave thanks *For a Mercy Received*:

> Thank God who spared me what I feared!
>   Once more I gird myself to run.
>   Thy promise stands, Thou faithful One.
> Horror of darkness disappeared
>   At length: once more I see the sun,
>
> And dare to wait in hope for Spring,
>   To face and bear the Winter's cold;
>   The dead cocoon shall yet unfold
> And give to light the living wing;
>   There's hidden sap beneath the mould.

The poem was of course devotional, but seems to contain also a secular meaning: this year, as William wrote, the bay had begun to sprout, and now the sap began to rise again in her heart. Spring was a figure of emotional as well as spiritual rebirth, an image of simpler unfurling joys, for the dead cocoon of love was once again ready to unfold. Or at least so it seems, though Christina was so reticent in matters of the heart that the clues are not easy to discern.

The new object of her affections was Charles Cayley, her father's last pupil, who had remained an intermittent friend of Gabriel and more especially William. He was an accomplished linguist, whom Gabriel thought a dry-as-dust scholar, but William regarded with more affection, as a nervous fogey old before his time, though wholly good-natured and exceedingly well-read.

The first hint of Christina's growing friendship is seen in the fund-raising anthology for the Lancashire textile workers, issued by the Victoria Press at the end of 1862. This was another feminist enterprise under the aegis of the Langham Place group, run by Emily Faithfull and dedicated to demonstrating the typographical and bookbinding skills women were capable of. Christina, as a yet-unpublished author, had not been invited to contribute to the first anthology, edited by Adelaide Procter. Now, Isa Craig placed her *Royal Princess* in place of honour, registering her change in status. At the same time Christina volunteered Charles Cayley's work, saying it was 'not impossible' she could procure his services, and at Christmas she gave William a copy of the anthology with handwritten corrections to his contribution *Ad Sepulchrum: A Fragment* a cod medieval ballad about a lady and her false Crusader knight.

She also drew Macmillan's attention to the volume, adding rather inconsequentially: 'Last autumn there was a plan for my attending the meeting of the Royal Society in Cambridge. Had I done so I should have hoped for the pleasure of an introduction to Mrs Macmillan, but after all I did not leave town.'

Had she visited Cambridge, Macmillan would of course have welcomed her to his house, but scarcely needed to know of a non-event some months before. He may idly have wondered what reason she had to attend the Royal Society, and the answer can only lie in Cayley's unprepossessing figure, for his brother Arthur was a celebrated mathematician, soon to become Sadlerian Professor.

Charles Bagot Cayley – or 'CBC' as he often featured in Christina's later correspondence – was a timid, reclusive and in some ways foolish man despite his erudition. He was slightly older than the Rossetti siblings, having been born in 1823 in Russia, where his father represented British trading interests. He was now bald, with a high domed head and pink cheeks, and both his outdated tail-coat and general absentmindedness became legendary. Absorbed in scholarly matters, he had little interest in anything else, but was 'sociable too in a shy way', though socially inept, as William recalled. He smiled furtively as if at some joke he alone appreciated, and when spoken to would often pause so long before replying that his interlocutor gave up waiting. Then, 'at last the answer came in a tone between hurry and confusion, and with an articulation far from easy to follow. In truth one viewed his advent with some apprehension, only too conscious that some degree of embarrassment was sure to ensue.'

Having lost his capital in an unwise advertising investment, Charles lived frugally in lodgings, or sometimes with his sisters and widowed mother in Blackheath, spending most of his time in the British Museum Reading Room. In the 1850s he published a three-volume translation of the *Divine Comedy* in *terza rima* (handsomely acknowledging Professor Rossetti's works) and alongside philology he had poetic ambitions, in 1857 issuing at his own expense a volume called *Psyche's Interludes* though nothing he wrote belonged to the 'readable order', as William commented. Indeed most was lamentable, ranging from choice specimens on Ovidian themes to sub-Tennysonian ballads, sometimes distressingly coarse, as on Hypatia's martyrdom:

> They pounded me with fists and stones,
> The murderous monks of old;

They scraped with oyster shells my bones
  They'd rent my inmost fold!

That face of which in lecture-hall
  I veiled the maddening light –
To blue and black they mashed it all!
  They made it such a fright.

He had a cloth ear, and the frequent falseness of his poetic measure must have made the Rossettis squirm; at a later date Christina made several emendations to his version of Dante, in order to correct the *terza rima*.

In 1860, having added Hebrew to his studies, Cayley produced a translation of the Psalms, in metre if not quite verse. The subscription list reveals that his social world was headed by the Leifchild family, closely followed by the Rossettis (Frances subscribed for four copies, William for three and aunt Charlotte for one) and it was perhaps this apparently devotional enterprise that first aroused Christina's interest in the author.

If so, she kept it very quiet. Writing to thank Mamma for another of Cayley's books in mid-1862, Gabriel remarked that he seemed 'lower in the scale of creation than ever', evidently unaware of his sister's growing partiality. Some few months before, Cayley had introduced his sisters, Henrietta and Sophie, whom Christina ambiguously described as handsome and striking, 'in a bonnet and not very good light', and with whom she discussed the Great Gorilla Controversy, for it emerged that the Cayleys were connected with the Dr Gray who challenged the claim of an explorer to have killed a gorilla in self-defence. The following year, she was invited to Cambridge, strictly speaking not to the Royal Society but the closely-allied British Association for the Advancement of Science, for whose proceedings in 1862 Arthur Cayley's subjects were dynamics, curves and Gauss's theory of terrestrial magnetism. The topics were too abstruse for Christina's comprehension, but the BAAS issued special ladies' tickets for relatives and friends, and no doubt Miss Rossetti was invited to join Charles and his sisters on an excursion to Cambridge, which had been Charles's own university and which she had never visited.[22] In the event however she did not go, having only just returned from Eastbourne.

Biographers have found it hard to credit Charles Cayley with inspiring the second of what William called his sister's 'affairs of the heart'. Lucy Charlmont, Christina's fictional heroine who is disappointed in love, finally finds happiness with a previously despised admirer who is worthy but unromantic, reflecting meekly on her own thirty years that 'one cannot have everything' and it is surely no coincidence that this dull but estimable fellow has bestowed upon him the name of Arthur, borrowed from Charles's brother. Moreover, acknowledging that Cayley was 'not at all the sort of man who would be attractive to the general run of women', William nevertheless added – since Christina had found him so – that 'the basis of his feelings and the tone of his mind were such as a woman of an exceptional order might genuinely admire'. Just as with James, Charles's unworldliness and lack of sexual presence may have been his most appealing features; for whatever reason, Christina seems to have been frightened by aggressive masculinity. Indeed, Cayley was so abstracted that he did not at first perceive her partiality. This can only be seen in a sequence of love poems in Italian that Christina now began writing which opened in December 1862, with *Amor Dormente?* (*Is Love Sleeping?*) and traces the awakening of her feelings:

> Goodbye, dear friend;
>   I may not love,
> For a lover that I love
>   Has already slain my heart.
>
> But for the next life
>   I reserve my hopes for you;
> For this life, memories
>   So many, and then more.

Hesitantly, the speaker offers hope, having believed her own heart dead – or asleep, as in her New Year poem. Was it about to wake from its cocoon?

Amor Dormente and the pieces that followed must have a private meaning, because they were not transcribed into the notebooks but discovered after Christina's death in a ribbon-tied bundle 'in the jealous seclusion of her writing desk'. William had no doubt all were addressed to Cayley.

This was the start of a tentative dialogue that Christina conducted with Cayley through the medium of poetry, as if both were too shy for direct speech. It came in response to a long poem Cayley composed in 1862 called *The Purple of the West*, an ambitious production that gradually discloses itself as a love sequence addressed to a fair mistress. The forms are too conventionalised to be personally revealing but suggest that Cayley was not a total stranger to timid, buttoned-up desire; indeed, poetic convention probably offered him the best means of expressing emotion, lacking as he did Christina's skill in direct and simple utterance. 'How could I sleep, unless I dream'd of her?' inquires one section. 'How dar'd I waken, when I dream'd no more?' It is far from clear that *The Purple of the West* was addressed to Christina, but it certainly stirred some answer in her heart, for her Italian sequence was called *Il Rosseggiar dell'Oriente: Canzoniere all' Amico Lontano*, which translates as the 'Reddening of the East: Songs to a Distant Friend'. It is thus a sunrise sequence, in response to Cayley's purple sunset, which was published in 1863, in the third Victoria Press anthology, issued to commemorate the marriage of the Prince of Wales to Princess Alexandra of Denmark. There being no charitable objective for this volume, Christina merely looked up and retitled something from among her old items. Soon afterwards, she wrote a second lyric marking the dawning of new love: *Amor si Sveglia?* (*Is Love Waking?*):

> With a new spring
>   The old spirit is reborn
> Love whispers to you 'Hope'
>   Still I'll not say it.
>
> If Love bids you 'Love',
>   He may encourage you, my friend,
> Swearing 'That heart is yours' –
>   Still I'll not say it.
>
> And in truth who can say
>   If that heart's worth a fig?
> I believe, at least I hope it:
>   Yet still not say it.

The subtleties of this were beyond Cayley's skill as an author but perhaps as a translator he appreciated the way the sense-stresses of each fourth line vary the meaning, conveying a delicate madrigal of feeling that might be designed to encourage a diffident lover. If Cayley's heart like her own had once been wounded, and he feared to hope again, she was here hinting at mutual reawakening.

Christina assured Macmillan that her own contribution to the Princess of Wales album was not new, for by courtesy he had prior claim on new pieces. She added, in her self-deprecating manner, that her 'scribbling facility' still appeared to have 'come to a long stop'. But this was disingenuous, if not untrue, for her inspiration had in fact returned, and in the first three months of 1863 she completed ten poems which seem to usher in a distinctly buoyant mood, in keeping with her reawakening heart. *The Queen of Hearts*, dated 3 January, was an exceptionally adroit performance of wit and oblique disclosure:

How comes it, Flora, that, whenever we
Play cards together, you invariably,
  However the pack parts,
    Still hold the Queen of Hearts?

I've scanned you with a scrutinizing gaze,
Resolved to fathom these your secret ways:
  But, sift them as I will,
    Your ways are secret still.

I cut and shuffle; shuffle, cut, again;
But all my cutting, shuffling proves in vain:
  Vain hope, vain forethought too;
    That Queen still falls to you.

I dropped her once, prepense; but, ere the deal
Was dealt, your instinct seemed her loss to feel:
  "There should be one card more"
    You said, and searched the floor.

I cheated once; I made a private notch
In Heart-Queen's back, and kept a lynx-eyed watch;
  Yet such another back
    Deceived me in the pack:

The Queen of Clubs assumed by arts unknown
An imitative dint that seemed my own;
  This notch, not of my doing,
    Misled me to my ruin.

It baffles me to puzzle out the clue,
Which must be skill, or craft, or luck in you:
  Unless, indeed, it be
    Natural affinity.

February began with a clutch of pieces looking forward joyously to summer – to Christina, swallows were always birds of promise and June always the 'month of months' – together with the thoughtful *Helen Grey*, in which the heroine is admonished in terms that might be directed at her own supercilious manner:

  Because one loves you, Helen Grey,
    Is that a reason you should pout,

And like a March wind veer about,
And frown, and say your shrewish say?
Don't strain the cord until it snaps,
  Don't split the sound heart with your wedge,
  Don't cut your fingers with the edge
Of your keen wit; you may perhaps.

In *Purple of the West*, Cayley had included a sonnet in which the fair mistress was a proud lily, and the poet himself too diffident to speak. In real life, as William described, talking to Cayley could sometimes be like a dialogue with the deaf, and now a long pause in the unfolding relationship occurred, with a correspondingly long gap in the *Rosseggiar* sequence, almost as if Christina had given it up. One has the impression of two shy persons, conscious of their age and of the possible ridicule their relationship might invite, anxious not to attract attention, and unsure of each other's feelings. Who would be the first to speak? Neither did, it appears. 'I loved you first,' Christina wrote later; 'I loved and guessed at you . . .' Much like Cayley's conversation, this was a relationship that would unfold only very slowly: his responses could not be hurried.

22

Admirers and Rivals

DESPITE THE GOOD reviews, sales of *Goblin Market and Other Poems* were slow. And after the excitement had subsided, Christina felt dismayed that the book had not established her more securely. When Macmillan asked why she sent no new poems to the magazine, she replied frankly, saying 'Truth to tell I was disappointed at drawing no more funds or fame from the Magazine, but I thought you were so well aware of my literary existence that if I was wanted, the same might be notified to me.' She promised to send Masson something immediately. But as regards a second collection, she wrote, in a rare account of her poetic practice:

> A rather longer book will I doubt not be possible should the demand arise but I know myself too well to forsee that even were I ever so successful, I should always be a worry to the publishing world.
>
> Write to order I really can*not*: not of course that I could not then produce somewhat in bulk; but if I have yet done aught worth doing, it has been by simply taking what came when it came. Indeed, if I may at all hope to be remembered, I would rather live as a single book writer than as an only-one-readable book writer.

This confirms the seriousness of Christina's literary ambition, only partially masked by the conditional subjunctive phrases. She certainly wished for funds and fame, and sometimes regretted not being able to write in bulk or to order like many contemporaries from Tennyson downwards, but she also knew that in her case good poems did not come from trying. Nor did they arrive as spontaneous utterances, as the conventional view of feminine inspiration held, and as William misleadingly believed, no doubt from hearing her describe the process as 'taking what came when it came'; they had to be waited for rather than willed. When they arrived, they were worked upon until satisfactory, or at least as good as she could make them. Of course, in youth, Christina had sometimes written virtually to order, with charades and *bouts rimés*, and this proved valuable training; but as her voice matured she feared the temptation to write for the sake of publication. Much as she liked praise and fame, she looked to quality, and her preference to be remembered rather 'as a single book writer than as an only-one-readable book writer' is crucial to an understanding of her career.

The poems she sent to Masson included *Light Love*, the moral ballad of a seduced woman nursing her child and appealing for divine justice. It chimed with *Macmillan's* social conscience and appeared in the February issue, closely followed by *The Bourne* in March. Both were old items not selected for *Goblin Market* (though presumably Macmillan did not know this) that restored her self-esteem and indeed brought a touch of arrogance, for in acknowledging receipt of two guineas for *Light Love* she complained about the level of payment. 'Let me however, observe that *Maude Clare* (before I could rank as "anybody") and *Apple Gathering* were £2-2-0 each,' she wrote, with reference to pre-*Goblin Market* earnings; 'and that I don't think that I ought to afford much longer pieces than the latter chosen from among my best, losing copyright as of course I do.' And, she concluded: 'for the future I think I must be more careful'.

This prickliness points to a less than ideal relationship with Macmillan which is rather difficult to understand, for he was an honourable businessman. Now she was a published author, Christina was aware her next collection would be judged by its previously unpublished items and therefore took care to give magazines her slighter rather than strongest pieces. But why did she feel Macmillan liable to underpayment? She was not otherwise mercenary of mind. Gabriel, however, always pushed for higher fees, and one suspects that, having decided 'Mac' was mean and his sister over-modest, he urged her to ask for more. Macmillan however had a standard system, of two guineas per page, or one guinea for a short poem, and she had not yet achieved such eminence as to command a better rate. Copyright was a related issue: under existing law it passed from author to publisher in respect of single items, and this could create difficulties when a collection was issued. Along with other authors Christina seems to have felt she should be paid both for the contribution and for the loss of copyright – just as, at this date, artists were beginning to negotiate both the outright sale of a picture and a fee for its reproduction rights.

But what surprises most about her letter is its aggrieved tone and the sense that she now considered herself 'somebody' in the literary world. When Macmillan was evidently also surprised, she hastily apologised. What he called her 'pet grievance', she insisted, was not that she wished to be paid more than two guineas a page – only that if *Light Love* had not been printed in columns it would have covered two pages. Moreover, she grovelled

No one is more aware than myself that what slight footing I have gained in the world of letters has its foundation in your magazine; indeed I had encountered too many rebuffs elsewhere to leave room for doubt.

She had also mistaken his position regarding copyright. 'As to keeping your written permission to reprint when and what I please, be sure that to me your word is as good as your bond,' she continued, 'and that whilst you generously forego your rights in this matter, I have neither present inclination nor money to plan second editions, nor indeed conceit to fancy them called for.'

The following month, Macmillan sent two guineas for *The Bourne*. Still smarting from her own presumption, Christina inquired with studied politeness whether Macmillan's 'system' involved such a rate of over-pay? If not, she would conclude that he sent it 'for other reasons', and refund half the fee. True, the little poem occupied only half a page, but this punctiliousness – which William later identified as a real defect in his sister's character – might also be received as sarcasm. It is to be hoped that Alexander Macmillan took no offence, but simply smiled at his over-sensitive contributor and her carefully-returned guinea.

The episode is one example of her changing sense of status as a writer. Hitherto, her career had been virtually private; now, people were always asking what she was writing, comparing her work to others', and inviting her to contribute to their magazines. This was gratifying, but sometimes worrying, when for whatever reason her disparaged 'scribbling facility' remained dormant. To stimulate it, and stay in touch with fellow writers like Adelaide and Bessie, Christina kept up her contributions to the Portfolio Society. Although largely a circle of mutual support, this also inevitably contained an element of competition. In May 1863, for instance, telling Barbara that the group was due to meet the next evening at Emily Faithfull's house, Bessie confided that though she did not want to see Miss Faithfull, she nevertheless felt 'inclined to go and beat' Barbara's cousin Mrs Willy, who was evidently giving herself airs.

This year, Bessie had a new book out, so she had grounds for self-congratulation. Poor Mrs Willy (wife of William Smith) was a mainstay of the Society, who eventually accumulated a large collection of its manuscripts from which Christina's contributions can be identified. In February this year, for instance, contradicting her own claim not to be able to write to order, she produced *A Year's Windfalls* expressly for the Portfolio (it shows, in the stodgy trot through the seasons like a nature-study exercise). Mostly however she looked out old items, and eighteen such fair-copy manuscripts survive, circulated between September 1862 and May 1864, and showing how new titles corresponding to Portfolio themes were added to existing or slightly amended texts: *A Soul* (17 February 1854) became *A Study*, *A Burthen* (16 July 1858) became *My Old Friends*, and *A Shadow of Dorothea* (11 November 1858) became *Rivals*. Not all were apt, but some thought went into the selection most strikingly when the Portfolio theme was 'A Coast'. For this Christina copied out her powerful Nightmare poem of 1857 with its mysterious dream-scape of islands and cities peopled with dead men, altering the first line to turn the 'love' in ghostland into a mere friend.

Other poems, though not surviving as Portfolio manuscripts, seem also to have been inspired by its themes. Both A Bird's Eye View and A Dumb Friend, which followed A Year's Windfalls sound like Portfolio titles, suitable for painting or poetry. So too does A Return, under which title Christina circulated a dialogue between the living and dead, copied into the notebook in July as The Poor Ghost. Clearly, the Portfolio was a valuable aid to composition.

Barbara used it for networking. When she came to Britain in summer 1864, for example, she called to present Christina with another picture, in return requesting copies of Christina's poems. Christina replied:

> I am quite ashamed that in the delight of securing your beautiful gift I forgot that you had paid me the compliment of bargaining that my last season's Portfolio papers were to be yours. If you still think them worth having pray reclaim them from Mrs William Smith in whose custody they remain. One or two of the series will I fear not be forthcoming. If you will oblige me with the missing subject, I will copy and send you the pieces.

Some months before, Emily Faithfull had also approached Christina, asking for a contribution to the new feminist Victoria Magazine launched by the Press, which was then advertised with the promise of 'A Poem by Christina Rossetti' in the first number – another register of status. In response, Christina sent LEL, the poem linking herself to Letitia Landon and Elizabeth Barrett Browning – an appropriate salute to the female tradition being carried on by the magazine – and attended the magazine's launch party in June, accompanied by Ellen Heaton.

Bessie, not unnaturally, was vexed by Emily's action, for the new magazine was in direct competition with the English Woman's Journal, which was struggling financially. She promptly invoked her own claim of friendship by also requesting a poem. Christina obliged by resurrecting Gone Before, an unpublished piece from 1856, which appeared in the ailing journal in October.

And in pursuit of further 'funds and fame', she kept Macmillan's regularly supplied, with The Prince who arrived too late in May and A Bird's Eye View in July. Both, rather curiously, were about brides who wait in vain for their bridegrooms. For some reason, David Masson turned the tardy suitor of the first poem into a 'Fairy Prince', which pointed up its folkloric provenance. 'I am glad you like my reverse of the Sleeping Beauty,' Christina wrote to Dora Greenwell; 'except in fairyland such reverses must often occur, yet I don't think it argues a sound or grateful spirit to dwell on them as predominantly as I have done. Bessie Rayner Parkes' last volume, with its healthy cheerfulness, has rebuked me.' This typical self-deprecation suppressed more than it said: though Christina regretted the melancholy of her verses, she hardly considered Bessie a competitor – except perhaps insofar as Bessie's new book received attention: in this respect her comment was an indirect acknowledgement of rivalry.

Earlier in the year, Dora Greenwell had sent an 'overboiling kettle of enthusiasm' which despite a 'vexatious amount of fizz' was truly perceptive of the special quality of Christina's work, and heralded a long and unbroken friendship between the two women, marked by mutual admiration and rueful recognition of female rivalry in respect of other writers. Unfortunately neither Dora's fizzing kettle nor Christina's response have survived, because as Miss Greenwell's biographer explained in 1885, Miss Rossetti did not like to 'accept in public the very high praise of her own genius and poetry which Dora expresses' and the letters subsequently disappeared. But despite modesty, Christina was gratified – Dora Greenwell was a well-respected poet in her own right, whose work regularly appeared in *Good Words* – and she responded by complimenting the 'lofty and profound' theme of one of Dora's recent poems. In return, Miss Greenwell ('am I right in addressing you as Miss *Dora* Greenwell? I really require my C. as otherwise letters appertain to my sister') requested a *carte*, which Christina was not 'conceited enough to send quite unabashed', and indeed unable to supply, for a a new studio portrait – presumably taken for the very purpose of sending to admirers – had been pronounced so bad that no prints were ordered. Despite their mutual acquaintance, they seemed fated never to meet, however. 'If our dear Scotts move away altogether from the North, I fear my prospect of making your personal acquaintance must dwindle to the altogether vague,' Christina wrote at the end of the year. But, she added, 'your kindness has made us no strangers, even though we should never meet – or rather never meet *here*; for on the last day of the year these separations and meetings of time should not alone be thought of'.

Another concomitant of fame was the anthologiser's request, and this year Christina also commended Dora to Mr Orby Shipley, a reverend editor with whom she was herself already in correspondence, pleased to assist his holy work and at the same time discharge her own religious duty of alms-giving; as she had so little money at her own disposal, the free gift of a poem represented a devotional offering.

Rev. Shipley, a young cleric of ritualist persuasion, was an assiduous anthologiser, and for a while Christina's involvement was relatively intense. To his first venture, *Lyra Eucharistica*, on the central rite of communion, she set two unpublished pieces, one a favourite beginning 'I am pale with sick desire' written in February 1856 and the other called *God be merciful to me a sinner*, both of which Shipley retitled and indexed as 'original poems by Miss Christina G. Rossetti'. There followed *Lyra Messianica*, on the Christian year, published at Easter 1864, and finally *Lyra Mystica*, the following Christmas. Altogether Christina submitted fourteen pieces of her own, including two already published items, on which Macmillan had to be consulted. 'Of course, what I give to Mr Shipley, I *give*: I do not receive money,' Christina explained earnestly, lest any suspicion of venality arise.

She also solicited contributions from other authors, forwarding some of Charles Cayley's translations on sacred themes, including one from her own father's *Arpa Evangelica*, which appeared in *Lyra Mystica*. Shortly after this, Shipley abandoned the enterprise, apparently in response to charges that the anthologies were too Romanist for an editor in Anglican orders. But it set a pattern: in the course of her career, Christina responded to many such requests, always willing to allow her work to be used for religious purposes and indeed regarding it as her duty to do so. At the same time, through these contributions her work reached a larger audience, for whom buying sacred anthologies was also a devotional act. Sales of her book might be slow, but magazines and anthologies kept her name before the public, steadily widening her readership.

Social invitations also increased as a result of her fame, for correspondence reveals that her social diary was relatively full of evening parties and at homes. Perhaps this modest degree of lionising was partly responsible for two short devotional poems in a style she was to make especially her own, written when she was most involved with Shipley's projects. The first, in May 1863, was a verbal 'variation' on a scriptural theme, aiming not to elaborate but to freshen the original:

> Consider
> The lilies of the field whose bloom is brief:
> We are as they;
> Like them we fade away
> As doth a leaf.
>
> Consider
> The sparrows of the air of small account;

> Our God doth view
> Whether they fall or mount –
> He guards us too.

The second, *The Lowest Place*, was to be viewed as her main 'signature'
poem:

> Give me the lowest place; not that I dare
>   Ask for that lowest place, but Thou hast died
> That I might live and share
>   Thy glory by Thy side.
>
> Give me the lowest place: or if for me
>   That lowest place too high, make one more low
> Where I may sit and see
>   My God and love Thee so.

This was certainly one of Christina's own favourites – she placed it in
a keynote position in subsequent volumes – but like its near namesake
The Lowest Room it does not seem to bear the full weight of self-
abasement ascribed to it, for if the request is submissive in formula-
tion, it is not so in aspiration, which is no less than the desire to share
God's glory in heaven – the acme of Christian hope. Rather than
representing what now seems excessive Heep-like humility, the poem
is surely a self-addressed admonition against pride. The often exaggerated self-denial in Christina's life and work stemmed partly from
Puseyism, but also from the conflict over ambition and the need to
reconcile being a good writer, a good woman and a good Christian,
without sacrificing the first of these aims.

　　Her ambivalent need for literary recognition was linked to her
father's unabashed desire for it. He, William wrote, 'was fond of name
and fame and would gladly have seen ten times as much published
about himself as he ever did see', while Christina though 'wholly
averse' to being a celebrity was not at all indifferent to fame, and
certainly proud to see her work published. The distinction is nice –
pride in one's work is never wholly separate from pride in oneself –
but important, and one Christina tried to draw by invoking humility.

　　This autumn her difficulties over photographs were solved when
Charles Dodgson contacted Gabriel with a view to securing celebrities
for his camera at Cheyne Walk. 'My dear Mamma,' wrote Gabriel the
same day, getting his visitor's name slightly wrong:

The photographer (Revd. W. Dodgson) is coming here on Wednesday to
do the lot of us – this day week. Will you stay dinner that day and I will

ask the Munros – Mr. and wife – who are the means of bringing Mr D. I
suppose Wm will be back by then will he not? If not, we must put it off.
Maggie is also available I trust.

Dodgson was unpacking his apparatus when Christina arrived, a day
ahead of the others. 'She seemed a little shy at first, and I had very
little time for conversation with her, but I much liked the little I saw of
her,' he recorded. She sat for two pictures, followed by Gabriel and
two friends the photographer did not know or, it seems, expect: 'a Mr
Cayley and a Mr le Gros' (the French painter Alphonse Legros, now
living in London). In the evening William and other guests arrived. 'A
memorable day,' noted Dodgson.

The following morning Maria and Mamma arrived. 'Spent the day
at Mr Rossetti's photographing,' Dodgson recorded. 'Took groups and
some single ones, of himself, his mother, two sisters and brother
William, and also of a very fine curly-headed boy (a model) and of Mr
and Mrs Munro . . . Both the sisters seem clever, and are very pleasant
to converse with.'

'It was our aim to appear in the full family group of five,' Christina
explained later, 'but whilst various others succeeded, that particular
negative was spoilt by a shower and I possess a solitary print taken
from it in which we appear as if splashed by ink.' This showed
Mamma and Maria at chess, William leaning over as if contemplating
his mother's next move, Gabriel looking on, hat in hand, and Christina seated beside him, turning towards the others with downcast eyes.
Only Maria looks towards the camera, with moonface and rotund
figure wrapped in a wide-sleeved mantle. For the occasion all three
women wore wide silk crinoline dresses, with fashionably flounced
pagoda sleeves, although their hair was severely dressed and there
were no concessions to simpering prettiness. In William's view, one
solo portrait of Christina gave her 'an intellectual profile' while the
other showed 'a cheerful and somewhat bantering air', though in
truth this is hard to detect – as always the female Rossettis presented
an austere image, in which humour and self-mockery are invisible.

They liked the results, however, continuing to order prints and
vignettes for distribution to friends and family, and Christina in particular remained on very cordial terms with the mathematical photographer. As it happened, Dodgson, who appeared to William merely
donnish, with an external appearance of polite propriety, had a particular reason for wishing to meet the author of Goblin Market, for this
had helped inspire his now-famous tale of 'Alice's Adventures Underground', which he was hoping to publish. Perhaps he mentioned this
at Chelsea, or asked about publishers: shortly afterwards Alice was
accepted by Macmillan. Dodgson's admiration was life-long. 'I regard

her as a *genuine* poet,' he later wrote emphatically. *Goblin Market* seems to me a work of real genius.'

He offered to show Maria and Christina around Oxford, should they visit the city. Christina was tempted, having never seen the murals painted by Gabriel and his friends. 'Delightful it would be, that possible visit to Oxford,' she replied:

> We contemplate it in a spirit of vague approbation. Stirred up by the kind offer of such a showman, and by a wish to see the sights of Oxford in general and Gabriel's handiwork in particular; weighed down by family immobility; – we tremble in the balance, though I fear the leaden element preponderates. It is characteristic of us to miss opportunities. A year or two ago I had a chance of seeing Cambridge, and of course missed it.

Dodgson does not seem to have pressed the invitation, though in his experience the Misses Rossetti were not especially immobile; following their visit to Chelsea, he met them again the next summer at a charity event in Surrey. In other respects, however, they were distinctly leaden: with few exceptions, the furthest Christina travelled was an annual visit to a sedate seaside resort, and even when not constrained by housekeeping and other duties, she showed little inclination to explore, or even visit friends within easy reach of London. The reasons for this are not clear, but lack of disposable income and the dangers of self-indulgence perhaps played a part. William would have provided the cash, but Christina would always have had to ask; unless Mamma showed a desire to move, her own wishes often remained unfulfilled.

If Dodgson's photographs confirmed her status as literary celebrity, she was also gratified by a belated but warm review of *Goblin Market* alongside Patmore's latest, *Angel in the House*, written by Caroline Norton – all the more so because to her secret dismay a new star had risen in the poetic firmament. According to the *Athenaeum*, the poems of Miss Jean Ingelow's first volume would 'make the eyes of all lovers of poetry dance with a gladder light than if they had come upon a treasure-trove of gold':

> Here is the presence of Genius which cannot easily be defined, but which makes itself surely felt in a glow of delight such as makes the old world young again. Here is the power to fill common earthly facts with heavenly fire; a power to gladden wisely and sadden nobly; to shake the heart and bring the mist of tears into the eyes ...

The panegyric occupied five and a half columns. Worse, it welcomed especially the poet's genial spirit, which brought just what the critic had lately asked for – in a comment that may have been the origin of

Christina's self-critical remark to Dora Greenwell about her own mournfulness – 'a little more of the blithe heart in our singers, a little more cheeriness in our poetry'.

Christina was neither anxious to read such a rival, nor to betray any sense of envy, as she discreetly acknowledged in December on receipt of Macmillan's latest payment. 'Miss Procter I am not afraid of,' she wrote: 'but Miss Ingelow (judging by extracts; I have not yet seen the actual volume) – would be a formidable rival to most men, and to any woman. Indeed I have been bewailing that she did not publish with you.' Issued by Longman in July, Jean Ingelow's *Poems* reached its third reprint in September, and finally went into twenty-six editions. *Goblin Market* had still not sold out its first.

'What think you of Jean Ingelow, the wonderful poet?' Christina asked Dora, letting a jealous tinge creep into her epithet; 'reviews with copious extracts have made me aware of a new eminent name having risen amongst us. I want to know who she is, what she is like, where she lives. All I have heard is an uncertain rumour that she is aged twenty-one and is one of three sisters resident with their mother. A proud mother, I should think.'

This was curious, for Jean Ingelow was a member of the Portfolio Society, and must have been already known to Christina at least by repute. Moreover, her book had been warmly hailed by the *English Woman's Journal* and though Christina may not have read the magazine regularly, she surely heard Jean's name mentioned among her Langham Place friends, and knew that, far from being a young star, Jean was ten years older than herself. There were several obvious links between them, for Miss Ingelow's volume contained poems on Portfolio themes, to which Christina had also written, such as *Strife* and *Peace and Reflections*, together with a much-praised lyric entitled *Divided* that offered a variation on her own favourite theme of death's separation:

> Sing on! we sing in the glorious weather
>   Till one steps over the tiny strand,
> So narrow, in sooth, that still together
>   On either brink we go hand in hand.
>
> The beck grows wider, the hands must sever,
>   On either margin, our songs all done,
> We move apart, while she singeth ever,
>   Taking the course of the stooping sun . . .

This was indeed, the very theme of the latest poem Christina had published in *Macmillan's*:

When shall they meet? I cannot tell,
Indeed, when they shall meet again,
Except some day in Paradise:
For this they wait, one waits in pain.

Of course, Christina's expressions of jealousy towards Jean were partly ironic and self-mocking; she was unsettled rather than consumed by envy. But the new rivalry gave an edge to her sense of poetic identity and she was quietly gratified when, the following year, an article in *Fraser's* magazine coyly titled 'Our Camp in the Woodland: A Day with the Gentle Poets' declared Mrs Browning fanciful and hectic, Miss Procter didactic and rhetorical, Miss Ingelow elastic and as 'fresh as dew' but Miss Rossetti more original and racy than all these:

She is the slave neither of forms nor ideas. She is bold, vigorous, peculiar, daring ... her feelings are strong and in command; she does not weep openly; though at times a touch of careless sadness wanders across the strings. Certain of her poems are marked by an air of composure, of quiet scorn, of tender trifling – rare in a woman's poem and possibly assumed as the mask of a mood of deeper feelings which she cannot afford to disclose.

Thus, in Gabriel's words, 'the palm among living poetesses is given to Christina'. She herself was never heard to make any such claim, but such was her implicit ambition.

23

Bleak Mid-Winter of the Soul

ADELAIDE PROCTER, whom Christina admired but did not fear as a rival, died early in 1864, lovingly nursed and mourned by Bessie. Christina herself fell sick, with what she described to Barbara as 'a fit of illness' that kept her 'languid and much at home' and William called 'a period of spiritual depression'. Within and without, all was wintry:

> What would I give for a heart of flesh to warm me through,
> Instead of this heart of stone, ice-cold whatever I do!
> Hard and cold and small, of all hearts the worst of all.
>
> What would I give for words, if only words would come!
> But now in its misery my spirit has fallen dumb.
> O merry friends, go your way, I have never a word to say.
>
> What would I give for tears! not smiles but scalding tears,
> To wash the black mark clean, and to thaw the frost of years,
> To wash the stain ingrain, and to make me clean again.

(28 January)

> Oh for the time gone by when thought of Christ
>   Made His yoke easy and His burden light!
>   . . .
>   When my soul watched for Him, by day, by night:
>   When my lamp lightened and my robe was white . . .

(23 February)

> God strengthen me to bear myself;
>   That heaviest weight of all to bear,
>   Inalienable weight of care.
>
> All others are outside myself;
>   I lock my door, and bar them out,
>   The turmoil, tedium, gad-about.

I lock my door upon myself,
And bar them out; but who shall wall
Self from myself, most loathed of all?

If I could once lay down myself
And start self-purged upon the race
That all must run! Death runs apace.

If I could set aside myself
And start with lightened heart upon
The road by all men overgone!

God harden me against myself,
This coward with pathetic voice
Who craves for ease, and rest, and joys:

Myself, arch-traitor to myself;
My hollowest friend, my deadliest foe,
My clog whatever road I go . . .

(1 March 1864)

Eloquently, Christina or someone else in the family called these 'the groans'. Their recurrent imagery of frozen feeling and self-loathing returns to the major motifs of her poetic symphony, recalling the verses of her breakdown such as *Hope in Grief* and *Will these Hands ne'er be Clean?* They express deep psychological distress, yoked to an inalienable burden within the self. The poet locks out everything else, and finds to her horror that she is still invaded by a strangling load – from which, paradoxically, stemmed much of her best verse.

Such a weight of inner care manifested in repeated depression is one typical symptom of incest survivors. Its intensity at this date suggests that this may have been the second occasion when spiritual self-disgust prevented Christina from going to confession. 'I have borne myself till I became unbearable to myself, and then I have found help . . . and relief inexpressible,' as she wrote later to Gabriel on the benefits of absolution, reminding him of the second time 'when circumstances had led me (rightly or wrongly) to break off the practice'. This is puzzling: what circumstances could have been considered right? There were no major changes at Christ Church, where Rev. Burrows remained in the post, steadily developing the pastoral work of the parish. Maybe the source was only a slight occurrence, when Christina, contracting a winter ailment, accepted advice to stay indoors during bad weather and subsequently fell into a trough of self-loathing that, as in adolescence, prevented her from seeking spiritual counsel. This was not rational – depression does not respond to reason – but the sense of a 'dark double' within her soul ('traitor', 'deadliest foe') lay close to the surface of Christina's personality. It was, moreover, almost exactly ten years since her father's death, an anniversary that whatever the cause of her teenage breakdown might arouse much retrospective sorrow and guilt.

Though she managed a half-cheerful paschal hymn at Easter, on 7 April another familiar, haunting spirit made its appearance, just half a year after the last corpse-cold ghoul. Here, a young wife waits for her dead husband, who appears 'like a puff of air', white and cold and boneless. He cannot rest while she mourns, and she is somewhat reproachful, and also afraid. She was followed in October by *Jessie Cameron*, who falls victim to a demon lover and is drowned:

> Only watchers by the dying
> Have thought they heard one pray
> Wordless, urgent; and replying
> One seem to say him nay:
> And watchers by the dead have heard
> A windy swell from miles away
> With sobs and screams, but not a word
> Distinct for them to say:
> And watchers out at sea have caught
> Glimpse of a pale gleam here or there
> Come and gone as quick as thought,
> Which might be hand or hair.

More unquiet spirits toss and howl amid a watery coastland. Another spectral lover is resisted and pitied, but draws his beloved to her doom. And once again, there is a wordless appeal, and in the end only a ghostly memory of something that may or may not have been witnessed. The poem has folklore origins in the tales of seal-wives, but was also a variation on one of Christina's obsessional melodies. Similarly, the restless ghosts that stalk her poetry so mournfully and yet so accusingly always seem to be trying to say something that the poet cannot quite hear, hinting at a secret knowledge. 'Lie still, my troubled heart, lie still,' she told herself on 6 May. 'God's word to thee saith "Wait and bear": The good which He appoints is good ... Thy hurt a help not understood.'

'Not that I am by any means very ill,' she hastened to assure Barbara: 'but I seem to require rest of various kinds in conjunction with medicine: in fact for the present even necessary business has to be postponed and I bide my time.' There are no further references to the Penitentiary in her correspondence, and though William believed she continued working there until 1870, it seems likely that in 1864 this also lapsed – perhaps causing additional guilt.

She dropped out of the Portfolio Society too, and worried herself into a knot with regard to her practice of submitting old compositions; 'now was this allowable?' she asked anxiously:

> If not, I very sincerely apologize for having infringed a rule never expressed to me: and I would ask you, if not asking too much, to express my regrets to my quondam colleagues. Again; would they, on these same lazy terms, admit me as a member? For in case you join, the temptation to me will be great; though I protest against your bestowing on me more than *one* of your noble works in the course of the term, and for that I shall indeed feel your debtor. I must also remind you that I was a corresponding member, not an attendant at the meetings . . .

'What a deal about myself,' she went on, compounding the tortuous self-criticisms.

There were some changes at home, for after uncle Philip's death earlier this year aunt Margaret came to live at Albany Street, occupying the whole of the second floor, with her own servant. Her advent was disturbing, for she suffered from what William described as hysterical fits, when she cackled like a hyena and endless peals of 'quasi-laughter' rang through the house; nevertheless, she seems to have been able to manage adequately with the aid of a maid.

Though her heart was hardly in it, Christina began to put together a new collection. *Goblin Market* had begun to show a profit and Macmillan was interested in a second volume. As encouragement, Gabriel read through her proposed selection, and sent comments. 'Thanks many,' she replied laconically. 'On almost all points I succumb with serenity: now for remarks.'

Most of these concerned what he considered weaker elements, such as the choice of names in *Maiden-Song* or the metre of *Last Night*, which she admitted but did not feel inclined to alter. She more vigorously disputed his criticisms of *A Royal Princess*, saying ' "Some to work on roads" etc is by so much one of the best stanzas that I am loth to sacrifice it. Is it so very like Keats?' (it was) and claiming never to have read the whole of *Isabella*. She also defended the violence of the peasants' revolt, arguing that the soldiers might have escaped roasting: 'a *yell* is one thing, and a *fait accompli* quite another', and contested his judgement of *The Bourne*, 'partly because Mac likes it and it is already in the Magazine, partly because *I* like it' and partly because it had been so prettily set to music by Georgie Burne-Jones's sister. *I am pale with sick desire* from *Lyra Eucharistica* was another 'special favourite'. In any case, quantity was going to be a problem, especially if she dropped any more. Her only further recourse would be to 'launch forth into the rag-and-bone store' (the old notebooks) and pull something out 'by main force'.

A sense of despondency rises from her letter. 'I hope after this vol. (if this vol. becomes a vol.) people will respect my nerves and not hint for a long while at any possibility of vol. 3,' she concluded. 'I am sure my poor brain must lie fallow and take its ease, if I am to keep up to my own mark.' And a day or two later she abandoned the attempt altogether. 'Don't think me a perfect weathercock,' she wrote. 'But why rush before the public with an immature volume?' Not even suicidal thoughts of untimely death should be 'a bugbear to scare me into premature publicity'.

She then told Macmillan. 'I have weighed and measured but alas! vol. 2 is not ready,' she wrote. 'Pray pardon my delay in letting you know this, but I only today arrived at the final conclusion.' So the matter rested. Gabriel turned his attention to persuading Macmillan to publish Swinburne's verses – in vain, for the publisher tried reading them aloud to his wife and not surprisingly turned them down, being 'inexorable against any shade of heterodoxy in morals'. He agreed however to issue William's translation of the *Inferno*, at author's expense, and meanwhile a second printing of *Goblin Market* went ahead.

It was now two years since her first hesitant hopes of a relationship with Mr Cayley. Polite, even cordial friendship persisted – he was busy translating Homer, and sending each instalment to Albany Street, to Maria's delight – but no romance flourished. In a situation of such delicacy, as a woman Christina could do little to initiate courtship, but with a pipe-stem that Cayley inadvertently left behind she sent some discreetly flirtatious lines:

> Far be from me the thought
> Of keeping the object
> That once aroused
> Love in your breast.
>
> If you use it no more,
> – if you can't even smoke it –
> Let it be your tender duty
> To preserve it for ever.

But the hint was ignored and a few weeks later Christina expressed her frustration in a rueful but sharp little *Sketch* on Cayley's obtuseness:

My blindest buzzard that I know,
  My special mole, when will you see?
  Oh no, you must not look at me,
There's nothing hid for me to show.
I might show facts as plain as day:
But, since your eyes are blind, you'd say,
  'Where? What?' and turn away.

In publishing this poem after Christina's death, William commented
on Cayley's abstracted wool-gathering demeanour, adding that any
man of 'ordinary alertness' would not have failed to see the favour
with which his sister clearly regarded Cayley at this date. Whether he
was wilfully choosing to ignore the signals, or simply unable to see
what was 'within his reach' is hard to tell; perhaps having reached the
age of forty without any open attachments, Cayley was deeply unwilling to forgo his single status, while greatly enjoying the attention he
received at Albany Street.

In June Christina completed a poem headed simply *Twice*:

I took my heart in my hand,
  (O my love, O my love),
I said: Let me fall or stand,
  Let me live or die,
But this once hear me speak –
  (O my love, O my love) –
Yet a woman's words are weak;
  You should speak, not I.

You took my heart in your hand
  With a friendly smile,
With a critical eye you scanned,
  Then set it down,
And said: It is still unripe,
  Better wait awhile;
Wait while the skylarks pipe,
  Till the corn grows brown.

As you set it down it broke –
  Broke, but I did not wince;
I smiled at the speech you spoke,
  At your judgment that I heard
But I have not often smiled
  Since then, nor questioned since,

Nor cared for corn-flowers wild,
  Nor sung with the singing bird.

I take my heart in my hand,
  O my God, O my God,
My broken heart in my hand:
  Thou hast seen, judge Thou.
My hope was written on sand,
  O my God, O my God:
Now, let Thy judgment stand –
  Yea, judge me now.

This contemned of a man,
  This marred one heedless day,
This heart take Thou to scan
  Both within and without:
Refine with fire its gold,
  Purge Thou its dross away –
Yea hold it in Thy hold,
  Whence none can pluck it out.

I take my heart in my hand –
  I shall not die, but live –
Before Thy face I stand;
  I, for Thou callest such:
All that I have I bring,
  All that I am I give;
Smile Thou and I shall sing,
  But shall not question much.

This is one of Christina's most memorable poems and one which, because of its open address and illusion of personal feeling, has been taken to be plainly autobiographical. But it is unwise to assume that it reflects any actual experience of Christina's. She was notoriously shy of revealing 'love personals' in print, yet published *Twice* soon after it was written. Nor did anyone caution her against doing so. Its wonderfully direct voice certainly sounds like a real experience of heartbreak – verbally enacted across the line-break in 'As you set it down it broke – Broke, but I did not wince'. But the poet is dramatist not autobiographer, speaking on behalf of all those whose love has been spurned by smiling, condescending men, and creating a female speaker whose life has been thus blighted ('I have not often smiled') and who now turns towards religion, offering her ardour to God and trusting to divine love to make good the mortal damage. There is of course an elision here between holy and human love, yet strikingly the poem links them, so that the speaker's submission to God's scrutiny is likened to her acceptance of the unnamed man's critical eye.

'I smiled at the speech you spoke, At your judgment that I heard,' she says. But she does not wince, or cry, or protest. Indeed, she is reluctant to speak at all, and proud of keeping silence. For, like many of Christina's poems, *Twice* contains an implicit protest against gender inequality that is not negated by but paradoxically asserted within the female mode of humble submission. The woman who loves protests against being silenced – 'but this once hear me speak' – but accepts the verdict with a patient and even grateful smile. In fact, the smile is subversive: a mutely sarcastic reply to the arrogance that presumes to pronounce on the 'unripe' state of her heart. To read this as a plain complaint against patriarchy and the male prerogative may be too feminist an interpretation of its authorial intent, but it is certainly part of its message. As the reader may feel, the speaker is better off with God, who is all things his human counterpart fails to be, and offers the only hope of fulfilment: 'Smile Thou and I shall sing'.

At the same time, the poem has clear personal significance, coming in the same season as her critique of Cayley's blindness. This was indeed the second time in her life she had offered her heart to a man, and the second time it had been effectively spurned.

This summer she accepted a long-standing invitation to visit Anne Gilchrist, widow of the author of a book on Blake that William and Gabriel had helped complete. With her four children, Percy, Beatrice, Herbert and Grace, Mrs Gilchrist now lived near Haslemere in Surrey. In William's words, she was loquacious, keenly interested in people and ideas, and 'in manner remarkably cordial, without "gushingness" . . . genial, courageous, steady in all her likings and habits . . . never out of temper, querulous or languid – not even fidgety'. Upon occasion, she could be honestly indignant in a good cause, and proved an ardent admirer of Walt Whitman when his work was first introduced to Britain. She had a cultivated mind and, according to another friend, 'ready sympathy with the studies or occupations of others; and a persistent kindness in endeavours to be useful'.

'My dear Mrs Gilchrist, I have indeed often thought of my prospective visit to Brookbank. Thank you so very much for remembering me and preparing for me this pleasure,' wrote Christina on 21 May, offering half-seriously, to 'instil the elements' of Italian into the Gilchrist children during her stay, and promising that, though she had been unwell, she would enjoy the 'charming walks in three different counties' available from the Gilchrists' cottage.

But she was still depressed and nervous. Upon arrival in late afternoon she was shown to her room, and when she did not appear for dinner, Anne tapped at the door, to find Miss Rossetti too shy to venture down alone to face the guests invited to meet the acclaimed authoress. She much preferred playing with the children, particularly five-year-old Grace, who long afterwards recalled Christina's visit. 'I have a vivid impression of playing a game of ball with her one summer afternoon upon a sloping lawn, under the branches of an old apple tree,' she wrote. 'To my child's eyes she appeared like some fairy princess who had come from the sunny south to play with me . . .' Together they investigated the wild life, and Grace was amazed at Christina's readiness to hold clammy frogs or furry caterpillars in the hollow of her hand. Perhaps they brought back memories of Holmer Green.

Anne was also charmed. 'There is a sweetness, an unaffected simplicity and gentleness, with all her gifts, that is very winning – and I hope to see more of her,' she wrote afterwards. 'She was so kind to the children and so easy to please and make comfortable that though a stranger to me, she was not at all a formidable guest.'

But if Anne was in awe of Christina's gifts, she herself was easily the more widely-read. She endeavoured, as Christina did not, to keep up with philosophical and scientific debates, and broaden her knowledge. 'For after all,' as she wrote to a friend, 'when youth and growing time are left behind and *ripening* time comes – if there is anything to ripen – reading is not enough.' Active thought was also required, to prevent mental somnolence. And so at Brookbank Christina not only at last read the whole of Miss Ingelow's celebrated *Poems*, but also dipped into a volume of Plato, offered by her hostess as if to rouse her mind. She returned from Surrey laden with books, gifts and flowers, and her thankyou letter was lively and warm.

The visit stimulated her poetic impulse too, prompting Ingelow-inspired verses about a milkmaid whose 'country ditty' may be suspected of satire, followed by *Songs in a Cornfield* in which summer heat is contrasted with the inner chill of grief, as the heroine realises her true love will not come, and *Bird or Beast?* in which the natural world is imaged as sorrowing for expulsion into the 'thorny thistly world' outside Eden:

> Did any bird come flying
>   After Adam and Eve,
> When the door was shut against them
>   And they sat down to grieve?
>
> I think not Eve's peacock
>   Splendid to see,

And I think not Adam's eagle;
But a dove may be . . .

A couple of weeks later, Christina and Maria were at a church fete in
Mitcham, where 'croquet and haymaking were the order of the day'
and they saw Rev. Dodgson again, together with Ellen Heaton, Holman Hunt, the Munros and Jenny Lind, and also met a young student
named Gerard Hopkins, whose sister was Maria's associate at All
Saints. 'When next I see you I have great things to tell. I have been
introduced to Miss and Miss Christina Rossetti,' he wrote proudly to
an Oxford friend. Later in the year Christina visited Cheltenham and
Malvern with uncle Henry, and in London finally met Jean Ingelow,
whom she found 'as unaffected as her verses, though not their equal
in regular beauty', as she reported to Anne. The invitation seems to
have come from Jean, who lived with her mother and unmarried
siblings in Kensington. Their situations were in many ways comparable, for Jean had started writing at a young age, and was believed
to have lost an admirer at sea, though this was never spoken of and
may have been simply 'read off' her verses. She lived modestly – the
failure of her father's business interests had twice brought the family
to bankruptcy – and gained little recognition until the publication of
Poems, dedicated to her brother with an expression of sisterly affection
that Christina admired though did not publicly emulate. Less given to
gush than Dora, she was almost as shy as Christina. 'I was very sorry
to be from home the other day when you called, I should much have
liked to see you,' she wrote on one occasion. 'My mother hopes you
will come and dine with us in a friendly way next Thursday; it would
give us so much pleasure to see you.'

Probably as a gift, Christina now received her own copy of Jean's
Poems, whose reprints so outnumbered her own and lent 'a becoming
green tinge' to her complexion, as she joked to Mrs Gilchrist; 'imagine
my feelings of envy and humiliation!' Reserve and rivalry notwithstanding, a genuine liking and esteem followed, for the two women
had much in common besides family affection, sharing a serious
commitment to their art with a clear sense of religious duty. Jean used
her literary earnings to rent rooms across the street in which to work
and also to provide what she called 'copyright dinners' for elderly
paupers, chosen by the parish; indeed, as a friend recalled, 'I think it
is probable that the pleasure of giving away much of what she earned
by her pen was even greater than the pleasure of composition.' In
verse, both she and Christina preferred simplicity over grandilo-
quence. Imagination was such a great faculty, Jean asserted, that 'it
should repose on things most simple and universal'; if tempted to
elevation, poetry 'should make haste to come down like a lark on the

grass and never concern itself with rank or riches or luxury'. Both also had experience of becoming sudden celebrities, and the consequent pressure to produce a new volume. When they met, Jean had just published a collection of moral stories for girls in the mode of Charlotte Yonge, but no subsequent book advanced her reputation beyond that of *Poems*. As Christina feared for herself, though rich and famous, Miss Ingelow remained more or less a 'one-readable-book writer'.

She was however helpful in practical matters, recommending to Christina her own American publisher Roberts Bros of Boston, and possibly also offering spiritual counsel, for a surviving letter to an unidentified recipient discusses the very issues that troubled her new friend:

> I wish to say to you that I don't think you should be so severe on what God so much loves (yourself). We are complete in Him. There is no need of so much 'compunction and contrition'. It is agreed that we are nothing; but we never shall be, here, however much we may improve. We, His dear children, are so constituted that we shall never be any great credit to Him. Let us cast this care too upon Him.
>
> Surely it is a fine thing for us that we are never satisfied with ourselves. This is by no means meant as a reproof. You want a good deal of loving encouragement especially just now when you are physically tired and overstrained. We can all delight ourselves in thinking that God is Love; but that the love to us should be the indulgent love of a father to me, to you, one is sometimes afraid to acknowledge.

Whoever this was addressed to, it was equally relevant to Christina, who was still deeply in need. On 10 October, she completed a desperate poem called *Despised and Rejected*, in which she described herself as dwelling in darkness. Repeatedly, she refuses to open her heart to Christ, whose voice finally dies away. Then

> On the morrow
> I saw upon the grass
> Each footprint marked in blood, and on my door
> The mark of blood for evermore.

Despair was absolute and self-lacerating, supporting the inference that this was the period when Christina felt unable to seek absolution. It also illustrates her characteristic invocation of the suffering Christ as a wounded supplicant, whom she is both guilty of rejecting and with whom she identifies, as a victim. In Christina's theophany, God was seldom the indulgent Father of Jean Ingelow's imagination, but the 'despised and rejected' Son, crucified, scourged and spat upon.

A similar perspective was articulated in *A Voice from the World*, which young Gerard Hopkins was currently struggling to complete:

> This ice, this lead, this steel, this stone,
> This heart is warm to you alone;
> Make it to God. I am not spent
> So far but I have yet within
> The penetrative element
> That shall unglue the crust of sin.
> Steel may be melted and rock rent.
> Penance shall clothe me to the bone.
> Teach me the way: I will repent.

This, as its language suggests, was conceived as 'an answer to Miss Rossetti's *On The Convent Threshold*, which had spoken most powerfully to Hopkins from the pages of her book, and led him to boast of the introduction at Mitcham. Like Christina he had responded to High Church doctrines of sin and contrition to expiate a troubled sense of sexual guilt, and her example encouraged him to seek publication for his intense, and awkward verses. Submitting *Barnfloor and Winepress* to Macmillan's some little while later, he explained to a friend that it was always printing such things by Miss Rossetti. His were rejected however; the literary world was not ready for Mr Hopkins's innovations, however much they might enjoy Miss Rossetti's.

The two writers shared more than technical affinity. Ten days after *Despised and Rejected*, Christina wrote *Weary in Well-Doing*:

> I would have gone; God bade me stay:
>   I would have worked; God bade me rest.
> He broke my will from day to day;
>   He read my yearnings unexprest,
>   And said them nay.
>
> Now I would stay; God bids me go:
>   Now I would rest; God bids me work;
> He breaks my heart tost to and fro;
>   My soul is wrung with doubts that lurk
>   And vex it so.

Here, the Christian soul is a servant whose self-will must be broken, in a spiritual experience that Gerard Hopkins would learn to recognise well.

Doubt was on the ascendant. Geological science, archaeology and Darwin's evolutionary theories had already undermined biblical ideas of the creation. Now even theologians were beginning to question scriptural certainties. The historical accuracy of the gospel was challenged and the temporal origins of the Judeo-Christian tradition revealed. As the *Westminster Review* pointed out, whatever the scholarship, to the ordinary believer the message was plain: 'All the bases of his creed are undermined; the whole external authority on which it rests is swept away; the mysterious book of Ruth fades into an old collection of poetry and legend; and the scheme of Redemption in which he has been taught to live and die turns out to be a demoralizing invention of man.' And all had happened with surprising speed: as free-thinking William noted to Scott, attitudes that had seemed destined to last the century had radically changed in just three or four years.

In response, many believers redoubled their faith by invoking an unknowable mystery at the heart of the divine order, whereby contradictions and perplexities were signs of human limitations, not heavenly impotence. And on the surface, this was Christina's attitude; there is no hint, in her writing or others' recollections, that her belief in God's beneficent ordaining of the universe faltered. But frequently in her work belief seems impelled by will rather than faith, and it is at least plausible that like so many others she too was troubled by doubt, fearing that her scheme of belief had no basis outside herself. Her response was always reaffirmation, but the repetitious need to reaffirm argues against certainty. In poem after poem she castigated herself for failing to respond to Christ, and the spiritual distress of a soul who felt unworthy of divine love was surely comparable to that of one who could no longer believe in that divinity. Though her poetry is usually read as unproblematically devotional, its spiritual anguish suggests a darker night of the soul, struggling against despair as well as sin. When she prayed, Christ did not often answer, and when he spoke, she could not always respond.

24

Prince and Alchemist

TOWARDS THE END of 1864 Christina's condition gave rise to such concern that she was sent to winter by the sea, at Hastings, with uncle Henry and cousin Henrietta, who was also sickly. 'There I stood on the platform, girt by my three boxes, one carpet-bag, strapful of shawls and bundle of umbrellas,' she wrote later in fictional voice, remembering weakness, for 'the journey down had shaken me, I was hungry and thirsty for my tea and, through fear of catching cold, I had wrapped up overmuch.' Physically, her worst symptoms were wracking headaches and a persistent cough that alarmingly suggested consumption. Cousin Teodorico, who had taken up homeopathy, suggested it had already reached a terminal stage, and prescribed remedies from a distance, but Christina preferred orthodox medicine, which relied on clean air and copious rest, together with a soothing jelly she later described as efficacious in easing the 'extreme irritation at her chest'; this was made 'by boiling down a whitish seaweed (the carrageen, or Irish moss) which washes up in abundance on the Hastings coast, and adding a little sugar and lemon juice to make it palatable'.

Like many Victorian women, Christina was shy when obliged to consult doctors, preferring those with an urbane, imperturbable manner, who did not poke or probe too deeply, or show surprise when told of her symptoms. As far as we can tell, the treatment she received was general and non-invasive, relying on tranquillity and tonics – in her lifetime Christina consumed vast quantities of medically-prescribed sherry – and was meticulously observed. It is difficult to judge whether any serious illness assailed her at this date. She did not have tuberculosis or pneumonia however and her nagging cough sounds like a *tussis nervosa* similar to those found by Freud and Breuer in several cases of hysteria or, as might be said today, a symptom of stress, relieved by the long rest beside the wintry sea.

She lodged in the High Street, and found Hastings full of invalids, including Georgie Burne-Jones, several Ingelows and 'some of the de Morgans', as she told Anne, explaining also to the Howitts that she was therefore not lacking in congenial company. Gabriel had been in Paris (with Fanny, though he did not tell the family this), visiting studios and hoping to meet Baudelaire; back in London, he and Swinburne were among the loudest fans of Adah Mencken, currently thrill-

ing the crowds at Astley's theatre with her semi-naked bareback performances, in a demi-monde far removed from Christina's experience.
He and William however combined to buy an engraving of crocodiles
for their sister's birthday, which Gabriel followed up with another,
whom he nicknamed Prudentius, in tribute to her poem. She was
sorry to miss the family party at Christmas, heeding medical advice to
protect her 'peccant chest' from London smoke and fogs, but jokingly
imagined herself making a spectral appearance in the manner of *At
Home*, 'if unbeknown I could look in upon you sucking (metaphorical)
plums and peaches'.

From Hastings she also negotiated a minor reconciliation with Henrietta Rintoul, who after the ending of the engagement had been
inclined to drop all acquaintance with the Rossettis. Christina had
tried to maintain the friendship and now tactfully offered to inquire
whether Henrietta still wished to accept the dedication of William's
Inferno, telling her brother that though by mutual consent he was
never discussed, she was sure that indifference was not Henrietta's
feeling. 'Being myself a woman,' she conjectured, it was rather 'a very
human bitter-sweet mixture'. Henrietta accepted the dedication.

In what she called her 'hermitage', Christina had plenty of other
occupation, taking daily walks, paying calls, devising amusements for
Henrietta and reading regular instalments of Cayley's *Iliad* with its
rolling periods and English hexameters. These were forwarded by
Maria, who revived her juvenile enthusiasm with breathless effusions
that make one weep for her lost ambitions: 'the doubt whether the sun
and moon were safe in heaven – the mourning of Achilles' horse – the
silent grief of Antiochus – the wonderful comparisons of the lion with
the curtaining eyebrows, of the river, of the promontory,' she wrote;
'really the more I think about it the more I warm to these heroes.'

Christina was also reading Plato, in the six-volume Bohn edition she
had received for her birthday. This began with Socrates' Apologia, the
Crito and the Phaedo, and suggests that Anne Gilchrist's advice
regarding serious study had borne fruit. And though she joked about
her envy of Jean's popularity, she was far from dissatisfied with her
own reputation, for early in January the *Times* ran a long article on
'Modern Poets', paying tribute to the renaissance of the art in recent
years (for the most part unreviewed in its pages, although Tennyson,
as Laureate, was never neglected), in which it was noted that 'Miss
Ingelow's work is full of feeling and bright with suggestions, but as
yet her style is wanting in form and decision of touch. She is apt to be
vague, and has not yet learnt to be brief', whereas

The poetical art of Miss Rossetti, although her book has as yet not
received the same favour from the public, is simpler, firmer and deeper.

Miss Ingelow is but a child of promise – of great promise certainly, but still only of the future. Her work as yet, with all its glow and radiance, is too nebulous, and much of it seems to come of that facility which is a young poet's greatest danger. Miss Rossetti, on the other hand, can point to finished work – to work which it would be difficult to mend. She is not so ambitious in her choice of subject as Miss Ingelow, and perhaps that is one reason why in what she attempts she is more successful.

'Of course I am crowing,' Christina told Gabriel, who sent the cutting (as did kind Mrs Heimann) together with a sketch in which he depicted his sister smashing furniture, in reference both to work it would be 'difficult to mend' and her longstanding reputation for tantrums. She and Henrietta were delighted.

The review did not of course damage her friendship with Jean Ingelow, which was now based on genuine esteem, but Dora Greenwell's correspondence with Jean reveals that a certain displaced rivalry was felt. Like most Victorian women, Dora and Jean exchanged gifts of their own making, and in response to Dora's kettleholder, Jean promised an embroidered workbag, joking that neither was likely to receive any comparable needlework from Christina; indeed, 'when I next see Miss Rossetti, I shall ask for proof that she can do hemming and sewing,' she wrote on 9 February. Neither fine nor plain stitching was a skill at which Christina excelled.

Jean was working on her second collection, and so, coincidentally, was Christina resuming the work abandoned nine months before. One motive, she told Gabriel, was the fear 'lest by indefinite delay I should miss the pleasure of thus giving pleasure to our dear Mother'. Frances was now sixty-four, so there were some grounds for anxiety, but one suspects a little maternal deception here, designed to lift Christina's spirits. Mamma cheerfully admitted her satisfaction at seeing her children's names in print – and there was now added cause for celebration, for William's *Inferno* was in production, and Maria's Italian language textbook had found a publisher. All four would thus soon be listed as authors, and in Hastings Christina undertook the additional task of searching out appropriate passages for her sister. 'Truth to tell, I have a great fancy for her name endorsing a book, as we three have all got into that stage, so I work with a certain enthusiasm,' she told Gabriel. One catches a sense of regret here, at the way Christina had displaced her elder sister by achieving the recognition Maria had always seemed to deserve. The ambition of authorship instilled in childhood cast a long shadow.

In a curious way, it is as if the four Rossetti children shared out aspects of their father's career. Maria followed his pedagogic footsteps; William shadowed in sober form his role as critic and scholar;

Christina gained fame as a poet; and Gabriel re-created Papa's position as cultural leader and hero. Young admirers and rich patrons made their way to Cheyne Walk, the former basking in the glow of his friendship, the latter paying large sums for the privilege of owning his pictures, so that he was now as wealthy and renowned as his father had always wished to be.

Papa's shade revisited the family on several occasions this winter, most notably with the publication of his poems in Italy, with a biographical preface based on Teodorico's account. At last, he wrote, Rossetti's name was being honoured in his own land. Old Thomas Keightley, meanwhile, lamented that William's *Inferno* contained no reference to his father's theories about Beatrice – hardly surprisingly, since William's aim was literal, translating only what was on the page. As Gabriel had done with the *Vita Nuova* and both Maria and Christina were also to do, he needed to distance himself from Papa's obsessional ideas, that had brought the family such misery.

As centrepiece and title poem for her new volume, Christina had accepted Gabriel's suggestion of developing *The Prince who arrived too late*, into a new long narrative called *The Prince's Progress*. This was plotted out so as to depict the dangers of procrastination: as the Princess waits, the Prince's arrival is delayed by various trials and diversions. When she unpacked the manuscript at Hastings, only one major episode remained to be written. 'True, O Brother, my Alchemist still shivers in the blank of possibility,' she told Gabriel, echoing the Arabian Nights; 'but I have so far overcome my feelings and disregarded my nerves as to unloose the Prince, so that wrapping-paper may no longer bar his "progress".' She was disciplining herself to disregard doubts, and finish the work.

At first however, she herself procrastinated, by working on Maria's book, sending three 'potboilers' to Macmillan, and calculating the remaining contents of the new collection. By her reckoning, the initial selection would exceed 120 pages, which 'cheers but not inebriates', she reported. She wanted however to reinstate several of those Gabriel disliked, especially at least one *terza rima*, 'in honour of our Italian element', and confessed to a superstitious, or in her words puerile, fancy for making the book the same length as its predecessor. That however had been the fruits of over ten years' work; by comparison, Vol. 2 (as she called it) had only four years to draw on, and she feared it would have to include some not 'skimmed as cream' by her brother.

Goblin Market was at last going into its second impression. Gabriel was confusing Macmillan's printer with additional proof corrections. Another religious anthologiser, Rev. Baynes, had asked permission to reprint *From House to Home*, while the composer Virginia Gabriel wished to set *Echo* to music, a compliment which especially gratified Christina because it was neither *Up-hill* nor *Birthday*, the two poems most frequently admired. 'I am truly pleased at the honour done me,' she wrote on 18 January. 'Echo, expectant, awaits her musical echoes.' As she told Macmillan, 'the more of my things get set to music the better pleased I am.'

On 16 January she finally sat down to finish *The Prince's Progress*. At first, she reported, 'the Alchemist makes himself scarce, and I must bide his time.' Two weeks later, however, he had arrived. 'My dear Gabriel, here at last is an Alchemist reeking from the crucible, she wrote. He dovetails properly into his niche. Please read him if you have the energy.'

In the text, an old wizard is bent over a seething cauldron, with grimy fingers, wizened features and a furtive, suspicious manner. For a century he has been striving to blend the elixir of life:

> The pot began to bubble and boil;
> The old man cast in essence and oil,
> He stirred all up with a triple coil
>   Of gold and silver and iron wire,
> Dredged in a pinch of virgin soil
>   And fed the fire.

But only when death comes to the alchemist is the elixir achieved:

> Thus at length the old crab was nipped.
> The dead hand slipped, the dead finger dipped
> In the broth as the dead man slipped –
>   That same instant, a rosy red
> Flushed the steam, and quivered and clipped
>   ·Round the dead old head.

> The last ingredient was supplied . . .

He was not precisely as planned, she confessed, 'but thus he came and thus he must stay: you know my system of work'.

The niche into which he fitted so neatly in the scheme of the poem was the barren land traversed by the prince on his journey. As the title suggests, this was something like that of Bunyan's Pilgrim; something like that of Poliphilius in the *Hypnerotomachia*; and something like countless medieval quest romances, where the hero is repeatedly diverted from his destined path. The germ of the poem, incidentally, seems to have come from *The Staff and Scrip*, in which a medieval queen waits for her pilgrim lover and which Christina nominated as her favourite among Gabriel's works. Perhaps she liked it because both form and content owed much to her own work, and certainly her collaboration with Gabriel over this new volume represented a renewal of their poetic partnership: there was no one else whose judgement she trusted more. As she noted later on the fly-leaf of one of her books: 'And here I would like to acknowledge the general indebtedness of my first and second volumes to my brother's suggestive wit and revising hand.'

Her tardy hero sets off with good intentions, but is first beguiled by a pretty milkmaid, before crossing the desolate land where he meets the Alchemist and sets to work as his assistant. When at length the wizard dies, the Prince fills a phial with the elixir and continues on his journey. But dangers, in crossing a turbulent river, and dalliance, with a family of winsome girls, and other difficulties delay him again and again, so that when he arrives at the palace he finds his beauty not sleeping but dying: as he enters, her corpse is carried out on its bier.

This is a sombre but familiar story, the 'reverse of the Sleeping Beauty' as Christina noted, taking us back to the nursery tales. As with *Goblin Market* however, the message is moral: those who dawdle on life's spiritual path will be doomed to eternal disappointment. Unlike *Goblin Market* the conclusion is unhappy, for there is no redemption, only endless regret. At one level a fairytale – 'once upon a time there was a Prince who was betrothed to a Princess who lived beyond the mountains...' – it is also homilectic: the Prince in symbolic terms representing the quotidian self, while the Princess is the immortal soul, which wastes and dies through neglect.

To Gabriel Christina explained that the phases of the poem were chosen with care. It was 'invested with a certain artistic congruity of construction not lightly to be despised', she wrote:

> 1st a prelude and outset; 2nd, an alluring milkmaid; 3rd a trial of barren boredom; 4th the social element again; 5th barren boredom in a more uncompromising form; 6th a wind-up and conclusion.

'See how the subtle elements balance each other and fuse into a noble conglom!' she declared, on 10 February in a misleadingly facetious tone that disguised her serious intent. But in truth the symbolic structure is far from clear. Without the author's gloss, one would not think that the stony landscape in section three or the mountainous terrain of section five represent the trials of 'boredom'; they seem rather the steep paths and narrow strenuous ways of Christian's pilgrimage. Christina's use of the word should give us pause, however, for 'boredom' indicates her perception of spiritual despair not just as anguish but as barren tedium. Her prince, who is in part a self-image, is beset by sensual and erotic temptations but even more sorely tried by ennui and the unrewarding effort that daily life so often demanded.

What of the Alchemist, whose episode is placed at the centre of the poem? In traditional terms he offers a mephistophelean bargain: the elixir of mortal life. This partly excuses the Prince's delay, for even if he tarries the Princess will live; together they will drink 'this draught of life'. But though he carries the phial triumphantly towards her, the magic potion does not save his Bride from death; in fact, by the time the Prince reaches the palace his precious gift is all but forgotten. As we suspected, it is no true elixir after all.

So is the Alchemist, with his reeking crucible, a diabolic figure? The poem seems to think he is more deluded than evil. He may be fool or villain or 'honest seeker'and falls into a 'self-chosen grave'. He stands perhaps for the pursuit of scientific knowledge, with its false promise of omnipotence, as contrasted with the spiritual quest for wisdom. The seething cauldron he stirs offers 'a world of trouble', and his shrivelled, stiff-necked appearance is a caricature of the mad scientist, 'buried alive from light and air', absorbed in vain experiments for the sake of an illusory goal.

Christina's comment that 'thus he came and thus he must stay' suggests that she herself had a less rigid symbolical scheme in mind, and was 'trusting the tale' to reveal its own story. In response, however, Gabriel felt the plot was still unclear and reverted to his original idea, whereby the Prince took part in a tournament. Christina was appalled. 'How shall I express my sentiments about the terrible tournament?' she began, playfully disguising her dismay:

> Not a phrase to be relied on, not a correct knowledge on the subject, not the faintest impulse of inspiration, incites me to the tilt; and looming before me in horrible bugbeardom stand TWO tournaments in Tennyson's *Idylls*. Moreover, the Alchemist, according to original convention, took the place of the lists: remember this is my favour, please. You see, were you next to propose my writing a classic epic in quantitative hexameters or in the hendecasyllabics which might almost trip-up Tennyson, what could I do? Only what I feel inclined to do in the present instance – plead goodwill but inability.

Christina's references both to Tennyson and to quantitative hexameters, which Cayley was producing at this moment, hint at a sense of rivalry which she was careful to deny; as a mere woman, she did not aspire to compete with epic works by the classical authors or current laureate. Nevertheless, hers was an ambitious poem, and on a major theme.

Gabriel remained unconvinced, but on 3 March Christina declared firmly that the plot was now 'obvious to mean capacities, without further development or addition'. Minor queries she dismissed im-patiently. The image of 'fields green to aftermath' was 'left for various reasons; the most patent I need scarcely give; but also I think it gives a subtle hint (by symbol) that any more delays may swamp the Prince's last chance,' she wrote. Moreover, 'now the moon's at full' was 'happily suggestive of the Prince's character' and would also stay. Her replies indicate how carefully the symbolic figures of the poem were built up, though some are not at all obvious to 'mean capacities'; how does the notion of the Prince delaying his departure until full moon happily or even obliquely reveal his character?

'Of course I don't expect the general public to catch these refined clues,' Christina continued, as if answering such obtuseness; 'but there they are for such minds as mine.' The delicacy and density of *The Prince's Progress* have not received the critical attention they deserve, but this was for Christina an important work, operating on simulta-neous levels of simplicity and sophistication according to the 'refine-ment' of the reader.

However, it may be too refined. The poem is driven by a powerful narrative engine – will the Prince reach his Princess in time? – that like *Goblin Market* carries a strong sexual charge, as in the lineaments of delayed desire. But the changes of pace and place are less successful. The reader becomes impatient with the postponements even though these are the subject of the story, and is not beguiled by the tempta-tions, which lack the allure of goblin fruit. As in traditional fable, the alternation is intentional: the hero now hurries, now dawdles, and we must follow at his pace. But he is tiresomely ready to loiter, and there is a pervasive sense in which he simply doesn't wish to reach his Princess, so the final outcome is not truly tragic. Although up to the last moment it is possible that by some miracle of grace he will reach his goal, the poem sets up such a dominant motif of failure, orches-trated through the parenthetical allusions to the waiting bride, that a happy conclusion could only be trite. By the same token, the predict-able ending is inevitably downbeat: the reader is not surprised that the Prince has fatally squandered his time. The Princess's passivity is a further problem: can she do nothing to save herself?

For these reasons, *The Prince's Progress* has never interested readers in the same way as *Goblin Market*. Christina was conscious of the difference. 'I readily grant that my Prince lacks the special felicity (!) of my *Goblins*,' she admitted. Yet she was not dissatisfied, clearly believing that 'fit audience though few' would appreciate the clues to its deeper meaning.

Gabriel's quibbles suggest an underlying anxiety that proved justi-fied. *The Prince's Progress* falls short of success. But how much was he to blame? For at the same time as Christina was receiving his constructive criticisms, she was also being put under the kind of pressure that was inimical to her art, as he urged her towards completion. He was concurrently keeping Macmillan informed of its progress, and talking up the volume among his friends, provoking unauthorised announcements of its imminent appearance. A good deal was therefore riding on Prince and Alchemist. Christina wanted to write an 'important' poem, as a worthy successor to the goblins. Her publisher and her public were waiting. She had a spiritual theme and a fairytale plot, and time at Hastings to do it. And it was done; the alchemist was slotted into his niche; the new poem was completed. After that she indulged 'in a holiday from all attempt at *Progress*', while Mamma came to visit, before setting to work again, attending to Gabriel's 'corrections'. The language is that of the schoolroom, and perhaps the writing of *The Prince's Progress* was too much of a task to be wholly delightful to read.

But if its relative failure was due to too much willing and too little waiting, Gabriel's role in composition was nevertheless facilitating. Christina welcomed and used his interventions because they were founded on a firm belief in her talent, which in many respects he rated above his own; she had, he told their mother later, more natural talent than himself. He wanted to ensure, too, that she publish nothing second rate, which critics could dismiss. His criticism thus set high standards, and helped her to see (and hear) how her verses would be read by others. If the pressure was ill-advised, this service was valuable.

The endeavour was brotherly in another respect, for in this poem on which he collaborated so closely, Christina painted the Prince in Gabriel's image. Once, Gabriel's art had shared his sister's idealism and sacred imagery. Now, he had embraced the fleshpots, both in art and life. His powers were great but his aims less so; like the Prince he was 'strong in joy' but 'of purpose weak'. Ruskin and Hunt were among those who deplored the carnality of his latest works – half-length images of females in variously alluring poses. Ruskin blamed Fanny Cornforth, but the cause lay rather in the coarse sensibility of Gabriel's male friends at this date – Swinburne, Whistler, Monckton Milnes, Charles Howell, Frederick Sandys. To some extent Gabriel concealed this from his family, inviting them to view a long-delayed altarpiece, for instance, but not a newer nude figure. But to some extent, too, Christina was aware of the change, though not perhaps of the full Baudelairean mixture of refinement and perversity, spiced with de Sade, scatology and visits to stripshows, that characterised the Cheyne Walk circle. A hint of Fanny's pink and buxom charms, for instance, informs the beguiling milkmaid who laughingly invites the Prince to linger under her apple tree.

Years before Christina had described her brother physically as of 'an easy lazy length of limb', with dark eyes and 'features from the South'. With the addition of a thick black beard, this perfectly describes the Prince, 'lazy of limb but quick of nerve', who is also 'apt to swerve' from his intended path, just as Gabriel ruefully acknowledged his inability to complete tasks once they became duties. The Prince dallies by the wayside for no better reason than reluctance to press on:

> He did what a young man can,
>   Spoke of toil and an arduous way –
> Toil tomorrow, while golden ran
>   The sands of today.

'Toil tomorrow' might have been Gabriel's motto, and these resemblances between real and fictional figures suggest a sisterly anxiety regarding the state of Gabriel's soul as well as his art.

As if the Prince's tardiness brought back memories of his own courtship, and a renewed desire to pay homage to his lost princess, Gabriel responded, a week before the third anniversary of her death, by making fair copies of Lizzie's fragmentary poems and offering them to Christina. 'I can't tell you the pleasure with which I welcome your kind loan of Lizzie's work,' she replied, adding impulsively that she would like to print them in her own volume, in a separate section. 'Such a combination would be very dear to me.' But when they arrived, she had second thoughts. They were full of beauty, but so painful '– how they bring poor Lizzie herself before one, with her voice, face and manner!' She especially liked one in which the poet chides her changeable lover, which was 'piquant with cool bitter sarcasm'. But altogether the verses were 'too hopelessly sad' (as well as perhaps too personal) for publication: 'talk of my bogeism, is it not by comparison jovial?' So the proposal was dropped. But Christina's initial response is revealingly suggestive of her regret for lack of earlier sympathy. As she knew, Gabriel still felt tenderly towards his wife. In memory of Lizzie he was working on a picture of her as Beatrice, and had hung her watercolours round the dining-room. The ghost of the bride for whom he had so fatally delayed lingered on in his life, and in his sister's work.

With *The Prince's Progress* completed, she returned her attention to the rest of Volume 2. It still lacked 'bulk', largely because of the 'squad' Gabriel had ousted, from which she at first hoped to reinstate several of her own favourite pieces, arguing

Unless memory plays me false, Mrs Browning's *My Heart and I* does not clash with my *To-morrow*: if it does, I could easily turn my own "heart" into "wish", and save the little piece, for which I have a kindness. Again, I am much inclined to put-in one *terza rima*; though whether my *Judgment* or *Captive Jew* I am not resolved. The *Judgment* is already published in one of Mr Shipley's books: and *Martyrs' Song* (in the same volume) was so honourably mentioned in a review we saw that that seems to constitute some claim on reprint.

However she promised not to spoil the volume or 'deal a death-blow' to her reputation by including really poor poems.

Gabriel's main objection was to over-fervid religious expression, with martyrs panting for the aureole and expiring in an ecstasy of immolation, or Babylonian captives fantasising about the rape of their conquerors' daughters. Christina favoured all three texts, evidently unembarrassed by the almost Swinburnian excess, contesting Gabriel's judgement on the grounds that the martyrs had 'won a word of praise from Mr Cayley' as well as a favourable review. In the end a bargain was struck: *Captive Jew* was suppressed and the others admitted.

A Fight over the Body of Homer gave greater trouble. Slightly pruned and retitled *The Lowest Room*, this had already been printed in *Macmillan's*. Gabriel wanted to eject it entirely, perhaps because it uncomfortably reminded him of Maria's youthful Greek passions, but officially because it was too stridently feminist, reminiscent of Isa Craig and Adelaide Procter, he alleged – it had of course been written before she had read or met either Isa or Adelaide. While disputing that this would therefore damage her reputation, Christina nevertheless accepted the veto, though warning that on the same grounds *A Royal Princess* should be omitted too: it was even more of 'a spite'. And if these two were ousted, the volume would be very slim.

Forseeing such need, she had written three 'little things which may help'. Now, in three days from 21 to 23 February, she produced three more: *Amor Mundi, From Sunset to Star Rise* and *Maggie a Lady*, followed by a fourth, despatched on 6 March – 'a longish thing (not only finished but altogether written just now and indeed finished since I last wrote to you) which no-one has yet seen'. This was expressly designed to replace *The Lowest Room* and in default of a better title, was called *Under the Rose*. 'I don't know whether you will deem it available; if not, let me have it again and I will fill deficit from the squad,' she continued; 'if on the other hand it passes muster, it will I believe stop the gap single-handed.'

Other points were matters of detail. Her spelling was always weak, she confessed, asking Gabriel to put the finishing corrections to her manuscript and forward it to Macmillan, trusting he would also undertake the 'business-details' as before, and assist with proofreading. Finally, she added, would he please preserve the rejected items? Even if unworthy of a place in Vol. 2, they might be published elsewhere.

But Gabriel had not finished. Having discussed the manuscript with Swinburne, he sent more comments, softening the blow with sketches for two woodcuts. Thanking him, Christina pointed out some criticisms of her own. He had drawn the Prince without his curly black beard, she wrote, upon which she would not insist ('though I won't record his waste of time in shaving') but the Bride's veil was symbolic and therefore essential: he must include it. As to his disparaging remarks on the other poems, it was comparatively flattering to be likened to Bessie Parkes: why did he not invoke the banal and popular Eliza Cook for good measure? Again she acquiesced in his exclusion of *The Lowest Room*, was glad *A Royal Princess* had passed muster, and somewhat wearily accepted further amendments, adding 'only don't make vast changes, as "I am I"'. She would not, for instance, alter the adjective 'hairy': though coarse it perfectly described poppy buds.

And now, she asked, was not the volume 'at last ripe for transmission to Mac? I feel a pardonable impatience'. If Gabriel thought she had in her yet another major piece, just waiting to be writen, he was mistaken:

> Do you know, I do seriously question whether I possess the working-power with which you credit me; and whether all the painstaking at my command wd. result in work better than – in fact half so good as – what I have actually done on the other system. It is vain comparing my powers (!) with yours (a remark I have never been called upon to make to anyone but yourself). However, if the latent epic should "by huge upthrust" come to the surface some day, or if by laborious delving I can unearth it, or if by unflagging prodment you can cultivate the sensitive plant in question, all the better for me: only please remember that "things which are impossible rarely happen" – and don't be too severe on me if in my case the "impossible" does not come to pass. Sometimes I could almost fear that my tendency is rather towards softening of the brain (say) than towards further development of mind.

'There's a croak!' she concluded cheerfully.

Hidden in this response, however (and in a parenthesis) was an important statement. As with the tournament, she disclaimed the power of writing Tennysonian epic, but nevertheless there was no poet besides her brother with whom she felt it vain to compare her own powers. Small wonder such overweening conceit required an ironic exclamation mark.

Gabriel liked three of the four new poems, and almost at once offered *Amor Mundi* to Samuel Lucas, now in charge of a new monthly named *The Shilling Magazine*. Of *Maggie a Lady*, a dialogue ballad about upward mobility, he immediately remarked that she must have been reading *Lady Geraldine's Courtship* – as indeed she admitted, though the similarities are not great. And though she herself claimed to have modelled *Under the Rose* on George Crabbe, the influence of Barrett Browning's *Bertha in the Lane* as well as *Aurora Leigh* is visible in its 'difficult' subject, for her newer poem was a dramatic monologue in the voice of a girl born illegitimate, or '*sub rosa*'. First reared by a foster-mother, Margaret is then taken to live with the Lady of the manor, whom she soon discerns to be her natural mother, though never a word is spoken. She pities her mother, curses her unknown father, mourns her nurse and determines never to marry.

As Christina feared, her brother thought this hardly an improvement on *The Lowest Room*. Illegitimacy was not a nice theme, as she freely admitted in response, trusting nevertheless that the treatment was not indelicate and that the poem would 'read its own lesson' – a bold challenge to the double standard of sexual morality and hypocrisy. 'I could almost curse My Father,' says her heroine bitterly:

> Why did he set his snare
> To catch at unaware
> My Mother's foolish youth;
> Load me with shame that's hers,
> And her with something worse,
> A lifelong lie for truth?

Later, Christina made the authorial view even plainer by changing her title to *The Iniquity of the Fathers upon the Children*. In her view, men were more to blame than women for sexual misconduct.

Like many men, Gabriel disliked women speaking on such subjects, about which he claimed they knew little. And in a very serious and spirited defence of her poem, Christina partly conceded the validity of his views and strongly contested them. If handled sensitively, illegitimacy was a perfectly proper subject for a female pen, she argued:

Even if we throw *U. the R.* overboard, and whilst I endorse your opinion of the unavoidable and indeed much-to-be-desired unreality of women's work on many social matters, I yet incline to include within female range such an attempt as this ... where the field is occupied by a single female figure whose internal portrait is set forth in her own words. Moreover, the sketch only gives the girl's own deductions, feelings, semi-resolutions;

granted such premises as hers, and right or wrong it seems to me she
might easily arrive at such conclusions: and whilst it may truly be argued
that unless white could be black and Heaven Hell my experience (thank
God) precludes me from hers, I yet don't see why "the Poet mind" should
be less able to construct her from its own inner consciousness than a
hundred other unknown quantities.

Her defence of imaginative freedom against those who would declare certain subjects off-limits for poetry or women writers was as
firm as the endorsement of her heroine's conclusions, which were
plainly designed to discomfit worldly readers:

> Of course the servants sneer
> Behind my back at me;
> Of course the village girls,
> Who envy me my curls
> And gowns and idleness,
> Take comfort in a jeer;
> Of course the ladies guess
> Just so much of my history
> As points the emphatic stress
> With which they laud my Lady;
> The gentlemen who catch
> A casual glimpse of me
> And turn again to see,
> Their valets on the watch
> To speak a word with me,
> All know . . .

In literary terms, *Under the Rose* is a weak poem – not because of its
subject or conclusions but because the jaunty rhythm frequently falls
into bathos. Christina was capable of better writing; in this instance
speed compromised quality. At a personal level, however, the resonances are disturbing, and all the more so for her emphatic denial of
any connection with the subject. For Margaret has a secret shame that
carries a lifelong stigma and can never be spoken of, but concerns a
seductive father whom no none holds responsible. In her early teens,
she falls into a deep grief that seems drawn from experience. Read
incest for illegitimacy and you have a comparable, if displaced, history. Of course, from her work at Highgate as well as numerous
contemporary novels from *Bleak House* to *Lady Audley's Secret*, Christina had enough knowledge of seduction and illegitimacy to create
Margaret's sad little story. Yet the recurrent motif of a secret linked to
sexual shame and emotional paralysis suggests that this poem, too, is

indirect evidence of a traumatic experience, deeply buried but waiting – when a new poem was needed in a hurry – for literary expression. In this regard, the final title *The Iniquity of the Fathers* had unwitting significance, and the filial curse, twice repeated, was uncannily apt.

The tussle with Gabriel continued. She agreed to let the *Shilling Magazine* have *Amor Mundi*, feeling 'rather triumphant' that she who had been 'the pariah' of *Once A Week* was now wanted by Mr Lucas. She accepted Mr Sandys as illustrator, too; though she would have preferred Gabriel, she well understood that he had neither time nor inclination. Poem and illustration duly appeared in the paper's second issue.

When finally all Gabriel's objections had been dealt with, Christina informed Macmillan that the manuscript would shortly arrive. Then to her dismay she received another screed of suggestions, which caused 'six well-defined and several paroxysms of stamping and foaming and hair-uprooting,' as she wrote, now almost out of patience with the continual emendations. Yes, he could suppress a 'screech' in *Under the Rose*. Yes, he could cut down *The Ghost's Petition*. Yes, there was a problem with one of the interludes in *Songs in a Cornfield*: would he choose and paste in one of the alternatives she enclosed. No, on second thoughts she would keep *Spring Fancies* as it was, and retain the second stanza of *Jessie Cameron*, which was essential to the plot. Now she trusted the text would at last go off. The illustrations were a separate matter. 'Your woodcuts are so essential to my contentment that I will wait a year for them if need is, though (in a whisper) six months wd. better please me,' she wrote tactfully. Both author and publisher knew of the procrastination to which *The Prince's* illustrator was prone.

To add to her embarrassment, Gabriel found fault with the second edition of *Goblin Market*. Eventually, however, he delivered the new volume to Macmillan, with instructions that proofs be sent both to Albany Street and Cheyne Walk, and that no printing take place without his express approval. Macmillan must have groaned at the prospect, but sent the manuscript at once to be set. Proof sheets appeared speedily, and by 26 April Gabriel was returning first corrections, explaining at the same time that the woodblocks would be delayed. Macmillan may have groaned again; he was in for a long wait. Perhaps Christina's complaints regarding the Prince's beard and Bride's veil (together with a teasing but acute inquiry as to whether he also had a tournament design on hand) had piqued her brother, who had difficulty accepting criticism; indeed in the end the illustrations appeared unrevised.

She was also impatient to be home, for the winter was over and she was getting bored. Towards Easter she was invited to lunch with

Barbara Smith's sister Bella, who like herself had been a corresponding member of the Portfolio Society. It was not a particularly congenial
event, though Bella was charming, and her husband General Ludlow
recounted an incident that stuck in Christina's mind for no worse
reason than it moved her heart. 'I have long remembered a story I was
once told as a party of us sat at luncheon,' she wrote later:

> The speaker, a General, had had a pet robin, a tame wild robin if I may call
> it so, a free familiar bird, fed and cared for by him and his.
>
> One day coming home from shooting he aimed his last random shot at
> a speck in the sky. No startling result ensued: what should ensue from
> such a shot aimed at such a safe altitude?
>
> Alas, a presumable result did ensue, not visible, but unalterably in-
> visible. The tame robin never came again; and the soldier, who loved it,
> and as he believed shot it, could not, when I listened to him, tell the story
> without emotion . . .

She also bumped into Jean Ingelow in the street, and another reason
for impatience may well have been the prospect of Jean's forthcoming
new collection. Christina would hardly have acknowledged such a
competitive aim, yet her eagerness to complete her own volume was
unaccustomed. Of course, given the nature of publishing – and her
princely brother's procrastinating habits – such despatch was unlikely and unachieved. Nonetheless, by the time Christina reappeared in
Albany Street in April, rather better in health, her new book was well
advanced and well advertised. There was little fear it would be overshadowed.

25

Italy and Beyond

THE CHIEF REASON Christina was anxious to finish work on her book was not rivalry, however, but her forthcoming visit to Italy. William had suggested mother and sister join his annual pilgrimage to their ancestral land, which neither had yet visited. It was a prospect so alluring that she was almost afraid to tempt fate by speaking of it, describing it as a *fata morgana*, and carefully qualifying her announcements. 'It seems not impossible (though so pleasant as to suggest improbability) that by the end of May I may go with William to get my first glimpse of Italy,' she told Macmillan, while to Anne Gilchrist she expressed the sort of self-postponing wish that came to infuriate William, saying she almost hoped the 'whole lovely scheme' would miscarry, thereby allowing him to travel alone and reach Naples. But this was holding her thumbs: there was no doubt of her eagerness.

Her excitement at the idea of going to Italy makes one wonder why, except for William, the family as a whole showed so little desire to visit the land of their fathers. They had grown up amid the constant aspiration of Papa's triumphant return, when tyranny would be defeated. Sometimes, recall had seemed imminent, only for hopes to be dashed and finally abandoned. After his death, continuing conflict made visits difficult but not impossible – there were comfortable British communities in Florence and Rome, and little risk to travellers. By now William was a seasoned tourist, feeling at ease as both an English gentleman and Italian expatriate. Gabriel on the other hand had baulked at all opportunities to visit Italy, and Maria showed no wish to do so, despite her language teaching. So only Christina and Mamma took up William's offer of a joint expedition, to be confined to the north in the interests of age and ease of transport.

Once the proofs were done, Christina showed little further anxiety over her book, knowing better than to hustle her brother regarding the illustrations. 'My *Prince*, having dawdled so long on his own account, cannot grumble at waiting yr. pleasure; and mine too, for your protecting woodcuts help me to face my small public,' she wrote. For his part, Gabriel continued to intervene in her affairs by trying to extract an advance from Macmillan, in what he evidently considered a persuasive manner. 'Now couldn't you be a good fairy and give her something down for this edition – say £100? You know she *is* a good poet, and some day people will know it,' he wrote. 'That's so true that it comes in rhyme of itself! She's going to Italy and would find a little moneybag useful.' But the contract was for half-profits, and Mac demurred, as Gabriel reported with disgust to his sister, who in turn wrote to her brother in dismay. 'Mr Macmillan writes under a complete misapprehension as to my Italian-tour-fund, precarious indeed if it depended on P. P. instead of on unfailing family bounty,' she wrote. 'However, now I will write direct to him and set matters as straight as words can set them.' She was happy with existing arrangements so would Gabriel please wash his hands of the vexatious business and leave her to deal with Mac? What on earth had made him connect the Italian holiday with her earnings from the new book? She thanked Gabriel for his 'brotherliness in business matters', but her firm reassumption of responsibility shows her awareness that this might more accurately be called meddling. Laughingly she also declined a half-case of Madeira, for medicinal purposes, procured by Gabriel's new acquaintance Charles Howell, saying it might be prized by connoisseurs, but was 'altogether lost on a Goth who knows not wine from wine'. Dr Jenner prescribed sherry and to sherry she would stick. William Jenner was a rising physician whom the family had first met around 1853; he ministered to the All Saints' Sisterhood and was Christina's preferred medical adviser; evidently he had declared her fit enough to travel.

On the eve of their departure, Christina sat to Gabriel for a portrait drawing, and on 22 May the travellers left London, on an inauspiciously dark and thundery morning. Stopping first in Paris, where they revisited Notre Dame and the Louvre as well as the international Exposition, and also met up with the Heimanns, they set off towards Basle on 26 May, via Langres high above the Marne valley, where Christina and William admired the view from the ramparts, and thence proceeded to Lucerne and Andermatt. As was his custom, William kept a dull travel diary, of places visited, sights seen and prices paid.

'Wherein lies the saddening influence of mountain scenery?' Christina wrote years later, evidently still puzzled by her reaction to the Alps. 'For I suppose many besides myself have felt depressed when approaching the "everlasting hills".' Was their sublimity too overwhelming? Hitherto, Christina had seen no landscape grander than the Malvern Hills, and for a grandchild of the Romantic generation she was unaccountably cast down:

Well, saddened and probably weary, I ended one delightful day's journey in Switzerland; and passed indoors, losing sight for a moment of the mountains.

Then from a window I faced them again. And lo! the evening flush had turned snow to a rose "and sorrow and sadness fled away".

A day or so later, they made their ascent of the St Gotthard by horse-drawn diligence. 'We did not tunnel our way like worms through its dense substance,' she wrote later after the rail link was opened; 'we surmounted its crest like eagles. Or, if you please, not at all like eagles: yet assuredly as like those born monarchs as it consisted with our possibilities to become.' But 'better to be the last of eagles than the first of worms.'

The eagle was of course her father's image of aspiration. For both Mamma and herself this was an important journey, and the entrance into Italy its keynote. Suddenly, at a certain point on the pass, came a minor but symbolic epiphany, when Mount St Gotthard 'bloomed into an actual garden of forget-me-nots', an 'unforgotten and never-to-be forgotten lovely lavish efflorescence which made earth cerulean as the sky', and retained its significance in a later sonnet:

> All Switzerland behind us on the ascent,
> All Italy before us, we plunged down
> St Gotthard, garden of forget-me-not . . .

'Could we forget that way which once we went?' she asked, whether or not one flower had bloomed to mark the spot. All her life, Italy had been a place of hearsay, imagination, idealism. William's previous travels had prepared them for something of everyday reality, but the actuality was almost certain to disappoint. Nevertheless they were so determined to find everything delightful, rejoicing as soon as they crossed into the Ticino in 'the loveable Italian faces and musical Italian speech', that all acquired glamour.

'Our small continental tour proved enjoyable beyond words; a pleasure in one's life never to be forgotten,' she reported to Anne Gilchrist. 'My Mother throve abroad, and not one drawback worth dwelling upon occurred to mar our contentment.' Indeed, everything was wonderful, she added, joking at their own enthusiasm. Even the exceptionally ugly pigs were turned to Italy's advantage, although not so the native poppies, whose colour was disappointingly pale.

At Como she and William went out on the lake in the evening, while nightingales sang and her brother talked politics with the boatman. This was truly Romantic, without Keatsian melancholy, and for once nature matched her mood:

> So chanced it once at Como on the Lake:
> But all things, then, waxed musical; each star
> Sang on its course, each breeze sang on its car,
> All harmonies sang to senses wide awake.

All things in tune, myself not out of tune,
Those nightingales were nightingales indeed:
Yet truly an owl had satisfied my need,
And wrought a rapture underneath that moon,
Or simple sparrow chirping from a reed;
For June that night glowed like a doubled June.

They stayed longest at Milan, where they witnessed the historic unveiling of a statue to Cavour, and visited the main hospital, noting happily that the children's ward was 'quite a pretty sight with its population of poor little patients'. 'I don't say a word about art treasures,' Christina confided to Anne, 'the truth being that I far prefer nature treasures', but they saw lots of paintings, William in particular being assiduous in pursuit of art. Exhausted, Christina spent the next day resting. They then travelled to Pavia, Brescia (where their guide was an ex-soldier who claimed to have known Papa) and to Verona, returning by Bergamo, Lecco and Chiavenna, before recrossing the Alps via the Spflugen Pass.

The itinerary however was less important than the emotions, which perhaps did not quite match the occasion. In an anecdote that has been taken to refer to this journey, Christina later recorded her disappointment at failing to see a rainbow in the spray when descending a mountainside next to a 'mountain torrent', adding 'In all my life I do not recollect to have seen one, except perhaps in artificial fountains.' This seems scarcely possible, though like her mother Christina had no liking for precipitous landscapes and can have seen few natural waterfalls. Slight as it was, her regret matches that for the unappreciated four-leaf-clover of her childhood, symbol of lost opportunities, and despite the forget-me-nots and nightingales, regret and disappointment were her dominant feelings, inscribed in lines written and headed *En Route*:

Life flows down to death; we cannot bind
    That current that it should not flee:
                    . . .
Why should I seek and never find
That something which I have not had?
    Fair and unutterably sad
The world hath sought time out of mind;
    For words have been already said,
Our deeds have been already done
    Yet life runs past . . .

What was she seeking in Italy? Was she sad because the dreams of her youth would now never be fulfilled, just as the real Italy could not deliver its ideal? Indeed, had not Italy always been a place she would seek and never find the undefinable something that she felt she had never had? Adulthood meant the relinquishing of dreams.

In the notebook, this piece began with even more gloomy thoughts:

> Men work and think, but women feel;
> And so (for I'm a woman, I)
> And so I should be glad to die
> And cease from impotence of zeal,
> And cease from hope, and cease from dread,
> And cease from yearnings without gain,
> And cease from all this world of pain . . .

With a few pious additions, this was later turned into a poem about an immured nun. It was, William opined, 'clearly a personal utterance' and he surmised that the title signified that 'by essential condition of soul' Christina felt she too was walled up. Yet with or without the conventual element, this seems more of a protest than a celebration of exclusion from the world, and its connection with the journey to Italy suggests the ambiguous nature of that experience.

In London, the Rossettis always felt partly foreign; in Italy they felt English. Christina was particularly charmed by the warmth of the people whose 'naturalness and freedom from self-centred stiffness struck a chord in her sympathies to which a good deal of what she was used to in England offered no response,' as William observed. But memory was also at work, for their childhood days had been filled with Italian warmth, among the host of histrionic exiles. Now, they seldom heard the language spoken in London. So this was, in a way, a nostalgic homecoming to their almost native country. 'Blessed be the land that warms my heart,' Christina wrote. 'Take my heart . . . Dear land, take my tears.'

William took her desire literally, writing later that it would have suited Christina 'much the best both for health and for mental satisfaction' to have settled permanently in Italy (so long as close to an Anglican church 'readily attainable in any large Italian city'). But this was to misunderstand. As Christina knew, inner contentment was not a matter of location, and such yearnings could be a snare. Later, in Time Flies, she recounted an anecdote of an artist who sought the most healthy place in which to settle, finally finding the perfect spot in Italy, where he promptly died. As she knew, Italy was a homeland of the heart, but she belonged to Britain. And in a number of poetic reflections she pondered the split inheritance, acknowledging both reality and loss:

To come back from the sweet South, to the North,
　Where I was born, bred, look to die;
Come back to do my day's work in its day,
　Play out my play –
Amen, amen, say I.

To see no more the country half my own,
　Nor hear that half familiar speech,
Amen, I say: I turn to the bleak North
　Whence I came forth –
The South lies out of reach . . .

Her sense of being born in exile, in the 'bleak North whence I came forth', shadows the melancholy weft running through her verse, with its lifelong desire for the unattainable home to which she might return, like swallows flying south at the end of summer – which always brought tears to her eyes, 'and the sweet name to my mouth'.

But if Italy was a motherland, symbolic of the sweet security of infancy, it was also 'strange, and not my mother'. For her English heritage was equally strong, or at least had its own virtues, like the pigs and poppies. Six days after her return to the 'northern' sphere, she articulated this poetically in verses about Enrica Filopanti, 'a very agreeable, bright-natured' woman introduced by Letitia Scott, who was 'eminently Italian in manner and character':

We chilled beside her liberal glow,
　She dwarfed us by her ampler scale,
　Her full-blown blossom made us pale
She summer-like and we like snow.

We Englishwomen, trim, correct,
　All minted in the self-same mould,
　Warm-hearted but of semblance cold,
All courteous out of self-respect.

Of semblance cold: the continuing self-criticism. Christina never ceased to regret her loss of natural warmth, the change from open-hearted 'Italian' childhood to trim, correct 'English' womanhood. The poem however ended on a different note, in praise of the stiff lip and quiet strength of her actual, adult nationhood, saying that if Enrica found them colourless and chill like the northern sea:

Rock-girt – like us she found us still
Deep at our deepest, strong and free.

English nationalism was also firm within her. The bleak North was her real homeland.

Soon after their return, Robert Browning called, specifically to make Christina's acquaintance. He sat in the parlour 'talking well and amusingly for an hour or so', and subsequently told William he was 'much gratified' by the meeting, though it appears Christina retreated behind her customary shyness, leaving mother and brother to converse. Yet Browning was speaking as a fellow poet, describing how he was currently engaged on a long historical poem concerning an Italian *cause célèbre* 'of an elopement of a suffering angel of a wife with an apostolic priest, and the machinations and murder enacted by the husband'. 'The mazes and conflicting appearance of right and wrong in the case,' William recorded, and 'the difficulty of finding out who deserved to be hung – the husband was so, and rightly, as Browning finally concluded – took possession of his sympathies.'

This, which became *The Ring and the Book*, does not quite sound the kind of story to take possession of Christina's sympathies, though she certainly possessed a Gothick imagination and much admired Browning. She had probably not yet read his latest volume *Dramatis Personae*, since William only started it a fortnight later, but it contained familiar subjects and styles, handled with metrical flexibility and irregular rhyme schemes such as she herself favoured. *Abt Vogler*, which she later listed as one of her favourites, was here, and so was *Mr Sludge the Medium*, an attack on the spiritualist hoaxer Daniel Home.

Spiritualism was a big issue of the day, for both believers and sceptics, and into the mouth of his medium Browning put some thought-provoking lines of defence. Why should spirit communication be so summarily dismissed? Were not such ideas the basis of religion? 'Go back to the beginning,' says Sludge:

> The first fact
> We're taught is, there's a world beside this world
> With spirits, not mankind, for tenantry.

On death were not all supposed to pass into the spirit world, watching over the living? The Bible, too, contained a fair number of messengers from 'the other side', from the ghost of Samuel onwards. Angels, too, spoke to the faithful, and from Aaron's Rod to the Raising of Lazarus the Bible was full of miracles. So there was a prima facie case for the manifestations produced in spiritualist seances, even if Sludge himself is an impostor, as he freely confesses.

'To me the whole subject is awful and mysterious,' Christina wrote, admitting that she could not otherwise account for the spirit messages, but trusting that 'simple imposture' would prove the true explanation. Like Browning she was profoundly distrustful of spiritualism, not least because it was opposed by the Church. Yet as Browning noted, its ideas were also partly in keeping with orthodox notions of the life beyond and the spiritualist craze obliged her to examine and formulate her beliefs regarding 'the world beside this world'. As she hoped, the apparently supernatural effects of spiritualist seances were proved fraudulent, but what of the supernatural itself? Ghosts and revenants and voices from beyond the grave, not to speak of angels in heaven, filled her poetic imagination. Did she believe in such phenomena? As a good Christian, she certainly believed in life after death; did she also believe in the continued presence of the dead, watching over and sometimes speaking to the living, as she so frequently portrayed them doing?

Victorian theology was not unclouded on this issue, even within the Anglican communion. It taught the doctrine of life everlasting – that physical death is but a transition, before the soul moves to another existence or plane, commonly called 'heaven'. But this concept was partly contradicted by the Adventist teaching to which Christina had been strongly exposed in youth, that at the Last Judgement Christ would come again to judge both the quick and the dead and assign all souls either to heaven or hell. This meant, among other things, that however holy in life the dead could not pass straight to heaven but had to wait until the End of Time.

This difficulty – ignored by the majority of the faithful – was reconciled through the theological doctrine of 'Soul Sleep', whereby souls after death were believed to rest in a limbo existence akin to earthly sleep, dreaming of paradise but not yet enjoying it. Death was thus seen to initiate a period of spiritual suspension, to be broken on the Last Day. Judging from her devotional works, Christina believed in soul sleep, which would not then allow for posthumous intervention in the lives of the living. The revenants in her poetry are therefore figures not of literal belief but of metaphorical imagination – ghosts symbolically speaking for and from the heart and the past, in the shape of dead lovers, betrayed women, lost children.

As she pondered these things, however, she became less and less certain, freely acknowledging that such matters were truly unknowable. In everyday terms, she retained her childhood beliefs in heaven as a place the dead 'go to', and where in due course all would be reunited. Towards the end of her life, she suggested that they were not allowed to communicate with the living, lest the living be thereby encouraged to strive heavenwards for the sake of reunion. 'Any of us who have lost our nearest and dearest may realize how keen would be the temptation to love – Alas! it may be to go on loving the creature more than the Creator,' she wrote. But this was merely a conjecture: the true meanings of the divine order remained always partly obscured – as in the Tractarian doctrine of Reserve – for the faithful to accept on trust.

Gradually, in her middle years, as a result of serious reading and study, the notion of the world beyond as a kind of great waiting room in the sky gave way to a more mystical vision. At first a paradisal dream land, where all sorrows and disappointments would fade into insignificance, heaven became an Ideal realm, dimly apprehended in life but representing the ultimate reality. Steadily, from Plato, St Augustine and seventeenth-century divines as well as latter-day theological writers like Isaac Williams and the work of William Blake, she constructed a religious and philosophical account of the relation between the earthly and divine, imperfect and perfect, actual and ideal. In her figuration, heaven remained an eternal promise but also a concept of everyday aspiration. 'On earth the possibility of harmony entails the corresponding possibility of discord,' she wrote later. 'Even on earth, however, whoever chooses can himself or herself keep time and tune: which will be an apt prelude for keeping eternity and tune in heaven.'

Increasingly, life came to seem the shadow, with the unseen ideality of heaven as the unknowable substance. And, she insisted, in the manner of a mystic, such questions could only be approached by imagery: the human imagination could not otherwise express what, in the words she so often quoted, 'eye hath not seen, nor ear heard, nor heart conceived'. Miracles she came to regard in rather the same light, as mysteries to be taken on metaphorical trust – though as a good Anglican she had little time for those ascribed to saints, nor their holy relics.

Christina's religious faith has been described as simple and unquestioning. In fact, it developed through deep and often difficult thought. And she was altogether less credulous than her brothers in respect of spiritualism, to which she became categorically hostile, believing that all such dabbling might pave the way for 'evil choice, imagination, conduct.' While she was developing her ideas of Christian Platonism, William and Gabriel and even the rationalist Scott were absorbed by seances. 'Last evening I went out to Albany St and saw William Rossetti and his sisters, and had a short walk and a smoke with him afterwards,' Scott told Alice in October, explaining that in the street William had asserted his belief in spirit communication because Lizzie was constantly appearing (that is, rapping out things) in séances at Cheyne Walk and communicating things such as only she could know.

William indeed took to attending professional séances, where he was a stranger, to keep a record of results. Once, the ghost of uncle John Polidori rapped for him, correctly identifying the manner of his death and his connection with Byron, but quite failing to remember his authorship of the *Vampyre*. Another medium succeeded in raising the spirit of Alice's brother Spencer Boyd, who had died earlier in the year, though on this occasion Scott's disbelief was undermined not so much by the message as by the fact that, on his inquiring whether he could look under the table for rapping mechanisms, the message came: 'mind your wig'. The rest of the company laughed, not knowing he was wearing one (though the medium may have been more observant), and both Scott and William were shaken. Another time, at an amateur séance at Thomas Keightley's home, a young friend named Louisa Parke transmitted garbled messages from Lizzie, but she had unaccountably failed to spot William attending a funeral in Highgate Cemetery the previous day (presumably ghosts were thought to maintain a perpetual vigil over their own graves). Moreover, she could not see into the future, being unable to tell William what would be the outcome of Christina's illness.

Such pathetic 'results' should have persuaded William of the futility if not fraudulence of spiritualism. On a later occasion when he and Scott tried to contact Pauline Trevelyan and Walter Deverell, they recognised the results as complete guesswork, and thereafter abandoned the whole endeavour. Clearly at some level, however, they wished to believe – at least temporarily.

With her poetic liking for voices beyond the grave, Christina might also have been intrigued by spiritualism's claims. Instead, like other women in her circle she was staunchly distrustful. Alice Boyd, for instance, had such a dislike of séances that Scott told William not to mention their experiences. Yet at the same time the men's willingness to believe undermined their atheism – where did they imagine the spirits spoke from? – in a manner that may have given their women-folk grounds for hope. The ghostly messages might succeed where human voices failed. For, as Scott conceded to Alice:

We cannot realize to ourselves any condition in the place of the body, and yet we are constrained to say, yes, we shall live for ever. This belief is inherent in our nature, it has existed always, and all the greatest intellects have assented to it. Of late years, I have been coming to a firm belief in a conscious future wherein we shall say to ourselves "I am the same". I do not speak of religion; it has been my misfortune to have it always presented to me in a way that made me impatient or contemptuous. I know this has been a great misfortune. I hope my misfortune will not be increased by my influencing you to feel the same.

On the contrary, Alice's faith was clearly influencing Scott. More silently, both Rossetti sisters hoped to save their backsliding brothers. Maria told William one reason for her joining All Saints Sisterhood was to obtain 'the grace of conversion' for him and Gabriel, while at a later date Ellen Heaton asserted that Christina strove for Gabriel's redemption by prayer and self-denial, 'bent on being Love's Martyr for his sake'. Both statements may be exaggerated, but there is no doubt that both Christina and Maria prayed and hoped for a miracle of regained faith.

The whole family took a sympathetic interest in Louisa Parke, the unsuccessful medium, whom they had known since the early 1850s when she was adopted by a family related to Keightley, and brought up as a prospective lady's maid. Being found to possess 'a very good brain', she was then educated to become a governess, and on several occasions the Rossettis assisted her search for employment. In 1861, for instance, she found a post through the recommendation of Maria's friends the Hollands, and in spring 1865 she stayed at Albany Street while seeking a situation. Christina invited Lucy and Cathy Brown to join them on a visit to the Zoo, and wrote on Louisa's behalf to Emily Seddon, who knew of a vacancy. To her vicarious relief, for she still harboured vivid memories of her own attempts at governessing, the position was not available after all. 'Miss Parke seems less appalled than I should be at the particular children in prospect,' she wrote. 'I return Miss Seddon's letter with grateful acknowledgements, and really cannot regret that my friend must perforce forego such a peculiar pupil.' She is believed to have corresponded with Louisa for the rest of her life, but no surviving letters are known.

Another new friend was the personable Charles Howell, who charmed everyone. Soon he was collecting stamps for Christina, promising to find a kitten and sending a portrait *carte* of his bride-to-be, in whom aunt Charlotte detected some likeness to the Princess of Wales (than which no higher compliment in aunt C's eyes). Christina forwarded Mr Howell's compliments to Mamma and Maria in Harrogate with Ellen Heaton, and looked forward, with a touch of that warm informality Howell seemed able to raise in friends and strangers alike, to meeting his 'Kate' personally. 'Pray pardon my unceremonious manner of naming her,' she concluded; 'but her surname is unknown to me, and "Miss Kate" is too hideous a way of expressing a pleasant idea.' Within a few weeks Kate Howell was introduced, and soon she too was in correspondence.

Young Golde Heimann also sent spare stamps. 'I only hope she does not deprive herself of what would be very good for barter,' wrote Christina to Amelia, when inviting the whole family to supper. 'Don't be late, please: ourselves and no ceremony.' Asked to meet the Heimanns was yet another new acquaintance named Caroline Gemmer, a fellow author and longstanding friend of Mr Burrows, whom Mamma and Maria had recently met. On being introduced, Christina received a copy of Mrs Gemmer's first book, *Poetry for Play Hours*, which she immediately despatched to Beatrice Gilchrist with instructions to pass it on to Grace if deemed too babyish.

Mrs Gemmer wrote under the pseudonym 'Gerda Fay', and her book of pretty verses displayed an unsentimental understanding of childhood. A more gushing adult collection followed, entitled *Lyrics and Idylls*. Coventry Patmore encouraged these endeavours, identifying Mrs Gemmer as a worthy successor to Mrs Browning and Miss Procter. 'You and Miss Rossetti' he wrote in 1863, 'are the only representatives of the late remarkable school of English poetesses.' But as her pen name suggests, Caroline Gemmer's hero was Hans Andersen, and her best work lay in children's literature.

So, it transpired, did that of the mathematical photographer from Oxford, Mr Dodgson, who towards the end of 1865 sent Christina a complimentary copy of *Alice's Adventures in Wonderland*. 'A thousand and one thanks – surely an appropriate number – for the funny pretty book you have sent me,' Christina replied:

> My Mother and Sister as well as myself have made ourselves quite at home yesterday in Wonderland: and (if I am not shamefully old for such an avowal) I confess it would give me sincere pleasure to fall in with that conversational rabbit, that endearing puppy, that very sparkling dormouse. Of the Hatter's acquaintance I am not ambitious, and the March Hare may fairly remain an open question. The woodcuts are charming.

Her delight was general, for *Alice in Wonderland* was an immediate success, and her ironical letter, singling out the unconversational rabbit and most unsparkling dormouse, indicates how warmly she responded to the spirit of the tale, as did her brother. 'Alice's perverted snatches of school poetry are among the funniest things I have seen for a long while,' Gabriel told the author. Dodgson's parodies tickled many brought up on Isaac Watts's ferocious verses, while the song to which the Lobster Quadrille is danced was recognisably based on one of Mary Howitt's best-known poems. The Rossettis perhaps also registered how aspects of Christina's now-public Prudent Crocodile were also incorporated into Alice's parody of Watts's busy bee:

> How cheerfully he seems to grin,
> How neatly spread his claws
> And welcome little fishes in
> With gently smiling jaws!

Jean Ingelow's *Stories told to a Child* were published this season, and when Christina was approached by Isa Craig, now editing of a monthly magazine called *The Argosy*, she therefore looked out her own earlier work in this genre. *Hero: A Metamorphosis*, the Andersen-derived fairytale about glory and contentment, thus appeared in February 1866. It was quite splendid, Gabriel observed, recognising its connection with *Alice* by also commending it to Dodgson as 'a capital fairy tale'. He urged Christina to write 'more such things'.

Instead, Christina offered two more quite different things to Isa, including the self-loathing *Who Shall Deliver Me?* written in 1864 but not chosen for the new book, followed by *If*. Miss Craig called on Gabriel to ask if he would illustrate. 'I couldn't do it,' he replied to his sister, 'but, as the poem seemed good for illustration, I sent her on to Sandys, and, failing him, to Hughes.' *Argosy* might baulk at Sandys's price, but 'Hughes perhaps might do it cheap for love of you. You know he's painted a capital picture from your *Birthday*, with the poem at full length on the frame. You ought to call and see it, which would please him.'

In the event *Argosy* agreed to Sandys's fee, rather unfortunately as it turned out, for his conception of the yearning *If* was a large blowsy figure, modelled from Fanny Cornforth, quite out of keeping with the wistful poem. For love of Gabriel however Christina seems to have accepted his promotion of Sandys as her illustrator, for he was also at work on a woodcut to accompany *Husband and Wife* destined for the anthology *A Masque of Poets*. Sandys's imagination proved unequal to the task: 'The only thing he could think of was to make a drawing of the woman lying dead, with some women preparing the grave-clothes and baby-clothes at the same time,' Gabriel wrote. This was fine, but would Christina mind changing the title to *Grave-clothes and Cradle-clothes*, to make this plain? It seems she did mind, or maybe the project fell through for other reasons, for no illustration appeared.

In personal terms, she much preferred Arthur Hughes, who had been a shy associate of the PRB in the early days, and whose pictures of young lovers were admired for delicate feeling and clear colour. Her response on this occasion is not recorded, and his picture is currently unlocated, but the choice of 'My heart is like a singing bird' for a painting is indicative of widening fame as well as friendship. So too was the invitation to contribute to a Christmas annual produced by the Dalziel firm, grandly entitled *A Round of Days: Original Poems by some of our Most Celebrated Poets [with] Pictures by Eminent Artists*. She sent her piece on Enrica Filopanti, rechristened *An English Drawing Room, 1865*, which appeared with a full-page illustration of crinolined ladies and mustachioed gentlemen, together with another item, originally entitled *A Yawn* but now retitled *By the Sea* and cut to render it impersonal; this was adorned with a vignette of waves, cliffs and stormclouds.

All these requests were gratifying and remunerative, although they placed Christina in an awkward position with Macmillan, since his magazine might justifiably have first refusal on unpublished items. In fact, when Mac made some such query towards the end of the year, Christina replied pointedly that Masson had held *Consider* for several months; she presumed it was unwanted and requested its return. It promptly appeared in the next issue.

Throughout the winter, Christina remained at home. 'With the geniality of ravens my friends talk of my going away for the winter, whereas I know not of it, last winter having been uniquely exceptional, she told Emily Newton, adding to Anne Gilchrist that her leaving London had not even been suggested doctorially'. However, she was able to accept evening invitations only if offered a bed: 'night air' was considered noxious to her lungs. Within these constraints, she was relatively active, paying regular visits to Chelsea and daytime calls on other friends. Early in the year Gabriel summoned the family to see his latest painting, of the Bride of the Canticles and her attendants, before despatch to its buyer. 'I should like you to see it, if you can, finished,' he wrote to his mother, 'as I know you nurse my productions in your dear heart. Sisters also of course if practicable'. Aunt Charlotte went too, recording a note about the young boy who sat for the figure of a black child, who wept copiously when obliged to keep still. 'G. suggested he might be thinking about his Mammy,' wrote aunt C, and behind this remark lay the forced separation of slave children from their parents, on which the abolitionists had built their campaign.

The American Civil War was over – William wrote a tribute to Lincoln and a long article on British responses, newly printed in the *Atlantic Monthly* – but the race issue was still in the public mind, for in October 1865 unrest in Jamaica had resulted in a punitive massacre and a subsequently angry debate in Britain between those who supported Governor Eyre and those who called for his arraignment. In the *Argosy* Isa Craig warned readers not to rush to conclusions; however much the unrest was to be deplored, the leader of the Jamaican protests, summarily executed, turned out to be an exemplary figure, the 'self-taught and self-bought' son of slave mother and white settler.

Slavery was also the theme of Madox Brown's new painting *The Coat of Many Colours*, which Christina saw on the easel in April, in the studio of the Browns' new home, 'a large and handsome house in Fitzroy Square,' as she told Anne, adding that Lucy was as nice as ever, Cathy quite grown up, and Nolly already exhibiting talent. She went to stay overnight with Alice and the Scotts, where she met

Swinburne, whom she found 'as surprizing as usual' – though in polite company Swinburne's manic behaviour was controlled and the tales of his intoxication, bawdy talk and sliding naked down the banisters at Cheyne Walk were largely concealed from well-bred ladies – and this month she and the family dined again at Cheyne Walk, together with the Heimanns and Ellen Heaton. Gabriel had decided to paint Mamma's portrait, and at the same time produced a new chalk drawing of Christina.

She herself was not producing much, despite the demand from anthologies. After the clutch of poems inspired by Italy, only twelve new pieces appeared in the succeeding twelve months. Through Jean Ingelow's good offices, however, she received an offer from Roberts Bros in Boston to publish *Goblin Market* in the United States, on generous terms. This was partly to prevent piracy, for no reciprocal copyright existed and, as she noted proudly, over two thousand copies of her book had already been bought by American readers.

At her request Macmillans forwarded proofs of *The Prince's Progress* and later in the year a double volume was issued in Boston, as *Poems* by Christina Rossetti. As Roberts Bros did not wait for any woodcuts, it so happened that American readers saw *The Prince* before those in Britain.

26

Penkill and Swinburne

WHEN HER NEW volume appeared, a year after the visit to Italy, Christina was in Scotland, staying with Miss Boyd and the Scotts at Penkill.

This was her first opportunity to really get to know and like Alice. The Scotts had moved to London in spring 1864, following the illness in which Scott had lost his hair and his subsequent retirement from the School of Design. For the time being Miss Boyd remained in Newcastle with her brother, but the long-term plan was to live *à trois*, and Scott's letters to Alice, filled with intimacies and endearments, demonstrate how close they had become. Both however were anxious to preserve her reputation from scandalous suspicions, so the house-share was openly arranged, on the basis that Alice would spend the winters living with the Scotts in London and the summers with her brother and 'WB' at Penkill. Had the Rossetti women imagined for a moment anything improper was afoot, they would neither have visited nor invited either Alice or Scott; instead, they welcomed Alice as a new and valued friend and must therefore have received assurances from Letitia that the arrangement had her blessing. Christina, as usual, was stiff and formal at first, having always liked Letitia better than Scott, but in time she numbered Alice among her dearest acquaintance, and in 1866 was happy to be asked to accompany Letitia for an early holiday at Penkill – an anticipated pleasure for one who had never yet visited Scotland. Spencer Boyd's untimely death meant that other visitors were now necessary to render WB's presence at Penkill respectable; as he told Alice, it was otherwise difficult for him to stay 'so long as we (you and I) have hoped'. Alice herself left for Ayrshire at the beginning of May, followed a couple of weeks later by Scott, he indeed being so anxious lest Christina think it improper that he contemplated delaying his own departure until she and Letitia were ready to travel.

This concern with proprieties looks suspicious, but was not un-necessary, as has been thought, 'given the common knowledge of the Scotts' household arrangements'. As yet there was hardly a *ménage à trois* – Alice had spent almost the whole of 1865 alone in Scotland – and though Christina was of course relatively innocent in the ways of the world, there is no reason for a more cynical age to doubt the basis of her trust, for Alice was an honourable and upright woman. She and Scott were in love, and therefore needed to preserve the proprieties

– not in order to disguise immorality but because gossip, without misbehaviour, would effectively finish their friendship.

Fortuitously, the invitation obliged Christina to decline two others, one from Anne Gilchrist, and another – more flattering but also alarming – from Julia Cameron, who had recently descended on Albany Street bearing a portfolio of photographs of Gabriel's paintings, five of which she graciously presented. Christina and Maria returned the call, to Little Holland House in Kensington, home of Mrs Cameron's sister, where as well as getting a brief glimpse of Browning they met the resident genius G. F. Watts and also Mrs Dalrymple, a third sister whose husband owned the neighbouring castle to Penkill. Mrs Cameron invited Christina to her home on the Isle of Wight, holding out the promise of a meeting with Tennyson. Christina confessed herself too shy to contemplate this prospect 'with anything like unmixed pleasure' but was perhaps more sorry than she admitted when the clash of dates made it impossible, for like all other poets at mid-century she stood in awe of the Laureate, and measured herself against him. What with her shyness and Tennyson's dislike of being lionised, however, a visit to Freshwater could well have been mutually awkward.

She therefore travelled north with Letitia, breaking the rail journey at Carlisle and proceeding along the coast to Girvan, where they were met by the Penkill carriage for the short drive to the Castle, an ancient peel tower hidden in the narrow Penwhapple glen. As castles go, it was small, hardly more than a double keep built perpendicular to the hillside. Spencer Boyd had renovated the original structure, rebuilt a circular staircase tower, and furnished the rooms with armour and ancient woodwork. Alice, inspired by embroidered wall-hangings at the Morrises' Red House, had covered the rough interior walls in dark blue serge stitched with red and white flowers, and Scott had begun an ambitious mural of the medieval Scottish poem *The Kingis Quhair* on the curving walls of the wide stairway. On arrival, Christina was recruited to sit for the figure of Lady Jane Beaufort. Somewhat ambiguously, the poem, written by James I of Scotland, is a celebration of married love.

'I hope you are amongst still finer surroundings, but you are not badly off if you are only in a country as fine as this,' Christina wrote to William, who had finally made the journey to Naples. 'As to room,' she continued:

> I expect I exceed you, inhabiting as I do an apartment like the best bedroom at Tudor House on a large scale . . .
>
> Ailsa Craig is a wonderfully poetic object continually in sight. Of small fry, jackdaws perch near the windows, and rabbits parade in full view of the house. The glen is lovely. And, to crown all, we are having a pleasant mild summer.

She had been at Penkill for just three days, and they had already been out for two drives and a visit to church.

Christina's bedroom, according to tradition, was at the top of the original peel tower, whose westward view from a turret-window towards the sea and the great rock of Ailsa Craig prompted a little *Song*, neatly filling the last page of the current notebook on 11 June:

> Oh what comes over the sea,
>   Shoals and quicksands past;
> And what comes home to me,
>   Sailing slow, sailing fast?
>
> A wind comes over the sea
>   With a moan in its blast;
> But nothing comes home to me,
>   Sailing slow, sailing fast.
>
> Let me be, let me be,
>   For my lot is cast:
> Land or sea all's one to me
>   And sail it slow or fast.

Here, early one morning, she replied to the sound of repeated taps, thinking herself called, only to find that the noise came from the jackdaws lodged in the loopholes. Scott, also sometimes thus wakened, described the silent early hours of summer, when everything was still and bright:

> the sky was white, the sun unspeakably white, making the shadows of the trees faintly chequer the smooth green terrace. On the point of one of the leaves of a great aloe below perched a thrush, silent and motionless; two wild rabbits were sitting on the green terrace still as if they were carved in stone . . .

On the floor of her room, Christina found a many-legged insect, whom she decided to eject. As she gathered it up, a swarm of baby millipedes was born into her hand. 'Surprised, but resolute, I hurried on, and carried out my scheme successfully,' she recalled, 'observing the juniors retire into the cracks outside the window as adroitly as if they had been centenarians.'

Short walks, in the grounds that Alice aimed to make into a pleasant garden, with alleys, arbours, fishponds and croquet lawn, or into the precipitous glen below the keep, were varied with local excursions to the coast or inland. The most spectacular sights were the evenings over the western sea; as she told Anne: 'when beyond the immediate greenness, a gorgeous sunset glorifies the sea distance, one scarcely need desire aught more exquisite in this world'. Together with Alice and Letitia, she attended the local episcopal church at New Dailly, and though Penkill was sufficiently remote to receive few visitors – the Dalrymples of Bargany were not in residence this June – Christina was responsible for one awkward encounter with the rector of Girvan. Before travelling north, she had anxiously written to inquire about services, in a manner that apparently led him to think, as she told Alice, that she was some kind of 'grandee residing awhile at your Castle'. He therefore called, to Alice's great annoyance – perhaps occasioned by greater anxiety regarding gossip.

The third week of Christina's stay was saddened by the death of Alice's little dog, which prevented her from joining the others for a two-day visit to the picturesque village of Barr. At the end of the month Christina and Letitia left, to wind up their holiday with 'a highly satisfactory week in Edinburgh' staying with Letitia's aunt. Scott had been rather prickly – not for nothing had Pauline Trevelyan nicknamed him Mr Porcupine – for, as he grumbled privately to William, living with three women with 'religion and ailments forming a large part of daily life and talk' was not exhilarating. Moreover, 'as for Christina and I, we fight like cats, as is our nature . . . especially at croquet.' This is the only record of antagonism between Christina and Scott and although partly self-mocking had a serious basis; he thought her narrow-minded and nervously over-cautious, with a sort of moral watching brief over her brothers. Though in later years she returned his teasing affection, her true feelings are harder to discern; it is likely that she still found Scott somewhat satanic, as well as grumpy. On this occasion much of his discontent clearly came from being outnumbered, and unable to spend his time alone with Alice. As an aspiring poet as well as painter, he may also have been a touch envious of Christina's renown, as manifested in her new book.

Gabriel's delays had again cost Christina the chance of pre-Christmas publication. It was March before he had sent the woodcuts for engraving and May before production could proceed, twelve months after the text was set. For her part, Christina had been alarmed to find some lingering proof errors, and was only pacified when Macmillan promised to have them corrected by hand. When bound copies of her 'laggard book' arrived however, at the beginning of June, she wailed that the book was still blemished 'by perhaps the worst misprint of all left uncorrected'. This was in fact merely an intrusive period in *Songs in a Cornfield* and as it turned out, the handwritten corrections appeared in all other copies, having escaped only the author's complimentary volumes, so her dismay proved unfounded.

Christina trusted her Scottish holiday made her 'all the braver to undergo the lash' of reviewing, but she probably expected better treatment than she received. As could have been foreseen, it was not a propitious time to bring out a new book, for Britain was in the midst of a financial crisis triggered by the spectacular collapse of a major banking and broking firm on 11 May – 'Black Friday' – that caused panic in the commercial world and decimated many individuals' savings. Moreover, June publication meant noticeably less publicity. By the time the book appeared, reviewers and readers were already beginning to disperse for the summer, and by the time they returned, new titles and topics commanded attention. The reviews that trickled in over July, August and September were therefore fewer, and lukewarm.

As could also have been predicted, whatever its quality her second book was bound to arouse less applause than the first. For one thing, there was no 'discovery' to announce, no 'new voice' to welcome. For another, even friendly reviewers offered a more serious critique, as befitted an established author. Thus the *Saturday Review* on 23 June:

Neither the *Prince's Progress* nor the shorter poems that follow can be said to open up veins of thought and feeling that are new . . .

A good many tame and rather slovenly verses have been left which ought either to have been cut out or polished into something more shapely. It is all very well to resist the temptation to substitute mere artificial emphasis instead of an idea, but a dull pointless cadence, such as now and again occurs in these verses, is almost as bad . . .

Thus the *Athenaeum*, on the same day:

We do not see the conflict of the heart, but the sequel of that conflict . . . Her saints and heroes have not the stir and dust of life about them; but they smile to us in a repose almost mournful, like effigies . . .

We cannot but lament that the tone of Miss Rossetti's poetry – always, be it remembered, religiously submissive – should be that of the dirge rather than the anthem.

If she was cast down, Christina did not show it. Writing to Anne, she claimed to have received no 'severe handling' from critics. Perhaps she recognised the judiciousness of their judgements; as she knew, the Prince lacked the Goblins' 'special felicity', and the volume as a whole undoubtedly contained too many pieces chosen for the sake of 'bulk'. It had its own hits, including *Jessie Cameron, Twice, Queen of Hearts,*

Bird's Eye View, Memory, LEL, Somewhere or Other and *Despised and Rejected* – but also too many poems that quite frankly fail, together with a meagre devotional section largely filled with straining martyrdom.

After she returned home, feeling well and plump and more than willing to take her share of housekeeping while Mamma and Maria went to Eastbourne, Christina stopped copying out her compositions, as she had done for over twenty years now, and even left the last notebook unindexed. This change in practice probably came about more by default than design – having been accustomed to 'wait' for poems, she found the critics of *Prince's Progress* had implicitly endorsed this method by their negative response to those very pieces written to bulk out the volume. She then reverted to previous practice, only to find herself waiting rather a long time. This had often happened in the past, and was not necessarily worrying, but when poems again began to appear, there perhaps seemed no compelling reason to purchase a new notebook – which was after all rather a juvenile procedure, and might in any case tempt fate, and scare her muse away again.

There was however another reason which may have inhibited her creativity more than she or anyone else realised – the outcry that greeted Swinburne's new book.

Over the past year, Swinburne had effectively displaced Christina as the new voice in verse. She returned from Scotland to find his *Poems and Ballads* the centre of literary attention and abuse, excoriated for its 'libidinous song', excited by 'shameless abominations' expressed with 'feverish carnality'. With copious quotations John Morley, in the *Saturday Review*, rather overdid the outrage in five columns.

> No language is too strong to condemn the mixed vileness and childishness of depicting the spurious passion of a putrescent imagination, the unnamed lusts of sated wantons, as if they were the crown of character and . . . the great glory of human life . . .
>
>   Is there really nothing in women worth singing about except 'quivering flanks' and 'splendid supple thighs', 'hot sweet throats' and 'hotter hands than fire'? . . .
>
>   . . . The bottomless pit encompasses us on one side, and stews and bagnios on the other.

The *Athenaeum* charged Swinburne with insincere immorality posing as decadence, and also implied that he was a ringleted, amorous-lidded pederast. The *London Review* castigated his blasphemy and gross depravity, the *Pall Mall Gazette* declared he was 'maudlin drunk on lewd ideas'. Personal and poetic judgements were intertwined, for

Swinburne's dissolute behaviour was well known in literary London, but this hardly mitigated the hostility.

This need not have affected Christina, but for the fact that her brothers were closely associated with Swinburne, who, when his publisher took fright and withdrew the volume, began drumming up support among his friends. Gabriel entered the lists cautiously, telling Tennyson, for instance, that while he hailed Swinburne's genius, he also 'strenuously combated its wayward exercise' and advised against publishing certain poems. Scott took a similar line, urging Swinburne not to compound the volume's notoriety by transferring to a less reputable publisher. But William went to the barricades, calling Swinburne 'the most glorious perhaps of living English poets' bar the Laureate, and composing a long defence, to be published alongside the reissued volume. Oddly, William seems to have had no personal liking for Baudelairean *fleurs du mal* or lust, and frankly warned Swinburne that his alcoholic behaviour was unacceptable. But he energetically supported poetic and pagan sensuality against parson and pedagogue and prude. And in doing so he drew into the argument other poets – including his sister, in what from anyone else would have been construed as a hostile paragraph. Christina Rossetti, he declared, was a 'natural' singer of the same order as Swinburne:

> There is no poet with a more marked instinct for fusing the thought into the image, and the image into the thought: the fact is always to her emotional, not merely positive, and the emotion clothed in sensible shape, not merely abstract. No treatment can be more artistically womanly in general scope than this, which appears to us the most essential distinction of Miss Rossetti's writings. It might be futile to seek for any points of direct analogy or of memorable divergence between Mr Swinburne and Miss Rossetti. The prevalent cadence of the poem 'Rococo', and the lyrical structure of 'Madonna Mia' may, however, suggest that the poet is a not unsympathetic reader of the poetess's compositions; nor is the 'Garden of Proserpine' much unlike some of these so far merely as lyrical tone is concerned.

Despite his qualifications, in plain terms (William's expression was often ponderous) this amounted to a claim that Swinburne had learnt his tones and cadences from Christina's instinctively sensuous and emotional verse.

This was partly true. Swinburne had undeniably echoed *An End* in the final lines of his most unreligious *Madonna Mia*, and had sung of world-weariness in the *Garden of Proserpine* in falling rhythms that matched hers. That motive and message were quite different did not make it less of a disastrous comparison, for though William's intention was of course to exonerate Swinburne, the indirect result was to infect Christina. If their work was similar, would not the public regard her in some sort as soul-sister to this notorious new-hatched poet, despite her reputation for devoutness and his for debauchery? Indeed, the critic of the *Examiner* tried to prove that Swinburne's sensuality was actually moral, in terms that might well remind readers of the goblin merchandise peddled by Miss Rossetti:

> He sings of Lust as Sin, its portion Pain and its end Death. He paints its fruit as Sodom apples, very fair without, ashes and dust within. In dwelling on their outward beauty, he is sensual. Men see that and say that he is a licentious writer. But again and again when he has dwelt as proper folk object to dwell on the desire of the flesh, the beauty drops away and shows the grinning skeleton beneath the fires of hell below.

A fortnight later, the same reviewer made this even plainer in a long notice of her work by 'identifying the gist of *Dolores* with that of *Goblin Market*!' as William told Swinburne. This was hardly mitigated by the reviewer's simultaneous comparison of Christina's work with that of George Herbert, or his attempt to crown her 'Queen of the living Shepherdesses in our British Arcadia'.

It was a doubly ambiguous linking, for Swinburne was regarded not only as depraved but also as perverted. As Scott opined, when proof copies of *Poems and Ballads* were prematurely circulated, his provocative depravity was partly a pose and partly the result of his 'unmanly' nature, a word which many suspected was 'physically correct'. As all agreed, and William had emphasised, Christina was the most feminine of writers. But for a 'womanly' poetess to be linked with an 'unmanly' poet was to imply that perverted femininity was somehow the cause of his corruption, as if she had leaked into his verse. And in the context of the attack on Swinburne's morality and versification, when everyone gave an opinion whether or not they had read the book, any comparison was at least unfortunate, and at worst contaminating. What, for instance, might readers think of the rippling feminine rhymes favoured by both poets? What of their shared interest in virgin martyrs like St Dorothea? What of Swinburne's notorious rendering of Sappho's distress on seeing her beloved in a male embrace – a specifically lesbian reading of the ode traditionally translated heterosexually? What, most unfortunately, of Christina's latest poem, which Gabriel had kept out of her book but which she had just published in *Macmillan*'s, in which the Jewish captive laments in wholly Swinburnian phrases:

Strangers press the olives that are mine,
Reap all the corners of my harvest-field,
And make their fat hearts wanton with my wine;
To them my trees, to them my gardens yield
Their sweets and spices and their tender green . . .

'I have read (did I say it before?) your sister's poem in M'millan with great admiration,' Algernon wrote on 13 October. In the circumstances, it was admiration she could well do without.

There is no evidence that Christina was openly or even consciously upset by her brother's remarks or the general linkage of her work with Swinburne's. Her subsequent relationship with the younger poet was friendly in tone, as he was always warmly respectful towards her. The following year, he made his admiration public, by inserting into a long article on Matthew Arnold in the *Fortnightly* a sudden paean of praise, listing her among 'immortal women' of artistic and religious eminence – 'St Theresa, St Catherine, Vittoria Colonna, Mrs Browning, Miss Christina Rossetti' – and hailing her poem *Passing Away* as 'so much the noblest of sacred poems in our language that there is none which come near it enough to stand second; a hymn touched as with the fire and bathed as in the light of sunbeams, tuned as to chords and cadences of refluent sea-music beyond reach of harp and organ, large echoes of the serene and sonorous tides of heaven.' This, one might feel, was sufficiently extravagant and foolish to do Miss Rossetti no good at all, but seems to have been welcomed. 'The praise is really too great, as you know she would be the first to say and feel,' wrote William to Swinburne, adding that it was 'not the less acceptable on all grounds'.

Alerted by the controversy, Christina probably did not read far into *Poems and Ballads*, though it is worth noting that she was not as extremely prudish as later generations have believed. She read and reread Plato with absorption, and after her visit to Penkill lent her copy to Alice, warmly commending 'the glorious *Apology*, *Crito* and *Phaedo*', and only warning her that the *Phaedrus* could not be read aloud in mixed company, and might be better avoided altogether. She herself had evidently not been so timorous, and though William later claimed that she pasted strips of paper over offensive passages in Swinburne's verse, this was on grounds of its 'irreligious taint'. For his part, William probably made no effort to persuade her otherwise, knowing that like others of his acquaintance, she was 'puritan enough to believe that good art cannot exist without good morals', as his friend Charles Norton in Boston put it, having read only the reviews.

One thing she could not escape however was the fact that Swinburne engrossed all critical attention. As *Fraser's* admitted in November, all available space had been occupied with this *cause célèbre*, so that amongst others, 'Miss Rossetti's quaint and characteristic volume ... must remain unnoticed till a more convenient season'. Such a time never came.

With the benefit of hindsight, it can be seen that both poets were aesthetic companions, so to speak, in the vanguard of the transition from the mid- to the dominant late-Victorian poetic mode, with its intense but dreamlike imaginative world. Ironically, just as Christina's *Lost Titian* anticipated Pater and Wilde, so in terms of form and style her verse led the way to an art for art's sake, whose amorality was wholly abhorrent to her sensibility.

27

Blumine

WHAT, ALL THIS WHILE, of Mr Charles Cayley? It was now four years since Christina had felt the stirrings of romance but there had been no recorded development in their hesitant courtship. He had finished his translation of the *Iliad* and begun work on *Prometheus Bound*. Despite his interest in the language he did not accompany the Rossettis to Italy. Nothing is visible in any surviving source, but some time in August 1866, while her mother and sister were at Eastbourne, Cayley asked Christina to marry him, and she declined.

On Mamma's return, she went to stay with the Polydores in Gloucester. William wrote generously, offering to provide a home, if lack of money was the obstacle to marriage, and inquired whether she would prefer him to stop seeing Cayley. 'I can't tell you what I feel at your most more than brotherly letter,' she replied on 11 September:

> Of course I am not *merely* the happier for what has occurred, but I gain much in knowing how much I am loved beyond my desserts. As to money, I might be selfish enough to wish that that were the only bar, but you see from my point of view it is not. Now I am at least unselfish enough altogether to deprecate seeing C. B. C continually (with nothing but mere feeling to offer) to his hamper and discomfort: but, if he likes to see me, God knows I like to see him, and any kindness you will show him will only be additional kindness loaded on me.

Money was one problem. Religious faith was another, for though William admitted to not knowing precisely where Cayley stood in such matters, he believed that Christina had 'probed his faith and found it either strictly wrong or woefully defective' – or, as he put it elsewhere, with a different emphasis, she 'made the whole affair a matter of conscience, inquired into his Creed and found he was not a Christian – either absolutely not a Christian, or else so far removed from fully defined religious orthodoxy that she could not regard him as sharing the essence of her own beliefs. She consequently, with a sore heart, declined to be his wife.'

But was this the whole truth? William also admitted to being 'never cognizant' of many details regarding Christina's affairs of the heart. In certain circumstances, she might not have regarded defective faith an insuperable obstacle to marriage. Her letter to William moreover regretted having only 'mere feeling' for Cayley, stating that it was unfair to continue seeing him on this basis, 'to his hamper and discomfort', which implies an imbalance in their affections. Maybe on receiving an explicit proposal Christina interrogated not just his faith but her own feelings and found they did not amount to love. Allied to religious indifference and lack of money – where, one wonders, did C. B. C. propose they should live as a married couple? With his mother and sisters? – this could have been the determining factor. Christina was not the woman to marry out of sympathy instead of love simply to avoid spinsterhood. 'I was so fond of him,' she told William on her deathbed, but though he translated this as meaning she had loved Cayley 'deeply and permanently', it was perhaps the love of friendship rather than matrimony. Nevertheless, her brother stoutly believed she should have married Cayley. 'She would have been far happier, and might have become rather broader in mental outlook, and no one would have been any the worse for it,' he asserted robustly, adding that 'after they had come to an explanation on religious questions, and she to a decision governed by her creed' she thought all the more highly of her suitor 'for having avowed the truth without disguise or subterfuge'. This was true, as her later writings show; no doubt she was grateful for no repetition of James's moveable allegiance.

Perhaps Christina cited religious difference to soften the blow, knowing her refusal would hurt. On one occasion later she referred directly to the pain she had caused Charles and the 'moment when – and no wonder – those who loved you best thought very severely of me', and added that she deserved severity, though 'I never seemed to get much at yours'. Another clue may lie in a short poem that Christina copied out and kept to the end of her life, with a marginal note indicating it was printed in *The Nation* on 6 September 1866, not long after she gave him her decision. Headed *Noli me tangere*, this reads:

> Luscious and sorrowful, bird o' the roses,
> To the vexed March winds prematurely singing,
> Would that with a warm hand I could have held thee,
> Kept from withering chill thy timid heart.
>
> Now have I terrified, now have I pained thee,
> Now with stiffening blood have I tangled
> All thy bosom's tremulous plumage,
> For a thorn, for a thorn was against it.

Gabriel once compared his sister to a startled bird, and these lines – possibly a translation – seem to offer an oblique comment on Cayley's desire to protect Christina, her withdrawal ('do not touch me') and his fear that she was distressed. More than that one would not like to hazard, except to note that a year later Christina answered the poem in her own *Rosseggiar* sequence with lines headed 'Luscious and sorrowful'; translated, these read

> Bird of roses and pain,
> Bird of love,
> Happy and unhappy: is that song
> Laughter or weeping?
> True to the untrue, in a cold land
> You guard your nest of thorns.

Was this how she perceived C.B.C. and herself?

Perhaps, in the time that had elapsed since her feelings first stirred towards 'the blind buzzard', she had come to accept that a true love relationship was not possible, and that it was neither sensible nor desirable to settle for less. Perhaps she looked for a more assertive response, which would reveal the strength of his feelings, and found none. But what she achieved by declining his proposal was a continuation of friendship. 'If he likes to see me, God knows I like to see him,' she wrote eloquently. She remained a single woman, with all the restrictions and freedoms this entailed, and he remained on good terms with her and the rest of the family. We can only guess whether any conscious or unconscious fear of a fully conjugal relationship shaped her decision, though it is clear that both men on whom she bestowed her affections were timid and physically unassertive. We cannot be certain that Christina was frightened of sex, but her affairs of the heart suggest she found masculinity in some way threatening, and that in the end she preferred not to marry. She was now thirty-five, and there would be no more offers.

Cayley's feelings may be inferred from two poems he wrote, one hailing her mixed national heritage – 'fine blood of England, Hellas, Italy' – and 'noble aspect, sweet and firm, and true', and the other hinting at greater distress, under the title *Wasted Footsteps*.

Christina spent nearly two months at Gloucester – a long stay that may fairly be ascribed to the need for a decorous lapse before seeing Cayley again. He dined with the family on 29 October, a sign that any awkwardness was now past. Christina began a translation on Italian architecture for John Murray, contracted earlier in the year, and also returned to her *Rosseggiar* sequence. 'I cannot tell you how dear the Italian language is to me, so dear that I will not attempt to compare it with my native English,' she wrote some time later to Elihu Burritt, an American linguist who had been too shy to pay his respects without a formal introduction, but was cordially invited to call on his next visit to Britain, 'only as I think in English I have naturally written in it also'. Indeed, she added modestly, she was 'a very imperfect Italian scholar, not a "scholar" at all, but a warm admirer merely'.

In December, Dora Greenwell dined at Albany Street in company with Fred Stephens and the wife to whom, it was now disclosed, he had been married for six years. On Christmas Day Gabriel came to Albany Street, and on New Year's Day entertained the whole family at Chelsea. It snowed heavily and they were unable to get home. Some while later he sent an unwanted Persian cat 'as a present to Christina if she likes to have it', saying it was impossible to keep the animal at Tudor House, where the menagerie now included two owls, a raven, a goat, several rabbits and seven or eight little waxbills – which was perhaps not the right company for a cat, although when one of the owls was found headless, the raven was blamed.

Other family news included the marriage of cousin Teodorico to a Scottish woman named Isabella, with whom he returned to Florence as a Protestant pastor. He hoped also to publish '*Il Mercato dei Folleti*, his translation of *Goblin Market*, wishing, as he wrote, 'to see what effect may be produced on the Italians by Christina's style of poetry, so daring and fresh and fine'.

She was pleased too when a composer called Travanti, of Neapolitan origin, who many years since had composed tunes for Papa's patriotic verse, requested permission to set to music her two most perfect lyrics, *A Birthday* and *When I am dead, my dearest*. She then had to refuse *When I am dead* to another aspirant, offering instead *Beauty is vain*. 'I hope to enjoy your music very much when it comes out, if I am so fortunate as to hear it,' she wrote graciously, when copying out the lines, and a year or so later, went with William to hear C. A. MacFarren's setting of *Songs in a Cornfield* performed at St James's Hall. In the visual arts, two exhibitors at the new Dudley Gallery had taken subjects from her poems: *Life is not good* by Eliza Martin, and *Lady Maggie* by Joseph Jopling, while Lady Waterford and the Hon. Mrs Boyle were preparing illustrations to *Maiden Song*. But when photographers Elliott & Fry asked Christina to sit for her portrait, for sale to the public, she declined this small concomitant of fame.

On 8 February aunt Margaret died, aged seventy-three; as was customary, Maria kept a deathbed diary of the final days. She herself was currently teaching Italian to the Heimann daughters, and at the end of the month, the contract for her *Exercises in idiomatic Italian through literal translation from the English* was finally signed to appear later in the year. In America an illustrated edition of Christina's poems was proposed; Gabriel suggested possible illustrators. Sales of the Roberts Bros composite volume had been good: of the 3000 print run all but

500 sold within a year, resulting in a royalty payment of £38.10s. To put this and her other earnings (some small amounts from Macmillan and 20 guineas for the architectural translation) into perspective, at the same date Gabriel informed the family that his income had been £2000 in 1865 and £1800 in 1866, while William had a salary of just under £500, which after two promotions rose in 1869 to £800. There seems no way of computing what Maria's teaching brought in, but it is unlikely to have exceeded £100 in a full year. With Mamma's inheritance this made the household comfortably but not lavishly well off, and they now employed two servants, and a laundress.

In April cousin Henrietta's mother, the enterprising Mrs Polydore, made a surprise appearance in Britain from New Orleans, where she now kept a hotel, confirming her reputation for unconventionality. 'She has gone through any number of singular adventures,' noted William in his diary. 'At one time she was near being exchanged to an Indian for a horse, as his squaw; and she actually some years ago, on hearing of her Father's illness or distress, came from Salt Lake to Liverpool, having in her pocket at starting only three dollars, and not spending any of it on the way.'

Aunt Margaret's death led to family discussions about moving to a quieter neighbourhood, with room also for Eliza and Charlotte. William and Maria inspected a number of properties, favouring the Bedford Estate in Bloomsbury, where streets were gated and public houses banned. Rents were higher, but eventually a 'very eligible house, freshly done up' was secured at no. 56 Euston Square. In May, Christina accompanied her mother, who had a lingering digestive complaint, to Tunbridge Wells, where there were few diversions but 'trees in leaf and blossom, gardens in gradations of beauty, green slopes, rocky interruptions, gorse-clad common and cloudy sky,' as she told the Heimanns, who together with Browns and Scotts were invited to dine at Albany Street for the last time. At the end of June they moved. She was glad to leave, though it had been their home for thirteen years, for the district had deteriorated, with 'reports not at all pleasing as to the character of our neighbourhood'.

The fashionable classes were moving west – the young Burne-Joneses had already left Bloomsbury for Kensington, though the Morrises were now not far away in Queen Square. On 12 June William went to buy printed chintz from the firm. He lined the drawing room walls with grasscloth and Japanese ukiyo-e prints.

In politics, the current issues were parliamentary reform, with the extension of the franchise to working men, the continuing case of Governor Eyre, and Cretan insurrection against Turkish rule. Gabriel and William had recently got to know the Anglo-Greek circle in London – the families of Constantine Ionides and Michael Spartali – where the charmingly free manners and intelligence of the young women was a matter of remark. They were especially well-informed on intellectual subjects, William noted – Miss Ionides had completed a quantitative translation of the first four books of the *Iliad*. Gossip on all subjects was circulated by Howell, but Sandys fell into disgrace, leaving Tudor House with many debts and a reputation for unsavoury anecdotes.

Earlier this year, Browning had accepted an invitation, updating the Rossettis on *The Ring and the Book*, and outlining his systematic working habits. He was unimpressed by the 'trifling affairs' Tennyson was currently publishing, though Christina thought it 'honourably formidable' to appear in company with *Lucretius*, as she did in the May issue of *Macmillan's*. Three pieces appeared in the spring, followed by a fourth in November. But her main occupation this year was not poetry but fiction, for a new religious monthly, edited by Robert Baynes, reverend editor of sacred anthologies similar to Shipley's, and aimed at 'all members of the Christian home'. Called the *Churchman's Shilling Magazine*, this proclaimed its fidelity to the established Church, and carried articles on religious and social questions, book reviews, poems and short stories. Christina's contributions began in April, with the first instalment of a long story called *The Waves of this Troublesome World: A Tale of Hastings Ten Years Ago*.

The working people of Hastings were all 'seafaring folk', and *The Waves* told the story of Henry Hardiman, a poor fisherman, and his sister Sarah, who breaks her father's heart by marrying a Methodist. Widowed, she returns to her brother's home, repenting of her apostasy. *The Waves'* message is that Sarah is a strayed sheep as in the parable on which her little niece Jane is catechised. According to the curate's wife, Mrs Grey, who acts as author's mouthpiece, she 'fell into grievous error when she turned her back on the church of her baptism' and followed her husband 'into schism'. Moreover, was it not possible that Sarah's return to Hastings was partly aimed at luring her family into the desert of Dissent? Yes, Jane, says Mrs Grey, 'this is just what many people do now. They fancy they can find better food for their souls out of the Church than in it, and so join the Dissenters; refusing to return, though they see written in the Bible that God added to the Church daily such as should be saved.'

The first instalment of this sectarian tale described Sarah's 'Departure' and the second her 'Return'. Reluctant to betray her dead husband, Sarah is finally brought back to the Church of her birth by the rescue of Jane and her little brother from certain death in a great storm. 'Back from meeting-house to church, through church up to the blessed Sacrament of the Altar, the grace of God led her,' intones the sanctimonious narrator and, as the story closes, Sarah is seldom absent from communion, 'partaking, whenever an opportunity offers, of the comfortable Sacrament of Christ's Body and Blood ... I truly believe this widow is one of the happiest: having chosen that good part which shall not be taken from her; thankful that her idol was removed for a season, if so she might receive him for ever.'

Parts of the story, mainly those set in the Hardimans' home, are charmingly written. But the theme is both unconvincing – Sarah is far more virtuous than anyone else in the tale – and puzzling: why should Dissenters be regarded as virtual unbelievers, 'out of the church', when all around actual irreligion was spreading? At times Wesleyanism is practically identified with Antichrist, and it is not just our more catholic age that finds the triumphing of one Protestant denomination over another uncharitable and even unchristian.

There is no evidence of any special proselytism against Dissenters in the pages of the *Churchman's Shilling Magazine*, though certainly it belonged to the High Church wing. Was there perhaps a displaced personal element here, relating in part to Christina's own subjective fear of religious backsliding and in part to the defective, wavering faiths around her, including that of C. B. C.? In the figure of Sarah she portrayed a woman torn between personal love and doctrinal duty, as to some degree was the case with herself and Cayley. Conjugal loyalty was held to be second only to religious conviction in moral importance, as *The Waves* explicitly states, and the emotional centre of Christina's story hinges on this conflict, resolved at length in favour of the Church. That the reader feels it to be something of a false wire-drawn conflict such as true love and true religion would soon have solved only suggests that perhaps Cayley's frayed faith was not quite the obstacle to marriage that Christina erected. By the same token, however, her choice was enacted in that of her heroine.

Later she was to become more ecumenical, but there is other evidence this year of a narrowing denominational position. When Emily Davies solicited her support for a proposed women's college at Cambridge, for example, she did not object to the enterprise as such, but simply 'declined joining anything that did not belong to the Catholic Church', – 'Anglo-Catholic, I supposed,' commented Miss Davies, knowing that Miss Rossetti was no Romanist. Ironically, though at the outset undenominational, the establishment that became Girton College in due course acquired an Anglican orientation, and indeed Emily Davies was anxious for High Church names on her College Committee. She was not surprised that Pusey should 'violently oppose' the idea, but was sorry to be refused by Charlotte Yonge on the grounds that 'home education' by 'sensible fathers' was more valuable. Higher education was a contested feminist field at this date, half a generation on from the skirmishes of the fifties, with many of the same warriors. Funds for the college, in this initial period, came primarily from Barbara Bodichon, who had suffered severely from fever in Algeria and now spent much time in Britain.

The second of Christina's *Churchman* tales, which appeared in July was a short, plain intervention in current ecclesiastical debates, entitled *Some Pros and Cons about Pews*, which dramatised the argument over pew-rents that had caused Mamma's dispute with the incumbent at All Souls so many years before and was a continuing issue within the Church. At Christ Church, Rev. Burrows finally succeeded in getting the parish to agree to abolition late in 1865. 'I hope our pews may be swept away next summer, but difficulties – apparent difficulties, at any rate – have been talked of,' Christina told Emily in November 1865, though it was late in the following year before they finally went. Out of the disputes she constructed her little story, a satirical dialogue between a rector and his opponents.

'I for one will never take it for granted that any good Christian is against the acknowledgement of our absolute equality before God,' announces Rev. Goodman. Ranged against him are various crusty and snobbish parishioners, each with an argument in favour of keeping their privileges intact. 'What hardship is it for a flunky or a clod-hopper to sit in a seat without a door?' asks Mr Wood. The poor are dirty neighbours, says Mrs Plume; indeed 'quite infectious ... one really couldn't risk sitting amongst them.' After all, adds fastidious Miss Crabbe, 'nobody wants to sit among smells, and cheek-by-jowl with more heads than one in a bonnet.' Mr Stone comes in strongly at the end, as conservative anchorman. Reform has gone far enough, he declares:

'We have borne with chants, with a surpliced choir, with daily services, but we will not bear to see all our rights trampled under foot ... The tendency of the day is to level social distinctions and to elevate unduly the lower orders. In this parish at least let us combine to keep up wise barriers between class and class, and to maintain that fundamental principle practically bowed to all over our happy England, that what you can pay for you can purchase'.

That may be the system of worldly England, comes the Rector's rejoinder, as his author's mouthpiece; but true Churchmen should have nothing to do with it. The only argument in favour of pews has been furnished, however, 'for it *is* hard upon our open-hearted poor that they should be compelled to sit by persons who, instead of viewing them as brethren beloved, despise the poor'.

The irony had a clear ecclesiastical purpose but also reflected the campaign to reform the franchise, which in 1867 was extended to include most workingmen. This controversy, fuelled by government reluctance and popular protest by urban workers – as well as some women, who put forward a mammoth petition for female suffrage – was essentially one of political democracy.

Christina's opposition to pew rents is clear. What of her views on political democracy? As a woman she had of course no personal interest in the proposed franchise reform, nor any platform from which to speak. William was very much in favour, however, so the political aspect of her parable can hardly have been unwitting. In other respects she did not regard herself as a Radical, although her position on such issues as slavery and national liberation suggests a distinctly Liberal perspective. She certainly did not endorse any revolutionary programme whereby the despised poor should, as it were, storm the pew doors and unceremoniously eject the bourgeoisie from their comfortable seats in society. But she did believe in the High Anglican disregard of rank, wealth and privilege – unlike Carlyle, for example, who was currently attacking democracy in his diatribe *Shooting Niagara: and After?*, which appeared in *Macmillan's* a month after Christina's thoughtful and temperate story, and ranted against "Manhood Suffrage" – Horsehood, Doghood ... in one brief word "the equality of men", any man equal to any other; Quashee Nigger to Socrates or Shakespeare; Judas Iscariot to Jesus Christ; – and Bedlam and Gehenna equal to New Jerusalem, shall we say?'

To some extent however Christina's concerns mirrored these, and her excursion into ecclesiastical politics through narrative parable marks the tentative start of a new role as critic of the age, following in the footsteps of Carlyle, Ruskin and Arnold, who were all currently attacking the soulless materialism, selfishness and philistinism with which society now seemed seized.

This was the subject of her third story for Rev. Baynes, published in November, neatly combining religious and commercial imagery. The financial prosperity of the mid-century had given way to economic recession and insecurity, signalled by the banking crisis of 1866. Investments were no longer 'as safe as houses' and material optimism faltered at the very time when faith was also losing ground to doubt and unbelief. As *A Safe Investment* begins:

> It was a pitchy dark night. Not the oldest inhabitant remembered so black a night, so moonless, so utterly starless; and whispering one to another, men said with a shiver that longer still, not for a hundred years back – ay, or for a thousand years – ay, or ever since the world was – had such gross darkness covered the land . . .

A solitary traveller enters the town by the eastern gate, riding a white horse. He has 'the air of one bound on some mission of importance'.

There follows a sequence of disasters – storms and shipwrecks, a fatal gas explosion, the embezzlement of railway funds – ending with a financial panic, as fearful citizens rush to the bank, clamouring for their money. The strange visitor inquires; each distraught individual tells the same tale of woe and ruin, of investments burst like bubbles. None offers hospitality but one woman, who alone is cheerful, for her money is 'not invested as so many in this town have invested theirs':

When I was yet young, One told me that riches do certainly make to themselves wings and fly away; and that gold perisheth, though it be purified seven times in the fire. Nevertheless He added that, if I chose, there could with my gold and silver be made ready for me an everlasting habitation, to receive me when the present fashion shall have passed away; and that I might lay up for myself treasure where neither moth nor rust doth corrupt, and where thieves do not break through and steal. So, when I was willing. He further informed me by what means I should send my deposits to that secure house whereof the Owner will be no man's debtor. On the first day of the week I was to go up to the branch-house upon the hill – you see it, sir, out to the East yonder; there, where a light shines to lighten everyone that goeth into the house; and according as I had prospered, I was to drop somewhat into the money-chest kept there. All such sums would be placed to my account, and would bear interest. But besides this, I was apprised that the Owner of the house employs many collectors, who may call at any moment, often at the most unlikely moments, for deposits. From these I was to take heed never to turn away my face, but I was to give to them freely, being well assured that they would carry all entrusted safely to my account. Thus, sometimes a father-less child calls upon me, sometimes a distressed widow; sometimes a sick case comes before me; sometimes a stranger, sir, as you have done this very night, demands my hospitality.

So, the story concludes, the traveller rose before daybreak, mounted and rode away, 'as one that carries back tidings to Him that sent him. Also this I know, that some, being mindful to entertain strangers, have entertained angels unawares.'

The parable was simple and even trite – the sort of commonplace truism commended by the *Saturday Review* a few months earlier in defence of what were slightingly called 'good books', on the grounds that despite platitudes it was still valuable to be told authoritatively that 'unselfishness and truth are good and excellent things'. Straight-forward moral values, linked to Christian faith, needed reiteration in an age of doubt and decay.

But if it reads like a sermon, *A Safe Investment* was accomplished and of obvious contemporary relevance. As with the bank collapse, behind

the gas explosion lay an actual event that befell the art dealer Gambart
– a greedy engrosser and profiteer, according to Gabriel – representative of new and conspicuous wealth, lavishly displayed. On the
eve of Derby Day in 1866, Gambart planned a spectacular ball at his
home in St Johns Wood, where marquees and a grand picture gallery
to exhibit Frith's painting of *Derby Day* and Holman Hunt's *Finding of
the Saviour* (an unintentionally apposite combination) were to be il-
luminated by a temporary gas supply. Early in the morning a huge
explosion ripped the back off the house, flinging rubble and furniture into the street. One servant died and several were injured.
It was the disaster of the year, sensationally reported in the press, and
the guests, who were to have included Gabriel, were regarded as
having had a miraculous escape. There were many who saw this as
retribution for overweening pride and extravagance. 'Hope nothing
of yours was blown up at Gambart's,' wrote Stephens to Hunt, asking
only partly in jest whether Satan had fetched away anything of
Gabriel's.

Indeed, the notion that such catastrophes were in some sense a
divine warning was generally aired. Economic depression, coupled
with an intensely cold winter and agitation over Reform, had led in
January 1867 to 'bread riots' in London, rousing middle class fear of
the hungry, violent mob. These were signs of very troubled times –
just as Christina had heard from Dodsworth twenty years before. The
message, biblically familiar in the mouths of prophets and preachers
urging Israel to return to holy ways, was also that of the secular
jeremiad, which as faith crumbled came to occupy a major place in
Victorian Britain, deploying the same rhetoric of analogy, warning
and promise. Christina presented her catastrophes and individual
misfortunes in just such minatory manner, as symbolic of spiritual
neglect. The address is general: through this medium Christina was
speaking out, albeit in a limited fashion, to the nation, adding her own
specifically Christian lesson to others' exhortations.

Christina's writing is often considered without reference to its historical context, but there were specific phases of her work, and the
increase in devotional writing visible from this time was clearly in
response to a perceived tide of rising godlessness and greed. In her
lexicon, 'worldliness' always spelt mortal danger. As a writer with a
certain reputation, she felt a growing responsibility to use this position – all the more so, one suspects, because in literary terms she was
allied with notorious anti-christians such as Swinburne. To some extent therefore *A Safe Investment* was also addressed to her brothers and
their friends – including no doubt Charles Cayley.

As it turned out, after declining his offer of marriage on the grounds of mere friendship, her feelings began to deepen. This at any rate is the inference of succeeding *Rosseggiar* poems, in the first of which she imagined meeting her beloved in heaven: 'Yet still I look to meet again one day, In everlasting, not this fleeting, life.' The sonnet answered one of Cayley's, also in Italian, beginning 'If I should meet her in the eternal peace', originally printed in *Psyche's Interludes*, which Christina was evidently rereading. She headed her own lines *Blumin replies*, in reference to Carlyle's imaginary Professor Teufelsdrockh, who in *Sartor Resartus* is enamoured of the lovely Blumine. Resemblances could easily be affectionately noted between Charles Cayley, erudite linguist, and this fictional Dr Devilsdung, who is Professor of Things in General, with no visible occupation but 'boundless learning' in all known tongues. Moreover, Cayley had prefaced one of his Dante volumes with a dedicatory poem addressed to Blumine. So was Christina sometimes 'Blumine' to Cayley's Teufelsdrockh? Among his papers found in her possession is one headed 'Her latest "Communication" ' and signed 'Blumine'. Though the text does not read as a poetic address by or to Christina, it does show that Carlyle's characters were shared figures in their friendship.

Through 1867, her Italian poems seem to rehearse her decision:

> Sweet heart, lost to me and yet not lost,
>   Sweet life, that leaves me in death,
> Friend and more than friend, I greet thee.
>
>   . . .
>
>   Do not disdain me for so hard a fate,
> But let me say: 'His hopes
>   Like mine languished in this chill winter' –
> Yet I will be resigned, what has been was . . .
>
> How much, how much I loved you! yet I might not
>   Express to you the love I feel:
> Far more than what I did not say,
>   I loved you in my heart.
>
>   . . .
>
> More than felicity, more than hope;
>   Than love I will not say it's of small account:
> Bitter-sweet you were in my memories
>   To jealous me.
>
> But you preferred virtue to me,
>   And truth, my friend: and shall you not know

Whom it was you loved? The flower only unfolds
  To the sun.

             . . .

If more than me you loved the Truth,
  Then Jesus was your unknown Love –
O Jesus, who spoke to him unknown,
  Vanquish his heart.

In public, their relationship remained formal: enclosing tickets for the
Botanic Gardens in early summer this year, Christina betrayed no hint
of intimacy or affection. But twelve months after his proposal, she
answered his sonnet *L'Amicizia* with her own, quoting his opening
phrase as epigraph and commending friendship as Love's sister –
kinder and more constant. 'Come Friendship, and be right welcome,'
she wrote. 'Come but let not Love depart.' Love might reign in secret,
undisplayed, but friendship could be unconcealed, today and tomorrow, and the day after . . .

Indirectly, her feelings were publicly avowed in an article on Dante
that she sent to the *Churchman's Shilling Magazine*. Purporting to be
about the difficulties of translating the great Italian author adequately,
this was in effect a plug for Cayley's *terza rima* version and a rebuttal
of criticism that had appeared in *Blackwood's*. It concluded:

> the beauty of the best translations goes far toward suggesting the surpas-
> sing beauty of their original . . . We appeal to our readers whether the
> quotations with which we ask leave to close our commendatory article do
> not show Mr Cayley in his translations as a master of vigour and beauty,
> of pathos and philosophy . . .

Friends and lovers have a long tradition of puffing each other's works
in the British press, but this is surely a rather touching example. It
reveals not only her affection, but also how much importance she
accorded to favourable reviews, even in unimportant journals. Cayley
does not seem to have sought fame, but Christina's article was a small
gift of this inestimable commodity.

28

Sing-Song and *Commonplace*

WHEN INVITED TO Charles Howell's wedding in the summer of 1867, Christina responded with unaccustomed eagerness. 'My dear Kate (for I count on your kindness to pardon the friendly freedom),' she wrote, on 2 July with thanks for 'so very kind an invitation to be with you on what will I hope be a happier day than you have yet experienced, and my heart warms towards you and Mr Howell and wishes you both every possible blessing'. She sent Mr Cayley's congratulations too, followed by a prettily carved card-case as wedding gift, and, after bringing her uncle and cousin back with her from Gloucester, not only succeeded in attending the wedding at St Matthew's, Brixton, but also called at the house before the ceremony, to wish Kate 'all happiness', and joined William and other guests in signing the marriage register.

It was all uncharacteristically gushing, and indicative of the warmth the Howells seemed able to raise in Christina as in others. Sadly, however, Charles Howell cheated and betrayed those he had previously charmed, and though for a while Christina sustained her affection for Kate, before long she too dropped the acquaintance that had begun so cordially.

Gabriel, to whom Charles was 'the darling of our circle . . . a treasure and a joy of our lives', did not attend the wedding. He was not well, suffering from eyestrain and 'confusion in the head', as he wrote in confidence to Allingham, afraid of the consequences to his work should rumours of failing sight get about. The occulist found nothing physically wrong, and ascribed the disordered vision to 'overwork' or, as we might say, stress. It may have been caused by high blood pressure, for it was accompanied by giddiness and insomnia; in retrospect, however, the mental confusion was most worrying, for it signalled the start of serious psychological disturbance. The family seem to have been aware of this, for when on 15 October, Allingham called at Euston Square, he recorded in his diary a hint of their concern:

At Mrs Rossetti's, Euston Square. The dear old lady looking strong still, with her handsome full-coloured face and rich-toned voice of sincere and touching intonations. She says nothing clever but it's always a pleasure to be near her. Miss R, Christina and Miss Heaton. Mrs R expresses her pleasure at Gabriel's having visited me, thinks it has done him good, talks as if I were a sort of mentor to him, which makes me feel rather ashamed.

On the surface, everything was well. Louisa Parke had again been staying with the family, prior to taking up a new post. Though Christina was writing little verse, her reputation was growing, particularly in North America. Earlier in the year Thomas Niles of Roberts Bros offered to publish a collection of her prose tales. Christina collected them: *Nick, Hero, The Lost Titian* and the three published by Rev. Baynes. But as a book it lacked both bulk and a centrepiece, and the project was not pursued.

She was starting to have a sense of status, which was partly gratifying – letters of appreciation and requests for autographs were graciously replied to – and partly alarming. Learning that the Heimann daughters cited her as a role model, she hoped earnestly that both would be 'wiser and happier'. But, she added, 'if they *will* study me in any light, then please assure them that, old enough as I am to be their mother and speaking from dearly-bought experience, there is scarcely perhaps a greater mistake either for this world or the next than disregard of one's parents' wise wishes on one's own behalf.' But when had she disregarded her parents' wishes? What, in this or any other context, was her own 'dearly-bought experience'? From the vantage of her thirty-six years, she was beginning to look back. When dear Dr Heimann sent belated congratulations on *The Prince's Progress*, she replied that she was pleased her second book had given him pleasure, adding:

We none of us stand still at any time: it is happiness enough if we go forward instead of backward – and certainly I would neither go backward nor stand still, even if I could.

Some months later, this reappeared as a thoughtful sonnet:

I would not if I could undo my past,
  Tho' for its sake my future is a blank;
  My past for which I have myself to thank,
For all its faults and follies first and last,
I would not cast anew the lot once cast,
  Or launch a second ship for one that sank,
Or break by feasting my perpetual fast.
I would not if I could . . .

Autumn 1867 brought a recurrence of low spirits, which William for once did not disguise as any physical ailment. On 12 November he told Anne Gilchrist that Christina's 'extremely low and depressed

state' had now lasted four or five weeks. The doctor told her to eat
well, and stay in bed until lunchtime, and after a while the worst
seemed to be over, though she was by no means restored. In this
condition, she wrote the last of the year's *Rosseggiar* poems, *Finestra
mia orientale* ('My eastern window'), subtitled *'in malattia'* ('in sickness'):

> I turn my face toward the east,
>   Toward the noonday where he dwells . . .
>
> O turn to the one who reveres you,
> Loves you, craves you, in her heart and with her mind.
> Faint and weary to you I turn:
>   What can this be I feel, my friend?
> I treasure every fond memory of you –
>   How much I would tell you! yet I do not tell . . .
>
> Would we were together!
> What would it matter
>   Where we built
>   Our nest?
> That land would be
>   Almost heaven.
>   Ah, if I could be with you
>   With my heart certain
>   Of being loved
> As it would wish!
>   Then the desert
> Would burst into bloom.

In the summer, Cayley had alerted her to watch out for a meteor
shower, which she characteristically missed seeing, logging it with the
four-leaved clover and waterfall rainbow as an emblem of the heart's
greater deferments. But, paradoxically, having declined to marry him,
her love was growing, at least in the secret *Rosseggiar* sequence.

Was she regretting her decision? It seems rather that she was using
these Italian verses to construct in her imagination a relationship of
true love that was founded on but far transcended the actual figure of
Charles Cayley and her feelings towards him – a true love that would
be fulfilled only in her heart and in heaven. In the sublunary world,
his failings and her reluctance made fulfilment imperfect and impossible, even undesirable; in heaven, all imperfections would be
erased in the Platonic essence of love, as she conceived it. This at least
is one explanation of what otherwise seems perversity on her part: to

have refused Cayley's love yet continue to love him, as it seems with more ardour than before. In August 1868 she wrote the last of the *Rosseggiar* poems, two sonnets addressed to 'Friend and more than friend', and alluding to 'she who said him nay, wishing it were yea', followed by two final quatrains:

> I loved you more than you loved me; –
>   Amen, if so God willed;
>   Amen, although my heart should break for him,
>   Lord Jesus.

> But Thou who knowest and and recordest all,
>   Thou who hast died for love
>   In the next world give me that heart
>   I loved so much.

Henceforth, her love poetry conveyed the recognition that the happiness she craved could not be attained in real life, but existed only in the Ideal or, in her words, *'nell'altro mondo'*.

Daily life could sometimes be dull but she was determined to stop complaining. 'Why should leisure be a blank, or quiet tedium or very easy household tasks a burden? See my philosophy and admire,' she wrote to Mrs Heimann when housekeeping for William while her mother and sister were on holiday. But she confessed nonetheless that she was prone to yawn occasionally in spirit, 'and fidget and grumble in the privacy of my own breast', while keeping up a courteous aspect towards her dear but sometimes impervious brother.

Soon her low state proved so persistent that in February she consulted Dr Jenner, who was now physician to the Royal Family. She found his manner discreet and sympathetic – he neither expressed surprise at any symptoms nor proved 'unpleasantly scrutinizing' in his questions – and placed full confidence in his diagnosis. This was that she had 'congestion of one lung, but certainly not consumption', and that her life might be 'prolonged indefinitely, but she must not relax in the precautions she has been taking of late years', as William noted in his diary – itself an indication of family anxiety. This was reassuring and non-invasive but hardly conclusive, and the effect was to turn Christina into a more or less permanent invalid, without any identifiable disorder. She followed the instructions to eat well, stay in bed all morning, never go out at night, and though not entirely housebound – daytime outings were permitted – sociability now depended more and more on visitors. It was a blessing, as she told Anne Gilchrist, that 'we are more central than we used to be, and proportionately more accessible'.

For change of air, she went with Mamma to Gloucester, and then to Scarborough, with one of the aunts. 'Would you believe that it was a real relief to me to find that your kind letter did not contain an invitation to Brookbank?' Christina added smilingly to Anne. 'A curious effect this of your kindness to me: but the truth is I have been so unwell that I must have said "no" had you asked me; and I was not ambitious of uttering the ungracious syllable.' Did Anne know Scarborough? 'We never were here before, and as yet are not enchanted; but some unexpected sunshine has just come out, and that may make a world of difference if we go and sit by the sea, for we have been having some dull mornings.' Making due allowance for illness, this is typical of Christina's letters: friendly but uninformative, with little but courteous surface meaning. From Scarborough she went on to Miss Heaton in Leeds, feeling better but not fully restored, and with her hostess took a drive out to a 'neighbouring seat' to view a fine collection of Turners.

Luckily, Gabriel seemed to be somewhat better. He had begun a new pictorial sequence – which was to last more or less for the rest of his life – composed of variations on an idealised portrait of Janey Morris, for whom he had conceived an extravagant passion. In addition to paintings there flowed an endless stream of portrait drawings, emphasising Janey's long neck, dark hair and soulful, inward-gazing eyes, which William said reminded him of the eyes of the little brahmin bull in the menagerie at Cheyne Walk. The Scotts were slightly scandalised, referring privately to Janey as Lucretia Borgia. But Gabriel's adoration was open, and Morris did not object – at any rate one of the large portraits was hung in place of honour in Queen Square. To celebrate its completion Gabriel gave a large and glittering dinner party at Chelsea to which Christina and Maria sent their excuses, it being Lent. For their part, Gabriel's mother and sisters seem to have liked Janey Morris, who occasionally dined at Euston Square and once requested a recipe. It seems too that she embarked on Italian lessons with Maria; though no details are known.

Christina spent the winter quietly, neither better nor worse in health and in the spring she went again to Gloucester, and then to Penkill, promising to trim up her hats for games of croquet on the shady lawn that had been laid above the steep-sided glen. She travelled north with the Scotts and as before enjoyed both the Castle and Alice's company. On the beach at Girvan, using a hairnet, they caught a fish and crab, carrying back both trophies for a sea-water aquarium. Se felt better and able to undertake 'goodish walks'. As a customary town-dweller, she took particular delight in the hedgehogs, deer and wild chaffinches of Penkill, a pleasure shared with Alice, who was painting a frieze of local birds and beasts on the ceiling of her bedroom. They went out for drives, too, prompting Christina to some doggerel lines about sitting back-to-back that elicited an affectionate riposte from Scott, and shows they no longer fought like cats.

At Penkill, too, she and Alice at last agreed to forgo 'Missing' each other, in keeping with the warm and easy affection they now felt. 'Only think of my humiliation at Killochnan,' Christina wrote in mock despair after travelling home, when 'an inexorable railway official defined Mrs Scott as nearly 1½ stone lighter than poor me! Let us hope, as in your case, that the overplus is brain.' (Jenner's advice was bearing fruit, or rather weight.) She imagined the scene at the Castle: 'What are you doing, I wonder, as I write (between 9 and 10 o'clock) – knitting perhaps or reading aloud; not snoozing let us hope after Mr Scott's strictures. My respects to him please.' Soon afterwards she wrote again, lamenting her own domestic incapacity while Mamma and Maria were away:

> You who are lady of castle and lands and deal justice not only to man and maid but likewise to fish and fowl, might be amused to witness the painstaking responsibility and toil with which I keep house for two . . .

She and William were reading Gabriel's new poems, which had been set in proof for him to amend. Only William was asked for comments, for Gabriel was uneasily aware that the distinctly sensual nature of many poems was hardly to Christina's taste; indeed he had asked William to remove one particularly indecorous piece from the packet before showing them *en famille*, on account of its post-coital theme. Soon after this, Gabriel's reading of one about Lilith drove both his sisters from the room.

The fact that Gabriel, with sincere artistic motives, was writing poems that his mother and sisters could not read, illustrates the wide gender gulf. A further indication came this autumn with contemporary revelations about Byron's incestuous relationship with his half-sister. William, in the throes of preparing an edition and memoir of Shelley, and in anticipation of similar work on Byron, felt obliged to discuss what he called a 'gross and ghastly story', which he hoped would prove untrue. Gabriel's view was more robust. 'Lastly, if Byron f—d his sister he f—d her [sic] and there an end – an absolute end in my opinion as far as the vital interest of his poetry goes, which is all we have to do with,' he wrote to William from Penkill. 'Scotus agrees – especially with the last sentiment.' But the subject was not to be discussed so frankly in mixed company, and even though the allegation had been raised by a woman – and by no less a woman than Harriet Beecher Stowe, in no less a publication than *Macmillan's Magazine* under the heading 'The Truth about Lady Byron's Married Life' –

it is possible that Christina did not read the offending article. Both the notoriety of the disclosure and the Rossetti family connection with Byron, however, make it more likely than not that she was aware of the nature of the 'private wrongs of the deepest kind' alluded to. She sent no new poems to Macmillan, which suggests that the indelicacy of this episode contributed to the subsequent cooling of relations between them.

As it happened, she had written no new poems for some time, apart from a few lines on the death of Alice's pet chaffinch. But 'when wombats do inspire, I strike my disused lyre,' she declared on learning that the Tudor House menagerie had acquired one of these antipodean creatures. 'He is a round furry ball with a head something between a bear and a guineapig, no legs, human feet with heels like anybody else and no tail,' Gabriel explained to Alice. 'His habits are most endearing . . . and he follows one about like a dog . . . if his leader hastens on, so does the wombat.' Cayley, sharing the general enthusiasm, sent a press clipping about Australian proposals to farm wombats for meat, and Christina composed a lyric in Italian urging the animal not to burrow its way home.

And perhaps inspired by the simple felicities of her verses on wombat and chaffinch, she now turned her hand to a new genre, in a collection of original nursery rhymes. This was somewhat surprising because, although Christina is now known partly as a children's writer, she was not so known in 1869, despite her use of 'fairy stories', any more than Tennyson was so known for his use of ancient legends. Nor had she previously shown any desire to write for children: though cast in the style of children's stories, both *Nick* and *Hero* were intended for adult readers.

A cluster of converging influences can be discerned. In August, *Tinsley's Magazine* began a series on contemporary writers with a critique of her work which although ostensibly laudatory took issue with her use of colloquial language, as for instance when the goblins were described as pulling faces and lugging baskets. 'If we met these passages isolated,' opined the critic, 'we should certainly inquire whose nursery-rhymes they were.'

Simultaneously, *Macmillan's* was running a series of articles on children's literature by Charlotte Yonge, who looked back with affection to the dog-eared volumes of her own childhood – works like Aikin's *Evenings at Home*, where 'the perfect precision and polish of language, even of the most simple renders them almost as complete epigrams as Aesop's fables, and contrasts with the slovenly writing of the present day', or Jane Taylor's *Original Poems* with 'their astonishing simplicity without puerility, their pathos, and arch drollery'. According to Yonge, the peculiarly lively lilt of Jane Taylor's verse made it so memorable that she could now 'never enter Cavendish Square without recollecting how "little Ann and her mother were passing one day" in that direction'. She also recalled that the only compositions that ever drew tears in childhood were 'The Lamentation of Poor Puss' and the 'Life and Adventures of Poor Dog Tray' – both of which she had hated accordingly.

Reading this at Penkill, perhaps Christina reminisced nostalgically with Alice about their own childhood literature. In subsequent articles, Mrs Yonge lamented the decline in children's writing, outlining her ideas of its essential qualities: delight, humour, morality and mystery. These were the very ingredients Christina brought to her collection, which was both traditional and innovative, paying homage to earlier writers and anonymous lyrics, but also giving original expression to nursery images and figures of her own.

When her poems were published, she dedicated them 'without permission to the baby who inspired them', whom William identified as the child of Professor Cayley of Cambridge, Charles's nephew Henry. This may have been displacement: as her love for Charles grew after she had refused to marry him, so the arrival of his nephew prompted maternal regrets in her heart. The true inspiration of her nursery rhymes was surely the children she herself would not now have.

Most importantly, however, she was writing to and for herself in a conscious return to her own infancy, structuring her whole sequence of 120 pieces – written in a single creative impulse during autumn 1869 – according to childhood experience. The title *Sing-Song* was suggested by her mother, 'and immediately adopted, and no doubt liked owing to its origin' as William noted, because at an important level the work was emotionally autobiographical. The melodious maternal speaking voice of the volume is that of the adult self 'mothering' the child within; imaginatively, therefore, the baby to whom the book was dedicated may thus also be Christina's own infant self, all those years ago at Charlotte Street and Holmer Green.

The poems were written to be read aloud, to an imagined audience whose ages range from birth to about five years. And this span was reflected in the sequence itself, which began with the return to the breast:

> Mother's arms under you,
> Her eyes above you;
> Sing it high, sing it low,
> Love me – I love you.

With an intuitive understanding of infant experience, the next poem introduced father and the possibility of separation. Then came her own father's cockadoodle noises to waken the children, followed by the postman's knock, bread and milk for breakfast, and memories of being dressed in a woollen frock on cold mornings. Throughout, happiness and security are balanced, and strengthened, by acknowledged grief and sorrow; for part of *Sing-Song's* purpose is to express and deal with pain. So the next poem recalled Maria's thrush, now buried under a tombstone of snow, and this in turn led to some strange but wisely consoling lines on the fruitfulness of sadness:

A city plum is not a plum brings us to the complexities of language beyond babytalk, and *Your brother has a falcon* to the trials of sibling rivalry. Cruel boys who steal birds' eggs introduce the pain selfishness will cause – that is, if we read the lines from the child's-eye-view – and are followed by a return to infant mortality, now in a less consoling manner. As the child grows out of babyhood it must learn what death means. This is hardly nursery fare in the accepted sense of jolly pieces for reciting with the bright 'diddums' voice commonly used when speaking to infants, but by the same token it acknowledges the full range of childish feeling.

And so the arrangement continued to mix and match the modes: *Hop o' my Thumb* followed by *Hope is like a barebell trembling from its birth*, and by a typical childhood question as to why the wind never stops blowing, which in turn precedes a 'carry me – cuddle me' piece, with daffodils in the valley, linnets in the trees, wrens and robins in the hedge – the world of nature contrasted with silly kisses to make the child laugh, just as mother stops turning the pages to indulge in a sudden cuddle. Violets, honeysuckles, cowslips and skylarks lead to a short story about Minnie and Mattie and fat little May, learning not just the names of animals but also how to enjoy the present moment.

Childish games of mock marriage – king and queen, sweetheart and lover – now precede a sequence of thoughtful, adult pieces. As William remarked, much of *Sing-Song* is 'truly in a high strain of poetry, and perfectly suited for figuring among her verse for adults, and even for taking an honoured place as such'. Charlotte Yonge had protested against Mrs Edgeworth's seemingly wise but exceedingly foolish maxim, that nothing should be taught to children that they cannot understand, observing rather the 'curiously disproportionate power of memory with which childhood is gifted, as if for the very purpose of accumulating stores for future use' and the almost equal delight in the mysterious and half comprehended. Some things were too strange and important to be reduced to a childish level. At the same time, in Christina's verses, they can be approached through the seemingly naive apprehension of ideas, as children struggle to bring language into line with experience:

> What are heavy? sea-sand and sorrow:
> What are brief? to-day and to-morrow:
> What are frail? spring blossoms and youth:
> What are deep? the ocean and truth.

Further into the book, lessons begin: numbers, time, money, months, colours. But soon play resumes: we go for a country walk and rest by a stile; we rescue an orphan lamb and watch Alice dance over the hills. We imagine fishes with umbrellas, lizards with parasols; we wonder why peacocks' eyes can't see; we tumble with the puppy and pat the cat. Then sorrow reappears, without any change of gear, moving easily from the domestic:

> The dog lies in his kennel
> And puss purrs on the rug

to the metaphysical:

> If hope grew on a bush
> And joy grew on a tree ...

Throughout *Sing-Song*, the mix of light and shade adds profundity to the silliest verses and lightness to the most sombre. For the most part, however, it invokes and explores a world of security, where there may be sorrow but no fear. Here, children expect to be happy. Here, men are not goblins and girls can safely ask for favours:

> 'I have a penny in my purse,
> And my eyes are blue;
> So ferry me across the water,
> Do, boatman, do'.

> 'Step into my ferry boat,
> Be they black or blue,
> And for the penny in your purse
> I'll ferry you'.

Glancingly, each poem picks up from the one before, mixing nonsense rhymes with mineralogical instruction, metaphysical speculation and moral injunctions. Gradually, sequences build up into a final series on sun, moon and stars, which naturally leads to bedtime:

> What do the stars do
> Up in the sky,

> Higher than the wind can blow,
> Or the clouds can fly?

The child's verses that began with waking thus draw to a close:

> Lie a-bed
> Sleepy head,
> Shut up eyes, bo-peep;
> Till day-break
> Never wake: –
> Baby, sleep.

Sing-Song is generally accorded little importance in Christina's life. But just as Jane Eyre's story is based on Charlotte Brontë's girlhood, or *David Copperfield* replays Charles Dickens's youth, so these rhymes are an autobiographical re-creation. And the genre is entirely appropriate: what better mode to invoke infancy than the songs and rhymes of the nursery – including the shadow side that children know so well but adults often ignore, especially when writing for children? It is as if, in middle life, this rediscovery of the child's viewpoint was necessary, valuable and even healing for Christina. But so well did the trifling forms, jingling rhythms and foolish wisdoms conceal their personal content, that few grown-up readers have guessed how significant these gossamer webs were to their author.

Out of the same impulse came *Vanna's Twins*, a story of surpassing sentimentality. 'You may recollect that I used not to be very tender hearted over babies,' Christina confessed to Alice, in recognition of the tale's mawkishness; indeed, at an earlier age she would no doubt have condemned it for gush. But it is all of a piece with the nursery verses.

It is set in Hastings, and narrated by a semi-invalid single woman – who at the beginning is standing like Christina at the station, with luggage and umbrellas, in search of lodgings. She has turned forty-five, and looks 'not a day younger' – but, as she says, this is 'an age at which there is nothing alarming at finding oneself alone in a strange place'. Accommodation is finally found – by this date Christina was an expert on seaside lodgings – in the clean and comfortable house of a family known as Cole, and the narrator settles in. She soon learns that her landlord's name is not Cole, but Cola (Nicola) Piccirillo; and his wife Fanny is properly Vanna, or Giovanna. They are Neapolitans, and when the narrator asks the name of their native town,

> they invariably answered me in a tone of endearment, by what sounded
> more like 'Vascitammò' than aught else I knew how to spell; but when my
> English tongue uttered 'Vascitammò' after them, they would shake their

heads and repeat the uncatchable word; and at last it grew to a standing joke between us that when I became a millionnaire my courier Cola and my maid Vanna should take the twins and me to see Vascitammò.

This is surely a memory of Papa's nostalgia for his native kingdom and birthplace, to which he had hoped to return with his *cara Francesca* and four dear pledges of their love. To Christina in childhood, Vasto must have seemed almost as fictional as Vascitammo, and Signor Piccirillo is certainly a denizen of Little Italy, transported to the coast – an optician who supplements the sale of spectacles and barometers with the 'marine trophies' that featured so frequently in his author's life.

Vanna is an Italian matron from the same stock, whose cuisine recalls the bi-national meals at Charlotte Street, where pasta was specially cooked for Papa, and with whose twins the narrator is soon besotted. 'What other babies were ever so fat and merry? To see their creased arms was enough till one saw their creased legs, and then their arms grew commonplace ... They chuckled at their father, mother, myself, or any stranger who would toss them, or poke a finger into their cushions of fat.' Well are they named Felice Maria and Maria Gioconda: just as in *Sing-Song*, the babies' names evoke the utter security of infancy. Vanna is even given to leaving them in the bath-tub while she serves a customer, and when the narrator suggests this may be dangerous, Vanna insists that in Italy all babies toddle in and out of the sea as soon as they can walk. '*E che male vi potrebb' essere? Non vi son coccodrilli,*' she asks – and what harm could come where there are no crocodiles? As the narrator admits, this was 'an argument no less apposite to the tub than to the sea', but hints at a deeper meaning for the author.

Mercifully, Christina's narrator has lost the strict ideas held by her predecessor in *The Waves of this Troublesome World*, and also her religious bigotry; Vanna and her husband, both good Catholics, are never once advised to attend the C of E. But like the earlier story this is in two parts; when the narrator next returns to Hastings, Felice and Maria are seven years old, merry and delightful as ever, and being taught by nuns in a neighbouring school. It is Christmas time, and while Cola is out on business, the twins are dispatched with a basket of fruit for a fatherless family on the east cliff. But it is snowing and they do not return. When three days later the thaw comes, they are found huddled together in a chalky hollow close to the edge of the cliff:

Gioconda with her head thrust into the market-basket, Felice with one arm holding the basket over his sister, and with the other clasping her close to him. Her fat hands met around his waist, and clasped between them was a small silver cross I had given her at Christmas, and which she had worn round her neck.

Lovely and pleasant in their lives, in their death they were not divided.

It is tear-jerking stuff – the reverse of the Babes in the Wood. Vanna and her husband decide to return home, and the story closes as the narrator sees them off by an early train on the first stage of the journey to Vascitammò, which now neither she nor the twins will ever see – just as the Rossettis would never return to Vasto.

Vanna's Twins and *Sing-Song* thus share the same ingredients: infant joy and intimations of its bleak opposite, imaged as cold snowy death. In both the poetry and prose the language is virtually identical. The 'song-singing thrush' is buried beneath a snow-tombstone just like Vanna's babes in the blizzard. And with this ending, Christina said farewell to her own happy childhood with loving, indulgent, Italian parents, preserved in her memory and verses of *Sing-Song*, but brought firmly to a close, as Vanna's twins experience the first snows of suffering, but are saved from any harsher endurance of pain. Dying, they live for ever in innocent infancy. Both works clearly sprang from the same creative impulse. Together, they represent the first steps in a self-healing process.

Christina made a fair-copy of *Sing-Song*, placing each poem on a separate page with a naive design to match (which she explained were not illustrations but 'merely my own scratches, and I cannot draw') to show the kind of book she had in mind. Jean Ingelow and Caroline Gemmer had achieved success in writing for children and though we cannot be sure that Christina's impulse was so calculated, at an early stage she saw the commercial possibilities of her rhymes.

She had evidently discussed progress with Caroline Gemmer, who on 4 February was informed that the rhymes had now 'so waxed in bulk as to justify their being shown to Mr Macmillan'. If he declined them, Christina intended to try another publisher and also to send them 'to my Boston publishers (how grand!)' She had of course already read Mrs Gemmer's baby-verses and, now that *Sing-Song* was complete, she also opened Jean Ingelow's *Studies for Stories*.

It's not clear precisely what happened next, but on 25 February, she accepted the contract offered by Gabriel's publisher, adding courteously: 'I hope for both our sakes the Rhymes may achieve some success.' Ellis had achieved success with William Morris's *The Earthly Paradise* and was evidently being led to see himself as publisher to a small but high-profile group of writers, who also included Swinburne. To increase the offer, Ellis suggested bringing out a new edition of her poems, if she could regain copyright.

There followed some negotiations, conducted by William on his sister's behalf. Macmillan made it clear that to retain his author he was willing to improve his terms in the future, and would not release copyright. Gabriel however was determined she should move, telling Allingham on 28 February that Christina had already decided to 'leave Mac altogether'. This was not exactly true: the new contract was only for *Sing-Song*. But at the same time Ellis also offered to issue her stories, to which she now added a new and longer piece, just completed – a novella in eighteen short chapters entitled *Commonplace* as if in response to *Tinsley's* reviewer. In mid-March she therefore despatched to Ellis a total of six tales (omitting *Some Pros and Cons* and *A Safe Investment*) for which she proposed the general title *Commonplace and Other Short Stories*. Ellis immediately offered a contract on the same terms as *Sing-Song*. But he didn't like the title. He also felt the book lacked bulk, and suggested she write an additional tale or two. This prompted Christina to confess that the six she had sent were virtually all the prose she had written since 1852, except for the two 'trifles' she had withheld owing to their 'special object' as items of Church propaganda. As to the title, she couldn't think of an alternative to *Commonplace* – unless it be Maria's suggestion of 'Births, Deaths and Marriages' – though they suspected this had already been used. Perhaps it had, or maybe Ellis thought it worse, for it was not adopted.

Her preface was datelined April 1870. Though an inexperienced publisher, Ellis moved with speed. *Commonplace and Other Short Stories* by Christina G. Rossetti, author of *Goblin Market* and *The Prince's Progress* was ready for publication on 7 May, in a small run of 250 copies.

It coincided with the appearance of Gabriel's *Poems*, which proved the sensation of the season, partly but not primarily for literary reasons. The previous autumn, using Charles Howell as his agent and Emily Seddon's husband H. V. Tebbs as legal advisor, Gabriel had arranged for the exhumation of Lizzie's coffin in Highgate Cemetery and the retrieval of his manuscript book. This was accomplished without the family's knowledge, though William was told almost at once and must at some stage have informed his mother and sisters – though in any case the rumour soon leaked out, undoubtedly increasing pre-publication interest in the volume. Indeed, the whole event was a perfect example of hype *avant la lettre*. Here, according to literary gossip, were the famous 'lost poems' buried with the author's wife, as well as new and exciting material. Moreover, author and publisher were busy 'working the oracle' (in Scott's words) to ensure favourable reviews. Gabriel retreated to Barbara Bodichon's cottage at Scalands, where he remained – sharing firstly with W. J. Stillman and then, discreetly, with Janey Morris – until publication was safely over.

The balance was more than reversed: whereas in 1862 *Goblin Market* had taken the lead, eclipsing *Early Italian Poets*, now *Commonplace* was utterly outpaced by *Poems*, in terms of column inches. Christina was neither angry nor envious, for she genuinely rejoiced in her brother's success, while Mamma's pride was almost palpable: invited to Euston Square, Mr Ellis was pronounced a 'fine-looking Englishman'. He was a fine payer, too and unlike Macmillan sent a cheque on publication, which gratified Christina.

Commonplace itself was something of a new departure, or rather a return to the satirical social observation of her epistolary tale of Angela -Maria, snobbish Emma and pious Clorinda. This time the main characters were three parentless sisters, Catherine, Lucy and Jane Charlmont, who respectively remain single, marry for love and marry for money. In style it was close to *Cranford* and *Scenes of Clerical Life*, though as Gabriel wittily told Alice, it was 'rather in the Austen vein ... and quite worthy of its title'.

Lucy Charlmont, whose feelings are ambushed when she learns that the man she loves has married another, is largely a self-portrait, while garrulous Mrs Tyke seems drawn from Letitia Scott and her genial husband from Dr Heimann. Miss Drum, who acts as chaperone and who despite an 'unflagging intention of being agreeable' is in fact 'rather tiresome', is surely based on one of the aunts, possessing more than a dash of *Emma's* Miss Bates, and aunt Charlotte's knowledge of Debrett. 'Now what Durham will this be, my dear?' she asks when Jane's engagement is announced. 'I used to know a Sir Marcus Durham – a gay, hunting Baronet. He was of a north-country family; but this may be a branch of the same stock. He married an Earl's daughter, Lady Mary; and she used to take precedence, let who would be in the room. 'No,' replies Lucy, suppressing a smile. Widowed Mr Durham is enormously wealthy, but his fortune has been made in the City.

With its sharp social commentary, *Commonplace* belies Christina's reputation as a pious recluse and poet of mournful imagination. It suggests that, like Jane Austen before her, the spinsterly vantage point gave good scope for witty, moral observation and storytelling. Certainly the story reveals wider participation in social events than Christina is usually credited with. Where, for instance, did she witness anything like the amateur theatricals staged with such elaborate preparation and rivalry as those in Mrs Hartley's drawing-room? The jealous jostling is waspishly described, and the acting cruelly mocked, especially that by a bevy of 'Anglo-Greek' girls whose originals must come from the Ionides and Spartali families. (Christine Spartali, incidentally, had married for rank, while her sister Marie, who studied with Madox Brown, was currently facing paternal opposition to her desire to marry Mr Stillman, for love.)

And beyond satire there is acute understanding of the workings of the heart. Lucy's inner vexation at the news of Jane's engagement, for example, is depicted as a struggle between conscience and self:

Conscience took alarm, and pronounced that envy and pride had a share in her vexation. Self retorted: It is not envy to see that Jane is mercenary, nor pride to dislike vulgarity. Conscience insisted: It is envy to be annoyed by Jane's getting married before you, and it is pride to brand Mr Durham as vulgar, and then taboo him as beyond the pale. Self pleaded: No one likes growing old and being made to feel it; and who would not deprecate a connection who will put one out of countenance at every turn?

Conscience wins, and *Commonplace* is indeed Austen-like in its dissection of Lucy's movement towards self-knowledge.

Its other set piece is a disastrous picnic party, at which Catherine tries vainly to chaperone Jane and Lucy sits miserably conscious of her fading looks. Partly inspired by the picnic in *Emma*, this also derived from Christina's own fern-hunting excursion with the Jervises in Staffordshire some twenty years before, for the picnic spot in *Commonplace* bears the same name as that of a glen close to Darlaston Hall.

Finally, the two contrasting weddings in *Commonplace* allow the author to give her views on modern marriage. Jane's banquet takes place in a large hotel (with pasteboard sentries borrowed, as Christina admitted to Alice, from those encountered on the overnight stop on the way to Penkill) and is an uncomfortable affair, the result of 'months of scheming and weeks of fuss', marred by an unseemly squabble over the regular and superstitious custom of throwing a shoe after the happy couple. Lucy's wedding is, of course, to be preferred, as Arthur Tresham and Lucy Charlmont took each other for better for worse, till death should them part:

No tears were shed, no stereotyped hypocrisies uttered, no shoes flung; this time a true man and a true woman who loved and honoured each other, were joined together; and thus the case did not lend itself to any tribute of lies, miscalled white.

Thus Christina treated herself to the fantasy of the wedding she would never have.

For into the social comment and humour she also interwove her own history, describing and thereby laying to rest the pain of reading of James's marriage in the newspaper, the fear of growing old and above all the long bouts of depressive melancholia that dogged her adult life, as Lucy paces along the rough, irreclaimable shingle beach 'to and fro, to and fro, at once listless and unresting'. Buried in this story too, is one of family blighted by the early, unexplained disappearance of a loving father, which was in essence that of her own. Through fiction, such experiences could now be faced, both inwardly and also publicly presented to the world, in a therapeutic process of description that distanced her inner self from the sources of injury which she had so long concealed. This inner compulsion may well explain why waspish mockery and social censure coexist in *Commonplace* with the long account of Lucy's depression, in particular her haunting visions of a drowned parent transformed into a monstrous image that functions metonymically to convey the cause of her trouble. Through such self-imaging, Christina was coming to terms, emotionally if not knowingly, with the pain of the past. Like Lucy, she was barely ten when her own father had figuratively drowned in his own despair. In *Sing-Song*, she had recreated the affectionate Papa of her childhood, playing pat-a-cake and making farmyard noises. In *Vanna's Twins*, she had drawn the bustling Cola in the same image with his *due maccheroni* and dreams of returning home. Here, in her heroine's nightmare fears, she was surely confronting her own traumas and whatever terrible memories accompanied her adolescent breakdown and recurrent depression. Lucy's morbid vision of her father's body lapping the shore, long dead but ever returning, drew something from her author's conscious or unconscious mind. Being once drawn, it might now lose its power to oppress her.

The reviews of *Commonplace* were generally poor. The *Athenaeum* compared the title-piece to *Cranford*, but dismissed the remainder as 'too manifestly designed to point a moral to be worthy of very high praise'. And the *Spectator* effectively demolished the book at length, dismayed that the author of *Goblin Market* had produced such dross – even *Hero* and *Nick* were disfigured by transformation too improbable even for fairyland. The remainder were tracts for the pious and 'gossipy commonplaces for quiet old maids', while *A Safe Investment* was mercilessly ridiculed for its 'very terrific account of what went on at a seaport town one stormy night when everyone seems to have declined to go to bed, and to have preferred roaming frantically about, knocking against each other in the pitchy darkness on their way to the bank to get their cheques cashed or in their desire to look on while the vessels on the coast were – one and all – being wrecked.' As to the title-story, it was preposterous that a deathbed instruction should have seriously prevented Catherine Charlmont from seeking a husband, for 'even the most conscientious of old maids' would hardly think it necessary to await the return of a deceased parent.

Whether because of this reception or more probably because it had fulfilled its purpose, *Commonplace* was Christina's last attempt at fiction. As she herself approached forty, Lucy's story closed a chapter in her own life.

'I can readily imagine that if *Commonplace* proves a total failure, *Sing-Song* may dwindle to a very serious risk', Christina wrote apologetically to Ellis, offering to release him from the contract to publish and pointedly congratulating him on the 'marked success' of her brother's book.

Ellis was fully occupied supplying the demand for Gabriel's *Poems* and keeping pace with the author's volley of promotional suggestions; he gladly took the opportunity to withdraw. Christina concealed disappointment with excessive courtesy in her reply from Folkestone, where she and Mamma were on holiday, adding philosophically: 'we are not all D. G. Rs!' Gabriel's poems were now into their third and fourth reprint.

There were other problems with *Sing-Song*, for it had been agreed that Alice would do the illustrations. Sadly, her skill was limited to animals and flowers, so the decision not to proceed allowed her role in the project to lapse too. 'Thank you for the great kindness, which relieves my uneasiness at the woeful miscarriage of *Sing-Song*. How very good of you to bestow cordial wishes on its future even divorced from your designs,' replied Christina.

In writing to Mrs Heimann this summer, she was not unduly cast down, musing that it would be handy to cut oneself in two, upon occasion ' – or if in two, why not in twenty?' so that she could cross the Atlantic to see Henrietta, dart into Euston Square to greet Maria, look in on Louisa Parke and a dozen more friends besides – a remarkably sociable desire from one usually full of excuses for 'stay-at-home' tendencies.

Her next letter dealt with graver matters – the 'awful reality of horror' that was the Franco-Prussian War. At first, most sympathies were with Prussia, as the victim of aggression. But the tide turned; as William put it, what began as 'Imperial France invading Germany' ended as 'Germany grinding down Republican France'. Christina's feelings were generally pro-French – paternal anti-Austrian prejudice rubbed off on all Rossettis – but she opposed war on principle and as the fighting proceeded public affairs stirred her pen as they had not done since the death of Prince Albert. The result was a two-part poem *On the German-French Campaign*, lamenting both the aggression and the defeat of France:

> As thou didst, men do to thee; and heap the measure
> And heat the furnace sevenfold hot:

As thou once, now these to thee – who pitieth thee
From sea to sea?

'O man, put up thy sword!' was an injunction Christina universally supported, deploring violent conflict.

'Of course, I think your proper business is to write poetry and not *Commonplaces*' Gabriel had told his sister a few months earlier. To this she replied in a letter whose opening page is now lost, defensively claiming that her poetic range was naturally narrow, and that it was 'impossible to go on singing out loud' to a 'one-stringed lyre'. Moreover, she wrote:

> It is not in me, and therefore will never come out of me, to turn to politics and philanthropy with Mrs Browning: such many-sidedness I leave to a greater than I and, having said my say, may well sit silent. 'Give me the withered leaves I chose' may include the dog-eared leaves of one's first, last, and only book. If ever the fire rekindles availably, *tanto meglio per me*: at the worst, I suppose a few posthumous groans may be found amongst my remains. Here is a great discovery 'Women are not Men', and you must not expect me to possess a tithe of your capacities, though I humbly – or proudly – lay claim to family likeness.

In this ambiguous and contradictory fragment Christina appears to say both that as a woman she could not write as well or as widely as her brother – though his *Poems* were by no means broader in scope, and Mrs Browning's political subjects came from an undeniably female pen – and also that although her inspirations seemed to have withered, yet she has (or would) compose a few more 'groans'. If not as prolific as others, she would still claim a place in the pantheon.

Like many poets, Christina suffered recurrent anxieties lest the 'poetic fire' die out. Any inquiry into what she was currently writing was liable to be met with evasion because, although justly proud of and eager to extend her reputation, she could not will poems into existence; the impulse still had to be waited for. She therefore took refuge in self-deprecating jokes about one-stringed lyres and withered leaves. The confusions in her letter also bear witness to conflicting self-images as poet, woman and sister. For all her seeming modesty, Christina wished to secure her place in the literary realm, where she had preceded her brother and now seemed in danger of being deposed – without challenging his traditional privilege. To this end, she therefore endorsed the prevailing view of women's lesser capacities, but reserved the right to excel, by saying that if she could not achieve 'greatness' she would rather 'sit silent' and leave her books to speak for themselves.

At the same time, Gabriel's stimulus was valuable, as always. And his brotherly advice that poetry was her proper business heralded a return to verse in the very mode she denied was within her grasp. In youth sibling rivalry had been a spur to composition; now Gabriel's success renewed the impulse. Indeed, fired by the reception of his book, Gabriel was now writing furiously, and was even inspired to emulate Christina's ode with his own sonnet on the current war, urging William to also do the same. This wind of enthusiasm fanned the embers of her muse, and around this time she imitated Gabriel's *Willowwood* quartet with four sonnets of her own, entitled *By Way of Remembrance*. Hitherto, she had used the sonnet mainly for devotional purposes; now she used it for love poems, in the classic tradition reaching from Dante, Petrarch, Spenser and Shakespeare down to Barrett Browning's *Sonnets from the Portuguese* and Gabriel's *House of Life* – a tradition that reminds us that the sonnet conventionally adopts an intimate address while not disclosing the beloved's identity and is traditionally addressed to an unresponsive beloved. In Christina's voice it expresses profound affection that is partly requited but without hope of fulfilment. Increasingly this was the poetic persona she constructed, looking forward to a Platonic or paradisal ideal with general as well as personal application.

This summer, when Mamma, the aunts and uncle Henry spent a pleasant at Chelsea, dining in the garden and feeding the deer, Gabriel told his mother that Christina was a 'more spontaneous' or natural poet than himself, crediting her with an instinctive talent. His own work was painstakingly composed, overpacked with adjectives and complex imagery. He seldom hit on a phrase with her unerring aim, and lacked the gossamer gift of profound simplicity as well as her unforced rhythms and lyric repetition. The comparison is visible in her answering *Echo from Willowwood* on lovers' separation:

> Two gazed into a pool, he gazed and she,
> Not hand in hand, but heart in heart, I think . . .

This was personally as well as poetically expressive, for it obliquely acknowledged Gabriel's unattainable passion for Janey Morris, which in concealed form pervaded his *Poems*.

To speak plainly, he was now besotted with the wife of one of his best friends, and was now looking for a country retreat where the idyll could continue away from inquisitive eyes. The relationship was not clandestine, however, and though one wonders how much Gabriel's sisters knew or guessed, they clearly did not regard Mrs Morris as a *femme fatale* or woman of loose morals. Christina's *Echo from Willowwood* suggests however that she interpreted Gabriel's passion as one like her own, destined never to be fulfilled on earth.

Maria, who at this date was perhaps giving Jane lessons in Italian, had herself plunged into the field of Dante studies with an explicatory essay on the *Divine Comedy* aimed at elucidating it for beginners. 'Dante is a name unlimited in place and period. Not Italy, but the Universe, is his birthplace,' she began, with characteristic energy; 'not the fourteenth century but all Time is his epoch.' But how many English readers were familiar with his work? How many – or indeed how few – shared her own vivid interest? Dante's text was dense and difficult, so his 'momentous' truths remained unread. Her task was straightforward: to outline and explain his life and ideas.

She knew, of course, that this was her father's territory, and paid tribute in her book's dedication to his 'beloved memory'. But she firmly refused to enter into any abstruse debates: where experts differed, she simply adopted the reading that made most sense, and in any case advocated tolerance of multiple meanings on the grounds that this added depth and breadth to textual interpretation – a tacit rebuke to her father's 'decoding'. She also regarded Beatrice as actual rather than allegorical, despite acknowledging her symbolic aspect as the personification of all beauty and nobleness.

Almost unconsciously, it seems, the Rossettis were drawn back to the banshee of their childhood, subject of Papa's obsessional theories, as if each had painful memories to expunge. Gabriel had translated the *Vita Nuova* and William the *Inferno*; now Maria offered a plain students' guide that cut through the conundrums and was above all concise, by comparison with Papa's endlessly unravelling exegesis. At the same time, however, her enterprise was a filial reassurance that his life's work was not worthless: Dante was undoubtedly a figure of major significance.

Being discussed over tea and supper and especially whenever Charles Cayley called, Maria's *Shadow of Dante* made Christina ever more familiar with Dante's text, which once more occupied a prominent place in daily life, no longer as an incubus of awesome, misunderstood power but as a poem dealing with some of her own closest interests regarding heaven and hell, figuratively rendered. She understood the appropriate punishments suffered by the various sinners, and also the attempt to portray the Nine Heavens of the *Paradiso* as a celestial Lake of Divine Light, circling a mystical White Rose that represents the godhead. As Maria explained:

> Petals upon petals, petals upon petals; the narrowest circuit encompasses the Sun-outmeasuring Lake ... What should be hidden, what withheld from the enthroned Souls who form those petals, seeing that they gaze into the Very Light?

The imagery is Dantean, but the rhythms are fervently Rossettian.

PART FOUR

1871–94

29

Disease and Derangement

IN THE CENSUS of 1871, the Rossetti family in Euston Square presented an impressive appearance to the enumerator, for William, now listed as head of the household, had been promoted to be 'Assistant Secretary (Excise Branch) Board of Inland Revenue', while Maria Francesca was described as 'Teacher of Languages & Authoress of educational & other works', Christina Georgina was 'Authoress of books, chiefly poems', and Charlotte Lydia was 'Salaried Companion to Lady of Title'. Mamma and aunt Eliza were listed as having 'income from dividends', and the household was supported by three servants: Grace Stephens, aged 66, cook; Eliza Stephens, aged 30 (presumably Grace's daughter), housemaid; and Eliza's faithful pensioner Sarah Catchpole, 60, underhousemaid.

The house was large enough for Eliza to occupy separate quarters on an upper floor, and also to accommodate uncle Henry on his regular visits. For general use the family had a drawing room, dining room, parlour and 'library', where William did his literary work in the evenings. The neighbours were equally superior to those at Albany Street – lawyers, law stationers, and stockbrokers. At no. 57 lived a schoolmistress with a solitary boarder, and at no. 59 an 'archaeologist and philologist'. Euston Square was comfortably close to the British Museem, where 'CBC' (now lodging nearby in Hunter Street) spent much of his time, and where, around this date the Rossettis also made the acquaintance of young Edmund Gosse, assistant librarian.

In February Christina finally retrieved *Sing-Song*. Ellis sent £35 in compensation, which she returned. 'It has been a tiresome affair and I think not well managed on Ellis's part,' noted William – a judgement confirmed by the fact that when Christina looked through the manuscript with a fresh 'business eye' on 2 March, she found twenty-two of the poems were missing. Though her tone was apologetic – 'I fear my poor little book is troublesome to you even as it were in its grave' – Ellis was clearly at fault. She then opened negotiations with Messrs Dalziel and Roberts Bros, with a view to simultaneous British and American publication. On 20 March Mr Niles called to collect the manuscript, in order to obtain costings for the illustrations. He sent favourable reports, as did Dalziels, who prepared the book for publication by George Routledge. By the end of April terms were agreed, and Arthur Hughes accepted the commission to provide illustrations, much to Christina's delight.

Suddenly, however, her health deteriorated, and this time the symptoms were alarming, though difficult to diagnose. Dr Jenner called it neuralgia and suggested change of air, thinking she would benefit by joining Mamma on a trip to Leamington. Three days later he was summoned again: Christina was much worse, unable to climb stairs or even to hold a pen steadily – leading to 'intolerable hideousness' of handwriting in a brief note to Gabriel. She had acute weakness and tremor in all limbs, together with high fever. Jenner now identified 'severe internal inflammation' as the cause and, seeing no immediate danger, left her in the care of Dr Fox, an abdominal specialist, during his own absence abroad. But there was no improvement, and for some days the family were convinced she was at death's door.

In retrospect, she had not been well since mid-1867, nearly four years before. And for the past twelve months or so she had suffered from 'very persistent weakness without exertion', as she had told Alice, though without corresponding lowness of spirits. 'If I was weakly in youth I must not expect to become athletic in middle age,' she joked to Anne Gilchrist. Over the autumn and winter of 1870–1 she had visited the Cayleys in Blackheath, and had remained cheerful and sufficiently fit for some social engagements, despite continuing exhaustion. She dined at Fitrroy Square before Christmas, for instance, to meet Cathy Brown's prospective husband, music critic Franz Hueffer, whom she described as 'a learned German ... but despite his learning only 25, so appropriately young for his fiancée of 20'. But now her condition had rapidly become acute. 'It must be getting on to a month since an attack of fever and other plagues began with her: she is in bed and very prostrate, and not likely to be out of doors this long while yet,' William told Anne in May. Occasionally, she managed to leave her bed, but only to lie on the sofa; anything else was beyond her very feeble powers. By mid-June she was still in bed – 'progressing, or at any rate not retrogressing,' as William told Swinburne with more hope than conviction.

Returning, Jenner pronounced her 'free from fever', and again prescribed a change of air. Plans were laid to return to Folkestone, but she had no strength to travel. On 17 June he brought a surgeon to examine her, saying the condition was possibly dangerous, but still making no clear diagnosis. William dealt with the correspondence over *Sing-Song*, and family life went on around her, Maria busy with the proofs of *A Shadow of Dante* and aunt Charlotte negotiating to buy the Euston Square lease. At Chelsea 'the great Russian novelist' Turgenev dined with Gabriel, and admired the animals. From Florence Teodorico wrote to say that the Italians wanted to remove Papa's remains for reburial in his native land. All the family except Gabriel were strongly opposed.

She went out for the first time on 24 June, in a wheelchair, and on 6 July was sufficiently strong to move for an 'improving fortnight' to lodgings in Hampstead, with Mamma. By 20 July she was back home, preparing for Folkestone. William did not feel it necessary to cancel his annual holiday on the Continent, and in many respects Christina's spirits remained good. On 28 July she wrote a long and chatty letter to William, listing the mail that had arrived since his departure and telling him that she was well enough to attend to the second proofs of *Sing-Song*. She was so charmed with the illustrations – Hughes had worked relatively closely, though not slavishly, to her suggestive 'scratches' – that she insisted his name be set in larger type on the title page, declaring that his designs alone deserved to sell the volume. Ellen Heaton, Charles Cayley and Henrietta Rintoul had called, Dr Heimann was doing well after a serious operation and Maria had received proofs of her frontispiece, showing Giotto's portrait of Dante and his supposed death mask. In view of the pain and weakness she was suffering, this letter contained little about her own state of health, and she wrote to Kate Howell with equal understatement, saying only that she had fallen ill in April and was now convalescent. She had seen Gabriel but twice, she joked, his 'nocturnal habits' not being adapted to sickroom visiting. In fact, Gabriel was now staying with Janey in an old manor house in Oxfordshire, rented as a rural retreat by himself and Morris – who was currently travelling in Iceland, apparently content to leave his wife and children with her admirer at Kelmscott. 'Please dear Janey, be happy,' he wrote.

William meanwhile travelled to Venice and Ravenna, where he visited Dante's tomb. Calling at Folkestone on his return, he found Christina still deplorably ill, suffering now from an abscess in the mouth and a grievously swollen throat. Back in Euston Square, she saw Dr Fox (Jenner was away attending the Queen at Balmoral) who diagnosed circulation problems, and prescribed digitalis, but the condition worsened and by early November was very frightening. Her throat and neck were goitrously enlarged, and she had difficulty in swallowing (though Fox held this to be nervous in origin). She had heart palpitations, stifling sensations, and breathing difficulties; occasionally she lost consciousness. Her nights were very bad, and additionally she suffered severe neuralgic headaches, which she ascribed to the glasses of wine and brandy Fox told her to take throughout the day. As regards appearance, she looked a 'total wreck' in William's words: her hair fell out, her skin discoloured, and her eyes bulged. Her voice became a rasping croak, and she looked suddenly ten years older, as Gabriel remarked on his return in October. Scotus reported to

Alice that she had 'lost all the beauty she had, her eyes seem so queerly exaggerated'.

She endured all these catastrophes stoically, though she was in no condition to celebrate the first copies of *Sing-Song* on 18 November, in good time for Christmas. The following day William wrote on her behalf to Macmillan's, who had incorrectly given her Maria's birthdate in a handbook of contemporary biography; one imagines that this was the least of Christina's worries. Still no clear prognosis was possible. On 25 November Jenner called, back from Balmoral, and agreed with Fox that she had 'a very rare malady'. To reduces stress on the heart he insisted she should not climb stairs – all meals were moved to the drawing room on the first floor, where she and Mamma were sleeping in the rear room – and advised against dental treatment for the abscess, which was causing great pain. Then he left to attend the Prince of Wales.

She survived. Finally, in the New Year, nearly nine months after the acute onset, a medical friend of Maria's recognised the symptoms as those of Graves' disease or exophthalmic bronchocele, first identified in 1842. This is a thyroid condition, characterised by exhaustion, goitre, tremor, feverish sweating, tachycardia and protruding eyeballs. It also causes mood changes, irritability and erratic ill-temper, though such psychological effects were not yet perceived as physiological in origin – or at any rate not by Christina, who no doubt ascribed them to her own, imperfect character. More seriously, there was no effective cure, and a high risk of permanent damage to the heart, liver and other organs. Later, William wrote that his sister's life 'hung by a thread' during this period, and there was certainly no assurance of full recovery.

One established cause of goitre is iodine deficiency in the diet. Less frequently iodine surplus also triggers thyroid malfunctioning. Seaweed is a natural source of iodine, and Christina was in the habit of taking the seaweed preparation carageen moss for her cough; could this have adversely affected the thyroid?

Henceforth, her looks were permanently altered, and her natural shyness was exacerbated, for strangers tended to stare, not knowing the cause, seeing her as a grotesque and prematurely aged woman. She also lived in constant fear of a relapse.

Sing-Song was the one bright strand in a doleful time. She loved Hughes's drawings of 'the apple tree casting its apples – also the three dancing girls with the angels – also the crow soaked grey stared at by his peers'. And she was not too ill to welcome the advance of £25 paid on publication, or the appreciative reviews. As usual, the *Athenaeum* was the most significant, saying that though she had written 'some of the saddest as well as the sweetest verses of our time', the book was altogether 'the perfection of this sort of verse – a something which would be as hard to explain as it is easy to feel and enjoy'. The woodcuts received equal commendation, comprising praise of a high order in a serious paper which did not generally review baby books. It is a mark of Christina's achievement; she was now a writer of whom good work was expected. Increasingly, critics referred to her work as a sort of benchmark, and many pieces in her first book were approaching classic status. *Goblin Market*, for instance, featured on a programme of readings at the Queen's Concert Hall in Hanover Square attended by Mamma and Maria. Christina herself was prevented by the 'usual night-air reason' but flattered to note that her work stood 'sandwich-wise between two specimens of Shakespeare'.

In recognition, she was asked for a Christmas poem by the American *Scribner's Monthly*. The resulting piece, reminiscent of the mood of *Sing-Song* and of Vanna's Italian carol, is now best known by its first and last stanzas:

> In the bleak mid-winter
>   Frosty wind made moan,
> Earth stood hard as iron,
>   Water like a stone;
> Snow had fallen, snow on snow,
>   Snow on snow,
> In the bleak mid-winter
>   Long ago.
>
>   . . .
>
> What can I give Him,
>   Poor as I am?
> If I were a shepherd
>   I would bring a lamb,
> If I were a wise man
>   I would do my part –
> Yet what I can I give Him,
>   Give my heart.

Scribner's editor advertised this piece somewhat coyly, claiming to have 'a little poem in my breast-pocket – wise in a sort of child-wisdom, sweet and clear and musical as the sunset chimes that were sounding a moment ago from the belfry of St John's – yes, and cheerier, for it celebrates that first Chrstmas morning'. But he sent a liberal fee of ten pounds, in advance, which is one illustration of why despite American recalcitrance over copyright, British authors were very pleased to deal with transatlantic publishers.

Christina's rising literary status was also demonstrated by the changes made by *Tinsley's* critic H. B. Forman, when revising his article for publication in *Our Living Poets* (1871) which appeared before *Sing-Song*. It was five years since Miss Rossetti's last delicate offering of verse, Forman wrote, and her public were getting impatient. She was he added, without question 'the poet of female poets' in England, whose best lyrics came close to perfection. He even half withdrew his earlier cavils, saying *Commonplace* was actually 'as far from commonplace as her accustomed audience would anticipate', and concluded with the hope that she would return to poetry and delight readers 'once more with some of her imperishable lyric masterpieces'.

When she recovered sufficiently to read this – Christina never affected to despise reviews, though in time she learnt to be less sensitive – her elation at the high praise must have been tempered by the fact that Forman printed her name throughout as 'Christina Gabriela Rossetti'. Furthermore, while she was the best of living English poetesses, second place was awarded to Menella Bute Smedley – who, whatever the merits of her verse, has never been accorded a leading position in Victorian literature. Christina may also have been wryly amused that Forman's determination to elevate Gabriel as founder of 'the Pre-Raphaelite poetic school' relegated her to a lesser place, as her brother's 'best disciple'. In some moods, Christina would accept such an assessment, but both she and Gabriel knew that, poetically, she was no follower.

In May 1872, after some months of remission, Christina was once more laid low with an acute recurrence of the thyroid condition. Again dangerously ill, she was nursed by Mamma and Maria. A couple of weeks later, another grave blow hit the family when Gabriel's mind gave way. William was summoned to Chelsea and later described Sunday 2 June as the most miserable day of his life, as he witnessed his brother raving wildly – 'past question, not entirely sane' – as he was to do 'for many months ensuing'.

The symptoms were those of paranoid mania: a conviction that he was the victim of a general conspiracy, accompanied by demented fantasies and aural delusions of voices whispering against him. He suffered unceasing mental agitation and distress, so that he could never relax and seldom sleep soundly. With increasing despair, he also knew that he was insane – aware that his delusions were imaginary but unable to escape them.

With hindsight, it can be seen that his condition began as early as 1867, when he complained of insomnia and 'confusion in the head'.

He had for some time been using soporifics – firstly alcohol and lately the new drug chloral, which was safer than opiates but did nothing for the mental agitation except blot out consciousness for a few hours; now he was convinced he did not sleep at all. With hindsight, too, his erratic behaviour over the past few years indicated loss of rationality, as with the manic collection of exotic animals, for instance, and the egregious decision to exhume his wife. There was his belief that Lizzie's soul had migrated into the song of a chaffinch at Penkill, and the frenetic anxiety over reviews of his book, as he tried to discover which paper would be the one in which his 'enemies' struck. There was also his largely unreasonable passion for Janey, a respectably married wife and mother, and his extravagant claims that 'beauty like hers is genius'. To a large extent this adoration was intended precisely as an unrealisable passion, with Janey as a *princesse lointaine* and Gabriel as her knight errant. Perhaps unfortunately, Jane was more than flattered. She returned Gabriel's love and encouraged the affair so they might be together in romantic solitude – either in the country or in the studio, where he never tired of drawing her face and hands. Just before they were about to go to Kelmscott for another season, Gabriel's mind snapped.

The immediate cause was continuing controversy over an adverse review of *Poems* by Robert Buchanan, which had originally appeared in October 1871 under the title 'The Fleshly School of Poetry'. Combining an attack on Swinburne and (most unjustly) Morris for indecency in verse, this labelled Gabriel as leader of the dirty lyricists, and was subsequently expanded into a pamphlet. Gabriel responded, and the subject kept simmering as papers reported attack and counter-attack. On 18 May one taunted the 'fleshly' poets with cowardice. Gabriel came three times to Euston Square the following week to discuss tactics. William's advice was to do nothing. But on 1 June the *Saturday Review* sneered at the 'Fleshly School' for 'their sickly self-consciousness, their emasculated delight' and their 'utter unmanliness which is . . . so disgusting'.

This insult to his virility tipped the balance of Gabriel's sanity. He became obsessed with the notion that there was 'a widespread conspiracy for crushing his fair fame as an artist and man, and for hounding him out of honest society'. Buchanan led the conspiracy, but distressingly Gabriel also identified as sworn enemies men he liked and admired, including Browning and even Swinburne and the wholly inoffensive Rev. Dodgson, whose *Hunting of the Snark* he construed as a hostile lampoon.

Initially, Euston Square was not informed of how grave the situation was. To Mamma, William wrote merely that Gabriel was 'hippish and out of sorts to some extent'. He took time off work to be with his brother, grateful also to Scott, who delayed his departure for Penkill. On 5 June medical help was summoned, and Gabriel's physician, John Marshall, called in young Dr Maudsley, then at the beginning of his career in mental disorders. Gabriel denounced him as 'no doctor but some one foisted on him with a sinister purpose', but agreed to leave Cheyne Walk, for the house of a new acquaintance, Dr Hake at Roehampton. The next day, he took a large dose of laudanum, intending to kill himself. He did not wake, and on Sunday afternoon a local doctor diagnosed his condition as that of an apoplectic seizure, saying that if Gabriel survived his brain would be irreparably damaged.

It was William's harrowing duty to inform the family of all that had happened, their shock aggravated by hearing Gabriel was near death. Mamma and Maria hurried back with him to Roehampton. Christina could not travel, being herself very sick; aunt Eliza took over the nursing duties. In deep despondency, William predicted that the effect on both his mother and Christina would be fatal. They found Gabriel still unconscious but alive. William despatched a note to Euston Square, and on Monday morning Christina replied, thanking him warmly for the note, which with 'its comparatively hopeful news' had helped her to sleep. 'I know not (having heard of one fearful alternative) what to hope: but with my whole heart I commit our extremity to Almighty God,' she wrote, sending all love and sympathy.

The 'fearful alternative' was presumably commitment to an insane asylum. Gabriel regained consciousness, but his 'gloomy and exasperating fantasies' were as bad as ever. A week later he was moved to the Browns' before being taken to Scotland, where a generous patron provided a sequence of secluded houses; Brown, Scott and Dr Hake's son George acted as his companions and minder.

Now William also gave cause for concern. He was both stunned by grief and overcome with anxiety, for Gabriel's collapse meant that he was responsible not only for mother, sisters and aunts, but also for his insane brother, and his brother's chaotic financial affairs, servants, creditors, models, mistresses and sundry hangers-on. Fortunately Janey Morris was level-headed; although distraught, she made no demands on William beyond asking if there was any way she could help.

There was an extra reason for distress, for to all the family Gabriel's condition must have revived memories of Papa's collapse and his paranoid suspicions that he was the subject of conspiracy and vilification. Now Gabriel too, at the height of his powers and acclaim, had fallen victim to similar delusions, which would surely destroy his career. It was as if a curse lay on the family; and for William, whom Papa's illness had condemned to hard labour in the Revenue Office (where only now was he reaping any reward) despondency and despair seemed an appropriate response.

Long-term arrangements had to be thought of, for Gabriel could not live at Euston Square, 'with Christina on a bed of sickness, perhaps of death' and William out all day at the office. At the least a strong, resourceful and discreet male servant was needed in case restraint was required. 'Ominous colloquies' were held about the benefits of an asylum, and though some spoke optimistically of recovery, William consistently refused to raise false hopes. It was a very dark period.

As it transpired, Gabriel did show improvement during his weeks in Scotland, and in September transferred to Kelmscott Manor, with George Hake in attendance. He paid a brief visit to Euston Square on the way through London. 'All this past cursed state of things began on my birthday,' he lamented to William. 'May the spell be removed now that yours is past!'

Christina, meanwhile, had been sent to Hampstead to recuperate, installed in a cottage at the top of the hill, where she welcomed a number of visitors, including Charles and Kate Howell, bearing a case of restorative sherry. Her handwriting remained palsied, however. 'You will have to pardon lodging house deficiencies of a marked character, please' she warned Mrs Heimann and her daughter. 'Excuse shaky letter as I am still weak', but she was able to sit out on a balcony, and by mid-July she was back home, feeling a shade better. Writing to thank Barbara Bodichon for friendly inquiries – Barbara's current involvement in the first university women's college did not crowd out old friends – Christina inquired whether her old offer of accommodation still stood. 'Now again my doctor bids me leave town, and we are in doubt whither to go,' she wrote. 'Of course it is not now that you could lend me your cottage as you once so kindly proposed?' As it happened, Barbara and Dr Bodichon were themselves at Scalands, but although unable to make her own house available, she helpfully commended lodgings in nearby Glottenham. Writing to Gabriel in mid-August, Mamma said Scottish air was no doubt more invigorating, but that Sussex was so agreeable that Christina seemed to thrive on it. They played croquet with the landlady and her daughter, until exertion made Christina's feet swell, and one day accepted an invitation from Barbara:

Mrs Bodichon sent her pony chaise, and we paid her a very pleasant visit, taking luncheon with her and a Miss Edwards, authoress, we conjecture, of two stories – My Little Lady – and Kitty – both of them very readable and original. Perhaps you know her . . .

I should like to live at Scalands; such a nice little house in a wood; everything in good taste, and the grounds well laid out. She has had built a nice large studio over Dr Bodichon's study. We had a few glimpses of the Dr, a singular looking and older man than I expected. Did not every day marriage prove that no one can be judge in the case of another I should wonder how his wife could choose such a husband: she is so different, a most favourable specimen of a true Englishwoman both in person and character . . .

The recollections of their fellow guest, Matilda Betham Edwards, were less generous in spirit, if more gushing in style. 'The season was midsummer,' she wrote, 'and the weather was both pictorial and poetical':

Tea [sic] was spread on a little lawn bordered with carelessly-kept, old-fashioned flowers . . . Little footways – paths there were none – led into coppice woods, wild strawberries, now ripe, gleaming ruby red among the moss, hazel trees showing ripe clusters, honeysuckle and wild rose scenting the air . . .
  Our little party numbered four. These were our hostess . . . her abundant golden hair a glory to behold, with a nobility of face much more striking than mere beauty, Mrs Rossetti, the poetess, and myself.
  Of her mother I remember nothing. Christina was at this time about forty, a plainly-dressed, gaunt, rather jerky woman, shy in manner and very reticent.

Barbara talked volubly, of 'gardening, flowers . . . the beauty of her environment' and of a beautiful sunrise she had lately seen.

Then the poetess by her side broke silence. "I have never seen the sun rise in my life", she observed quietly.
  The confession came to me as quite a little shock. That a poetess could reach middle life without having once beheld Nature's great pageant seemed unbelievable.

It was even more astonishing of one who had written *By fits and starts looks down the waking sun*, but so it proved: the author of the 'winning little poem' in which motherless lambs were fed from teapots, which so seemed to derive from experience, was 'not only town-bred but townish, the last person in the world from whom one could expect a pastoral'. How one wished Miss Rossetti had lived more in the country, for it was 'surely one of the strangest admissions ever uttered by a poet "I have never seen the sun rise in my life." '
Perhaps Christina spoke thus to puncture the effusions flowing from Miss Edwards; the tea (or luncheon) party has a distinctly Carrollian flavour. Her fellow guest was clearly unaware of Christina's illness and the cause of her gaunt appearance and jerky movements. But in view of her uncharitable account, one can sympathise with Christina's

dislike of meeting strangers – and particularly rival authors with preconceived notions of how poetesses should look and behave. As Nature replaced God as a shared object of worship, and as Britain became a predominantly urban nation, the notion that poets should be country-dwellers and nature-lovers was growing widespread. It was a form of cultural pastoralism from which Christina would more than once dissent, insisting it was not necessary to live in the country to write poetry, and that she did not take inspiration directly from nature.

She was fatter from her month in the country, but the 'fearful brownness' of her skin was not diminished; indeed the discolouration caused by illness made her face permanently sallow. She still felt languid and sometimes low, with 'another inconvenient symptom' too delicate to name, which may have been urinary. Towards the end of September she and Mamma returned home, to allow Maria – who had kept house at Euston Square through a long and difficult summer – to enjoy a short visit to Eastbourne, where the All Saints' Sisterhood had established a convalescent hospital.

The most encouraging sign of Christina's recovery came in the autumn when she once more took up her pen, in response to the faithful Cayley, who around the beginning of October saluted her return with a short poem on *The Birth of Venus*. Christina wrote an answer, entitled *Love-lies-bleeding* in which the poet laments that, meeting Love again after a long absence, she sees 'no recognition in his look, no trace Of memory in his eyes'. Cayley then rebutted this with another piece, received on 13 October, and Christina wound up the exchange with *Venus's Looking Glass*, tracing a movement from hope in spring through despair in summer to renewed hope in autumn. Both her pieces reflect her experience this year, though cast in a formal and classical mode that served to mask personal utterance. Indeed, both sonnets were considered sufficiently impersonal in tone to be sent to the *Argosy* magazine, where they were printed in January 1873. And thus, with something approaching normality, the worst period of her adult life closed.

30

Lucy Arrives and Maria Leaves

CHRISTINA'S ILLNESS MARKED a turning point in her life, for at its worst moments she had fully expected to die. She regarded her recovery as a deliverance and was conscious too of how much selfless love and care she had received from her mother, sister and aunts. Not surprisingly her religious faith deepened. So did her sense of literary responsibility. Henceforth she was always generous and welcoming to aspiring poets, especially if they shared her faith, and most especially if they were American, where her reputation seemed so much greater than at home. 'Waifs across the Atlantic always give her peculiar pleasure, and so sympathising a reader is already an unseen friend,' Maria wrote on Christina's behalf during her illness, on receipt of an unsolicited volume. The correspondent was Margaret Junkin Preston, author of *Beechenbrook: A Rhyme of the War* (1865) and *Old Song and New* (1870) and at Christmas Christina returned her own greetings:

> Let me thank you for a letter full of good will, and a volume in which I find form for admiration; and spirit for sympathy. It is a most blessed variety from the prevalent tone of the day when one finds distinct Christianity in combination with intellect and finds it not ashamed to assert itself ... My letters from America are usually friendly and pleasant, and yours takes rank amongst them. Pray do not think of feeling towards me as towards a stranger.

Another correspondent was Sarah Chauncey Woolsey of Baltimore, who wrote under the name of Susan Coolidge and who at the end of 1872 sent her children's story *The New Year's Bargain* to Miss Rossetti. Replying politely, Christina said she had heard from her cousin that Miss Coolidge's book had been well received in America. Her next – *What Katy Did* – was even more so.

Around this time, too, Christina received a visit from Mary Mapes Dodge, founding editor of the renowned children's magazine *St Nicholas*. Mrs Dodge called when Christina was still invalid, presumably after reading *Sing-Song*, and with the first issue of *St Nicholas* in May 1873, sent an emissary with a repeated request, whom Christina willingly received. 'Dear Sir, Pray carry out the promise of your letter, and favour me with a call,' she wrote. 'I am so much at home, especially in the afternoons, that there is more prospect of my being on the spot to receive you.' She liked the appearance of *St Nicholas*, and hoped to fill a 'nook in its pages' though she could not immediately find a suitable piece. 'Pray let this be my excuse to you,' she concluded 'tho' I will hold myself at liberty to send some little thing, should one I like to offer occur to me.' Not long afterwards, one did thus 'occur', and she sent Mrs Dodge the alphabet poem containing the 'black Bear and brown Bear both begging for Bun', which was duly printed under the title *An Alphabet from England*.

But though always courteous, Christina was not always equally cordial. To a fellow *Scribner's* contributor identified only as 'H. H.' she sent thanks for a volume that had arrived at an opportune moment 'when sickness was in our house and a new entertaining book was most welcome', but firmly dissociated herself from some of its 'utterance [with which] I neither think nor feel'. She was equally frank with young Nolly Brown, who published a precocious novel; despite friendly feeling towards the author, she did not hesitate to tell him how 'detestable' she found many of his characters. And as the years went by, she began to dread the receipt of unsolicited books, wishing neither to give offence nor disguise her opinion.

In April, she and Mamma went to Hastings, hiring a wheelchair to enable Christina to take the air. When they returned, Maria, who had another attack of erisypelas, went again to Eastbourne. Gabriel remained at Kelmscott through the winter, and in early May was rejoined by Janey and her daughters. He was still morose and insomniac – rising late, painting till dusk, joining the others in the evening and then dosing himself with whisky and chloral – but Jane's solicitude helped to keep his demons at bay. 'That Gabriel *was* mad was but too true,' she commented after his death; 'no-one knows it better than myself.'

William planned to take an early holiday, heading as always for Italy, but this time accompanied by the Scotts, Alice Boyd and Lucy Brown. Christina was 'a good bit better than a year ago' he told Anne Gilchrist, but 'still a miserable wreck'. When Edmund Gosse saw her for the first time since her illness, she was 'so strangely altered as to be scarcely recognisable' but well enough to be working in the British Museum. On 23 June she told Barbara happily: 'Indeed I am better beyond what I had a right to look for'.

At the end of the month, when Janey and her daughters returned to London, Christina and her mother went to Kelmscott, a small sleepy village on the road to nowhere amid the water meadows of the upper Thames. 'My dear Ellen, what would you say to our quiet life here, after the gaieties of your London season?' she wrote to Miss Heaton, who had met various 'European Royalties' at a function in the Guildhall:

Our greatest gaieties are being rowed in the boat by amiable Mr Hake, or playing a stakeless rubber [of whist] at night. But to me the boat is delightful: and I don't think gold and glitter in Guildhall can have been more beautiful than the gold and enamel of our river flower-banks here. Then water sounds are so delightful – and so are bird's notes in native freedom – and so are all sorts of things in the country.

The manor was an old and virtually unaltered stone house, with farm buildings, a walled garden with a great yew hedge, and small hedged paddocks. As Christina had recently written to Caroline Gemmer, 'of all flowers known to me I would least give up roses; and of all roses (what say you?) least give up the dog-rose of our hedges. Does any cultivated thing quite come up to its shades, its shapes, its proportions? Wild honeysuckle is lovely indeed, but not like wild roses.' At Kelmscott in June there were both in profusion for her delight, together with George Hake's dogs and a fat pony in the paddock.

Within the house, Gabriel used an upstairs room with ancient tapestry hangings as a studio, where he was painting a model named Alexa Wilding, as a sort of stand-in for Janey. Miss Wilding was goodnatured and respectable but not very bright, Gabriel warned his mother, and would have to join the family for meals, as she could hardly be locked in a closet when not sitting. Mamma and Christina were gracious, for however much they admired intellectual eminence they were also well accustomed to less elevated conversation – as *Commonplace* had made clear.

Gabriel was pleased to see that Christina's protruding eyeballs had sunk back, and she herself felt so much better that she even thought of going on to visit some friends named Edgecombe living outside Oxford, though in planning her return home she was also anxious to see Ellen. 'Does either day afford me a hope of seeing and chatting with you again? *Yes*, please' she wrote sociably. The horrors of the past year were receding, for Gabriel too seemed much improved. In fact, he managed to conceal the full extent of his mental disorder – as Scott noted, 'neither in writing nor viva voce was he confidential to members of his own family' regarding his schizophrenic delusions, and it is possible that they felt his malady was much exaggerated. They were grateful nevertheless to Mrs Morris and young George Hake, who shouldered many responsibilities in looking after Gabriel.

On 6 July William and the Scotts returned home, and on 9 July unexpected news reached Kelmscott: William and Lucy Brown were engaged to be married. 'My dear, dear Lucy,' Christina wrote at once:

I should like to be a dozen years younger, and worthier every way of becoming your sister; but, such as I am, be sure of my loving welcome to you as my dear sister and friend. I hope William will be all you desire; and, as I know what he has been to me, a most loving and generous brother, I am not afraid of his being less than a devoted husband to you. May love, peace, and happiness, be yours and his together in this world, and together much more in the next; and, when earth is an anteroom to heaven (may it be so, of God's mercy to us all) earth itself is full of beauty and goodness . . .

William had brought a 'fresh spring of happiness' into the family, she told him:

Who shall wish you well except the sister whom you have cared for all her life? If dear Lucy and you are as happy as I would, (if I could) make you, earth will be the foretaste and stepping-stone to heaven. Her sweetness, amiability, and talent, make her a grace and honour to us – but I need not state this to you . . .

They had been taken by surprise – the prospect 'dawned on me only with the proposal,' Christina told Caroline Gemmer – but they had long liked Lucy. Sadly, in their view, Maria's religious instruction had failed to take, and like William she was an avowed agnostic – but all paled beside the prospect of his happiness. He was now forty-three. Lucy was thirty, and over the past couple of years had established an enviable reputation as a painter, exhibiting ambitious and dramatic subject pictures – Romeo finding Juliet in the tomb, and Margaret Roper rescuing the severed head of her father Sir Thomas More from its traitors' spike on London Bridge.

The engagement led to another major decision, for Maria announced her intention to join the All Saints Sisterhood as a professed religious – a move made possible by the advent of Lucy, whose responsibility it would henceforth be to keep house for William.

The All Saints' Sisters of the Poor, under Harriet Brownlow Byron, now ran an orphanage, ragged school and infirmary in Marylebone, a convalescent hospital at Eastbourne, and a mission house and girls' school in Bristol. But it was the formal life that most drew Maria, with its Rule of regular prayer, worship and work. She dismissed the idea that being a nun involved any severance or division. 'This most blessed life, though outwardly it produce a separation, draws one closer than ever in heart to all old friends,' she wrote to some acquaintances, reminding them that 'before taking the Habit I told you that the Rule here does not cut daughters off from their parents, or I could never have entered'.

She began her novitiate on 11 September. 'Dear Maggie' wrote William from the office, 'I said little this morning, but felt much.' The family would miss her dear and familiar presence, but he knew her desire was 'to die to the world, and live to Christ' and he sincerely hoped she would find 'the peace which passeth all understanding'. The effect on the family was mixed. 'Though I am glad that Maria should carry out her long desire of becoming a Sister, I miss her company and conversation very much,' Mamma told Gabriel, and he in turn regretted her departure. Maria was 'much the healthiest in mind and cheeriest of us all', William came next, 'and Christina and I are nowhere,' he wrote. 'I suppose of course she will appear duly at our Christmas gathering, will she not?'

After her induction, Maria bade another farewell to the world, with 'the last dinner she would share with the family', at which Scott was the only guest. This was not strictly true: All Saints was not a closed order, and Sisters were allowed a weekly home visit. Henceforth, however, Maria was obedient to conventual authority and no longer a free agent with regard to social pleasures or family obligations. Gabriel continued to press her to spend Christmas with them, apparently unable to grasp the meaning of her vows. He grieved 'to think how lonely she will be on Christmas-day without her family'. To Maria, of course, Christmas was a highlight of the whole 'life of intense spiritual joy' she now experienced and she arranged instead to come home at New Year.

As it happened, the Sisterhood was in some turmoil, for Rev. Upton Richards, the order's founding father, had died in June, and his successor Rev. Benson was opposing certain 'Romish' practices, as it appears in order to impose his authority over Mother Harriet. Maria proved a steady and valued member, in due course using her scholarly training to translate the Day Hours of the Roman Breviary, which with some revisions became a standard text for Anglican orders. Sister Caroline Mary Short, novice mistress at the time of Maria's admission, recalled her as 'notable for saintliness', a great example of a true, holy Religious, and 'a thorough Italian', who used to make her confession weekly and had a great gift of tears'.

For Christina, Maria's departure represented the first major change in domestic life for many years, and one that was closely followed by William's change of status. The three siblings who had lived together for twenty adult years were now separated, and it is hard to judge whether Christina felt more fearful or released, as she lost both close companionship and also that inevitable restraint that living with others entails. Where previously Maria's spiritual guidance – on questions of alms-giving, for instance, or Lenten observance – had been daily available, now Christina was responsible for her own decisions. Edmund Gosse (soon to marry young Nellie Epps) recalled Maria as a far stronger character than her sister, 'though of narrower intellect

Maria, Christina and Mamma. Studio photograph
taken around 1855

Studio photograph of Christina,
early 1860s

John Brett self-portrait

Charles Bagot Cayley

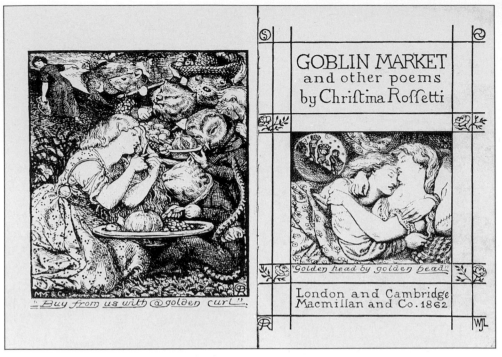

ABOVE Frontispiece and title page of Christina's first collection *Goblin Market*.
Woodcuts by Gabriel Rossetti

BELOW King Arthur and the Weeping Queens. Woodcut by Gabriel Rossetti to illustrate
The Palace of Art in Moxon's edition of Tennyson's *Poems* published 1857. The head of the
second queen from the left is thought to have been drawn from Christina, and the head of
the fourth from left facing viewer from Elizabeth Siddal.

The Rossetti family, 1863,
photographed by C. L. Dodgson
in the garden at Tudor House,
Cheyne Walk

John Everett Millais by William Holman Hunt

Robert Browning by Francis Talfourd

Ford Madox Brown by Gabriel Rossetti

Algernon Swinburne by G. F. Watts

Adelaide Procter by Emma G. Richards

Henrietta Polydore by Gabriel Rossetti

Jean Ingelow studio photograph

Amelia Heimann by
Gabriel Rossetti

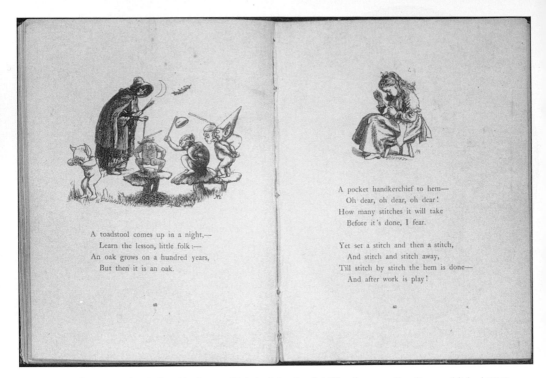

A toadstool comes up in a night,—
Learn the lesson, little folk:—
An oak grows on a hundred years,
But then it is an oak.

A pocket handkerchief to hem—
Oh dear, oh dear, oh dear!
How many stitches it will take
Before it's done, I fear.

Yet set a stitch and then a stitch,
And stitch and stitch away,
Till stitch by stitch the hem is done—
And after work is play!

ABOVE Illustrations by Arthur Hughes to Christina's book of children's verses *Sing-Song*, published 1872

BELOW The Mouth Boy: illustration by Arthur Hughes to Christina's book of children's stories *Speaking Likenesses*, published 1874

hastily shutting her basket, she turned to see who was approaching.

A boy: and close at his heels marched a fat tabby cat, carrying in her mouth a tabby kitten. Or was it a real boy? He had indeed arms, legs, a head, like ordinary people: but his face exhibited only one feature, and that was a wide mouth. He had no eyes; so how he came to know that Maggie and a basket were standing in his way I cannot say: but he did seem somehow aware of the fact; for the mouth, which could doubt-less eat as well as speak, grinned, whined, and accosted her: "Give a morsel to a poor starving beggar."

"I am very sorry," replied Maggie, civilly; and she tried not to stare, because she knew it would be rude to do so, though none the less amazed was she at his aspect; "I am very sorry, but I have nothing I can give you."

"*Nothing*, with all that chocolate!"

"The chocolate is not mine, and I cannot give it you," answered Maggie bravely: yet she felt frightened; for the two stood all alone together in

the forest, and the wide mouth was full of teeth and tusks, and began to grind them.

"Give it me, I say. I tell you I'm starving:" and he snatched at the basket.

RIGHT Christina, 1866. Pencil portrait by Gabriel Rossetti (Private Collection)

BELOW LEFT Maria Rossetti photographed as a member of the All Saints Sisterhood, 1874–5

BELOW RIGHT Christina, 1877. Engraving from chalk drawing by Gabriel Rossetti, used as autograph card in 1880s and 90s

(After the Drawing by DANTE GABRIEL ROSSETTI, by kind permission of W. M. Rossetti, Esq.)

Sincerely yours
Christina G. Rossetti

Christina and her mother, 1877. Chalk drawing by Gabriel Rossetti done in Kent and presented by William Rossetti to the National Portrait Gallery in 1895 (National Portrait Gallery)

Christina's funeral in Highgate Cemetery, January 1895. William Rossetti (wearing skullcap) in front of coffin

and infinitely poorer imagination', and formed the view that her extreme High Church views 'starved the less pietistic, but painfully conscientious nature of Christina', with an influence he likened to that of 'police surveillance exercised by a hard, convinced mind over a softer and more fanciful one'.

Gosse of course had his own painful memories of spiritual surveillance amid the extreme piety of the Plymouth Brethren community in Devon, together with strongly inculcated anti-Catholic views. No one else recognised his as an accurate sketch of Maria, and yet in some degree the perception was acute, for Christina undoubtedly revered and deferred to her sister, whose virtuous example admonished her own failings. In their teenage years Maria had led the way, with her ardent espousal of religion under Pusey and Dodsworth that now culminated in the taking of vows – a saintly step that Christina could never hope to emulate.

Maria's decision was not entirely selfless, however, in the way it affected others, for as well as depriving Mamma of care and companionship in her increasingly infirm old age, it placed the whole of this duty on Christina, who was – or seemed likely to be – herself in need of invalid care. From the outset William had proposed that he and Lucy continue to live with his family. 'Any other course would be out of the question' he told Mamma, adding that Lucy fully and warmly supported this idea. But it meant displacing aunt Eliza, who moved with Charlotte to an apartment a few streets away, in Bloomsbury Square. Always independent, both aunts were now approaching eighty; whose duty would it be to care for them?

We do not know the details of Maria's discussions with her sister, or whether All Saints was sufficiently flexible to prevent outright conflict between religious and family obligations in the case, say, of terminal illness. Christina neither felt nor uttered any complaint, but Maria had effectively left those who loved and needed her. The fact that this was not perceived as such only conceals the unacknowledged cost to Christina, at the same time as she found herself wanting in comparison with her sister's holiness.

So it may have been suppressed grief and resentment that led to an outburst of anger some six days after Maria's departure, directed against Lucy, the person ultimately responsible for the imminent upheaval at Euston Square. She wrote instantly to William to apologise for the 'ebullition of temper' over proposed household arrangements:

My sleeping in the library cannot but have made evident to you how improper a person I am to occupy any room next to a dining-room. My cough ... not to speak of other far worse matters of noise which with a habitual invalid are inevitable makes it unseemly for me to be continually and unavoidably within earshot of Lucy and her guests. *You* I do not mention, so completely have you accommodated yourself to the trying circumstances of my health: but, when a 'love paramount' reigns amongst us, even you may find such toleration an impossibility.

She certainly did not want their dinner guests to hear her coughing or using the commode. With unsisterly stiffness and a certain degree of submerged menace, she went on:

I must tell you that not merely am I labouring under a serious relapse into heart-complaint and consequent throat-enlargement (for which I am again under Sir William Jenner's care) but even that what appeared the source of my first illness has formed again, and may for aught I can warrant once more have serious issues.

Her first illness was the 'peccant chest' that had threatened consumption, now recurring alongside the thyroid disorder. 'The drift of all this,' she continued, was that she and Mamma proposed to leave Euston Square and join the aunts. This was not because Mamma preferred daughter to son, but 'because of my frail state which lays me open to emergencies requiring help from which may you long be exempt'. And she concluded:

Dear William, I should not wonder if you had been feeling this obvious difficulty very uncomfortably, yet out of filial and brotherly goodness had chosen not to start it: if so, I cannot rejoice enough that my perceptions have woken up to some purpose.

I do not know whether any possible modification (compatible with all our interests, and not least with Lucy's) may occur to you as to arrangements; to me, I confess, there scarcely seems any way out of the difficulty short of a separation. Perhaps in a day or two you will let Mamma or me know what you judge best.

Of course Mamma is in grief and anxiety; her tender heart receives all stabs from every side. – If you wonder at my writing instead of speaking, please remember my nerves and other weak points.

Sudden irritability is a side-effect of thyroid disorder, but something also evidently touched a raw emotional nerve, and it is hard not to feel that albeit unconsciously Christina was using ill-health as a weapon against unwelcome changes and especially her own displacement. While William was a bachelor, they had shared near-parity of importance in the household; now she would be a 'superfluous' female relative, and her own needs would necessarily yield to new dispositions. Hence her use of the term 'reigns' in respect of Lucy's arrival and her sense that she was being forced out. Her status was threatened: in response she threatened to leave.

William insisted that they stay. He would continue to provide – his self-image of masculinity was involved here – so living arrangements were altered, and Christina moved to share Mamma's bedroom on the first floor, no longer within earshot of dinner guests. It was only a partly satisfactory solution.

The wedding was scheduled for the end of March. All rooms in the top half of the house were cleared for Lucy and William to decorate and furnish. In the process Maria's residence at Euston Square was effectively erased from the record. It must have been rather like a bereavement, without any allowable grief.

Christina was not drawn to follow Maria's example. 'So you think I once trembled on "The Convent Threshold"? she wrote later to Caroline Gemmer. 'Not seriously ever, tho' I went through a sort of romantic impression on the subject like many young people. No, I feel no drawing in that direction.' She would prefer a hermitage to a nunnery. Hermits and writers, of course, have a good deal in common, in their solitary lifestyles and – in Christina's case – devotional habits. And the two traits came together at this time in her little pocketbook volume of prayers entitled *Annus Domini*. Issued by a religious publisher in April 1874, it reads like a thanksgiving, perhaps the outcome of a sacred obligation self-imposed during her illness. As an impressionable girl, she had been taught that sickness and suffering were sent for her correction, with a holy purpose. While ill, she had been unable to attend church, and therefore dependent on domestic devotions and private prayer, founded on daily Bible reading as an aid to holy meditation. She had also been much prayed-for; indeed, given the relatively ineffectual doctoring, her recovery may have seemed as much the result of prayerful intercession as medical treatment.

The book also marked a new departure, that Christina was able to make only after Maria's departure, when she took over the responsibility of leading daily prayers for the household, and it is possible that compiling such a calendar – in effect a day-book of private devotions – led her to think of publication. Though each entry in *Annus Domini* is short, the selection was based on a sequential reading of the Bible, showing that Christina worked her way steadily through scripture from Genesis to Revelation, choosing texts on which to hook her collects. At the rate of, say, five entries a day, the whole composition would have taken nearly four months; though straightforward, the task was not therefore speedy.

The most frequently selected books were the Psalms, Isaiah, Revelation, Epistle to the Hebrews and the Gospel of St John, and the texts chosen were typically prophetic or symbolic (or one might say poetic) linked to the prayers by homilectic analogy. The 'seven golden candlesticks' of Revelation ii : 1, for example, were accompanied by a prayer comparing the image to the branches of the Holy Catholic Church:

> Make her light shine to Thy Glory throughout all lands, illuminating the darkness of heathendom, rekindling the fire of Thy love in Christendom: and with light give the seeing eye, and with fire bestow final perseverance. Amen.

A large number of the prayers build on a word or image in a frankly meditative and mystical manner, projecting the symbol inward using scriptural phrases as signals of spiritual meaning. And if the language and links were familiar from sermons, they were not therefore routine or shallow; each required reflective thought and understanding.

There are prayers for the conversion of unbelievers, prayers for orphans and widows, for world peace, dead babies, fallen women, convicts and condemned prisoners. There are prayers for the Church and the priesthood; and for patience, humility and diligence in placing one's talents in the service of God. There are prayers for grace 'not to question or cavil at those mysteries which Thou revealest in Thy Word', prayers against rash or uncharitable judgements, and even a prayer for the ugly, which may be read as in part a prayer for her own altered appearance, trusting that all such be nevertheless graced with spiritual beauty.

There are also interesting prayers about scientific knowledge. 'May we be not misled by false science from holding fast those truths which Thou hast revealed' says one. 'Suffer us not to be seduced from the faith by miscalled reason, or apparent facts of science, or wit and learning of misbelievers, or subtleties of Satan. Have compassion on those that err' says another, firmly dismissing the challenge to biblical truth.

Above all, however, there are prayers for contrition and deliverance from sin; for the strength to 'withstand the allurements of the world, the seductions of the flesh and the suggestions of the devil'. O Lord Jesus Christ, Christina pleaded, 'preserve us from the sins of the flesh and of the spirit, wilful or inadvertent, of presumption, habit or surprise, from sins scarlet or crimson ... fill us with awe and shame, us sinners, us foul sinners, us miserable sinners, full of wounds and bruises and putrifying sores...'

Beside Pusey, the chief clerical models were the recently republished devotional works of seventeenth-century divines like Jeremy Taylor,

William Loe and Lancelot Andrewes, of which Andrewes's *Private Devotions*, with prayers for each hour of the week, was perhaps the most familiar. It was also a favourite of Maria's – she gave a copy to Letitia in 1857 – which Christina probably reread during her illness, for her prayers owed much to Andrewes's style:

> Remember what my substance is,
>   dust and ashes,
>   grass and a flower,
>   flesh and a wind that passeth away,
>   corruption and the worm,
>   as a stranger and sojourner upon earth
>   inhabiting a house of clay,
>   whose days are few and evil,
>   to-day and not to-morrow,
>   at morning and not till evening,
>   now and not presently,
>   in a body of death
>   in a world of corruption
>   that lieth in wickedness,
> Remember this.

If not earlier, she had also recently read Donne, whose 'large and keen intellect and fervid poetic sense' William had commended.

Her text was accepted by James Parker & Co on condition (or so one infers) that a practising clergyman be invited to commend its contents. Christina therefore asked her old friend Rev. Burrows to provide a preface, in which he wrote:

> I have had great pleasure in looking over these Prayers as they passed through the Press, for they seem to me valuable in themselves from their fervour, reverence and overflowing charity, and also because they are suggestive of the use which should be made of Holy Scripture in our devotions. Each little Prayer may be considered as the result of a meditation, and as an example of the way in which that exercise should issue in worship.
>
> It will be observed that all the prayers are addressed to the Second Person in the Blessed Trinity, and are therefore intended only to be used as supplementary to other devotions.

This put Christina in her place, doctrinally. But neither in verse nor prose had she ever been able to address God the Father. It was always Christ whom she prayed to, and certainly so throughout *Annus*

Domini – even when an Old Testament text was invoked, with occasionally strange results, as when Christ rather than Jehovah is the figure with whom Jacob prevaileth. Although in keeping with the prophetic nature of the invocation, nevertheless a clear bias against paternal divinity is visible, as Burrows perceived.

His advice that her prayers be not used on their own also contained a warning against independent witness. Piety was to be commended, but in subordination to clerical authority. By not only compiling but also publishing her devotions, Christina was tacitly laying claim – in all due humility – to a genre traditionally the preserve of the priesthood. At this date almost all authors of homiletic literature were members of the clergy, with the dual authority of anointed vocation and masculinity. However pious and orthodox in her beliefs, the poetess Christina Rossetti was here presenting herself publicly as a religious guide, in a manner not frequently found in the Victorian Church.

'I do not see much purpose in the note by Burrows,' wrote Gabriel with his customary acuity, commending the prayers as 'fervent and beautiful' and worthy of wide acceptance. With customary self-disparagement Christina replied, thanking him for 'finding what to say of my book', though disappointed he had said nothing about the single poem it contained.

She pressed a copy on William, as he returned from honeymoon, trusting it would receive a 'fraternal welcome', if not a devotional one. Tactfully, she also cited the good opinion of Dr Littledale, one of the few clergymen William tolerated.

Littledale was a High Church friend of the Scotts and a ritualist colleague of Rev. Shipley until a doctrinal quarrel divided them, who had included a poem of Christina's in his *People's Hymnal* in 1867. He was 'a priest of many parts', according to a church chronicler: 'a brilliant theologian and liturgiologist, a controversialist whose two-edged sword was tempered by wit and charity, and author of many volumes, stories, acrostics. He wrote on souls as well as parchments, as the father-confessor of many who influenced their generation, notably the second bard of the Oxford Movement, Christina Rossetti'. If this was so, it was presumably during her illness that Littledale came to hear Christina's confession and administer the sacrament. He lived in Red Lion Square and was chaplain to the London house of the East Grinstead Anglican Sisterhood, with which Letitia Scott was involved. With his deep-set eyes and long grey beard, he looked like a medieval monk, William recalled, but was also an excellent raconteur, with an Irish brogue and keen sense of humour. Perhaps he encouraged *Annus Domini*, for he was not only himself an energetic author and editor but also a supporter of religious study for women. Women should not be brought up as devout simpletons, he wrote forthrightly;

their subordinate status in the New Testament derived from Roman law not Holy Writ, and the early Church welcomed female learning. Therefore:

> woman as well as man must look up directly to her Creator, for we read of woman, as of man, that she was created in the image of God. Conformity to that image, therefore, not to the blurred and defaced impression of it left still faintly traceable on man's battered soul, is to be her ideal.

At Littledale's request Christina also wrote a poem for 'one entering her novitiate'. Entitled *The Master is Come, and Calleth for thee*, it was for an East Grinstead postulant, but applied equally to Maria.

Christina did not of course expect payment for *Annus Domini*, but she certainly looked upon its publication with the same professional eye as any other book. She had, it seems, no thought of abandoning her career. Indeed, the literary impulse seems to have been so strong that it was almost as hard for her not to write as it was to write to order; the urge was simply too satisfying. And her return to the literary world was marked at the end of 1873 with what she called *A Dirge*, but was typical of the plaintive lyric figure of uncertain feeling she was now so skilled at weaving, with its accomplished assonance, anaphora and falling rhythm. The content was slight, but the polished surface, as so often, covers a depth of mysterious, unexplained emotion in a dialogic movement from question to ostensible answer, creating a lament for transience and mutability whose power lies like a shadowy current somewhere below the sound and sense of the words.

She made her first appearance in a textbook at this date, featuring among the poets represented in the *Student's Treasury of English Song*, edited by W. Davenport Adams and published by Nelson & Sons, with the full texts of *The Bourne*, *Summer*, and *Gone for Ever*, and extracts from *Up-hill*, *On The Convent Threshold* and *Old and New Year Ditties*. Unfortunately the accompanying critical note again identified her as Christina Gabriella, got her birthdate wrong, and devoted most of its space to the achievements of her father and brothers.

But her fame was spreading. A couple of years later, when the young Vincent van Gogh was working in London as schoolteacher and lay preacher, he delivered a sermon on Psalm 19 at the Methodist church in Richmond, ending his address with the first stanza of *Up-hill* – lines he had copied out a year earlier in a letter to his brother Theo. Though he got the words slightly wrong, quoting from memory or maybe translation, it shows what wide currency the poem had attained.

31

Speaking Likenesses

CHRISTINA'S NEXT BOOK was 'a little prose story, such as might I think do for a child's Xmas volume', which she offered to Macmillan at the beginning of February 1874. 'Properly speaking, it consists of 3 short stories in a common framework – but the whole is not long'. It was called *Nowhere*.

For some time she had been contemplating a collection of fairy tales, although as she confessed to Caroline Gemmer a year earlier, these remained as misty as 'the heaps of golden coin they would procure me'. Sadly nothing came of this plan, though occasional references in correspondence to Red Riding Hood and Bluebeard hint at the direction this imaginative return to childhood might have taken. Instead, she wrote her own group of original tales, about eight-year-old Flora and her fictional companions Edith and Maggie, which describe the birthday party that goes horribly wrong, the picnic fire that won't light, and the frightening journey on a winter's night to deliver a basket of Christmas goodies.

Retitled *Speaking Likenesses* for publication, the book is now quite out of favour. It has been described as a 'peculiarly revolting' text for children, savouring more of Isaac Watts or the Brothers Grimm than Lewis Carroll or Hans Andersen. Biographers have been embarrassed by it: Mackenzie Bell in 1898 said it could 'not be ranked high among its author's books', and misrepresented the nature of Flora's nightmare; Mary Sandars in 1930 ignored the book altogether; Georgina Battiscombe in 1980 called it simply an illustrated fairy story, which suggests she had not read it with attention. Lona Packer in 1965 detected the 'demon lover' of William Bell Scott concealed behind the figure of Quills, who raises his spikes like a porcupine, while to Frances Thomas in 1992, Flora's fate seemed 'merely sadistic fantasy'. Even the editor of a modern reprint describes the work as self-defeating, in 'a sad and sometimes bitter parable of a lonely lady'.

It is true that *Speaking Likenesses* is not a charming book. But this is all the more reason for taking it seriously, to discover what impelled Christina to write it.

In the first place, it formed the sequel to *Sing-Song* and *Vanna's Twins*, being written for and about slightly older children, up to the age of Flora and Maggie. It is structured as a sequence of tales within a tale, related by an aunt to five nieces busy with needlework, whose interruptions form part of the narrative, and thereby returned auto-biographically to Christina's childhood, when she herself listened to tales while hemming handkerchiefs. She dedicated the book to her 'Dearest Mother in grateful remembrance of the stories with which she used to entertain her children', but of course the Rossetti young-sters had also been well supplied with aunts, and it is likely that Christina's illness, with its enforced return to childish dependency, together with the impending break-up of the household at Euston Square, prompted the imaginative re-creation of a time when she herself was a small story-demanding niece.

The irascible aunt's fantastic fables are more exemplary than enter-taining – an aspect emphasised by the change of title, for while *No-where* invokes imaginary realms *Speaking Likenesses* points a moral lesson; as Christina explained, her small heroines 'perpetually en-counter "speaking (literally *speaking*) likenesses" or embodiments or caricatures of themselves or their faults'. In this sense little Flora, Maggie and Edith are self-images, whose adventures also embody the story of her own moral life, and the lessons she had learnt. The spinster aunt is also a self-image, however. Once, Christina had looked for-ward to being an aunt to Lizzie and Gabriel's child; now, with the marriage of William and Lucy, she was again in prospect of becoming one.

The stories she had to tell thus had a strong autobiographical ele-ment, as may be guessed from Edith's wandering into the wood, or Flora's position as youngest child and her birthday bliss that turns quarrelsome. As well as drawing on Christina's own experience how-ever they also had literary antecedents, most evidently in the books of her friend Mr Dodgson. Christina's aunt is a literary companion to the avuncular narrator of the *Alice* tales, her sharpness contrasting with his sentimentality towards little girls, though each possesses a similar understanding of how arbitrary the world appears to children. More-over, Christina made direct and deliberate borrowings from Carroll, taking the moving tables and perambulating pictures of Flora's party from the *Looking Glass* world with its live furniture and chesspieces, and placing the dream in which Flora is attacked by Angles, Hooks, Quills and the rest in a looking-glass hall. There is an autocratic Queen very like Carroll's and large parts of both tales take place in woods and forests where figures appear and disappear at whim. Flora's hateful tea party matches that of the Mad Hatter, where the heroine gets nothing to eat, and the voracious Mouth-Boy who demands Mag-gie's chocolate is surely step-brother to Tweedledum and Tweedledee. The comparison need hardly be argued further: writing to Gabriel later in the year Christina described her book as 'a Christmas trifle, would-be in the *Alice* style, with an eye to the market'.

Alice's success had been phenomenal, and many were inspired to emulation, but 'the market' (of which she was no judge) was hardly Christina's main concern. Instead, she entered into a moral dialogue with Carroll, making the unpredictable figures who assail her heroines into tormentors that represent moral failings to be confronted and eventually defeated. The game in which Flora is terrorised harks back to the earlier fantasy assault of the goblins against Lizzie, as

> Quills with every quill erect tilted against her, and needed not a pin: but Angles whose corners almost cut her, Hooks who caught and slit her frock, Slime who slid against her and pressed her, Sticky who rubbed off on her neck and plump bare arms, the scowling Queen and the whole laughing scolding pushing troop, all wielded longest sharpest pins, and all by turns overtook her . . .

Playfulness swiftly changes to pain. In the second 'game' the girls are victims, the boys deploying 'every natural advantage' in such a violent manner that the aunt is obliged to apologise. Well may she do so: because the nature of the game is unspecified, the Freudian nature of the boys' advantage is underlined by their quill or hook or phallic protuberance. Just as the goblins' assault was metaphorically sexual, so here we have something approaching rape, speaking figuratively.

Marooned in her nightmare, Flora is forbidden to taste the alluring treats of childish desire: strawberry tea and festive supper of turkey, lobster, mushrooms, raspberry tart, meringue, champagne, ices, pineapples, greengages and melons – how quickly the list reverts to the fruits Christina always invoked as symbols of tempting cupidity. Once more, goblin baskets are dangled before the girl, and withheld. Then, fantastically, the fruits turn into glass houses that become prisons of fear:

> Picture to yourselves golden twinkling lamps like glowworms down almost on the ground; lamps like illuminated peaches, apples, apricots, plums, hung about with the profusion of a most fruitful orchard. Should we not all have liked to be there with Flora, even if supper was the forfeit?
>
> Ah no, not with Flora: for to her utter dismay she found that she was being built in with the Queen. She was not called upon to build: but gradually the walls rose and rose around her, till they towered above her head; and being all slippery with smoothness, left no hope of her ever being able to clamber over them back into the road home, if indeed there was any longer such a road anywhere outside.

The Birthday Queen is like a tyrant king, in a sort of Bluebeard's castle on which the other characters rain stones and insults. Soon Flora is hysterical with horror. In a 'paroxysm of terror' she sobs 'don't, don't, don't!' As the transparent wall shatters, she wakes.

She is duly chastened, but the punishment is surely out of all proportion to her earlier snappishness. Not surprisingly, readers feel a disturbing element of sadism pervading the tale.

But critics have missed an essential aspect of the book, to which Christina gave the clue in her letter to Macmillan describing the text as three stories in a common framework. Read as a single work, *Speaking Likenesses* is not a harsh, didactic work in the mode of Isaac Watts but a traditional tale in which pain and fear are overcome, as in Hansel and Gretel, or Peter Rabbit. It is a cathartic narrative with a happy ending, in which Christina's heroines learn to withstand monstrous figures and failures – representing 'bad' external or internal forces – in order to defeat them. The third tale, in which Maggie makes her journey through the wild wood, is of course the chapter of resolution, and its moral not only inscribes the rewards of virtue but also the healing power of storytelling itself. For the hateful children who turn play into persecution reappear in the third episode, in which Maggie takes up Flora's role (indeed the village shop kept by Maggie's grandmother is explicitly identified as the source of Flora's sugar plums and Edith's doll; the three girls are soul-sisters). It is now no longer a birthday, when selfish desires are paramount, nor a summer afternoon when picnic pleasures are planned, but a dark winter evening when duty calls – for Maggie is a reluctant though obedient delivery-girl. Her passage through the wood is beset with trials and temptations, and in a green glade she meets a group of joyful jumping children who invite her to play:

'Yes,' she answered eagerly; 'yes, yes; what shall we play at?'

A glutinous-looking girl in pink cotton velvet proposed 'Hunt the Pincushion'.

'No, Self-Help,' bawled a boy clothed in something like a porcupine skin.

'Oh Aunt, are these those monstrous children over again?' the narrator's nieces interrupt. 'Yes, Ella, you really can't expect me not to utilize such a brilliant idea twice' she replies. But the apology is deceptive: the aunt's failure of invention is not her author's (despite the glancing satire on Carroll's reintroduction of March Hare and Mad Hatter as Heigha and Hatta in *Through the Looking Glass*). For this time Sticky, Quills and Co are quickly despatched. Maggie remembers her promise to make haste: 'her fatal promise, as it seemed to her' remarks aunt to her audience; 'though you and I, who have as it were peeped behind the scenes, may well believe that it kept her out of no delightful treat'. So she refuses to play, and continues on her errand, pursued by mocking laughter but safe from harm.

Her second encounter is straight from the Land of Grimm, with the eyeless boy whose mouth is filled with tusks. He is large and strong, and whines for the chocolate in Maggie's basket. But she stands up to the Mouth's demands:

> 'I don't believe you are starving,' cried Maggie, indignantly, for he looked a great deal stouter and sleeker than she herself did; and she darted aside, hugging her basket close as the beggar darted out a lumpish-looking hand to seize it. 'I'm hungry enough myself, but I wouldn't be a thief!' she shouted back at her tormentor, whilst at full speed she fled away from him wondering secretly why he did not give chase, for he looked big enough and strong enough to run her down in a minute: but, after all, when she spoke so resolutely and seemed altogether so determined, it was he that hung his head, shut his mouth and turned to go away again, faster and faster, till he fairly scudded out of sight among the lengthening shadows.

Again, Maggie is safe, having simply said 'No'.

Her third encounter is with a group of sleepers around a warm gipsy fire in the middle of the wintry wood, barely recognisable as the site of young Edith's summer picnic. Maggie longs to stop and rest, but with 'one last desperate effort' she attends to her task, to reach her destination at last. Spitefulness, greed and sloth are thus overcome in turn.

And thus Christina made the three stories into the 'progress' of a young princess – the victory of duty over self-indulgence, another version of the moral tale she spent her life telling. Maggie's staunchness is rewarded, for although the family to whom she delivers the basket offer her no morsel of chocolate or fruit, on the way home her antagonists have vanished, their places taken at each site of encounter by three helpless creatures. Each of course corresponds: the playful puppy to the unplayful children, the mewling kitten to the whining Mouth, the frozen wood-pigeon to the sleepers round the fire. She carries back all three vulnerable creatures to the loving warmth and welcome of her grandmother's house, and the happy, comforting end to the story.

Insofar as the unity of *Speaking Likenesses* has been invisible to readers, Christina's storytelling was defective. Was this because moral fable was only its ostensible purpose? At a deeper level, the tale retraced her own emotional journey, following *Sing-Song* as part of a recuperative process. In its pages childhood suffering and discontent were revisited and vanquished, just as the tired, cold, frightened Maggie of the outward journey or past is comforted by a 'maternal' self on the return, rescuing the kitten, nursing the pigeon in her bosom, and skipping home alongside the puppy. Simultaneously, the 'child within' is cradled and protected by the adult aunt-author – who at the end of the book displays a quite uncharacteristic sentimentality towards dumb creatures.

Flora's nightmare, with its tempting treats and playful games that turn to terror, is thus an unconscious re-telling of some trauma that led to a feeling of being trapped in a glass castle or bubble – an image often used by incest survivors to describe their dissociated emotions. Edith's inability to light the picnic fire when she is lost in the wood suggests the isolation and impotence of the girl no one could help. And it hardly needs a Freudian understanding to see the fat beggar with large mouth and no eyes (Papa said he was going blind) not just as personified greed but as a powerful figure of insistent male sexuality, whose wheedling demands are matched by the 'lumpish-looking hand' like a clammy fin that darts out to snatch Maggie's basket. When denied, he hangs his head and turns away.

In new guise, he is the crunching crocodile who dwindles back to size. He is a goblin, too, threatening and pleading for something the girl is not permitted to give, though she too desires it and is all alone and vulnerable. Thwarted by her courteous but steadfast refusal, Mouth-Boy droops and disappears, to be replaced by a soft, small, mewling creature she can love and cherish. In this story, all phallic figures are defeated.

Thus tamed, adult sexuality loses its power to scare. In real life, the tabby kitten warmed its belly at the fireside fender as it shared the hearthrug with Christina's tired but always affectionate father, and in later life there was always a tabby cat in every house she occupied. And if as conjectured the psychological trauma of her adolescence had a sexual component, causing fear, self-loathing and guilt, the final story in *Speaking Likenesses* was therapeutic, re-creating fear and desire in order to purge their power. In this configuration, the romping children suggest that playful excitement may sometimes turn to terror; the fireside sleepers that drowsiness may lead to danger; and the Mouth that an adult man may behave like a wheedling child, asking for 'food' he does not need and ought not to take.

Ironically, but in another sense truly, Christina described this tale as 'the exciting and veracious history of Maggie'. Perhaps the small brave heroine does what her creator had been unable to do in real life: by saying no to each encounter and particularly to the Boy, she can complete her journey in safety. Her antagonists are rendered impotent, and she is rewarded with an epiphany, as she finally emerges from the forest of darkness and the wintry night sky flushes from horizon to zenith with a rosy glow, while the northern lights came out and lit up each cloud as if it held lightning, and each hill as if it smouldered ready to burst into a volcano. Every oak tree seemed turned to coral, and the road itself to a pavement of dusky cornelian.

Safe and sound in her grandmother's house after this glimpse of paradise, Maggie is warmed and fed with tea and buttered toast before falling securely asleep in her own snug bed. So, it would seem, Christina used her creative gifts to absolve herself of a burden of guilt she had carried for so long.

Christina sent the manuscript to Macmillan because, after a two-year gap in their correspondence she had received a final statement for *Goblin Market*. She thereupon resumed business relations, with unspoken recognition of her mistake in having taken her work elsewhere. Mac replied by return, sending a cheque for fifteen pounds, as if in comparable recognition of his meanness, but which she was obliged to return as unearned. He also offered a new edition of her complete poems in single volume – a 'really gratifying offer', she replied on 4 February, meanwhile forwarding her little story for his consideration.

Macmillan took his time to respond, but in April accepted the story, to her surprise and pleasure. He offered an outright payment of thirty-five pounds, as was standard with illustrated children's books, which she accepted, adding only the supplementary condition that it be issued by 31 December; she did not intend to miss the Christmas market again. She also undertook her own negotiations, without relying on fraternal agents, and stated plainly that she would like Arthur Hughes as illustrator.

Ten days later, she heard that the book was already announced in the *Athenaeum*. 'Funnily enough, I did not know matters were concluded between Mac and me, but now I hope they are,' she wrote to Gabriel. By 15 May, however, all was formally agreed.

The only problem was the title. As Gabriel said, *Nowhere* was 'unlucky' owing to Samuel Butler's irreligious *Erewhon*; and also a stale idea. Macmillan was not taken with *Speaking Likenesses* either. But it had 'met with some approval in my circle,' his author wrote, firmly; very likely he had not pondered the text deeply enough to remark its aptness.

Despite this touch of asperity, relations with Mac were mended. But there were still some problems however, for the title page was amended without her approval, and the list of illustrations included several howlers. The Birthday Queen was called 'the Cross Fairy', as if children's books came interchangeably off the peg, while the encounter with the romping children was described as 'Maggie meets the fairies in the wood'. Whoever compiled the list was slovenly too, in captioning the last picture as Maggie drinking tea and eating buttered toast with Grannie when it clearly showed her dancing along with pigeon, puppy and kitten. 'Gabriel writes me that I ought to beg a *cancel* of the *title-page*,' Christina wrote to Macmillan when finished copies appeared at the end of October. 'Then the *List of Illustrations* treats my subjects as I should not have treated them: the word "fairy" I should altogether have excluded as not appropriate to my story ... What shall we do? Cannot something be done to remedy these oversights and soothe my anxiety?'

It was too late: nothing could be done. She exhibited a new-found serenity however, telling Gabriel simply that she had failed to check the title page and never thought of checking the illustration list. This was her sixth book, and perhaps she now realised that proof errors did not determine readers' responses.

It appeared in time for Christmas, ensuring relatively healthy sales, though perhaps readers expected something altogether more delightfully like *Sing-Song*. Writing to thank Macmillan for her six complimentary copies, Christina added jokingly: 'I only hope the public appetite will not be satisfied with 6 or 60, but crave on for 600 or 6000 at least!' and by January she was genuinely pleased to hear that more than a thousand copies had been sold, for, 'truth to tell, I had feared the reviews might this time have done me a very real injury with the buying public; but, for me, such a sale is certainly not bad'.

In fact, reviewers were more baffled than hostile. The *Athenaeum* noted that the 'fanciful little stories would have been more original if Alice had never been to Wonderland', while the *Academy* more acutely noted that the whole tale gave 'the uncomfortable feeling that a great deal more is meant than appears on the surface, and that every part of it ought to mean something, if only we knew what it was'. This underlines the submerged element of autobiography or Freudian narrative in the text, an interpretation strengthened by the fact that Christina felt no further urge to write for children. *Sing-Song* and *Speaking Likenesses* had served their creative purposes.

By this date there had been more changes at Euston Square. When William and Lucy returned from honeymoon, Christina, Mamma and the aunts stayed on in Eastbourne, to be near Maria and to leave the newly-weds time to settle in. 'To think that you two now have one home and one heart – may they be full of peace, love and happiness,' wrote Christina lovingly to her brother. 'What a year of pleasure this will have been to you, dear Will – or indeed I should rather say of happiness.' Gabriel was upset, however, that his mother and sisters had not come to Kelmscott. 'The weather is divine here now and everything lovely,' he wrote. Was Maggie not allowed to go so far afield as to a brother's roof? 'It would have been so nice to see her here as well.' Christina replied soothingly, adding in passing that their sitting room reminded her of Kelmscott, though her brother would probably loathe the wallpaper. Oddly enough, she herself was producing designs, one of which she submitted to the Morris firm. Her apple trees proved fruitless however, as she reported a month later: 'Mr Morris has written me a truly obliging letter, finding something to praise, but setting up a standard of such complicated artistic perfection as (I fear) no alterations of mine can ever by possibility attain.'

At Euston Square there were still some domestic matters to sort out, including housekeys, linen supplies, cutlery and the mysterious question of William's missing bath: Christina advised the housemaid to look in the lumber room. But the main advantage of the changes was the new-found freedom. 'One thing I thoroughly enjoy,' she told Mrs Gemmer, 'that my Mother and I can now go about just as we please at our own sweet wills, without any consciousness of man resourceless or shirt-buttonless left in the lurch!' Returning to London, they lodged with the aunts in Bloomsbury Square, which had the advantage of proximity to the British Museum, as well as delaying the date at which she and Lucy would have to share the same house. 'I do not suppose we are altogether congenial, but we do very well together,' she went on: 'she is clever in her way, and I think she would (oh vanity!) say as much for me in mine; and her way being art, and mine literature, our fields are all our own.' Truth to tell, one would not have suspected professional rivalry to be uppermost in this relationship; evidently Christina was glad Lucy was not a poet. She even looked forward to the benefits of an enlarged social circle, for Lucy was already quite at her ease as hostess.

But at Kelmscott agitation and paranoia once more gained on Gabriel. He quarrelled and dismissed the servants, and had to be restrained from attacking anglers on the riverbank. By the end of July he was back in Cheyne Walk, as it turned out never to go back to the Manor. In August Morris announced plans to restructure the firm, with himself as sole owner and managing director. Expansion was needed for future profits, but the partners no longer functioned as a team and indeed one might soon be certified insane, with all the problems this would bring to a company with mutual liability. The newly-formed Brown-and-Rossetti clan nevertheless perceived this as a hostile act, and as the restructuring took place all social contact with the Morris and Burne-Jones families virtually ceased. Before this happened, however, Christina had been in correspondence with Jane, who sought a place at the All Saints Hospital on behalf of a young Icelandic woman in need of convalescent care, and it may be surmised that she went along reluctantly with the dissension. As her wallpaper submission to Morris suggests, she felt no hostility on her own account.

In mid-August Lucy suffered a miscarriage in early pregnancy. Soon afterwards she and William accompanied the Browns to Margate, while Nolly was suffering with an infected foot. News between the households dwelt much on ailments, for Mamma had a severe nose bleed which the doctor claimed had averted a fit. The aunts were capable nurses, however, and she was soon well enough to accompany them to Chelsea, in the first week of October, to see Gabriel's new paintings. 'We will arrive in caravan' wrote Christina happily. 'Where in England or its studios is your peer?'

Both families, however, were soon overcome with renewed distress, for Nolly Brown's condition rapidly worsened. 'I even think it possible he may not live till this reaches you,' Christina told Gabriel on 5 November. 'He did survive last night, and this morning Sir W. Jenner and Mr Marshall are making one more effort to save his life, but I know not whether with real hope of success.' He died the same day, of blood poisoning, aged twenty. This year too saw the death of Henrietta Polydore, which though foreseen was a sadness to Christina, who had been closest to her cousin.

She was now financially responsible for her own affairs, and began keeping records of income and expenditure, as well as detailed housekeeping accounts on her mother's behalf. Given her slender means, her own affairs were simple, though she wryly admitted to William at the year's end that even so she could not make them balance. In 1874, her personal income totalled £38. 15. 5d, with most of the money coming from investments bequeathed by aunt Margaret and uncle Philip and apparently managed by the family solicitor or bank. In this first year, for instance, her Russian Bonds, which yielded about £25 in a full year, were exchanged for City of Boston shares, which brought in £40. By comparison, she had £4. 2s. 11d from *Goblin Market* and £2. 5s 2d from Roberts Bros' edition of *Poems*, plus a birthday gift of five pounds from aunt Charlotte; and this virtually concluded Christina's sources of income.

'The fire has died out, it seems; and I know of no bellows potent to revive dead coals. I wish I did,' she had told Macmillan in respect of a new collection, employing again her favourite metaphor. But she was encouraged by the inquiry, and when he raised the subject again early in 1875 she replied with some eagerness, saying 'one nice fattish volume takes my fancy' and lamenting how few new pieces she had to offer. Four days later, she accepted his proposal for 'a general reprint of my verses,' in one volume, writing:

> So soon as I hear from you quite conclusively, I will look up what waifs and strays I can from magazines, and forward them to you: of *never-printed* pieces, I fear I shall scarcely find one or two for use. I shall like to make the arrangement of pieces carefully for myself, and suppose the fresh matter had better be introduced amongst the old, as suits subjects or what not. Of course I like to correct my own proofs, as heretofore: an author's privilege I cling to.

She at once contacted a clerical anthologiser to retrieve a small contribution on the grounds that it was now needed for the new edition and set to work on the arrangement, using proof sheets from the earlier volumes. Soon she informed Macmillan that fusion was under way. Alas, she added, *The Germ* had 'already contributed what it had to contribute, curious old book that it is'; perhaps he had forgotten how few of her poems had been published there.

In the new volume, which was honestly but unexcitingly titled *Goblin Market, The Prince's Progress and Other Poems*, she disposed the contents of her previous collections in new order, intermingled with thirty-seven additional pieces. These were either poems previously published in magazines – and she firmly inserted *The Lowest Room* again, in defiance of Gabriel's veto – or newly-written. Of these the most significant was that on the Franco-Prussian war. Several available items, including the *Echo from Willow-wood* and the whole *Il Rosseggiar* sequence, were omitted, underlining their personal aspect. Some titles were altered, but the most striking change was the deletion of six poems from the earlier volumes, which dealt with sexual themes in what she now considered a coarse manner. Those she excised included *A Triad* with its flushed mistress, *Cousin Kate*, with her bastard son, and *Sister Maude*, cursed for spying on her sister's lover. One can sympathise with some of the other omissions, but the loss of these subtly altered the tone of the whole collection, reducing the racy and vigorous elements that reviewers had praised.

'Here, at last, is my book' she told Macmillan on 16 March. Ten days later she was correcting galleys, and requesting extra sheets so that a uniform edition might be issued in the United States. Final proofs however were not ready until August, when she made an unidentified substitution of 'a short new thing for a correspondingly short old thing'; which may well have been *Confluents*, a gossamer lyric heralding the influence of the new Aestheticism:

As rivers seek the sea,
  Much more deep than they,
So my soul seeks thee
  Far away;
As running rivers moan
On their course alone,
  So I moan
  Left alone . . .

Its goal the river knows,
  Dewdrops find a way,
Sunlight cheers the rose
  In her day:
Shall I, lone sorrow past,
Find thee at last?
  Sorrow past,
  Thee at last?

Walter Pater is almost the last writer one would associate with Christina, but perhaps she had been reading his *Studies in the History of the Renaissance* (1873) with its famous assertion that 'All art constantly aspires towards the condition of music . . . [It] comes to you, proposing frankly to give nothing but the highest quality to your moments as they pass, and simply for those moments' sake.' In her lyric mode, this was precisely Christina's experience.

She wrote from Bristol, where she and Mamma were visiting Maria at the All Saints Home in Clifton, 'comfortably lodged and entertained' apart from the 'austere' absence of carpets. Clifton was rather 'Cheltenhamy', she told William, yet refreshingly full of trees, with the Downs for carriage drives, a zoo for her special delectation and doubly agreeable because Mamma's cousin Mrs Austin was living nearby with her two daughters, and so was Dora Greenwell, on whom Christina paid 'private and personal' visits (as distinct from the formal, card-leaving kind), remarking how large-minded and truly likeable Dora was, though 'far more delapidated than myself, poor thing'. So the two poetesses compared ailments.

When Gabriel saw the new book in November, he had some remarks. The retitling of *Under the Rose* was better but unwieldy; she should have called it simply *Upon the Children*. The first part of the Franco-Prussian poem was 'just a little echoish of the Barrett-Browning style', and there was a 'real taint' of the same 'modern vicious style' in *The Lowest Room*, which he was sorry to see printed, marred as it was in his view by 'what might be called a falsetto muscularity'. He also complained of the witty *Queen of Hearts* and *No*

Thank You, John!, for more or less the same reasons, believing that everything in this particular tone was 'utterly foreign' to her true poetic instincts. And he concluded, as if to reprimand her for not consulting him beforehand,

> If I were you, I would rigidly keep guard on this matter if you write in the future, and ultimately exclude from your writings everything (or almost everything) so tainted. I am sure you will pardon my speaking so frankly.

'The whole subject of youthful poems grows anxious in middle age, or may at some moments appear so,' she replied equably; 'one is so different, and yet so vividly the same.' She was sorry if she had made a mistake in reprinting *The Lowest Room*, but it had after all long ago appeared in *Macmillan's*; and in any case was in her view 'by no means one of the most morbid or most personal of the group'. As regards *John*,

> as no such person existed or exists, I hope my indiscretion may be accounted the less; and *Flora* [*Queen of Hearts*] surely cannot give deep umbrage. The latter I hardly think as open to comment as *My Secret*: but this last is such a favourite with me that please don't retort "nor do I". Further remarks, if any, when we meet.

Yet it was not indiscretion but muscularity that Gabriel found objectionable, and on this aspect she was silent, though more conciliatory when she next wrote, claiming 'after impervious density' to have understood his complaint. She now apologised for reprinting *The Lowest Room*, claiming it had been included mainly for the sake of 'bulk'. But in any case it was done, and could not be mended.

Gabriel conceded defeat but, evidently still smarting, expressed himself in a glancingly scatalogical remark to Theodore Watts, about 'that vile trashy poem "The Lowest Room" I told her was only fit for one room viz, the bog', which she had printed without telling him. 'So now the world will know she *can* write a bad poem.'

This is very curious. Christina assuredly could write a bad poem, but though imperfect *The Lowest Room* is not bad, and certainly not for the reasons adduced by Gabriel. Women's rights and women's suffrage were now insistently on the political agenda, and though its conclusion, with its approbation of female docility and subservience should surely have indicated how far Christina was from endorsing any such feminist cause, yet the articulation of protest at the heart of her poem must have made him uncomfortable. Gabriel was in a position to know how the culture of male supremacy had curtailed the personal ambitions of both his sisters. Looking at Maria and Christina now, twenty years after the poem's composition and forty after his drawings of the Homeric heroes, he may well have felt uneasy with its prophetic stanzas:

> While I? I sat alone and watched;
>   My lot in life, to live alone
> In mine own world of interests,
>   Much felt but little shown . . .
>
> So now in patience I possess
>   My soul year after tedious year,
> Content to take the lowest place,
>   The place assigned me here.

He pursued his attack indirectly, using Gosse. Being essentially a reissue, the book was no sort of publishing event, but in consultation with Gabriel Gosse managed to place a long and flowery notice in the *Examiner*, in which he praised 'the rare genius of Miss Rossetti':

> delicate and yet strong, circumscribed but fathomless, small in scope but perfect within its own limits, the gift of this poet seems in comparison with the sea-like or river-like genius of her most eminent contemporaries to resemble nothing so much as a well of water apart among the woods . . .

He commended the sonnets, regretted the deletions, and attacked *The Lowest Room* as 'a bad imitation of Miss Ingelow', adding gratuitously: 'failure with Miss Rossetti always means complete failure. Either her poem is clear, round and faultless, like a dew-drop, or it is a shapeless passage of fallen thoughts.'
  'Save me from my friends!' Christina replied directly. 'You are certainly up in your subject.' She acknowledged that 'the pen you use for me has always a soft rather than a hard nib', and added:

> As to the lamented early lyrics, I do not suppose myself to be the person least tenderly reminiscent of them; but it at any rate appears to be the commoner fault among verse writers to write what is not worth writing, than to suppress what would merit hearers.

Privately to Gabriel she protested that *The Lowest Room* had been composed well before 'Miss J I misled me anywhither', and restated her personal liking for the poem. She evidently felt that the *Fight over the Body of Homer* had gone on long enough.

32

Public Cause and Private Grief

' WE HAVE A niece!' Christina announced to Gabriel on the birth of Lucy and William's daughter on 20 September 1875. Named Olivia Frances in honour of her grandmother and lamented uncle Nolly, she was not baptised, her parents being unbelievers, though this was a subject on which Mamma as well as Maria and Christina held strong views. They knew better than to intervene, however and in any case still maintained a tactful distance, lodging with the aunts until after Lucy's confinement and moving in early November, at the end of Maria's novitiate, to stay with Gabriel, who had rented a large and gloomy house in Bognor, a sedate resort on the south coast.

The faithful George Hake was in attendance, and Alexa might also be there. 'The presence of good-natured Miss Wilding would be agreeable to us instead of the contrary,' replied Mamma graciously. They found Gabriel occupied with a large painting of Venus Astarte, based on Jane Morris. There had been great gales and a tall elm lay uprooted on the lawn. Mamma had a troublesome cough, and after ten days they returned to London, shortly before Janey and her daughters arrived in Bognor. Christina was asked to send some books, but her first parcel was returned with the information that Mrs Morris took no interest whatsoever in the Royal Family, and had already read both the *Vicar of Wakefield* and Macaulay's *Lays of Ancient Rome*. Fanny Burney was more successful, followed by six volumes of Walpole's Letters. With these, Christina sent news of the death of old Mrs Harrison, whom they had known since 1845. Emily, the youngest daughter, brought the news, saying her mother had worked almost to the last and died peacefully in her armchair. 'The kind old lady whilst I was so ill sent me at different times 2 of her own drawings – wild roses and violets,' Christina added affectionately. The weather was cold and she trusted Gabriel and George were continuing to feed the garden birds. Since the snow set in, Gabriel joked, George had been most attentive to the 'feathered tribe', quite contrary to his usual practice, which was to shoot them.

Gabriel badly wanted his family to come back for Christmas, with Maria but without Lucy's baby. In the end the aunts agreed to go to Bognor, where they joined George Hake's father and brothers. But Maria could not go. On Christmas eve she wrote again, aware her position was difficult for him to understand, 'considering the sacredness of family affections' but trying to explain the 'intense spiritual joy' of her present life. If Gabriel failed to understand her reasoning, it is certain that Christina did.

Christmas dinner was a great failure, as Gabriel wrote after all visitors had departed, for 'George had put all the comfortable chairs on one side of the table backing the fire, and on these the four ladies were deposited with the four gentlemen grimly facing on the opposite side and myself at the top. It looked as if I was going to preach a funeral sermon.' The carving was very slow, so at least two minutes elapsed between each guest receiving their plate. Vegetables and sauces followed after a further delay, and no second helpings were offered. The plum pudding was poor, and the whole meal a mortifying and stupid mess.

It was a sad and rather grotesque end to the year, caused, in Dr Hake's view, by Gabriel's unbalanced state of mind but redeemed by his retrospective gratitude for his mother's good health and spirits. 'Your dear face always brightens things when I look at it,' he told her in mid-January, adding however some gloomy remarks prompted by reading the Life of Benjamin Haydon, the painter who had shot himself in despair, and noting that poor Mary Haydon, whom they used to know, had been the first to enter the studio and find her father's body. Mamma asked if there were any reference to Papa in Haydon's letters, and this glancing memory raised another filial tribute from Gabriel. 'I assure you that your first inculcations on many points are still the standard of criticism with me, and that I am often conscious of being influenced correctly by those early-imbibed and still valuable impressions,' he wrote. It was a sentiment all Frances's children shared.

Some months earlier Christina had tried to interest her brother in the campaign against cruelty to animals, a cause in which she was now active. Did Gabriel take any interest in that 'horror of horrors' – live dissection? she enquired, enclosing a petition form. He duly sent his name, together with some reservations which she addressed in her next letter. 'I used to believe with you that chloroform was so largely used as to do away with the horror of vivisection,' she wrote; 'but a friend has so urged the subject upon me, and has sent me so many printed documents alleging and apparently establishing the contrary, that I have felt impelled to do what little I could to gain help against what (as I now fear) is cruelty of revolting magnitude.' The details alleged were such as to cut to the heart, she added, enclosing a leaflet.

This was almost certainly supplied by Caroline Gemmer, who also kept Christina supplied with copies of the anti-vivisection magazine *Animal World*. The leading figure in the movement was feminist Frances Power Cobbe, author this year of *The Moral Aspects of Vivisection*, as well as numerous articles and pamphlets calling for legislation.

Christina had long been sympathetic, as her concern over French veterinary dissection of live horses in 1863 indicated, and like others she was shocked to learn that British regulations established in 1870 to provide for anaesthesia in animal experimentation were not being implemented. As time passed, Cobbe recalled, 'we were surprised to find that nothing was done to enforce these rules'; moreover, live dissection for teaching was as flourishing as before, and indeed proudly advertised by medical schools. In 1874 anti-vivisectors began pressing for legislation, collecting signatures from influential persons, including Tennyson, Browning, Carlyle and Ruskin, for a parliamentary petition which, with mass meetings and press coverage, was a favoured method of pressure group campaigning.

In February 1875 the *Morning Post* carried a description of vivisection by a former laboratory assistant, who claimed that up to three dogs were sacrificed daily, in the interests of scientific supremacy: 'The saddest sight I ever witnessed was when the dogs were brought up from the cellar to the laboratory for sacrifice,' he wrote:

> When an animal had endured great pain for hours without struggling or giving more than an occasional low whine, instead of letting the poor mangled wretch loose to crawl painfully about the place in reserve for another day's torture, it would receive pity so far that it would be said to have behaved well enough to merit death; and as a reward would be killed at once by breaking up the medulla with a needle, or 'pithing' as this operation is called.

In May an anti-vivisection bill was introduced into the House of Lords, countered by one promoted by experimental physiologists. There followed a parliamentary Commission of Inquiry, and in response Cobbe and her colleagues organised a campaign under the patronage of Lord Shaftesbury, Cardinal Manning, Lord Mount Temple and other eminent names, which in March 1876 sent a deputation to the Home Office.

Christina was thus an early recruit to the ranks of those who circulated leaflets and solicited signatures in this cause. The female culture of formal calls came into its own, as did the habit of regular correspondence with relatives and friends. Defenders of vivisection caricatured their opponents as dessicated old maids, whose emotions were unhinged by spinsterhood and whose minds were ill-informed on the scientific need for animal experiments. Victorian anti-vivisection was indeed strongly supported by women and partly seen as a woman's cause – presumably because animal protection was a logical development of the caring role ascribed to women, extending their traditional responsibilities for the young, the weak and those unable to speak for themselves.

Above all, however, it offered a political role to those who were otherwise disfranchised. Middle-class women were customarily excluded from political life not only because they were voteless but also because parliamentary affairs were held to be an area unsuitable for the female sex. Like war, politics was necessary but not nice, and the 'true woman' did not sully herself with involvement in such matters. Anti-vivisection, however, was largely an extra-parliamentary campaign based not on party or class interest but on moral feeling – a truly disinterested protest against cruelty. It was passionate and clear-cut, and had honourable antecedents in earlier campaigns against child labour, slavery, baby-farming and the like. And if women could not put pressure on their elected representatives, they could and did raise funds and urge the ostracism of their opponents – any eminent medical practitioner who came out publicly for vivisection.

In May 1876, a bill prohibiting live dissection and unanaesthetised experiments was introduced in Parliament, supported by a large public meeting at the Westminster Palace Hotel. But owing to the medical lobby this became law only in a mutilated form that protected vivisectors by licensing them. 'The world has never seemed to me quite the same since that dreadful time,' wrote Cobbe. 'My hopes had been raised so high to be dashed so low as even to make me fear that I had done harm instead of good, and brought fresh danger to the hapless brutes for whose sake, as I realised more and more their agonies, I would have gladly died.'

The campaign for total prohibition continued, and though largely unsuccessful kept the issue on the political agenda until the end of the century. As Christina's correspondence shows, she remained committed to the cause for the rest of her life, on one occasion alerting Ellen Heaton to a forthcoming AV event in Brighton, for instance (in exchange for Ellen's petition on the protection of Thirlmere in the Lake District, illustrating how animal rights and environmental protection shared an affinity in this extra-parliamentary political field) and on another, having 'nothing else to contribute' she sent a dozen autographed copies of a specially-composed poem for an AV bazaar. Later she wrote a moving elegy after reading a newspaper report of a mistreated dancing bear. Suffering animals always claimed her sympathy.

Her standpoint was always moral, or ecclesiastical, and stories were told of her scrupulous interrogation of would-be petitioners, for as her fame increased, so her name acquired added value to campaigners. Collecting influential signatures against the proposed destruction of part of the New Forest, for example, Edmund Gosse was promised Swinburne's if Christina also signed. So Gosse asked her and reported:

at last she was so far persuaded of the innocence of the protest that she wrote *Chr*, and then stopped, dropped the pen and said very earnestly: 'are you sure they do not propose to build churches on the land?' After some long time I succeeded in convincing her that such a scheme was not thought of, and she proceeded to write *istina G. Ros*, before stopping again. 'No schoolhouses?' she asked, fluctuating with tremulous scruple.

Finally, she was convinced, and Gosse bore away her full signature. She had no difficulty, it may be noted, in supporting the campaign of Morris and the SPAB to preserve St Clement Danes church in the Strand.

She continued to see Mr Cayley, meeting him in the British Museum and when he made up a four for whist with herself, Mamma and aunt Eliza. He was now living in South Crescent, a short walk from Bloomsbury Square, where Christina and Mamma were frequently installed with the aunts. Early in 1876 he was responsible for getting Christina, William and Maria to contribute to a collection of translations of the late Latin poem called *Hadrian's Death Song*, but in most respects the friendship settled down into a conventional groove. Christina's affections now turned more and more in Mamma's direction, as if to compensate her for the loss of Maria and William. In January 1875 she wrote fervently to Caroline Gemmer of her conviction that 'Mothers – or shall I use large words? and say the Maternal Type is to me one of the dear and beautiful things which on earth help towards realising that Archetype which is beyond all conception dear and beautiful' – an emblem of divine love 'patient, forgiving, all-outlasting'. Three weeks after Gabriel's endorsement of Mamma's 'first inculcations', she presented her own affirmation in a poem:

> Fairer than younger beauties, more beloved
>   Than many a wife,
> By stress of Time's vicissitudes unmoved
>   From settled calm of life;
>
> Endearing rectitude to those who watch
>   the verdict of your face,
> Raising and making gracious those who catch
>   A semblance of your grace;
>
> With kindly lips of welcome, and with pleased
>   Propitious eyes benign,
> Accept a kiss of homage from your least
>   Last Valentine.

The occasion was Frances Rossetti's chance remark that she had never received a valentine. She was seventy-five years old and it was nearly thirty-four years since Christina's first poem, so carefully copied out on her 'natal day' in April 1842, with its wish for long life and happiness.

By casting herself – at the age of forty-five – as her mother's 'least last valentine', Christina was returning to her role as youngest child, now that she was the last one left at home. She was also, less happily, standing in the role of sweetheart, praising Frances's beauty and offering a kiss in place of those not received in the past. Later she told William that she felt their mother's life had not been happy, and though no member of the family, least of all Frances herself, referred to the dark years around 1845, it is as if, thirty years later Christina still wished to console Mamma for the troubles she had borne, and continued to bear, now that Gabriel was similarly afflicted. Once again, the two women were required to comfort and cheer the family member by whom, according to custom, they themselves should have been cared and protected. By tradition and practice in many Victorian households, wife, widowed mother and sister were dependent relatives; with both Papa and Gabriel the emotional roles were reversed.

Christina now had every prospect of spending the rest of her active life caring for mother and aunts, all comparatively fit and likely to survive until she herself, less physically robust, was nearing sixty. She embraced the responsibility willingly, devoting herself to ensuring their comfort and never regretting the fact that her own social life was thereby restricted; indeed she correctly blamed such constraints on her own illness rather than their needs, for neither Mamma nor aunts wished to be a hindrance. At some level, no doubt, she felt resentment, but it was nowhere visible, and to all intents and purposes Christina accepted and even enjoyed her necessary and valued role as caring niece and daughter.

This became more overt in the middle of 1876 when the combined household at Euston Square split up. Christina, whose 'ebullition of temper' in 1873 was a forewarning, had never been sanguine about the possibility of domestic harmony when Lucy reigned as 'love paramount', and since the marriage smooth relations had been maintained by means of long absences. But the inherent strains were not easy to overcome. Christina has been blamed, but the fault lay neither wholly nor even largely on her side. For one thing, it was William who insisted on his mother and sister continuing to live in what had long been regarded as 'his' house, instead of allowing them to join the aunts. However, he was at work all day and not subject to the domestic friction inevitably felt when three women and their servants shared a home. Now there was also a baby and nursemaid, and by midsummer

Lucy was again pregnant. Christina was more or less obliged to put her mother's needs first, and Lucy naturally did the same with little Olivia's. Nor was she the biddable girl she had been when Maria had been her teacher. Extremely sociable, for some unexplained reason she 'viewed with disfavour' several of the Rossettis' oldest friends, including Allingham, Woolner and Amelia Heimann, who, like Christina's clerical visitors, were not made welcome at Euston Square. Instead, Lucy cultivated new friends, particularly persons of intellectual and political eminence. William enjoyed the increased acquaintance, listing many names in his memoirs and dwelling especially on the Robinson family, first known in 1876, through whom he met leaders of the Irish Nationalist movement.

All this might not have mattered, except that it was not always possible to avoid each others' visitors, especially as women were accustomed to pay daytime calls without prior invitation. Lucy's daughter Helen later attributed the break-up of the household to an unfortunate visit from Holman Hunt's second wife, Edith, whose marriage, being a deceased wife's sister, was not regarded as legal by the narrow English law of the day, when

> Edith – surely the soul of all propriety – was shown into the drawing room where Christina and her mother were also at the moment. On Mrs Holman Hunt being announced by the maid, Christina got up and walked out of the room without greeting her. My poor mother – who was expecting a baby at the moment – was naturally very greatly upset and the baby consequently went awry.

'I would only add that Lucy Rossetti had the greatest admiration for her sister-in-law's genius,' continued Helen in allusion to other allegations of dispute between the two. 'The notion that she put up counterclaims as a writer is nonsense. She may not have found Christina an easy housemate but she never wavered in admiration of her genius.'

But the anecdote is puzzling. Edith Waugh married Holman Hunt (in Switzerland) in November 1875 and travelled thence with him to Jerusalem, only returning to Britain in the spring of 1878, well after the house-sharing at Euston Square was given up. She can therefore have been announced in the drawing room as 'Mrs Holman Hunt' in Christina's presence only at a later date. Maybe this was the case, and Christina felt immediately obliged to leave the house, for her principles made it difficult to accept a marriage that was explicitly forbidden by her Church; she could only remain loyal to her faith by being offensive to both Edith and Lucy. Whether such an incident could cause Lucy to miscarry is another question. It was evidently felt that the events were connected, which perhaps suggests that the contretemps occurred early in the house-sharing period, during the summer of 1874, when Lucy is known to have lost a baby. At this point, Edith had announced her intention of marrying Hunt, and was as a result estranged from her family and ostracised by friends. If at this time she called on Lucy she may well have received a frosty reception from Christina, though one suspects that in either case Christina's aim was to avoid direct confrontation.

She and Mamma took extreme care never to encroach, in William's words, on 'the rightful rule that the wife is mistress of the house'; yet however hard they tried they could not meet her approval, nor she theirs. Underlying everything was their dismay at Lucy's lack of religion. For, as her husband continued,

> It was obviously a great grief to my relatives to find that Lucy, to whom they had been looking as a possible corrective of my heterodox opinions, was just as far from orthodoxy as myself. Not that they either badgered or slighted her upon this account; but the feeling existed on their side, and on the other cognizance of the feeling.

The most grievous aspect of this, from Christina's viewpoint, was the refusal to bring children up in the Christian faith, without Lenten or sabbath observance. The decision to separate households was therefore inevitable. The initiative seems to have come from Frances: writing to inform Gabriel on 18 July, Christina described herself as partly ignorant of the plans. 'On the whole, I suppose it may be best to regroup ourselves, and of course we part friends,' she said; 'but I am evidently displeasing to Lucy, and, could we exchange personalities, I have no doubt I should then feel with her feelings.'

Reluctantly, William agreed, and Christina, with a humility that must have been additionally annoying, wrote to Lucy to ask forgiveness:

> I hope, when two roofs shelter us and when faults which I regret are no longer your daily trial, that we may regain some of that liking which we had as friends, and which I should wish to be only the more tender and warm now that we are sisters. Don't, please, despair of my doing better.

They moved at Michaelmas, on the ending of the aunts' lease at Bloomsbury Square, finding a new residence at 30 Torrington Square, halfway between Euston Square and the Museum. William's assistance with the rent was declined; the resources of the four women were sufficient for the modest lifestyle they preferred.

But the move was overshadowed by Maria's sudden and unexpected decline. The first symptoms became visible towards the end of July, when she was sent to Eastbourne, where Christina and Mamma watched with growing alarm as her strength waned. In September, she was brought back to London, but she had cancer and the sad outcome was chronicled in family letters:

SEPTEMBER
Christina to Gabriel,
Mamma and I saw her this afternoon, and at the first moment were very painfully impressed by her exhausted condition; but she rallied somewhat as we sat with her and was most heartily glad to see us . . .

William to Lucy,
Fox is to see Maria on Monday; and on Tuesday he wishes to return with his most trusted surgeon, who will perform an operation . . . Of course we are all considerably dejected about this painful state of things: that the case is a truly serious one is not at all disguised . . .

Christina to Gabriel,
She is so very good and patient that we need only regret her state for our own sakes, not for hers. Mamma and I are going continually to and fro to sit with her.

William to Lucy,
The news of Maria today is not at all good. Yesterday she was put under chloroform and the Doctors made the requisite examination: they say there is certainly a tumour . . .

Christina to Gabriel,
We were able to stay with her perhaps a quarter of an hour yesterday, she was talking feebly . . . The All Saints Mother, talking to Aunt Charlotte, intimated (as I understand) quite clearly her hopelessness of recovery . . . Surely through the darkness God compasses her around.

OCTOBER
Christina to William,
There is no great change from day to day in our dear Maria, but all I believe tends in the direction we dread. If I do not write again very soon, please conclude that it is because her condition does not vary very appreciably.

Christina to William,
I make haste to assure you that dear Maria went happily through the second operation this morning, and has experienced great consequent relief. Today she must be kept extremely quiet: tomorrow our Mother and I hope to see her in the afternoon.

Christina to William,

That Maria enjoys seeing you is quite certain, and the only uncertainty is whether at a given moment she could indulge herself so far . . .

NOVEMBER

Gabriel to Mamma,

It is terrible indeed to think of that bright mind and those ardently acquired stores of knowledge now prisoned in so frail and perishing a frame. How sweet and true a life, and how pure a death, hopeful and confiding in every last instant! Her expression to me as to the relation she now felt herself to bear to her Lord, and her certainty of seeing him in person, were things hardly to be counted as intercourse with a soul still on earth . . .

Christina to Gabriel,

You see my black edge. This afternoon (at between half past 1 and a quarter to 2, about) our dear Maria died peacefully. Part of the morning she suffered a good deal of distress, and her mind seemed to wander: but before quite the end she was quiet, with no more sign of suffering than must go with such a transition . . .

William to Gabriel,

Letter written to me yesterday by Christina says 'At 9 the funeral service will commence in the Sisters' Private Chapel at the back of the Home . . . All of us who desire to go (of us relatives, I mean) are quite welcome. Any flowers brought will be available . . .'

Maria had hoped her approaching funeral would not be in the gloomy, old-fashioned 'hood and hatband' style:

'Why make everything as hopeless-looking as possible?' she argued.

And, at a moment which was sad only for us who lost her, all turned out in harmony with her holy hope and joy.

Flowers covered her, loving mourners followed her, hymns were sung at her grave, the November day brightened and the sun (I vividly remember) made a miniature rainbow in my eyelashes. . . .

The untimely death of such an 'irreplaceable sister and friend' was however all the more grievous for being so unexpected; until it happened, William told Anne Gilchrist, they had no reason to suppose Maria unlikely to live out an ordinary term of life.

The depleted family gathered at Christmas as Lucy's guests, hardly more cheerful than at Bognor. Gabriel was again deteriorating, having had false walls inserted in his studio, convinced the neighbours were spying on him. He used an alarming amount of chloral in pursuit of rest, and became so quarrelsome that he even dismissed the faithful George Hake, to the family's dismay. 'I am sure you have had to bear and have good humouredly borne, a great deal of unpleasant and capricious demeanour on his part,' wrote William to George. 'For all this please accept the apologies of myself and I might say all the rest of my family.'

Endeavouring to cheer her brother, Christina sent him a new poem, which she thought amongst her best. 'If I remember the mood in which I wrote it, it is something of a "genuine lyric cry" – and such I will back against all skilled labour,' she wrote on 1 January, underlining her belief that good poems were written without laborious effort. The poem was perhaps an elegy for Maria, entitled *A Life's Parallels*:

> Never on this side of the grave again,
>   On this side of the river,
> On this side of the garner or grain,
>   Never –
>
> Ever while time flows on and on and on,
>   That narrow noiseless river,
> Ever while corn bows heavy-headed, wan,
>   Ever –
>
> Never despairing, often fainting, rueing,
>   But looking back, ah never!
> Faint yet pursuing, faint yet still pursuing
>   Ever.

Grief filled other poems of this period, including *Death-Watches*, with its 'funeral moon lit in heaven's hollow', which was an appropriate symbol for her 'moony' sister, and the more self-referential lament *Soeur Louise de la Miséricorde*.

The same feeling was poured into another poetic valediction, a long sequence of mourning images called *Mirrors of Life and Death*:

> As Waters that drop and drop,
> Weariness without end,
> That drop and never stop,
> Wear that nothing can mend,
> Till one day they drop –
> Stop –

> And there's an end,
> And matters mend . . .
>
> As Wind with a sob and sigh
> To which there comes no reply
> But a rustle and shiver
> From rushes of the river;
> As Wind with a desolate moan,
> Moaning on alone . . .

'Happily in proportion as earthly hope dies out heavenly hope glows and kindles, so evident is the Grace of God in our dear Maria's patience and loving conformity to the Divine Will,' she had written to one of Maria's friends in the last weeks of her sister's life. She endeavoured to add the same ultimate hope to her poem, but grief overshadowed all religious optimism.

Gabriel suggested *Mirrors of Life and Death* be sent to the *Athenaeum*, though he also proposed some amendments and cuts, objecting to two stanzas about a mouse and a mole, which he thought inappropriate to a lament. Christina demurred, making some changes but saying she could not wean herself of the furry pair and defending her odd account of the mole grubbing underground, 'feeling no bias of fur' by explaining that like velvet moleskin has no nap. 'Now my little piece satisfies myself,' she wrote firmly to avoid further tampering, 'and I shall be very glad if it goes under your auspices to the *Athenaeum*, though I would have spared you further trouble by acting for myself now I am old enough and tough enough'; at the worst, a rejection would not be her first. The poem was printed on 17 March, exactly a month after what would have been Maria's fiftieth birthday.

She took the mole and mouse indirectly from Charles Cayley, whose own sorrow and sympathy was comforting, though sometimes quaintly expressed. With New Year greetings from Hastings, where his mother and sisters were now permanently resident, he sent a pickled creature known locally as a sea-mouse, an iridescent marine worm also called *aphrodite aculeata*. Christina thanked him with a little poem, ending:

> Venus-cum-Iris Mouse
> From shifting tides set safe apart,
> In no mere bottle, in my heart
> Keep house.

In February 1877, Lucy and William had a second child, Gabriel Arthur, born on the same day as his paternal grandfather and destined,

in the eyes of the family, to carry on the Rossetti name. It was a burden
he would carefully evade as he grew older, choosing instead to train
as an electrical engineer. 'A Rossetti addicted to science seems an
oddity,' William wrote when his son was twenty, adding a comment
which shows how strongly the parental desire for 'name and fame'
had been absorbed by all: 'but I would much rather he did something
in science than nothing or little of any serious account in art or
literature'.

Less than a year after their vigil at Maria's bedside, Christina and
her mother were urgently summoned to Chelsea, where Gabriel's
chloral dependency was up to a dangerous level. According to the
doctors, as 'an absolutely essential step' he was to be forced to leave
London and take exercise. He wanted them to join him, so as Christina
told William 'once more all *our* plans are altered, and we are now
ready at any moment to precede, accompany, or follow him as the case
may be.' Returning from holiday, William had a serious talk with his
brother, urging him to rouse himself. Gabriel asserted that it was
impossible to leave the house, as he was continually harrassed and
insulted outside. Brother, mother and sister then took turns to visit the
invalid in a vain attempt to raise his spirits, though one day Christina
managed to get him to play chess. Dr Marshall held an anxious
conversation with Mamma, plainly telling them that Gabriel would
not survive if nothing was done, and two days later, 'by a great effort'
he was persuaded to leave Cheyne Walk for Herne Bay in Kent, where
he was eventually lodged in a secluded farmhouse. On 24 August,
Christina and Mamma joined him and the professional nurse Mrs
Mitchell, ready to stay as long as need be.

'His depression is very painful,' she reported a fortnight later:

> though sometimes a shadow of the old fun breaks out and lights up all the
> moment. Yet some positive advance seems to have been made if we look
> back a few weeks. The rooms are no longer kept in semi-darkness, he does
> not now sit in that attitude of dreadful dejection with drooping head, he
> perspires less and, if I am not mistaken, the pains in his limbs have
> lessened. He looks stout, his complexion is florid; only his eyes have a
> peculiar appearance which cannot, I fear, be favourable . . .

In the evenings they played whist and as a respite from the sickroom
she and Mamma went out for regular drives. For a week or two they
welcomed the company of Frederick Shields, a Manchester-born artist
whose faith as well as friendship commended him. 'It is balm to my
Mother and me to hear a man of genius who is also a Christian, who
speaks of the personages and facts of the Bible *as* of personages and
facts, and who brings love and devotion to his work for the glory of

God,' Christina wrote to Shields in December. 'Pray do not think me overbold in expressing myself, but you well know how many men of genius speak and think otherwise.'

After Shields left, Theodore Watts arrived. He later recalled taking walks with Christina, conversing upon poetry, though this may have been exaggerated, for he also confessed that though 'the verse of any poet or poem that she enjoyed above the others were always, you may be sure, the best', nevertheless 'she never attempted to say a word as to why she thought them the best'. Watts was a gossip: perhaps Christina suspected any inadvertent opinions would swiftly make their way into print. In any case most of their talk concerned Gabriel, whose maladies Watts thought partly imaginary. Many anxious discussions were held as to the best means of grappling with his delusion that he could no longer paint or draw, before an accident disclosed lines on which they could work. They were talking of W. B. Scott's sudden hair-loss when Watts said 'Sketch Scotus's bald pate for us'. Gabriel drew a rapid and perfect image. 'Of course we made no comment upon the fact of his powers of work being suddenly restored,' commented Watts,

> but the next day Christina was seized by a burning desire to have her portrait drawn in chalk. Simultaneously Mrs Rossetti was seized by a burning desire to possess a portrait of Christina in chalk. When Rossetti declared that he could not even hold a piece of chalk, Scotus's bald pate was pointed to. The result of the little plot was a very successful chalk portrait group, of Christina and her mother ... followed by another portrait of Christina, then by a portrait of Mrs Rossetti and then another of Christina.

At last there was a visible symptom of recovery, though the results convey the gauntness of Gabriel's mood as much as his sister's appearance.

Watts talked to Christina about Nature, too, which he believed to be sentient. Did that, she replied teasingly, explain the disgraceful state of the garden at Cheyne Walk, where he could not bear to see the weeds cut, even when Gabriel spoke of getting a gardener? What about the cultivated flowers who were choked to death, she asked:

> 'To you, I suppose, a beautiful flower garden is as uninteresting as a flower in wax or in Morris's wallpapers, compared to one of your beloved weeds?'
> 'Not so entirely', I said, 'and yet ... it recalled to my mind those unhappy victims of Chinese cruelty, those children who are imprisoned from their infancy in some fantastic mould, such as a vase, and compelled to grow into its shape'.

'A new horror for my imagination', said Christina; 'don't tell Gabriel of such a thing. It will keep him awake.'

Amid such subjects, she disclosed as she had done to Matilda Edwards that she had never seen the sun rise. Watts was veteran of many dawns on Wimbledon Common and accordingly one morning they rose and went out just as the chilly breeze rose and the eastern sky began to grow pale:

> Christina was not much interested at first, but when the grey became slowly changed to a kind of apple green crossed by bars of lilac and then by bars of pink and gold, and finally when the sun rose behind a tall clump of slender elms so close together that they looked like one enormous tree, whose foliage was sufficiently thin for the sunbeams to pour through it as through a glittering lacework of dewy leaves, she confessed that no sunset could surpass it.
>
> And when the sun, growing brighter still and falling upon the silver sheet of mist in which the cows were lying, turned it into a sheet of gold and made each brown patch on each cow's coat gleam like burnished copper, then she admitted that a sunrise surpassed a sunset. She stood and looked at it, and her lips moved, but in a whisper I could not hear.

According to Watts, Christina's 'ever-present apprehension of the *noumenon* underlying the phenomenon' dimmed her eyes for more objective observation of the natural world. This high Romantic approach, espoused by Shelley and eloquently articulated by Ruskin, had latterly become debased into a sort of generalised nature-worship, which frequently substituted for the loss of transcendental religion, as it seems to have done for Watts. For Christina, of course, it was part of her fundamental faith that all creation had a divine purpose, but their conversations fed into poetry at this mournful season, and on 11 October Christina informed William that the obliging Mr Watts had just forwarded her latest piece to the *Athenaeum*.

This was *An October Garden*, published the following week, invoking the faded roses and asters of their present lodging. Her own flower emblem was the subject of the accompanying *Summer is Ended*:

> To think that this meaningless thing was ever a rose,
>   Scentless, colourless, *this!*
> Will it ever be thus (who knows?)
>   Thus with our bliss,
> If we wait till the close?

Following these came a sad sonnet, inspired partly by Watts's view of sentient nature, and the pathetic fallacy that human moods are shared by the natural world, but mainly by Gabriel's sad condition, isolated and self-chained by his own fears:

> The irresponsive silence of the land,
>   The irresponsive sounding of the sea,
>   Speak both one message of one sense to me: –
> Aloof, aloof, we stand aloof, so stand
> Thou too aloof bound with the flawless band
>   Of inner solitude; we bind not thee;
>   But who from thy self-chain shall set thee free?
> What heart shall touch thy heart? what hand thy hand? –

She felt grievously about Gabriel's lack of faith, believing that his troubles would be assuaged if not cured by return to the Church. And indeed Gabriel was desperate enough to agree, except that nothing could reach his despair.

From this dismal period, too, came a major poem of spiritual despair, entitled *An Old World Thicket*, a symbolic narrative whose exact date of composition is not known but into which Christina bound both her experience of the sunrise and the idea of sentient nature, as well as her dual inheritance, for it begins with Dante and ends with Abraham (as the title suggests) and the typological promise of Christ as Redeemer.

In the opening stanzas, a dawn chorus of birds who 'seemed to speak more wisdom than we speak' serves to contrast natural joy with personal sorrow:

> Sweetness of beauty moved me to despair,
>   Stung me to anger by its mere content,
>   Made me all lonely on that way I went,
>   Piled care upon my care,
>   Brimmed full my cup and stripped me empty and bare:
>
> For all that was showed what all was not
>   But gave clear proof of what might never be . . .

Closing her eyes to nature, the poet hears the birds fall silent and the waters of the world weep in harmony with her mood. Her heart then rises rebelliously, full of anger and despair:

> Ingathering wrath and gloom,
> Ingathering wrath to wrath and night to night.

Ah me, the bitterness of such revolt,
   All impotent, all hateful, and all hate,
That kicks and breaks itself against the bolt
   Of an imprisoning fate,
And vainly shakes, and cannot shake the gate.

Agony to agony, deep called to deep,
   Out of the deep I called of my desire;
   My strength was weakness and my heart was ire;
   Mine eyes that would not weep
Or sleep, scaled height and depth, and could not sleep . . .

In this dark night, her soul is gnawed by grief, passing back from desolation to rage and self-pity, and finding a mournful echo in the sounds of nature. Then, at last, comes a vision of hope, as a sunset glow fills the forest:

   Each twig was tipped with gold, each leaf was edged
      And veined with gold from the gold-flooded west;
   Each mother-bird and mate-bird, and unfledged
         Nestling, and curious nest
      Displayed a gilded moss or beak or breast.

Filing peacefully between the trees she sees a home-bound flock of sheep, the sun full in their faces, led by a patriarchal ram. As Christ's flock, they amble peaceably towards the sunlit land that stands for heaven.

   In this poem Christina included many of her favourite images, but also significantly reversed the nightmare vision of that much earlier dream in which sheep and goats featured as fearsomely depraved. Using nature in a frankly symbolic manner, she described a movement from natural joy through suffering and sorrow to Christian resignation as a journey of spiritual healing achieved through the poetic rendering of a mystical vision. It was and is an important poem in her life story, being at once a meditation on mourning and an affirmation against desolation, offering hope but no certainty. Written around the same time as Hopkins's *Wreck of the Deutschland*, which has a comparably epiphanic ending, *An Old World Thicket* reveals how sorely Christina's faith was tried by sorrow, and how keenly she needed affirmation.

   Her own near-fatal illness, followed so soon by Maria's death, led her to a revaluation of her life and its more purposeful consecration to Christ. Hitherto her main objectives had been poetic; now they were primarily pious. The distinction may be delicate, insofar as much of her verse was always religious, but the shift was important as she strove to place all her gifts in the service of her faith, for general as well as personal ends – her grains of sand in the balance. Henceforth, her literary career gained a new dimension from her religious writing, a development which may be loosely compared with that of John Donne. Out of suffering, Christina sought to create a new role for herself that was both private and public.

33

Equal in Christ

CHRISTINA'S DEVOTIONAL WRITINGS have never attracted the study they deserve in relation to their importance in her life, just as her last two decades have received scant attention from biographers content to describe her as an invalid and recluse who seldom moved further than the short distance between home and church. But this modern impatience with her doctrinal beliefs has ignored her engagement with the world through devotional writing and in doing so missed the emotional struggle with private and public grief that was played out in her work as well as her life, once Maria was dead and Gabriel's malady incurable. Even as Maria was dying, Christina completed a new book, which she sent to Macmillan, in the hope that she would be able to offer the dedication to her sister. It was, she explained, 'a sort of devotional reading-book for the red-letter Saints' Days, which is of course longing to see the light' and which she had called *Young Plants and Polished Corners*. If it were accepted she would ask Mr Burrows for a foreword.

A more ambitious devotional project than *Annus Domini*, this derived from the idea of making each saint's day the basis for contemplative thought in a sequence of scriptural and meditative passages. To each 'red letter' day of the Anglican calendar – the feasts of the nineteen Gospel saints, Michael and All Angels, Holy Innocents, All Saints and the Presentation and Annunciation, the only two feasts of the Virgin celebrated in the English Church – she added seven subsections, consisting of a biographical continuation of each saint's story beyond scripture (excluding relics and miracles); a prayer for an appropriate grace; a complex 'memorial' linking episodes of the saint's life with analogical passages from elsewhere in the Bible and a parallel text taken from the Psalms, re-arranged to echo the saint's narrative; an account of the saint's Emblem (for the Evangelists) or precious Stone (for the Apostles); and finally a description of a common wild flower appropriate both to season and saint.

Taking her title from Psalm 144: 'that our sons may grow up as young plants: and that our daughters may be as the polished corners of the temple', she aimed the book at young people. Its origin lay in her own meditations during church services – with whose offices she was now so familiar that it was perhaps hard to keep the mind from straying – where she had noted that the phrases of each prescribed

Psalm might be reordered to relate, literally or symbolically, to the saint's life being celebrated. Thereby, anecdotal or analogical correspondences could be unravelled for purposes of holy contemplation.

Much diligent research and theological reading went into the project. There survives, for example, a note from Maria quoting J. M. Neale on the Carmelite scholar Ayguan with medieval references to chalcedony, one of the semi-mythical stones cited in Revelation. Throughout Christina followed orthodox teaching, except that where scriptural authority was lacking, she invented her own systems, choosing for instance to link the saints to the apocalyptic gemstones in the same order as their place in the Church calendar. Thus, St Andrew – first saint of the Christian year because the first Apostle, whose feastday falls on 30 November – was allocated jasper, while SS. Simon and Jude (28 October, the end of the Church year) were given jacinth and amethyst.

The flower sections were even more wholly her own idea, having no biblical precedent and indeed being chosen exclusively from British wild flowers such as daisy, cowslip, honeysuckle, holly, groundsel, bracken, grass and chickweed. This was based on personal choice, as she explained in her preface, but also drew on secular examples such as the 'language of flowers' so popular in the Victorian age, or the schoolroom staples of general knowledge: 'flowers of Britain', 'rivers of Europe', 'animals of Africa', 'gemstones of the world'.

As with the gemstones, the botanical elements serve only as the beginning of holy meditation. Thus, for example, the scarlet pimpernel, chosen for St Matthew, whose blossom opens or closes in accordance with the promise or threat of the atmosphere, thus earning for it the pretty homely name of Shepherd's or Poor Man's Weatherglass:

> The scarlet pimpernel grows freely in the valley of the Nile, and perhaps when Moses, being a babe, wept in his ark of bulrushes, not far off glowed these wide-open flowerets; as if the sky had lent a galaxy of stars to cluster beside his cradle and in a symbol reveal the hosts of heaven keeping watch with Miriam.
>
> And the servant said unto him, Peradventure the woman will not be willing to follow me unto this land: must I needs bring thy son again unto the land from whence thou camest? (*Genesis 24, 5*)

She claimed no original scholarship either in hagiography or textual explication: the aim was purely devotional, such learning as was required being cited only as an aid to meditation, in a frankly mystical manner. Christina believed in the absolute and divinely-revealed truth of the Bible, but from outside holy writ she borrowed many hagiographic details from wholly uncertain traditions, to which she explained she attached 'no binding faith nor even necessarily any credence'. The legends were simply used as the starting-point for contemplative thought. 'If some points of my descriptions are rather flights of antique fancy than lore of modern science, I hope that such points may rather recall a vanishing grace than mislead from a truth,' she continued, adding that should anyone object that many of her suggestions were 'exploded superstitions' or mere fancies – and that 'if I have fancied this another may fancy that'

> till the whole posse of idle thinkers puts forth each his fresh fancy, and all alike without basis; I frankly answer, Yes: so long as with David our musings are on God's works ... and so long as with St Timothy our meditations are on charity, faith, purity, which array the Saints of Christ in a robe more excellent than the glory of Solomon or the loveliness of a lily. And whereinsoever I err I ask pardon of mine own Master to whom I stand or fall, and of my brother lest I offend him.

But the ultimate phrase is disingenuous: this author answers only to God for her interpretations.

For as all her devotional writings demonstrate, Christina held a firm Protestant belief in the primacy of the Word, as revealed in the New Testament, and its direct relation to the pious individual. In this tradition, each woman could be her own theologian. Her book on the saints' days therefore partly constituted a commentary on the Book of Common Prayer, the great English text created by Cranmer in the sixteenth century, and also lay within a tradition that stretched back beyond the Reformation to mystical writers such as the fourteenth-century Englishwoman Julian of Norwich, as well as to seventeenth-century divines associated with the Anglican community at Little Gidding, pointing forward to works like *Ash Wednesday* and *The Four Quartets*. As such it formed part of her own spiritual autobiography. In adolescence she had responded out of her immediate sense of suffering and sin to the doctrines propounded by Pusey; now, in her maturity, she endeavoured to create and share with others a contemplative understanding of the divine order.

She was careful, even anxious, to disavow any overt competition with clerical authority, insisting on the 'secondhand' and deferential nature of her work. 'No graver slur could attach to my book than would be a reputation for prevalent originality,' she wrote, 'For the learned, I have no ability to write, lacking as I do learning and critical practice.' But though sincere this too was disingenuous: much study and thought went into the work, despite its position in the subordinate lay tradition, and it was the first of several books in which Christina strove to complement the teachings of ordained men.

Young Plants and Polished Corners was overlong and over-dense, especially for the young. It consisted of repeated quotations, analogies and textual allusions that spiral down the pages as if composed in a dialect derived entirely from biblical phrases that do duty for a multiplicity of meanings. Silently, however, she added original poems to twelve of the Feasts, in a manner that suggests they arose naturally from meditation rather than being written in accordance with a chosen scheme. They are, not surprisingly, among the most attractive elements in the book, and that for the Baptist – with fugitive echoes of Herbert and Blake – is one further illustration of how biblical language of itself held for Christina the magical verbal power that poetry sought to capture and create, in an indivisible fusion of idea and image, simple structure and multiple meaning:

> Sooner or later: yet at last
> The Jordan must be passed;
> It may be he will overflow
> His banks the day we go;
> It may be that his cloven deep
> Will stand upon a heap.
> Sooner or later: yet one day
> We all must pass that way;
> Each man, each woman, humbled, pale,
> Pass veiled within the veil;
> Child, parent, bride, companion,
> Alone, alone, alone.
> For none a ransom can be paid,
> A suretyship made:
> I, bent by mine own burden, must
> Enter my house of dust;
> I, rated to the full amount
> Must render mine account.
> When earth and sea shall empty all
> Their graves of great and small;
> When earth wrapped in a fiery flood
> Shall no more hide her blood;
> When mysteries shall be revealed;
> All secrets be unsealed;
> When things of night, when things of shame,
> Shall find at last a name,
> Pealed for a hissing and a curse
> Throughout the universe:
> The Awful Judge, most Awful God,

Then cause to bud Thy rod,
To bloom with blossoms, and to give
Almonds; yea, bid us live.
I plead myself with Thee, I plead
Thee in our utter need;
Jesus, most Merciful of Men,
Show mercy on us then;
Lord God of Mercy and of men
Show mercy on us then.

The unexpected almonds come from Aaron's rod, which 'brought forth buds, and bloomed blossoms', and the commercial imagery perhaps derived from the recent house removal. Above all, however, this was a meditation on the loss of Maria and the prospect of death, in keeping with those of the puritan divines who were Christina's spiritual ancestors.

Despite the poems, Macmillan declined to publish the book. A year later, soon after spending the bleak Christmas of 1877 alone with her mother and brother, at Gabriel's insistence Christina offered her manuscript to a second, unidentified publisher, who also returned it with regrets that the 'time was not right'. She told Dr Littledale, who replied in doggerel:

'Tis but too true, dear Miss Christina,
  What publishers to you reply,
A time like this has always been a
  Time when frighted Muses fly . . .
The public likes a *Prince's Progress*
  But only in the *Morning Post*,
And makes a *Goblin Market* ogress
  Of Russia's or of Turkey's host. . . .
'Twon't last for ever, never fret 'ee
  But wait till war's alarums fail:
Such is the rede, dear Miss Rossetti,
  of your true friend,
                            R. Littledale.

As the 'Eastern Question', war's alarums between Turkey and Russia had been troubling British politics for over a year, following the suppression of rebellions within the Ottoman empire, carried out with particular savagery in the case of Bulgaria. Prime Minister Disraeli

and the Queen, who supported Turkish rule, were vigorously opposed by Gladstone and the Liberal and Radical parties, even at
the expense of seeming to encourage Russian ambition – for behind
the immediate issues lay British imperial interests in the Middle East.
In April 1877, Disraeli mobilised the navy to guard the Suez Canal
and Dardanelles and to threaten Russia. 'O shame and double shame,
if we march under such a leadership as this in an unjust war against
people who are not our enemies,' proclaimed William Morris,
who took a leading role in the protests. But 'patriotic' forces – whose
theme song 'We don't want to fight but by jingo if we do' helped to
coin a new term for national bellicosity – rabidly supported 'the
gallant Turk' against 'the Russian bear' and in December, when Ottoman forces suffered a setback, there were renewed calls for British
action. 'Oh, if the Queen were a man,' wrote Victoria, 'she would
like to go and give those Russians ... such a beating!' Anti-war meetings were attacked by jingoistic crowds. 'People go about in a
Rule Britannia style that turns one's stomach,' Morris reported in
disgust.

Christina left no recorded opinion of her own on the Eastern
Question or the threat of war against Russia. Later, she professed
herself sufficiently patriotic to admire the tune of *Rule Britannia*, but
by pointedly omitting to admire the words she perhaps conveyed
her dislike of jingoism and war-mongering; quite possibly she shared
William's sentiments when he told the increasingly bellicose Swinburne that he loathed war, 'be it of England against Russia or Afghans
or Zulus', and felt no inclination to be anti-Russian merely by virtue of being British. Indeed, she may have been more positively
anti-Turk, because the Bulgarian victims were Christian communities,
whom Russia claimed to be liberating from their infidel oppressors.
Certainly she pondered such matters, and at the outset of hostilities
she cut and kept a magazine article by Charles Cayley in which he
laboured in typically convoluted manner over the philosophical problem of selflessness, inter alia discussing patriotism and political partisanship of the kind currently dividing the nation, and concluding
with a quotation from Pope comparing true self-love to that of others,
like a pebble creating ever-widening circles:

> Friend, parent, neighbour, first it will embrace,
>   His country next, and next all human race,
> Wide and more wide, the o'erflowings of the mind
>   Take every creature in, of every kind.
> Earth smiles around with boundless beauty blessed
> And heaven beholds its image in his breast.

It was a sentiment Christina implicitly endorsed and informed her next project undertaken in Lent 1878, by which time peace negotiations were under way. This was a Harmony on Charity and though it does not mention war, the text chosen, *I Corinthians XIII* – 'now abideth faith, hope, charity: these three; but the greatest of these is charity' – seems to have been prompted by the belligerent atmosphere and her own fervent hope that disputes be settled by lovingkindness rather than aggressive militarism or mob violence.

A Harmony is a collation of passages on the same subject, arranged so as to exhibit their consistency and offer an implicit commentary. For her Saints' Days, Christina had used Isaac Williams's Harmony on the Gospels; here she compiled her own, in three sections, comprising the text, alongside examples from the sayings and life of Christ and quotations from the apostles.

The idea of making a Harmony, she explained later, was suggested to her as a Lenten exercise – possibly by Littledale. It was primarily intended for private devotional purposes, but, true to her literary vocation, within a few months Christina submitted it to the editor of *New and Old*, a church magazine run by Rev. Charles Gutch, rector of St Cyprian's, Dorset Square.

Later, the Torrington Square household had a subscription to *New and Old* and would have read in its pages a quantity of short meditative and didactic pieces, poetry, fiction and polemic, highly flavoured with Ritualism and a distinctly intemperate defiance respecting church controversies over confession, altar candles and suchlike. It also ran a curious agony column for those in religious dilemmas, such as how to avoid breakfast when staying with friends who did not fast before Holy Communion (one answer being to get up in time for early mass). Gutch's views – and the paper was largely a vehicle for these – were strongly representative of the High Church wing, and far from progressive on secular affairs, though he was a rousing antivivisectionist, which may have been the basis of his acquaintance with Christina. On gender issues, he was firmly reactionary, holding that women needed no more education than would fit them 'to be intelligent companions, to manage households, train children, nurse the sick, and so on'. If women ever succeeded in gaining 'what a few mad enthusiasts style "women's rights" ', they would in Gutch's view, or wish, find they had paid a dear price for something that promoted neither social, political or domestic peace, nor prosperity. Therefore, 'the motto for women, at any rate for Englishwomen, should be "Rest and be thankful" '.

He knew a 'name' when he saw Christina's, however, and in his magazine published not only her *Harmony* but also the letter that came with it, in which the author, with customary self-deprecation, hesitantly suggested he might find her piece 'worth looking at' if ever *New and Old* suffered an 'empty season'. It was printed in the first issue of 1879, appropriately looking forward to Lent.

A year earlier, Christina had enrolled in a course of lectures on Dante's *Inferno* at University College, London. Perhaps she felt the deficiencies of her education more keenly now she was no longer able to benefit from the scholarly endeavours of Maria or William. As her surviving annotations to the *Shadow of Dante* indicate, Maria's death had by no means closed down her interest in the *Divine Comedy*. She was moreover, also engaged in the related literary task of tracing references and quotations from Dante, Petrarch and Boccaccio for Grosart's scholarly edition of Spenser's *The Faerie Queene*. We do not know how this commission emerged, but it may have been passed on from William. It overlapped with work by Francis Hueffer, Cathy Brown's husband, whose article on Petrarch's friendship with Boccaccio Christina read this summer in *Macmillan's*, and whose book on the Troubadours was favourably reviewed at the same time. Simultaneously, Christina was also following Cayley's progress with his current translation of Petrarch's songs and sonnets, much of which she read in manuscript during 1878 and which would in due course influence her own writing. Cayley dedicated his version of sonnet 22 to Maria's memory, presumably aware of the family tradition that claimed descent from Laura, as described in Christina's own essay on Petrarch for the Dictionary of Universal Biography.

In addition to these intellectual interests, she agreed to contribute poems to the *Dublin University Magazine* (despite its title, published in London) whose new editor, Keningdale Cook, was an acquaintance of William's. She sent *Yet a Little While*, but when the magazine arrived, she was horrified to find it in company with writers whose freethinking 'school of thought' she suspected of being antagonistic to her own. 'If so, I am sure you will kindly set me free from my quasi-engagement to write on demand for the Magazine,' she told Cook: 'for I never could be at my ease or happy in literary company with persons who look down upon what I look up to.I have not *played* at Christianity, and therefore I cannot play at unbelief.' In reply, Cook argued that her work would set an example, unhappily describing her as a 'poetic angel' who would influence the 'publicans and sinners' among the readership. This was exactly the kind of playful remark she loathed. It had been her lot so often to disagree with people she liked that she was beginning to think it must be salutary, she returned even more firmly,

Were I of the authoritative sex, and thus a born teacher and preacher, I might perhaps advantageously take up a position at once of protest and of fellowship on your staff: as it is, I think it is as much as I am competent to do to hold my own without either compromise or gratuitous self-assertion. You see whither this conviction cannot but lead me: and to avow it to you, who honour claims of conscience, is so far a pleasure.

It surely needs something far more edifying than "a bright poetic angel" to influence those whom you (not *I*) characterize as "publicans & sinners". Moreover, if I took it into my head that I wore a halo, I think one of the first texts for my study would be S. Mat. 21. 31.

'Verily I say unto you that the publicans and harlots go into the kingdom of God before you' was the text here cited, and with this rebuke Keningdale Cook was silenced. Once more her disavowal was ambiguous, however: though neither male nor a born 'teacher and preacher', she took seriously her role as an influential and Christian writer. Though all her life Christina denied intellectual ability, her close reading of Plato, Dante and authors such as Spenser as well as Christian theology warn us against collusion in such self-disparagement.

From these strands she wove together a new long poem called *A Ballad of Boding*, which drew on a famous ode translated by Spenser as *The Visions of Petrarch* and was similarly allegorical:

> There are sleeping dreams and waking dreams;
> What seems is not always as it seems.
>
> I looked out of my window in the sweet new morning
> And there I saw three barges of manifold adorning . . .

Petrarch's second vision was of a tall ship, with sails of gold and tackle of silk, wrecked by a sudden storm. Christina's first boat has sails like fire, the second like glittering wire, the third sails of sackcloth. The first two are devoted to revelry, with figureheads symbolic of pleasure and power, folly and evil, while the sackcloth crew carry harps and trumpets sounding notes of alarm, as they labour at the oars against contrary winds. The poet weeps for pity when those weary of the task abandon their hard ship and are welcomed on board the others. As they drive on over the ocean, a grim spectre appears in the guise of a waterspout:

> With a horny hand it steered,
> And a horn appeared

On its sneering head upreared
Haughty and high
Against the blackening lowering sky.
With a hoof it swayed the waves;
They opened here and there
Till I spied deep ocean graves
Full of skeletons
That were men and women once . . .

Only the third ship stays clear of the cloven hunter with his abominable smile, until he lands on its deck, laying his hand on the helm. The crew cry out, pleading for deliverance. The mast bends, the planks strain, wind and rain rouse up the waves: shipwreck seems inevitable. Then an angelic form swoops to the rescue, grappling with the satanic figure, who, cast into the sea, turns his attention back to the first and second crews, catching them with hook, net and fiery breath, till their ships founder and are engulfed. Only the third ship crosses the bar safely into the haven, as the storms abate, amid sunset splendours.

The religious allegory is perhaps too plain for this poem to take its place alongside *Goblin Market* or *The Prince's Progress*, though that is where it belongs, not least for the sake of its free rhythms and pulsating lines, figuring forth vivid pictures of tempest-tossed vessels. The goblins' cries may be somewhat ambiguous, or the prince's diversions too subtle, but no reader could mistake the meaning of these distinctive ships.

In the midst of such serious undertakings, Christina took a literal and literary holiday, at Walton-on-the-Naze in Essex, the 'ultra-unfashionable resort' that the Rossetti women chose to visit in 1878 and where, reading Cayley's translations of Petrarch, she witnessed no real or fantastic sea-storms from the boarding-house window, but was busy rendering her own work into Italian. Prompted by Teodorico's announcement that he was translating *Sing-Song*, Christina tried versions of her own, under the title *Ninna Nanna*, or lullaby.

Hers were 'so free and easy' that they were 'not translations but imitations', she insisted, but they were of course those of a poet, concerned with more than exact transmission of meaning. As she herself noted, citing Gabriel, whatever else translation involved it did not mean making a bad poem out of a good one. Thus for the *Sing-Song* rhyme on the white horses of the sea, she wrote:

Cavalli marittimi	The horses of the sea
Urtansi in guerra	Rear a foaming crest

E meglio ci servono	But the horses of the land
Quelli di terra.	Serve us the best.
Questi pacifici	The horses of the land
Corrono o stanno;	Munch corn and clover
Quei rotolandosi	While the foaming sea-horses
Spumando vanno.	Toss and turn over.

The last two lines were onomatopoeic, she explained, conveying 'the accumulative on-come of the waves, mounting on each other's backs', as indeed their assonance suggests.

If a pig wore a wig was her triumph, however, its punning tail/ tailoress transformed into a delightful Italian joke about a lawyer to make a codicil for the missing coda:

'Porco la zucca fitt in parucca!	If a pig wore a wig
Che gli diresti mai?'	What could we say?
'M' inchinerei, l'ossequierei –	Treat him as a gentleman
"Ser Porco, come stai?"'	And say 'Good-day'
'Ahi guai per caso mai	If his tail chanced to fail
Se la coda andasse a male?'	What could we do?
'Sta tranquillo – buon legale	Send him to the tailoress
Gli farebbe un codicillo.'	To get one new.

Teodorico's versions do not seem to have been published, though other of Christina's poems were translated this year by Luigi Gamberale, for inclusion in an anthology of English and German verse published in 1881 under the title *Poeti Inglese e Tedeschi* – a linking that must have caused a wry smile, remembering the exiles' furious denunciation of the hated *Tedeschi*. And the whimsical tendency that blossomed so suddenly in *Ninna Nanna* also bubbled up in *Freaks of Fashion*, a comic poem satirising the sartorial plumage of birds and by extension current fashions, which Christina sent in response to a request from Routledge's *Every Girl's Annual*, showing that her sense of humour was still alive, if rather curiously expressed. Indeed, despite bereavement and distress, she also felt an obligation to be as cheerful as she could manage. Inner grief was compatible with courteous cordiality towards others.

Her relations with Macmillan were again a little strained, for the firm was not punctilious in sending statements of account when no money was payable. In its first two years Christina received no profits from the English edition of *Poems* (1875), though small but worthwhile sums came from Roberts Bros. At the end of 1877, she wrote to ask Mac how the book was faring – or whether it had 'suffered under the general trade depression and failed'. Virtually by return came a 'final

payment' for the second edition of *Goblin Market*, with information
that income from the new volume was being set against the still
unearned balance of *Prince's Progress*. By the end of 1878 *Poems* was
showing a profit, earning Christina 17s. 1d in January 1879 and £9.
17s. 8d in October, and a few months later a bookshop inquiry revealed that a reprint was planned. She had been neither informed nor
consulted, and the edition also appeared without courtesy: the first
she knew was when the book was seen in the shops in December 1879.
Mindful of previous history, she was anxious not to alienate Macmillan, but a note of puzzled irritation sounds in her correspondence.
Gabriel at once consulted Watts, who as a lawyer offered to put her
relationship with the publisher on a formal footing. Christina replied
gracefully but firmly. If Mr Watts and Gabriel and William were all
convinced of its necessity and it would not involve expense, she
would allow Watts to speak to Macmillan, she wrote,

> But only and absolutely in the most amicable manner; as being quite
> certain that no wrong has been done or dreamt of, as knowing that I am
> satisfied with actual arrangements, and as bearing in mind that I stick to
> my position of cordial personal friendship with my friendly publisher . . .
>   Nothing however, not proof positive that I had been pillaged! would
> make me have recourse to law: this is a statement at once preliminary and
> final.

The 'ensuing colloquies' were satisfactory to both parties, according
to William, but Gabriel and Watts were denied the legal skirmish they
had looked for.
  She was equally firm and conciliatory with regard to an incipient
quarrel with Lucy, over some remark regarding young Olive, who
with her nursemaid and baby brother paid regular visits to their
grandmother and aunt. Arthur received all the favour due, in their
eyes, to a firstborn grandson; as Christina commented ruefully, it was
the lot of females to sing second in life. But Olive was apparently
rebuked or criticised, causing Lucy to take offence. Hastily, Christina
apologised:

> My dear Lucy,
>   I am heartily glad you have written, because it gives me a chance of
> doing away with an impression I never meant to create. I quite admire our
> clever little Olive . . . and the more at her ease she is among us, some of her
> nearest relations, the better . . . You do not know how much pleasure,
> moreover, you will retrench from Mamma's quiet days if you check
> Olive's coming here, or her perfect freedom when she is here. *That* is a
> truly motherly heart, full of warm nooks for children and children's

children: and she could not bear *her* gratification in seeing and hearing
your little ones to be doubted or misunderstood. This with her love to you
and to them. And mine too, please, to all three: not a crocodile love!

'Kiss and be friends' is a very sound old exhortation: get Olive to be my
proxy, and I shall not fear to miss the result. Need I?

She responded equally tactfully to William's curious offer of a mum-
mified human relic. For if Lucy could be touchy, William's brotherly
sympathy also had its limits. He noted, for instance, that Christina
spent inordinate amounts of time making up scrapbooks for hospital
patients and children, remarking that nine times out of ten when he
called she was engaged in this trivial activity, and he refused to take
any interest in her devotional writing, presumably for fear of encouraging it. Though he himself was not squeamish, (he already possessed
a burnt fragment of Shelley's skull) he surely might have anticipated
his God-fearing sister's response to an Egyptian relic given to him as
a gift. Her calm and courteous wit barely masked the palpable disgust. 'Had I an oratory, I might willingly accept the loan of "head and
hand" as a *memento mori*,' she wrote; 'but as it is I could not feel easy
at keeping bits of fellow human-creatures as curiosities; my preference
would be to give them reverent burial.' Further to remind without
offending him of her literal belief in the resurrection, she quoted
Maria's fear of being caught in the Mummy Room of the British Museum when the Last Trump sounded. She was genial, but not joking;
like her sister she took such matters seriously.

In 1879, she began work on a new devotional project, shorter and
simpler than the now-shelved Saints' Day calendar, but more complex
than the Harmony, in which she allowed herself scope for ethical as
well as meditational observation. This took the form of a commentary
on the Benedicte, originally entitled *Treasure Trove* and probably also
begun as a Lenten exercise, for the Benedicite is an alternative canticle
appointed by the Prayer Book for use during Lent.

Its full title *Benedicite, Omnia Opera*, comes from the opening words:
'O All ye Works of the Lord, bless ye the Lord', which in turn is taken
from the Song of the Three Holy Children cast into the fire by Nebuchadnezzar. There follows a litany of God's creation – heavens, waters,
sun, moon, stars, rain, wind, fire, seasons, day, night, light, darkness,
ice, snow, lightning, clouds, earth, mountains, plants, fountains, rivers, fish, birds, beasts, men – on which framework Christina built her
own praise-poem, saluting the divine order and joy in all creation.

This was a lesson to herself, about willing acceptance of all that was
divinely ordained, which in her theology meant all that was, however
painful. As with the saints' calendar, her method was analogical, and
the aim homiletic:

Whatsoever we contemplate, this is the true end of all contemplation: to
'see Jesus'.

Again, knowledge was marshalled not for its own sake but for contemplative use: angels, for example, were discussed in terms of the
lessons such immaterial beings might teach mere mortals – their
actual or supposed existence was not at issue.

She treated similarly objects that had arrived in the world since the
appearance of the Bible and Prayerbook, such as electricity, which she
discussed under the heading of 'Powers', as both 'the dangerous
element of the storm, announcing its awful passage by lightning flash
and thunder clap' and also as 'man's servant; available in the physician's hands for treatment of disease and in the telegraph and telephone for communication of intelligence'. Such modern inventions
(the first practical use of the telephone was demonstrated by Alexander Bell in 1876, while a few years before aunt Charlotte had
benefitted from medical treatment involving galvanism, which had
greatly impressed Christina) were then glossed in terms of divine
dispensation.

In the same context of scientific discovery, she also paid tribute to
the mental faculties that enabled mankind to 'plot the orbit of a planet
as yet undiscerned' – such as Pluto, whose existence was inferred but
not yet astronomically confirmed. To this she attached a sententious
moral, however. 'In a more or less degree every one of us inherits this
awful birthright of intellectual power,' she wrote. 'With Esau we may
despise and squander this birthright; with Reuben disgrace and forfeit
it; but ours it is,' as such it represented a tremendous responsibility,
which might bring down a curse or a blessing. 'Let us be content to
remain ignorant of many things,' she continued, 'lest amid the shal-
lows (not the depths) of science we make shipwreck of our faith.' Yet
no longer did she regard science as the site of error in *Annus Domini*;
instead, faith must be content not to understand the dilemmas posed
by scientific discoveries. And from somewhere she picked up a curious and unscientific 'fact', namely that the moon might emit light. 'It
used to be supposed that "the moon walking in brightness" ... is no
more than a mirror reflecting the Sun's radiance,' she wrote, but 'now
careful observation leads towards the hypothesis that she may also
exhibit inherent luminosity.'

Mindful of his last response, she did not submit this manuscript to
Macmillan, but to the SPCK, which had published Maria's *Letters to
My Bible Class* and where Littledale had influence. In July it was
accepted for publication under a revised title. 'Sad to say,' she told
Gabriel, 'my little book *Seek and Find* is exclusively prose: yet I flatter
myself some of it is that prose which I fancy our Italian half inclines

us to indite ... I took a keen interest in writing it, and I hope some may feel an interest in reading it.'

But if there was no verse in the text, it left its trace in *All Thy Works Praise Thee O Lord*, a long poetic litany which must originally have been intended for the book, and where the works of creation speak in turn, expressing their essence as an emblem of the divine order.

To Keningdale Cook, Christina had expressed a wholly orthodox disavowal of masculine authority regarding religious preaching, and following biblical precedent her poem contained wholly scriptural views of gender:

> WOMEN
> God makes our service love, and makes our wage
> Love: so we wend on patient pilgrimage,
> Extolling Him by love from age to age.

> MEN
> God gives us power to rule: He gives us power
> To rule ourselves, and prune the exuberant flower
> Of youth, and worship Him hour after hour.

Explicitly disclaiming all ambition, she also insisted that *Seek and Find* was 'of course, but a simple work adapted to people who know less (!) than I', but this statement is contradicted by the text itself: with increasing confidence Christina was voicing the female right to speak and be heard in religious discourse. And in this respect *Seek and Find* is a far more interesting text than it first appears to our irreligious age, both in terms of Christina's self-appointed role, and her own ongoing argument with feminism.

As she well knew, gender was a political as well as devotional issue, for although women's ordination was not on the ecclesiastical agenda (and none would have been more affronted than Christina had it been), the question of women's rights in general and in particular women's right to vote were very much on the political order of service at this time.

From 1871 equal franchise bills were annually defeated in parliament, in the context of a sustained campaign whose weapons included the public support of any woman with a measure of national fame. As a literary celebrity, Christina was asked to add her name to the cause of women's suffrage by Augusta Webster, a fellow poet Christina greatly admired. Author of several verse dramas, translations from Greek and three volumes of poetry in the Robert Browning mode dealing with spinsterhood and the marriage market, she was also a Macmillan author, a neighbour of Gabriel and the Scotts in Cheyne Walk, and a regular contributor to the *Examiner*, where she wrote, in her own words, 'one of those lighter columns which everyone reads and no one recalls', under the self-deprecating title 'A Housewife's Opinions'.

The tone was light but the opinions weighty. In 1878 Webster wrote earnestly on the current suffrage bill, arguing for the extension of the parliamentary franchise to women ratepayers on the grounds of natural justice. The vote was now enjoyed by all male householders but still denied to all women, even those who were ratepayers in their own right, without a husband or brother to 'head the household'. It was 'commonplace justice', therefore, to grant the franchise on the basis of the same qualifications, regardless of sex: women householders bore an equal burden of taxation and had an equal right to representation. If the state allowed single and widowed women to live independently, as it manifestly did, it must accept the notion of Eve without an Adam and grant her equal citizenship.

Formulated in this way for tactical reasons the bill had drawbacks, not the least being that under its provisions married women such as Mrs Webster herself would still be denied the vote. Some women therefore objected to the bill as seeming to cast a slur on wives and mothers, who were otherwise pre-eminently worthy of the franchise. This, in part, was Christina's position, and to Augusta Webster she sent a reply at once emphatic and confused, containing strong views both for and against female suffrage. 'I write as I am thinking and feeling, but I premise that I have not even to my own apprehension gone deep into the question,' she wrote, though in one sense she had done so, for her objection was 'a fundamental one underlying the whole structure of female claims':

> Does it not appear as if the Bible was based upon an understood unalterable distinction between men and women, their position, duties, privileges? Not arrogating to myself but most earnestly desiring to attain to the character of a humble orthodox Xtian, so does it appear to me; not merely under the Old but also under the New Dispensation. The fact of the Priesthood being exclusively man's, leaves me in no doubt that the highest functions are not in this world open to both sexes: and if not all, then a selection must be made and a line drawn somewhere.

The double negatives and denials betray some understandable discomfort, for the suffrage bill did not propose to abolish the God-given distinction between male and female, nor to open the priesthood to women, only to open the franchise to householders. Since God allowed women to be householders, this was a line that could very properly be drawn without challenging any divine dispensation.

And, she continued, suddenly taking up a quite contrary position, if on the other hand female rights were likely to be 'overborne for lack of female voting influence', then she would 'feel disposed to shoot ahead' in favour not just of female voters but female MPs as well, as 'only right and reasonable'. Moreover,

> I take exception at the exclusion of married women from the suffrage – for who so apt as Mothers – all previous arguments allowed for the moment – to protect the interests of themselves and their offspring? I do think if anything ever does sweep away the barrier of sex, and make the female not a giantess or a heroine but at once and full grown a hero and a giant, it is that mighty maternal love which makes little birds and little beasts as well as little women matches for very big adversaries.

But then she backtracked again, invoking the lame contemporary argument that women should not vote because not called upon to defend the nation. 'I do not know whether any lady is prepared to adopt the Platonic theory of female regiments,' she joked; 'if so, she sets aside this objection: but I am not: so to me it stands.'

Mrs Webster wrote again, apparently arguing that many good women were in the suffrage movement. So be it, replied Christina:

> Many who have thought and done much more than myself share your views – and yet they are not mine. I do not think the present social movements tend on the whole to uphold Xtianty, or that the influence of some of our most prominent and gifted women is exerted in that direction: and thus thinking I cannot aim at 'women's rights'.
>
> Influence and responsibility are such solemn matters that I will not excuse myself to you for abiding by my convictions: yet in contradicting you I am contradicting one I admire . . .

So Christina declined to support women's suffrage. And by her silence she implicitly endorsed the traditionalist position. Ten years later she went further, offering her name to the notorious anti-suffrage women's petition organised by Mary Ward, thereby placing herself firmly in the reactionary camp.

Yet the tenor of Christina's arguments is surely more *pro* than *contra*. Her objections were threefold: biblical authority on distinction between the sexes; male responsibility for national defence; the failure of prominent suffragists to uphold and promote Christianity. But no one of these arguments is as firmly conveyed as that in favour of female votes as an influence for good, or that on the merits of mothers in defending the interests of the weak – one of the major duties of national legislators – which Christina even took as far as the advanced opinion that women had the right to stand for election as well as to vote. And her wish, occluded by the involutions of syntax but nonetheless heartfelt, for the barrier of sex to be swept away is strongly phrased: women have, in their very nature, the qualities of strength and courage to stand alongside men – in national government and defence – not as oddities but equal heroes and giants, 'at once and full grown'. They could not be priests, but they could certainly fight, for their rights and those of others.

The Anglican Church did not promulgate a position on suffrage as such, which was a secular matter on which churchmen might differ. Littledale, for instance, was firmly in favour of women's education and may have been so regarding the franchise. Gutch was opposed, as his indignant assertion that suffragists were 'mad enthusiasts' made clear. And some while later he too solicited Miss Rossetti's support. In reply, she sent a rather dismaying poem for his magazine, on female subordination:

> Woman was made for man's delight:
>   Charm, O woman, be not afraid!
> His shadow by day, his moon by night,
>   Woman was made.
>
> Her strength with weakness is overlaid;
>   Meek compliances veil her might;
> Him she stays by whom she is stayed.
>
> World-wide champions of truth and right,
>   Hope in gloom and in danger aid,
> Tender and faithful, ruddy and white,
>   Woman was made.

But the fighting imagery again makes this more ambiguous than it seems: as champion of truth and right, woman has the 'might' to withstand male power. The anti-slavery movement would not have prevailed without its many female activists, she may have reflected, and those opposed to vivisection knew their cause would not be such a hard struggle if women had direct legislative influence.

One may infer that it was primarily for religious reasons that Christina felt unable to ally herself with those in the forefront of the feminist campaign, which had the fatal defect in her eyes of not being guided by scriptural concerns. Nevertheless, she grappled with the problem of gender, and in the pages of Seek and Find set forth a subversive resolution of the ostensible position she adopted elsewhere.

On the one hand, in the section on Men and Women, she repeated the orthodox view, as propounded in her poem. But she devoted the section on the Sun and Moon to a meditation in which she described the female role as only symbolically subordinate:

> In many points the feminine lot copies very closely the voluntarily assumed position of our Lord and Pattern. Woman must obey: and Christ 'learned obedience' ... She must be fruitful, but in sorrow: and He, symbolised by a corn of wheat, had not brought forth much fruit except He had died . . . He came not to be ministered unto but to minister; He was among His own 'as he that serveth'.

Obedience, suffering, subordination, service: the duties enjoined on women were also the highest Christian virtues, as expressed by Christ. Woman, not man, was therefore made in His image. Moreover,

> her office is to be man's helpmeet; and concerning Christ God saith 'I have laid help upon One that is mighty' ... And well may she glory, inasmuch as one of the tenderest of divine promises takes (so to say) the feminine form: 'As one whom his mother comforteth, so will I comfort you' ...

From which it may be inferred that God is not so much Our Father as our protective, loving Mother – just as elsewhere Christina described maternal love as the earthly copy of transcendent or ideal Love and as Julian of Norwich expressed in her famous meditation on the mothering role of Christ derived from Revelations. And thus Christina reached a sort of heavenly equality, for 'In the case of the twofold Law of Love', we are taught to call one Commandment 'first and great', yet to esteem the second as 'like unto it'. And 'the man is the head of the woman, the woman is the glory of the man' just as 'there is one glory of the sun and another glory of the moon'.

In this context, the erroneous supposition that the moon was also luminous was a claim for women's independent power, and Christina's conclusion was indirectly addressed both to discontented feminists and to their clerical opponents:

> But if our proud waves will after all not be stayed, or at any rate not be allayed (for stayed they must be) by the limit of God's ordinance concerning our sex, one final consolation yet remains to careful and troubled hearts: in Christ there is neither male nor female, for we are all one.

Whose heart was 'careful and troubled' on the subject but her own? This was not her last word on the subject of gender, but in Christina's theology, woman was subordinate to man as Christ was to God, and therefore in no way inferior but by analogy equal or 'like unto' man. Each had glory. Finally, of course, she believed in transcendence, for sacred language was both literal and metaphorical: however it might be in the secular sphere, heaven and religion recognised no distinction of sex. Always acknowledging the subordination of the secular to the sacred realm, these were the words of a woman who saw her own image in Christ, modest and humble but also proud to speak with His ministers in order to comfort and inspire the faithful. Her vocation was literary, but it was also holy.

The SPCK paid £40 for *Seek and Find*, and proof corrections were finished by midsummer 1879. Published in the autumn, it was somewhat surprisingly mentioned in favourable terms by the *Saturday Review*, which William dismissed as the reading-matter of vulgar and idle Clubmen. If so, Christina would have been pleased to reach them, by whatever means.

34

Monna Innominata and Later Life

SEAFORD, WHERE CHRISTINA and her mother spent four weeks in summer 1879, was 'very quiet, but so are we', and rather empty at first, she wrote from her campstool on the beach to William, *en famille* at Broadstairs. Her latest literary project was a dramatic pageant called *The Months*, intended for drawing-room performance, rather in the style of those popularised for family performance by Louisa Macdonald, wife of the author of *At the Back of the North Wind* and *The Princess and the Goblin*, whose works Christina knew by repute if not directly. In a manner of speaking her own pageant was commissioned, being written at the request of a colleague of Maria's at All Saints', for 'something performable by her sister's family', as a Christmas entertainment. Christina therefore constructed her text with twelve speaking parts, equally divided for girls and boys, with non-speaking parts for smaller children, and a simple scene of a cottage interior, set as for the stage.

Her theme, of the months and seasons, was appropriately bland for a domestic entertainment, though in the event proved too elaborate for the designated family. It was distinctly secular, especially when set beside her other writings, and seems to reflect the contemporary passion for 'Nature' as a self-sufficient literary subject. The concept was technically innovative as far as Christina was concerned, for she had never before tried a dramatic mode, but the pageant form is essentially that of rehearsed recitation, and she included no dramatic action or plot.

The Months has its charms – including an allusion to November as the 'youngest sister, looking dim And grim, With dismal ways', which Christina gleefully quoted to remind her brothers of her mournful reputation. But it is at best a failed companion to *Sing-Song*, and at worst a piece of decorative banality, the verbal equivalent of Kate Greenaway. According to William, it was performed 'on quite a striking scale' at the Albert Hall, but more often in the sedate setting of girls' schools, where it made a suitable platform piece. Standing by itself, it would suggest that the true poetic fire had indeed died out, replaced by imitation coals.

'I for my part am a great believer in the genuine poetic impulse belonging (very often) to the spring and not to the autumn of life, and some established reputations fail to shake me in this opinion; at any rate, if so one feels the possibility to stand in one's own case, then I vote that the grace of silence succeed the grace of song,' she had observed at the time of her last volume. But if *The Months* confirmed this self-judgement, it was belied by her subsequent work, for over the next few months Christina embarked on a new and major literary project, the fourteen-sonnet sequence (a 'sonnet of sonnets') entitled *Monna Innominata*, which more than secured her mature reputation.

The exact genesis of this is hard to date precisely. At Christmas 1879, leaving the aunts with William and Lucy, she and Mamma again kept Gabriel company at Chelsea, and on Boxing Day she confided that she was 'hugging hopes of getting together before long enough verse for a *small* fresh volume' – this being another reason why she did not wish to quarrel with Macmillan. A few weeks later she combined with her brother to present David Main's *Treasury of English Sonnets* to their mother on her eightieth birthday, for which each wrote an accompanying poem. 'Sonnets are full of love', Christina's lines began: 'so here now shall be One sonnet more ... To her whose heart is my heart's quiet home.' Their mother was happily surprised with the gift, not having had the slightest suspicion of their conspiracy.

It was thirty-eight years since she had given Mamma her first birthday poem, as she glancingly recalled in a note to her niece, saying

> if at some future day a 'golden glory' of art or of poetry should alight on your 'head of golden tips', then (if you are at all like old Auntie) you will find that almost if not quite its brightest point is that it kindles a light of pleasure in your own Mother's eyes.

Paying a birthday visit, four-year-old Olive had demanded a share in Grandmamma's poem, and been rewarded with one of her own, about flowers as golden as her hair.

Love and sonnets were thus much in the air. Gabriel was currently adding to the *House of Life* and composing sonnets on Chatterton, Keats, Shelley and others. Christina's sequence however sprang from an older tradition. As the quotations from Dante and Petrarch that form fourteen double epigraphs for *Monna Innominata* indicate, it had its origins in her work for Grosart and interest in Cayley's translations, together with her own continuing study of Dante. At University College in 1879 and 1880 she was among the most assiduous attenders at the subsequent lecture courses on the *Purgatorio* and *Paradiso*, given by Charles Tomlinson, whose wife Sara had been known to the Rossettis in the 1850s, when she organised parochial work at Christ Church under Rev. Burrows, including volunteer ministry to the women of the St Pancras workhouse. Later the Tomlinsons moved to Highgate and employed girls from the Penitentiary to complete their training as

'respectable domestics'. On Sara's death in 1873 her widower assuaged his grief by translating Petrarch's laments for Laura, and
published a short study of the sonnet's origins which stressed the
formal structures of Italian models.

Christina owned a copy of this and was also given Tomlinson's next
book, a collection of original and translated sonnets. Her own sequence
is notable for its accomplished yet never servile adherence to Petrar-
chan formalities. There were other echoes, too, especially of Cayley's
versions, which almost suggest she tried her hand at translating, or
improving, his texts. As her annotated copy of his Dante shows, she
sometimes corrected his English verses, and his sonnet 285, for instance, with its opening line 'Oh day and hour and moment of my
cross!' was echoed in her own lines:

> I wish I could remember that first day,
> First hour, first moment of your meeting me!

while in one of Cayley's own poems, privately published this spring,
Petrarch's words 'Love made me love God less' reappear in the argument of *Monna*'s fifth sonnet.

But her project was more ambitious than mere imitation. To make it
plain, she wrote a preface to her sequence, which opened by stating
that both Beatrice and Laura, immortalised by the great poets, had
come down to posterity 'resplendent with charms' by virtue of their
idealisation, but in her view 'scant of attractiveness' as women. There
were many others, too, whose names were not known, *donne innom-
inate* celebrated by less famous writers. Moreover, 'in that land and
that period' which produced the Albigenses and the Troubadours
(that is twelfth century Languedoc or Provence), she could imagine
'many a lady' sharing her lover's poetic aptitude, who might have
spoken for herself in verse, when the barrier to their love was one
'held sacred by both, yet not such as to render mutual love incompatible with mutual honour'. The unnamed lady of her title is therefore not the object of distant adoration but the speaking subject: a
woman writing to a beloved man. At a stroke this subverted the
sonnet's gender convention, and allowed Christina, as a woman
writer, to take the active role in love poetry.

There were two immediate sources for this idea. One came from
Francis Hueffer's book *The Troubadours*, which as well as noting the
'scanty information' on the poets' objects of desire as individuals, also
contained a chapter on 'Lady Troubadours', identifying some 'fourteen gifted women' – a 'very modest figure seeing that the entire
number of the troubadours is close on 400' – whose work had survived. *Monna Innominata* has, of course, fourteen sonnets.

With a very Victorian notion of sexual difference, Hueffer went on to state that quite properly none of these ladies was a professional poet. Male troubadours made their livelihood from literature, whereas for the women 'poetry was not an employment but an inward necessity. They poured forth their mirth or their grief and after that relapsed into silence'. Even the brilliant and beautiful Clara of Anduse, who was described as ambitious of literary fame, 'does not seem to have sinned by over-production. Only one of her songs remains to us, and there is no reason to believe that time has been more than usually destructive to her works', while Beatrice de Die, the only female troubadour with a reasonably large number of surviving songs, had but one theme – the story of her love:

> without this passion she would have remained mute. Her first song is the embodiment of new-awakened happiness; her last a dirge over hopes dead and lost.

The poignancy of leaving only one work would not have been lost on Christina, who tried not to be ambitious of literary fame and also believed poetry to be an 'inward necessity' rather than a form of employment. A similar movement from hope to silence informs *Monna Innominata*.

'Had such a lady spoken for herself,' she continued of the imagined unnamed woman in her preface, 'the portrait left us might have appeared more tender than any drawn even by a devoted friend.' Indeed, as she remarked to Gabriel, it was surprising the device had not already been used. 'I rather wonder that no one (so far as I know) ever hit on my semi-historical argument before for such treatment – it seems to me so full of poetic suggestiveness,' she wrote.

In one non-historical form it had been deployed, by Elizabeth Barrett Browning, to whose example Christina also referred:

> had the Great Poetess of our own day and nation only been unhappy instead of happy, her circumstances would have invited her to bequeath to us, in lieu of the 'Portuguese Sonnets', an inimitable 'donna innominata' drawn not from fancy but from feeling, and worthy to occupy a niche beside Beatrice and Laura.

Christina was always a writer of exact meaning. In her 'semi-historical' argument she intended to use the circumstances of an unnamed poet like one of the fourteen 'lady troubadours', unhappily separated from her beloved, as the mask for a modern poetess of unfulfilled love, drawn from the feeling heart not historical fancy, whose work would match the joyful poems of her great predecessor. She did not mean to imply, as she explained to Gabriel, that her *donna innominata* surpassed the Lady of the 'Portuguese' sonnets, whose circumstances were unlike those of the 'traditional figures' she had in mind; no barrier separated Mrs Browning from her love.

In courtly poetry the love between poet and mistress was conventionally impeded either by her disdain or her marriage. In 1880 the gender roles could be reversed, but the idea of a female writer pursuing an unresponsive or, worse, a married man was compatible neither with poetry nor honour. In *Monna Innominata* the barrier is purposefully undefined: all we know is that the lovers have often been parted and can now never be united. Thus a modern woman laid her claim to immortality in a great tradition that stretched back to include her 'own ancestress' Laura.

Sonnets from the Portuguese was a decoy title, given to the poems on publication in 1850 and using the grammatical ambivalence to imply that they were translations – such as the 'Portuguese Letters' from Caterina to Camoens, themselves concealed behind a fiction – when in fact they were personal expressions of love to Robert from Elizabeth, whom he sometimes called 'my Portuguese'. Was Christina's 'nameless lady' a comparable disguise for the poet's own self? If so, who was the beloved object of *Monna Innominata*'s affections?

William had no doubt. He described the preface as a similar decoy: 'a blind – not an untruthful blind, for it alleges nothing that is not reasonable ... but still a blind interposed to draw off attention from the writer in her proper person'; and declared that it was 'indisputable that the real veritable speaker in [the] sonnets is Christina herself, giving expression to her love for Charles Cayley'.

But was this so? As befits the genre, the beloved person is nowhere identified within the verse, and over the years critics and biographers have hunted for the ghosts of supposed lovers who might be hovering between the lines. In the absence of other evidence, most have finally accepted William's statement, with varying degrees of reluctance based on the imperfect fit of the poems to what is known of the relationship. The slim volume of Cayley's *Poems and Translations* issued in spring 1880 offers few further clues, for though it contained the sonnet on Gabriel's portrait of Christina that the Scotts interpreted as revealing 'the secret throbbings of Cayley's heart', this merely praised her noble aspect and triple inheritance, and the remainder of the volume, despite some items that can be linked to *Il Rosseggiar*, is far from offering any overt declaration of passion to which *Monna* might be a response.

Much about Christina's emotional life remains enigmatic; perhaps her sonnet sequence was indeed a response to Cayley's little volume: it describes a mutual love that nevertheless came to nothing, which seems to accord with their relationship. But the sonnets are infinitely more than that. They are the culmination of a literary creation tied not to affection for any particular man, but articulating love in all its aspects – romantic, wistful, steadfast, self-denying, painful, heroic, serene – as it was alive in her heart and her imagination. Unlike earlier poems, she intended this sequence for publication, not as a 'love personal'; yet within its framework, she was able to express all her feelings, apparently anchored in some instances to the relationship with 'CBC', but not defined or limited by that and certainly not meant to describe or disclose its details. Into *Monna Innominata*, Christina poured all her hopes and experiences of love; the result was emotionally autobiographical, yet not confessional.

Her unnamed but speaking self looks back to the dawning of love:

> If only I could recollect it, such
>   A day of days!
>
> If only now I could recall that touch . . .

and its first, tentative expressions:

> I loved you first, but afterwards your love
>   Outsoaring mine, sang such a loftier song
> As drowned the friendly cooings of my dove.
>   Which owes the other most? My love was long,
>   And yours one moment seemed to wax more strong;
> I loved and guessed at you, you construed me
> And loved me for what might or might not be –

She explores the pains and joys of expectation:

> Thinking 'Now when he comes,' my sweetest 'when':
> For one man is my world of all the men
> This wide world holds; O love, my world is you.

and resolves the conflict between love and religion:

> I love, as you would have me, God the most;
> Would lose not Him, but you, must one be lost . . .
> This say I, having counted up the cost –
>
> Yet while I love my God the most, I deem
>   That I can never love you overmuch;
>   I love Him more, so let me love you too;
> Yea, as I apprehend it, love is such

> I cannot love you if I love not Him,
>   I cannot love Him if I love not you.

She recounts her love for posterity, delineating its strength, endurance and selflessness, looks forward to fulfilment (or fulfilling transcendence) in heaven, and ends by bidding farewell to earthly love and lover:

> Youth gone, and beauty gone, if ever there
>   Dwelt beauty in so poor a face as this;
> Youth gone and beauty, what remains of bliss?
> I will not bind fresh roses in my hair,
> To shame a cheek at best a little fair –
>   Leave youth his roses, who can bear a thorn –
> I will not seek for blossoms anywhere,
> Except such common flowers as blow with corn.
> Youth gone, and beauty gone, what doth remain?
>   The longing of a heart pent up forlorn,
>   A silent heart whose silence loves and longs;
>   The silence of a heart which sang its songs
>   While youth and beauty made a summer morn,
> Silence of love that cannot sing again.

So the nameless lady falls silent. Momentarily, however, the mask seems transparent. If she will never again sing of love, she has left a supreme expression of its joys and pains.

Christina always insisted that *Monna Innominata* be read as a single sequence, not a collection. As a 'sonnet of sonnets', its structure echoes that of two quatrains making an octave, followed by a sestet, all parts combining into a whole. Sonnet 8, in which the lady offers to lay down her life to save her beloved, represents the 'volta' on which the meaning turns, the ultimate expression of love. Both poetically and emotionally *Monna Innominata* is thus an astonishingly subtle, layered creation, both intimate and universal, and Shakespearean in its accomplished fusion of melody and simple surfaces with depth of thought and feeling.

She was now nearly fifty, and 'quite wonderfully recovered', as Gabriel told an old friend in May, so that she could no longer be viewed as an invalid. Though never entirely free from anxiety that the thyroid condition might recur, she was certainly better, and already lamenting her increasing stoutness – generally regarded as a sign of health – by joking that a 'fat poetess' was hardly an appropriate sight. She still invoked her condition to excuse her from some of the many social obligations others now wished to heap upon her, but was far from unsociable; indeed, there were many regular and occasional visitors at Torrington Square, who were warmly and courteously welcomed. She saw many old friends, including Ellen Heaton and Alice Boyd, and on 21 June dined with the aunts and uncle Henry at William's house, now renamed 5 Endsleigh Gardens, following a murder on the far side of the Square, and where she now had a second niece, named Helen Maria.

Early in the season she took Mamma to Eastbourne. 'I think it worthwhile to date this letter,' she explained to Gabriel, 'as illustrating that even in 1880 our dearest Mother was able to leave home on a little holiday excursion, to stroll and sit out for about 3 hours daily, and to be amused on the Parade.' Others would no doubt hate the crowds, the fashions, brass bands, blacked-up 'nigger minstrels of British breed' and other tourist attractions or horrors, according to taste, but she was sufficiently frivolous to find some entertainment in it all. Visiting the Royal Academy, she had bumped into Burne-Jones, whom she had not seen for so long and who was now a star among British artists. How his kindly face and genius carried her back to times now twenty years past! There was good news too of Swinburne, who had renounced all alcohol except pale ale and was devouring food – an entire pie containing five pigeons at one meal. 'Anything is such an improvement on inebriety that I am ready to rejoice,' she commented, conjecturing that 'old habits have left a craving which must be satisfied by a quite exceptional supply of some sort!' She was sorry to hear of old Tom Taylor's death: 'may his "charities" follow him,' she wrote.

Other deaths reminded her of advancing years and prompted her own potential epitaph. 'May I deserve remembrance when my day comes, and then remembered or forgotten it will be well with me,' she told Gabriel in July.

She was looking back, as *Monna Innominata* suggests, but by no means withdrawing from moral engagement with the world. She was still active in the AV movement for instance, and also ready to voice her opinions on matters of art or conduct. One example, which helps to explain why relations with Lucy were still strained despite the separation of households, related to a poem forwarded by her sister-in-law. Author and theme remain unidentified, but according to Christina the subject was simply 'diabolical' and indeed worsened by the finesse of the treatment. 'I wish it had never been written,' she wrote plainly: 'this failing, I wish it may never be published. Of course, this is not criticism even according to the weakliest feminine standard: but what would be the use of my attempting to criticise what I should like to expunge?' ('Weakliest' here was ironic: to Christina moral standards were higher than aesthetics.)

To William her scrupulous puritan sense came to seem a positive defect. 'The narrow path was the only one for her, and a lion in the same path made no difference,' he wrote in his memoir. 'A small point she was the first to concede; but as soon as a jot of duty seemed involved, tenacity was in the very essence of her being.' Such extreme uprightness had its limitations; increasing over-scrupulosity straitened her character and closed up her mind. Yet flexibility could not be a virtue to one with high standards and a literal belief in the encroachment of evil. And simultaneously William wrote that no one felt more strongly than his sister 'the Christian obligation of being in charity with all men', and that as time passed she found this a pleasant duty. Furthermore, as he explained in a perceptive account:

> No precept of the Christian religion was more indelibly impressed upon her mind and sympathies than 'judge not, that ye be not judged'. She never – not even in thought, so far as thought was under her control – imputed a bad motive to anyone; and to hear her talking scandal or indulging in ill-natured gossip would have been equally impossible as to see her putting on a pair of knickerbockers . . .

At the same time, he continued, she 'had a large fund of discernment, and speedily fathomed defects in her acquaintances which she never announced'.

This keen sense of judgement – not always unvoiced – was illustrated in her response, this summer, to the news that the wealthy philanthropist Angela Burdett Coutts had married a much younger man. The news was 'startling, portentous, quasi-incredible,' she wrote. 'Can such ends come of such beginnings! if so, may I never have gift, grace, or glamour to woo me a husband not half my age!!'

She was similarly discerning with regard to Fred Shields, whose piety gave Christina much comfort but whose personality she found trying. 'One may walk the world as one's own wet blanket; and perhaps such is our friend's tourist costume,' she wrote after hearing his complaints about Scotland. And on another occasion she took a very severe line when Shields brought round some drawings by a young artist, evidently thinking that the author of *Goblin Market* would like pictures of 'exquisite child fairies, attired only in gauzy wings'. He was mistaken. 'Dear Mr Shields,' she wrote the next morning, apologising for having allowed politeness to mask her true views:

> I think last night in admiring Miss T's work I might better have said less, unless I could have managed to convey more. I do admire the grace and beauty of the designs, but do not think that to call a figure a 'fairy' settles the right and wrong of such figures . . .

Child nudity was not acceptable in any form, and 'last night's blunder must not make me the slave of false shame this morning'. Shields would surely agree that all should 'forbear such delineations, and that most of all women artists should lead the way'. She would have been dismayed to know that Gertrude Thomson's 'little nudities' were also ardently admired by other men she respected, including Ruskin and Dodgson, though her sense of their indecency would have been confirmed by the latter's coyly flirtatious request that the artist make friends with 'any exceptionally nice little nudity' who was willing to be victimised for his photographic benefit.

A third text Christina held constantly in mind was the injunction 'not to do anything whereby thy brother stumbleth or is offended or is made weak'. William thought this trammelled her writing, for

> she would in some instances have expressed herself with more latitude of thought and word, and to a more valuable effect, but for the fear of saying something which would somehow turn to the detriment of some timorous or dim-minded reader. She certainly felt that to write anything for publication was to incur a great spiritual responsibility.

He believed this narrowness of mind to stem from enslavement to 'old women in cassocks', as he unkindly described her clerical friends, principally Gutch. But this was to deny her independence. Whatever prudery or rigid views she espoused were those of choice, shaped by her understanding of the world. Her objections to naked fairies, for example, were based on the perceived spread of pornography and the demand by clients of high-class brothels for the sexual services of young girls. Christina's views may have been narrow, but they were not foolish, and they were shared by the many women and men at this date who supported the Social Purity movement, opposing pornography and sexual licence and advocating a single, high, moral standard for both sexes – which in the context meant primarily men.

Christina gave most thought to artistic responsibility. Had she written a sonnet on Chatterton, she told Gabriel, she would have pitied his poverty but not pardoned his suicide, and she was greatly relieved to be able to praise her brother's ballad on the drowning of the Plantagenet Prince Henry in 1120. For *The White Ship* was a moral tale – at the last moment the cruel Prince redeems his soul by sacrificing his life in an attempt to save his sister's. 'I wish you would write more such, and on such subjects: surely they are well worth celebrating, and they leave no sting behind,' she wrote. Gabriel suspected criticism. No, she replied, she was not thinking of arousing envy and spite in speaking of the innocuous nature of historic ballads '– but rather of one's own responsibility in use of an influential talent'. It was his talent she referred to, but the observation was also self-directed.

As it happened, William was right regarding her poetry: the sense of moral responsibility was inhibiting. It led to innocuous banalities like *The Months*, whereas the power of *Goblin Market* and other early work lay precisely in the vigour of her uncensored imagination, vividly portraying the taste and smell of temptation. Now she was no longer likely to take such risks.

Another moral issue arose when Lord Henry Somerset, son of the Duke of Beaufort, asked and received Christina's permission to set one of her lyrics to music. Hearing this, Gabriel warned that scandal was attached to Somerset's name, and it would be unwise to let it be in any way connected with hers. Christina wrote at once to withdraw permission, and was distressed to receive an answer in which Lord Henry asserted his innocence, saying he would 'not affect to misunderstand' her reason. He seemed 'justly hurt' and legitimately resentful of the damage done to his reputation by the circulation of slanderous gossip. 'I am very much pained,' she told Gabriel,

> and think I will write once more – FINALLY – not of course to reconsider the question of the music, but to make myself less uncomfortable in case (however blindly) I have been unjust.

She asked Gabriel not to mock her scruples, for she was, as always, 'weighed upon by the responsibility of all one does or does not do', and wrote what William described as 'rather a long letter of Christian magnanimity' to Somerset, in which she defended her decision without imputing any guilt to her correspondent.

Gabriel assured her the rumours were true, but meanwhile Somerset wrote again, enclosing two documents to prove his case: 'one I think any candid person would admit carried great weight; the other goes far with me,' she wrote; and Mamma agreed. She was therefore going to return all the correspondence so that Lord Henry could be assured that neither within nor after her lifetime would the accusations reach other hands. To make doubly sure, she left his name blank in her letter to Gabriel, lest it too unwittingly contribute to the gossip. It is not clear what she thought of the supposed facts – Lady Henry Somerset had left her husband in 1877, alleging homosexual misconduct, and had recently defeated his attempt to regain custody of their son – but far from demonstrating prudish homophobia her scruples reveal sympathy and concern. 'Poor fellow, whatever his case may be, he is infinitely to be pitied,' she told Gabriel, and William noted she was much perturbed by the matter, and inclined to believe Somerset had been unjustly treated.

Ironically, in view of his concern for Christina's reputation, Gabriel also felt it would be damaged by the Society for the Promotion of Christian Knowledge, which at the end of the year agreed to publish her Saints Calendar. Courteously, she corrected him. 'I don't think harm will accrue from my S.P.C.K books, even to my standing,' she wrote on New Year's Day: 'if it did, I should still be glad to throw my grain of dust into the religious scale.'

It snowed at Christmas, and aunt Eliza was ill, so they stayed at home. The diary Christina began keeping on her mother's behalf in 1881 gives a glimpse of daily life, showing that neither fog nor frost curtailed social activity at Torrington Square. On 4 January, she and Mamma called on Lucy, who was once more pregnant, and the following day received visits from William, Rev. Nash (incumbent of Christ Church, Woburn Square, where they now worshipped), anti-vivisectionist Mr Willmer and two women named Lauretta Warnes and Katherine Aspinell, who called by appointment and may have been admirers. After church on Thursday, Louisa Parke came to lunch and Charles Cayley to tea, which was followed by whist. On Friday Christina went to church, for a short walk and to the bank by cab with aunt Eliza; on Monday aunt Charlotte arrived from Lady Bath's. Then Christina made the journey to Chelsea, lunching with Letitia Scott, whose husband had been ill, before calling on her brother, whose condition gave rise to renewed anxiety. He was gloomy, and wrote afterwards to apologise, inviting aunt Charlotte to see his new picture. Christina replied, promising to fix an early date and hoping for milder weather. 'I say *we* because I hope to accompany her,' she added. 'At the worst, however, we can face a fair amount of cold, for this day we were cabbing and shopping about together for just 3 hours!'

The following week, however, a very severe cold spell kept even 'hardy Aunt Charlotte' indoors; only Christina managed to get to church, and then when the thaw set in it brought down part of the drawing-room ceiling. Eliza was still poorly, and old Sarah Catchpole was also in bed. Nevertheless, on 29 January Christina and Charlotte made the trip to Chelsea. Three days later, Eliza received the last sacrament, and began gifting her personal possessions, in the belief that she was near death. However, she recovered and by the beginning of March was able to go for a short drive in Regents Park.

On 24 January the death was announced of James Collinson, reviving memories of the ill-fated engagement thirty years before. Christina was already thinking about the past, for *Monna Innominata* had been succeeded by a new sequence, a double sonnet of sonnets, entitled *Later Life*. This was also part of an attempt to rouse Gabriel's dangerously low spirits, for verse was one of the few subjects on which he became animated. He had increased the *House of Life* to one hundred sonnets, and encouraged William to aim for a similar target in his *Democratic Sonnets*, on the political events of their lifetime. Christina's sequence ranged more deeply over memory and desire, comprising a sort of spiritual autobiography in which she acknowledged all regret and dissatisfaction, and contemplated the prospect of mortality. She was now fifty, having crossed this latest rubicon in December, and Collinson's death – followed within weeks by that of his sister Mary, who had so intimidated her on that visit to Pleasley Hill – surely contributed to her mood of retrospection. 'What see we glancing back?' she asked in Sonnet 6:

> Lost hopes that leave our hearts upon the rack,
>> Hopes that were never ours yet seemed to be,
>> For which we steered on life's salt stormy sea . . .

Recently she had spoken to Littledale on the subject of resignation and he, of more cheerful disposition, had urged obedience to God's will, which partakes rather of acceptance than endurance. But the poet of *Later Life* – who speaks in her own voice – is overburdened by distress, toiling forward wearily. There was much to regret, with many hopes still unfulfilled:

> We lack, yet cannot fix upon the lack:
>> Not this, nor that; yet somewhat, certainly.
>> We see the things we do not yearn to see
> Around us . . .

Maturity brought some gains, however. Now, love could be summarised with a few wise words:

> To love and to remember; that is good.
>> To love and to forget; that is not well.
>> To lapse from love to hatred, that is hell
> And death and torment, rightly understood.

Rightly understood, life was like a nightmare in which the dreamer wrestles silently with an adversary who turns out to be the self:

> And much of all our waking life, as weak
> And misconceived, eludes us like the dream.
> For half life's seemings are not what they seem . . .
>> . . .
> When I was young I deemed that sweets are sweet:
> But now I deem some searching bitters are

> Sweeter than sweets, and more refreshing far,
> And to be relished more, and more desired . . .

These were the lessons of middle age: that rightly understood shame was also a virtue – a 'stinging salve so fierce it seems that we must die', a cauterising blade thrust ino the heart. Shame and sorrow are sent for our correction: at last, these sonnets seem to be saying, she understood Pusey's puritan message without its masochism.

If *Monna Innominata* was inspired by *Sonnets from the Portuguese*, *Later Life* seems to draw on John Donne's nineteen *Holy Sonnets* with their alternation between despair, self-laceration and faithful hope. Donne was not much read by the Victorians, but he was included in Main's anthology, and Gabriel had become a confessed admirer, especially of the *Holy Sonnets* and *Progress of the Soul*. 'Do you know Donne?' he asked a young correspondent. 'There is hardly an English poet better worth a thorough knowledge.'

Like Donne, Christina placed her faith in God with an intensity that almost betrayed its desperation. But in many of her moods this faith was firm and uplifting, and her sequence was partly in answer to Tennyson's *Despair*, published in November 1881, for *Later Life* is underpinned by a mature voice that has passed anguish, and has many happy memories. The foggy weather of Sonnet 17, for instance, sets the speaker dreaming of 'somewhere' that sounds like Hastings and is also a synonym for desire:

> Ah pleasant pebbly strand so far away,
> So out of reach while quite within my reach,
> As out of reach as India or Cathay!

This recognition led on to other memories, of winter and summer, robins and nightingales, the lake at Como and the forget-me-nots on the St Gotthard. Places visited gave way to lands unseen and, in an unforced progression, to contemplation of the next world. The speaker then begins to take leave of life, proceeding to imagine her own death with Donne-like allusions to its ghastly adjuncts, taking refuge in no poetic dreamings or heavenly consolations:

> While I supine with ears that cease to hear,
> With eyes that glaze, with heart-beat running down
> (Alas, no saint rejoicing on her bed)
> May miss the goal at last, may miss the crown.

In thus imaging her own end, Christina was no doubt thinking of Maria, and perhaps also of James, for in her last sonnet she affirmed the continuing presence of loved ones, in the heart if not in life:

In life our absent friend is far away:
  But death may bring our friend exceeding near,
  Show him familiar faces long so dear
And lead him back in reach of words we say.
He only cannot utter yea or nay
  In any voice accustomed to our ear;
  He only cannot make his face appear
And turn the sun back on our shadowed day.
The dead may be around us, dear and dead;
  The unforgotten dearest dead may be
    Watching us with unslumbering eyes and heart
Brimful of words which cannot yet be said,
  Brimful of knowledge they may not impart,
  Brimful of love for you and love for me.

The virtual disappearance of such belief in the afterlife causes today's readers some difficulty with Christina's verse in this mode. Though lack of belief is not seen as an obstacle to the appreciation of seventeenth-century literature, Victorian expressions of faith are felt to represent foolish adherence to ideas that were on the eve of extinction. But to a poet like Christina, heaven was as real as to any medieval or Jacobean writer. This life was a preparation for the next, and the articulation of this spiritual truth her most valued message. It is perhaps easier now to dismiss Victorian religion than to understand it.

She prepared her new collection for publication, shortly before an anxious five-day visit to Chelsea attended by some misunderstandings. She and Mamma would not usurp his bedroom, Christina assured Gabriel, but sleep wherever beds could be conveniently placed; indeed they would happily share a bed and hope that their habit of early rising would not disturb him. She soothed his fear that they would attract visitors, saying 'I don't think you need apprehend a flood ... I don't expect anybody to pursue us to Chelsea'; it was unlikely Dr Littledale would come all the way from Bloomsbury to see her. On her own behalf she was anxious to find a suitable church for her Lenten observances, and on the third day of their stay, she and Mamma trailed off on a roundabout quest that exhausted and disappointed them. The following day Gabriel read out his new ballad, but though Christina had promised to bring 'a small mass of verse' to Cheyne Walk, he does not seem to have taken any interest in her current work. Indeed, the previous autumn he had told a hopeful anthologiser that she had no unpublished sonnets, and when informed otherwise dismissed these as a just few 'new scraps' she was hoarding for a fresh volume.

He was however involved in the compilation of this same anthology, being edited by a young admirer in Liverpool called Thomas Hall Caine. Amongst suggested contributors, he had given Caine the name of Rev. R. W. Dixon, an old friend of Burne-Jones. As it happened, Dixon was in correspondence with Gerard Manley Hopkins, currently working in Liverpool, and with his own work forwarded two of Hopkins's sonnets, *Starlight Night* and *Caged Skylark*, urging him to submit others. Hopkins sent three more, effusively acknowledged by Caine. When these reached Gabriel, however, his verdict was instant. 'I cannot in any degree tolerate Mr Hopkin's [sic] sonnets, though perceiving well that he is an able man,' he wrote on 31 March. So Christina lost the opportunity of seeing sonnets by her own poetic admirer – which may have included *God's Grandeur* and *Spring*. Or did she perhaps read them, for the sonnets were at Cheyne Walk during her Lenten visit? Had she been advising Caine, her verdict would surely have been more sympathetic.

Gabriel also reacted adversely to William's sonnets, of which there were now nearly fifty, alarmed by incendiary subjects like 'Tyrannicide' and 'Fenianism'. William was after all a civil servant; prosecution would mean absolute ruin for his family, he told Lucy. William retorted that no one else would object except perhaps Mamma and Christina, whose great age and 'isolated devoteeism' respectively reduced the practical significance of their views. As it happens, the one on the Fenian martyrs had 'touched a sympathetic cord' in Christina's heart a few weeks earlier, so neither isolation nor 'devoteeism' prejudiced her judgement. William however was sufficiently discouraged by his brother's response to abandon his whole project.

After her return home, Christina wrote to tell Macmillan she had a new collection ready. He replied swiftly, enclosing a standard 'half-profits' contract, which she was sufficiently businesslike to note appeared to assign copyright to the publisher. 'But copyright is my hobby' she wrote: 'with it I cannot part. If it is of any value I think I have the first claim upon it, and if it is of none it may gracefully be left to me!'

This matter was quickly settled in her favour, but there remained a query regarding Roberts Bros, to whom she wished to give first refusal. Macmillan's now had an American office; did this complicate matters? Within a week however everything was cleared, and she despatched the manuscript 'all ready', adding: 'perhaps you suspected I was not quite so ready!'

She presented a less businesslike attitude to William, saying she was 'somewhat in a quake, a fresh volume being a formidable upset of nerves'. But, she added, 'at any rate, it cannot turn out TWINS!' This referred to the unexpected arrival of Mary Elizabeth and Michael Ford, making a total of five children for Lucy and William and finally completing their family. Christina and Mamma visited at once and wrote to Cheltenham, where aunt Charlotte was visiting uncle Henry.

Her book was set, proofed, printed and bound within thirteen weeks, and publication was announced for 25 July – rather to the author's surprise. 'I should have fancied this moment [fell] between 2 publishing seasons,' she wrote to William, 'but it seems unlikely that a sane publisher should not understand his own business better than I do.'

She had chosen *The Months* as lead poem, and the book was therefore titled *A Pageant and Other Poems*, which in retrospect seems a mistake; a lead poem needs to be impressive. Moreover, *The Months*, essentially a poem for children, set the wrong tone for the volume. Perhaps it was chosen simply on grounds of length, though *Later Life* occupies more pages and was surely more appropriate. Indeed, Christina's reputation would today stand higher if this, her third major collection, were known as *Later Life and Other Poems* and seen as the poetic harvest of her maturity. Instead of being flagship, *The Months* could then have brought up the rear – which would also have enabled the usual order of the book to be reversed, with the sacred poems preceding the secular. Whatever Gabriel's anti-devotional bias, this would have worked to the collection's advantage.

Another mistake was her dedicatory *Keynote* poem, implying that all were the last, fading leaves of a dying muse:

> Where are the songs I used to know,
>   Where are the notes I used to sing?
>   I have forgotten everything
> I used to know so long ago;
> Summer has followed after Spring;
>   Now Autumn is so shrunk and sere,
> I scarcely think a sadder thing
>   Can be the Winter of my year.
> Yet Robin sings through Winter's rest,
>   When bushes put their berries on;
>   While they their ruddy jewels don,
> He sings out of a ruddy breast;
> The hips and haws and ruddy breast
>   Make one spot warm where snowflakes lie,
> They break and cheer the unlovely rest
>   Of Winter's pause – and why not I?

The notion of ruddy berries does not do justice to the major jewels of the book – *Monna Innominata, Later Life, An Old-World Thicket*. In writing to Gabriel on the eve of publication, Christina explicitly hoped that the sonnet sequences would 'claim attention', but she had done nothing to signpost them. Moreover, her superstitious desire to make each volume the same length led her to include a considerable quantity of what can only pejoratively be called light verse, such as *Freaks of Fashion*, together with some very feeble efforts like the quasi-Tennysonian *Brandons Both*, and the surpassingly sentimental *Johnny*. If Gabriel thought *The Lowest Room* a bad poem, one wonders what he made of these.

The true keynote was valediction. For here are the mourning poems for Maria, the explicit farewell to Italy, the lines in which an immured nun celebrates her state, various verses bidding goodbye to youth and beauty, and a new invocation of martyrdom, in which a sequence of gory images that hark back to teenage imaginings is followed by a maturer lament on approaching age:

> For flesh and blood are frail and sore afraid
> And young I am, unsatisfied and young,
>   With memories, hopes, with cravings all unfed,
> My song half sung, its sweetest notes unsung,
>   All plans cut short, all possibilities. . . .

She could still describe herself as having cravings that would never be achieved. Her songs were not so much wintry or withered, but still unsung, still governed by desire, and now heightened by the sense of closing possibilities – a regret held in check by an insistent but not assured belief in full satisfaction hereafter. Nor is this merely the familiar *tempus fugit* theme, but a keener menopausal poignancy induced by age.

The triple sonnet sequence *The Thread of Life* may legitimately be regarded as a personal utterance in this same vein. It opens with a reverse assertion of the pathetic fallacy which states that the 'irresponsive silence' of nature on land and sea speak 'one message' of inner solitude; and continues:

> Thus am I mine own prison. Everything
>   Around me free and sunny and at ease . . .
> Then gaze I at the merrymaking crew,
>   And smile a moment and a moment sigh
> Thinking: Why can I not rejoice with you?
>   But soon I put the foolish fancy by:
> I am not what I have nor what I do;
>   But what I was I am, I am even I.
>
>   . . .
>
> Therefore myself is that one only thing
>   I hold to use or waste, to keep or give;

> My sole possession every day I live,
> And still mine own despite Time's winnowing.
> Ever mine own, while moon and seasons bring
> From crudeness ripeness mellow and sanative . . .

' "Surviving" is the lot of old age,' Christina wrote to Caroline Gemmer some while later:

> No, I don't exactly take the *tantalization* and *delusion* view of past years. They all have led me up to what now I am, and the whole series is leading me to my final self. I trust all I have vainly wished for here will be more than made up to me hereafter if – an all-momentous if! – I endure to the end. After all, life is short, and I should not immerse myself too deeply in its interests. Please note that I say "I should not" – I dare not pretend "I do not".

Into her third sonnet she placed a statement of future intent, saying that though the past has created the present, yet she still has herself 'to use or waste', in shaping her final being. In response to what she perceives as Christ's bidding, she will therefore 'sing A sweet new song of His redeemed set free' – a song of the victory of redemption over death. This is the clearest announcement of Christina's understanding of her poetic task henceforth, and one that governed the rest of her career.

35

Gabriel's Death

IN PUBLISHING *A Pageant and Other Poems* in mid-July, Macmillan probably regarded this as a book that would sell steadily rather than in a blaze of publicity, but certainly his timing delayed and damaged its prospects with reviewers. On publication day the author was on vacation with her mother and aunts, in Sevenoaks, after several tiring days spent searching for accommodation in Edmonton (where Rev. Burrows was now resident) and Hampstead. They took drives and a walk in Knole Park, 'of such an extent as might well beforehand have seemed quite out of the question,' she told Amelia triumphantly. They saw deer and squirrels and sat under a great beech tree whose wrinkled grey bark reminded Charlotte of an elephant. Moreover, their landlady had been a close friend of Geraldine Jewsbury – one of the literary heroines of Christina's youth – and altogether the lodgings were 'the very nicest we ever occupied'.

Receiving his copy of *A Pageant* at the end of July, Gabriel at first refrained from detailed reading, complaining only of the self-deprecating *Keynote* sonnet. 'Considering that I was "old and cold and grey" so many years ago,' Christina replied, 'it is (as you suggest) no wonder that nowadays I am "so shrunk and sere".' Then she added with a burst of humour: 'If only my figure would shrink somewhat! For a fat poetess is incongruous, especially when seated by the grave of buried hope.'

She was not sulking beside the grave of twice-buried hope because he had not read her book she added, five days later. 'In fact, there is a certain sense in which delay respites one's nerves, however in the long run one wants to be read . . . No reviews have reached me as yet.' She was disappointed to learn that the American edition was delayed, and was indeed more eager to be read than to protect her nerves for her fear of criticism was now more apparent than real.

The first review came from Gabriel's young friend Mr Caine, who had been invited to live at Cheyne Walk. Amongst other things, he misread her preface, arguing that she was wrong to state that cheerful verse must be drawn from fancy while sadness was 'of necessity drawn from feeling', and adding that she was mistaken in saying that Mrs Browning would, if unhappy, have created a lady 'more worthy' to stand beside Beatrice and Laura. She had not meant that at all, Christina replied to Gabriel, misreading this in her turn as a criticism of the 'Portuguese' poems. 'Surely not only what I meant to say but what I do say is, not that the Lady of those sonnets is surpassable, but that a "Donna innominata" by the same hand might well have been unsurpassable,' she wrote.

Gabriel sent his own comments via Mamma. The *Pageant* was 'most lovely', and *Monna Innominata* beautiful and impressive. *A Ballad of Boding* was 'grimmish on the whole', while *Behold a Shaking* (a double sonnet on the Last Judgement) might 'keep youngsters awake' at night. To this Christina replied succinctly: 'I cannot joke on that subject'. But she was pleased to hear, via Mr Watts, of Swinburne's 'dancing and screaming ecstasy' on reading the *Pageant* and from Letitia (immured by rain with her husband and Alice at Penkill) of Scott's warm admiration for *Monna*. It was, he told Gabriel, 'equal or superior to anything she has done, or anyone has done', while reading *Summer is Ended* prompted him to send a dried rosebud, with two stanzas in memory of time past:

> Once a rose, ever a rose, we say,
> A loved one who loved us . . .
>
> Sere and sealed for a day and a year,
> Smell it, Christina, I pray.

Watts was predictably respectful when his notice took the lead review in the *Athenaeum*, praising the sonnets, whose 'cadences seem to recall a nightingale note, which will ring in every English ear as long as there are English ears to listen'. But it was his remark on *The Months* that gave most pleasure. 'To get back a moment to my book –,' she wrote to Gabriel, 'I cannot forbear adding how delighted I am at the favourable verdicts on the *Pageant*. I fancy it among the best and most wholesome things I have produced.'

It was certainly among the most wholesome, but the remark betrays some anxiety, for the moral responsibility incurred by fame and influential talent was not always easy to reconcile with good writing, and she needed the reassurance of 'favourable verdicts' on pieces that might otherwise miss her high targets. At some level, she knew these were not the best she could do.

Called to be Saints finally appeared in the autumn, as *Young Plants and Polished Corners*. It sold well, which was more than could be said for her poems, though their first American review had proved favourable. Augusta Webster sent a copy of her latest volume, and duly received *A Pageant* in return. Mr Swinburne got *Called to be Saints* and professed himself delighted with the poem on St Bartholomew. The

SPCK's editorial director was brought to tea by Dr Littledale and the book received an unexpected review in the *Academy*. On Holy Innocents, Mamma and aunt Eliza, attending All Saints, heard the preacher begin with an allusion to her work. Such was the wholesome influence she sought.

The autumn also saw the publication of Gabriel's new collection, *Poems and Ballads*, and the purchase by Liverpool Corporation of his huge canvas, *Dante's Dream on the Anniversary of the Death of Beatrice*. But it was a painful fact that 'no scintilla of pleasure or cheerfulness seemed to come from this double achievement,' William recalled; 'the curtains were drawn round his innermost self and the dusk had closed over him and was fast darkening into night.' The metaphor concealed William's reluctance to acknowledge this, for he had now become rather impatient with his brother's gloomy hypochondria.

Sin and guilt became oppressive. 'I can make nothing of Christianity, but I only want a confessor to give me absolution for my sins,' Gabriel told Scott when the latter paid a rare visit to Tudor House, though living only doors away. Sleeping or waking, he was troubled by disturbing dreams and memories. 'Matters of very old date agitated his mind,' explained William, referring in particular to an incident in the 1840s when filial insolence had provoked their father's anger. Behind this lay the unresolved distress of that time, and Gabriel's refusal of responsibility when, in order to retain his privileges as an art student, he had obliged the others to shoulder burdens and shown scant sympathy for his father's illness. Shame therefore haunted his mind. 'Have I not heard and seen those that died long years ago?' he told Scotus, apparently in reference to Lizzie. But there were also other skeletons in Gabriel's closet.

Alarmed by his tendency to cancel visits, Christina and her mother took to calling without pre-arrangement. On 26 November, for example, Christina invited herself to dinner at the Scotts' and made this the excuse to call on her brother, whom she found in a sad state. Two days later she returned with Mamma, relieved to find Caine and Watts in attendance. Then William disclosed the reason for Gabriel's distress. 'I seem to recover a shadowy recollection of the incident,' Christina replied; 'and, if I am right, Mamma used her influence successfully to get the words unsaid. No wonder that in weakness and suffering such a reminiscence haunts weary days and sleepless hours of double darkness.' She could not herself speak to Gabriel, who had confided in his brother, but perhaps William could induce him to seek counsel from someone like Mr Burrows; 'you must laugh at me if you will, but I really think a noble spiritual influence might do what no common sense, foresight of ruin, affection of friends, could secure.'

They were all acutely aware of the morbid nature of his imaginings, which brought uncle John Polidori's suicide to mind. So two days later she wrote directly, offering her own counsel:

My Dearest Gabriel,

I write because I cannot but write, for you are continually in my thoughts and always in my heart, much more in our Mother's who sends you her love and dear blessing.

I want to assure you that, however harrassed by memory or by anxiety you may be, I have (more or less) heretofore gone through the same ordeal. I have borne myself till I became unbearable to myself, and then I have found help in confession and absolution and spiritual counsel, and relief inexpressible. Twice in my life I tried to suffice myself with measures short of this, but nothing would do; the first time was of course in my youth before my general confession, the second time was when circumstances had led me (rightly or wrongly) to break off the practice. But now for years past I have resumed the habit, and I hope not to continue it profitlessly.

" 'Tis like frail man to love to walk on high.
But to be lowly is to be like God"

is a couplet (Isaac Williams) I thoroughly assent to.

I ease my own heart by telling you all this, and I hope I do not weary yours. Don't think of me merely as the younger sister whose glaring faults are known to you, but as a devoted friend also.

This heartfelt letter is the most direct acknowledgement Christina made of her teenage breakdown, and though it does not identify the 'memory or anxiety' that had harrassed her, it is clear that she felt affinity with Gabriel's haunted suffering, and that his mental return to the troubled 1840s rewoke her own experience of that distressful decade, which it eased her heart to speak of.

She certainly sympathised more with Gabriel than did William. 'Don't you think neither you nor I can quite appreciate all he is undergoing at present?' she wrote, urging him not to ascribe all their brother's 'doings and non-doings to foundationless fidgetiness'. She added compassionately: 'It is trying to do with him at times, but what must it be TO BE himself? And he in so many ways the head of our family – it doubles the pity.'

Gabriel then suffered a minor stroke, which left him partly paralysed, though the family were reassured by medical opinion that this was a hysterical symptom. The doctor had also replaced chloral with morphia, causing the recurrence of violent delusions, nightmares, hallucinations and confused speech. These would diminish, Gabriel was told, with 'a proper exertion of will' and vigorous exercise. From this distance, the diagnosis appears woeful: whatever the cause, he was now very sick physically as well as mentally.

'My dear Mr Watts,' wrote Christina:

I am glad your hopes have rallied thus encouraging ours – for indeed the alarm was terrible. Next week perhaps we may be readmissible to the sick room, for neither my Mother nor I have seen poor Gabriel since Sunday when I went alone. I am writing this same post to Mr Maudsley to ask him whether there is a chance for us: I do hope dear Gabriel does not by chance miss us and fancy himself neglected.

In the New Year, he agreed to travel to Birchington in Kent, to stay in a newly-built holiday house offered by Tom Seddon's architect brother, on condition his mother and sister come too. Both had been unwell with winter coughs and colds aggravated by stress, but on 2 March they joined him, Caine and nurse Mrs Abrey, grieved to find Gabriel much weaker and in pain. 'Pray do not doubt the reality of poor dear Gabriel's illness,' Christina told William on 14 March. 'With all my wish to send you news, I really cannot say whether [he] is gaining or losing ground':

Wherever he is, Mamma and I sit with him a great deal; and he reads not novels only, but occasionally he takes up a newspaper. I spoke to Mrs Abrey this morning, aiming to arrive at her real opinion: – she cannot account for the continued wasting away which goes on in spite of food and in some measure of tonics.

Indeed, he was worse than when he arrived. This was 'sad indeed, but the not saying it is vain'. And she unintentionally admitted more in writing to a friend, saying 'nor do I know when Mamma and I are likely to return home . . . and the strain upon her and upon me is not small'.

Both London and local doctors continued to hold out hope, even when they diagnosed 'brain-softening' and kidney failure. She and Mamma divided the night watch, Mamma sitting up till midnight and Christina till six a.m., with Nurse Abrey and Caine taking charge during the day. On 7 April William and Watts were summoned by telegram. It was Good Friday, and the local rector Mr Alcock came and prayed with the invalid, who did not object. With Watts's help, Gabriel made his will, leaving everything to his brother and sister. Christina protested vehemently, and succeeded in getting her name replaced by Mamma's. With Mrs Abrey she sat with Gabriel through Saturday night, causing her to miss church on Easter Sunday, and in the evening, as they were planning the night shifts – Mamma, William and Christina in turn – Gabriel suddenly threw his arms out, screamed loudly, and fell back insensible. The nurse raised the alarm, the doctor was sent for, and all assembled round the bed. At 9.31 p.m. he was pronounced dead.

More telegrams were despatched. They chose a spot for the grave in Birchington churchyard (Gabriel refused to be buried at Highgate), and the funeral was fixed for Friday, when aunt Charlotte joined the depleted family and more than a dozen of Gabriel's friends and fellow artists. Christina gathered woodspurge and forget-me-nots from the garden. Before the interment Fred Shields made a tearful drawing of Gabriel's head, and a professional firm took a deathmask. On the day of the funeral, the *Athenaeum* printed an obituary composed by Watts, announcing the death of 'one of the most rarely gifted men of our time ... wonderful as an artist and poet, yet still more wonderful as a man'.

Christina wrote a commemorative poem, which was published a fortnight later. Her description of the graveyard demonstrates that even in bereavement she preferred accuracy to idealisation.

> A lowly hill which overlooks a flat,
>   Half-sea, half countryside;
>   A flat-shored sea of low-voiced creeping tide
> Over a chalky weedy mat.

She concluded without reference to immortality:

> A lowly hope, a height that is but low,
>   While Time sets solemnly,
>   While the tide rises of Eternity
> Silent and neither swift nor slow.

Relieved that his earthly sufferings were over, she had no hope that Gabriel had joined Maria in heaven. She had prayed hard, but there was no evidence of grace. Indeed, to Caine's young sister, who had spent part of March at Birchington, Gabriel had told a macabre joke of a dying man. 'Do you know why Christ died?' asked the vicar. 'Oh sir!' replied the man, 'is this the time to ask conundrums?' And this grim jest was matched by a new poem Gabriel had begun on the Dutchman who wagered his soul in a smoking match with the devil – a 'grotesque-horrid ballad' in Christina's words – as well as by his very last sonnet on the Sphinx's question, indicative of a final, desperate desire for the non-existent key to the meaning of human life. To Christina there was no mystery, but a straight promise in the words of Christ, and it was grievous that Gabriel died unbelieving.

*

As Gabriel lay dying, Christina received a request to contribute to the biographical series *Eminent Women*, being offered a list of possible subjects including Elizabeth Fry, Mary Lamb, George Sand, George Eliot, Harriet Martineau and Adelaide Procter, with the suggestion that the last of these might prove most suitable.

She was both interested and willing. She would gladly try Mrs Fry, or Mary Lamb, who was 'both manageable and well worth writing', she told William. But she would not consider 'the 2 Georges' or Miss Martineau, with whose views she did not sympathise. The proposed fee of fifty pounds was ample, she told the commissioning editor John Ingram, recommending also three more potential authors 'adapted and willing to contribute biographies': Letitia Scott, Caroline Gemmer and 'most of all Henrietta Rintoul'.

She was much tempted to tackle Adelaide Procter, whom many years ago she had known personally, together with 'one or two of her intimate friends', though it was so long since she had mixed in that literary circle that she doubted her ability to get at private sources of information. She surmised that 'a great part of the volume of from 150 to 200 pages must in the case of a quiet life, such as I suppose Miss Procter's to have been, be made up of quotations from her unpublished verse or of available correspondence should such come to light'. At the same time, however, she told Ingram that the ideal author for this book was Anna Mary Watts (née Howitt) – who had been 'in the heart of that social set', instead of like herself 'on its merest outskirt'. Anna Mary had long dropped out of the public eye, but the successful reissue of *An Art Student in Munich* in 1880 may have suggested she was about to resume a literary career. Christina herself could not promise speedy delivery. 'I am but a slow worker, and could not prefix a time for sending in,' she explained; therefore 'it might (might it not?) suit us both better if instead of one of the *earlier* lives of the series being assigned to me one of the *later* should be selected'.

Gabriel's death postponed further consideration, but within weeks Ingram returned to the project, this time suggesting Elizabeth Barrett Browning. Again Christina was interested:

> I should write with enthusiasm of that great poetess and (I believe) loveable woman, whom I was never, however, so fortunate as to meet. But before I could put pen to paper it would be necessary for me to know what would be Mr Browning's wish in this matter – and by his wish, whatever it might be, I should feel bound; both because he as her husband seems to me the one person entitled to decide how much or how little concerning her should during his lifetime be made public, and because having long enjoyed a slight degree of acquaintance with him I could not

but defer to his wish. On the other hand I would far rather you (if you think proper to do so) should feel the way on such delicate ground.

Unfortunately for us, Robert Browning did not wish for such a biography, which effectively cancelled the project as far as Christina was concerned. She could not 'embark on the memoir of E.B.B' without his co-operation, and strongly sympathised with his reticence.

Ingram persisted, some months later proposing that she write a life of Ann Radcliffe, Gothick author of *The Mysteries of Udolpho* and *The Italian*, which had thrilled Christina in her teens. 'She takes my fancy more than many, tho' I know next to nothing about her,' she replied:

And I will try my pen upon her, if you please. Are any hopes to be indulged of private letters, journals, what not, becoming accessible to us? or must I depend exclusively on looking up my subject at the British Museum?

Research began, and the fee was accepted, subject to sufficient material being discovered. Christina then wrote to the *Athenaeum* asking for unpublished materials, and contacted her old acquaintance Professor Masson, now at Edinburgh, who recommended the keeper of the British Museum Library Richard Garnett, who 'knew all about everything'. But it proved fruitless: there was not enough information on Mrs Radcliffe's life, and in the fall of 1883 Christina reluctantly abandoned the project. 'Returned from the seaside I can only say I have done my best to collect Radcliffe material and have failed,' she told Ingram. 'Some one else, I dare say, will gladly attempt the memoir, but I despair and withdraw. Pray pardon me for having kept you so long in suspense.'

Though no biography resulted, Christina's readiness and professionalism were considerable, and even extended to asking for a specimen sheet in order to calculate how many pages of manuscript were needed for a book of the requisite length. A sense of literary sisterhood rises from the project, too, both in terms of the subjects – Christina's literary mothers and cousins as it were – and in her recommendation of friends as fellow authors. In the event, none contributed to the *Eminent Women* series. As it happened, Lucy Brown did, writing on Mary Shelley, and it may have been this essay into authorship that gave rise to her daughter's belief in a certain literary resentment between her mother and aunt.

Christina was approaching potential eminence herself, as her critical reputation and anthology representation show, though her ultimate fame was by no means assured. In 1883, for example, a study of

English Poetesses: A Series of Critical Biographies with Illustrative Extracts from Aphra Behn to the present, allocated a full chapter to Barrett Browning but included Christina in an assorted group containing Jean Ingelow, Augusta Webster, newcomer Alice Meynell and now-forgotten Emily Pfeiffer and Harriet Hamilton King. And once more the biographical sketch was largely devoted to Gabriel, merely giving details of her birth and the titles of her books. The editor was however good enough to send Christina a proof copy of her entry, thereby allowing her to correct errors of fact and syntax and complain of his outline of *Goblin Market*. Why 'goblin curl' instead of 'golden curl'? she asked; 'also why "delicious" dream? Nothing can be further from my intention (*see* original text!).'

A couple of years later, Elizabeth Sharp, preparing an anthology of women's writings, was more flattering. 'I need hardly say that, in common with all who know as well as love English Poetry, I recognise your work as belonging to the first rank,' she wrote in January 1885. She proposed to give as much space as she could to Christina and Mrs Browning, who both had 'a special right thereto'.

In general Christina did her best to accommodate anthology re-quests, though she opposed the use of extracts. 'I do not mind what piece you select, subject only to your taking any piece in question *in its entirety*,' she wrote to an American anthologiser in 1883, insisting that all components of a sequence such as *Monna Innominata* had a unity which was intended by the author. And was it possible that the compiler of a school anthology wished to reprint 'the *entire* text' of *Goblin Market*? she asked Macmillan on another occasion. 'If this is indeed her and your wish I consent – but on no account if any portion whatever is to be omitted.'

But this principle was often bent, or ignored. Elizabeth Sharp was refused permission to take one sonnet from *Monna Innominata*, but allowed to extract two from *Later Life*. Religious editors were hard to oppose, and more usually won the argument. Indeed, Christina took special pains to assist sacred anthologies, particularly in her extensive relations with Rev. W. G. Horder, editor of the popular *Poets' Bible*, which contained poems from all periods on scriptural subjects. Sur-prising though it may seem, she herself had seldom written on biblical incidents, so no work of hers was included in Horder's first volume. As she told the reverend editor in 1881, 'If any of my own pieces could find place in your proposed volume they would be quite at your service. But they are so prevalently in a subjective vein that I fear they may not repay you for a sifting.' Her 'suggestions and counsel' were acknowledged in the preface, however, for she had sent recom-mendations, including one that suggests tender memories had been awakened by the death of her former sweetheart; this was 'a blank verse poem of some length on the "sorrowful mysteries" of our Lord's life, written by James Collinson, an artist not long deceased, and published in a now rare magazine entitled *The Germ* about the year 1849 . . .'

Politely, Horder called to convey his thanks in person. He did not avail himself of *The Child Jesus*, but when the following year he compiled a new work called *Intimations of Immortality* he asked for *Later Life* 24 and *Monna Innominata* 13 – apparently also requesting her to alter the reference to God's foreknowledge in the latter poem on the grounds that this denied free will. 'Dear Mr Horder,' she replied courteously but firmly:

> I am very glad if you can utilise 'The Wise do send . . .' I heartily wish I could answer quite the same to 'If I could trust . . .' – but here you have already (have you not?) felt that convictions and principles are involved – I cannot unsay what I hold to be absolutely true, even if originally I might have expressed myself better. And if one of the illogical sex may without offence argue with one of the logical, I would venture to illustrate my point by observing that my prescience that you will take all kindly does not *compel* you to do so!

In 1883, for an enlarged *Poets' Bible*, Horder picked two poems from the *Pageant* volume, and for an Old Testament anthology in 1885 he selected several more, including *By the Waters of Babylon* and the sonnet on Esther from *Monna Innominata*. In return Christina sent a copy of her latest devotional work. 'Thank you for your kind words about my new little book,' she replied to his acknowledgement. 'Be sure that not one of my readers would be more genuinely pleased than myself if I could always write poems!' 'But just because poetry *is* a gift – I scarcely dare to follow your allusion to prophets in company with poets – I am not surprised to find myself unable to summon it at will and use it according to my own choice.' She was gratified nonetheless: this was her conception of the responsibility of fame.

To William fell the responsibility of winding up Gabriel's estate and approving suitable memorials. A retrospective exhibition was planned at the Royal Academy (somewhat ironically, enmity having existed between Gabriel and the Academy during his life) and after personal mementoes had been distributed to family and friends, the contents of Tudor House, excluding works of art, were auctioned in early July, realising sufficient funds to meet Gabriel's debts, and leaving sufficient within the estate to provide a handsome inheritance.

Madox Brown was asked to design a headstone, and Fred Shields a memorial window. Then there was the question of biographies, as authors rushed into print. The first was relatively harmless, being by a stranger with little knowledge of Gabriel's life, which appeared in July. Caine's recollections of Gabriel's last months, published in early autumn, were much less to the family's taste, being marked by unctuous and morbid sensationalism. William, who had objected to large parts, tried not to let his feelings show. True to her principles, Christina tried not to impute base motives to Caine. 'Considering the circumstances under which his experiences occurred, I think it may be fairly pronounced neither unkind nor unfriendly,' she told Lucy. But she hoped one day to see her brother's life written 'by some friend of older standing and consequently of far warmer affection towards his hero; who, whatever he was or was not, was loveable'.

No older friend came forward; instead a very recent acquaintance named William Sharp began a book for Macmillan on Gabriel's work. Declining the dedication, Christina agreed to answer a few questions. Though coloured by a sort of misleading reverence whose effect is subtly derogatory, Sharp's recollections over a decade later show how the somewhat forbidding 'fat poetess' appeared in these later years.

They had first met in the autumn of 1880 when Sharp paid a formal call at a house in Bloomsbury on a rapidly darkening afternoon. Other guests were present, and the lamps were not yet lit, he recalled, and his arrival caused only a momentary interruption in the conversation, dominated by a woman giving a vivid account of her experiences with slum children in the country, who was convinced it was 'not possible for anyone to live a happy life unless they have a brief sojourn in the country at least every year'.

At this point a singularly clear and rippling laugh interrupted the speaker. The voice had a bell-like sound, like that of resonant crystal. The pronunciation was unusually distinct . . .

'Ah,' she said, 'there comes in the delightful enthusiast. But Mrs — I assure you that your good heart is mistaken. There are hundreds and thousands of us who for one reason or another never escape from London. I may speak for myself, alas, who am not only as confirmed a Londoner as was Charles Lamb, but really doubt if it would be good for me, now, to sojourn often or long in the country, and you must remember there are more Lambs than Wordsworths among us townfolk, and that as we are bred so we live.'

'But,' said the lady, 'You yourself must admit that you would be far happier in the peace and beauty of the country which is so infinitely more poetic, in every way so much more beautiful than the town!'

How cool and quiet the bell-like voice sounded now!

'I am one of those who think with Bacon that the Souls of the living are the Beauty of the world!'

'That is a beautiful saying ... but now let me ask, do not you yourself find your best inspiration in the country?'

'I? ... oh dear no! I know it *ought* to be so. But I don't derive my inspiration, as you call it – though if you will allow me to say so, I think the word quite inapposite, and to be used of very few, and then only in the most literal sense – I don't derive anything from the country at first hand! Why, my knowledge of what is called nature is that of a town sparrow or, at most, that of the pigeon which makes an excursion occasionally from its home in Regents Park or Kensington Gardens. And, what is more, I am fairly sure that I am in the place that suits me best. After all, we may enjoy the majesty and mystery of the ocean without ever adventuring upon it; and I and thousands of other Londoners, from the penniless to those who are as relatively poor as I am, are in the position of those who love the sea, and understand, too, in a way, its beauty and wonder, even though we reside in Bloomsbury or Whitechapel.'

As far as Sharp was concerned, the speaker of these words was a short, stout woman of advancing years, with strangely protruding eyes. He was not introduced and when the lamps were lit she veiled herself abruptly, rising to leave.

Some time later, he was told that Miss Rossetti the poetess was a gloomy, bigoted religionist and recluse, morbidly sensitive to her appearance following a severe illness. From Gabriel he heard anecdotes about *The Germ* and the *Verses* of 1847, and was encouraged to call at Torrington Square, where he received a courteous and friendly reception. Opening the door Christina recognised his face and resumed the conversation about Bacon before leading him upstairs to meet Mamma, to whom he was introduced as 'Gabriel's young friend'. This time, Sharp was struck by Christina's sallow, heavily lined face, dark hair thickly threaded with white, Quakerish plainness of dress, and her constant fingering of a watchchain below the mauve ribbon that fastened her lace collar. When Sharp failed to know the source of Bacon's remark on the souls of the living she replied smiling: 'Do you know Mr Garnett of the British Museum? He knows everything, I am told, fortunate man!'; and finally, when conversation flagged, she asked if he would like to hear Southwell's *Burning Babe*, which she was reading to Mamma.

They met again briefly at Birchington and then when Sharp began his book. Christina volunteered a number of tales about Gabriel's youth, including the story of their visit to the Zoo when he invented fanciful biographies for the animals, and also her dream of escaped canaries, which Gabriel had promised to paint. 'He was always like this as far back as I can remember, though less whimsical and more moody as a youth than as a boy or a man,' she explained. Of herself, as was appropriate, she said little. 'She was too humble to speak much opinionatively unless directly challenged or skilfully allured,' Sharp noted later; 'while it seemed natural in herself to consider that the centre of interest was in her companion of the moment and not herself'. Socially speaking, he added, she was shy, remote, silent and gloomy.

One would like to have an account from Elizabeth Sharp, compiler of the *Women's Voices* anthology, who accompanied her husband on at least one visit to Torrington Square. Other visitors noted that her opinions were often distinctive and surprising. 'She paid more attention to social questions than one would be apt to suppose, and respecting them her attitude was often highly individual,' wrote Mackenzie Bell, her first biographer. Neither silence nor remoteness would seem an exact description of Christina at this date.

POLITICALLY, CHRISTINA'S VIEWS could be quite pronounced. In the summer of 1882, for example, insurrection in Egypt was suppressed by the British government according to its imperialist lights, with gunboats, a naval bombardment of Alexandria, the evacuation of British residents ('fate of remaining Europeans and Christians unknown' according to the *Illustrated London News*) and the eventual occupation of the city by British troops. Prime Minister Gladstone asked Parliament to approve extra expenditure to cover the cost of this operation, which led William to protest against paying increased income tax for this purpose, and Christina to add:

> How willingly would I *incur* Income Tax for the sake of *not* murdering Egyptians or anyone else!

She also penned a curious poem – the latest example of public events provoking her to protest verse. The *St James's Gazette*, an evening newspaper of Conservative views ('Alexandria evacuated in Flames – Horrible Atrocities – Landing in force ordered') carried an irregular column of political comment in verse, and on 21 July poured scorn on the resignation of veteran Radical John Bright, while elsewhere attacking Gladstone for his handling of the crisis. Bright had resigned as a matter of principle in protest against the shelling of Alexandria, but the squib charged him with hypocrisy, in parodic lines beginning 'When raged the conflict fierce and hot'. Christina responded with a parody of her own poem *No Thank You, John!*, under the title *Counterblast on Penny Trumpet*:

> If Mr Bright retiring does not please,
>   And Mr Gladstone staying gives offence,
> What can man do which is not one of these?
>   Use your own common sense.
>
> Yet he's a brave man who abjures his cause
>   For conscience' sake: let byegones be byegones:
> Not *this* among the makers of our laws
>   The last and least of Johns.

> If all our byegones could be piled on shelves
>   High out of reach of penny-line Tyrtaeus!
> If only all of us could see ourselves
>   As others see us!

Though probably not written with publication in mind, this evidently relieved Christina's own indignation.

Her verses chimed with the views on India that she expressed to Mrs Heimann regarding the 'terrible Indian news' following the British victory at Kandahar in 1880. 'I do think our Indian crown is in great measure the trapping of a splendid misery: and how should it be otherwise when so much injustice and bloodshed have (I believe) founded and upheld our rule?' she wrote. ' "All the perfumes of Arabia cannot sweeten this little hand": and the riches and influence of such an empire would be a world well lost, if thus we could learn to do justice and love mercy and walk humbly.'

This is the most explicit example of Christina taking upon herself as a British citizen (in her use of 'our' and 'us') the responsibility for imperial injustice. William claimed that his sister 'knew and cared next to nothing about party politics' and 'in all her later years her feeling leaned more towards the Conservative than the Liberal cause', but the impression this gives of detachment and an increasingly reactionary position is misleading. Christina felt keenly and independently about issues such as slavery, military conquest, animal welfare, so in certain respects her views were distinctly more Radical than Conservative. Far from distancing herself from political responsibility, she included herself among those who would benefit morally from a 'well lost' empire.

In one sense, however, William was right about his sister's dislike of party politics, for she also denounced party feeling, 'whether called religious zeal or national antagonism or political creed', each of which became in her view 'simply devilish when it leads us not only to condemn opponents (or it may even be those merely to whom we are opposed) but to wish that they may really be as unworthy as history or rumour makes them' and to 'court and hug and blaze abroad every tittle of evidence that tells against them'.

This came from her new book called *Letter and Spirit*, completed over the autumn and winter of 1882–3, which took moral conduct as its starting-point in a study of the Commandments and confirmed her steady access of confidence in the role of religious writer. No longer content merely to marshall holy writ, Miss Rossetti was now ready to interpret it, and offer her own lessons regarding personal and political morality, in the manner of any preacher. She was, for instance, bold in taking a prophetic stance regarding contemporary injustice and godlessness, in Old Testament style. ' "Therefore now shall they go captive with the first that go captive",' she quoted, '– words which speak to us of the nineteenth century and not least in England with an awful omen. Surely for us, as for Nebuchadnezzar of old, it is high time to "break off our sins by righteousness and our iniquities by showing mercy to the poor" '. She prayed that 'we in England may penitently consider and amend our ways', suggesting that the current diminution of national wealth and honour (through economic recession and military defeats) was already a sign of imminent chastisement and '(unless we repent) the beginning of the end'.

In such admonitions, she was without apology assuming the mantle of Victorian sage, urging national repentance to cure present ills. This was a role Carlyle had filled until his death in 1881, followed by Ruskin, Arnold and a host of lesser commentators in the periodical press. In more strictly religious guise it was of course the chiliasm derived from Dodsworth and his 'signs of the times' – and for those reared in this tradition there was undeniable proof of unrighteousness not only in poverty at home and oppression in India or Egypt, but above all in the steady growth of unbelief. For religious as well as political reasons, Christina's faith urged her to intervene in secular affairs.

Though didactic in purpose, however, the mode of her new book was ruminative, as she deliberated on her subjects in a manner that drew them into a spiritual unity. Her basic texts were the ten commandments of the decalogue and the two of Christ, on loving God and thy neighbour, but her commentary was not for beginners, being addressed to a more sophisticated audience who like herself were accustomed to complex and subtle homiletic reading. She did not therefore write on the wrongness of murder, but provided instead an extensive discourse on ignoring God, the spiritual equivalent, together with a good deal on unintentional error by the devout, who might be misled by zeal into forsaking the spirit of Christian teaching. Hence, of course, her title.

Not surprisingly, many of the warnings in *Letter and Spirit* were self-directed, especially those analysing the faults of over-scrupulosity – the wire-drawn desire to avoid sin at all costs – which she identified as something to which the devout were especially prone. Thus, she warned the punctilious that even while toiling along the narrow path, they were likely 'to graze the hedge on one side or other at every step':

> thorns catch them, stones trip them up, a perpetual dust attends their footsteps, grace and comeliness of aspect vanish. Though they dare not shut themselves up comfortably indoors with the slothful man, they are haunted by the "lion without" and dwell on the probability of his catching them at every corner . . .

William regarded over-scrupulosity as the 'one serious flaw' in Christina's character, having the full practical bearings of a defect that weakened the mind and chilled the spirit. This testimony from an affectionate and always judicious brother demonstrates how Christina's tight piety marred her relationships with others, to whom she could seem a sort of moral monitor, openly or tacitly judging their conduct. But the tendency to narrowness and self-righteousness in her Church, and not only among the laity, was clearly one of her chief concerns.

Daringly, she ventured to correct other religious teachers, in evident reference to sermons she had heard or read. 'Who has not seen the incident of the Young Ruler utilized as a check to extravagant zeal?' she asked in allusion to the rich man whom Jesus told to sell all and give to the poor, contesting the view that the story 'does not, by any means require us to sell all' and that differences of rank, of position, of circumstances, were providentially ordained, and not lightly to be set aside.

Then there was the question of over-elaborate scriptural exegesis which mistook the trees for the wood:

> Take the history of the Fall. The question of mortal sin shrinks into the background while we moot such points as the primitive status of the serpent: did he stand somehow upright? did he fly? what did he originally eat? how did he articulate?

Similarly with the flaming sword at the gate of Paradise. Was it a blade flashing and swaying towards each point of the compass, or a sort of blazing discus? What was Cain's motive for murdering Abel? What exactly was his mark? What was the precise architecture of Noah's Ark?

> At every turn such questions arise ... Were the Cherubim of the Tabernacle of the first Temple and of the second Temple of similar or of diverse aspects? Clear up the astronomy of Joshua's miracle. Fix the botany of Jonah's gourd. Must a pedestal be included within the measurement of Nebuchadnezzar's "golden image"? In the same vein we reach at last the conjecture which I have heard quoted: In which version was the Ethiopian Eunuch studying Isaiah's prophecy when Philip the Deacon met him?

Of these and similar diversionary inquiries, Christina's injunction was from Ecclesiastes: ' "By these, my son, be admonished: of making of many books there is no end" '.

On the making of her own book, she was characteristically modest yet also confident. 'I feel it is a solemn thing to write conjectural sketches of scriptural characters,' she began; 'filling up outlines as I fancy ... making one figure stand for this virtue and another for that vice, attributing motives and colouring conduct.' Yet she trusted to forgiveness for any mistakes, and earnestly hoped that all persons described were in truth superior to her depiction.

Among her targets was 'that mean virtue', secular economy, as she compared thriftiness with niggardly spirituality. Unlike other dramatised figures in the book, such as the Idler and the Money-grubber, Economy is conceived as female, who pretends to save in order to give to the poor but falls into stinginess and, worse, self-congratulation:

> The sordid Economist walks the world unabashed and says her say complacently in company. She keenly realises and relishes the distinction between elevenpence threefarthings and one shilling ... and frequents remote shops in honour of this distinction. Her remarks turn on prices and linger in the store-room or the coal-cellar. She gossips about the extravagance of this dinner-giver and the watsefulness of that household, frittering away her own and her neighbour's time, not to speak of her neighbour's patience. To save a halfpenny she will squander time recklessly ... Her tastes, aims, contemplations, standard, are of the earth, earthy.

Who was she thinking of? The vigour of the writing here surely indicates that Christina's own patience had been sorely tried by just such price-consciousness and fault-finding, and that she knew her own tendency to be careful with money led to dangerous miserliness. She commended instead the 'heavenly-minded Economist', who was mean only with herself, but who would 'find scarlet for her household and wine for her friends – or if not wine at least a cup of cold water sweetened with sympathy'.

Generosity is a keynote of *Letter and Spirit*. Truth-telling, for example, must be tempered with sympathy and the censorious habit of dwelling on others' faults must be silently turned into intercessory prayer. Moreover – and here the generous tone becomes ironically a little fierce – 'it is no light offence to traduce the dead, to blacken recklessly their memory, to cultivate not tenderness for them, helpless and inoffensive as they now lie...' Was she thinking perhaps of Gabriel, whose character some envious persons were tempted to slander, or of older, earlier dead, whom she had been reared to traduce, like the Austrians and Pio Nono? She was surely also thinking of religious hatred between churches, for the remark developed from the passages in which she denounced party and sectarian feeling.

As regards private faults, she was more forgiving of Anger than Envy, noting (with obvious relevance to her own outbursts) that anger was often warm-hearted and open, and easily defused by family affection, whereas envy was like blood-poisoning, corrupting invisibly from within. She also devoted two full pages to celebrating spinsterhood over wifehood, describing the latter as 'doing well' but the former as 'doing better'. Thus

> She whose heart is virginal abides aloft and aloof in spirit ... If she rejoices, it is on spiritual heights, with blessed Mary magnifying the Lord; if she laments, it is still on spiritual mountain-tops, making with Jephthah's daughter a pure oblation of unflinching self-sacrifice.

The reference to Jephthah's daughter is significant, for she is the biblical type of the girl who submits to being murdered by her father in obedience to his vow. And above all in this book Christina acknowledged and overcame her own dislike of God the Father. For the first time in her devotional work she quoted extensively from both parts of the Bible rather than seeing all in a New Testament light, observing that 'we are accustomed in the Old Testament pages at every turn to seek for and revere the types of God the Son; – is it so that we sometimes overlook types as luminous of God the Father?' Now she warned against attending too exclusively to Christ, for

> to view in fact even if not avowedly the Three Persons as Three Gods leads towards arraying them in opposition to each other; till we feel towards the Divine Son as if he alone was our Friend, the Divine Father being our foe; as if Christ had not only to rescue us from the righteous wrath of His Father but to shelter us from His enmity.

This was a surprising but revealing admission of having appealed to Christ while cowering from God, aligning herself as his victim, pleading for intercession. Here, she explicitly named the paternal God as one to be feared and appeased.

Whatever the theological import, this suggests that Christina had indeed had problems with fathers, literal and spiritual. Spiritually, her acknowledgement was a mature, if belated, recognition of the power of Puseyite doctrines imparted to impressionable young people. Psychologically, it represents her reparative understanding that it was no longer necessary to be afraid of paternal displeasure. Fathers, whether divine, spiritual or actual, were no longer to be seen as hostile, and her burden of guilt for disobeying their commands, provoking their wrath, disregarding their desires or resisting their chastisement was thereby lightened.

Whatever the precise cause of Christina's emotional injury in adolescence it is plain that she suffered from both Dodsworth's minatory teaching and Papa's self-pitying demands. Both were manipulative, commanding not only obedience but love, and thus causing guilt and fear. Now, at long last, she could indirectly acknowledge this, in recognising that she had looked to Christ as if He alone were her Friend and the Divine Father the one from whom she needed protection and shelter. It was surely not coincidental that this recognition occurred in the wake of her attempt to console Gabriel for the filial disrespect that had aroused paternal wrath, and at a time when, having seldom mentioned her earthly father in published writing or private letters, Christina was invited to revive his memory by reading and contributing to the various memorials of her brother which dwelt on their childhood. It is as if through writing and religion she had now succeeded in healing whatever injury she had suffered all those years before.

Coincidentally, Papa's posthumous rehabilitation was now assured. Thirty years past, he had died a failed and foolish scholar; now he was a famous Italian poet and patriot. The centenary of his birth on 1 March 1783 was approaching, and in Italy cousin Teodorico urged Vasto to erect a statue to the town's celebrated son, in the already-named Piazza Rossetti. In London a commemorative plaque was proposed. 'Dear Sir,' replied Christina, 'I am happy to say I am a daughter of that Gabriele Rossetti who so truly loved his country and who after long years of exile died a patient Christian.' She attached a list of his residences, added that British practice frowned on effusive inscriptions, and pointed out a fault in the proposed verses – 'my Father's taste dictating a smooth and musical flow of verse'. For the first time she assumed a proud and happy position as his daughter and poetic heir, incidentally claiming credentials that honoured the living as well as the dead, for 'patriot, poet, patient Christian' were her own qualities.

And as if in direct acknowledgement of her patrimony, she agreed to write an article on Dante, requested by Gosse for the *Century* in New York. 'Family feeling stirs within me – the tradition of my race!' she joked, nervously agreeing to enter the 'opened door into the circle of (humblest) Dantesque literature.' 'I do not know how long I shall be, but sooner or later I will write to you again, even if all I have to write of is failure,' she added. Within a week or two, however, she wrote again to ask whether she would be allowed to 'weave in a word here and there from the *original*?' feeling that so much beauty evaporated with the loss of the 'musical Italian' text. She also wanted to use Cayley's translation, rather than the more familiar version by Longfellow, and though she told Cayley that progress was at a snail's pace, the piece was duly completed and despatched before the end of April.

It was a formidable undertaking, she began – and 'if formidable to others, it is not least formidable to one of my name, for *me* to enter the

Dantesque field and say my little say on the Man and his Poem'. She commended her father's *Commento* on the *Inferno* for giving beginners a clue and experts a theory regarding the poem's profundity, and Maria's *Shadow* as an eloquent exposition of the *Divine Comedy* 'as a discourse of most elevated Christian faith and morals'. William's translation she described as a 'strenuous endeavour' to achieve close verbal accuracy in English blank verse. She mentioned also the 'rare felicity' of the *Vita Nuova* translation by Gabriel (whom she called 'my brother Dante', in deference to the general public's adoption of this as his first name, and in part to distinguish public from private references). Of her own endeavour she was characteristically self-disparaging, saying she could lay claim to no long study or family learning, only her own 'great love' of the subject.

She was not a natural critic. As in her articles on Petrarch and others for the Biographical Dictionary, she filled her piece with information on Dante's ancestry, education, political career and exile. She revealed a certain dismay, which clearly dated from her youth, at his switch of allegiance from Guelph to Ghibelline, becoming an 'ardent champion of that Imperial power that aspired to rule over Italy', before exonerating him on the grounds of political confusion and in-fighting. On the vexed question of Dante's love for Beatrice, her views were clear and unhistorical, for she interpreted it in terms of present day romantic love, saying it was to be hoped that Dante's passion for Beatrice at the age of nine was neither returned nor guessed at, since Beatrice had gone on to marry another, at the age of twenty. She regarded Dante's own marriage to Gemma Donati as unhappy, noting that though seven children were born and Gemma rescued Dante's manuscripts when his house was torched, she did not join him in exile, which Christina surmised was because she felt eclipsed by Beatrice. If so, Gemma was 'truly to be pitied in her thankless and loveless lot'. Moreover, Dante had been untrue to Beatrice, according to her own stinging words in Purgatory.

This unscholarly but interesting feminine response to the supposed plot of Dante's emotional life concluded with a brief reference to the many puzzles in the poem, and the esoteric interpretations of (unnamed) critics who saw in Beatrice 'an impersonation rather than a woman' and in the Divine Comedy a concealed political meaning. 'So obscure a field of investigation is not for me or for my readers,' she concluded; 'at least not for them through any help of mine.' Thus, she disposed of the task to which Papa had devoted her own childhood years. One has the impression quite a few ghosts were being laid.

Other memories of the past were now much in evidence. Some months before, Christina had acknowledged receipt of Scott's valedictory volume of verse: *Poet's Harvest Home,* in which he printed both the *Rose-Leaves* lyric written to Christina and a sonnet on his own advancing years. Christina responded with some of the doggerel lines that always marked their friendship, alluding to their respective ages:

> My old admiration before I was twenty
> Is predelict still, now promoted to se'enty;
> My own demi-century, plus an odd one
> Some weight to my judgement may fairly impart.
> Accept this faint flash of a smouldering fire,
> The fun of a heavy old heart.

As Scott did not need to be told, her heart was heavy with the loss of Gabriel. And in turn this prompted Scott's memory of his first visit to the Rossetti home when, as he told Alice, he had found only 'the old man with a shade over his eyes and a great snuff box, and Christina standing writing at a small high desk'.

Alice was at Penkill, while Scott had stayed in London to attend Gabriel's sale, dismayed to find that William had set aside only worthless items as mementoes of long and staunch friendship. Christina made amends in the autumn, offering Alice a brass sundial plate 'perhaps the very one in the old Cheyne Walk garden ... May we send it you down to Penkill? – and think of it as marking time somewhere in the beautiful place?'

Mamma had kept all Gabriel's letters from the earliest days, and now began sorting through them to select material for an authorised 'Life and Letters' that Theodore Watts had offered to compile. Reading the letters was a tearful business, but on 7 November Mamma's task was complete. 'The accompanying parcel makes up the entire number she offers you to choose from (marked here and there with the monitory blue pencil)', Christina told William, explaining that once the final selection was made she herself would copy out the texts for the printer, 'so that the dear sheets with their eliminated passages need not come under a strange eye. I am a fairly quick and diligent scribe, so do not take fright at your prospect.' Soon afterwards, she was busy with the task – 'such good old letters some of them, so loving – and some so funny,' she told Lucy. It was a sad but pleasant occupation, and meant that, rather strangely, she was looking back in quasi-autobigraphical mode at her own family history as it would be seen by others. Not long before, in *Harper's Magazine*, she had read a vivid account of her own childhood, recreated by Mary Robinson from conversations with William.

Earlier in the year, she had been asked by Ella Pratt, editor of the American children's magazine *Wide-Awake*, for a Christmas poem

which she also offered to the current editor of *Macmillan's* in order to
secure British copyright. But when *Wide-Awake's* payment (five
pounds, in advance) and proof arrived on 2 October, she returned the
text with a worried inquiry as to whether the poem was embargoed
from appearing in Britain before Christmas. It so proved, and the
poem was then withdrawn from *Macmillan's*, being replaced with *A
Wintry Sonnet*, which was duly, though unseasonably, printed in the
April issue.

The American carol was an untitled hymn on the Incarnation describing the Christ-child's soft small hand and 'voice which is but
baby-noise'. Less than a month into the new year, the family was
distressed by the sudden sickening of little twin Michael, who at the
age of twenty months had barely begun to speak more than baby
noises. On 24 January 1883, in response to an urgent message, Christina
went round to Endsleigh Gardens, where she 'found all in grief, and
sat with poor William and Lucy till the baby died at 1 o'clock'. During
this time she asked and received permission to baptise Michael with
her own hands, fearing that heaven would be closed to him as to a
chrisom child. Baptism, she wrote to Lucy afterwards, was 'the sole
door' she knew of whereby entrance was promised into that heavenly
happiness 'which eye has not seen nor ear heard neither heart of man
conceived', and which in her view little Michael deserved to enjoy.

In the circumstances, one's sympathies are all with Michael's
parents, who sanctioned this intervention, so evidently for Christina's
benefit, and did not take offence at the implied rebuke of having
neglected baby Michael's soul. Surely his aunt read the service to
convey her own love and grief rather than because she truly believed
unbaptised infants were excluded from heaven – or perhaps God the
Father still retained some punitive attributes. And she composed
a commemorative poem for Michael, which was published in the
Athenaeum on 17 February.

To Caroline Gemmer's letter of condolence, which suggested that
had Michael lived, he might have proved another genius in the Rossetti line, Christina replied with emphatic dissent. 'Oh, my dear
friend, don't let us wish for any more geniuses!' she wrote. This was
not the moment so soon after losing Gabriel, and recalling his sufferings – and also those of her dear Father. Genius was 'near allied to
madness' in popular imagination, and to Christina the two were
evidently entwined.

She touched on other family affairs in a reply to aunt Henrietta
Polydore, now living in Louisiana, who had sent a photo of the grave
in which cousin Henrietta rested, in Christina's words 'until (please
God) we meet again in a far different world'. Christina now sent
news of aunt Eliza, whose sight was failing sadly, but daily set an

example of patient cheerfulness, which her niece sententiously asserted was 'truly a better thing than the enjoyment of strong health'.
She also mentioned 'a little namesake' of hers in America, towards
whom she felt 'great good will'. Who was this? Despite her sojourn in
Utah, it is unlikely that Mrs Polydore had taken a new husband and
borne another child, for in all correspondence she retained uncle
Henry's name. But somewhere near New Orleans was a child explicitly named after Christina Rossetti.

The two exhibitions of Gabriel's work in 1883, which provided the
fist public opportunity for assessment, also enabled Christina to express her views on her brother's art. She was not an uncritical admirer,
she assured Mrs Gemmer, remarking on certain unappealing aspects
of *La Bello Mano*, a voluptuous painting of 1875, though not specifically mentioning the mix of symbols pertaining to both Virgin and
Venus, that conflated spiritual and carnal virtues. She also remarked
rather sharply that the picture of *Lilith* 'ought surely to make her
admirers recoil!' and by asserting that Lizzie's beauty 'was of a rarer
type' she implicitly criticised Jane Morris's looks. Identifying *Sea Spell*
as one of her favourites, she added a nostalgic reminiscence regarding
the yellow iris, Gabriel's favourite flower which 'abounded at Kelmscott' – where, she added, she and her mother had enjoyed a summer
visit, doing 'various things pleasant in the doing and pleasant to look
back on'.

Of *Letter and Spirit*, which was just being delivered to the SPCK, she
wrote:

> I endorse with my whole heart your remark on the paramount burden of
> responsibility; when one is strong one can by God's grace bear it; but
> when one is weak, the pressure at times, or the *hauntingness* may become
> fearful. And the books I write make me more and more glaringly inexcus-
> able for my faults of all sorts, and shortcomings, and cowardice especially.

'Each volume heaps up responsibility,' she added. Amendments and
additions were attached to a proof copy and the book appeared at the
end of April, rather before it was expected.

Literary composition thus remained her chief occupation, around
which domestic duties were disposed – on one occasion she joked to
Mrs Gemmer that the arrival of the laundry demanded her attention,
and 'so my *poet steps* must trudge upstairs to the humble work'. Some
while later she told Rev. Nash that 'there were times when the power
to write had apparently passed away', but it was poetic composition
to which she referred, for as we can see she was seldom without some
literary work in hand. Many writers find that one type of sustained
work will often drive away other kinds of writing, particularly poetry

that depends not so much on 'inspiration' – a commodity Christina was always sceptical of – as on a certain leisure of the mind. So it seems no coincidence that while she was working on *Letter and Spirit* she wrote no more than occasional verses. She lacked, too, the spur of competition, now that Gabriel was no longer sending his productions for her comments.

37

Girls' Protection

WHILE VISITING CHRISTIE'S for a final look at Gabriel's pictures in May, Christina bumped into her old friend Bessie Parkes, now Mme Belloc, together with her daughter Marie. It was a long while since Christina had seen Bessie, who had married and been widowed in France; now a pious Catholic and no longer an active feminist, she lived in Sussex, devoting part of her time to nursing Barbara Bodichon, who had suffered a disabling stroke in 1877.

There were other intimations of mortality, for early in the year Charles Cayley suffered a short but serious illness, prompting him to make his will and ask whether Christina would accept a personal bequest and agree to be his literary executor. 'My dear old Friend, I will not dwell too much on the sad possibility you hint to me,' she wrote, hoping he would soon be well, and saying that the bequest of 'some trifle that you had been fond of and perhaps had used' would be precious. She would also willingly watch over his literary affairs, in order to promote his posthumous 'name and fame', as a memorial to their friendship. (Alas, Cayley would be saved from oblivion only by his friendship with Christina, not by his books.) His will, dated 3 May 1883, specified that she receive his 'best writing desk'.

Christina's niece Olive long remembered the impression Mr Cayley made in these last years, with his old-fashioned tailcoat and habit of paying formal calls. On one occasion she recalled a chance meeting when he got lost in a symbolically apt manner inside the skeleton of a fossilised dinosaur in the Natural History collection of the British Museum, which was kept in a long narrow corridor, entered at one end and left at the other. When they came out Lucy was walking on chatting with the keeper when Olive suddenly piped up: 'Mamma, where is Mr Cayley?' They looked around; no Mr Cayley in sight; they retraced their steps but he was not to be found. Then the home of the ichtyhosuarus was reopened and Mr Cayley was found standing there, wrapped in his thoughts . . .'

In the summer of 1883 while their house was being redecorated Christina and her mother spent two months at Birchington, where wranglings over Gabriel's grave betrayed deeper tensions within the family. William, who elected to pay for the headstone, commissioned Madox Brown to produce a suitable design, similar to that erected for

Nolly, and emphatically not in the shape of a cross. Mamma and Christina conveyed their dismay, but William proved oddly stubborn, even when Brown suggested that a large Irish cross in granite might look very much in keeping. 'As my mother wants a cross and I don't,' William replied, he was 'strongly minded to say that she might have the cross if she liked, but then she herself must order it.' Mamma however refused to usurp his project, and he was therefore caught between acting on his own wishes and ignoring his mother's. So he succumbed.

Christina sent Mamma's warm thanks, adding on her own account:

I am only trying to make matters easy, pleasant, manageable; I am not attempting to meddle where you have and I have not rights. Whatever monument is erected, I hope you will not reject £10 or £15 as my contribution towards honouring our dear brother's memory.

In the event Brown's Celtic cross, with bas reliefs of St Luke, patron saint of painters, the mystic marriage of Dante and Beatrice and a curiously-chosen depiction of the temptation of Adam and Eve, proved acceptable. 'How fine the Cross looks,' Christina told William after seeing it in position. But William surrendered with ill-grace, placing an inscription on the cross stating that 'this cruciform monument' was bespoken by his mother, designed by Gabriel's lifelong friend Ford Madox Brown and erected by himself and Christina – all of which, he told Watts, was intended 'to suggest to the discerning agnostic that I myself would not have had a cross, but that I conceded the point to my mother's wish...'

What a fuss! Funerals and memorials are often areas of family disagreement, but one ponders the subtext of this particular stand-off. William's resistance, in the face of his mother's and sister's wishes, suggests that the dispute concealed a deeper 'fight over the body' than Gabriel's last resting place merited. As it turned out, William prevailed in other ways, for it was his account of his brother and indeed all the family, that was raised for posterity.

The memorial window proved equally troublesome. Christina was obliged to mediate between the artist – her neurotic friend Mr Shields – and Mr Alcock the rector, who vetoed the proposed depiction of Mary Magdalene. In the end Shields gave way.

At Birchington, Mrs Seddon lent them Ruskin's latest lectures on the state of contemporary painting. These began with 'D.G. Rossetti and W. Holman Hunt', and contained a tribute 'in the reverence of sorrow' to the much loved friend who stood first in the list of those who had 'raised and changed the spirit of modern art'. But Ruskin also made many criticisms of Gabriel's technique and subjects and ended by awarding the palm to Hunt. Shields was indignantly on fire in Gabriel's defence, but after a burst of irritation Christina refused to be angry, joking that even Ruskin's description of the Chatham Place apartment as a garret would not be allowed to upset her patience. And, she added in her next letter to Lucy:

> It is such a triumph for ME to attain to philosophic calm that, *even* if that subdued temper is applied by me without commonsense, "color che sanno" may still congratulate me on some sort of improvement! Ask William, who knew me in my early stormy days . . .

Though William honourably denied that he knew of anything beyond 'mere casual fractiousness in infancy', Christina was evidently thinking of her reputation for rage, and it was perhaps around this time that she told her niece of the arm-slashing incident with the scissors. And she added renewed apologies to Lucy, saying she was 'sorry to recollect how much you yourself have undergone from my irritability, and how much there is for you to bury in kind oblivion'. Not that all was subdued; on another occasion around this time Christina again apologised, for an unkindly-meant remark on the pitch of Cathy Hueffer's voice. The remark may have been true: what mattered to Christina was her malice in making it.

She had other reasons to admire Ruskin who, though intermittently insane, had been reappointed Oxford Professor of Art. He had taken a stand on vivisection and when a year later he resigned his Professorship over the establishment of an experimental laboratory at the university, she was jubilant.

The campaign was again active, and Christina was again circulating petitions, for new legislation was again before Parliament, and London was plastered with posters graphically proclaiming the horrors of the practice. But though she sent a poem entitled *Hope Deferred* to an AV annual, she did not keep up with campaign literature, as she confessed to Mrs Gemmer. 'Having made up my mind, I do not feel bound to go over the ground continually,' she wrote; and she only glanced at the rest of the volume. She had a new cause, 'perhaps even more urgent', to which she now lent her support.

'My dear Mrs Heimann, have you seen the little book I enclose on a most painful and shameful subject?' Christina inquired in May, explaining that she and Mamma had stocked themselves with copies for distribution, and adding

> I am trying to get signatures to the "Protection" Petition to both Houses of Parliament, and must send in my papers at least by the end of this month unless I am told otherwise.

The subject was the 'Protection of Minors', urging that the age of consent for sexual intercourse be raised, to outlaw child prostitution and protect girls against sexual expliotation. This was 'a dreadful subject to look into, but still more dreadful to leave alone, spreading corruption and festering in our midst', she wrote.

For some time public opinion had been stirring, alongside the long-running protests against the inspection of prostitutes under the Contagious Diseases Acts (on which, incidentally, there is no evidence of Christina's support). In 1871 a commission of inquiry had concluded that the traffic in children for infamous purposes was considerable and that the age of consent should be raised to fourteen instead of twelve as under existing law. As a compromise, in 1875 the age of consent was raised to thirteen, but further attempts foundered, until in 1880 the topic again became newsworthy with the activities of 'social purity' campaigners regarding the alleged 'traffic in girls' between Britain and Belgium, where in certain brothels, according to Josephine Butler,

> there are immured little children, English girls of some twelve to fifteen years, lovely creatures (for they do not care to take any who are not beautiful), innocent creatures who, stolen, kidnapped, betrayed, got from English country villages by artifice, are sold to these human shambles . . .

Challenged to provide proof, Butler laid an official deposition which obliged the British government to investigate the allegations. In May 1881 a Select Committee of the House of Lords was appointed. Numerous 'anti-vice' campaigns then flourished, under the leadership of Mrs Butler, veteran of the anti-Contagious Diseases campaigns, and Ellice Hopkins, self-appointed 'rescue worker' and founder of female missions and vigilance societies, who was instrumental in the formation of the White Cross League, dedicated to male chastity, and the Church of England Purity Society. In 1882, with money from a benefactor, she began a specific campaign to alter the age of consent and protect children from procurers, which was responsible for the parliamentary petition Christina asked Mrs Heimann to sign.

What kind of evidence was this based on? The alleged 'white slave' traffic proved less substantial than supposed – in most cases girls were found to have travelled to Belgium in full knowledge of the employment offered – and much of the evidence heard by the Select Committee related instead to juvenile prostitution in London, on which there were differing views. One metropolitan police inspector, for instance, told the committee there were few girls under sixteen involved in prostitution, but the head of London's CID was convinced that juvenile prostitution was 'rampant at this moment, and in the streets about the Haymarket, Waterloo Place and Piccadilly from nightfall there are children of 14, 15 and 16 years of age going about soliciting'.

The Lords Committee felt more information was required. In June 1882 Ellice Hopkins therefore brought new evidence, from rescue workers in the East End, and refuges like the Highgate Penitentiary, which claimed to be admitting younger and younger inmates. Indeed, as Rev. Oliver lamented to Christina and her mother, on their visit this year he now commonly received girls of twelve and thirteen – and one as young as ten. Hopkins, who favoured twenty-one as the age of consent, claimed that 'this proved there was a large and unfortunate demand for children now, on the streets'. The Lords then recommended that the age at which it should be an offence to have or attempt to have carnal knowledge of or indecently assault a girl be raised from thirteen to sixteen and in May 1883 a bill was therefore introduced, backed by the petition signatures showing the strength of its support in the country. It was however blocked by the House of Commons, amid warnings of entrapment and blackmail by sexually precocious girls.

To what extent the moral panic of this period accurately reflected the extent and style of sexual commerce is hard to determine. Somewhat ironically, the social concern of the 1850s and the CD campaign in the '70s resulted in fewer 'gay women' plying their trade on the streets and more such activity in brothels, though by 1880 the number of streetwalkers was again on the increase – or perhaps simply more visible in the same areas as middle-class women did their shopping. At the same time, fear of disease (also increased by the CD propaganda) made men more anxious about the health of those whose sexual services they purchased; crudely, the younger the girl, the less likely to be venereally infectious. Among certain groups, too, there was a salacious preference for 'green fruit', although how far this was practised rather than merely bragged about is again difficult to say. However, all factors increased public concern and presented a prima facie case for trying to cure 'youthful vice'.

Causes were widely held to include overcrowded housing and low moral standards among the poor, as well as the debauched desires of upper-class 'swells'. Lurking behind this was a submerged concern, largely again focused on the poor, over sexual promiscuity in general and incest in particular. One magistrate told the Select Committee: 'I can see how evil influences are early brought to bear upon them; and there are assaults committed upon them by their very near relatives, by brothers and even by fathers.' The young Beatrice Potter, working

in a sweatshop later in the decade, was horrified to hear her companions joke about having babies by their fathers and brothers. Incestuous activity does seem to have been common among the urban and no
doubt also the rural poor, but some historians now suspect the social
concern was in part a displacement, and that the campaign reflected a
general but unspoken concern over the sexual abuse of children in all
ranks of society, as a poem published by Louisa Bevington in 1882
sems to confirm.

The reintroduced Criminal Law Amendment bill failed again in
1884, as did a subsequent prosecution against a 'notorious procuress'
in Chelsea, where former servants claimed thirteen-year-olds were
regularly deflowered by high-ranking clients. The CD acts were finally repealed, but Girls' Protection seemed to hang fire. Christina
continued to gather signatures and attended at least one public meeting on the subject, in February 1884. In March 1885, when legislation
was again proposed, this time setting the age of consent at fifteen, Mrs
Percy Bunting (whose husband edited the *Contemporary Review*) called
at Torrington Square with petition papers. 'We failed in 1884 but that
is our spur to try again in 1885,' Christina explained to one correspondent. 'Please send me back the *Lords* petition for "Minors Protection". I do not want the *Commons* yet, if there is any hope of your
kindly getting us some more names,' she wrote to another supporter
in April. By the end of May, however, the bill failed yet again.

The issue then erupted when maverick journalist W. T. Stead con-
spired with Josephine Butler and others to 'procure' a thirteen-year-
old virgin for ostensible debauchery, and ran a series of sensational
articles entitled *The Maiden Tribute of Modern Babylon* through July,
with headlines on the Violation of Virgins, Confessions of a Brothel
Keeper, Strapping Girls Down, and the International Slave Trade in
Girls.

Within two weeks the Salvation Army had 400,000 signatures on a
petition to raise the age of consent to eighteen. Noisy public meetings
were held, and the government hastily reintroduced the bill, which
rapidly completed its progress. As William noted after attending a
mass demonstration, Stead had created a 'frightful commotion', over-
shadowing all other news. Christina's response may be inferred from
Mamma's donation to the campaign earlier in the month, but once the
legislation was passed, her concern lapsed; unlike other social purity
campaigners, she did not pursue further aspects of the cause, and
some three years later declined an invitation to become honorary
patron of the Women and Children's Protection Society.

When I first discovered Christina's involvement in 'this most painful and shameful subject', with its emphasis on 'lovely and innocent'
girls aged twelve to fifteen, I was disturbed by its relevance to the

apparent evidence of sexual trauma at the same age in her own history. Did Christina unconsciously take up the cause because of her own experience of seduction or abuse? In the context of what can be called the culture of petitions, it may carry no such significance; and certainly not all those who circulated pamplets and petitions can themselves have been victims of sexual abuse. Christina's support for child protection clearly grew out of her earlier work at the Penitentiary, when she had endeavoured to help young women withstand the temptations of vice and folly. But she was not an indiscriminate supporter of worthy causes, showing no interest for example in the very vocal Temperance Movement, another field in which women of her class were prominent. So girls' protection would seem to fit a repeated pattern of concern for young and vulnerable beings, from the linnets whose nests were destroyed by wanton boys, through the horrors of live dissection, to the dangers that beset young Maggie in her meeting with the Mouth Boy, and including those that threatened 'little English girls' in the brothels of Belgium. And in the same way, Christina's work with the girls at Highgate and Maggie's rescue of puppy and kitten can be seen alongside Minors' Protection as elements in a reparative process.

Her theological thinking on Eve also has its place in this process. After her juvenile identification with Mary Magdalene and the Virgin Martyrs, the main biblical figures to whom Christina was drawn were Esther, who risked her life to save her people, and Eve, mother of mankind and original sinner, whose story she had first dramatised in poems in the early 1860s. In *Letter and Spirit* she returned to the topic, trying to tease out whether Adam or Eve was most to blame for the Fall. Eve made a mistake, she argued, whereas Adam made no mistake, but simply disobeyed God; each had 'an especially vulnerable point, but this was apparently not the same point'. Both courses however led 'to one common result, that is, to one common ruin'.

This seems plain enough, yet Christina interrupted her lesson to introduce an unexpectedly imaginative account of Eve in the Garden:

indulging quite innocently sundry refined tastes and aspirations, a castle-building spirit (if so it may be called), a feminine boldness and directness of aim combined with a no less feminine guessiness as to means. Her very virtues may have opened the door to temptation. By birthright gracious and accessible, she lends an ear to all petitions from all petitioners. She desires to instruct ignorance, to rectify misapprehension: "unto the pure all things are pure", and she never suspects even the serpent. Possibly a trace of blameless infirmity transpires in the wording of her answer, "*lest ye die*" for God had said to the man "... in the day that thou eatest thereof thou *shalt surely* die"; but such tenderness of spirit seems even lovely in the great first mother of mankind; or it may be that Adam had modified the form, if it devolved on him to declare the tremendous fact to his second self ... With Eve the serpent discussed a question of conduct, and talked her over to his own side: with Adam, so far as appears, he might have argued the point for ever and gained no vantage; but already he had secured an ally weightier than a score of arguments. Eve may not have argued at all: she offered Adam a share of her own good fortune, and having hold of her husband's heart, turned it in her hand as the rivers of water.

The picture of Eve, looking for occupation in Eden with 'a feminine directness of aim combined with a no less feminine guessiness as to means', is delightful and cunning; for what is here proposed is virtually an exculpation of original sin in woman. Eve listened to the serpent out of sympathy and innocence; being innocent, she had no apprehension of evil. Far from wishing to disobey God's prohibition, she wanted only to share her knowledge and good fortune.

Letter and Spirit also contains a passing reference to Adam's 'meanness' in trying to excuse himself by blaming Eve, and among Christina's surviving rough manuscripts forming a commentary on Genesis which may be a preparatory study for this work is a much-corrected draft beginning 'Let us in imagination go back to Eve', which states:

> That Eve sinned and earned her own death is clear, but we are not told that she brought death on the human family. "In Adam all die", writes St Paul, taking no notice of the guilty woman.

By this stage, Christina evidently did not believe Eve was guilty, either. Indeed, Eve herself was subordinate, whereas Adam was 'exclusive head and stock of mankind', with ultimate responsibility. And finally, she concluded:

> Following out which idea it seems to ensue that all we inherit, all the spiritual corruption entailed on the human family by the Fall, descends to us thro Eve indeed, but from Adam.

The inference of her argument is that men rather than women must take responsibility and blame, if unto them is allocated superior knowledge and power.

In thus absolving Eve, Christina was contesting traditional theology, and also the age-old tendency to 'blame the woman' in much the same way as the Contagious Diseases and Social Purity campaigners argued. We may also detect a belated assessment of those in authority who blamed the wayward girls at Highgate for their fall, putting apples in their way and then threatening them with expulsion. And later in *Letter and Spirit* she concluded the topic by presenting Adam and Eve as models of conjugal loyalty, adding 'Nor need we attempt to settle which (if either) committed the greater sin'. Maybe not, but she had raised the question. Again, this was in part self-healing, as she shifted the blame for 'original' sin from the weaker female to the stronger male, from the innocent to the one in authority and by implication from herself to her father. The burden on woman was not thereby lifted, but it was considerably lightened.

38

Time's Flight

TWO DAYS AFTER her fifty-third birthday, as she returned from morning Litany, Christina found Arthur Cayley and his wife waiting with the news that Charles had been discovered dead in his solitary lodgings. She went immediately to see her 'dear friend' lying just as he was found, his hand to his face: he had died in his sleep on the night of 5 December. His sister Sophie, summoned from Hastings, was also there, with information on the will. 'He has left you all his own works that are now at his publishers, and a large writing-desk, in which is an envelope with a letter of yours to him, and a ring: there is also a large packet of your letters,' she explained. Would Christina like them returned? 'You were I know *the* friend he valued most.'

Christina went on at once to Somerset House to tell William. 'I shall not easily forget the look of her face, and the strain of self-command in her voice,' he recalled. In Covent Garden she bought a funeral wreath, which she placed on Cayley's bed, beside the family flowers. His last recorded visit to Torrington Square had been a week before his death.

Sophie asked if she wished to attend the funeral, but Christina declined, though both she and Mamma sent more flowers. Charles was buried at Hastings on 11 December and two days later Arthur Cayley brought round the desk; he also destroyed her letters, as she requested. The separate letter mentioned by Sophie, in an envelope, was presumably that in which Christina agreed to become literary executor, which would have been kept with the will. The ring was probably Charles's own signet ring, though speculations as to its being the engagement ring Christina returned when declining his proposal have a more romantic appeal. Among other scattered items, she kept CBC's last letter to herself, dated 30 October, with thanks for unidentified 'Vasto sweets', including a 'rare pear' and 'others whose names I can't divine'. Earlier this year, the civic authorities in his birthplace had honoured the centenary of Gabriele Rossetti's birth. 'My husband would have been 100 today,' Mamma noted when Cayley had called to add his congratulations.

Christmas was saddened by the loss of so dear a friend, Christina told Shields, quoting the text 'They shall perish, but Thou remainest' and adding: 'one ought to be able to say so even when death does its momentary worst: but how easy the words are to utter, and how difficult their meaning to attain.' So the year closed rather sombrely. On 15 January Christina made a solitary pilgrimage to pay her personal respects at the Hastings graveside. She was now accustomed to writing memorial verses, but in this instance resurrected a very old piece, copied into the notebook over thirty years before; abridged and retitled as *One Seaside Grave*, it was sent to the *Century*, and published in May. This, however, was a private tribute, for the poem was not publicly linked to Cayley and to all appearances their relationship ended as it had begun, unknown to the outside world.

A year later, for the anniversary of his passing, she composed a longer mourning poem, lamenting the burial of hope:

> Brief was the day of its power,
>   The day of its grace how brief:
> As the fading of a flower,
>   As the falling of a leaf,
> So brief its day and its hour . . .

followed, in her next devotional work, by a summary of the theme that had informed *Monna Innominata*:

> Now and again two who have differed – and two who differ cannot both hold the entire truth – have loved on faithfully, believing and hoping the best of each other, one (perhaps each) praying for the other . . .
>   In such a case, where both have loved the Truth and have accounted it "great and mighty above all things", there surely remains a strong consolation of hope to flee unto . . .

As literary executor, Christina was responsible for sales and management of Cayley's books and translations. In 1884 these brought in just under five pounds, and in subsequent years smaller amounts trickled into her accounts – no doubt earmarked for charitable purposes – but there was never a great demand, and no call for reprints. Her own financial position, as she had explained to Charles, was still minimal – 'perhaps you may recollect my telling you that even now I am not so much as independent, so little indeed have I' – and she also calculated that she owed William at least two thousand pounds for household support over twenty years, which she was far from possessing. No money came to her directly from Gabriel's estate but, as of course she recognised, on the deaths of her mother, aunts and uncle she would be 'amply provided for'. If she did not survive them, there would be no problem.

In 1883 for the first time her literary earnings of over £80 exceeded investment income, which this year was less than £35. Macmillans and Roberts Bros paid over profits from *A Pageant* and *Poems 1875*, the SPCK paid £26 for *Letter and Spirit*, and *The Century* twenty guineas for the Dante article. It is sometimes supposed that Christina earned no money from her writing until her works began to sell rather belatedly, but the figures show that it came, in the main, from current rather than past endeavours.

Cayley's death was followed by intimations of new life, for in the New Year George Hake brought Rose Donne, his prospective bride, to meet Mrs and Miss Rossetti. Though cordial, the visit may have been rather daunting to Rose, who the following day received further, modified congratulations from Christina. 'I feel that to complete my good auguries something more is wanting, without which by me they cannot be fully expressed,' she wrote:

> Nothing seems to me of first importance except the question of piety and goodness. This I hope crowns all in your and his case, and renders all valid. Do you know I should be not cowardly merely but hypocritical if I shrank from saying that this seems to me the turning point of all, the root from which all true happiness springs. I so truly wish this to be both yours and his that the ardour of my good will may (I hope) excuse to you any mistake or indiscretion in my manner of expressing it.

and she added as a postscript a large arrow pointing to her signature with the words 'You see, even my name binds me not to be ashamed to appear a *Christ*ian'.

Luckily, Rose proved sufficiently committed to goodness and piety to validate the good wishes, and when a daughter was born the following year, Christina was pleased to be asked to stand godmother to little Ursula Gordon Hake – 'a beautiful name, recalling one hero and one (imaginary) saint' she wrote (with a typically scrupulous parenthesis). Having ascertained the parents took baptism seriously, she hoped graciously that they would add 'Christina' to the baby's names. On the appointed day, she made her way by cab to the church in Campden Hill, declining to stay to dinner but offering Ursula a coral necklace – a relic of her own infancy, perhaps presented at her own christening. But 'what must you have thought of me!' she wrote after returning from the ceremony:

> I went *and I returned* with the beads in my pocket. Not till some time after Mr Hake had alighted at the Albert Hall did it dawn upon me that I was carrying away little Ursula's property – and then I was too far on my way to turn back. Please receive them now, and lay the blame of my forgetfulness on the pleasure and interest I was enjoying amongst you all.

Thereafter she kept in regular contact with the Hakes, welcoming the births of a son and second daughter while retaining a soft spot for her goddaughter. 'My love to darling Ursula the deposed baby,' she wrote in 1889. 'Guys and Marjories are preferable to solitude, however dignified, as I hope she will admit one day.' Her gifts included *Sing-Song* as well as a wooden alphabet and Noah's Ark, and when in the spring of 1890 she received a reciprocal bunch of primroses and violets from the country, she returned a charming poem to little Ursula, first alluding to the flowers appropriate to Easter and then saying:

> No primroses like these from Ursula,
>   No violets sweet as her's –
> For love comes with them, and love Godmamma
>   Even to all flowers prefers.

When Ursula was seven, Christina sent a bible, saying it was similar to the one her own 'kind Father gave me at the age of 6', which she still possessed.

Other childhood memories were aroused early in 1884 when Edmund Gosse asked if he might interview Miss Rossetti for the *Century*. Christina, who some months before replied to an anthologiser that ' "C.G.R. born December 5 1830" ' was 'pretty well the only "biographical fact" I feel disposed to volunteer', showed herself surprisingly receptive to the idea. She was habitually at home in the afternoon, she replied, warning however that during Lent she was 'somewhat pre-engaged' by other duties. Thus, she continued:

> So far your enterprise is easy. The difficulty will encounter you – if, that is, you ever nerve yourself to encounter it – one stage further on, when even your skill as an interviewer may fail to discover my poetic schooling. When was it, and what was it?

She referred him to the *Harper*'s article on Gabriel's childhood, saying that for herself too literary influence was more a matter of atmosphere than schooling. As always, she insisted that she was the 'least and last' of the group, lagging behind her 'clever and cultivated parents' and 'clever sister and two clever brothers'. So durable was infant experience, it seems, that even now Christina felt herself the baby of the family, though a customary degree of protective camouflage may be suspected here, designed to head off too many inquisitive personal inquiries. But she was sufficiently impelled by nostalgia to describe to Gosse the happiest parts of her childhood at Holmer Green, and to these she ascribed the origins of her literary impulse.

But her first recorded poem was written at the age of eleven, some time after the loss of Holmer Green. Her statement suggests that Gosse's request had set her pondering the 'origins of her poetic schooling', to identify her earliest inclinations towards metre and rhyme, perhaps prompted by Maria's verses for the thrush and by Grandfather Polidori's prophecy that Christina '*avrà più spirito di tutti*', which she had recently recalled for William. Certainly, in this account, she did not claim poetic talent as a paternal inheritance, but rather located it as a shining domain within Grandpapa's garden, a long stage-coach ride from Charlotte Street. And as if in recognition of this, she offered Gosse a copy of *Verses*, adding that she was willing to respond to 'any definite question', but feared he would find no 'definite point' to start from. And she finished off with a self-excusing postscript: 'Pray don't imagine I have often written so long a letter about myself!' More's the pity, the biographer as well as interviewer might reply. Baulked of easy answers, Gosse did not pursue the interview.

Christina was now 'very plump' and lived in 'extreme quiet' with her mother 'and an aunt or two', William told Barbara Bodichon. But scarcely a day passed without visitors at Torrington Square, and Christina's social life included lunch with the Scotts, the Ruxtons and the Sadlers, various tea parties, 'at homes' and even the occasional evening party. She took Mamma to the SPCK, accompanied aunt Eliza to a charitable bazaar, and visited Highgate for the last time in 1884, to pay her condolences to Rev. Oliver's widow.

Regular visitors included various vicars – Revs. Nash and Godson (aunt Eliza's favourite), as well as Mr Burrows (soon to leave his parish for a canonry at Rochester Cathedral) and Dr Littledale, who usually called on Sunday afternoons. Rev. Dodgson came at intervals, often with a small girl to introduce to the plump poetess. Mrs Scott and Mrs Heimann called, as did a number of Mamma's regular friends, and the grandchildren once or twice a week. Ellen Heaton called frequently when in town, and Christina exchanged regular visits with Henrietta Rintoul, Louisa Parke, the Misses Harrison and a new friend Miss Conway. She also received a steady stream of admirers and American visitors, who were graciously welcomed – for though Christina confessed to a relative lack of interest in 'transatlantic literature', she welcomed callers from across the ocean. Among those who came to pay their respects were the writers Sarah Orne Jewett and Annie Fields (who received a handwritten copy of *A Dirge*) three artists named as Miss Ball Hughes, Miss Green and Miss Hale, and one 'Miss Perkins, an American', who may have been the writer better known as Charlotte Perkins Gilman. Once, Jean Ingelow brought Louise Chandler Moulton, a literary hostess from Boston, who recalled Miss Rossetti as tall, dignified and very formal. Urged to take a low chair, Mrs Moulton replied that she preferred a high one; 'in fact,' she joked unwisely, 'I have gone so far as to hope that when I get to heaven, if I ever do, the chair allotted to me will be high.' Gravely, and to the mortification of her visitor, Christina replied: 'For my part, I shall be content with whatever chair the Almighty may choose for me.'

When aunt Eliza's faithful retainer and friend Sarah Catchpole – whose son George seems to have been sometimes employed as odd man – completed forty years with the family, she was finally pensioned off in lodgings of her own. It was a sign of advancing years all round. In June 1883 cousin Teodorico collapsed and died in mid-sermon, while discoursing to his Florentine congregation on the Book of Revelations. Isabella promptly remarried, somewhat to the family's consternation. Christina did not really approve, having earlier looked forward to Isabella's heavenly reunion with Teodorico. 'I quite see that the marriage is under all circumstances a brilliant one,' she wrote ambiguously to William and Lucy, rather wickedly adding a couplet contrasting the 'fair and fickle South' with the 'true and tender North'.

In autumn 1884 Eliza suffered a slight stroke, after which Charlotte finally decided to retire from Lady Bath's service to the bosom of her family, where her nursing services could only be more and more in demand. This was immediately proved, for on Christmas Day uncle Henry had a severe stroke, and Charlotte travelled down to care for him until his death on Twelfth Night, only to return after the funeral suffering from exhaustion; one of the All Saints' nurses was engaged to look after her, Christina being fully occupied with Mamma and Eliza. 'My uncle was turned 77,' she replied to Scott's letter of sympathy, 'so don't give yourself airs of superior age! I wish I could have seen him again, but it was impossible for me to quit my precious Mother. 'And to her fell the task of informing Henrietta Polydore of her official widowhood.

With their condolences, the Scotts invited Christina to drop formality in favour of first names, or initials, or even nicknames. 'My dear W.B.' she replied. 'I reject "Hedgehog!" But she valued the gesture. 'I almost think I must take to "My dear L.M."; for so says my heart in full proportion.' After so many years' friendship this move might seem tardy were it not for the very real formalities of early Victorian relationships. Christina and Alice had been reared in an age when spinsters might mutually dispense with 'Miss', but married couples remained 'Mr' and 'Mrs' to all except relatives. Customs were now changing, however, and around this time Christina carefully consulted Lucy as to whether she wished to be known by her own name, or continue as 'Mrs W. Rossetti'. For herself she preferred to use no title, as she explained when inscribing a book. 'I have ventured to write your name without the formality of "Miss",' she wrote; '– an omission I like towards myself often, so I hope you do not dislike it.'

In April Scott suffered a near-fatal heart attack. Christina and her mother called twice before he was taken, by Alice, to Penkill for the summer. He barely made the journey and never returned. This year also saw the death of Anna Mary Howitt Watts, breaking a link with the long gone Pre-Raphaelite past, and in June Mamma's cousin Mrs Austin died, aged ninety. Mamma herself grew frail and increasingly went out by cab instead of walking, though for as long as she was able she tottered with Christina to church. 'It was a sight to be remembered by many,' wrote an unidentified acquaintance '– the sweet gentle-faced old and feeble mother leaning on the arm of her devoted daughter.' Once or twice weekly they drove out, round Regents Park, to Hampstead or Battersea Gardens. When Lady Bath was in town, they dropped Charlotte at Prince's Gate before a circuit of Hyde Park. Henry's death left them better off: Mamma's income rose to over £1000, and Christina benefitted by some £400, roughly divided between her uncle's legacy and her mother's gift.

'What old women our reminiscences make us!' she wrote to Caroline Gemmer in 1883, noting that both had known Canon Burrows for over thirty years. Now in her early fifties, she was scarcely old and her comment partly expressed ironic awe at the thought of adult acquaintance of three decades' standing. But the unrelenting passage of time was the subject of her new book, *Time Flies*, published in May 1885, and written over the preceding year as a 'reading diary', with prose reflections and original poems, for each day of the year.

Six months earlier, writing politely to Swinburne with another glancing reminiscence, Christina had described herself as 'an escaped governess' – for had she only learnt her lessons properly she would have been obliged to teach 'some one something'. This made her solicit support for distressed governesses – 'my sisters-that-should-have-been'. Instead she had become a writer, and yet not a prolific one. 'Pray believe that dumbness is not my *choice*', she added – nor would she excuse herself by citing the parrot who screamed 'But I think the more!' But she could safely say that she was well pleased when 'by fits and starts' the poetic impulse returned.

As usual she was less than candid, for *Time Flies* is a fully original work. Her biographer, Mackenzie Bell, observed that many of 'the original thoughts and pregnant sayings that enrich the book must have had their root in her own experience'. And, indeed, parts of *Time Flies* are the closest of all Christina's writings to autobiography, complementing the fragmentary recollections in her correspondence. Here, for instance, she included her memory of being overcome with shyness at Madame Tussauds, her account of the centipedes and jackdaws at Penkill, and the sunset flush on the Swiss Alps. Here too is the story of the two frogs at Holmer Green, together with the wild strawberry, dead mouse, and four-leaved clover. But there are only a handful of such direct anecdotes, and their purpose was devotional – the strawberry incident leading, for example, to the observation that while she rejected the half-eaten fruit as 'good for nothing', a less fortunate child might not have disdained the final bite, and in any case, why should not snails have a share in strawberries? In other instances, the personal element of a reminiscence was quite insignificant – as, for example, an ivory elephant that formed one of the ornaments at Torrington Square, a possession of longstanding sentimental value, here serving merely as a moral peg. Similarly, too, with antique and Venetian glass in Emily Seddon Tebbs's drawing-room, which recalled a broken bottle Christina had rescued from a roadside ditch – of which no further details are given.

Yet nevertheless the book was autobiographical: as Bell noted 'having to write something about each day in the year ... she fell back, unconsciously, on her own wide experience – wide not in the outer but in the inner sense'. So though not conceived as a Romantic autobiography, nor even an Augustinian one, *Time Flies* was a personal testimony, containing the fruit of a lifetime's spiritual experience and self-knowledge, and as such the most subjective and effective of her religious works.

Read carefully, her text offers a complex and thoughtful history of her inner life, presented not in narrative or chronological form, but as aspects of her current self. For as she wrote to Caroline Gemmer, the past years 'have all led me up to what I am now, and the whole series is leading me to my final self'. In this spirit, *Time Flies* represented her past and present self, looking both backward and forward, as in its pages she traced out the emotional landmarks of her life, beginning with earliest intimations of security:

> A nest implies size in comfortable proportion to inhabitants, warmth, softness, sleep, pure air, sunshine, leafy shade, a windy branch whereon to rock safely. Wind and rain heard yet little felt ... overhanging presence of love. A brooding breast sheltering its cherished nestlings. A love ready to confront death in their defence ...

These, in turn, led to anticipations of danger and death:

> In a certain little nest, built almost if not quite upon the grassy ground, having a sheltering bush behind it, and not far in front a railing, I one day saw three naked young birds consisting mainly of three gaping beaks.

Neither father nor mother in sight, there sat three wide open birds and beaks . . .

There seemed a thousand chances that these particular nestlings should never attain to feathers and years of discretion; for like their own beaks their nest spread wide open, and any passing cat might in a moment "finish the birds with the bones and the beaks". Occasional cats were known to haunt these grounds . . .

Was this possibly in Regents Park? Feather by feather, the birds became safely fledged, yet she remembered her fear on their behalf, which now seemed an apt figure for shaky faith.

Elsewhere, she recalled a childhood humiliation, as when a small girl she heard the saying that oil calmed troubled waters, and earnestly suggested this remedy for storms at sea – remembering also that 'her suggestion fell flat, as from her it deserved to fall'. Here, too, she gave her considered verdict on Maria's hero Achilles and her own preference for Ajax; and here, obliquely, she invoked her paternal inheritance with Italian proverbs on diligence and ambition – '*Fra Modesto non fui mai Priore*, say the Italians: Brother Modestus never became Prior' – as well as memories of unruly verbal games, stating firmly that

Puns and suchlike are a frivolous crew likely to misbehave unless kept within strict bounds. "Foolish talking" . . . writes St Paul, "is not convenient". Can the majority of puns be classified as wise talking?

Unmistakably attached to Mamma's birthday were her sternly consoling words on the Cross being the Tree to satisfy heartsickness, as a means of annealing disappointment. And though no individuals were identified by name, there was a personal tribute to aunt Eliza as 'a good unobtrusive Christian' whose anxieties were eased by the thought that no day lasted more than twenty-four hours. Papa's birthday was marked by a lesson drawn from prisms and pigments, which seems as if it should relate to Gabriel, and may be a buried memory of the paints their indulgent father bought when Mamma was away. Her brother's own day was commemorated by the legend of Joseph's beauty making the lily of the Nile rise as to the sun – surely a half-concealed image of Gabriel's dazzling glory as a child. More obliquely, the plant curiously called impious cudweed gave rise to a familial analogy, its flowerhead surrounded and in time overtopped by flowerets being compared to 'a father encircled by his children'. Here, the term 'overtopped' suggests an unconscious analogy.

Time Flies also contains over seventy entries devoted to hagiography, each attached to the saint's name-day, which take us back to

Christina's teenage years, when the virgin martyrs were so vivid in Dr Neale's writing and Dr Pusey's preaching. Here, for instance, is Prisca, aged thirteen, who went up to 'her glorious death by decapitation', Agnes, also thirteen, who refused marriage in order to serve God and became 'His burnt offering', and Agatha who resisted sexual advances and suffered torture and cruelty to her body, while setting her face as a flint.

'One day long ago, I sat in a certain garden by a certain ornamental water,' began the entry for 10 April, which seems to re-create her teenage experience of depressive apathy, perhaps at Longleat:

> I sat so long and so quietly that a wild garden creature or two made its appearance: a water rat, perhaps, or a water-hunting bird. Few have been my personal experiences of the sort, and this one gratified me.
>
> I was absorbed that afternoon in anxious thought, yet the slight incident pleased me. If by chance people noticed me they may have thought how dull and blank I must be feeling: and partly they would have been right, but partly wrong . . .

With maturity, the recollection of wretchedness was lightened by the memory of 'some small secret fount of pleasure . . . lit by a dancing rainbow'. She had learnt to overcome despair.

She turned the familiar nightmares of her youth to new uses, so that the sensation of falling endlessly into a bottomless pit became an image of eternal damnation, while a spider encountered one night in the All Saints Hospital at Eastbourne was a figure of fear and evil, inescapably linked to the self, like the clutching creature in *The World*: 'The gas was alight in my little room with its paperless bare wall,' she wrote.

> On that wall appeared a spider, himself dark and defined, his shadow no less dark and scarcely if at all less defined.
>
> They jerked, zigzagged, advanced, retreated, he and his shadow posturing in ungainly indissoluble harmony. He seemed exasperated, fascinated, desperately endeavouring and utterly helpless.
>
> What could it all mean? One meaning and one only suggested itself. That spider saw without recognising his black double, and was mad to disengage himself from the horrible pursuing inalienable presence.
>
> I stood watching him awhile. (Presumably when I turned off the gas he composed himself).
>
> To me this self-haunted spider appears as a figure of each obstinate impenitent sinner, who, having outlived enjoyment, remains isolated irretrievably with his own horrible loathsome self . . .

Yet Christina had now succeeded in turning off the gas of Puseyite commination, and was no longer helplessly tied to the shadow of her own 'black double'. For *Time Flies* was generally a cheering text, in which she counselled against mournfulness and self-castigation. 'A gloomy Christian is like a cloud before the rainbow,' she wrote; 'but the heavenliest sort of Christian exhibits more bow than cloud, walking the world in a continual thanksgiving.'

As if James Collinson's death had prompted a final reconciliation with the pain he had caused, she here printed his sonnet of rejection, reproduced from memory after thirty years and appended to the anniversary of his death – a secret long nursed and now silently revealed. Her own poem for 24 April seems also to record her recognition of his withdrawal of love, in its allusion to 'sickening fear And a heart-breaking loss', while the untitled lyric attached to 11 May may well commemorate the date on which James formally asked her to release him from the engagement, containing as it does a direct response to his sonnet:

> Lord, when my heart was whole I kept it back
>   And grudged to give it Thee.
> Now then that it is broken, must I lack
>   Thy kind word 'Give it Me'?
> Silence would be but just, and Thou art just
> Yet since I lie here shattered in the dust,
>   With still an eye to lift to Thee,
> A broken heart to give,
> I think that Thou wilt bid me live,
>   And answer 'Give it Me'.

Hidden thus among various moral, devotional and anecdotal entries are many significant memories and reflections. They included more recent events such as Maria's funeral, with the rainbow teardrop, together with tributes to her piety, goodness and cheerful self-abnegation. And the entry for 23 December referred to the very recent task of copying out Gabriel's letters:

One day I caught myself wishing what I felt convinced would not be the case – that a certain occupation at once sad and pleasant and dear to me, and at that very moment inevitably drawing towards a close, could have lasted out through the remainder of my lifetime . . .

Naturally, many of the most characteristic entries were self-directed. Temptation, she wrote, was a sieve, to discover the vices of 'pride, vanity, self-confidence, contempt of others, discontent, envy, rebellion'.

And 'scrupulous Christians' like herself needed 'special self-sifting' for they too often resembled translations of the letter in defiance of the spirit, lacking all proportion. And the scrutiny of motive prompted several other autobiographical glimpses such as this:

> Interruptions are vexations.
> Granted. But what is an interruption?
> An interruption is something, is anything which breaks in upon our occupation of the moment. For instance, a frivolous remark when we are absorbed, a selfish call when we are busy, an idle noise out of time, an intrusive sight out of place.
> Now our occupations spring? . . . from within for they are the outcome of our own will.
> And interruptions arrive? . . . from without. Obviously from without, or otherwise we could and would ward them off.
> Our occupation, then, is that which we select. Our interruption is that which is sent us.
> But hence it would appear that the occupation may be wilful while the interruption may be providential.
> A startling view of occupations and interruptions!

She also criticised those who, perhaps like herself, were intolerant of well-intentioned but annoying guests (perhaps like Mrs Moulton) who aimed at repartee and jocularity. 'Our pet nerve they grate upon,' she wrote; 'a hint as broad as a scowl suffices not to suppress them.

> Well, dense they may be, but they mean well by all men.
> *We* are highly strung, sensitively refined, our tact amounts to intuition, not one weak point would we exhibit but for super-fine delicacy. Only do we . . . mean well by *all* men?

'How easy it is to talk!' she acknowledged to Caroline Gemmer. 'Yet I assure you it is not out of a light heart I write my commonplaces, nor do I find it at all easy to illustrate them in practice.'

The kind of moral advice contained in *Time Flies* is out of fashion today, but sanctimoniousness is softened by its sympathy and our knowledge that all flowed from personal experience. And she concluded her meditative self-examination with remarks that inter alia likened an elephant's trunk to an episcopal crozier – with the accompanying exclamation 'But Bishops should write for me, not I for Bishops!' – she was now not loth to assume the role of religious teacher. Every Christian was 'king and priest' in God's kingdom, she wrote, with a concomitant pastoral responsibility towards every soul within reach – the more so, perhaps, owing to her discovery that not all clergy were 'unselfish saints and undaunted heroes'. She had had a lifetime in which to assess them.

Time Flies was not to be the last of her meditations, but it was her most important, as well as her favourite, and to all intents and purposes marked a spiritual reckoning. Time might fly, but she had rendered a timely account and for once her title was exactly right, interweaving literal and symbolic, personal and general meaning.

She was surprised how much emotional energy it cost, observing to Mrs Gemmer that the completion of a new book often took a good deal out of the author. Hearing that Anne Gilchrist was gravely ill, she despatched a copy, noting that the title was apt to an acquaintance of twenty years, and also sent one to Alice Boyd, then in the midst of anxiety over 'WB'.

Not all friends were old, however, for the admiration and friendship of younger women brightened Christina's life in her fifties. One was 'Miss Katharine Tynan, an Irish poetess', who in 1885 sent Miss Rossetti a copy of her first book, inscribed 'with humility and reverence to the first of living women poets by the last and least'. Later, Katharine Tynan invoked the mellifluous excitement of Swinburne and Gabriel as chief influences, but her title poem *Louise de la Vallière* shared the same subject as Christina's *Soeur Louise de la Miséricorde*, and her letter expressed profound homage. For once, Christina postponed replying to the impatient author until she had read the volume, when she returned 'sincere admiration' for its poetic qualities, and added

> But beyond all *gifts* I account *graces,* and therefore the piety of your work
> fills me with hopes far beyond any to be raised by music of diction. If you
> have honoured my form by thinking it worth imitating, much more may
> I your spirit.

She also sent a copy of *Time Flies*, inscribed to 'Katie Tynan'.

Tynan, now in her early twenties, lived with her widowed father outside Dublin and had published in various magazines. Like her friend young Willie Yeats she took themes from Irish mythology and was counted in the ranks of the Celtic Revival; her subjects, according to a later critic, were Nature, mothers and children, religion and Irishry. Visiting England in the autumn, she arranged to call on both William and Christina. She was 'an agreeable clever woman', William told Lucy, with a perceptible Irish intonation but 'no exceptional amount of gush'. For her part, Christina found her visitor 'deferential enough to puff me up like puff-paste'.

Katharine, who was in fact pushy as well as deferential, was staying with Alice Meynell. She took the Meynells' daughter Monica to visit the renowned poetess, and later wrote various accounts of the meeting. 'I remember that the Meynells envied me going to visit her, saying "You will have the privilege of seeing a saint,"' she wrote in 1913. She was therefore disappointed that their hostess wore skirts of iron-grey tweed and stout boots, instead of the 'trailing robes of soft beautifully coloured material like all the writing and painting world of the day'. She also felt Miss Rossetti 'made the worst of herself, perhaps as a species of mortification', and 'affected a short, matter-of-fact way of speaking' that dampened the desire to sit at her feet. 'I wrote such melancholy things when I was young,' she explained in response to Katharine's gauche remarks on the disjunction between verse and appearance, 'that I am obliged to be unusually cheerful, not to say robust, in my old age.'

Tynan's earlier account, 'Santa Christina', written in 1911, was openly hagiographic and also lazy, even managing to confuse the heroine of *Maggie A Lady* with that of *Brandons Both*. 'One poem we discussed was "Milly a Lady",' she wrote. 'Is that the title, I wonder?' But she remembered that the verse she quoted, about lacking a mother, provoked an affectionate murmur from Mamma, sitting at the other side of the fire. This was the occasion when Christina revealed Gabriel's correct deduction that before writing *Maggie A Lady* she had been reading *Lady Geraldine's Courtship* and almost imperceptibly we glimpse another link being forged in the chain of the female tradition, as a new woman poet was welcomed to the ranks; Katharine Tynan was born in the year of Elizabeth Barrett Browning's death. When in 1887 Katharine asked permission to dedicate her second book *Shamrocks* to Christina and William jointly, she inscribed the presentation copy to 'Miss Christina Rossetti from her disciple the writer'. The sense of inheritance is clear.

'I doubt whether the woman is born, or for many a long day, if ever, will be born, who will balance, not to say outweigh Mrs Browning,' Christina had written in 1891, to a literary admirer who rated her the greater artist. She would not show such conceit, but the lineage was not denied. 'Now my juniors may take their turn and write,' she wrote to Katie, after a second visit. But when on another occasion Miss Tynan, perhaps wishing to establish some claim to the succession, asked if she might interview her illustrious elder, Christina owned she found 'this modern fashion highly distasteful', and claimed to be tenacious of her obscurity, adding that anyone could write what they pleased about her work, without her assistance. When they met, she compared interviews to photographs, with the subject turning 'their best side' to the public. Embarrassed and baulked, Katharine promised not to publish, whereupon Christina was more forthcoming, disclosing for instance that she might have married 'two or three times' – a remark which seems to confirm the relationships with James Collinson, Charles Cayley and John Brett – although this seemed highly improbable to young Miss Tynan, who felt an atmosphere of 'very old age' blanketed the house at Torrington Square, with a heavy silence that seemed to darken as well as muffle sound.

'Now that Christina Rossetti is dead, you have no woman rival,' Yeats told Tynan in 1895, but the evidence suggests that Katherine did not sustain her early promise. She married, settled in London, raised five children and dissipated her talents in a torrent of popular novels and journalism.

Alice Thompson Meynell, who became Christina's effective literary heir, displayed more discipleship in her work than in person. Indeed, in 1880 she had published a series of articles on 'Our Living Authors' in which she described Christina as a 'quaint, spiritual and gently emotional poetess', before awarding highest honours to Gabriel. 'Don't think me such a goose as to be keenly mortified by being put below you,' she responded, curious as to the anonymous author: 'who can it be who knows so much about our family, and yet in one or two points is positively at fault – as when he leaves us *no* English element, and seems to make you the eldest of the group?' The closest Mrs Meynell came to meeting Christina was when Miss Tynan took her daughter Monica to tea with the eminent poetess, no doubt bearing expressions of esteem in both directions, for in print Meynell's homage was unmistakable: indeed, her 'signature' poem *Renouncement*, was all too evidently in the Rossettian mode.

A slightly younger poetic successor was Charlotte Mew, twenty-five when Christina died, whose life was shadowed by poverty and family trouble, but who lived not far away in Gordon Square. To these names should be added that of Michael Field, pseudonym of the literary couple, aunt Katherine Bradley and niece Edith Cooper, who from the 1880s produced a stream of poems and poetic dramas; and those of Margaret Henderson, Rosamund Marriott Watson, and Anne Patchett Martin, all of whom sent Christina their volumes of verse and received gracious thanks, but failed to make a lasting mark in literature.

'Sad to say, another unknown has presented me with a volume of sonnets of which (so far as I have waded) the less said the better as *poetry*,' wrote Christina to Lucy early in 1886, warning her never to publish a volume 'unless you are quite sure you can excel (say) Mr. W. Shakespear; or if not, at least don't bestow it on poor disconcerted me! a warning to be early and with absolute impartiality brought home to Olive, Arthur, Helen, Mary, who exhibit alarming tendencies.' For in her endeavour to 'mean well by all men', she hated to hurt any aspiring author's self-esteem, yet also to tell untruths in any degree.

As William wrote, she was resolute in setting a demarcation line between poets and versifiers, unable to see 'any good reason why one who is not a poet should write in metre'. But she did her best to advise, maintaining a long correspondence, for example, with a would-be versifier and invalid named Miss Newsham, who first wrote in 1889, enclosing her verses after reading one of Christina's poems in a religious magazine. 'If the Queen of the Night is clothed in royal blue, should not the sky be bluer?' Christina asked, in a tactful criticism, pointing out also that *dawn* and *born* were not true rhymes. She professed herself happy so to advise, saying

> I assure you, my brother Gabriel did, in old days, so much of the same kind for my poems, that they came out materially the better for his care. I like to imitate him in my turn. And here I am at your service.

Alas, Gabriel had better material on which to work, but Christina's was the more gracious impulse. 'If my strictures please you I am happy in offering them, and if my letters cheer you at all in so much illness and suffering, they are doing a blessed work – blessed to myself,' she wrote, insisting too that her correspondent drop 'all stately forms' of address and write simply to 'Miss Rossetti'.

In personal terms, the most important admirer, who became Christina's close friend and companion, was Lisa Wilson, an aspiring poet and artist of whom virtually nothing is known. She first called in May 1885, full of gratitude for Christina's poems 'which I loved and admired so much and wanted so badly to say "Thank you" for all the loveliness of thought and exquisite pictures she had filled me with,' as she wrote later. 'Don't expect me to be as nice as my poems or you will be disappointed,' replied Christina with a twinkle. Lisa had been 'a very invalidish girl, obliged to lie down a great deal', but admiration enabled her to collect a promised copy of *Time Flies* in person, and after reading about the unappreciated four-leaved clover, she sent some pressed specimens gathered in Cornwall, which Christina inserted into the volume. To Lisa, Christina became a 'dearest friend', while to Christina Lisa proved a loving and devoted friend – one of those, in William's words, 'who saw my sister most frequently and affectionately in her closing years'. When in 1892 Lisa presented a decorated book of her own poems, Christina lovingly inscribed a short verse *To my Fior-de-Lisa*, playfully casting Lisa as a lily and herself as a rose – their respective flower emblems. William added that Miss Wilson had 'a graceful touch of her own both in published verse and in painting', but again the promise was unfulfilled, for Lisa Wilson's work seems to have been mainly published in magazines, and research has so far failed to rediscover her career.

Younger writers Christina herself admired included the American poet Sarah Piatt, in some of whose works she would have found echoes of her own verse. And, in 1890, she received a copy of Emily Dickinson's posthumous *Poems*, issued by her own publisher Roberts Bros of Boston.

'She had (for she is dead) a wonderfully Blakean gift, but therewithal a startling recklessness of poetic ways and means' she wrote admiringly. There may have been direct influence, for Christina's work was widely read in the United States, and both poets, born the same year, shared not only a natural gift for language and metaphor, but a direct speaking voice and similar themes: hope deferred, love denied, ambition, emotional pain and secret desires, with a comparable touch of wit and whimsicality. Several of Dickinson's poems contain echoes of Christina's – her lines beginning 'One dignity delays for all' recall *Up-hill*, for example, and *If you were coming in the fall* is reminiscent of Rossettian lines on longing:

> If certain, when this life is out,
> That yours and mine should be,
> I'd toss it yonder like a rind,
> And taste Eternity.

> But now, all ignorant of the length
> Of time's uncertain wing,
> It goads me like the goblin bee
> That will not state its sting.

Most strikingly, however, Dickinson's expression of something undisclosed at the heart of verse responded to Christina's teasing yet serious refusal to reveal:

> I asked no other thing,
> No other was denied.
> I offered Being for it;
> The mighty merchant smiled.

> Brazil? He twirled a button,
> Without a glance my way:
> "But, madam, is there nothing else
> That we can show to-day?"

Had Christina, like Emily, given up all pursuit of publication, her verse might have retained more quaintness and innovation, for their work sprang from similar impulses, and it is nice to know that despite the recklessness of form, Emily Dickinson's little book was not a volume by yet another 'unknown' that Christina wished had not been bestowed on her, but one she genuinely welcomed and admired.

39

Narrowing Grooves

IN 1886 FRANCES Rossetti's life drew to a close. In 1885, for the first time, she was too frail to take a seaside holiday, though her sisters (in rather worse health) took themselves to Brighton. Over the winter the most frequent visitors at Torrington Square were doctors and clergy (the daily diary kept by Christina for her mother frequently records a 'home service' when the old ladies were unable to get to church). On 25 February Mamma had a fall in her room and from then on visibly weakened. By the end of March Charlotte was also confined to bed, and two nurses were employed to help Christina. On 3 April Mamma's condition was such that Christina summoned William in the middle of the night, and though she lingered a little longer, unconsciousness supervened, and at midday on 8 April she died quietly.

Long foreseen, the loss was grievous, for at the age of fifty-five Christina had always lived under the same roof as her mother, and for the past decade or more had devoted herself to Mamma's care and comfort. And the strain told: in the weeks that followed she was troubled by old symptoms – choking fits and headaches that perhaps threatened a return of the thyroid condition. In August she was sent to Brighton for restorative change of air, accompanied by Olive. Here they 'haunted the aquarium', to watch the evil-looking octopus spread his tentacles and spurt the contents of his ink bag.

To Christina, indeed, the creature was a living symbol of evil, a 'ghastly, lothly, emblematic likeness of Satan'. She admitted having seen only this one small specimen, but as Olive observed, the Brighton octopus exercised a fearful fascination over her aunt. 'Inert as it often appeared, it bred and tickled a perpetual suspense,' wrote Christina:

> will it do something? will it emerge from the background of its water den? I have seen it swallow its live prey in an eyewink, change from a stony colour to an appalling lividness, elongate unequal feelers and set them flickering like a flame, sit still with an air of immemorial old age amongst the lifeless refuse of its once living meals . . .

If the octopus was Satan, its tank was clearly hell. 'I had to remind myself that this vivid figure of wickedness was not in truth itself wickedness,' she added hurriedly – but the creature's symbolic nature was evidently more real to her. It prompted a meditation on human wickedness. 'There is a mystery of evil which I suppose no man during his tenure of mortal life will ever fathom,' she wrote:

> I pursuing my own evil from point to point find that it leads me not outward amid a host of foes laid against me, but inward within myself; it is not mine enemy that doeth me this dishonour, neither is it mine adversary that magnifieth himself against me: it is I, it not another, not primarily any other; it is I who undo, defile, deface myself. True, I am summoned to wrestle on my own scale against principalities, powers, rulers of the darkness of this world, spiritual wickedness in high places; but none of these can crush me unless I simultaneously undermine mine own citadel . . . Nothing outside myself can destroy me by main force and in my own despite . . . my own inherent evil is what I have to cope with . . .

This was the familiar problem, entrancingly enacted in *Goblin Market*, now sombrely, inexorably restated. And this sombre mood suggests that Christina was again visited by depression – a natural accompaniment to grief. Indeed William felt that her mother's death formed the 'practical close' of her own life. 'All that remained for her was religious resignation for a sorrowful interval and a looking forward to the end,' he wrote morosely; 'the nursing of two invalided aunts (eventually one) occupied her hours and sapped her remaining forces.' But this was with hindsight, and while her own strength lasted Christina showed no such melancholy decline. 'Happiness is in our power even when continual pleasure is out of the question,' she wrote firmly to Caroline Gemmer. 'In *will* at least, I am that contented "droner" who accounts her assigned groove the best. Here I can, if I choose, please God: and what more could I do elsewhere?'

And she was always conscious of those less fortunate. Economic recession in 1886 resulted in unemployment, distress and militant demonstrations in London, which heavy policing turned into riots. As it happened, William Morris was now among the leaders of the Socialist League, which took a major role in the agitation. Christina disliked both the militancy and secularism of the movement, but was sympathetic to the causes; as she wrote to Lucy, exiled from London by ill-health:

> It is just as well too that you escaped the alarm of the riots, which were serious enough as they were, and alarmed one lest they should become yet more so. But, however much one may deplore lawlessness, it is heart-sickening to think of the terrible want of work and want of all things at our very doors – we, so comfortable.

Emigration, not socialism, was the only remedy she could propose, while fearing this would leave Britain weakened. Nevertheless 'no one can call upon people to starve today lest England should prove powerless to hold her own tomorrow. You see, my politics are not very intricate...'

Elsewhere, she condemned socialism when divorced from Christianity, which suggests that she saw it as misguided. On Irish self-government, the other great question of the day, which was currently splitting the Liberal party, her opinions are not recorded, unless one declaration of 'loyal principles' refers to a request to support Home Rule (William did so, but as a government employee was precluded from overt declaration). On the other hand, Katherine Tynan, who was dismayed to find Jean Ingelow vehemently hostile to Ireland and the Irish, did not record any such obstacles to friendship with Christina. Christina herself expressed surprise that Swinburne, who this summer launched a 'slashing denunciation' of Gladstone's Irish policy, now listed himself as a Conservative, finally laying to rest his earlier reputation for radicalism. Always more cautious, her views had also remained more stable. It appears too that at one stage Christina assisted 'the Irish Peasant Poet' named O'Conor, for he wrote now and then from his new home in Canada where in 1886, she was gratified to learn, he was awarded a state pension; no doubt she believed emigration the answer to Ireland's problems too. Some little while later she wrote wistfully of an unfulfilled desire to visit that 'near-at-hand island', qualified by fear of the sea-crossing and the understandable 'alienation' of the inhabitants.

To young Olive, watching the octopus in the aquarium, her aunt appeared almost as repulsive a companion, dressed in dowdy out-of-date clothes, and wearing the 'hideous cap then donned by maiden ladies over thirty (held to be elderly)'. She had, too, 'a rather grim cast of countenance, and chilly austere manners that never unbent, even to a small niece', so that despite goodwill there was little spontaneous affection. Christina's letters give a rather different impression, for in large part her love was now directed towards William's children – 'my children, I may almost say, as none other can be so near to me,' she told Lucy this year. Immediately after her mother's death she made her will, leaving to William the amount she computed owing to him and making the children her ultimate heirs. In terms of feeling, she favoured Arthur as the only boy – it was the the lot of girls to play second fiddle, she noted ruefully – but also resurrected Grandpapa's long ago comment on herself to apply to little Helen, whom, she prophesied, would be the most spirited of the lot – 'allowing, that is, for the inborn preponderance of man over woman!' And as it turned out, she was right.

So to the best of her ability she was a loving and generous aunt, always welcoming their visits and remembering their birthdays. 'What a beautiful thing to be no more than 5 years old!' she wrote with a birthday kiss for '*aged* Mary' in 1886. She took them on outings and sent Arthur riddles and on one occasion the rules of a card game devised by herself, saying 'I daresay you never suspected your sober old aunt of having invented a game'. She was pleased in 1890 when Lucy's wish to move to Primrose Hill left the family temporarily houseless, and they accepted her invitation to lodge at Torrington Square. As Olive recalled:

> Frugal in her habits and sparing in her diet, there was nothing mean in her composition and when in 1890 she took under her roof my parents and us four children while a monumental move was being made from the Endsleigh Gardens house, she was the soul of hospitality. She had given the old retainers – the word describes the denizens of her kitchen much better than the word 'servants' – standing orders and one day a large roast leg of mutton, the next a sirloin of beef with all the usual trimmings appeared on the board, followed by puddings and tarts and biscuits galore . . . and at high tea, over which she presided, a Yorkshire ham would face a pickled tongue.

For the first time in her life, Christina was of independent means and responsible for her own expenditure. Her income from investments was ample for herself, but required prudent handling owing to the 'somewhat expensive' scale on which she and the aunts kept house – or rather that she kept on their behalf. This was, she told her brother, only right – 'especially considering all Aunt Charlotte has done for me' – but sometimes meant drawing on capital.

Nevertheless, despite her goodwill, the children were always a source of tension between herself and William. From Brighton, for instance, she reported that Olive was an intelligent companion, both 'docile and independent, which is a very fine combination of qualities', but inwardly perhaps harboured a 'jealous disposition' – a tactless charge indignantly refuted by Olive's father. And she was always fearful regarding any tendency to 'worldliness'; as Olive recalled, 'of all people Mr Worldly Wiseman was the most hateful' to her aunt.

For her concern was not to amuse, but to guide and, if possible, to save. Only with difficulty could she refrain from instructing her nieces and nephew in the faith that was the base and centre of her own existence. She prayed for them daily – and even once asked the unbelieving William if he would do the same for her – for in her eyes to fail to seek the salvation of others was a dereliction of Christian duty, akin to ignoring poverty and pain. 'It seems unnatural to love you so much and never say one word about matters which colour my life,' she explained sadly to her brother.

Shortly before their mother's death, she and William discussed the future, anticipating that the aunts would also soon be laid to rest.

Christina thought of moving out of London, maybe to Rochester, where Burrows was a Canon, and taking a large house, to accommodate the family whenever they wished. But the 'great stumbling-block', as William made clear, was her tendency 'to proselytize the kids'. Christina protested, claiming she 'would herself openly practise her religious duties and leave the kids to see and think what they liked of them', but such limitation was hardly compatible with her own faith. The children recalled her avoidance of treading on any scrap of paper, lest it be printed with the name of God, and her rule that holy words like 'eternal' and 'almighty' should not be used in a secular sense. Indeed, she wrote, to say 'the almighty dollar' was simply blasphemous, however unintentionally – an objection that smacks of fanaticism. She could not therefore keep religion within bounds, as she wrote equally plainly to Lucy after a conversation about how happy the children seemed. And so they were, in an everyday sense, Christina concurred, but she herself could not use the word *happy* without meaning something beyond the present life. 'Please do not take offence at what I say,' she added lamely.

Lucy's health deteriorated, and at the end of 1886 it was decided that she and the older two children should winter on the Riviera. Christina declined to join them, unwilling to leave the aunts, but early in February she herself was medically bidden to quit London, and went, alone, to Torquay, where it was cold but sunny and quiet. It was hilly, she told aunt Eliza, with steps and steep slopes and houses perched at all angles. The bay was so enclosed as to resemble a lake, when her own preference was for a 'boundless expanse' of ocean, and the beach was sandy, rather than her favoured shingle; 'still, one must be very prejudiced and thankless not to enjoy what it *is* without cavilling at what it is not'. She found two suitable churches and two very old acquaintances – the widow of Swynfen Jervis, and Sara Coleridge's daughter Edith. 'If "not the rose", these "yet have been near it",' she remarked. Shortly before her mother's death, they had enjoyed reading Mrs Coleridge's biography, compiled by Edith.

The tranquillity at Torquay was disturbed only by news of an earthquake on the Riviera, where she feared for Lucy and other acquaintances known to be wintering in the sun – old Mrs Townsend, the friend of long ago, Isabella and her new husband, and some connections of cousin Sarah Austin. Other old friends were present in July when a memorial to Gabriel was unveiled on Cheyne Walk and Tudor House was opened to guests. Browning, Hughes, Stephens, Shields, Alfred Gurney and Augusta Webster were there – but not Christina, presumably because the ceremony was performed by Holman Hunt,

and Edith was unavoidably present. Aunt Charlotte was Christina's
excuse, but in her absence aunt Eliza gamely made the excursion,
supported by two servants from Torrington Square.

Later this month Christina received from Penkill a copy of Scott's
illustrated edition of the *Kingis Quhair* – an 'unexpected and kind gift'
that also sent her mind back to former days, which she was glad to
have enjoyed, though without wishing their return. She recalled sitting for Lady Jane in the *Kingis Quhair* mural, and how Scotus had
'always excelled in rousing up my precarious spirit of fun', reminding
him too of the visit to Wallington when she had looked so pensive at
luncheon as if 'sitting by the grave of buried hope?!!!'. And she was
pleased to know that all three dear friends – Sun, Moon and Star –
were in conjunction at the Castle, so that 'the full constellation occupies one astronomical House at present'.

Her own 'assigned groove' was narrowing perceptibly, for though
the house at Torrington Square was 'uselessly large and inconvenient-
ly expensive,' as she noted towards the end of 1887, the aunts' age and
infirmity made it impossible to move. Early in 1889 Eliza suffered a
seizure that left her mentally and physically helpless, and after this
geriatric invalid care became Christina's full-time occupation. There
was 'no fear of my not being in town, as I now never leave home on
account of my infirm old Aunts – so do not *hope* to find me gone away
if you come!' she told Katharine Tynan. And to Miss Newsham she
wrote frankly and firmly, refuting the idea that she was especially
miserable because confined to London:

> Thank you for thinking of and desiring my happiness. I am surrounded
> by blessings, and am not tried by any severity of health. Yet I am not
> strong and I suppose I have a natural tendency to despondency. My home
> circle too is less cheerful than in old days, consisting as it now does of two
> very aged Aunts (87 and 80) one bedridden, the other still more seriously
> diseased. But against all this must be set that I am exactly where I should
> choose to abide were all the world laid open to my choice. Both my Aunts
> are truly good and have been very kind to me.

To little Juliet Hueffer, youngest of Cathy Brown's children, Torrington Square was a gloomy place, where Christina greeted Helen, Mary
and herself warmly – 'Welcome, merry little maidens!' – providing
cakes for tea and making dolls' furniture out of conkers and pins, but
also took them up to see 'two very ancient ugly aunts who lay in beds
on the opposite side of the room, separated by a thin strip of carpet.
They were so old they couldn't stand up, and they could hardly talk.
They always seemed to me to be waving their long skinny hands...'

They wore large frilled nightcaps and flowered bedjackets, and put Juliet inescapably in mind of the Wolf in Red Riding Hood.

Money was 'a great cheerer of spirits and lightener of loads', Christina told Caroline Gemmer. This was no shocking admission, she continued, as long as others' spirits and loads were regarded as having an equal claim on one's cash; 'only the consideration must be acted upon honestly, or alas for a "barren fig tree" '. Endeavouring to observe this second duty of benevolence, however, she fell foul of a wheedling, dishonest supplicant named William Bryant, whose continual appeals sorely tried her charity and patience. Introduced by Hall Caine, Bryant was a failed author and professional beggar, who over nine years caused Christina great distress.

When her mother died, he pressed his own needs, for instance, and repeatedly asked for 'loans' that were never repaid. He claimed 'business openings' that might fail for want of ready cash, but never showed the slightest intention of working. Christina sent regular gifts of money, stamped envelopes and other 'trifles', including a copy of *Verses* for Bryant to sell. Characteristically, he complained of the 'low price' it fetched. She recommended him to Macmillans and Professor Sidgwick of Cambridge (similarly afflicted by Bryant's importuning but possibly less soft-hearted) and supported his applications to charitable institutions including the All Saints Hospital. Only slowly did she grow impatient. 'I am pained both for you and by you. Alas! all your needs make me none the richer or the better able to meet them,' she wrote in November 1886, enclosing a small sum. 'As to *charwomaning*, I can sympathize with you, being myself something of a Joan-of-all-trades to save odd pence!' But when he began sending representatives to call in person on his behalf, and requests on a weekly basis she was dismayed. 'I am sorry for your sickness, pains, sorrows, want of work (10/- enclosed) ... But I beg you to realize that it is quite impossible I should respond unboundedly to unbounded appeals, heartily as I wish well to you and your wife. Do spare me having to go over the same ground again and again ...'

Because Bryant drank, her assistance was vain, as she eventually acknowledged. 'Please do not take trouble to answer me: I think it most imprudent policy to bore (more than one can help) those of whom one asks favours!' she wrote in one undated note, and in April 1894 she finally brought the correspondence to a close, with a characteristic double message:

> And now I plainly add that I wish no longer to receive applications directly from you or your wife. I wish you both well, but I have thought the matter over and this is the conclusion I arrive at.
>
> None the less, your sincere friend, Christina G. Rossetti.

To William, Christina's inability to cast Bryant off was a symptom of spinsterish weakness, but having once expressed sympathy she was unwilling to withdraw it. Her numerous letters are strewn around the globe, for when the funds dried up Bryant sold the notes to auto-graph-dealers. And though no similar details survive, William re-corded that another supplicant whose appeals also amounted to persecution was Luigi Polidori in Italy, grandson of Gaetano's brother, whom aunt Charlotte subsidised for many years and Christina felt duty-bound to assist.

On 8 January 1890 aunt Charlotte died. 'One good old Aunt still claims my care,' wrote Christina to Watts a little later, adding

> Meanwhile I live, so to say, in a circle of the absent who inhabit either this world or the next: and if absence does not deprive me of their sympathy, never may it deprive them of mine!

What of her writing? In 1884, Swinburne had issued a public *Ballad of Appeal* in the pages of his own new volume, repeating in a letter the same wish 'which all your readers must share, and to which I trust you will not always turn a deaf ear – long as it seems since you have given us any fresh cause to thank you for a fresh gift of such verse as only you can give . . .' In return, she sent a copy of *Time Flies*, trusting he would appreciate the verse it contained. But she feared it was the last. In the autumn following its publication she declined the invita-tion to become a regular contributor to a magazine she admired, saying

> I never had my verse-writing power so under command as to be able to count on its exercise, and my last little book pretty well exhausted my last scrap. Now I am feeling as if I may have written my final book – notwith-standing a hope that it may not turn out so after all!

She had of course often invoked the notion of exhausted powers in the past, and though it was true that she had little talent for writing to order, *Time Flies* itself showed that the fire still kindled. Moreover, in its prose passages she had given a glimpse of her compositional practice. 'Suppose our duty of the moment is to write: why do we not write?' she inquired rhetorically:

> Because we cannot summon up anything original, or striking, or pic-turesque, or eloquent, or brilliant.
> But is a subject set before us? – It is.
> Is it true? – It is.

> Do we understand it? – Up to a certain point we do.
> Is it worthy of meditation? – Yes, and prayerfully.
> Is it worthy of exposition? – Yes, indeed.
> Why not then begin?

She now plainly saw her role as that of Christian writer, and if in the past she had wished always to write in an original, eloquent, brilliant vein – as who does not? – she also recognised a devotional duty, to write prayerfully and helpfully for others.

She was therefore willing when able, and in 1886–8 happily answered a request from the art-oriented magazine *Hobby Horse*, launched in self-conscious succession to *The Germ*, to which, despite its total lack of religious commitment, she sent two carols and a moving Easter hymn, which revealed that she was becoming reconciled to the dark and now 'not unlovely' season:

> Wintry boughs against a wintry sky;
> Yet the sky is partly blue
> And the clouds are partly bright: –
> Who can tell but sap is mounting high
> Out of sight,
> Ready to burst through?
>
> Winter is the mother-nurse of spring,
> Lovely for her daughter's sake,
> Not unlovely for her own:
> For a future buds in everything;
> Grown or blown,
> Or about to break.

She contributed a poem to the *Athenaeum* on the death of Cardinal Newman in 1890 and had also set herself a new devotional task, pursued in the intervals of nursing and housekeeping, as she explained, when Watts inquired what she was currently writing:

> all I am doing is reading and thinking over part of the New Testament, writing down what I can as I go along. I work at prose and help myself forward with little bits of verse. What I am doing is (I hope) for my own profit, nor do I in the least know that it will ever become an available 'book'. At present, as you may divine, I am not likely to draw much upon the simply imaginative.

The text was the Book of Revelation, and her prose pieces and 'little bits of verse' were eventually published as *The Face of the Deep*, a lengthy commentary on this most opaque and figurative of sacred texts – St John's vision of the final struggle of good and evil commonly known as the Apocalypse. It thus contained her considered meditations on the essential relation of 'this world and the next', or the quotidian and the ideal, within an eschatalogical framework. It appears that the task was inspired by sisterly piety, for Maria was the 'dear saint' and 'dear person' who once remarked on Patience being the lesson of Revelation. 'Following the clue thus afforded me,' Christina explained in her preface, 'I seek and hope to find Patience in this book of awful import, and along with that grace whatever treasures besides God may vouchsafe me . . .' Patience was the virtue most needed, one may surmise, in caring for confused and incontinent old aunts.

But Revelation had of course been a favourite text of the chiliastic Dodsworth, and the approaching millenium was also in mind at the start of her commentary, which opened

"Things which must shortly come to pass". – At the end of eighteen hundred years we are still repeating this "shortly" because it is the word of God . . . For truly the end of all flesh is at hand, whether or not we possess faith to realize how a thousand years and one day are compatible in the Divine Sight.

Christina did not literally expect the End of the World at the end of the century; but with death all around, she preached eternal vigilance, lest the soul be caught unawares.

As it progressed, her text was a mix of contemplative thoughts, ethical observations, mystical quotation and scriptural exegesis that waded both deeply and widely into the ocean of John's visionary images. Like *Time Flies*, though less easily or extensively, it can be read biographically as a partial record of her spiritual experience in these narrowed years. 'What wearied me once, must I do yet again?' she asked, responding in Christ's words as she had frequently done in verse.

"Yes."
Is there no alternative?
"None, except destruction . . ."
Is there no help?
"Not until thou begin to help thyself."
Is there any hope?
"Yea, assured and boundless hope . . ."
Nothing on earth is a substitute for performance of duty, be that duty what it may.

Supporting the inference that the book was started shortly after
Mamma's death, Christina's first topic was bereavement. The dead
were yet alive in Christ and those who had 'lost our nearest and
dearest' should pray for patience in sorrow:

> Love, to be love, must walk Thy way
>   And work Thy Will;
> Or if Thou say "Lie still";
>   Lie still and pray.

Meditating on the spiritual strength needed to carry out duties took
Christina poetically back to happier times, and a plaintive protest:

> Other hearts are gay –
> Ask not joy today:
> Toil today along thy way
> Keeping grudge at bay –
>
> On a past May day
> Flowers pranked all the way;
> Nightingales sang out their say
> On a night of May –
>
> Dost thou covet May
> On an Autumn day?
> Foolish memory saith its say
> Of sweets past away –

which concluded with a firm admonition against lingering ambition:

> Gone the bloom of May,
> Autumn beareth bay:
> Flowerless wreath for head grown grey
> Seemly were today –
>
> Dost thou covet bay?
> Ask it not today:
> Rather for a palm-branch pray;
> None will say thee nay.

When Lucy reported that a bookseller professed no knowledge of
Sing-Song, Christina joked that her renown was evidently 'under
eclipse', and perhaps the circumstance prompted her poem, with its
faint echoes of *Maude* and the sprig of bay.

'Patience is its own reward,' she wrote a few pages later. 'It preoccupies the soul with a sort of satisfaction which suppresses insatiable craving, vain endeavour, rebellious desire' and this chapter ended with a mystical image of the soul's relation to the eternal, as rivers running into the divine sea. Increasingly she anticipated her own death.

But ethical issues were not ignored, and buried within the dense text of this book is a full account of Christina's philosophy of life, for her Platonic concept of heaven led directly to considerations of present conduct. She therefore again defended animal rights, linking this to an environmental plea to abuse neither the earth nor the beasts upon it; and counselled those engaged in penitentiary and reformatory work not to tell others to suffer patiently but rather assume fellowship of suffering. Perhaps reflecting current social unrest, she also attacked class superiority. In the ideal realm, she wrote, such questions as 'Are they common folk or gentry? learned or illiterate? vulgar or refined? in or out of society? worth or not worth knowing?' would be unseemly and unnecessary; so too in daily life. Similarly, she wrote of ethnic and national divisions, which ideally should not be obliterated but welcomed: 'Every kindred, every tongue, every people, every nation ... French with Germans, Italians with Austrians, English with Irish, whites with blacks, all ranks with all ranks, all men with all men'.

Furthermore, present divisions in the Church were to be utilised rather than attacked, she argued, for 'cannot we learn much from the devotion of Catholic Rome, the immutability of Catholic Greece, the philanthropic piety of Quakerism, [even] the zeal of many a Protestant?' But she firmly condemned spiritualism, and its associates mesmerism, hypnotism, and fortune-telling, fearing they led to the surrender of free will or the road to evil choice, imagination, conduct. And she also castigated a small host of contemporary positions because they were not informed by faith, with a warning against 'fairseeming superstructures which are not founded upon the one only Rock', listing

> Philanthropy divorced from dogma.
> Socialism in lieu of Christian brotherhood.
> Indifferentism to truth simulating charity.
> Charity degraded into an investment ...

Somewhat startlingly, she was even tempted to identify 'Godless philanthropy' with Antichrist, evidently feeling that to do good for wrong motives was tantamount to evil.

Some other observations were equally fundamentalist, especially as the decline in churchgoing and Sunday observance was grievous to

Christina. But her excoriation of greed and selfishness sounds radical as well as reactionary:

> Now are they the wicked who stand callous amidst the fears, torments, miseries of others; not investigating human claims, not mourning with them that mourn, not moving burdens with one of their fingers, not heeding the burning questions of their day, neighbourhood, nay sometimes of their own hearths . . .
>
> Alas England, full of luxuries and thronged by stinted poor, whose merchants are princes and whose dealings crooked, whose packed storehouses stand amid bare homes, whose gorgeous array has rags for neighbours!
>
> . . . well may arrogant England amid her seas quake and lament betimes . . .

And she assumed a prophetic mantle in seeing contemporary events as 'signs of the times':

> Glance at recent troubles in Ireland: mark boycotting and its resuts. Look at home; at strikes and unions, so far as any terrorism resorted to is concerned. God in His mercy restrain men from misusing tremendous edge-tools, launching out on unfathomed waters . . .

Nevertheless she warned, though the mighty would be laid low and the rich excluded from heaven, on earth social position was allotted primarily as a means of glorifying God and serving others. Monarchs and subjects, employers and employed, masters and servants existed equally and complementarily, and it behoved all 'in our several stations' to be affectionate, loyal, and helpful to each other.

The vexed gender question received a good deal of consideration under various clauses of the apocalyptic vision. Here, for instance, Christina saw sexual equality as a heavenly ideal where woman would 'be made equal with men and angels; arrayed in all human virtues and decked with all communicable divine graces'. And now she fully rehabilitated Eve, whom she trusted would stand 'amongst all saints of all time' before the throne of God.

Elsewhere, however, she saw woman as the traditional personification of worldly evil, just as in her old poem *The Three Enemies*. For Satan 'understands how to tint her mists and bubbles with prismatic colours, hide her thorns under roses and her worms under silk. He can paint her face and tire her head, and set her on a wall and at a window . . . and so has she her men singers and women singers, her brazen wind instruments and her hollow drums . . .' Moreover, a 'perverse and rebellious woman' was liable to a particular foulness and degradation, precisely because this violated her femininity. Whatever else the Scarlet Woman of the Apocalypse might represent, she was also a figure of this rebelliousness against God. Similarly, if like Jezebel a woman, aiming to establish her equality with man, posed 'as prophetess to his prophet', she could only do so by false pretension and imposture' – to which judgement Christina added a contemporary comment: 'History repeats itself'.

Nevertheless, 'we daughters of Eve' were not bound to be inferior, for woman was 'a mighty power for good or for evil'. And, she added,

> I think that in these days of women's self-assertion and avowed rivalry with men, I do well to bear in mind that in a contest no stronger proof of superiority can be given on either side than the not bringing into action all available force. As yet, I suppose, we women claim no more than equality with our brethren in head and heart: whilst as to physical force, we scout it as unworthy to arbitrate between the opposed camps. Men on their side do not scout physical force, but let it be.
>
> Does either man or woman doubt where superiority resides, when at chess one player discards a pawn in favour of the other?
>
> Society may be personified as a human figure whose right hand is man, whose left woman; in one sense equal, in another sense unequal. The right hand is labourer, acquirer, achiever: the left hand helps, but has little independence, and is more apt at carrying than at executing. The right hand runs the risks, fights the battles: the left hand abides in comparative quiet and safety; except (a material exception) that in the *mutual* relations of the twain it is in some ways far more liable to undergo than to inflict hurt, to be cut (for instance) than to cut.
>
> Rules admit of and are proved by exceptions. There are left-handed people, and there may arise a left-handed society!

Christina's old 'Fight over the Body' was still urgent, and still inconclusive: for while she accepted natural inequalities and therefore separate spheres, yet she observed how men abused their power – and the images of injury here remind us that in 1888, when she was writing, five women were murdered and cut open in London's East End by the unidentified Jack the Ripper, who still stands as archetype of male violence against women.

A year later, Christina put her muddled principles into practice by volunteering her signature to the infamous women's Protest against Female Suffrage, organised by novelist Mrs Humphrey Ward at the behest of the editor of the *Nineteenth Century*, in whose pages the original petition was printed, with an appeal for others to add their names:

The undersigned protest strongly against the proposed extension of the Parliamentary Franchise to women, which they believe would be a measure distasteful to the great majority of women of the country – unnecessary and mischievous both to themselves and the state.

Among the signatories were some who might have known better, such as the future Beatrice Webb, acting also from muddled motives. Those known to Christina included Laura Epps and two of Georgie Burne-Jones's sisters, as well as a number of eminent church wives, whose views may have influenced her own. But her signature seems to have been sent independently, for when the additional 1200 names were printed many came in groups – with significant batches from both Girton College and Lady Margaret Hall, incidentally – while Christina's was singly and randomly listed, as were those of her friends Ellen Heaton and Emily Tebbs, and others she knew by reputation, such as Ellen Terry and Eliza Cook. She was therefore in respectable if not commendable company. As Millicent Fawcett pointed out in her rejoinder, however, the names of those who had done most for for women in education, social reform, philanthropy, legal rights, guardianship of children and professional training were conspicuously absent. But the Protest was a severe blow to the suffrage cause. Christina's signature must have pained Lucy, who like William supported votes for women and no doubt also Augusta Webster – for whom incidentally Christina retained a high regard. When in early 1890 Gladstone compiled a list of 'distinguished poetesses', the one omission Christina noted with regret was Mrs Webster's.

The Face of the Deep was published by the SPCK in 1892. It was Christina's last major project, and is today the least read of all her works, though it contains over two hundred poems. It also links back to both the Adventism of her youth and indirectly to the endlessly unravelling textual exgesis of her father's work on Dante. Somewhere in its five hundred pages, one feels, Christina lost herself in abstruse meditations that drew her backwards forty years, for the main devotional thrust of the book is fear of evil, without and within. The terrifying scarlet woman of St John's vision, for instance, prompted a quotation from the Divine Comedy, and a sonnet that recalls the cloven-footed female figure of The World, from 1849:

> Foul is she and ill-favoured, set askew:
>   Gaze not upon her till thou deem her fair,
>   Lest she should mesh thee in her wanton hair,
> Adept in arts grown old yet ever new.

Her heart lusts not for love, but through and through
  For blood, as spotted panther lusts in lair;
  No wine is in her cup, but filth is there
Unutterable, with plagues hid out of view.
Gaze not upon her; for her dancing whirl
  Turns giddy the fixed gazer presently:
  Gaze not upon her, lest thou be as she
    When at the far end of her long desire
Her scarlet vest and gold and gem and pearl
  And she amid her pomp are set on fire.

Reading through Christina's work some thirty years later, Virginia Woolf commented that if she were bringing a case against God, Christina Rossetti would be her first witness. For the defence, we might ask what impelled Christina to choose such a fearful religion – and why, in her last years, she found in it so little consolation. Hers was assuredly a careful and very troubled heart.

40

Lost Laureate

AUNT ELIZA LINGERED on in such a frail state that Christina seldom left the house for more than an hour or so, dividing the invalid care with her devoted servant Harriet Read. When a friend sent wild hyacinths and primroses to Torrington Square, packed in moss, she replied: 'as I no longer go to the country . . . I may say that the country very graciously comes to me'. After William and Lucy moved to Primrose Hill, her groove became even narrower, for the children paid fewer visits to their aunt, and were anyway growing up into interests of their own, Olive and Helen achieving a certain notoriety in their teens through their involvement in Russian revolutionism and espousal of Anarchist views. By the end of 1891 they were producing an incendiary magazine called *The Torch* from the basement of their new home, though this is likely to have been presented to aunt Christina as a juvenile enthusiasm not to be taken too seriously.

William called at Torrington Square once a week, and from time to time Christina went to St Edmund's Terrace. Here, in April 1891 fellow guest Arthur Munby noted that she was 'looking charming with her white hair and beautiful complexion'. But she was not at ease in large gatherings, and left without saying goodbye to Lucy because, as she was making her way into the room, the door shut in her face; she was 'still sufficiently shy to lose heart under such a rebuff', she wrote. So it is not surprising that she declined the next invitation, politely explaining that she felt 'loth to come out of my hole'. She was seeing *Face of the Deep* through the press, and also compiling a collection of her devotional verse, to be issued in 1893 by the SPCK under the title *Verses* – an incidental echo of her first little book printed by Grandpapa nearly half a century before. Here she arranged some three hundred poems into eight sections, in a unified sequence to indicate spiritual progress, under headings that included 'Some Feasts and Fasts', 'Gifts and Graces', 'The World', 'Songs for Strangers and Pilgrims'. As her last collection, it was a valedictory volume, and 'looking back' was the theme of the final poem:

> Looking back along life's trodden way
>   Gleams and greenness linger on the track;
> Distance melts and mellows all to-day,
>   Looking back.

> Rose and purple and a silvery grey,
>   Is that cloud the cloud we called so black?
> Evening harmonizes all to-day,
>   Looking back.

> Foolish feet so prone to halt or stray,
>   Foolish heart so restive on the rack!
> Yesterday we sighed, but not to-day
>   Looking back.

Appropriately, the verse form was one she had made her own, with a fading last line. And among the reprinted items were a few unpublished pieces, which show that once again Christina had been looking into her old notebooks. Rather surprisingly, she resurrected the long *Nightmare* poem of 1857, which was not originally devotional in intent. Now, the ghostly lover who bids the poet keep a secret was dropped, leaving only two of the original stanzas, under a new title and epigraph:

> A CASTLE-BUILDER'S WORLD
>   'The line of confusion, and the stones of emptiness'
> Unripe harvest there hath none to reap it
>   From the misty gusty place,
> Unripe vineyard there hath none to keep it
>   In unprofitable space.
> Living men and women are not found there,
>   Only masks in flocks and shoals;
> Flesh-and-bloodless hazy masks surround there,
>   Ever wavering orbs and poles;
> Flesh-and-bloodless vapid masks abound there
>   Shades of bodies without souls.

In *Face of the Deep*, she had warned against 'castle- building', saying 'a world of mere opinions and fancies, of day-dreams and castles in the air' was 'antagonistic to the true and substantial world of revelation', and it appears that in reviving these lines, she was cautioning against fantasies and unprofitable dreaming.

With Mr McClure of the SPCK she carried on a cordial correspondence regarding proofs, corrections and bindings – 'as to colour, my own taste inclines to black' she wrote rather morbidly; 'but if that might repel a cheerful purchaser I should at any rate vote for something dark and grave not to say sombre'. They discussed other matters too, for McClure kept her supplied with devotional reading matter, including his own sermons, which she was pleased to find echoed her own feelings with regard to class divisions and class conflict. And, she added:

> It is so easy from an armchair to exhort a man on a bench: I wish the scene could be varied occasionally, and that instead of a roomfull of 'Labour' to appease some heart and tongue of fire faced a roomful of 'Capital' to abate.

Christina's revolutionary nieces might not have found their pious aunt as reactionary as they supposed.

Mr McClure was courteously keen to introduce his wife to Miss Rossetti, a request she equally courteously evaded, pleading 'anxieties of various sorts'. But then she relented. 'It is out of my power to present myself in Eccleston Square', she wrote in November 1892, 'so now my indulgent friends come to see me without exacting a return visit. Will Mrs McClure some day make herself of this obliging number? I am usually able to see my visitors.'

Tennyson died in October 1892, and there was no obvious successor. On 23 October, when the Garnett family dined at Edmund Terrace, the laureateship was the chief topic of conversation. According to young Olive Garnett, William was 'of the opinion that Swinburne and Wm. Morris should have the refusal of it, after them perhaps Coventry Patmore. He thinks Sir Edwin Arnold will probably get it, and would keep out Lewis Morris at any price. Christina Rossetti, possibly Augusta Webster should be the choice among women. As I entirely agreed I said nothing.'

Cathy Hueffer's son Ford proved more feminist, at least in Christina's presence, by proclaiming that 'hundreds of people' thought the honour should go to her. She disputed the figure, but the anecdote shows the question was discussed. Nor was it mere family partiality that put her name forward. Pondering the succession and noting that both Swinburne and William Morris were 'impossible' (the one because of his past notoriety, the other because of his present politics), Arthur Munby wrote firmly: 'Christina Rossetti is *my* choice'. And a little later Lewis Carroll was forthright. 'If only the Queen would consult *me* as to whom to make Poet Laureate! I would say "for once, Madam, take a *lady*!" ' he told a friend. 'But *they never consult the right people.*' So Clearly her name was canvassed, among the public if not the Palace. 'Little did I think that anyone had bestowed 1000 votes on me,' Christina herself wrote to Miss Newsham. 'I wonder who will at last be Laureate: not Mr Ruskin, I wish, as I see no reason why the laurel should pass from poetry to prose, however poetical.'

She was indeed the best candidate – the poet of finest moral sensibility, technical excellence and high principles. And it may be that talk of the succession in part prompted her to write – or the editor to request – a poem on the death of the infant Duke of Clarence and Avondale entitled *A Death of a First-Born* and published in *Literary Opinion*. As it happened, however, the Queen left the laureateship vacant until 1896, when the jingoistic critic Alfred Austin was appointed, to widespread mockery. A bare five years older than Austin, Christina was already sick when the vacancy arose, but gender prejudice undoubtedly cost Britain the best poet laureate available.

It would be good to relate that as Christina crossed the rubicon of sixty life's trials diminished. Sadly however, as Lucy's health worsened so did her temper, into querulous, demanding and unhappy invalidism, from which her family were the chief sufferers. 'It gave a swerve to her feelings and to her construction of persons and occurrences and made her look at all sorts of matters with a resentful bias,' explained William. 'Mentally it was the same kind of thing as if she had gazed with the physical eyes through blackened spectacles.' This became particularly bad at the end of 1892, when Lucy turned against her husband, ousted him from their bedroom, and made no secret of her feelings. 'Poor Mrs Rossetti is in a fearful state of irritation, hardly responsible, I should say,' reported young Olive Garnett after helping to tidy the *Torch* room. 'She will not have a nurse, or anyone but the children to nurse her, and she cannot be left alone ... "Anarchy" alone helps to keep the children's spirits up.' By June Lucy was virtually unrecognisable, looking 'almost a skeleton', with her skin brown and shrunken, and her eyes very large and bright. The rest of the family was not much better: 'It was terrible to sit still quietly and talk about things that didn't matter,' wrote Olive Garnett.

> Mr Rossetti hung his head down over the side of [his] chair and literally forced himself to speak and smile... The girls had packets of cigarettes and began to smoke. "We have taken to this" they said, "it makes us feel happy and keeps us up, we smoke a great deal now." I remonstrated. "Ah, it's all very well to talk but if you lived in this house for half a year, you'd smoke and drink too ..."

Among her most welcome callers Christina counted Olive Garnett's mother, a regular purveyor of flowers, and Olive's older sister May, whose Anglo-Catholic piety so consoled Christina for her nieces' unbelief that on May's wedding in July 1893 she gave her an antique gold ring set with turquoises and an appropriate garnet, evidently an heirloom.

A less rewarding acquaintance was Ellen Proctor, a woman of Christina's own age whom she had met around 1880 at the home of a fellow churchwoman named Katherine Conway, when Miss Proctor, who had family in Ireland and South Africa, waxed eloquent on the Zulu War and its disasters, having known many of the British officers who died in the battle of Isandlwana. When she described 'the dash for the Queen's Colours made by Coghill and Melville', Christina remarked, perhaps with less admiration than Miss Proctor assumed, that she made it sound 'like knights of old doing battle for a lady's favour'. At length Miss Proctor realised she was talking too much, and also discovered the name of her fellow guest. 'Are you Miss Rossetti?' she asked. 'Yes, I am.' 'Miss Christina Rossetti?' 'Christina Rossetti at your service' (with a smile). 'Did you really write *Good Friday* ('Am I a stone and not a sheep')?' 'Yes, I did', and her face became at once grave and solemn. 'This was what cemented our friendship, the sympathy with Christ's sufferings' concluded Miss Proctor perceptively; 'none could touch the core of her heart like that.'

Ellen was involved in parish work in London's East End, helping run a club for factory women, including the matchgirls whom more politically active women like Eleanor Marx and Annie Besant were aiming to rouse to industrial action. According to Miss Proctor, 'Miss Rossetti took a deep interest in the welfare of these young people and would herself have liked to become a working member of the club, had her nursing duties allowed it.' She also expressed sympathy with the child actors whom Ellen encountered walking home late at night after their performances were over. 'London makes mirth,' she quoted, 'but I know God hears The sobs in the dark and the dropping of tears.'

The following year Ellen was in Ireland, prompting Christina to express her desire to visit that 'near-at-hand island', and her sorrow towards its troubles – a view Miss Proctor probably did not share, as some while later she was involved in a long and painful process to evict three peasant families from her land. She also revisited the Cape, and Christina's surviving letters display a determined optimism in the face of Ellen's complaints regarding climate, finances, health and other matters. She wrote kindly and sympathetically, but sometimes drily. 'I have seen the bank failure announced in the paper and am sorry for all whom it involves in ruin or distress; even to a wealthy person £3500 is a serious loss,' she wrote in 1890. 'Really it is sometimes a comfort not to possess a fortune, so that one cannot lose it.' And in January 1894, when harsh weather exacerbated unemployment, she commented that 'the contrast between London luxury and London destitution is really appalling – all sorts of gaieties advertised, and deaths by exposure and starvation recorded, in the same newspaper'.

Lisa Wilson proved the most truly sympathetic friend, providing staunch and loving support. She was indisputably the most important of Christina's later friends, despite the almost complete erasure of her presence from the historical record. Lisa's story is only fragmentarily known, but it appears that she had spent some years in Rome before making Christina's acquaintance and after Christina's death her own little book of verse revealed how much the friendship meant to Lisa. Her original visit to Torrington Square to collect *Time Flies*, on 27 May 1885, for instance, was emotionally recalled in a sonnet entitled *First Meeting*:

> Let me recall the time when we first met
> O my lost darling! 'Twas the end of May,
> The month of flowers and such a lovely day . . .
>
>   Can I forget
> Of what we spoke? I watched your grave dark eyes,
> Your lips, with their sweet melancholy curve
> And rare swift smile. Your musical low voice
> Thrilled through me. Ever since, through life's rude noise
> It calms me.

'Did you guess, through my reserve, what now you fully know in Paradise?' Lisa concluded, alluding to the feelings she never expressed face to face, but which she collected under the heading 'Love Songs' in a little volume dedicated to 'the sweet and gracious memory of Christina G. Rossetti, who honoured me with the name of friend'.

Though we have no distinct evidence of how often they met, the course of their friendship is celebrated in Lisa's halting but heartfelt verses, addressed to an unnamed fair lady whose beauties are spiritual:

> Since first she took my hand within her own
> My hand, please God, my work, have purer grown . . .
>
> Since she has called me Friend, beyond all need
> My life is crowned; and I am proud indeed.

In one lyric, Lisa commemorated Christina's birthday in December, and in another she confessed her 'whole Heart's worship'. Though she never told her love, Miss Wilson was deeply smitten. And, lest any should doubt that her love poems were inspired by Christina, the last has for title her own words '*And if thou wilt, Remember*', and addresses her as 'my heart's darling'.

'And still she keeps my heart, and keeps its key' was the epigraph Lisa chose for her verses. Many years later, she told an inquiring biographer that Christina was her 'spiritual mother', but it would

seem to have been a more sisterly, or even spiritually sapphic relationship – tacitly acknowledged in Christina's verses to Lisa on their
complementary flowers, lily and rose:

> The Rose is Love's own flower, and Love's no less
> The Lily's tenderness.
> Then half their dignity must Roses yield
> To Lilies of the field?
> Nay, diverse notes make up true harmony;
> All-fashioned loves agree:
> Love wears the Lily's whiteness, and Love glows
> In the deep-hearted Rose.

Lisa's love was most valued when, early in 1892 Christina discovered
she had cancer. She told William only when surgery was imminent.
'What she tells me is this,' he reported to Lucy in May:

> For some little while past . . . she has been conscious at times of a certain
> sensation in the left breast: it has never once amounted to what she would
> call pain: and a double lump can be felt. She spoke to [Dr] Stewart, who
> has as yet treated the case with medicines, and she referred to cancer: he
> did not definitely say that such it is, but she understands him to imply it.
> She is now told that severe pain may shortly be expected unless an
> operation is performed: so now on Wednesday it *is* to be performed (I
> presume the breast, or some large part of it, will be removed) . . . She looks
> ill, but not *extremely* ill; spoke calmly and firmly, without concealing some
> natural sinking of the heart at what waits her; and even branched off into
> ordinary talk at times . . .

She wished no one else to know, from 'a very natural dislike of
publicity in newspaper-paragraphs – "we regret to understand that
the distinguished poetess" etc etc.'

Medically, the mastectomy was pronounced successful, and Christina rallied, telling Ellen Proctor from Brighton that she hoped soon to
resume her post beside her aunt's bed. 'Do you wonder that I feel life
a saddened period? Surely not,' she had written to Caroline Gemmer
some weeks earlier. 'Look without or look within, *feel* without or feel
within, and it is full of trial.' Mrs Gemmer had suggested that fame
outweighed other disappointments in life, but Christina disagreed.
'As to literary success I am fully satisfied with what has befallen me,
but literary success cannot be Mother, Sister, dear friend to me,' she
wrote, presumably in veiled allusion to Charles Cayley. Two years
later she received a courteous call from his niece Mary, who informed
her that Sophie and Henrietta had died some years before, and that

Professor Cayley was now rather frail; his wife sent daffodils and Mary's brother Henry – he who may have inspired the baby poems of *Sing-Song* and was now a tall student of architecture – called to escort his sister home.

In June 1893 aunt Eliza finally died, aged eighty-three. It was a blessed release, though Christina herself was now too sick to enjoy much freedom. In August she was again sent to Brighton. The cancer had recurred, though the doctors were reluctant to fully inform her. 'I suppose my health may have much broken down for a permanence, but I do not know, I am not told, that I am in present danger, or that it is impossible I should live to a great old age like several of my family,' she wrote to Mrs Gemmer. 'I am most wonderfully and graciously spared pain. As to wishing for life or death, I wish to wish only for God's will.' And by the end of the year she was thinking positively of leaving Torrington Square for a more convenient cottage-style home closer to Primrose Hill. But the decision was deferred until the next Michaelmas, by which time she was too sick to go anywhere.

In October 1893 Madox Brown suffered a stroke and died, the day after Lucy left London with her daughters to winter in Italy. There she grew worse and at one stage Christina even proposed going out herself, accompanied by a nurse to be whatever use she could. 'Perhaps the girls might find some sort of support in the presence of one who might be their grandmother,' she told William at Christmas. In March he was summoned by telegram, and left immediately with Arthur. After Lucy's death on 12 April the depleted family returned home, further burdened by the fact that she had left all her property, including the lease of their house, not to her husband but her children, whose tenant William therefore became. 'I will not venture to say I regret anything in Lucy's will,' wrote Christina tactfully, 'and I will not suppose it possible that any trouble can arise about the house.' But if for any reason William wished to move, she was available and willing should any combination of residences appeal to him – 'available, that is, if life lasts so long. But, if not, I have the comfort of knowing that your income would be increased.'

'Do not suppose by this that I have fresh reason to anticipate a speedy end,' she went on hurriedly, 'but you and I know how precarious is all life and how doubly precarious mine has become ... and now put me out of your dear old thoughts so far as to feel that I can contentedly wait till you have heart and leisure to look me up: you will not, I think, distort this sentence into meaning that I do not care to see you!'

Verses was selling exceptionally well: Mrs Garnett reported that one bookshop had received twenty or thirty vain inquiries, and a reprint was ordered. As Ellen Heaton's friend Bishop Westcott noted later, it was good to think 'how widely Miss Rossetti's influence is now reaching through her "Verses". I see the book everywhere and find that it speaks to the heart whenever a reader listens to the words, and waits, as a poet must be read.' But Christina had fallen out with the SPCK, to the extent of cancelling her subscription and returning the payment for *The Face of the Deep*, because they had published a work defending, or at least accepting the need for vivisection. This was the subject of some anxious correspondence with McClure. 'Please pardon my writing in this Holy Week of Supreme Mercy to plead thus far the cause of the helpless,' she wrote at Easter 1894, asking the Society to publish an amended edition. Six months later, when her writing had deteriorated to a mere scrawl, she offered twenty pounds to destroy all remaining copies – 'not that I think this the best method of cleansing our hands but that I hope under the circumstances it would be allowable' – invoking the figure of Achan, the troubler of Israel who trangressed in the thing accursed, stealing and hiding treasure for his own use. In her very last weeks however she relented, and renewed her subscription.

By August her state was so low that she was confined to bed in the first-floor front room and was not expected to rise again. 'Spoke to Stewart, who gives a very gloomy and alarming account of her condition. I don't care to enter into the details,' William noted in his diary. Subsequent entries show the sad and long drawn out sequel:

August 19. Her bed is now removed into the front drawing room. She was not in pain to any serious extent, but drowsy – must have had a sleeping-draught . . .

September 3. Gradual, though not very marked, worsening . . .

September 30. Suffering and weak, but perfectly conversible. She never utters a syllable of complaint, nor even, unless questioned, of information as to her troubles. A good deal of coughing of late.

October 6. She confesses now, but only if she is asked, to pain that must be called severe, especially in the left shoulder . . .

November 15. Her condition of weakness and prostration is so extreme, and her voice so near to extinction, that I hardly understand how it could be possible for her to live more than a day or two . . . Her last words today were 'Good-bye, dear William'.

December 7. Today again Christina was very placid, and capable of attending to whatever was said. It is remarkable how much her articulation has improved beyond what it was some fortnight ago.

She was comforted by regular visits from Lisa Wilson and gentle Mrs Garnett and pain was eased by opiates – or so it seemed. But lodging next door was a woman who heard and wrote otherwise to William at the end of October, saying she and her daughters were disturbed by distressing and 'long-continued fits of hysterical screaming' sounding loudly through the wall in the evenings. We do not know how William replied, but perhaps he asked Dr Anderson (who had replaced Stewart) to increase the morphine, for a day or so later Mrs Stopes sent her thanks and apologies. 'I did not think you could do anything but perhaps give instructions to her attendants not to leave her alone,' she wrote. 'I did not know she was *so* ill. I trust you will pardon my letter, and receive my sympathy.' It is hardly likely that the faithful Harriet Read, assisted by a professional nurse, left Christina alone to any degree; but she was perhaps not authorised to administer anodynes.

The cries were probably caused by pain, though there is a darker possibility. During William's visits, Christina frequently returned to the 'curious vein of sprightliness' that had made her so facetious in youth. He was composing a memoir of Gabriel – having given up waiting for Watts – and found his sister sometimes alert and able to recall details he had forgotten, such as her lines on the Chinaman's pigtail and those locating Frome beyond the Styx. In the last stages of illness, however, all intervals of cheerfulness and detachment vanished. He feared she was literally afraid of hell. 'Assuredly my sister did to the last continue believing in the promises of the Gospel,' he wrote later; 'but her sense of its threatenings was very lively, and at the end more operative on her personal feelings ... She remained firmly convinced that her Mother and Sister are Saints in heaven, and I endeavoured to show her that, according to her own theories, she was just as safe as they; but this ... did not relieve her from troubles of soul.' He blamed Gutch, who now constituted himself Christina's spiritual confessor, and came as frequently as did Rev. Nash. The latter, who was her parish priest, ministered to her 'on her passage through the shadow of death' with all the judicious kindliness that was natural to him and due to her 'as an exalted Christian as well as a suffering woman'. By contrast, Gutch took it upon himself to be austere – 'a course as foolish as it was unfeeling,' according to William, who found the visits always left Christina more rather than less gloomy. After one such, when Gutch had evidently spoken of damnation, Christina commented 'How dreadful to be eternally wicked! for in hell you must be so eternally – not to speak of any question of torments.' This must have been the occasion when William wrote in his usually mild-mannered diary: 'Gutch. Eternally wicked. Wicked old man', which presumably relieved his feelings.

The text 'I will trust and not be afraid' was hung where she could see it constantly, but she approached the end, William concluded – for she knew she was dying –

> with a more imminent sense of unworthiness and apprehension than acceptance and confiding hope ... Her lifelong motto might have been 'Though he slay me, yet will I trust in Him'; and she thought that she had a 'Father in Heaven' not incapable of slaying her for ever.

God the Father was still a figure to be feared. In some recess of her soul, did Christina also fear to meet again her earthly father – not in heaven with Maria and Mamma waiting to welcome her, but perhaps in hell, where she and he belonged in eternal torment?

It is a distressing thought: let us hope that morphine was responsible for Christina's morbid imaginings and continual 'prayer without ceasing' on her deathbed. On her birthday, 5 December, when she reached sixty-four – older than both Maria and Gabriel, but twenty years younger than both mother and aunts – she was able to see both William and Mrs Garnett, as well as the faithful Lisa Wilson. But 'I fear her mind is always now possessed by gloomy ideas as to the world of spirits,' William noted on 17 December. On 21 December she showed signs of agitation, but on 24 December she was calm, and seemed to understand the letter from Henrietta Rintoul that William read out to her. On Christmas Day she was 'gloomy and distressed' but tactiturn: William surmised that religious ideas were dominant. On 26, 27 and 28 she was half-conscious, constantly praying. Towards five in the morning of 29 December she 'turned quite blue' according to Harriet Read, but continued praying until 7.20 when she let out a great sigh and died. It was a painful and sadly comfortless end.

Lisa Wilson remembered Christina's last words in lines of grief:

> 'Farewell, until tomorrow', thou didst say
>   And, clasping close my hand, didst still delay
> My going, till the shadows round us lay
>   Dark on thy face and mine.
>
> 'Until tomorrow'. In the eventide
>   We parted; in the darkness I could hide
> My tears – and so I left thee, satisfied.
>   No tears, O friend, were thine.
>
> 'Until tomorrow'. When the morrow came
>   We did not meet; thy flickering, fading flame
> Of life went out; as on thy lips a name
>   Was breathed, with one Divine.

> 'Until tomorrow'. And I spake to thee
>   And thou wert silent; silent even to me
> Kneeling beside thee. Silent even to me,
>   No word, no smile, no sign . . .

The great poet of mortuary verse had found a loving disciple to commemorate her death in cadences borrowed from her own. And perhaps with this affection – felt if not openly voiced – Christina's end was not quite comfortless.

In *The Face of the Deep* Christina had composed her own epitaph:

> My harvest is done, its promise is ended,
>   Weak and watery sets the sun,
> Day and night in one mist are blended,
>   My harvest is done.
>
> Long while running, how short when run,
>   Time to eternity has descended,
> Timeless eternity has begun.
>
> Was it narrow the way I wended?
>   Snares and pits was it mine to shun?
> The scythe has fallen so long suspended,
>   My harvest is done.

'May I deserve remembrance when my day comes,' she had told Gabriel twenty years earlier; 'and then remembered or forgotten it will be well with me.' There is today no prospect of Christina Rossetti being forgotten, but we are only beginning to understand her complex and contradictory personality, and the experiences that led her to choose a narrow way. Her harvest, in terms of poetry, was both full and lasting; it was also of greater range and depth than has commonly been thought. The combination of emotional pain and literary talent gave her life and work a unique quality. As both a woman and a writer she deserves remembrance.

Acknowledgments

A large number of people have helped in the research, writing and production of this book. The author wishes to thank them all, including: Gillian Allnutt, Karen Armstrong, Mary Arseneau, David Bentley, Florence Boos, Ruth Brandon, Martin Brett, Susan P. Casteras, Diane D'Amico, Anna Davin, Kamilla Denman, Elton P. Eckstrand, Dick Fredeman, Alicia Faxon, Antony H. Harrison, Anne Harvey, Michael Hickox, Peter van de Kamp, Mark Samuels Lasner, Fred Leventhal, Ian Mackillop, Mary Louise and Frederick Maser, Lucy and Roderic O'Conor, Kate Perry, Jean F. Preston, John Purkis, Len Roberts, Frank Sharp, Elaine Showalter, Sarah J. Smith, Janet and Oliver Soskice, Ann Summers, Frances Thomas, Judith Walkowitz, the William Morris Gallery.

Particular thanks go to Michael Wardle, Carolyn Matthews, Barbara Elliott and Jill Wilson for information and insights regarding adolescent breakdown and sexual abuse. The author is also grateful to the Authors Foundation and to Jesus College Cambridge for residence and research facilities as a Professional Fellow Commoner. Thanks go also to Jennifer Kavanagh, Philippa Brewster, Mindy Werner and Marion Steel for editorial advice and assistance. The index was compiled by Helen Smith.

Abbreviations

Individuals referred to by initials in the References and Bibliography are as follows:

AB	Alice Boyd
ABH	Amelia Barnard Heimann
ACS	Algernon Charles Swinburne
ABG	Anne Burrows Gilchrist
AM	Alexander Macmillan
AW	Augusta Webster
BLS	Barbara Leigh Smith [later Bodichon]
BRP	Bessie Rayner Parkes
CAH	Charles Augustus Howell
CBC	Charles Bagot Cayley
CG	Caroline Gemmer
CGR	Christina Georgina Rossetti
CL	Charles Lyell
CLD	Charles Lutwidge Dodgson [Lewis Carroll]
CMB	Catherine Madox Brown
DG	Dora Greenwell
DGR	Dante Gabriel Rossetti
EAP	Ellen A. Proctor
EBB	Elizabeth Barrett Browning
EES	Elizabeth Eleanor Siddal
EG	Edmund Gosse
EH	Ellen Heaton
EMB	Emma Madox Brown
FGS	Frederic George Stephens
FJS	Frederick James Shields
FLR	Frances Lavinia Rossetti
FMB	Ford Madox Brown
FSE	Frederick Startridge Ellis
GGH	George Gordon Hake
GMH	Gerard Manley Hopkins
GR	Gabriele Rossetti
HRA	Helen Rossetti Angeli
JB	John Brett
JC	James Collinson

JEM	John Everett Millais
JI	Jean Ingelow
JM	Jane Morris
JR	John Ruskin
KH	Kate Howell
KT	Katharine Tynan
LMB	Lucy Madox Brown [later Rossetti]
LMS	Letitia Margery Scott
MB	Mackenzie Bell
MFR	Maria Francesca Rossetti
PJT	Pauline Jermyn Trevelyan
RDH	Rose Donne Hake
RFL	R. F. Littledale
TGH	Thomas Gordon Hake
THC	Thomas Hall Caine
TK	Thomas Keightley
TPR	Teodorico Pietrocola Rossetti
TW	Thomas Woolner
TWD	Theodore Watts Dunton
WA	William Allingham
WBS	William Bell Scott
WHH	William Holman Hunt
WMR	William Michael Rossetti

References

Most references are cited in abbreviated form: for full details see Bibliography. See also list of Abbreviations for identities of persons cited by initials. A complete edition of CGR's letters is currently being published by the University Press of Virginia (see Bibliography); page numbers were not available as this book went to press, but dates and recipients are given here. A new and complete edition of DGR's letters is currently being prepared by W. E. Fredeman; until this is available scholars must rely on the 1965 collection edited by Oswald Doughty and J. R. Wahl, listed in the Bibliography along with WMR's letters, published by Penn State University Press, and other sources.

PART ONE: 1830–50

1 Nursery Days

3   earliest memory: in *Sing-Song*, as with most of the nursery rhymes and images cited in this chapter.

3   little butterfly: GR to FLR 21 May 1832, Waller 53

4   small greed: GR to FLR 15 May 1832, *Autobiography* 120

4   Italian intonation: *SRs* i, 16

4   demure little boy: *PWs* xlvii

5   topped us all: Sharp 1912, 73

5   fiery spirit: *SRs* i, 19.

5   rocking horse: see Surtees 1971, no.1

5   maternal store: CGR to DGR 8 Feb 1882

5   angelic little demon: *SRs* i, 20, and GR to FLR Jan/Feb 1836, Vincent 31 and Waller 122, 128. CGR and DGR spent the first three months of 1836 at Holmer Green with FLR, who had been ill.

5   all the outcry: Vincent 30

6   colouring books: *FLM* i, 15

6   paws on fender: *FLM* i, 15

6   antelope: *FLM* i, 38

7   speak English: *SRs* i, 9

8   My first: CGR to WMR 14 Jan 1886

8   Cecilia: *PWs* xlix

8   *cosa fatta*: TF 22

8   if any one thing: CGR to EG 26 Mar 1884

9   grounds quite small: ibid; also *TF* 45
9   four-leaved trefoil: *TF* 63
9   children's story: *Speaking Likenesses*.
10   frogs: *TF* 128–30
10   the way in which: Frend 1896, 823
10   experience of death: *TF* 45
10   to this hour: *TF* 136–7
12   nominal whipping: *SRs* i, 20
12   to have a temper: ibid
13   moderating self-control: *FLM* i, 22
13   if we cannot do: Battiscombe 23. See Waller 46 for the original French proverb: '*Quand on n'a pas ce que l'on aime, Il faut aimer ce que l'on a'*.
13   quite at home / tree of life: *TF* 80
14   She had told Maria: FLR to HP Sept 1830, UBC

2 Family Life

15   certainly born: *PWs* lxvi
15   neither nursery: CGR to unidentified correspondent 23 Jan 1888
15   independent character: *FLM* i, 28
17   passion for intellect: *FLM* i, 22
17   another niece: Waller 50–1
17   Lady Dudley Stuart: she died in 1842. The family also recalled visits from Prince Louis, later Napoleon III, whom WMR noted dismissively did 'not excite any admiration for intellect, demeanour or person in our house; and was often disadvantageously contrasted with Prince Pierre Bonaparte', also a frequent visitor; see *Notes & Queries*, 22 Feb 1862, 157–8.
17   Four children: *Autobiography*, 86
18   rare a woman: GR to FLR 29 May 1832, Autobiography 125
18   I love above all: GR to FLR 16 Jan 1836, Waller 128. See also *FLM* i, 24, and Waller 38.
18   young couple: GBJ i, 236
18   most womanly: *FLM* i, 32
19   on her deathbed: *SRs* 541
19   all my earliest years: *FLM* i, 15
20   woman in Naples: in *Il Veggente in Solitudine* GR denied earlier marriage and fatherhood; see Waller 37
20   King Ferdinand: *Autobiography* 77
20   in the long run: Vincent 2
21   regular system of life: Waller 37
22   Oxford St: Waller 48
22   physically affectionate: see *SRs*, Autobiography and letters to FLR quoted in Waller

22   clustered round: see Sandars 31; *SRs* i, 16

22   not fretting: Waller 122–3

22   This morning: Thomas 23

22   chest of drawers: Vincent 30

22   Not one of us: *SRs* i, 22

23   *carissima* etc: Waller 152

23   no beauty: Waller 122–3; Vincent 31

23   short ode: Bell 7

24   fond of name and fame: WMR typescript PUL Troxell I

24   natural temper: *SRs* 16 and *FLM* i, 12

24   eminent callers: *PRDL* 66; Waller 61

25   My father: *FLM* i, 54

25   *un cercatore*: *FLM*, i 46

26   dead weight: CGR to EG 26 Mar 1884; and CGR to unidentified correspondent 23 Jan 1888

26   rather indolent: *PWs* lxvii

26   hit her fancy: Bell 13

27   collection of tales: *Speaking Likenesses*

28   only child: CGR to RDH Mar 1889

29   unsavouriness: *FLM* i, 69

29   Maria and Greek: Waller 141–3

29   lifelong passion: *SRs* 18

29   magnificent passage: MFR to CBC 1864, PUL Troxell III

29   Bravo!: GR to FLR 5 Sep 1839, Waller 142. This letter also recounts a more recent visit to the Jervises' house in Richmond, when CGR accompanied her father and was entertained by the Jervis daughters.

30   *Domestic Medicine*: 1840 edition, 44; see also Elaine Showalter, *The Female Malady*, 1987, 124–6

30   settled down: *SRs* 18

30   Ajax: *TF* 72

31   My dear sister: Sharp 1912, 77

3 First Poems

32   Myrtle Cottage: Vincent 32

32   pent up: Sharp 1912, 70

32   Maria's first book: CGR to Buxton Forman 26 Oct 1885. The translation, done in 1841, was later described by GR as the work of his '14-year-old Sappho': see Waller 173.

33   *Sir Hugh the Heron*: *FLM* i, 85

33   *Rivulets*: see Waller 174.

33   *To my Mother*: on the back FLR added 'This was written for me April 27th 1842 and given with a nosegay by C'. The printed version of this, purporting to come from Gaetano Polidori's

printing press, has long been exposed as one of T. J. Wise's forgeries.

33   light of pleasure: CGR to Olive Rossetti 27 Apr 1880

33   NB These verses: BL Ashley 1362

33   born leader: Sharp 1912, 73

35   poet in the family: ibid

35   perfect nonsense: see Waller, chapter 5, for contemporary and modern critiques of GR's scholarship.

36   as Lyell explained: see Charles Lyell, *The Poems of the Vita Nuova and Convito*, London 1842, and *The Lyrical Poems of Dante Alighieri*, London 1845. Lyell also provided a 200-page foreword to the *Anti-Papal Spirit of Dante*.

36   his biographer: Waller 77–8

36   Eco: 'Some Paranoid Readings', *TLS*, 29 Jun 1990

37   crazy interpreter: *Disquisitions on the Anti-Papal Spirit* ii, 200

37   audacious thought: *Autobiography* 68

37   letters to patrons: see Waller 98

37   banshee: *FLM* i, 64

38   summer of 1840: Waller 109–11; Vincent 32

38   the pot can only: Charles Lyell to GR 23 Feb 1841, Vincent 70

38   republican slogan: see Bod. MS Eng. Misc. d. 330

39   GR's health: *SRs* i, 35 and *FLM* i, 10

39   first letter: CGR to GR 26 Jun 1843

39   Amelia Barnard: *FLM* i, 110

39   poetic effusions: DGR to FLR 14 Aug 1843

41   mantle of gloom: *SRs* i, 35

4 Breakdown

42   I thank God: MFR to GR Jan 1846, Waller 17

46   to live and nought: *Autobiography* 102

46   Both girls: *Il Veggente in Solitudine*, 1846, 344

46   imitated from Herbert: BL Ashley 1362

47   temperamentally unable: *FLM* i, 93

47   always alone: GR to Guiseppe Ricciardi, Waller 157

47   good at chess: *PWs* lxvi and *FLM* i, 41

47   an old gentleman: Scott i, 247

48   young clergyman: *PWs* 465

48   resentment: see R. Seidenberg and C. Papathomopoulos, 'Daughters who tend their Fathers', in *The Psychoanalytic Study of Society*, vol. 2, 1962

48   unusual deference: *PWs* lxvi

49   leeches: see below chapter 8

49   innate character: *PWs* lxvi

49   quick tempered: Battiscombe 28

50 Ask William: CGR to LMB 24 Aug 1883
50 passionate temper: Helen Rossetti Angeli, quoted Packer 10
50 angina pectoris: *PWs* 1
51 shaky letter: CGR to WMR 17/18 Sep 1845.
52 I knew her: CGR to WMR 25 Mar 1887. In June 1846 MFR left the Reads, when Mrs Read fell ill.
52 Hare's memorandum: see James A. Kohl, 'A Medical Comment on Christina Rossetti', *Notes & Queries*, 1968, 423. The note was written in Jan 18uary 1898 on a blank page of a presentation copy of Bell, by L. Godfrey Bilchett of Epsom, who had the story secondhand, not directly from Bell.
53 exaggerated piety: see Doughty 1949, 18
53 fond of society: *PWs* lxvi

5 Sin and Sisterhoods
55 slave of irrational dogma: *SRs* i, 127
57 telling eloquence: Burrows 1887, 10
57 we have had Pusey: Coleridge 1874, 173–4
58 God grant: Neale 1846, 414. Neale's influence prompted ACS to describe him to WMR as the 'Rev Alexandre Dumas–de Sade – alias J. M. Neale – who applied an almost matchless gift of exciting dramatic narrative to such refreshing subjects as (for instance) a girl tied naked to a red-hot chair or a matron laid down naked on a bed of red-hot iron nails ... he was an absolutely unsurpassed writer of short stories; and a burning and shining light in that particular uppermost "high" branch of the Anglican Church to which our mothers and sisters belonged': see Lang vi, 1962, 178.
58 opinion of Dodsworth: Burrows 1887, 16
58 people have no business: William Dodsworth to E. B. Pusey, 20 Feb 1845, Williams and Campbell 16
59 romantic impulse: CGR to CG c. 1880
60 I want to assure you: CGR to DGR 2 Dec 1881
60 I am scarred: quoted H. P. Liddon, *Clerical Life and Work of E. B. Pusey*, 1907, iii, 96
61 two poems: these included Hartley Coleridge's *Multum Dilexit*
62 audience with Pusey: N. F. Cusack, *The Story of My Life*, 1891, 63
63 miraculously changed: quoted Keith Denison, 'Dr Pusey as Confessor and Spiritual Counsellor', in *Pusey Rediscovered*, ed. Perry Butler, SPCK, 1983
63 hairshirt: see Butler 1983
64 awful sense: *PWs* liv

6. Portrait of the Artist As Young Poetess
65 load of books: CGR to WMR 11 Aug 1846

65   lonely: CGR to ABH, 1846 *The Waves of this Troublesome World*
65   never-failing pleasure: CGR to PJT 1860; CGR to WMR 14 Jan 1886; and CGR to LMB Jan 1886
66   sea-anemones: *TF* 198
66   Sappho: see Joan Dejean, *Fictions of Sappho 1546–1937*, University of Chicago Press, 1989
66   de Stael: see Leighton 1992, 30
68   eminent female poets: see Frederic Rowton, *The Female Poets of Great Britain*, London 1848
68   Mrs Hemans's effusions: for this and a discussion of the strategic 'spontaneity' of early Victorian women's verse, see Leighton 1992, 28–30
69   Crabbe's *Poems*: see Sotherans sale catalogue 1920, lot 1351; the volume later returned to CGR
69   casual and spontaneous: *PWs* lxviii; *NPs* xiii; *PWs* lxix
71   Thou hast green laurel leaves: *The Works of Mrs Hemans*, vi Edinburgh 1839, 182
71   Mrs Harrison: CGR to DGR 1875
72   pencil portraits: Surtees nos. 420 and 421
75   remarkable granddaughter: copied into FLR's Commonplace Book now in Bod. MSS (original in Italian)
75   Rev. Bray: see Bray 1857
76   equivocal compliments: see CGR to WMR 10 Aug 1847
76   consign the fool: DGR to FLR Aug 1847
76   not without company: see CGR to WMR 10 Aug 1847, and Newton Family archive in Guildhall Library.
77   Mourn not: *"I do set my bow in the Clouds"*
78   *Sognando*: see *PWs* 494. As the lines were copied into CLP's copy of *Il Tempo, ovvero Dio e l'Uomo* (presented and inscribed by the author in 1843) WMR believed they were composed after CLP's death in 1890, when CGR came into possession of the volume. This may have been so, but it seems more likely that they are from an earlier date.
78   God has seen fit: CR 28 Apr 1847, Waller 254–5
78   Remember me: translated by CBC as *The Power of Contrition*
78   old, toothless: GR 27 Oct 1848, Waller 157

7 The PRB

80   so leave London: Gen. Pepe 26 Apr 1848, Waller 69
80   uneasy: GR 24 May 1848, Waller 156
80   Horrible, horrible! GR to FLR 14 Aug 1848, and to CL 27 Oct 1848, Waller 156–7
81   Reynolds thinks: see Weintraub 1978, 19
81   visit to Zoo: Sharp 1882, 11

82   William Bell Scott: WB Scott i, 247
83   Brighton: CGR to ABH n.d., GR to FLR 21 Aug 1848, *Autobiography* 131
84   'display': DGR to WHH Aug 1848. This must be earlier than September as proposed in DW, since it refers to the initial meeting of the literary society which WMR's letter of 11 Aug 1848 refers to taking place the following day.
84   Hunt's lines: WHH 1905, i, 114
84   adept and speedy: *PWs* 490
84   seven of twenty: see MS notebook (Bod. MSS) and R. W. Crump, 'Eighteen Moments' Monuments': Christina Rossetti's *Bouts Rimés* Sonnets in the Troxell Collection', *Essays on the Rossettis*, ed. Robert Fraser, Princeton, 1972, 210ff. Fair copies of sonnets by CGR and WMR dated 21 Aug 1848 are at Duke University.
85   Christina's *Plague*: DGR to WMR 30 Aug 1848
86   list of Immortals: ibid
86   rigid transcripts: WHH 1905, i, 128
87   imperative prophet: see Stephens, 7
87   Hunt's impressions: WHH 1905, i, 133
88   talk of beaus: CGR to WMR 25 Aug 1849
88   Papa's response: GR 27 Oct 1848, Waller 291
88   Tennysonian mannerisms: see Thomas 81. See also CGR to WMR Nov 1848, saying another poem might be acceptable if suitably embellished with a 'real live castle', tumbling battlements and moss-grown stones.
89   JC at Christ Church: *SRs* i, 65
89   took possession: WHH 1905, i, 129; also Stephens, 17
90   *The Child Jesus*: DGR to FLR Sept 1848
91   William's account: *SRs* 72–3
92   quenched in blood: *Autobiography*, 98
92   anti-Papist Protestantizing religionists: see *Autobiography* 71
92   unforeseen effect: *SRs* 72
93   self-portrait: Chloe McLoughlin, 'James Collinson: Vision d'un préraphaélite', *Bretagne: images et mythes*, ed. D. Delouche, Presses universitaires de Rennes, 1987
93   not unintelligent: *SRs* 65
93   tame and sleepy: WHH i, 162–3

8 James and *The Germ*
95   true likeness: *PWs* lxi
95   Gabriel's portrait: Surtees no. 423
95   thoughtful and pleasing: CGR to WMR 23 Nov1848
97   love personals: CGR to WMR 28 Apr 1849
97   Take ye heed: Dodsworth 1849, v and 16

98   day of fasting: see Coleridge 1874, 233
98   flagellate himself: see 'Bernhard Smith and his connection with Art, or "The Seven Founders of the P. R. B" ' by Minnie Bernhard Smith, 1917, BL
98   Scott: *FLM* i, 114–5; *SRs* i, 59, 131
98   Mephistophelean: WHH 1905, i, 230
98   particular affinity: Scott ii, 247; see also WBS's obituary of MFR in *Examiner*, Dec 1876
99   lifetime's anguish: see Packer 1963
99   banishment: CGR to ABH Apr 1849
99   double sisterhood: CGR to WMR 28 Apr 1849
99   *Athenaeum* critic: WHH 1905, i, 178–9
100 charades: Marshall's pocket diary for 1850, in which CGR's lines appeared, thanked contributors for sending in puzzles and solutions before 1 June the previous year
101 Mrs Collinson: CGR to ABH 28 Aug 1849
101 local converse: CGR to WMR 25 Aug 1849
102 picnic party: based on description in *Corrispondenzia Famigliare*
102 inflated state: CGR to WMR 8 Sep 1849. Mrs Charles's full name was Anne Mowbray Collinson (her middle name was also appropriated for *Maude*). She was a local girl, in her early 20s at the time of CGR's visit; her daughter Mary Maud was one year old. Anne's sister was named Carrie Maltby.
103 unvarying kindness: CGR to WMR 19 Sep 49
103 picture of a young woman: now in Yale Center for British Art, New Haven
104 Kingsley's aim: Charles Kingsley, *The Saint's Tragedy*, London 1848, xxiii
104 nothing more important: CGR to WMR 26 Sep 1849
107 even at that early age: see *Germ* reprint, 1900, 21
108 literally freezing: CGR to ABH and CGR to WMR 10 Jan 1850
109 an amusing tale: CGR to ABH 1850
109 should all other articles fail: CGR to WMR 25 Jan 18 1850
110 all details: ibid
111 C. C's silence: ibid
112 influential Catholics: WMR to FGS 16 Jan 1850
112 much about the time: *PWs* 479
112 even sarcasm: *PWs* lxviii
112 JC's letter: to DGR May 1850, in *PRBJ* 71

9 Heartbreak

113 some such date: see *FLs* 12
113 blight on her heart: *SRs* 73, *PWs* lii
114 JC's sonnet: *TF*, 26

115 Many years ago: ibid; Bell identified the friend as JC. He had been told of the engagement by WHH.
115 mystic letters: *PRBJ* 70–1
115 pictorial blasphemy: *Athenaeum*, I Jun 1850, 592
115 in debt: JC to WMR 21 May 1850, quoted *PRB* 230
117 to Gloucester: see CGR to WMR 23 Aug 1851, showing CGR had already visited the city and its environs
117 distrust the resort: CGR to DGR Nov 1876
117 clandestinely: CGR to WMR 8 Aug 1850.
118 Priscilla Townsend: CGR to WMR 3 Sep 1850
118 high praise: see *Germ* reprint, 1900, 14
118 I was surprised: TW to WBS 1850, PUL
119 constantly talking: *SRs* i, 132
120 changes at Christ Church: Burrows 1887, 23–30
121 WMR on 1851: *SRs* 168
121 WMR on *St Elizabeth*: *Spectator*, 19 Apr 1851, 377
121 *Athenaeum*: 19 Apr 51; FGS to WMR 21 Apr 1851, *PRBJ* 242–36; *Times*, 7 May 1851

PART TWO: 1850–60

10 *The Bouquet*
127 such melancholy things: Tynan 1913, 158
127 on summer Sundays: see Flora Masson, *Cornhill*, 1910, 641–7. Flora Masson was a daughter of Rosalind Orme, who married David Masson.
128 shy: CGR to AM 7 Jan 1863
128 Allingham, Cayley, Charley Collins: see WMR to WA 22 Oct 1850; and WHH 1905, i, 288, 304
128 Dr Epps: WMR to WBS 4 Dec 1851; *SRs* 71
129 Teodorico: see CGR to ABH 21 Jun 1853; Oliva Chapter 10; *FLM* i, 34
129 Lady Bath on *Maude*: CGR to WMR 21 Jul 1851
129 Back in London: CGR to WMR Aug 1851
130 Mrs Grey: *The Waves of this Troublesome World*
131 Friendly Society: Burrows 1887, 94
133 William's dismissal: *PWs* 493
135 Robert Browning: DGR to WHD 30 Aug 1851
136 family anxieties: CGR to ABH 20 Jul 1852
136 many thanks: CGR to WMR 30 Jul 1852. CGR had met Agnes Jervis in 1842
138 *After a Picture*: retitled *Books in the Running Brooks* when submitted for publication in an as-yet unidentified magazine; see Crump iii, 384

141 working brother: *PRBJ* 23 Jan 1853
142 ploddingly enough: WMR to WBS 10 Mar 1853
142 our London school: CGR to ABH 31 Mar 1853

11 Frome Forlorn Hope
143 we have discovered: CGR to WMR 22 Apr 1853
143 in my cottage: DGR to FLR 12 May 1853; *NPs* 381; Bell 172
143 my precious Mamma: CGR to FLR 28 Apr 1853
144 the vicar: see Bennett, 1909
144 70 years old: GR May 1853, Waller 243–4
145 so you are alone: Pistrucci to GR 7 Jul 1853, Waller 251
145 by far the happiest: Keightley to GR 23 Oct 1853, Waller 250
145 in better spirits ... baby thrush: CGR to ABH 6 Jun 1853
145 Juvenile author: CGR to ABH 13 Jul and 25 Aug 1853
146 financial fantasy: CGR to WMR 13 Aug 1853
146 Sara Coleridge obituary: see Coleridge 1937, 115–6
146 Charley Collins: *SRs* 152; WHH i, 271, 288, 294; Catherine Peters, *Wilkie Collins*, 1991
147 Pray remember: CGR to WMR 19 Sep 1853
147 *Beautiful Poetry*: CGR to WMR 3 Oct 1853
147 Something like Truth: DGR to CGR 8 Nov 1853
148 Barbara Smith: DGR to CGR 8 Nov 1853
148 the third night: GR to FLR 15 Dec 1853, Waller 246
148 Oh my dear Grandpapa: GR to FLR 16 Dec 1853, Waller 247
148 DGR on Gaetano: DGR to WBS Dec 1853, Scott i, 303
149 more warmth: *SRs* 6
149 when are you going to return: GR to FLR 22 Dec 1853, Waller 247
149 decision to return: DGR to TW 5 Feb 1854
149 wherever we settle: CGR to WMR 23 Feb 1854
150 a patient Christian: CGR to unidentified correspondent 26 Sep 1882
150 large feet: *TF* 35; this must refer to MFR, as it is the entry for the day after her birthday
150 Charley Collins's proposal: see Tate Gallery exhibition catalogue *The Pre-Raphaelites*, 1984, 29
150 Gug's emanations: DGR to WMR 28 Mar 1854
151 Bessie Parkes: DGR to BRP 9 May 1854; Parkes 1895, 26
151 old Mrs Howitt: CGR to Miss May 14? May 1894
152 Oh how terribly: AMH to BLS c. 1848, CUL Add MSS 7621 (transcript)
152 Leith Hill / Hermitage: see Parkes 1856, 25 and Parkes 1895, 86
153 beautiful sisterhood: Howitt 1853, 91
153 sharp stones: Howitt 1853, viii
153 stripped and sorrowful: Lee 1955, 211

154 Bessie and Barbara in Wales: see BRP 3 Sep 1854, Girton College
156 had so long: CGR to BRP 4 May 1855
156 As an unknown: CGR to W. E. Aytoun 1 Aug 1854
156 misconceived: see *Germ* reprint, 1900, 23
157 *Fraser's*: WMR 31 Oct 1854, Troxell 184
157 *Our Paper*: see Crump iii, 400
157 labour and discipline: EBB to Mary Minto Oct 1843, BL Add 41 323

12 *Hero*
159 battle of Alma: FMB Diary, 97. The first *Times* despatches from Scutari appeared on 12 Oct 1854
159 Don't you find: WMR to WBS 15 Nov 1854
159 Hundreds dying: Mary Seacole, *The Wonderful Adventures of Mrs Seacole in Many Lands*, 1857, ed. Audrey Dewjee, Bristol 1984, 122
159 Sarah Terrot: see Sarah Terrot, *Reminiscences of Scutari Hospitals in Winter*, Edinburgh 1898
160 Need I be ashamed ... these ladies: Seacole, 122 ff.
161 whirlpool: EHP's letters home are in UBC
161 If Miss N goes: FN 5 Jul 1855, Goldie 1987
161 since siege of Troy: EBB to Anna Jameson 24 Feb 1855, *Elizabeth Barrett Browning's Letters*, ed F. G. Kenyon, 1897, 189
164 two kinds of ambition: Thomas Carlyle, *On Heroes*, 1844
164 aunt Henrietta: WMR to ABG 24 Aug 1876,
164 party at Seddons': FMB Diary 118.
166 not a real dream: *PWs* 479
167 de Quincey: *Confessions of an Opium Eater*, 1822, 248
167 night but clear: *RRP* 49
168 scapegoat: WHH to JEM 10 Nov 1854, Millais i, 236. JEM continued to visit the Rossettis; see JEM to WHH 7 Jul 1854, JPM
168 constantly invalid: *PWs* 1

13 Wrestlings in the Soul
170 no joke: DGR to WMR 12 Apr 1855
170 she and Guggums: FMB Diary 155
171 portrait photos: *PWs* lxii; CGR to AM c. 1862
171 Ruskin's generous words: in *Academy Notes*, 1855.
171 new man: DGR to WA 11 May 1855
171 assuredly dark hours: JR 3 Jun 1855, Daly 174
172 Your name: WMR to WBS 14 Apr 1856
172 Lady Frances Lindsay: CGR to ABH 22 Nov 1855 and CGR to WMR Nov 1855.
173 indolent: *PWs* lxvii
174 flurry and skurry: DGR to WA 25 Nov 1855

175   elixir of life: ibid
175   own favourites: CGR to Lilian 7 Apr 1891
175   great poetess: CGR to John Ingram 29 Apr 1882
175   delightfully unliterary: DGR to WA 8 Jan 1856
176   Ellen Heaton: see Virginia Surtees, *Sublime and Instructive*, 1972
179   without love of fame: Joshua Reynolds, *Discourse V*
179   pure rage: DGR to James Smetham 1865
179   to *The Crayon*: WMR to W. J. Stillman 23 Apr 1856
180   call on Emma: FMB Diary 118
183   Annie snatched the letter: Lee 217. The painting of Boadicea no
      longer exists.
184   falsetto muscularity: see below
185   O the wonder: DGR to WA 18 Dec 1856
185   I doubt whether: Bell 93
186   off to Algeria: FMB Diary 191

14   Full Powers
188   Upon her reputation: *PWs* lvi
188   nicest young fellows: DGR to WA 6 Mar 1856
188   enough poetry: DGR to WA 18 Dec 1856
188   *Oxford & Cambridge* contributions: CGR to unidentified corres-
      pondent 6 Mar 1882
188   'Staff and Scrip': CGR to Lilian 7 Apr 91
190   Mamma unites: CGR to FMB / EMB 22 Jul 1857
191   few things: *PWs* 472
192   the same thing: Griggs 199
193   less peculiar: LMS to WBS Jul 1857, PUL Troxell
193   Indian Mutiny: quotations here come from *Illustrated London
      News* and sources cited by Edwardes 1973. Bp Blomfield died
      shortly after issuing his prayer, but the instructions were pres-
      umably followed by the London clergy.
194   Jhansi: *ILN* 8 Aug 1857, 147; 5 Sep 1857, 242. See also my paper
      in *JPRAS*, Spring 1992. The final version of CGR's poems had an
      extra, central stanza, added in 1861 when CGR prepared her first
      collection. The notebook version does not survive but must have
      been written between 5 and 7 Sep 1857
195   *Punch*: *Retribution* by E. A Armitage, later a large oil painting
      now in Leeds City Art Gallery
199   something unknown: McGann 1980, 244; see also Leighton 1992, 146

15   No Thank You, John
201   *Charity Boy's Debut*: *National Magazine*, 22 May 1857
201   two new pictures: see *Spectator*, 20 Feb 1858, 218, and Roger
      Peattie, 'WMR's Reviews of James Collinson', *JPRS*, 1985, 100–3.

201 portrait of his wife: see McLoughlin (above) 79
203 no such person: CGR to DGR 14 Dec 1875; *PWs* 483
203 somewhat smitten: *FLs* 54
203 Brett's early career: *SRs* 90; Tate Gallery catalogue, 1984, 147; and information from M. H. S. Hickox and the Watson family
203 JB and Epps: see JB to Ellen and Amy Epps and Laurens Alma Tadema in CUL Gosse MSS
204 study of Marian Erle: Phillipps 6 Apr 1992, lot 58
204 pencilled notes: David Cordingley, 'The Stonebreaker', *Burlington Magazine*, Mar 1982, 141; and Hickox 1982, 108
205 will you remember: WMR to JB 31 Jan 1858
205 Ruskin's appreciation: *Academy Notes*, 1857
206 proposed to and been refused: Violet Hunt, *Wife of Rossetti*, 1932, 272
207 have been quite artistic: CGR to Mary Haydon 1861
208 insufferable: 12 May 1862, Hudson 160–1
209 grand Arctic picture: CGR to ABH 20 Jul 1864. The full title of JB's picture was *A north-west squall in the Mediterranean*
209 historical fragment: CGR to LMS 24 Jun 1858
209 quiet face: Thomas Dixon to WMR, Weintraub 101
209 cordial words: Thomas Dixon to WMR 16 Jan 1868, *RPs* 341
210 Trevelyans: see DGR to PJT n.d. NUL, WCT 66; also Surtees 66
210 every book and ballad: Augustus Hare, *The Story of my Life*, 1893, i, 276–7, 347–8; Hare was at Wallington in 1861 and 1862
210 at luncheon: CGR to WBS 25 Jul 1887
210 well and waggish: CGR to PJT 1858
210 Olaf: CGR to LMS 24 Jun 1858
210 south of the city: at Marsden; see WBS to PJT 13 Jun 1858, NUL, WCT 74
210 Dora Greenwell: WMR to MB 10 Sep 1896. See below for CGR's friendship with Greenwell.
211 travelling companions: CGR to LMS 24 Jun 1858
211 William noted: *PWs* 473
215 wombat: *SRs* 285
215 Simeon Solomon: WMR to FLR 1 Sep 1858
215 I cannot bear: CGR to ABH 4 Apr 1862
216 manifest masterpieces: *PWs* 461 and liii
216 reply to Dr Heimann: CGR to Adolf Heimann 29 Apr 1862

16 Highgate Penitentiary
218 women must work: Barbara Leigh Smith, *Women and Work*, 1856, 6; for this and other quotations, see Hollis
218 escaped governess: CGR to ACS 19 Nov 1884
219 bricklayer's daughter: *Times* 24 Feb 1858

219   diocesan prospectus: this and other information comes from the St Mary Magdalene Home's Annual Reports 1855–70 now in the Guildhall Library; *EWJ* vol. 1 no. 1, 13 ff; Census returns for 1861, 1871, 1881; library of Highgate Literary and Scientific Institution. Other references are found in Burrows's history of Christ Church Albany Street, and histories of Highgate by John Lloyd, 1881, and John Richardson, 1983, as well as *VCH* for Middlesex, 1980. A photograph of Park House around 1880 is in L. B. Haringey archives. The Penitentiary, renamed a House of Mercy, was taken over by the Anglican Clewer Sisters in 1900, and closed in 1940, when Park House was demolished.

221   WMR on Highgate: *FLs* 26

222   almost whole time: CGR to ABH 3 Aug 1859

224   influx of funds: CGR to PJT 14 Aug 1860

224   very becoming: LMS to WBS 1860, Scott 59

226   a true woman: see Hollis 236

226   spirited defence: CGR to DGR 13 Mar 1865

227   weak generosity: *Westminster Review*, 1850, 149

227   *The Magdalen's Friend*: see vol. i, 1860, 13–14.

17   Girls and Goblins

230   In the first instance: 7 Dec 1893, Iowa State Archives, Des Moines.

231   *Fairy Family*: Archibald Maclaren, *The Fairy Family*, Oxford 1857, reprinted Dailrymple Press London 1985, 3–4. I am indebted to John Purkis for this suggestion.

231   Hone: *Hone's Everyday Book for 1827*, London 1826, 452

232   Laura's susceptibility: B. Ifor Evans, 'The Sources of Christina Rossetti's "Goblin Market"', *Modern Language Review*, xxviii, 1933, 156–65

232   certain destructions: CGR to PJT c. 1859

232   infantile libido: Germaine Greer, introduction to *Goblin Market*, Stonehill Publishing NY 1975, xxxii

233   more than once: *PWs* 459

235   night side of the nursery: see Ellen Moers, *Literary Women*, 1977, 104–5; also Greer and Leighton

235   tale for Penitentiary: this interpretation was first raised conjecturally by David Bentley in 'The Meretricious and the Meritorious in *Goblin Market*: A Conjecture and an Analysis', in Kent 1987, when CGR's association with the Highgate Penitentiary was thought to date from 1860, precluding the possibility of the poem (written in April 1859) having been specifically composed for the penitents. Now that it has been shown that her work at Highgate was well underway by mid-1859, the link can be more firmly inferred.

235 evening class: AM to DGR 28 Oct 1861, *Letters of Alexander Macmillan*, ed G. A. Macmillan, Edinburgh 1908, 95
235 incidents at Park House: *EWJ*, Mar 1858, 19–20
237 disclosing the dedication: *PWs* 460; see also Bell 207
237 sensational speculations: see Violet Hunt and Packer 1963, 150–1
237 avoid obscurity: CGR to unidentified correspondent 23 Jan 1888

18 Sister and Sisters

239 so devoted: LMS to WBS 1858, PUL Troxell V
239 to Olaf: MFR to B. W. Olaf [WBS] n.d. PUL Troxell III
240 textbook: MFR 1867
240 William not leaving town: CGR to ABH 3 Aug 1859
242 Bible Class: MFR 1872
242 women's ministry: see Helsinger et al, 174–91. My thanks also to Elaine Showalter for information on Catherine Booth
242 *True in the Main*: 'True in the Main: Two Sketches', *The Dawn of Day*, an illustrated monthly for Sunday school and parish use, May and June 1882. From WMR Diary 11 Oct 1882 (*FLs* 212) it would appear that the real names of the families featured were Baker and Meader, and that WMR mistakenly believed they were families of CGR's acquaintance and charity rather than MFR's, which suggests that his knowledge of his sisters' charitable work was limited, like that of CGR's work at Highgate.
243 rubicon of thirty: Dora Greenwell, 'Our Single Women', *North British Review*, Feb 1862, reprinted in *Essays*, 1866, 1–68
244 married life: 'Queen Bees or Working Bees', *Saturday Review*, 12 Nov 1859
244 WBS on MFR: WBS to WMR 25 Nov 1876, Peattie 347, n. 1
244 WBS on AB: WBS to PJT 31 May 1859, NUL, WCT 74 and Scott, ii, 293
247 where are the poetesses: *Letters of Elizabeth Barrett Browning*, ed. F. G. Kenyon, 1899, i, 230
247 some poem of your sister's: JEM to WMR 13 Jul 1859, *RRP* 231
248 WMR on Perugia: see WMR to MB 6 Aug 1895. The poem was written between 27 Aug and 18 Nov 1859
248 Gabriel intervened: conjecture based on CGR's description of herself as 'the pariah of *Once a Week*' (see below) and DGR to FLR n.d. DW 450. There is no evidence that CGR was in contact with *Once a Week* after 1859.
249 perfect gem: James Marshall 5 Apr 1860, Allingham 1911, 222

19 The Rubicon

250 Napoleon III: CGR to CG 13 Feb 1873 or 74
250 DGR marriage: DGR to FLR 14 Apr 1860

250 if not: DGR to WMR 17 Apr 1860

251 WMR on wedding: WMR to WA 23 May 1860

251 some years ago: CGR to PJT Jul 1860

251 dreary summer: CGR to PJT 14 Aug 1860

252 the first picture: CGR to BLSB 15 Aug 1860

253 another trifle: neither this nor 'Refuge' has been identified. Possibly, BLS was exchanging gifts with all her friends and 'Refuge' was the work of another friend such as BRP or AAP, whose gift CGR was asked to emulate.

253 intense curiosity: TW to PJT 25 Aug 1860, NUL

253 everything in disorder: DGR to FLR 28 Nov 1860,

254 Henrietta Rintoul: *SRs* 261

254 celibate marriage: Weintraub 114

254 I never saw: CGR to WMR 30 Nov 1860

254 repressed virgins: Weintraub 115

255 relieved and exhilarated: CGR to WMR 6 Dec 1890

255 perhaps the best tale: *FLM* ii, 162

255 submitted her story: CGR to *Cornhill* 24 Feb 1860; CGR to *Blackwoods* 12 Oct 1860. According to Bell (279) it was DGR who found something in the story that more worldly readers would take to mean something improper.

256 good looks: *PWs* lx

258 symptoms of incestuous abuse: see Denise J. Gelinas, 'Persisting Negative Effects of Incest', *Psychiatry* vol. 46, Nov 1983, 312–32; J.L. Herman & L. Hirschmann, *Father-Daughter Incest*, Harvard 1981. See also Association for Child Psychology and Psychiatry (ACPP) London, occasional paper 3, *The Consequences of Child Sexual Abuse*, 1990. An illuminating first-person account of incest, forgetting and recovery is Sylvia Fraser, *My Father's House*, Doubleday Canada 1987.

262 enjoyment and need: letter from Jane O'Brien, *Guardian* newspaper, 16 May 1991

263 unremembered plight: Miller 1985, 245; see also Miller 1990

PART THREE: 1861–70

20 Towards Publication

267 bay kept waiting: *PWs* 472

267 aphorisms: see DGR to FGS 4 Sep 1873, Weintraub 206

267 *Folio Q*: DGR to WMR 18/19 Jan 1861

267 dear Mr Masson: CGR to David Masson 19 Jan 1861. In *The Rossetti-Macmillan Letters*, 1963, 60, this is mistakenly ascribed to 1866.

268 Gabriel surprised: DGR to CGR Jan 1861

268 irregular measure: JR to DGR 24 Jan 1861, Cook & Wedderburn, vol. 36, 354–5

268 most senseless: DGR to WMR 25 Jan 1861

269 a chance: DGR to CGR Jan 1861

269 many and many thanks DGR to CGR 28 Jan 1861

269 grammarian's quibble: ibid

269 public attention: *PWs* 472; CGR to Macmillan & Co 5 Feb 1861

270 pennyworth of wheat: DGR to WA 10 May 1861

270 subject of annoyance: CGR to AM 5 Apr 1861 and 4 Apr 1861

270 in great hopes: CGR to AM 8 Apr 1861.

270 conciseness and clarity: see Jerome McGann, introduction to Kent 1987, 5–6; and Harrison 1988, Ch. 2

271 Auntship: CGR to Mary Haydon end Jan 1861

272 quite in confidence: DGR to WA Jan 1861,

272 bad news: DGR to FLR and DGR to FMB 2 May 1861

272 Hush, Ned: GBJ i, 222

273 Boulogne, Rouen: CGR to WMR 26 Oct 1861

276 American War: CGR to CG c. 1883–4

276 appropriate theme: CGR to Isa Craig 13 Nov 1862. This concluded with 'hearty wishes for a blessing on our common cause'.

276 first fortnight: CGR to WMR 25 Oct 1861

277 my brother: CGR to AM autumn 1861

277 I was hoping: AM to DGR 28 Oct 1861, *Letters of Alexander Macmillan*

277 No doubt: DGR to FLR 4 Nov 1861

277 was she to choose: CGR to AM, probably 13 Nov 1861, the date of her return from Highgate

278 where was he? : DGR to Charles J. Faulkner 28 Nov 1861 and 2/9 Dec 1861, WMG

278 Have you seen: CGR to AM c. Dec 1861

278 Please expunge: CGR to AM 9 Dec 1861

21 Fame

280 you will see: WMR to FGS 11 and 15 Feb 1862

280 cause of notoriety: Doughty 1949, 297

280 you are perhaps: CGR to AM 26 Feb 1862

281 marvellous boldness: Charles Faulkner to Cormell Price Apr 1862, J. W Mackail, *William Morris*, 1899, i, 157

281 no small satisfaction: CGR to AM 1862

281 already commenced: CGR to AM in two undated letters c. Apr 1862

282 *Spectator*: 12 Apr 1862, 414–5

282 *Athenaeum*: 26 Apr 1862, 558

282 faring very well: CGR to AM, probably 22 Apr 1862

283 *EWJ*: May 1862, 206–7
283 Julia M. Cameron: to WMR 13 May 1862, *RPs* 4
283 F. T. Palgrave: to WMR 1 Jun 1862, *RPs* 6
283 *Saturday Review*: 24 May 1862, 595–6
283 Boston weekly digest: *Littell's Living Age*, nos. 947 and 961
284 well-attested tendency: see Norma Clarke, *Ambitious Heights*, London, 1990, 53–4
284 I wish I had: CGR to AM 7 Apr 1862
284 forwarding: CGR to AM summer 62, from Eastbourne
285 great affair: BLS to WA 4 Jun 1862, *Letters to William Allingham*, 1911, 78. WMR left for Italy on 2 Jul 1862.
285 so seedy: DGR to FMB 3 Jul 1862
285 unsystematic expenditure: WBS to WMR 8 Mar 1862, Peattie 122
286 we should have missed: CGR to BLS Sep 1862
286 I used: CGR to BLS 1864
286 amiable and quaint: CGR to ABH 17 Jan 1860
288 *Ad Sepulchrum*: see CGR to Isa Craig 13 Nov 1862. My thanks to Mark Samuels Lasner for additional information on this.
288 last autumn: CGR to AM 2 Jan 1863
288 sociable in a shy way: *SRs* 174–5
289 emendations: see article in *Victorian Poetry*, 1994 by Sarah W. R. Smith and Kamilla Denman
289 lower in the scale: DGR to FLR summer 1862
289 Henrietta and Sophie: CGR to WMR 25 Oct 1861
289 BAAS: My thanks to Mary Sampson, archivist of Royal Society, for information enabling this to be sorted out, as well as for pointing out that 'Ladies Tickets' to meetings accounted for a sizeable proportion of BAAS' annual income
290 not at all the sort: *SRs* 311. Elsewhere WMR with elaborate circumlocution identified CGR's long poem *From House to Home* (19 November 1858) as having been inspired by her love for CBC (*PWs* 481) although as in the same book he also wrote that after GR's death the pair hardly met until around 1860 (*PWs* liii), this can hardly have been the case. I cannot see that any special friendship existed prior to 1861/2.
291 *Il Rosseggiar*: my thanks to Hugh Shankland of Durham University, for translations
291 scribbling facility: CGR to AM Feb 1863

22 Admirers And Rivals

294 Truth to tell: CGR to AM 7 Jan 1863
295 let me observe: CGR to AM 3 Feb 1863
295 apologized: CGR to AM 5 Feb 1863
296 other reasons: CGR to AM 2 Mar 1863

296 International Exhibition: CGR to ABH 22 Sept 1862
296 telling Barbara: BRP to BLS 19 May 1863, Girton College Archive. For a preliminary account of the Portfolio Society and CGR's contributions, see my notes lodged with Girton College Archive. My thanks as ever to Kate Perry, College Archivist, for assistance with research on this and associated matters.
296 CGR's contributions: see Sotheby's 10 Feb 1970, lot 256, now in PUL. Other titles by CGR include *A Discovery, A Hopeless Case, A Prospective Meeting, A Return, Summer, Autumn, Winter, Sunshine, Solitude.* Though existing as fair copy MS and as such cited by Crump, these titles do not represent authorial intentions. Later in the Portfolio's life, themes were similar – 'A Cool Retreat', 'A Pleasant Path', 'A Winter Morning', 'Evening, 'Tranquillity' etc. See Sotheby's 10 Feb 1970, lots 257–8. My thanks to Diane d'Amico for drawing my attention to these lots.
297 I am quite ashamed: CGR to BLS 1864
297 launch party: CGR to ABH 1 Jun 1863
298 reverse of Sleeping Beauty: CGR to DG Jun 1863
298 kettle of enthusiasm: see WMR to WBS 24 Feb 1863
298 Greenwell's biographer: W. Dorling, *Dora Greenwell*, 1881, 241
298 our dear Scotts: CGR to DG 31 Dec 1863
299 *Lyra Eucharistica* etc: the first of these volumes was completed in June and published in July 1863
299 What I give: CGR to AM 2 Jul 1863
300 name and fame: WMR typescript, PUL Troxell I
300 the photographer: DGR to FLR 30 Sep 1863; see also 29/30 Sep 1863 in *The Diaries of Lewis Carroll*, ed. R. L Green, 1953, 202
301 little shy: 6 Oct 1863, Green 203
301 it was our aim: Bell 134
301 intellectual profile: *PWs* lxiv
301 liked the results: see list of 44 items ordered by CGR in 1864–5, Troxell 1935, 152
301 Dodgson's admiration: CLD 18 Oct 1893. Cohen, 1979, ii, 986
302 delightful it would be: CGR to CLD c. 1863–4
302 warm review: *Macmillan's Magazine*, Sep 1863, 398–404 by Caroline Norton
302 make the eyes: *Athenaeum*: 25 Jul 1863, 106–8
303 Miss Procter: CGR to AM 1 Dec 1863
303 what think you: CGR to DG 31 Dec 1863
304 'Our Camp in the Woodland', *Fraser's Magazine*, Jul 1864, 204–13
304 the palm: DGR to FLR 16 Aug 1864

23 Bleak Mid-winter of the Soul
305 fit of illness: CGR to BLS 1864; *PWs* 484

306   I have borne myself: CGR to DGR 2 Dec 1881
308   Not that I am: CGR to BLS summer 1864
308   Thanks many: CGR to DGR? Apr 1864
309   Don't think me: CGR to DGR 7 May 1864
309   I have weighed: CGR to AM May 1864
309   against heterodoxy: see Lang i, 59
310   ordinary alertness: *PWs* 484
312   Mrs Gilchrist: see WMR introduction to Gilchrist 1887
312   visit to Brookbank: CGR to ABG 21 May 1864
313   vivid impression: Frend 1896, 822–3
313   Anne also charmed: see Gilchrist 1887, 145
313   reading is not enough: see Gilchrist 1887, 154
314   Mitcham: see CLD Diary 25 Jun 1864, Green 218; and GMH 14
      Aug 1864, *Further Letters of GMH*, ed. C. C. Abbott, OUP, 2nd
      edn., 1956, 214. Martin, 1991, 72, says that this meeting took
      place at 'a grand literary party' in London; but this does not tally
      with CLD's diary entry, though the dates coincide. The Mitcham
      fete was hosted by Russell Gurney MP, whose family was known
      to MFR and GMH.
314   as unaffected: CGR to ABG ?Dec 1864
314   I was very sorry: undated letter from Jean Ingelow in PUL
314   imagine my feelings: CGR to ABG, Dec 1864
314   copyright dinners: see Ingelow 1901, 80
315   I wish to say: ibid, 151–2
317   all the bases: 'Neo-Christianity', *Westminster Review*, Oct 1860,
      296
317   surprising speed: WMR to WBS 14 Aug 1865

24 Prince and Alchemist
318   There I stood: *The Waves of this Troublesome World*
318   soothing jelly: ibid
319   congenial company: CGR to Miss Howitt 26 Dec 1864
319   peccant chest: CGR to DGR 23 Dec 1864
319   myself a woman: CGR to WMR 2 Jan 1865
319   breathless effusions: MFR to CBC 27 Mar 1865 etc, PUL Troxell III
319   'Modern Poets': *Times*, 11 Jan 1865, 12
320   I am crowing: CGR to DGR 16 Jan 1865
320   comparable needlework: JI to DG 9 Feb 1865, *Athenaeum*, 7 Aug
      1897, 193. This has given rise to an erroneous notion that the
      'three poetesses' engaged in 'a great sewing competition'. In fact
      JI's letter shows only that she and DG exchanged gifts of needle-
      work and that CGR did not.
320   indefinite delay: CGR to DGR 30 Jan 1865
320   Truth to tell: CGR to DGR 16 Jan 1865

321 True, O Brother: CGR to DGR 23 Dec 1864
321 puerile fancy: CGR to DGR 16 Jan 1865
322 I am truly pleased: CGR to DGR 18 Jan 1865; CGR to AM Dec 1864
322 Alchemist makes himself scarce: CGR's letters to DGR in this period are in *RP*
323 general indebtedness: see Crump i, 234
328 three little things: *Dost Thou not care? Grown and Flown, Eve*
328 Lady Geraldine's Courtship: Tynan 1912, 186
329 at last ripe: CGR to DGR Mar 1865
330 even if we throw: CGR to DGR 13 Mar 1865.
333 General and robin: *TF* 92–3

25 Italy and Beyond

334 *fata morgana*: CGR to DGR 31 Mar 1865; CGR to AM 30 Mar 1865; CGR to ABG Apr 1865
334 My Prince: CGR to DGR Apr 1865
334 be a good fairy: DGR to AM 28 Apr 1865
335 complete misapprehension: CGR to DGR 3 May 1865
335 sherry: CGR to DGR Apr 1865
335 saddening influence: *TF* 111
336 St Gotthard: *TF* 112
336 enjoyable beyond words: CGR to ABG Jul/Aug 1865
337 children's ward: ibid
337 spray rainbow: *TF* 178, where the reference to a single companion, and the date to which this incident is allocated do not tally with the 1865 journey. Possibly the incident did not take place in Switzerland, as has been assumed, but in Britain.
338 personal utterance: *PWs* 487
338 the best for health: *SRs* 348–9
340 Browning: WMR to WBS 14 Aug 1865
341 awful and mysterious: CGR to DGR 23 Dec 1864
341 any of us who have lost: *FD* 44
342 on earth: *FD* 321
342 evil choice: *FD* 274
342 last evening ... Scott conceded: WBS to AB 3 Oct 1865, *Pictor Ignotus* 93–4
343 we cannot realize: ibid
344 grace of conversion: Thomas 293; for the words attributed to Ellen Heaton see *Works and Days: From the Journal of Michael Field*, ed. T. and D. C. Sturge Moore, John Murray London, 1933, 115, where the conversation appears to date from 26 Apr 1889 – after DGR's death. That both CGR and MFR prayed for their brothers'

REFERENCES

return to the Church is undeniable; whether their other devotions were directed at this aim is more speculative.

344 Miss Parke: CGR to LMB Apr/May 1865; see also Surtees no. 405, and letter from A. J. K. Todd to Virginia Surtees 23 May 1963, according to which Louisa Parke carried on a correspondence with CGR all her life. If preserved the letters have not yet come to light.

344 Pray pardon: CGR to CAH 9 Aug 1865

344 Don't be late: CGR to ABH 25 Oct 1865

345 You and Miss Rossetti: Coventry Patmore to CG 9 Feb 1863, in *Memoir and Correspondence of Coventry Patmore*, ed. B. Champneys, 1900, i, 236

345 thousand and one: CGR to CLD, Nov/Dec 1865

346 capital fairy tale: DGR to CLD 2 Feb 1866 and DGR to CGR 5 Jan 1866

346 I couldn't do it: DGR to CGR 5 Jan 1866

346 Grave-clothes etc: ibid

347 *Consider*: CGR to AM 5 Dec 1865

347 geniality of ravens: CGR to Emily Newton Nov 1865 and to ABG Apr 1866

347 I should like: DGR to FLR 26 Feb 1866

347 thinking about his Mammy: CLP in *RPs* 175

347 large and handsome house: CGR to ABG Apr 1866

348 chalk drawing: Surtees no. 429, inscr. Sep 1866

348 Roberts Bros: CGR to Roberts Bros 3 Jan 1866. Her correspondent here was probably Thomas Niles, brother-in-law of Lewis Roberts, who had successfully marketed Ingelow in the USA; see also CGR to ABH 10 Oct 1865

26 Penkill and Swinburne

349 difficult to stay: WBS to AB 12 May 1866, *Pictor Ignotus* 95

349 common knowledge: *Pictor Ignotus* 95

350 too shy: CGR to WMR 4 Jun 1866

350 I hope: ibid

351 sky was white: Scott ii, 292

351 surprised but resolute: *TF* 62

352 spectacular sights: CGR to ABG Jul 1866

352 grandee: CGR to AB 1879, see *TLS*, 26 Jun 1958, 389

352 fight like cats: WBS to WMR Jul 1866, *Pictor Ignotus* 98

352 only pacified: CGR to AM 5/16 Dec 1865

352 laggard book: CGR to ABG Jul 1866

352 worst misprint: CGR to WMR 4 Jun 1866

353 handwritten corrections: see Crump i, 274

353   all the braver: CGR to ABG Jul 1866. AB's diary shows CGR and LMS at Penkill 1–27 Jun 1866.
353   *Saturday Review*: 23 Jun 1866, 761–2
353   *Atheneaum*: 23 Jun 1866, 824–5
354   no language: *Saturday Review*, 4 Aug 1866, 145–7
354   maudlin drunk: see *Swinburne: the Critical Heritage*, ed. C. K. Hyder, London 1970
355   strenuously combated: DGR to Alfred Tennyson 6 Oct 1866
355   the most glorious: WMR, 'Swinburne's *Poems and Ballads'*, 1866, reprinted *Swinburne: the Critical Heritage*, 79–80
356   sings of Lust: *Examiner*, 22 Sep 1866, 597
356   gist of *Dolores*: WMR to ACS 7 Oct 1866, and *Examiner*, 6 Oct 1866, 629–31.
357   I have read: ACS to WMR 13 Oct 1866, Lang i, 201
357   immortal women: ACS, 'Mr Arnold's New Poems', *Fortnightly*, 1 Oct 1867, 441
357   praise too great: WMR to ACS 10 Oct 1867
357   *Phaedrus*: CGR to AB 30 Jul 1866
357   puritan enough: Charles Eliot Norton to WMR 12 Sep 1866, Peattie 154, n.1
357   irreligious taint: CGR to Miss Hayward 17 Jan 1867
357   *Fraser's*: Nov 1866, 648

27 Blumine

359   I can't tell you: CGR to WMR 11 Sep 1866
359   probed his faith: *PWs* liii; *SRs* ii, 312–3
360   would have been far happier: *SRs* ii, 313
360   moment when: CGR to CBC 26 Feb 1883
361   I cannot tell: CGR to Elihu Burritt autumn 67
362   *Il Mercato dei Folleti*: TPR to WMR 22 Dec 1866, *RPs* 217
362   I hope to enjoy: CGR to Helen Melville 24/28 Jan 1867
363   singular adventures: WMR Diary 5 Apr 1867
363   Tunbridge Wells: CGR to ABH 26 Apr 1867 and 17 May 1867
364   honourably formidable: CGR to AM, May 1868. David Masson was no longer *Macmillan's* editor.
365   declining joining: Emily Davies to Anna Richardson 28 Dec 1867, Barbara Stephen, *Emily Davies & Girton College*, 1927, 167
366   I hope our pews: CGR to Emily Newton 8 Nov 1865 and summer 66
367   Horsehood, Doghood etc: Thomas Carlyle, 'Shooting Niagara: and After?' *Macmillan's*, Aug 1867, 321
368   commonplace truism: 'On Twaddle', *Saturday Review*, 23 Jun 1866, 744. Since this issue contained the review of *PP*, it was probably read by CGR.

369   blown up: FGS to WHH 17 May 1866, Jeremy Maas, *Gambart*, 1975, 198. Regarding the other catastophes in CGR's story, there were a number of famous shipwrecks in mid-century which might have been the model for that in *A Safe Investment*, among them the wreck of the *Royal Charter* off Anglesey in 1859 and that of the *Birkenhead* near the Cape of Good Hope. The embezzlement of railway company funds is an oblique reference to a scandal in Jamaica, involving fraudulent conversion of funds during the building of a rail line.

369   speaking to the nation: see G. P. Landow, 'Elegant Jeremiahs: the Genre of the Victorian Sage', *Victorian Perspective*, ed. J. Clubbe and J. Meckier, 1989 (which does not however mention CGR)

370   rereading: see Sonnet vi, reprinted with some alterations in CBC, 1880, 59

371   the beauty: 'Dante: an English Classic', *Churchman's Shilling Magazine*, Oct 1867, 200–3

28   *Sing-Song* and *Commonplace*

372   My dear Kate: CGR to KH 2 Jul 1867

372   darling of our circle: DGR to KH 31 Aug 1867

372   in confidence: DGR to WA 30 Sep 1867, 10 Oct 1867

372   at Mrs Rossetti's: 15 Oct 1867, Allingham, 1911, 165

373   collection of prose tales: WMR Diary 11 Jun 1867

373   Heimann daughters: CGR to ABH 21 Dec 1866

373   none of us stand still: CGR to Adolf Heimann 22 Jan 1867

373   low spirits: WMR Diary 20 Oct 1867 and WMR to ABG 12 Nov 1867, Library of Congress

376   more central: CGR to ABG 14 Jun 1868

376   would you believe: ibid; see also CGR to ABH summer 1870, in Scarborough.

376   Italian lessons: possible inference from MFR to JM n.d. BL Add 45346

376   Gloucester and Penkill: CGR to ABG May 1869 and CGR to AB? 14 May 1869

377   Only think: CGR to AB 1869

377   *Lilith*: WBS to AB 1 Oct 1869, *Pictor Ignotus* 108

377   Lastly, if Byron: DGR to WMR 15 Sep 1869

378   round furry ball: DGR to AB's aunt 21 Sep 1869

378   colloquial language: *Tinsley's Magazine*, Nov 1868, 392

378   Charlotte Yonge: 'Children's Literature of the Last Century', *Macmillans*, Jul 1869, 233–4

379   *Sing-Song* suggested: *PWs* 489

384   waxed in bulk: CGR to CG 4 Feb 1870

384 contract: CGR to FSE 25 Feb 1870

385 negotiations: see WMR diary 28 Feb 1870; DGR to WA 28 Feb 1870; CGR to FSE 5/7 Mar 1870; CGR to AM 29 Mar 1870

386 Austen vein: DGR to AB 23 Mar 1870 (in DW 818 dated 16 Mar 1870; but see DW 824 where DGR acknowledged receipt of *Commonplace* on 22 Mar 1870)

388 *Athenaeum*: 4 Jun 1870, 734

388 *Spectator*: 29 Oct 1870, 1292–3

389 readily imagine: CGR to FSE 1 Jun 1870

389 Thankyou: CGR to AB 7 Jul 1870

389 cut oneself in two: CGR to ABH 28 Jul 1870

389 Franco-Prussian War: CGR to ABH Aug 1870; WMR to ABG 4 Dec 1870

390 Of course: DGR to CGR 23 Mar 1870

390 one-stringed lyre: CGR to DGR Mar/Apr 1870

391 more spontaneous: FLR to CGR 19 Aug 1870, *FLs* 32.

392 Dante is a name: MFR 1874, preface

392 Mystical Rose: ibid., 204–5

PART FOUR: 1871–94

29 Disease and Derangement

395 tiresome: WMR Diary 9 Feb 1871; CGR to FSE 2 Mar 1871; CGR to Dalziels 26 Apr 1871

396 intolerable hideousness: CGR to DGR 28 Apr 1871

396 symptoms: see WMR Diary for this period

396 persistent weakness: CGR to AB 7 Jul 1870

396 very prostrate: WMR to ABG 17/28 May 1871, Duke 1934, 73, 76

396 progressing: WMR to ACS 15 Jun 1871

397 chatty letter: CGR to WMR 28 Jul 1871; to Dalziels 3 Aug 1871; to KH 28 Jul 1871

397 dear Janey: WM to JM 16 Jul 1870, BL Add. 45338.

397 total wreck: WMR Diary 16 Nov 1871; DGR to Miss Losh 28 Oct 1871; WBS to AB 19 Nov 1871, *Pictor Ignotus* 110

397 Hughes's drawings: CGR to WMR 1 Sep 1871; to Dalziels 25 Nov 1871

398 reviews: *Athenaeum* 6 Jan 1872, 11

399 Queen's Hall: CGR to DGR c. 1868

399 *Scribner's*: Nov 1871, 239 and Jan 1872, 278; see also WMR Diary 1 Nov 1871

400 *Tinsley's*: H. B. Forman, *Our Living Poets: An Essay in Criticism*, Tinsley Bros, London 1871, 248–50

400 Gabriel's mind: see *FLM i*, chap. xxxiv; WMR to FLR 1 Jun 1872, immediately following *Saturday* article; and Fredeman, *Last Decade*

402 comparatively hopeful: CGR to WMR 10 Jun 1872

403 all this past: DGR to WMR 27 Sep 1872

403 shaky letter: CGR to ABH 24 Jul 1872; and to BLS 29 Jul 1872

403 Mrs Bodichon: FLR to DGR 29 Aug 1872, BL Ashley 3865

404 fellow guest: see Betham Edwards 1911, 131–5

30 Lucy Arrives and Maria Leaves

406 waifs across Atlantic: MFR to Margaret J Preston 21 May 1872, Maser 69; CGR to Margaret J Preston 27 Dec 1872; CGR to Dear Sirs (Susan Coolidge's publishers) 24 ?Jan 1872

406 Dear Sir: CGR to unidentified correspondent c. 1873 Maser 70

407 H. H.: CGR to unidentified correspondent 31 Mar 1873. It is possible that the offending author was the same 'H. H' mentioned on opening page of Emily Dickinson's *Poems* (Roberts Bros Boston, 1890) as 'the author's fellow townswoman and friend'.

407 rebuke to Nolly Brown: see CGR to Oliver Madox Brown 1873

407 Gabriel was mad: JM to TWD 1883, BL Add MSS 45353

407 good bit better: WMR to ABG 13 May 1873, Duke 81; Gosse 1895, 160; CGR to BLS 23 Jun 1873

407 at Kelmscott: CGR to EH 1 Jul 1873

408 dog-rose: CGR to CG 5 Dec 1872

408 neither in writing: WBS to WMR 22 Oct 1885, *Last Decade* 82

408 dear, dear Lucy: CGR to LMB 10 Jul 1873 and WMR 10 Jul 1873

409 most blessed life: MFR to the Misses Bevir 25 Dec 1874 and 13 Aug 1875, PUL, Troxell III

409 novitate: WMR to MFR 11 Sep 1873; FLR to DGR 16 Sep 1873, Packer 1963, 305; DGR to FLR 13 Sep 1873

410 last dinner: WBS to AB 31 Oct 1873, *Last Decade* 279

410 lonely at Christmas: DGR to FLR Dec 1875; MFR to DGR 13 Dec 1875, Packer 1964, 618

410 novice mistress: see Peter Mayhew, *All Saints: Birth and Growth of a Community*, Oxford, 1987

411 police surveillance: Gosse 1895, 160

411 any other course: WMR to FLR 9 Jul 1873

411 ebullition: CGR to WMR 5 Nov 1873

413 So you think: CGR to CG c. 1885

415 Donne: see *Humorous Poems* edited by WMR for Moxon in 1872 (which did not of course include any of Donne's sacred poems, but shows his secular work was well-known in the family)

416 *People's Hymnal*: ed. R. F. Littledale, 1867 and numerous reprints.

416 Littledale: see D. M. Boycott, *The Secret History of the Oxford Movement*, 1933, 122–3; and D. M. Boycott, *Lead Kindly Light: Saints and Heroes of the Oxford Movement*, 1932, 124 (a book that incidentally includes CGR as one of its 'saints')

417 female learning: R. F. Littledale, *The Religious Education of Women*, 1874, 12

417 van Gogh: see Martin Bailey, *Young Vincent* ,1990, 61, 97

31 *Speaking Likenesses*

418 prose story: CGR to AM 3 Feb 1874

418 fairy tales: CGR to CG 13 Feb 1873

418 out of favour: *TLS*, 29 May 1959, xi; Bell 271; Battiscombe 157; Packer 187 and 252; Thomas 297; R. L. Taylor, ed., *Sing-Song, Speaking Likenesses, Goblin Market*, NY 1976, xviii

419 literally *speaking*: CGR to AM 27 Jul 1874

419 Christmas trifle: CGR to DGR 4 May 1874; see also Knoepflmacher 1986, 299 ff.

423 veracious history: CGR to CG 1874

424 gratifying offer: CGR to AM 4 Feb 1874

424 funnily enough: CGR to AM 20 Apr 1874 and to DGR 4 May 1874

424 unlucky title: DGR to WMR 20 May 1874. Samuel Butler's satirical romance had been published in 1872; CGR to AM 27 Jul 1874

425 Gabriel writes: CGR to AM Oct/Nov 1874; and to DGR 5 Nov 1874

425 public appetite CGR to AM Nov 1874; and 25 Jan 1875

425 reviews: *Academy*, 6 Dec 1874; *Athenaeum* 27 Dec 1874, 878–9

425 To think: CGR to WMR 15 May 1874

426 The weather is divine: DGR to FLR 23 Apr 1874

426 fruitless: CGR to DGR Jun 1874

426 new-found freedom: CGR to CG late 1874

427 miscarriage: it has been said that this was caused by dissension within the combined household and specifically by CGR's priggish and unfriendly behaviour towards LMB's guest, Edith Holman Hunt; see Charlotte Yeldham, *Women Artists in C19 France and England*, New York 1984, i, 312–5, citing a note by LMB's daughter. But WHH's marriage took place in November 1875 and cannot have caused a miscarriage in Aug 1874. In any case CGR and LMB were scarcely in occupation at Euston Square simultaneously during 1874.

427 Nolly Brown: CGR to DGR 5 Nov 1874

427 housekeeping accounts: preserved in UBC

427 fire has died out: CGR to AM 4 Feb 1874

427 one fattish volume: CGR to AM 26/30 Jan 1875

428 here at last: CGR to AM 16/25 Mar 1875

429   Clifton: CGR to WMR 11 Aug 1875 (dated thus by WMR in *FLs*)
429   DGR's remarks: DGR to CGR 3 Dec 1875
430   CGR's reply: CGR to DGR 4 and 22 Dec 1875
430   vile trashy poem: DGR to TWD 19 Dec 1875
431   Gosse: 'Miss Rossetti's Poems', *Examiner*, 18 Dec 1875, 1418–9
431   Save me: CGR to EG 20 Dec 1875; and to DGR 22 Dec 1875.

32 Public Cause Private Grief
432   Wilding: see DGR to FLR 31 Oct 1875
432   kind old lady: CGR to DGR Nov 1875
432   George Hake: DGR to CGR 3 Dec 1875
433   intense spiritual joy: MFR to DGR 24 Dec 1875, Packer 1964, 619
433   great failure: DGR to Fanny Cornforth 5 Jan 1875
433   Hake's view: see Hake 1892, 230
433   Your dear face . . . inculcations: DGR to FLR 19/21 Jan 1876
433   used to believe: CGR to DGR Sep 1875
434   live dissection for teaching: see Cobbe ii, 251
434   saddest sight: *Morning Post*, 2 Feb 1875, quoted Cobbe ii, 263–4.
434   woman's cause: see Mary Ann Elston, 'Women and Anti-
      vivisection in Victorian England 1870–1900', in N.A. Rupke ed.,
      Vivisection in Historical Perspective, 1987, 259 ff.
435   my hopes: Cobbe ii, 280
435   specially-composed poem: CGR to Mrs Ruxton 1879
435   Gosse asked her: Gosse 1895, 160
436   Mothers: CGR to CG 26 Jan 1875
438   with disfavour: *SRs* 431
439   Edith HH: HRA to *TLS* 2 Jul 1964, 571
439   rightful rule: *SRs* 422
439   inform Gabriel: CGR to DGR 11 Jul 1876
439   ask forgiveness: CGR to LMB Sep 1876
439   Maria's decline: from *FLs*, *FLM* ii, and Peattie. The funeral is
      described in *TF* 213.
441   irreplaceable sister: CGR to LMB 18 Feb 1886
441   no reason to suppose: WMR to ABG 8 Jan 1877
442   unpleasant and capricious: WMR to GGH 12 Jan 1877
442   genuine lyric cry: CGR to DGR 1 Jan 1877
443   happily in proportion: CGR to Edith Bevir end 76; see also CGR
      to Mrs White 7 Dec 1876
443   my little piece: CGR to DGR Jan/Feb 1877; *Athenaeum*, 17 Mar 1877,
      350
444   addicted to science: WMR to C. E. Norton 9 Sep 1897
444   once more: CGR to WMR 6/15 Aug 1877
444   His depression: CGR to WMR 30 Aug 1877
444   It is balm: CGR to FJS Dec 1877

445 walks with CGR: Watts-Dunton, 'Memories of CGR', *Nineteenth Century*, Feb, 1895, 361–2

446 her latest piece: CGR to WMR 11 Oct 1877

33 Equal in Christ

450 devotional reading book: CGR to AM 4 Nov 1876

454 Littledale's doggerel: 7 Feb 1878, *FLs* 72

454 Eastern Question: see E. P. Thompson, *William Morris*, 1976, ch. 5

455 William's sentiments: WMR to ACS 28 Jan 1877

456 Harmony: *New & Old*, Vol. vii, Jan 1879, 36–9. My thanks to Mary Arseneau for alerting me to the existence of this otherwise lost text by CGR and thereby enabling me to spot its presence in the *New & Old* index. A printed copy was included in FLR's 'maternal store' of press clippings sold by Sotherans in 1920 and 1931, whose current location is unknown.

456 mad enthusiasts: *New and Old*, iii. 1875, 152

457 Hueffer's article: see CGR to WMR 9 Aug 1878

457 CBC's translation: CBC to CGR 4 Sep 1878, *FLs* 76–7; and CGR to David Johnston 5 Dec 1879

457 free thinking school: CGR to Keningdale Cook 14/21 Jun 1878

459 *Ninna-Nanna*: *PWs* 494 says that TPR's versions inspired CGR's, but the correspondence in *FLs* 77–8 makes clear she had done several of her own before his appeared

460 Routledge's Annual: identified from an anthology of comic verse which reprinted *Freaks of Fashion* in 1881

460 wrote to Mac: CGR to AM 12 /18 Dec 1877

461 bookshop enquiry: see CGR to DGR 26 Dec 1879

461 But only: CGR to DGR 17 Dec 1879

461 CGR apologised: CGR to LMB Jun 1878

462 Had I an oratory: CGR to WMR 21 Aug 1878

463 sad to say: CGR to DGR 25 Jul 1879

465 current suffrage bill: Auga Webster, 'The Parliamentary Franchise for Women Ratepayers', 1878, reprinted in *A Housewife's Opinions*, 1879, 275–9. The previous year AW had argued on similar lines saying the suffrage bill had been six times rejected.

465 I write as I am thinking: CGR to AW c. 1878

34 Monna Innominata and Later Life

470 Seaford: CGR to WMR 21 Jul 1879

470 I for my part: CGR to EG Dec 1875

471 hugging hopes: CGR to DGR 26 Dec 1879

471 if at some future: CGR to Olive Rossetti 27 Apr 1880

471 Tomlinson: see Tomlinson, 1900; Tomlinson, 1874; Sotheby's 30 Jul 1895, lots 741

472   that land: several critics have identified this as Italy in the time of Dante. But the birthplace of the Albigensian heresy was not Italy but Albi, and the troubadours were distinctively provençal. CGR was a writer of exact meaning, who would not have written thus had she meant to invoke the Italy of Dante and his school, although Petrarch's (and Laura's) association with Provence allows for a certain linking of the two locations. See William Whitla, 'The Preface as Pre-Text', in Kent 1987, for the most useful discussion of *Monna Innominata* to date.

473   Beatrice de Die, etc: see Hueffer 1878, 281 ff

473   I rather wonder: CGR to DGR 5 Sep 1881

473   'The Sonnet in England': J. A. Noble, *The Sonnet in England and Other Essays*, 1893, 52–6

474   a blind: *PWs* 462; *FLs* 97

474   secret throbbings: WBS to AB 1 Jun 1880, *Pictor Ignotus*, 331.

474   My thanks to Wayne H. Phelps and to Florence Boos for assistance with CBC's *Poems and Translations*.

476   wonderfully recovered: DGR to Miss Munro 21 May 1880

477   Eastbourne: CGR to DGR 16 Jul 1880

477   may I deserve: CGR to DGR 20 Jul 1880

477   diabolical subject: CGR to LMB n.d.

478   narrow path: *PWs* lxiii

478   no precept: *PWs* lxvii

478   startling, portentous: CGR to DGR 9 Aug 1880

478   Fred Shields: see CGR letters to FJS in Mills 1912

479   little nudities: CLD to Emily Gertrude Thomson 10 Aug 1897, Cohen, 1979, ii, 1134–5. CLD's voyeurism was also curiously linked to CGR's work, for this letter about naked children romping on the beach also contains the following sentences: 'Then think what an embarrassing thing it would be to begin an aquaintance with a naked little girl! what could one say to start the conversation? Perhaps a poetical quotation would be best ... we *might* begin with Keats' [sic] charming lines "Oh where are you going with your love-locks flowing, And what have you got in your basket?" The lines quoted are of course from CGR's *Amor Mundi*.

479   spiritual responsibility: *PWs* lxviii

479   Chatterton: CGR to DGR 20 Jul 1880

480   influential talent: CGR to DGR 9 Aug 1880

480   Lord Henry Somerset: see CGR to DGR 6 Sep 1880 and WMR Diary 13 Sep 1880, where he noted that CGR was 'much occupied with the affair of Lord H. Somerset and is disposed to believe his letter of self-vindication'. Publicly, Lord Henry was accused of misconduct with a footman, but according to WMR the true scandal was his relationship with his wife's cousin, who

as it happens was the son of Sophia Dalrymple – Julia Cameron's
sister – and thus indirectly known to DGR.

481   I don't think harm: CGR to DGR 1 Jan 1881
481   cabbing and shopping: CGR to DGR 14 Jan 1881
483   Do you know Donne: DGR to THC 11 Apr 1880, Manx Museum
      typescript
484   apprehend a flood: CGR to DGR 1 Apr 1881
484   new scraps: DGR to THC 10/22 Nov 1880
485   Mr Hopkin's sonnets: DGR to THC 31 Mar 1881; see also GMH
      to R W Dixon 6 Apr 1881, *GMH Selected Letters*, ed. Catherine
      Phillips, OUP 1990, 149, where GMH wrote 'I sent Mr Hall Caine
      a choice of three sonnets, which he acknowledged and is to write
      "at some length shortly". 'Martin, 330, states that THC replied to
      GMH saying 'a critic of utmost eminence' had blackballed his
      sonnets, and that GMH took this to be Matthew Arnold. It was
      clearly DGR.
485   isolated devoteeism: DGR to LMB 12 Apr 1881; WMR to DGR 13
      Apr 1881
485   copyright is my hobby: CGR to AM 20 Apr 1881
485   despatched the manuscript: CGR to AM 27 Apr 1881
485   somewhat in a quake: CGR to WMR 28 Apr 1881. A surviving
      notebook now in HRC Texas, inscribed by CGR for FLR's birth-
      day, presumably in 1881, contains all the poems in *A Pageant and
      Other Poems* exzcept the sonnets of *Later Life*; it raises the possi-
      bility that CGR had reverted to her earlier practice of copying
      out poems when completed.
486   should have fancied: CGR to WMR 20 Jul 1881
486   claim attention: CGR to DGR 26 Jul 1881
488   "Surviving": CGR to CG n.d

35 Gabriel's Death
489   Knole Park: CGR to ABH 4 Aug 1881; to DGR 26 Jul 1881
489   Considering that: CGR to DGR 4 Aug 1881
489   not sulking: CGR to DGR 9 Aug 1881
489   first review: *Academy*, 27 Aug 1881, 152
490   surely not only: CGR to DGR 5 Sep 1881
490   Gabriel's comments: DGR to FLR 4 Sep 1881; CGR to DGR 5 Sep
      1881
490   Scott's admiration: WBS to DGR 25 Aug 1881, Packer 341
490   Watts's review: *Athenaeum* 10 Sep 1881, 327–8; CG to DGR 5 Sep
      1881
490   To get back a moment: CGR to DGR 5 Sep 1881
491   no scintilla . . . sin and guilt: *FLM* i, 375–9
491   shadowy recollection: CGR to WMR 30 Nov 1881

492 My dearest Gabriel: CGR to DGR 2 Dec 1881
492 Don't you think: CGR to WMR 19 Feb 1882
493 I am glad your hopes: CGR to TWD end 1881
493 Pray do not doubt: CGR to WMR 14 Mar 1882
493 nor do I know: CGR to Mrs Ruxton Mar 1882
494 obituary: *Athenaeum* 14 Apr 1882
494 Relieved: CGR to Mrs Ruxton 3 May 1882
495 Adelaide Proctor: CGR to WMR 8 Mar 1882; to John Ingram Mar 1882
495 EBB: CGR to Ingram 29 Apr 1882, 8 and 13 May 1882
496 Mrs Radcliffe: CGR to Ingram 24 Apr 1882 and 17 Sep 1883
497 Why goblin curl: CGR to E. R. Robertson 27 Aug 1883
497 I need hardly say: Elizabeth Sharp to CGR 20 Jan 1885, UBC
497 in its entirety: CGR to Dear Sir 1883
497 entire text: CGR to AM 24 Nov 1886
497 reverend editor: for CGR'S relations with W. G. Horder, see his anthologies and DGR to FLR 2 Mar 1881; CGR to WMR 11 Jul 1881; FLR Diary 13 Jul 1881; CGR to Horder 29 Jul 1882 and 20 May 1885
499 considering the circumstances: CGR to LMB late 1883
499 at this point: Sharp 1912, iii, 66 ff
501 paid more attention: *The Author*, Mar 1895, 269

36 Letter and Spirit

502 incur Income Tax: CGR to WMR 26 Jul 1882
503 terrible Indian news: CGR to ABH 29 Jul 1880
503 nothing about party politics: *PWs* 493
505 one serious flaw: *PWs* lxxiii
508 I am happy to say: CGR to Dear Sir 26 Sep 1882
508 family feeling: CGR to EG 4 Jan 1883 and 30 Jan 1883; CGR to CBC 26 Feb 1883
510 the old man: WBS to AB 7 Jun 1882, *Pictor Ignotus* 343
510 sundial plate: CGR to AB 23 Oct 1882
510 accompanying parcel: CGR to WMR 7 Nov 1882
511 the sole door: CGR to LMB Jan/Feb 1883
511 genius: CGR to CG 27 Feb 1883
511 little namesake: CGR to Henrietta Polydore 18 Feb 1883
512 DGR's paintings: CGR to CG 26 Jan 1883
512 I endorse: CGR to CG 27 Feb 1883
512 poet steps: CGR to CG 27 Jun 1884
512 told Rev. Nash: Bell 145

37 Girls' Protection

514 My dear old Friend: CGR to CBC 26 Feb 1883

514 dinosaur: Jularo 65–6
515 gravestone: for this correspondence see *FLs* and Peattie
515 memorial window: see Mills 280 ff and Bell
516 such a triumph: CGR to LMB 22/24 Aug 1883
516 jubilant: CGR to CG 6 May 1885; here CGR identified CLD as 'another anti-V'
516 circulating petitions: see CGR to Margaret Hunt (novelist wife of artist Alfred Hunt) and CGR to ABH 3 Apr 1883
516 my dear Mrs Heimann: CGR to ABH 11 May 1883 and 11 Feb 1884
517 Minors' Protection: see Edward Bristow, *Vice and Vigilance: Purity Movements in Britain since 1700*, Dublin, 1977; Michael Pearson, *The Age of Consent: Victorian Prostitution and its Enemies*, 1972; Judith Walkowitz, *City of Dreadful Delight*, 1992. My thanks also to Judith Walkowitz's analysis of these issues.
519 we failed in 1884: CGR to George Catchpole 13 Mar 1885 and to Francis Draper 14 Apr 1885
519 frightful commotion: WMR to LMB 23 Aug 1885
519 honorary patron: CGR to WMR 5 Nov 1888

38 Time's Flight

523 CBC's death and will: Sophie Cayley to CGR 7 Dec 1883, *FLs* 139
523 CBC's ring and last letter: see Thomas 342 and CBC to CGR 30 Oct 1893, Boston Public Library
523 Christmas saddened: CGR to FJS 26 Dec 1883
524 amply provided for: CGR to CBC 26 Feb 1883
525 good auguries: CGR to RDH 6 Jan 1884; other letters cited here are also to RDH
526 C. G. R. born December 5: CGR to Dear Sir 8 Jun 1883
526 poetic schooling: CGR to EG 26 Mar 1885
527 *avrà più spirito*: CGR to WMR 23 Sep 1884
527 extreme quiet: WMR to BLS 29 Aug 1884, Ashmolean typescript
527 *A Dirge*: see Annie Fields Album, JPM
528 low chair: Louise Chandler Moulton, *Bookman*, NY, Feb 1909, 603
528 my uncle: CGR to WBS 26 Jan 1885
528 omission I like: CGR to KT 19 Aug 1885
529 old and feeble mother: M. Johnson, 'Christina G. Rossetti', *Primitive Methodist Quarterly*, July 1895, 480
529 old women: CGR to CG 26 Jan 1883
529 escaped governess: CGR to ACS 19 Nov 1884
530 spiritual autobiography: Bell 304
530 my final self: CGR to CG 4 Mar 1887
535 her favourite: ibid
535 humility and reverence: inscribed by KT in the presentation copy

535 beyond all gifts: CGR to KT 19 Aug 1885. For KT see Ann Fallon, *Katharine Tynan*, Boston 1979. My thanks also to Peter van de Kamp for information on Tynan.

535 deferential enough: WMR to LMB 30 Dec 1885; CGR to LMB 11 Jan 1886

535 seeing a saint: Tynan 1912, 158

536 I doubt whether: CGR to Patchett Martin 23 Sep 1891

536 now my juniors: CGR to KT 23 Apr 1888

536 tenacious of obscurity: CGR to KT 23 Apr 1888 and 14 Sep 1893

537 such a goose: see *Pen* 3 Jul 1880, 207; and CGR to DGR 20 Jul 1880

537 Margaret Henderson etc: my thanks to Linda K Hughes of Texas Christian University for information on Anne Patchet Martin and Rosamund Marriott Watson who wrote as Graham R Tomson and was listed by the *Athenaeum* in 1894 as one of CGR's poetic heirs

537 sad to say: CGR to LMB 11 Jan 1886

538 demarcation line: *PWs* lxix

538 Miss Newsham: see Sandars 257; this was presumably the Louisa Newsham who around 1897 had a long poem issued by Mowbray & Co as a sort of devotional greetings card, a copy of which survives in BL Printed Books

538 Lisa Wilson: see Sandars and *PWs* 489; also CGR's copy of *TF* with pressed trefoil now at Delaware Art Museum. Jones 219 says CGR's correspondence with LW was destroyed on LW's death, presumably at her request. My thanks to Diane d'Amico for sharing her researches (and frustrations) into the elusive history of LW.

539 Emily Dickinson: CGR to WMR 6 Dec 1890. In this edition of Dickinson's *Poems*, from which I have quoted, the versification was in fact smoothed out from the originals.

39 Narrowing Grooves

541 octopus: CGR to RDH Sep 1886; Jularo 22

541 will it do something: *FD* 470

541 meditation on wickedness: *FD* 189–90

542 all that remained: *SRs* ii, 526

542 happiness is in our power: CGR to CG 3 Jan 1888

542 just as well: CGR to LMB Feb 1886

543 O'Conor: my researches have so far failed to identify this figure

543 near-at-hand island: CGR to EAP 1888

543 hideous cap: Jularo 75

543 my children: CGR to LMB Mar 1886

543 little Helen: CGR to WMR 23 Sep 1884

544 aged Mary: CGR to LMB 21 Apr 1886

544 card game: CGR to Arthur Rossetti 26 Feb 1889
544 frugal habits: Jularo 70-1
544 somewhat expensive: CGR to WMR 23 Nov 1886
544 jealous disposition: see *FLs* 156–7
544 Worldly Wiseman: Jularo 67
544 it seems unnatural: CGR to WMR 8 May 1888
545 stumbling block: WMR to LMB 5 May 1886
545 Please do not take offence: CGR to LMB 1887
545 Torquay: CGR to EHP Feb 1887
546 lunch at Wallington: CGR to WBS 25 Jul 1887
546 invalid care: CGR to Miss Newsham 11 Oct 1889
546 infirm old aunts: Soskice 1921, 8
547 hermitage or den: CGR to ABH 23 May 1887; Bell 163
547 barren fig tree: CGR to CG 3/23 Jan 1888
547 Bryant: over 60 letters to the Bryants survive, in various loca-
      tions. For Luigi Polidori, see *SRs* ii, 511
548 one good old Aunt: CGR to TWD Jan 1890
548 Swinburne's wish: ACS to CGR 17 Nov 1884, *FLs* 147
548 verse-writing power: CGR to Mrs Kingsley 24 Nov 1885
549 *Hobby Horse*: my thanks to Mark Samuels Lasner for this infor-
      mation
549 Brother Bruin: CGR to Sarah Bolton 7 Jul 1885
549 all I am doing: CGR to TWD 22 Nov 1886
551 under eclipse: CGR to WMR 9 Jan 1889
556 Virginia Woolf: *The Diary of Virginia Woolf* ed. A. O. Bell, 1977, i,
      178

40 Lost Laureate
557 a friend: Ellen Proctor
557 Anarchist views: a letter now in Cornell University Library
      dated 18 Feb 1892 from Kopotkin to 'Miss Rossetti' was presum-
      ably addressed to Olive, not CGR
557 looking charming: Hudson 415
557 door shut: CGR to LMB 23 Apr 1891; CGR to WMR 4 Jul 1891
558 as to colour: CGR to McClure 25 Feb 1892
559 class conflict: CGR to McClure 3 May 1892
559 out of my power: CGR to McClure 16 Nov 1892
559 on laureateship: Olive Garnett Diary 23 Oct 1892, Johnson 1989, 127
559 Munby: 3 Mar 1891, Hudson 415
559 Lewis Carroll: CLD to Miss Moberly Bell 13 Oct 1893, Cohen
      1979, ii, 986
559 little did I think: CGR to Miss Newsham, quoted Sandars 263–4
560 swerve to her feelings: *SRs* 444

560 Poor Mrs Rossetti: Olive Garnett Diary 22 Apr 1893, Johnson 1989, 180

560 almost a skeleton: Olive Garnett Diary 9 Jun 1893, Johnson 1989, 196–7

561 Ellen Proctor: see Proctor 1895

561 bank failure: CGR to EAP 30 Oct 1890; there are discrepancies between the MS and that printed in Proctor 1895, 53

561 London luxury: CGR to EAP Jan 1894

563 cancer: WMR to LMB 22/24 May 1894

563 saddened period: CGR to CG 20 Jan 1892

564 wish only for God's will: CGR to CG 1893

564 proposed going: CGR to WMR 24/29 Dec 1893

564 Lucy's will: CGR to WMR 18 Apr 1894

565 as a poet must be read: *Life and Letters of Brooke Foss Westcott*, 1903, ii, 262

565 anxious correspondence: CGR to McClure 21 Mar 1894 and 24 Oct 1894

566 hysterical screaming: Charlotte Stopes to WMR 31 Oct 1894 and 4 Nov 1894, Packer 1963, 399–400

566 eternally wicked: *SRs* 532

566 afraid of hell: WMR to MB 12 Feb 1895

566 Gutch: *SRs* 532

566 I will trust: Proctor 82. For CGR's death see also *SRs* and Bell

Bibliography

This Bibliography is organised in three sections: first, works by Christina Rossetti; second, works cited in the References by author, title or abbreviation, in alphabetical order, together with other published sources; third, manuscript sources consulted.

WORKS BY CHRISTINA G. ROSSETTI

Verses, privately printed London 1847

Corrispondenzia Famigliare, in *The Bouquet from Marylebone Gardens*, privately printed London 1852

Goblin Market and Other Poems, Macmillan London 1862

Poems, Roberts Bros. Boston 1866

The Prince's Progress and Other Poems, Macmillan London 1866

'Dante: an English Classic', in *Churchman's Shilling Magazine*, London 1867

Commonplace and Other Short Stories, F. S. Ellis London and Roberts Bros. Boston 1870

Sing-Song: A Nursery Rhyme Book, Routledge London and Roberts Bros. Boston 1872

Annus Domini: a Prayer for each Day of the Year, James Parker London and Roberts Bros. Boston 1874

Speaking Likenesses, Macmillan London and Roberts Bros. Boston 1874

Goblin Market, The Prince's Progress and Other Poems, new edition, Macmillan London 1875

Poems, new enlarged edition, Roberts Bros. Boston 1876

'Harmony on 1 Corinthians XIII', in *New and Old*, London 1878

Seek and Find: a Double Series of Short Studies of the Benedicite, SPCK London 1879

A Pageant and Other Poems, Macmillan London and Roberts Bros. Boston 1881

Called to be Saints: the Minor Festivals Devotionally Studied, SPCK London 1881

Poems, Roberts Bros. Boston 1882

'True in the Main: Two sketches', *The Dawn of Day*, London May and June 1882

Letter and Spirit: Notes on the Commandments, SPCK London 1883

TF: Time Flies: A Reading Diary, SPCK London 1885 and Roberts Bros. Boston 1886

Poems, new and enlarged edition, Macmillan London and New York 1890

FD: The Face of the Deep: a Devotional Commentary on the Apocalypse, SPCK London, Young and Co New York 1892

Verses, SPCK London 1893

NPs: New Poems, ed. W. M. Rossetti, Macmillan London 1896

Maude: a Story for Girls, ed. W. M. Rossetti, James Bowden London and Herbert S. Stone Chicago 1897

PWs: The Poetical Works of Christina Georgina Rossetti with Memoir and Notes, ed W. M. Rossetti, Macmillan London 1904

FLs: The Family Letters of Christina Rossetti, ed. W. M. Rossetti, 1908

Crump: *The Complete Poems of Christina Rossetti: a Variorum Edition*, ed. R. W Crump, 3 vols., Louisiana State University 1979–1990

CLs: The Collected Letters of Christina Rossetti, ed. Antony H. Harrison, 2 vols., University Press of Virginia 1995–

PUBLISHED SOURCES BY AUTHOR OR SHORT TITLE

Place of publication London unless otherwise stated

Allingham 1860: *Nightingale Valley*, ed. William Allingham, 1860

Allingham 1907: *A Diary*, ed. H. Allingham and D. Radford, 1907

Allingham 1911: *Letters to William Allingham*, ed. H. Allingham and E. B. Williams, 1911

Battiscombe: Georgina Battiscombe, *Christina Rossetti: A Divided Life*, 1981

Bell: Mackenzie Bell, *Christina Rossetti: a Biographical and Critical Study*, 1898

Bennett: *The Story of W. J. E Bennett*, ed. F. Bennett, 1909

Betham Edwards: Matilda Betham-Edwards, *Friendly Faces of Three Nationalities*, 1911

Boyce: *The Diaries of George Price Boyce*, ed. Virginia Surtees, Norwich 1982

Bray 1838: Anna Eliza Bray, *By the Borders of the Tamar and Tavy*, 2 vols., 1838

Bray 1854: Anna Eliza Bray, *A Peep at the Pixies, or Legends of the West*, 1854

Bray 1859: *Poetical Remains of Edward Atkyns Bray*, ed. A. E. Bray, 2 vols., 1859

Bryson & Troxell: *The Letters of Dante Gabriel Rossetti to Jane Morris*, ed. John Bryson and Janet Troxell, Oxford 1976

Burrows 1887: H. W. Burrows, *A Short History of Christ Church Albany Street*, 1887

Burrows 1894: *Memorials of Henry William Burrows*, ed. Elizabeth Wordsworth, 1894

Butler 1983: *Pusey Rediscovered*, ed. P. Butler, SPCK 1983

Cline: *The Owl and the Rossettis: Letters of Charles A Howell and Dante Gabriel, Christina and William Michael Rossetti*, ed. C. L. Cline, Pennsylvania State University Press, Philadelphia and London 1978

Cayley 1851: *Dante's Divine Comedy*, translated by C. B. Cayley, 4 vols., 1851–5.

Cayley 1857: C. B. Cayley, *Psyche's Interludes*, 1857

Cayley 1879: *The Sonnets and Stanzas of Petrarch*, translated by C. B. Cayley, 1879

Cayley 1880: C. B. Cayley, *Poems and Translations*, privately printed by Brain & Co, 1880

Cobbe: *The Life of Frances Power Cobbe*, 2 vols., 1894

Cohen: *The Letters of Lewis Carroll*, ed. M. N. Cohen, 2 vols., 1979

Coleridge 1873: *Life and Letters of Sara Coleridge*, 2 vols., 1873

Coleridge 1937: *Sara Coleridge's Letters to Henry Reed*, ed. L. N. Broughton, Cornell University Press 1937

Cook & Wedderburn: *The Complete Works of John Ruskin*, ed. A. Cook and A. W. Wedderburn, 36 vols., 1903–12

Daly: Gay Daly, *The Pre-Raphaelites in Love*, New York and London 1989

D'Amico 1994 (i): Diane D'Amico, 'Christina Rossetti's "Helpmeet" ', *Victorian Newsletter* no. 85, 1994, 25–29

D'Amico 1994 (ii): Diane D'Amico, 'Christina Rossetti and *The English Woman's Journal*', JPRAS new series 1994, 20–23

Dodsworth 1849: William Dodsworth *Signs of the Times: sermons preached in Advent 1848*, 1849

Dorling 1885: William Dorling, *Memoirs of Dora Greenwell*, 1885

Doughty 1949: Oswald Doughty, *Dante Gabriel Rossetti: the Last Romantic*, Oxford 1949

Duke: *The Letters of W. M. Rossetti to Anne Gilchrist*, ed. C. Godhes and P. Baum, Duke University Press North Carolina 1934

DW: *The Letters of Dante Gabriel Rossetti*, ed. Oswald Doughty and J. R. Wahl, 4 vols., Oxford 1965–7

EWJ: *English Woman's Journal*, 1858–65

FLM: *Dante Gabriel Rossetti: His Family Letters with a Memoir*, ed. W. M. Rossetti, 2 vols., 1895

FMB Diary: *The Diary of Ford Madox Brown*, ed. Virginia Surtees, Yale University Press, London and New Haven 1981

Frend: Grace Gilchrist Frend, 'Christina Rossetti', *Good Words*, December 1896

GBJ: Georgiana Burne-Jones, *Memorials of Edward Burne-Jones*, 2 vols., 1904

Germ: *The Germ: Thoughts towards Nature in Poetry, Literature and Art*, ed. W. M. Rossetti, 4 issues 1850, facsimile reprint 1901

Gilchrist 1887: *Anne Gilchrist: Life and Writings*, ed. H. H. Gilchrist, 1887

Gosse 1895: Edmund Gosse, *Critical Kit-Kats*, 1895.

GR *Anti-Papal Spirit*: Gabriele Rossetti, *Disquisitions on the Anti-Papal Spirit*, translated by Caroline Ward, 2 vols., 1834

GR *Autobiography*: *The Autobiography of Gabriele Rossetti*, translated and edited by W. M. Rossetti, 1901

GR *Il Veggente*: Gabriele Rossetti, *Il Veggente in Solitudine*, Paris 1846

GR *Beatrice*: Gabriele Rossetti, *La Beatrice di Dante*, 1842

Green: *The Diaries of Lewis Carroll*, ed. R. L. Green, 2 vols., 1953

Griggs: E. L. Griggs, *Coleridge Fille*, 1940

Hake: T. G. Hake, *Memories of Eighty Years*, 1892

Harrison 1988: Antony H. Harrison, *Christina Rossetti in Context*, University of North Carolina and Harvester Brighton 1988

Harrison 1990: Antony H. Harrison, *Victorian Poets and Romantic Poems*, University Press of Virginia 1990

Hickox: M. S. H. Hickox, 'John Brett and the Rossettis', *JPRS*, 1980

Hollis: *Women in Public 1850–1900*, ed. Patricia Hollis, 1979

Howitt 1853: Anna Mary Howitt, *An Art Student in Munich*, 1853, reissued 1883

Hudson: Derek Hudson, *Munby: Man of Two Worlds*, 1972

Hueffer 1878: Francis Hueffer, *The Troubadours*, 1878

Hunt 1932: Violet Hunt, *The Wife of Rossetti: Her Life and Death*, 1932

ILN: *Illustrated London News*

Ingelow 1863: Jean Ingelow, *Poems*, 1863

Ingelow 1901: *Some Recollections of Jean Ingelow*, 1901

JPRAS / JPRS: *Journal of Pre-Raphaelite and Aesthetic Studies / Journal of Pre-Raphaelite Studies*, various locations 1980–94

Johnson 1989: *Tea and Anarchy: the British Museum Diaries of Olive Garnett*, ed. Barry Johnson, 1989; see also *Olive and Stepniak 1893–1895*, ed. Barry C. Johnson, Birmingham 1993

Jones: Kathleen Jones, *Learning not to be First: the Life of Christina Rossetti*, Windrush Press Moreton-in-March 1991 and Oxford Paperbacks 1992

Jurlaro 1991: Felicita Jurlaro, *Christina Rossetti: the True Story*, Excalibur Press 1991

Kent: *The Achievement of Christina Rossetti*, ed. David A. Kent, Cornell University Press 1987

Knoepflmacher: U. C. Knoepflmacher, 'Avenging Alice: Christina Rossetti and Lewis Carroll', *Nineteenth Century Literature*, 1986, 299 ff

Lang 1959: *The Letters of Algernon Charles Swinburne*, ed. C. Y. Lang, Yale University Press, 6 vols., 1959

Last Decade: W. E. Fredeman, 'Prelude to the Last Decade: Dante Gabriel Rossetti in the Summer of 1872', *Bulletin of the John Rylands Library*, University of Manchester, vol. 53, 1970–1

Lee: Amice Lee, *Laurels and Rosemary*, Oxford 1955

Marsh 1989: Jan Marsh, *The Legend of Elizabeth Siddal*, 1989

Martin: Robert Bernard Martin, *Gerard Manley Hopkins: A Very Private Life, 1992*

Maser: *Christina Rossetti in the Maser Collection*, with essays by Mary Louise Jarden Maser and Frederick E. Maser, Bryn Mawr College Library, 1991

MFR 1867: Maria Francesca Rossetti, *Exercises in Idiomatic Italian through literal translation from the English*, and *Anedotti Italiani: Italian Anecdotes selected from II Compagno del Passeggio Campestre: a key to Exercises in Idiomatic Italian*, 2 vols., 1867

MFR 1872: Maria Francesca Rossetti, *Letters to my Bible Class*, SPCK 1872

MFR 1874: Maria Francesca Rossetti, *A Shadow of Dante*, 1874

Millais: *The Life and Letters of John Everett Millais*, ed. J. G. Millais, 2 vols., 1898

Miller 1983: Alice Miller, *The Drama of the Gifted Child*, translated by Ruth Ward, 1983

Miller 1985: Alice Miller, *Thou Shalt not be Aware*, translated H. and H. Hannum, 1985

Miller 1990: *The Untouched Key: tracing childhood trauma in creativity and destructiveness*, translated H. and H. Hannum, 1990. See also Alice Miller, *Banished Knowledge: facing childhood injuries*, translated L. Vennewitz, 1990

Mills: *The Life and Letters of Frederic Shields*, ed. Ernestine Mills, 1912

Moulton 1909: Louise Chandler Moulton, 'Christina Rossetti', *The Bookman*, New York, February 1909

Oliva: *I Rossetti tra Italia e Inghiltera*, ed. Gianni Oliva, Rome 1984

Packer 1963: Lona Mosk Packer, *Christina Rossetti*, University of California and Cambridge University Press 1963

Packer 1964: Lona Mosk Packer, 'Some unpublished letters from Maria Francesca to Dante Gabriel Rossetti', *PMLA* 1964, 615–7

Parkes 1856: Bessie Rayner Parkes, *A History of our Cat Aspasia*, 1856

Parkes 1895: Bessie Rayner Parkes Belloc, *In a Walled Garden*, 1895

Peattie: *The Letters of William Michael Rossetti*, ed. Roger Peattie, Philadelphia 1990

Pictor Ignotus: W. E. Fredeman, 'The Letters of Pictor Ignotus: William Bell Scott's correspondence with Alice Boyd 1859–1884', *Bulletin of the John Rylands Library*, University of Manchester, vol. 56, 1976

PRBJ: *The P. R. B. Journal*, ed. W. E. Fredeman, Oxford 1975

PRD&L: Pre-Raphaelite Diaries and Letters, ed. W. M. Rossetti, 1900

Pusey 1844: Edward Bouverie Pusey, *The Foundation of the Spiritual Life by Jean Joseph Surin*, translated from the French, 1844

Pusey 1893: H. P. Liddon, *Life of Edward Bouverie Pusey*, 3 vols., 1893–5

Pusey 1898: *Edward Bouverie Pusey, Spiritual Letters*, ed. J. O. Johnston and W. C. E. Newbolt, 1898

Procter 1858: Adelaide Anne Procter, *Legends and Lyrics*, 1858

Procter 1862: Adelaide Anne Procter, *A Chaplet of Verses*, sold for the benefit of the Providence Row Night Refuge, London 1862

Procter 1864: Adelaide Anne Procter, *Collected Poems with a Memoir by Charles Dickens*, 1864

Proctor 1895: Ellen A. Proctor, *A Brief Memoir of Christina G. Rossetti*, SPCK 1895

The Rossetti-Macmillan Letters, ed. Lona Mosk Packer, 1963

RRP: Ruskin, Rossetti, Pre-Raphaelitism: Papers 1854 to 1862, ed W. M. Rossetti, 1899

RPs: Rossetti Papers 1862–70, ed W. M. Rossetti, 1903

Scott: William Bell Scott, *Autobiographical Notes*, ed. W. Minto, 2 vols., 1892

Sandars: Mary F. Sandars, *Christina Rossetti*, 1930

Sharp 1882: William Sharp, *Dante Gabriel Rossetti*, 1882

Sharp 1912: William Sharp, *Papers Critical and Reminiscent*, ed. Elizabeth A. Sharp

Soskice: Juliet Soskice, *Chapters from Childhood*, 1928

SRs: W. M. Rossetti, *Some Reminiscences*, 2 vols., 1906

Stephens: F. G. Stephens, *Dante Gabriel Rossetti*, 1894

Surtees 1971: Virginia Surtees, *The Paintings and Drawings of Dante Gabriel Rossetti: a catalogue raisonnée*, 2 vols., Oxford 1971

Tate Gallery 1984: *The Pre-Raphaelites*, exhibition catalogue 1984

Thomas: Frances Thomas, *Christina Rossetti*, Self-Publishing Co, Hanley, Worcs. 1992 and Virago Press London 1994

Tomlinson 1874: Charles Tomlinson, *The sonnet, its origins, structure and place in poetry*, 1874

Tomlinson 1891: Charles Tomlinson, *Sonnets*, 1891

Tomlinson 1900: *Life of Charles Tomlinson*, ed. Mary Tomlinson, 1900

Troxell: *Three Rossettis: Unpublished Letters from Dante Gabriel, Christina and William*, ed. Janet Camp Troxell, Cambridge Mass. 1937

TLS: Times Literary Supplement, London

TWD: Theodore Watts Dunton, 'Reminiscences of Christina Rossetti', *The Nineteenth Century*, February 1895

Tynan 1895: Katharine Tynan, 'Christina Rossetti', *The Bookman*, New York February 1895

Tynan 1912: Katharine Tynan, 'Santa Christina', *The Bookman*, supplement 1912

Tynan 1913: Katherine Tynan, *Twenty-five Years*, 1913

Vincent: E. R. Vincent, *Gabriele Rossetti in England*, Oxford 1936

Waller: R. D. Waller, *The Rossetti Family 1824–1854*, Manchester University Press 1932

WHH 1905: William Holman Hunt, *Pre-Raphaelitism and the Pre-Raphaelite Brotherhood*, 2 vols., and 2 edns., 1905 and 1913

Weintraub: Stanley Weintraub, *Four Rossettis, A Victorian Biography*, New York 1977 and London 1978

Williams and Campbell: T. J. Williams and A. W. Campbell, *The Park Village Sisterhood*, SPCK, 1965

Wilson: Lisa Wilson, *Verses*, 1896

WMR Diary: part published in *The Diary of William Michael Rossetti*, ed. Odette Bornand, Oxford 1972; part published *Victorian Poetry*, 1980

MANUSCRIPT SOURCES

The majority of manuscript sources are not cited under References, since all known letters from CGR are published in *The Collected Letters of Christina Rossetti*, ed. Antony H. Harrison. How- ever, much of the research for the present study was done from MS sources, and I should like to thank the following collections for their assistance (abbreviations refer to non-CGR materials cited in References)

Ashm: Ashmolean Museum, Oxford; Bancroft Collection, University of California; Berg Collection, New York Public Library; BL: British Library – Addl MSS, Ashley Library and RPs; Bod: Bodleian Library Oxford; Boston Public Library; Brotherton Library, University of Leeds; Bryn Mawr College; Cambridge University Library; Colorado College; Columbia University Library; Cornell University Library; Delaware Art Museum; Fitzwilliam Museum Cambridge; Girton College Cambridge; Haverford College Philadelphia; HRC, University of Texas; Illinois University Library; Iowa University Library; Iowa State Archives, Des Moines; John Rylands Library Manchester; Johns Hopkins University Library; JPM: J. Pierpont Morgan Library New York; Kentucky University Library; Kings College Cambridge; Library of Congress; Louisiana State University; Loyola University Library; Manx Museum; National Library of Scotland; Newnham College Cambridge; NUL: Newcastle University Library; NYU: New York University Library; Penn State University Library; Pennsylvania Historical Society, Philadelphia; PUL: Princeton University Library; Rutgers University Library; Somerville College Oxford; Trinity College Cambridge; Wellesley College, Massachusetts; William Morris Gallery, London; Yale University Library.

Thanks are also due to the National Register of Archives, PRO, London and the University of Reading Register of English Literary Manuscripts. Individuals to whom especial thanks go for assistance with MS sources include Antony Harrison, Mark Samuels Lasner, Fred Leventhal, Mary Louise and Frederick E. Maser, Carolyn Matthews, Lucy and Roderic O'Conor, Kate Perry, Francis C. Sharp.

Index

Throughout the Index, 'CGR' stands for Christina Georgina Rossetti. Her works are listed under her name. For all other abbreviated names, see under Abbreviations.